THE CROWELL SERIES IN AMERICAN EDUCATION
JAMES C. STONE, *Advisory Editor for Education*

Readings in the

Foundations

of Education

COMMITMENT TO TEACHING, VOLUME II

COMMITMENT TO TEACHING
James C. Stone and Frederick W. Schneider

Volume I FOUNDATIONS OF EDUCATION, SECOND EDITION
Volume II READINGS IN THE FOUNDATIONS OF EDUCATION, SECOND EDITION
Volume III TEACHING IN THE INNER CITY: A BOOK OF READINGS

Edited by

James C. Stone
PROFESSOR OF EDUCATION
UNIVERSITY OF CALIFORNIA, BERKELEY

Frederick W. Schneider
PROFESSOR OF EDUCATION
SAN JOSE STATE COLLEGE

THOMAS Y. CROWELL COMPANY · NEW YORK · ESTABLISHED 1834

Readings in the
Foundations
of Education

Second Edition

COMMITMENT TO TEACHING, VOLUME II

L. C. Card 72-146069
ISBN 0-690-20198-2

First Printing, April, 1971
Second Printing, October, 1971

Designed by Barbara Kohn Isaac

Manufactured in the United States of America

Foreword

The title of this book includes the phrase "commitment to teaching"—an economical description of the one item of philosophical equipment that every teacher *must* have. Alfred North Whitehead, in his preface to *The Aims of Education,* has stated the requirement another way: "The students are alive, and the purpose of education is to stimulate and guide their self-development. It follows as a corollary from this premise that the teacher should also be alive with living thoughts."

The necessity for commitment is urgent, for the teacher's task in America is larger and more laden with mission than it has ever been before. American education has been challenged, over the last twenty years, by encompassing change. There is change at every point of contact between education and the community: in purpose, to educate in terms of a politically ordained equality of opportunity; in scope, to carry all students to the highest level of education their capacity permits; in support, to draw not only from the community and the state, but increasingly from the federal government; in method, to use equipment, specialized personnel, programmed instruction, independent study, team teaching and other new ways of presenting material and supporting the learning process.

The challenge is good. It gives validity to the school as an institution of our time and validity to those who teach in it.

The authors have recognized that the modern teacher must do more than know and present his subject. He must know and, what is more to the point, understand, the society which his students come from. Recognizing this, they have chosen well the readings that will draw the student from one viewpoint to another, from one discipline to another, and from one intellectual style to another, always to the purpose of establishing both the nature and the necessity of commitment to teaching.

FRANK BOWLES
Former Director
Education Program
The Ford Foundation

Preface

As the decade of the seventies gets underway, the condition of education in the United States continues to be discussed by persons in all walks of life. Laymen and professional educators all over the nation are still carrying on lengthy, and sometimes heated discussions of the pros and cons of educational strategies, learning activities, and organizational plans. Perhaps it was always thus; perhaps it shall always be so; unquestionably it has been, and will continue to be a healthy situation for the educational community when professionals and lay persons can sit side by side and work together on the solutions to the interminable problems that arise when the aim is developing the best educational programs possible for America's children and youth.

It is possible that, at times, these discussions have been, and are being, carried on without the benefit of certain important perspectives: historical, philosophical, sociological, and psychological. Additionally, the problem of offering the optimal educational program for the nation's school-age population continues to present new and increasing concerns for all persons who are, in one way or another, interested in the public schools of the nation and the provisions they are making for their students.

The editors of this volume have had a number of purposes in mind as they perused the literature for selections representing what, in their estimation, could be considered among the best thinking with respect to the many problems concerning education. Firstly, articles were chosen that would give evidence of the fact that many of the problems under discussion are rooted in the past as well as in the present, and in philosophical perspectives as well as in psychological and sociological theories and applications. Secondly, articles were selected because of their relevance or appropriateness to the interests and needs of today's students of education. Thirdly, it was felt that a careful selection of the literature that was published toward the close of the sixties and the opening months of the seventies will aid students who, for one reason or another, are unable to avail themselves of the best in representative literature in the field in any other way. It is hoped that this volume will make it possible for students to sample a wide range of the thinking of authorities and practitioners in education with a minimum amount of wasted motion on their parts. In short, the editors have attempted to select contributions which will provide guidelines for the historically-, philosophically-, sociologically-, and psychologically-based discussions between lay persons and professionals, regardless of whether the discussions are held in college classrooms, board of education meeting rooms, or in school cafeterias.

With a few notable exceptions, there has been no duplication of articles that appeared in the original edition of Volume II. The current book reflects the thinking of authorities and practitioners at the end of an action-packed decade, and at the beginning of another period of time that promises to be one of continued change, experimentation, and excitement. Both the original edition and this revised edition contain much of the finest thinking related to the foundation areas of the field of education published in the past few years.

Like its sister volumes in the Commitment to Teaching series, this one is student-oriented in its origin and content. In Volume II, *Readings in the Foundations of Education,* Second Edition, we have followed to some extent the organization used in the two companion books, Volume I, *Foundations of Education,* Second Edition, and Volume III, *Teaching in the Inner City: A Book of Readings*.

The editors of this volume wish to express their appreciation to the many authors and publishers who have given permission to reprint their articles.

JAMES C. STONE
FREDERICK W. SCHNEIDER

Contents

III. Teaching   117

VI. The Pupils: Color Caste and Social Class   269

VII. The Past 417

VIII. The Philosophies 465

IX. The System   515

X. The Profession   563

I. The Milieu

The worlds of 1950 and 1970 are different. Man's technology has done that. The students of 1950 and 1970 are different. A technological world has done that. The social environment in which our children and youth are living and learning will continue to change. We have moved into a present for which none of us was prepared by our understanding of the past. And we—learners and teachers—face a future for which none of us is prepared by our understanding of the past. Our social order today lacks the order, stability and structure it once had. As a nation we are rapidly becoming an apartheid, polarized society, with minorities against the majority and with large segments of our young incubated in hostility and reared to anger and rebellion. Most of the students in our schools will live the majority of their lives in the twenty-first century, the nature of which is at best speculative.

How can we analyze the changes taking place in our culture here and now in ways that will help us prepare our children today for tomorrow's world? What does education today say to students about a world whose most striking characteristic is constant change? And, by the way, which world? What can we say to youth about an environment so radically altered that we, the adults, must radically alter ourselves in order to survive in it? Will we teach children about the world we knew or the one they know? About the one our parents knew as children or the one our children will know? Will schooling help them to master a changed world or will education help them master a world of change? Education reacting to change or education causing change? Teachers following or teachers leading? Students striking or students creating?

The first part of this book focuses on the nature of our changing society and its impact on education. To understand our own past and our present culture is but the beginning of what will be a continuing job; for the newest thing about American culture is that it is in a constant state of change. Teachers cannot avoid facing the most vivid truth of this new age in which we live: "No one will live all his life in the world into which he was born, and no one will die in the world in which he worked in his maturity."

3

How we as teachers must learn to cope with this cultural reality requires the kind of "thinking ahead" that the noted anthropologist Margaret Mead has done for us.

Next comes Tom Wolfe's "What If He Is Right?" The *he* about whom Wolfe writes is Marshall McLuhan, the herald of a new multimedia world in which "the medium is the message." Wolfe not only interprets McLuhan's message for us, but in so doing takes us behind the scenes to show us McLuhan, the man. "What If He Is Right?" leads naturally to the basic philosophical question "What Kind of Society Do We Want?" as considered in the article by John W. Gardner. The reordering of our national priorities in an effort to control the direction of change is the subject of the excerpt from the *Final Report of the National Commission on The Causes and Prevention of Violence.*

One of the most significant questions raised by the articles in Part I is the extent to which the young themselves are qualified to direct changes in our society. Margaret Mead, in her "Youth Revolt: The Future Is Now," suggests that our culture is moving from the postfigurative, in which children learn from adults, to the prefigurative, in which adults also learn from their children. In another view, George S. Counts argues that the question is not whether we should impose anything on the child but rather what we should impose.

The reader will find no pat answers to questions we have raised, nor is it implied that he will necessarily find them in the selections he is about to read. He will find points of view from various perspectives. He will be provoked into probing for his own answers.

1. Thinking Ahead

Margaret Mead

When we look realistically at the world in which we are living today and become aware of what the actual problems of learning are, our conception of education changes radically. Although the educational system remains basically unchanged, we are no longer dealing primarily with the *vertical* transmission of the tried and true by the old, mature, and experienced teacher to the young, immature, and inexperienced pupil. This was the system of education developed in a stable, slowly changing culture. In a world of rapid change, vertical transmission of knowledge alone no longer serves the purposes of education.

What is needed and what we are already moving toward is the inclusion of another whole dimension of learning: the *lateral* transmission, to every sentient member of society, of what has just been discovered, invented, created, manufactured, or marketed. This need for lateral transmission exists no less in the physics or genetics laboratory than it does on the assembly line with its working force of experience and raw workmen. The man who teaches another individual the new mathematics or the use of a newly invented tool is not sharing knowledge he acquired years ago. He learned what was new yesterday, and his pupil must learn it today.

The whole teaching-and-learning continuum, which once was tied in an orderly and productive way to the passing of generations and the growth of the child into a man—this whole process has exploded in our faces. Yet even as we try to catch hold of and patch up the pieces, we fail to recognize what has happened.

Why should the businessman be concerned with this apparently academic issue? In our rapidly changing world, industry has taken the lead in practical consideration of problems of obsolescence and in many ways is capable of taking a position of leadership in the task of reorienting the training of people to live in this new world.

SOURCE: *Harvard Business Review*, XXXVI, 6 (November–December, 1958), 23–37, 164–70. Copyright © 1958 by the president and Fellows of Harvard College; all rights reserved. Reprinted by permission of the publisher.

In order to understand the issues, let us begin by looking at some of the features and underlying assumptions of our American educational system as it is today. Even a brief examination of the picture we carry in our minds of "education" and of "students" will indicate the state of confusion at which we have arrived and the immediate need for creative leadership in working out a more realistic system of education.

We have moved into a period in which the break with the past provides an opportunity for creating a new framework for activity in almost every field—but in each field the fact that there has been a break must be redis-covered. In education there has been up to now no real recognition of the extent to which our present system is outmoded. Meanwhile, as the turmoil over our educational system grows, the various responsible groups in the United States are jockeying for position. But some of them, particularly those representing industry, have as yet hardly entered the field.

Historians point sagely to the last two educational crises—the first of which ended with the establishment of the universal elementary school and the second with the establishment of the universal high school—and with remarkable logic and lack of imagination they predict that the present cri-sis will follow the same pattern. (And what is history for if not to tell us exactly how to make the same mistakes as in the past!) According to such present predictions, the crisis will last until 1970, when it will end with the establishment of universal college education, accessible in principle to all young Americans.[1]

Implicit in this prediction is a series of other ideas, such as:

The assumption that our educational system has fallen behind in some-thing (though it is not now clear what the "something" is—the work train-ing of German apprentices,[2] or the technical training of young Soviets,[3] or the linguistic mastery of Netherlands students), and that it should therefore arrange to catch up.

The explanation that our difficulties are due to the "bulge"—the host of babies that tricked the statisticians peacefully extrapolating their population curves and bedeviled a people who had decided that orphan asylums could slowly be turned into homes for the aged and elementary schools into high schools as a population with a falling birth rate aged into maturity. (Only a few people followed out the simile to senility!)

The thinking of the people who are sure that the pendulum is swinging

[1] See the resolution in favor of free education through college passed by the Na-tional Education Association, *New York Times,* July 6, 1958, Section 4.

[2] See, for instance, David Whitlock, "The Number of Apprentices Needed and How to Reach This Goal," an address presented at the 48th Annual Convention of the American Vocational Association, San Francisco, December 3, 1954.

[3] U.S. Office of Education, Division of International Education, *Education in the USSR,* Bulletin No. 14, 1957.

back to sense—to discipline and dunce caps, switches and multiplication tables, and the highly satisfactory forms of torture which somebody (they themselves or at least their grandfathers) once suffered in the cause of learning.

But in the midst of the incessant discussion and the search for scapegoats to take the blame for what everyone admits is a parlous state, extraordinarily little attention is paid to any basic issues. Everyone simply wants more of what we already have: more children in more schools for more hours studying more of something. The scientists want more students to be taught more mathematics, while the liberal arts advocates want more of their subject matter included in the curriculum. The planners want more school buildings built, and the educators want more teachers trained who have studied more hours and who will get more pay. Meanwhile, the child labor committees want more inspection and more attention to migratory children, and the youth boards want more social workers and more special schools and more clinics provided.

Likewise, extraordinarily little attention is paid to the fact that two great new educational agencies—the armed services and industry—have entered the field, and there is little awareness of the ways in which operations in these institutions are altering traditional education.[4] Recruitment programs of the armed services now include explicit statements of their role as educational institutions. For instance:

The United States Armed Forces Institute . . . has enabled thousands upon thousands of young men to finish their high school education and begin college-level studies. A second Army program enables young men to attend courses at many civilian schools and colleges in off-duty hours. . . . [A third program teaches soldiers—on their bases] such subjects as typing, stenography, foreign languages, literature, and many more.[5]

But most important, the pattern itself is hardly questioned. For we *think* we know what education is and what a good education ought to be; and however deficient we may be as a people, as taxpayers, or as educators, we may be actualizing our ideals. An occasional iconoclast can ask wistfully: "Wouldn't it be fine if we could scrap our whole school system and start anew?" But he gets no hearing because everyone knows that what he is

[4] U.S. Army Recruitment Service, "Pathway to Maturity: A U.S. Army Booklet for Parents." See also U.S. Army Recruitment Service, "The Army and Your Education" and "Reserved for You: Technical Training Opportunities in the U.S. Army for High School Graduates"; Harold F. Clark and Harold S. Sloan, *Classrooms in the Factories: An Account of Educational Activities Conducted by American Industries* (Rutherford, New Jersey, Institute of Research, Fairleigh-Dickinson College, 1958).

[5] "Pathway to Maturity," op. cit.

saying is nonsense. Wishful dreams about starting all anew are obviously impractical, but this does not mean that someone should not ask these crucial questions:

Is our present historic idea of education suitable for people in the mid-twentieth century, who have a life expectancy of 70 years, and who live in a world of automation and global communication, ready to begin space exploration and aware of the possibility that we can bring about the suicide of the entire human species?

As all these present and pressing concerns of the human race are new, is it not possible that a system of education may be out of date which was designed for small societies that were connected by horse-drawn coaches and sailing ships, and where any war could threaten only small sections of the human species at any one time?

Is it not possible that the problem of the educational system's obsolescence goes beyond such issues as methods of teaching reading or physics, or the most desirable age for leaving school, or the payment of teachers, or the length of summer holidays, or the number of years best devoted to college, or even the comparative advantages of working while going to high school or college?

Is not the break between past and present—and so the whole problem of outdating in our educational system—related to a change in the rate of change? For change has become so rapid that adjustment cannot be left to the next generation; adults must—not once, but continually—take in, adjust to, use, and make innovations in a steady stream of discovery and new conditions.

Our educational system, besides being the oldest system of universal free primary education in the world, bears the marks of its long history. But it is not possible to think that an educational system that was designed to teach what was known to little children and to a selected few young men (after which they could be regarded as "educated") may not fit a world in which the most important factors in everyone's life are those things that are not yet, but soon will be, known?

Is it not equally possible that our present definition of a pupil or a student is out of date when we define the learner as a child (or at best an immature person) who is entitled to those things to which a child is entitled —moral protection and a meager subsistence in a dependency position— and who is denied those things which are denied to a child—moral autonomy, sex and parenthood, alcoholic beverages, and exposure to hazards?

In the picture which we have of the student, we have muddled together *both* a conception of the young child who is unable to fend for himself or to protect himself against moral and physical hazards, and who is entitled to be fed and sheltered *and* our own historical conception of the scholar's role as one in which some few men could claim lifelong support provided they themselves accepted an economic dependency that was demeaning to other men and a type of life in which they were subject to supervision (and, until recently in Christian history, gave up sex and parenthood).

This composite picture is one into which we can fit the scholarly monk, the Cambridge don who was not permitted to marry, and the student who lives in college and whose degree depends on his sleeping there (a touchingly infantile method of attaining a degree). All of these match our conception of the learner as a dependent who is subject to supervision appropriate to a child and who must pay for his learning by abnegating some of the rewards of maturity.

Yet the combined ideas of the child and the monk do not complete our picture of the student; we have added still other things to it. With the industrial revolution there came new possibilities of exploiting human labor. Work, which through long ages had often been disliked by members of the upper classes and had been delegated to women, slaves, or serfs, became something different—more hazardous, more menacing. In this situation children were the most easily identifiable victims, and their fate was dramatized as a conflict between their right to an education and their subjection to dangerous and ruthless exploitation in the mines, in the factories, in dives, and in the street trades. The common school, born at a period in the United States when we were particularly concerned with extending the rights of the common man, was sponsored and fought for by labor groups. In this way the common school became doubly identified as the means of making all children literate and as the official enemy of child labor. A vote to raise the school-leaving age was a vote against child labor, and, like sin or cancer, child labor became something no one could be in favor of, officially.

So, as inevitably happens when different institutions in a culture become intertwined, raising the school-leaving age came to stand for several things: it was, on the one hand, a way of increasing the privileges of every child born in the United States and, on the other hand, a way of protecting children against the hazards of work to their health and morals.

That our picture of harmful labor is itself very complex can be seen even from a cursory examination of federal and state child labor laws.[6] Looking at these we find that work outdoors is better than work indoors, that work in small cities is better than work in large cities, that work in summer and during vacations is less harmful than work in winter or during school terms, that work done for parents does not count as work, and that there is one form of work in which all the rules can be broken about age, hours, places, hazards from the weather, weight of objects dealt with,

[6] U.S. Department of Labor, Wage and Hour and Public Contracts Divisions, "A Guide to Child-Labor Provisions of the Fair Labor Standards Act (The Federal Wage and Hour Law)," *Child-Labor Bulletin*, No. 101 (Revised), June, 1957.

being on the streets, going to strange places, and so forth—which, charac-teristically and in the best spirit of Horatio Alger, is delivering newspa-pers.

This one exception in our children's right to protection highlights the whole picture. In the American myth, men rise to success and greatness by working hard as children, and as we have progressively forbidden them this traditional preparation for greatness, we have left them the one sym-bolic activity of delivering newspapers. (Nowadays, however, it may be the father—bank president or chief justice—who actually delivers the papers because the son is in bed with a cold under the care of an expensive pedia-trician.)

Slowly, as a society, we have codified both the rights and the disabilities of minors and also the conditions under which a minor may take on the privileges appropriate to adults because they require maturity. These are problems which are dealt with in the most primitive societies, though the way in which they are thought of may contrast with ours. What has hap-pened in our contemporary society is that the codified rules, each intended to serve some specific need, fail to fit the contemporary situation—and the result is confusion.

The state of confusion that characterizes our attitudes toward maturity in students shows up in a variety of ways. For instance:

School regulations may forbid a married student to attend high school even though he or she may be below the age and the grade when it is legal to leave high school.

Even more quaintly, in one large city the schoolgirl who has an illegiti-mate child may go back to school after the child has been born, but the married girl who becomes a mother may not return.

In some school systems, not only expectant mothers but also expectant *fathers* are barred from the daytime high school.

The complexity of the total picture and the confusion about the relation-ship of being a child, a minor, a student, and a morally incapable individ-ual are further increased when we include, as nowadays we must, the armed services. For in different degrees the armed services permit a boy to enlist who is too young to marry, to leave school, to buy cigarettes or to drink beer, to vote, to make a legal contract, to bequeath property, to change his citizenship, to work in a hazardous occupation or in other occupations be-tween the hours of seven and seven, or to have contact with dangerous ma-chinery. Yet by enlisting he is enabled to operate the complex instruments of death and to die for his country.

So, when we think about education and try to identify the student, we have in our minds—whether or not we are aware of it—an exceedingly complex picture, the elements of which are compounded and confused in their historic connections. Yet we must identify what they are if we are to remodel our educational system so that it is devoted to the kind of teaching and learning that is appropriate to the United States today. For this purpose a look at education in other societies will be helpful:

Education which is limited to small children is appropriate in a very primitive society like that of the Eskimo. The nine-year-old Eskimo child has learned, from father or from mother, the basic skills of a spoken language, the handling of tools and equipment, knowledge of the weather, relevant personal relations, and religious taboos. He must wait until he is physically mature before he can marry; as he grows older he will gain proficiency in hunting, in religious practices, in his knowledge of time, the seasons, and the landscape; and he may come to exercise leadership. But his education, in the sense of learning whatever adults could teach him directly, was over long before.[7]

In other societies that are more complex, education may not be completed before adolescence, when some young people may elect, or may be chosen, to learn more complicated skills and may memorize the classics, master complex weaving skills, or become skilled craftsmen or leaders of ritual activities.

After the invention of writing and the development of mathematics and medicine, these did not become part of the whole tradition which had to be imparted to everyone. Like techniques of gold working or a knowledge of magical charms, they were taught by a few to a few in a long continuum of teaching-and-learning, in which the teacher responded as much to the pupil as the pupil did to the demands of the teacher, and both attempted not so much to add to the sum total of knowledge as to increase the skill of its manipulation.[8] Under these circumstances, new knowledge was added so gradually that the slow web of transmission of ancient skills was not torn.

Parallel to these developments was the special education given by specially chosen tutors and teachers to the children of the aristocracy; such an education was designed to ground the pupils well in many arts and graces and in a scholarship which they would not practice but would wear as an adornment or use for wise government.[9]

In a country governed by a conqueror or in a country to which large numbers of immigrants come, there are special problems of education as the government becomes responsible for people who speak a different language and have different customs. For, in these situations, the function—or

[7] Franz Boas, "The Central Eskimo," *Sixth Annual Report of the Bureau of American Ethnology* (Washington, 1888), p. 399.

[8] Margaret Mead, "Our Educational Emphases in Primitive Perspective," in *Education and the Cultural Process*, edited by Charles S. Johnson (Nashville, Fisk University, 1943), pp. 5–12.

[9] Thomas Woody, *Life and Education in Early Societies* (New York: The Macmillan Company, 1949).

at least one function—of the educational system is not the transmission to the next generation of something that all adults or that specialized groups of adults know, but rather the transmission of something the parents' generation does *not* know to children whom the authorities wish to have educated.[10]

So, looking at our educational system today, we can see that in various ways it combines these different functions:

The protection of the child against exploitation and the protection of society against precocity and inexperience.

The maintenance of learners in a state of moral and economic dependency.

Giving to all children the special, wider education once reserved for the children of privileged groups, in an attempt to form the citizen of a democracy as once the son of a noble house was formed.

The teaching of complex and specialized skills, which, under our complex system of division of labor, is too difficult and time-consuming for each set of parents to master or to hand on to their own children.

The transmission of something which the parents' generation does *not* know (in the case of immigrants with varied cultural and linguistic backgrounds) to children whom the authorities or the parents wish to have educated.

To these multiple functions of an educational system, which, in a slowly changing society, were variously performed, we have added slowly and reluctantly a quite new function: *education for rapid and self-conscious adaptation to a changing world.* Yet we hardly recognize how new this function of our educational system is. It is implicit in the demands of educators that schools develop flexibility, open-mindedness, and creativity; but such demands might equally well have been made 200 years ago, well before the rhythm of change had radically altered.

That we have as yet failed to recognize the new character of change is apparent in a thousand ways. Despite the fact that a subject taught to college freshmen may have altered basically by the time the same students are seniors, it is still said that colleges are able to give students "a good education"—finished, wrapped up, and sealed with a degree.

A student who is still in college can "go on" to a higher degree because he has not as yet "completed" his education, i.e., the lump of the known which he has decided to bite off. But a student who has once let a year go by after he is "out of school" does not "go *on,*" but rather "goes *back*" to school. And as we treat education as the right of a minor who has not yet completed high school (for the position of a boy who has completed high

[10] Margaret Mead, *The School in American Culture* (Cambridge, Harvard University Press, 1951).

school at the age of 14 is a different and anomalous one, in which he is exempt from most of the forms of protection accorded minors because a high school diploma is equated with physiological maturity, the capacity for parenthood, and the ability to resist the seductions of hostel and bowling-alley life), just so we equate marriage and parenthood with getting a diploma; both indicate that one's education is "finished."

Consistent with these ideas and with our conception of what a student is, our educational institutions are places where we keep "children" for a shorter or longer period. The length of time depends in part on their intelligence and motivation and in part on their parents' incomes and the immediately recognized national needs for particular skills or types of training—and as long as they are there, we treat them as minors.

Once they have left, we regard them as in some sense finished, neither capable of nor in need of further "education," for we still believe that education should come all in one piece, or rather, in a series of connected pieces, each presented as a whole at the elementary school, the high school, and the college level. All other behaviors are aberrant. So we speak of "interrupted" education—that is, education which has been broken into by sickness, delinquency, or military service—and we attempt to find means of repairing this interruption. Indeed, the whole GI bill, which in a magnificent way gave millions of young men a chance for a different kind of education than they would otherwise have got, was conceived of primarily as a means of compensating young men for an unsought but unavoidable interruption.

Thus we avoid facing the most vivid truth of the new age: *no one will live all his life in the world into which he was born, and no one will die in the world in which he worked in his maturity.*

For those who work on the growing edge of science, technology, or the arts, contemporary life changes at even shorter intervals. Often, only a few months may elapse before something which previously was easily taken for granted must be unlearned or transformed to fit the new state of knowledge or practice.

In this world, no one can "complete an education." The students we need are not just children who are learning to walk and talk and to read and write plus older students, conceived of as minors, who are either "going on" with or "going back" to specialized education. Rather, we need children *and* adolescents *and* young *and* mature *and* "senior" adults, each of whom is learning at the appropriate pace and with all the special advantages and disadvantages of experience peculiar to his own age.

If we are to incorporate fully each new advance, we need simultaneously:

The wide-eyed freshness of the inquiring child.

The puzzlement of the near-dunce who, if the system is to work, must still be part of it.

The developing capacities of the adolescent for abstract thinking.

The interest of the young adult whose motives have been forged in the responsibilities of parenthood and first contacts with a job.

The special awareness of the mature man who has tempered experience, skepticism, and the power to implement whatever changes he regards as valuable.

The balance of the older man who has lived through cycles of change and can use this wisdom to place what is new.

Each and every one of these is a learner, not of something old and tried —the alphabet or multiplication tables or Latin declensions or French irregular verbs or the rules of rhetoric or the binomial theorem, all the paraphernalia of learning which children with different levels of aspiration must acquire—but of new, hardly tried theories and methods: pattern analysis, general system theory, space lattices, cybernetics, and so on.

Learning of this kind must go on not only at special times and in special places, but all through production and consumption—from the technician who must handle a new machine to the factory supervisor who must introduce its use, the union representative who must interpret it to the men, the foreman who must keep the men working, the salesman who must service a new device or find markets for it, the housewife who must understand how to care for a new material, the mother who must answer the questions of an observant four-year-old.

In this world the age of the teacher is no longer necessarily relevant. For instance, children teach grandparents how to manage TV, young expediters come into the factory along with the new equipment, and young men invent automatic programing for computers over which their seniors struggle because they, too, need it for their research.

This, then, is what we call the *lateral transmission* of knowledge. It is not an outpouring of knowledge from the "wise old teacher" into the minds of young pupils, as in vertical transmission. Rather, it is a sharing of knowledge by the informed with the uninformed, whatever their ages. The primary prerequisite is the desire to know.

Given this situation, which of the institutions that are concerned with the revision of our educational system is to take the initiative: the educational world, the government, the armed services, citizens' voluntary organizations, churches, or industry? Each has a stake in the outcome; each has power to influence what happens; each has its own peculiar strengths and weaknesses.

Industry, however, has the peculiar advantage of understanding the major evil from which our whole educational system is suffering— *obsolescence*. Modern ideas of obsolescence have come out of studies of industrial processes, and industrialists have made these ideas so much a part of their thinking that making allowance for the costs of obsolescence and supporting continuing research on problems of obsolescence are a normal part of their professional behavior. In any major effort to modernize our educational system, of course, it would be appropriate for all the institutions to have a voice. It would be well, for example:

For educators to watch out so that all they know would not be lost in the shuffle.

For government to guard the needs of the nation.

For church and synagogue to protect the religious values of the past.

For the armed services to concentrate on our defense needs.

For citizens to organize means of protecting the health, safety, and welfare (present and future) of their own and the community's children.

In these circumstances, would it not be most appropriate for industry to take the lead in highlighting the obsolescence of our present educational system? In the United States, in 1958, approximately 67% of the civilian labor force are engaged in some kind of work in industry. Of the advances which account for obsolescence, a very large proportion have come out of industry. But, at the same time, much of the thinking that is holding up a real revision of our school system is based on an outmoded public image of industry as a monstrous and wicked institution which, if not restrained, would permit little boys to be sent down into coal mines or to work in conditions in which their lungs would be filled with powdered silicon.

In fact, industry has already taken the lead—within its own walls—in developing a new type of education that includes all levels of competence and training and that freely faces the need for education at the senior levels of management. In their recent survey, Clark and Sloan have presented a masterful picture of the very real contribution that education within industry is making to educational change.[11] The thinking that has gone into this contribution, however, has not yet become an articulate, leading part of our rethinking of the educational system as a whole. But if industry, as represented by individual leaders from management and labor in many parts of the country, would come forward with plans which dramatized our dilemma, such plans would be heard.

What might these plans be? First, in regard to work performed by young people, industry could say to all those who believe that children should be kept in school primarily so that they will not be on the streets or at work under bad conditions: "We will agree that young people need more supervision than older workers—that someone should know where they are each day, that their health should be protected and checked, and that they should be protected from organized attempts to deprave them.

[11] Harold F. Clark and Harold S. Sloan, op. cit.

We will undertake to train and supervise the young people who *at this time* cannot gain anything by remaining in school."

But this would not be enough. This offer would need to be accompanied by a second one: "As soon as *any* worker—of any age at any level—in our plant, office, or laboratory is ready to study again, we will facilitate his, or her, doing so."

This is, admittedly, a large order. But we cannot have one without the other. For as long as we continue to think that free and, when necessary, subsidized education is appropriate *only* when it is *preliminary* to work (though, exceptionally, it may be continued after some inevitable "interruption"), just so long the guardians of character, of political literacy, and of our store of talent that comes from all classes and in many cases shows itself only very slowly will argue for—and will get—longer and longer years of compulsory education and longer and longer years of free education.

Under these circumstances, the meaning of education and the purpose of schools—especially for young people between the ages of 14 and 20—will only become more confused. On the one hand, the education that is absolutely necessary for those who, at an early age, are ready to go on to become scientists, statesmen, philosophers, and poets will be hamstrung by the presence of those others who, at the same age, do not want schooling; and on the other hand, the lives and characters of the temporary nonlearners will be ruined, and they will be incapacitated as potential later learners.

What we need to do, instead, is to separate primary and secondary education—in an entirely new way:

By *primary education* we would mean the stage of education in which all children are taught what they need to know in order to be fully human in the world in which they are growing up—including the basic skills of reading and writing and a basic knowledge of numbers, money, geography, transportation and communication, the law, and the nations of the world.

By *secondary education* we would mean an education that is based on primary education and that can be obtained *in any amount* and *at any period* during the individual's whole lifetime.

By so doing, we could begin to deal effectively with the vast new demands that are being made on us. The high schools would be relieved of the nonlearners, among whom are found a large number of delinquents. But, more important, men and women, instead of preparing for a single career to which—for lack of any alternative—they must stick during their entire active lives, would realize that they might learn something else. The very knowledge that this was so would relieve much of the rigidity that now bedevils management. Women, after their children became older, could be educated for particular new tasks—instead of facing the rejection that today is related to fears about new learning that is acquired in middle age.

Whatever their age, those who were obtaining a secondary education at any level (high school, college, or even beyond) would be in school because they *wanted* to learn and *wanted* to be there—*then*. A comparison of GI and non-GI students has shown how great have been the achievements of students who have chosen to go to school.[12] Furthermore, the student—of whatever age—who was obtaining a secondary education would no longer be defined as someone without adult rights who must accept dependency and meager stipends and have a dedicated delight in poverty.

In an educational system of this kind we could give primary education and protection to actual children as well as protection and sensitive supervision to adolescents. We could back up to the hilt the potentiality of every human being—of whatever age—to learn at any level. And we could do this proudly.

The kind and amount of leadership that industry can best take in making individual plans for sending workers—*on pay*—to get more education, and the kind and amount of leadership that can best come from tax-supported activities is a problem that will have to be threshed out. In the United States, we usually depend upon private initiative to make the first experiments before tax-supported agencies pick up the check. So, too, we shall have to work out the problem of providing special work situations for adolescents and on this basis make our decisions as to whether tax-supported institutions—rather than individual industries—should become chiefly responsible for the employment of adolescents.

But we also need to recognize articulately that there are other routes to competence than the one route provided by the conventional school. Experimental cooperative-work plans in the public schools need to be supplemented by experiments in industry.[13] Such a plan is the one being conceptualized by Pylon, in which the sons of successful parents, who are financially able to continue their studies but find nothing rewarding in school work, are given a chance to learn under meaningful, money-making conditions.[14]

---

[12] Norman Frederiksen and W. B. Schrader, "The Academic Achievement of Veteran and Nonveteran Students," *Psychological Monographs,* Volume 66, No. 15.

[13] See Board of Education, City of New York, High School Division, "Our Public Schools: Cooperative Education," Part IV, *Report of the Superintendent of Schools 1954–1955;* and U.S. Office of Education, *Work Experience Programs in American Secondary Schools,* Bulletin, 1957, No. 5.

[14] Don A. Luscombe, *Pylon: A New Concept and a New Institution (a nonprofit organization chartered under the Laws of Pennsylvania),* (Gwynedd, Pennsylvania, no date).

The right to obtain a secondary education when and where the individual could use it would include not only the right of access to existing conventional types of schools but also the right of access to types of work training not yet or only now being developed—new kinds of apprenticeship and also new kinds of work teams (such as the "Day Haul," which is helping to solve our seasonal labor needs [15]).

In thinking about an effective educational system we should recognize that the adolescent's need and right to work is as great as (perhaps greater than) his immediate need and right to study. And we must recognize that the adult's need and right to study more is as great as (perhaps greater than) his need and right to hold the same job until he is 65 years old. Recent publications of the Department of Labor show that we are already beginning to recognize the importance of work for youth.[16]

Among the nations whose industrial capacities make them our competitors, the United States has a comparatively small total population. The more completely we are able to educate each individual man and woman, the greater will be our productive capacity. But we cannot accomplish the essential educational task merely by keeping children and young adults— whom we treat like children—in school longer. We can do it by creating an educational system in which all individuals will be assured of the secondary and higher education they want and can use any time throughout their lives.[17]

[15] "What Goes On Here," *Woman's Day,* June, 1958.

[16] See District of Columbia Department of School Attendance and Work Permits, *You May Employ Youth: A Guide to the Application of Child Labor Standards in the District of Columbia* (1957); U.S. Bureau of Labor Standards, *Employment Certificates—Help You Help Youth,* Bulletin No. 183, 1955; and U.S. Bureau of Labor Standards, *You CAN Hire Teenagers: Here's How* (Washington, September, 1957).

[17] Margaret Mead, "Closing the Gap Between the Scientists and the Others," *Daedalus* (American Academy of Arts and Sciences), in press.

2. What If He Is Right?

Tom Wolfe

Gentlemen, the General Electric Company makes a considerable portion of its profits from electric light bulbs, but it has not yet discovered that it is not in the light bulb business but in the business of moving information. Quite as much as A.T.&T. Yes. *Of-course I-am-willing-to-be-patient.* He pulls his chin down into his neck and looks up out of his long Scotch-lairdly face. Yes. The electric light is pure information. It is a medium without a message, as it were. Yes. Light is a self-contained communications system in which the medium is the message. *Just think that over for a moment—I-am-willing-to-be*—When IBM discovered that it was not in the business of making office equipment or business machines——

> ————but that it was in the business
> of processing
> information,
> then it began
> to navigate
> with
> clear
> vision.
> Yes.

Swell! But where did *this* guy come from? What is this—cryptic, Delphic saying: *The electric light is pure information.*

Delphic! *The medium is the message. We are moving out of the age of the visual into the age of the aural and tactile.* . . .

It was beautiful. McLuhan excelled at telling important and apparently knowledgeable people they didn't have the foggiest comprehension of their own bailiwick. . . .

SOURCE: Tom Wolfe, *The Pump House Gang* (New York: Bantam Books, Inc., 1968), pp. III–12, 118–22. Copyright © 1965 by the New York Herald Tribune, Inc.; copyright © 1968 by Tom Wolfe. Reprinted by permission of Farrar, Straus & Giroux, Inc.

"Of course, packages will be obsolete in a few years. People will want tactile experiences, they'll want to feel the product they're getting—"

But!—

McLuhan's chin goes down, his mouth turns down, his eyes roll up in his *of-course* expression: "Goods will be sold in *bins*. People will go right to bins and pick things up and *feel* them rather than just accepting a package."

Landor, the package designer, doesn't lose his cool; he just looks—*what if he is right?*

. . . *The human family now exists under conditions of a global village. We live in a single constricted space resonant with tribal drums. . . .*

McLuhan is fond of quoting Daniel Boorstin's dictum, "The celebrity is a person who is known for his wellknownness." That pretty much describes McLuhan himself. McLuhan is one of those intellectual celebrities, like Toynbee or Einstein, who is intensely well known as a name, and as a *savant,* while his theory remains a grand blur. Part of the difficulty is that McLuhan is presented to the world as "the communications theorist." His first book, *The Mechanical Bride,* was a book about communication. Since then McLuhan has barely dealt with communication at all, at least if you define communication as "interchange of thought or opinions." He is almost wholly concerned with the effect of the means of communication (the medium) on the central nervous system. His theory falls squarely in a field known as cognitive psychology, even though his interests cut across many fields. Modern cognitive psychology is highly scientific devoted to complex physiological experiments. McLuhan isn't. In fact, he is a theoretical cognitive psychologist.

This is made quite clear in *The Gutenberg Galaxy. Understanding Media* is really a chapbook for *The Gutenberg Galaxy*'s theory.

The theory, as I say, concerns the central nervous system. McLuhan makes a set of assumptions, à la Bergson, about how the central nervous system processes information. He believes that humans have a "sensory balance"—a balance between the five senses: sight, hearing, touch, smell, and taste. This balance, he says, changes according to the environment. For example, if the visual sense is dimmed, the auditory sense intensifies (as in the blind); if the auditory sense is increased, the sense of touch diminishes (as when a dentist puts earphones on a patient, turns up the sound, and thereby reduces his sensitivity to pain). Great technological changes, he goes on to say, can alter these "sensory ratios" for an entire people. McLuhan is concerned chiefly with two of these great technological changes: (1) the introduction of print in the fifteenth century (reputedly by Johann Gutenberg) and the spread of literacy in the next four hundred years: (2) the introduction of television in the twentieth.

Print, says McLuhan, stepped up the visual sense of Western man at the expense of his other senses. It led, he says, to "the separation of the senses, of functions, of operations, of states emotional and political, as well as of tasks." This, he says, had overwhelming historical consequences: nationalism and nationalist wars (cultural fragmentation); the modern army, industrialism and bureaucracy (fragmentation of tasks); the market and price structure (economic fragmentation), individualism and the habit of privacy (fragmentation of the individual from the community)—and schizophrenia and peptic ulcers (caused by the fragmentation of both intellect and action from emotion); pornography (fragmentation of sex from love); the cult of childhood (fragmentation by age); and a general impoverishment of man's intuitive and artistic life (because of the fragmentation of the senses). And those are but a few of the results he mentions.

Enter TV. Television and the electric media generally, says McLuhan, are reversing the process; they are returning man's sensory ratios to the pre-print, pre-literate, "tribal" balance. The auditory and tactile senses come back into play, and man begins to use all his senses at once again in a unified, "seamless web" of experience. (Television, in McLuhan's psychology, is not primarily a visual medium but "audio-tactile." The world is becoming a "global village," to use one of his happy phrases.

The immediate effects of TV on the central nervous system, says McLuhan, may be seen among today's young, the first TV generation. The so-called "generation gap," as he diagnoses it, is not a state of mind but a neurological fact. It is a disparity between a visual, print-oriented generation and its audio-tactile, neo-tribal offspring. School dropouts, he says, are but the more obvious casualties among a great mass of "psychic dropouts." These are children educated by the electric media to have unified, all-involving sensory experiences. They sit baffled and bored in classrooms run by teachers who fragment knowledge into "subjects," disciplines, specialities, and insist on the classification of data (rather than "pattern recognition," which is the principle of computers). This means, he says, that the educational system must be totally changed. In the long run, he says, the new neural balance will cause total change in everything anyway: "Total Change, ending psychic, social, economic, and political parochialism. The old civic, state, and national groupings have become unworkable. Nothing can be further from the spirit of the new technology than 'a place for everything and everything in its place.' You can't *go* home again." Many of the implications of the theory are very cheery, indeed: no more bitter nationalism—instead, the global village; no more shutout, ghetto-pent minority groups (racial fragmentation)—instead, all "irrevocably involved with, and responsible for," one another; no more tedious *jobs* (mechanistic fragmentation)—instead, all-involving *roles;* no more impoverished intuition (fragmented senses)—instead, expanded, all-embracing sensory awareness; and so on. Man made whole again!

MAN MADE WHOLE AGAIN

I gazed upon the printed page.
It tore me limb from limb.
I found my ears in Mason jars,
My feet in brougham motorcars,
My khaki claws in woggy wars—
But in this cockeyed eyeball age
I could not find my soul again.
Vile me.
And then—
                    I touched a TV dial
And—pop!—
                    it made me whole again.

To a clinical neurologist or psychologist, McLuhan's neurology is so much air. McLuhan's subject matter, as I say, is not communication but the central nervous system. The central nervous system is today perhaps the greatest dark continent of the physical sciences. Precious little is known about even the crudest neural functions. It was not until the 1950's that experimenters discovered, piecemeal, through experiments in several countries, the actual processes by which even so primitive an impulse as hunger is transmitted through the brain (Neal Miller in America, W. R. Hess in Switzerland, Konorski in Poland, Anand in India, *et alii*). It has taken half a century, since the development of the technique of stereotaxic needle implants, to reach even such tiny thresholds as this. It was not until 1962 that physiologists, using microelectrodes, discovered how the eye transmits shapes to the brain. To move from this level to the postulate that TV is altering the neural functions of entire peoples or even one person —this could only strike a clinician as romanticism.

McLuhan, however, was ready for the criticism. He insisted he was not presenting a self-contained theory but making "probes." He sees himself as trying to open up the dark continent for systematic exploration by others. He says he is not drawing conclusions but using what facts are available as "means of getting into new territories." He even says that if he could persuade enough investigators to study the effect of the new technologies systematically, he would gladly return whence he came, viz., to "literary studies." At the same time, he has sought to give his theory some scientific underpinning by setting up psychological studies of sample groups in Canada and Greece, studying their "sensory balance" before and after the coming of TV to their locales. The Canadian study has been completed, and I understand that the results, unpublished as of this writing (January, 1968), were inconclusive.

What, then, has been the nature of McLuhan's extraordinary splash? It certainly has not been scientific, despite the fact that he now characterizes himself as a scientist, speaks of the "clinical spirit," and compares his methods to those of modern psychiatry, metallurgy, and structural analysis.

A clue, I think, may be found in the parallels between McLuhan's history and Freud's. In any historical perspective the two men are contemporaries (Freud died in 1939). Both have come forth with dazzling insights in a period (1850 to the present) of tremendous intellectual confusion and even convulsion following what Nietzsche called "the death of God"; and Max Weber, "the demystification of the world." Both men explain *all* in terms of—*Santa Barranza! something common as pig tracks! under our very noses all the time! so obvious we never stepped back to see it for what it was!* Freud: sex. McLuhan: TV. Both men electrified—outraged! —the intellectuals of their time by explaining the most vital, complex, cosmic phases of human experience in terms of such lowlife stuff: e.g., the anus; the damnable TV set. The biggest howl Freud ever caused was with a two-page paper that maintained that anal sensations in infancy were capable of imprinting a man's mature personality in a quite specific way. Freud was the subject of as much derision in his day as McLuhan in his; and, like McLuhan, benefited from it. Freud said to Jung: "Many enemies, much honor"; McLuhan might well say the same. After all, where there's smoke, there's . . . *what if he is right?* McLuhan said to his disciple and amanuensis, Gerald Stearn: "No one believes these factors have any effect whatever on our human reactions. It's like the old days when people played around with radium. They painted watch dials and licked the brushes. They didn't believe radium could affect people."

Freud, of course, was a doctor of medicine and a trained clinician and a more certifiably scientific thinker than McLuhan. But Freud, like McLuhan, strove after the cosmic insight. The more rigorous psychologists today, as well as most research physicians, regard Freud as a romanticist, almost a metaphysician. They cast the old boy as a sort of Viennese Bishop Berkeley. There is a suspicion that Freud poked *around—aha! very significant!—* amid the plump velvet and florid warps and woofs of a few upperbourgeois Viennese households including his own—*Dad, that bugger, seduced my sis* —and then rerouted his insights through the front door of the clinic as findings explaining the behavior of all mankind. One cannot help but wonder something of the sort about McLuhan. Here sits the master out back at the ping-pong table. And there, inside the house, sit the kids, gazing at their homework—amid a raging, encapsulating sensory typhoon of TV sets, transistor radios, phonographs, and telephones—and yet they make it through school all the same—*Very significant!* Amazing, even. A neo-tribal unity of the senses. "The family circle has widened. The world-pool of information fathered by electric media-movies, Telstar, flight—far surpasses any possible influence Mom and Dad can now bring to bear."

3. What Kind of Society
Do We Want?

John W. Gardner

There are many ways in which a nation can die. It can die from internal strife, tearing itself apart. It can die of indifference, of an unwillingness to face its problems, an incapacity to respond to the suffering of its people. It can die of old age—a waning of energy and an inability to learn new ways which, little by little, cause a society to lose a commanding grip on its future.

In all of history, no people has seriously attempted to take into account the *aging* of institutions and to provide for their continuous renewal. Why shouldn't we of the United States be the first to do so?

As a nation, we have done quite a lot of social inventing and innovating. Among the consequences: the Bill of Rights, the land-grant college, the county agent, the Federal Reserve and Social Security systems. But we do not have to look far today to identify signs of age and rigidity in our institutions. The departments of the federal government are in grave need of renewal; state government is in most places a 19th-century relic; most municipal government is a waxwork of stiffly preserved anachronisms; the system of taxation is a tangle of dysfunctional measures. The unions, the professions, the universities, the corporations—each has spun its own impenetrable web of vested interests. And we seem to have steadily mounting difficulty in getting at all of our problems. Why?

One of the reasons is that people interested in improving our society never quite come to grips with the complex and technical processes by which it functions. They are preoccupied with specific evils that must be corrected. I don't blame them. So am I. But the result is that each re-

SOURCE: *Reader's Digest*, XCV, 569 (September 1970), 74–78. Incorporated from John W. Gardner, *The Recovery of Confidence* (New York: W. W. Norton, 1970). Copyright © 1970 by John W. Gardner. Reprinted by permission of W. W. Norton & Company, Inc.

former comes to his task with a little bundle of desired changes. The implication is that if his reforms are carried through, the society will be wholly satisfactory.

That is a primitive way of viewing social change. The true task is to design a society (and institutions) capable of continuous change, continuous renewal, continuous responsiveness.

Beehive or Pluralism?

What would be the attributes of a society capable of such continuous renewal? First of all, it would be characterized by pluralism—by variety, alternatives, choices, and multiple foci of power and initiative. We have just such pluralism in our society today. But it would be folly to ignore that the logic of modern, large-scale organization tends to squeeze out pluralism, and to move us toward one comprehensively articulated system of power.

In the private sphere, corporations merge, newspapers merge, and small colleges and small businesses find survival increasingly difficult. As I contemplate this, I find myself treasuring every remaining bit of pluralism, everything that stands between us and the one all-embracing System. So, when I hear young people recommending the abolition of private enterprise, I am inclined to question whether they have weighed the consequences. It may not have occurred to them that socialism, or any other alternative to private enterprise, would inevitably mean a vast expansion of the federal government. General Motors would not disappear; it would simply be lumped with Ford, Chrysler, Boeing, Pan American and so on in a vast Ministry of Transportation. And bureaucracy would conquer all.

No society that cares about its own vitality will permit that to happen. A society that deadens the individual cuts off its own sources of renewal and cements over the seedbed of its future growth. But, unfortunately, the end toward which all modern societies, whatever their ideology, seem to be moving is the beehive model, in which the system perfects itself as the individual is steadily dwarfed. Our ideology tells us that every person is important, that organizations and institutions exist for individuals. But the trend I have described transforms individuals into specialist-links in larger systems, increasingly incapable of autonomous functioning.

Even the alert, informed, exceptional American is farther down the path toward the beehive model, more securely "locked in" to a specialist role in the society, than he realizes. He is more cowed by the overarching systems that govern our lives than he would be willing to admit. The whole style of modern social organization tells him in a thousand ways, "You aren't important. What you do won't make a difference." So he works within the lines of his own specialty, plays his own highly defined role and hopes that somehow everything will come out all right.

Everyone has noted the passivity that results. Carried to its logical end, it could be the death of this "self-governing" society.

New Kinds of Local Leadership

The society capable of continuous renewal will be one that develops to the fullest its human resources, that removes obstacles to individual fulfillment, that emphasizes education, lifelong learning and self-discovery. We shall have to work simultaneously along two parallel lines: we must ask the individual to accept certain kinds of responsibility, and we must create the institutional framework in which individual responsibility and participation are feasible.

It is not essential that *everyone* participate. As a matter of fact, if everyone suddenly did, the society would fly apart! But the fact that opportunities exist and that a good many people are taking advantage of them will affect the attitude of those who don't participate. The essence of it is that participation should be an available option.

The possibility of participation is closely linked to the revival of local government and local leadership. It is hard to feel individually responsible with respect to the invisible processes of a huge and distant government. Responsibility comes most readily when one can see the consequences of one's actions. That implies participation in a vital local community.

Now comes a tough and decisive question: Can action on the part of the individual at the grass roots ever really be effective?

It all depends on how we design our society. Local leadership in the old-fashioned sense—wise in the lore of the locality, but intensely parochial in its perspective—is dead. We must create a wholly new form and style of local leadership, skillful in relating its own efforts and programs to larger systems. Local leaders must understand how the economy of their area relates to larger economic trends, patterns and programs. They must understand that the significant gains in the years ahead will come through a creative interplay of federal, state and local levels.

The Need to Be Needed

We must identify those features of modern organization that strengthen the individual and those that diminish him. Given such analysis, we can design institutions responsive to human need, institutions that will strengthen and nourish each person, that will permit each individual the fulfillment that comes with the exercise of his talents. In short, we can build a society to man's measure—if we have the will.

The struggle begins with preservation of the natural resources and natural beauty of the land, and with control of environmental pollution. It must extend to considerations of population control, to the use of leisure, to the pace and space of life.

One of the least recognized of human motives is the need to be needed. The experience of recent years suggests that the *service* idea, as exemplified in the Peace Corps and VISTA, taps a rich vein of motivation in the American people. When people are serving, life is no longer meaningless. They no longer feel rootless or unconnected; they feel responsible. As we enable the individual to enjoy greater freedom, we must at the same time provide him with opportunities for allegiance and commitment to goals larger than himself. Otherwise, individual freedom degenerates into a sterile self-preoccupation.

Faith in Our Ideals

We can make great progress in improving the functioning of our society and still not have anything that will live or last unless we concern ourselves with the *values* that underlie the enterprise. If a society believes in nothing, if it does not generate in its members a sense of moral purpose, there is no possibility that it can develop the high level of motivation essential to renewal.

We have in the tradition of this nation a well-tested framework of values: justice, liberty, equality of opportunity, the worth and dignity of the individual, brotherhood, individual responsibility—all supremely compatible with social renewal. Our problem is not to find better values but to be faithful to those we profess—and to make them live in our institutions.

We cannot speak of our values apart from the down-to-earth programs that are necessary to put them into effect. For example: if we believe in individual dignity and responsibility, then we must do the necessary, sometimes expensive, often complicated things that will make it possible for each person to have a decent job if he wants one. We must provide the kind of education that will enable him to hold a job, the kinds of work training necessary to prepare him for specific lines of work. If he has reached adulthood without learning to read and write, we must offer him basic literacy education. If he has a physical impairment, we must see that he gets medical attention or rehabilitation services. And we must take any and all of the measures necessary to ensure that there is a job available when he is ready for it.

Call to Action

To redesign our society, there is heavy work ahead—work for able and courageous men and women who are willing to tackle the evils of the day in a problem-solving mood. We have plenty of debaters, plenty of blamers, plenty of provocateurs, plenty of people who treat public affairs as an opportunity for personal catharsis or glorification. We *don't* have plenty of problem-solvers.

A relevant call to action would address itself first to that complacent lump of self-satisfied Americans who fatten on the yield of this society but never bestir themselves to solve its problems. It would address itself to the powerful men who rest complacently with outworn institutions when they have it in their power to redesign those institutions. It would address itself to those Americans who are still uncommitted to the values we profess to cherish as a people.

As a people, we still have a choice. If we want a society on the beehive model, all we need do is relax—we'll drift into it. If we want a society built around the creative possibilities of the self-directing individual, then we have tasks to perform.

I am not proposing new duties; I am recalling old duties. Remember the Preamble to the Constitution? "We the people of the United States, in order to form a more perfect union, establish justice, insure domestic tranquility, provide for the common defense, promote the general welfare, and secure the blessings of liberty to ourselves and our posterity . . ." Great phrases, and the greatest of all is "We the people of the United States." Not we the public officials of the United States. Not we the certified experts on public administration. Not we who happen to have time to think about these things when we're not busy running our businesses or practicing our profession. Just we the people.

We, acting in our own communities across the nation, can pull this fragmented society together again. We can re-create an America in which men speak to one another in trust and mutual respect, sharing common objectives, working toward common goals. We can return this nation to a path of confidence and well-being. We can design a society capable of continuous renewal.

We can do these things. No one can do them for us.

4. To Establish Justice
to Insure Domestic Tranquility

Final Report of National Commission
on the Causes and Prevention of Violence

Violence in the United States has risen to alarmingly high levels. Whether one considers assassination, group violence, or individual acts of violence, the decade of the 1960s was considerably more violent than the several decades preceding it and ranks among the most violent in our history. The United States is the clear leader among modern, stable democratic nations in its rates of homicide, assault, rape, and robbery, and it is at least among the highest in incidence of group violence and assassination.

This high level of violence is dangerous to our society. It is disfiguring our society—making fortresses of portions of our cities and dividing our people into armed camps. It is jeopardizing some of our most precious institutions, among them our schools and universities—poisoning the spirit of trust and cooperation that is essential to their proper functioning. It is corroding the central political processes of our democratic society—substituting force and fear for argument and accommodation.

We have endured and survived other cycles of violence in our history. Today, however, we are more vulnerable to violence than ever before. Two-thirds of our people live in urban areas, where violence especially thrives. Individual and group specializations have intensified our dependence on one another. Men are no longer capable of solitary living and individual self-defense; men must live together and depend upon one another to observe the laws and keep the peace.

The American people know the threat. They demand that violence be brought to a halt. Violence must be brought under control—to safeguard life and property, and to make possible the creation of the understanding and cooperation needed to remedy underlying causes. No society can re-

SOURCE: *Final Report of the National Commission on the Causes and Prevention of Violence* (Washington, D.C.: Government Printing Office, 1969), pp. xv–xxxii.

main free, much less deal effectively with its fundamental problems, if its people live in fear of their fellow citizens; it is ancient wisdom that a house divided against itself cannot stand.

In this Report we suggest a number of specific measures for the better control of violence. We urge, for example, that the nation should double its investment in the prevention of crime and the administration of justice, as rapidly as that investment can be wisely planned and utilized. We recommend that central offices of criminal justice be created at the metropolitan level to make all parts of the criminal justice process—police, courts, corrections—function more effectively, and that private citizens' organizations be formed to work as counterparts of these offices in every major city in the nation. We urge that public officials, including law enforcement officers, intensify their efforts to develop more effective tactics in handling both peaceful demonstrations and violent disturbances. As we show by comparing successful and unsuccessful strategies of control of major mass demonstrations of the past few years, official behavior may determine whether protest remains peaceful or erupts into serious violence.

Further, we recommend the adoption of a national firearms policy that will limit the general availability of handguns.

Necessary as measures of control are, they are only a part of the answer. They do not cure the basic causes of violence. Violence is like a fever in the body politic: it is but the symptom of some more basic pathology which must be cured before the fever will disappear.

Indeed, if measures of control were this society's only response to violence, they would in the long run exacerbate the problem. The pyramiding of control measures could turn us into a repressive society, where the peace is kept primarily through official coercion rather than through willing obedience to law. That kind of society, where law is more feared than respected, where individual expression and movement are curtailed, is violent too—and it nurtures within itself the seeds of its own violent destruction.

In this Report, we analyze basic causes which underlie the chief varieties of contemporary violence. We make a number of recommendations directed to removing these causes. They cannot be eliminated entirely; even in a perfectly just society in which all have a fair and nondiscriminatory stake, there will always be some violent individuals, in rural as well as in urban areas, and measures of control will always be required to restrain them. But we can improve the conditions and opportunities of life for all citizens and thus reduce sharply the number who will commit violent acts.

Thus, we urge that young people must be given a greater role in determining their own destiny and in shaping the future course of our society. Responsible participation in decision-making may, for many, be a substitute for the violence that is born in frustration. We propose lowering the voting age, reforming the draft, and providing a massive expansion in opportunities for youth to engage in public service activities whose goals young people wholeheartedly embrace.

While we categorically condemn all illegal violence, including group

VIOLENT CRIME IN THE CITY

Violent Crime by City Size (U.S. 1960 and 1968)

Rates per 100,000 Pop.

Cities:	1960	1968
Over 250,000	293.7	773.2
100,000–250,000	154.0	325.3
50,000–100,000	104.3	220.5
25,000–50,000	70.1	150.8
10,000–25,000	57.3	126.6
Under 10,000	47.7	111.4
Suburban	N.A.	145.5
Rural	N.A.	96.5

Reported Urban Arrest Rates for Violent Crimes by Age

Rate per 100,000 Population U.S. 1967	Age	Increase in Rate 1958 to 1967
123.0	10–14	222.0%
408.2	15–17	102.5%
222.1	10–17	138.8%
436.1	18–24	45.5%
127.3	25+	41.1%
189.1	All Ages (10+)	65.7%

- Violent crime in the city is overwhelmingly committed by males.
- Violent crime in the city is concentrated especially among youths between the ages of fifteen and twenty-four.
- Violent crime in the city is committed primarily by individuals at the lower end of the occupational scale.
- Violent crime in the cities stems disproportionately from the ghetto slum where most Negroes live.
- The victims of assaultive violence in the cities generally have the same characteristics as the offenders: victimization rates are generally highest for males, youths, poor persons, and blacks. Robbery victims, however, are very often older whites.

SOURCE: Task Force Report, *Crimes of Violence* (National Commission on the Causes and Prevention of Violence, to be published)

violence,[1] as incompatible with the survival of a just, democratic, and humane society, we state emphatically that aggrieved groups must be permitted to exercise their constitutional rights of protest and public presentation of grievances. Accordingly, we believe the President should seek legislation that would confer jurisdiction upon the United States District Courts to grant injunctions, upon the request of the Attorney General or private persons, against the threatened or actual interference by any person, whether or not under color of state or federal law, with the rights of individuals or groups to freedom of speech, freedom of the press, peaceful assembly, and petition for redress of grievances.

We must have the perception to recognize injustices when they are called to our attention, and we must have the institutional flexibility to correct those injustices promptly. To enable the less affluent to obtain effective and peaceful redress of grievances, we recommend that additional steps should be taken to meet their needs for lawyers, and that state and local jurisdictions should be encouraged to experiment with the establishment of grievance agencies to serve all citizens.

The way in which we can make the greatest progress toward reducing violence in America is by taking the actions necessary to improve the conditions of family and community life for all who live in our cities, and especially for the poor who are concentrated in the ghetto slums. It is the ghetto slum that is disproportionately responsible for violent crime, by far the most acute aspect of the problem of violence in the United States today.

To be a young, poor male; to be undereducated and without means of escape from an oppressive urban environment; to want what the society claims is available (but mostly to others); to see around oneself illegitimate and often violent methods being used to achieve material gain; and to observe others using these means with impunity—all this is to be burdened with an enormous set of influences that pull many toward crime and delinquency. To be also a Negro, Puerto Rican or Mexican-American and subject to discrimination and segregation adds considerably to the pull of these other criminogenic forces.

Safety in our cities requires nothing less than progress in reconstructing urban life. We must meet the 1968 Housing Act's goal of a decent home for every American within a decade. We must take more effective steps to realize the goal, first set in the Employment Act of 1946, of a useful job at a reasonable wage for all who are able to work. We must provide better educational opportunities for all our children. We must act on current recommendations that those American families who cannot care for them-

[1] In Chapter 3 we define group violence as the unlawful threat or use of force by any group that results or is intended to result in the injury or forcible restraints or intimidation of persons, or the destruction or forcible seizure of property.

selves receive a basic annual income. We must restructure our local governments, restore their fiscal vitality and accomplish a host of other major tasks of the kind discussed in this Report.

As these brief introductory comments indicate, we believe that the twin objectives of the social order must be to make violence both unnecessary and unrewarding. To make violence unnecessary, our institutions must be capable of providing justice for all who live under them—of giving all a satisfactory stake in the normal life of the community and the nation. To make violence unrewarding, our institutions must be able to control violence when it occurs, and to do so firmly, fairly, and within the law.

The Preamble of our Constitution does not speak merely of justice or merely of order; it embraces both. Two of the six purposes set forth in the Preamble are to "establish justice" and to "insure domestic tranquility." If we are to succeed in preventing and controlling violence, we must achieve both of these goals.

We are well aware that our recommendations for attaining these objectives—and the recommendations of other national commissions before us—will require far-reaching improvements in our institutions and unprecedented levels of public funding. We adopt as our own the verdict which the Kerner Commission pronounced upon the scope and costs of its recommendations:

[T]hey neither probe deeper nor demand more than the problems which called them forth. There can be no higher priority for national action and no higher claim on the nation's conscience.

For the past three decades, the primary concerns of the federal government have been the national defense, the conduct of wars and foreign affairs, the growth of the economy, and, more recently, the conquest of space. These problems have consumed the major part of the public attention. They currently devour more than two-thirds of federal expenditures and approximately 50 percent of federal, state, and local expenditures combined.

Traditionally we have left the problems of social justice, provision of essential community services, and law enforcement primarily to the states and cities. In recent years, the federal government has made some major efforts in diverse fields such as rural development, civil rights, medical care, housing, employment, and education, but these efforts have been subordinated to the claims of the "national security."

Yet the federal government still collects the lion's share (about 65 percent) of all tax receipts. Tax revenue available to the states and cities falls woefully below what is needed to discharge their responsibilities. Each one

ASSASSINATION ATTEMPTS AGAINST PRESIDENTS AND PRESIDENTIAL CANDIDATES

Year	Victim	Assailant and Professed or Alleged Reason	Method of Attack and Result	Location	Activity of Victim at Time of Attack
1815	Andrew Jackson	Richard Lawrence; declared insane, said Jackson was preventing him from obtaining large sums of money.	pistol, misfired	Washington, D.C.	Attending funeral service in Capitol rotunda
1865	Abraham Lincoln	John W. Booth; loyalty to the Confederacy, revenge for defeat, slavery issue.	pistol, killed	Washington, D.C.	Attending theatrical performance in Ford Theatre
1881	James Garfield	Charles Guiteau; disgruntled officeseeker, supporter of opposite faction of Republican Party.	pistol, killed	Washington, D.C.	Passing through train station to go on vacation
1901	William McKinley	Leon F. Czolgosz; anarchist ideology	pistol, killed	Buffalo, N.Y.	Standing in reception line at Pan-American Exposition
1912	Theodore Roosevelt (Candidate)	John Schrank; declared insane, had vision that McKinley wanted him to avenge his death.	pistol, wounded	Milwaukee, Wisc.	Leaving hotel to deliver a campaign speech
1933	Franklin D. Roosevelt (President-Elect)	Guiseppe Zangara; hated rulers and capitalists.	pistol, bullets missed the President	Miami, Fla.	Leaving after delivering speech in Bayside Park
1950	Harry S. Truman	Oscar Collazo and Griselio Torresola; Puerto Rican independence.	automatic weapon, prevented from shooting at President.	Washington, D.C.	Inside Blair House as assassins attempted to break in
1963	John F. Kennedy	Lee H. Oswald; motive unknown.	rifle, killed	Dallas, Tex.	Taking part in motorcade through Dallas streets
1968	Robert F. Kennedy (Candidate)	Sirhan Sirhan; opposition to U.S. mid-East policy.	pistol, killed	Los Angeles, Calif.	Leaving primary campaign headquarters through hotel kitchen after delivering speech

SOURCE: Task Force Report, *Assassination and Political Violence* (National Commission on the Causes and Prevention of Violence, October, 1969)

percent rise in the Gross National Product increases the income of the federal government by one and one-half percent, while the normal income of state and city governments increases by less than half that percentage. Concentration on "national" and international problems at the expense of "local" and domestic concerns has left us with an enormous deficit of unmet social needs and deeply-felt social injustices.

Ironically, this gap has appeared despite rapidly accelerating technological, economic and social gains. For the first time in man's history, this nation is nearing the capability of releasing all citizens from the poverty and social privation that hitherto have been accepted as the inevitable lot of mankind. We have also achieved an enormous capacity to communicate: the poor, the black, and other deprived groups among us can see daily on their television sets what they are missing, and how near their release from bondage can be. But our institutions have not yet made it possible for an expectant populace to achieve what our economy and technology are becoming capable of providing.

In our judgment, the time is upon us for a reordering of national priorities and for a greater investment of resources in the fulfillment of two basic purposes of our Constitution—to "establish justice" and to "insure domestic tranquility."

We solemnly declare our conviction that this nation is entering a period in which our people need to be as concerned by the internal dangers to our free society as by any probable combination of external threats. We recognize that substantial amounts of funds cannot be transferred from sterile war purposes to more productive ones until our participation in the Vietnam war is ended. We also recognize that to make our society essentially free of poverty and discrimination, and to make our sprawling urban areas fit to inhabit, will cost a great deal of money and will take a great length of time. We believe, however, that we can and should make a major decision now to reassess our national priorities by placing these objectives in the first rank of the nation's goals.

The decision that has the greatest effect on the level of our expenditures for these objectives is what we decide to spend on the national defense. For three decades, the national defense has ranked first by far in our scale of priorities, much of the time necessarily so. With occasional exceptions, whatever the Administration has requested for the Armed Forces has been readily granted. Since 1939 there have been a number of occasions when the Administration's budget requests for the Armed Forces have been exceeded by Congressional appropriations; for most other federal programs the opposite is true. For example, actual appropriations for the general welfare (health, labor, education, housing, pollution, and law enforcement) are currently running more than five billion dollars annually below the amounts previously authorized by the Congress.

Our Commission is not competent to recommend a specific level of national defense expenditures. We recognize that without the deterrent capability essential for security against external attack, internal freedom and security would not be possible. It is to be expected that our military leaders will, like other government officials, stress the extreme urgency of the programs under their charge. But we believe the time has come to question whether expenditures for the general welfare should continue to be subordinated to those for national defense.

Defense expenditures, stated in 1968 prices, fell from about 78 billion dollars in 1953 (at the end of the Korean War) to about 60 billion dollars in 1954 and remained at that level for the decade 1955 to 1964. But by 1968 they had risen again to the present 81 billion dollar annual level as the result of our major commitment of troops to Vietnam.[2]

Federal expenditures for the general welfare, while they have increased substantially over the past several years, are now approximately 60 billion dollars, of which $25 billion represents social security payments.

As a first step, we should try to reverse this relationship. When our participation in the Vietnam War is concluded, we recommend increasing annual general welfare expenditures by about 20 billion dollars (stated in 1968 dollars), partly by reducing military expenditures and partly by use of increased tax revenues resulting from the growth of the Gross National Product. We suggest this only as an initial goal; as the Gross National Product and tax revenues continue to rise, we should strive to keep military expenditures level (in constant dollars), while general welfare expenditures should continue to increase until essential social goals are achieved.[3]

Based on estimates of the Council of Economic Advisers,[4] the funds needed to achieve this goal without inflationary consequences could be obtained from two sources:

1. The end of the Vietnam war should reduce defense expenditures by 19 billion dollars annually. The Council anticipates that this reduction will be offset in part by war-end program adjustments and deferred weapons programs.

---

[2] For fiscal 1970, the budgeted figure is $77 billion.

[3] Some experts believe that since military expenditures were successfully held to an annual level of 60 billion dollars (in 1968 prices) for the decade from 1955 to 1964, a comparable plateau can and should be maintained for the decade of the seventies. Indeed, it has been urged that, assuming the success of strategic arms limitation talks and a reevaluation of our foreign commitments, it would be feasible to hold the military budget for the early 1970s to 50 billion dollars (at 1969 prices). See Kaysen. "Military Strategy, Military Forces and Arms Control," in *Agenda for the Nation* (Washington, D.C.: Brookings Institution, 1969), p. 549.

[4] Annual Report of the Council of Economic Advisers, January, 1969, pp. 199–200.

Hence, defense expenditures should go down to about 65 billion dollars (at 1968 prices).[5]

2. The Gross National Product is expected to increase over the next decade (in constant dollars) at the rate of about four percent a year. The same should be true of federal tax revenues, which should grow in real terms at an annual increment of approximately 15 billion dollars.[6] Of this amount, approximately half will be required to meet expected annual increases for "baseline" federal non-defense expenditures other than general welfare programs. Hence, about seven or eight billion dollars more each year than the preceding year should be available for new and expanded programs in the general welfare field.

Whether somewhat more or less than the amounts we have indicated should be provided to overcome social ills is not the important point.[7] What is important is that the people of this nation recognize both the possibilities and the need for choice. For an entire generation, we have necessarily been more aware of and responsive to the external dangers to our society than to the internal dangers. In this Commission's opinion, the internal dangers now demand a greater awareness and a more substantial response—one that can only be made if we face the need to reorder our priorities. It is time to balance the risks and precautions we take abroad against those we take here at home.

The Department of Health, Education, and Welfare has made a suggestion which merits careful consideration as a potentially valuable supplemental step toward reordering national priorities, namely, the preparation of an "Annual Social Report." [8] The Annual Social Report, comparable to the present Annual Economic Report, would provide us with a set of

[5] At estimated 1972 prices, for example, actual outlays would be 73 billion. At this point, defense expenditures would be at seven percent of forecast GNP, as compared to perhaps eight percent at present. In other industrially advanced democratic countries, according to the Institute for Strategic Studies, defense expenditures (in 1966) were 6.4 percent of GNP for the United Kingdom, 4.4 percent in France, 3.6 percent in West Germany, 3.3 percent in Italy, 2.2 percent in Canada and 1.1 percent in Japan. For Soviet Russia, the estimated figure is 8.9 percent, but this represents a total 1966 defense outlay of less than 30 billion dollars as compared to about 68 billion dollars for the United States.

[6] This estimate assumes that the present 10 percent surcharge will have been repealed, but that other tax reform measures will be neutral in their effect on aggregate revenues. Any substantial reduction in federal tax revenues incidental to tax reform will make it more difficult to reorder our priorities as we have proposed.

[7] We further note that the same point can be strongly made for other non-military categories of expenditure that have been built into the federal budget, including agricultural and maritime subsidies, the postal service as presently structured, and space exploration. See Schultze, "Budget Alternatives After Vietnam" in *Agenda for the Nation* (Brookings, 1969), p. 44.

[8] *Toward a Social Report,* Government Printing Office, 1969.

measurements—of "social indicators"—on how well we have done in providing housing, education, health care, public safety, and opportunities for
the upward advancement of all sectors of our population. It would tell us
whether the disadvantaged groups among us have been advancing at a rate
sufficient to foster hope and to quiet the desperation that drives men to
violence. It would significantly aid the nation and its leaders in establishing national priorities.

The Social Report would be prepared by social scientists recruited for
stated periods of public service from among the nation's best scholars, just
as the members and staff of the Council of Economic Advisers are today.
They could be organized as a Council of Social Advisers, as are the Economic Advisers, or in some other visible and independent form. A major
function of the social science staff would be to develop tools for measuring
the comparative effectiveness of social programs. While we have learned a
good deal about social stresses and the gross causative factors that require
correction, we still know very little about whether particular remedial programs work at all, which ones work better than others, and why. We lack
practicable means for measuring cost-benefit ratios, for establishing and
observing parallel programs with significant variables, and for putting an
end to programs which have failed to justify their continuance.[9] A central
staff charged with this responsibility could do much to improve the accuracy of our social planning and the efficacy of on-going programs.

Two decades ago, the Council of Economic Advisers was created by the
Full Employment Act of 1946, amid much skepticism about the "science"
of economics and particularly about the wisdom and effect of governmental efforts to stimulate or restrain economic activity. Today we recognize
the importance of the government's economic role and of national economic measurements, imprecise and imperfect as the economist's tools still
are. The other social sciences may now have as much potential for inform-
ing wise government policy as economics had twenty years ago.

In a democratic society, the citizens possess the basic social power, and
national priorities reflect the value judgments of the majority. Skeptics may
thus take a pessimistic view of this Commission's recommendation that our
national priorities be reordered. They will point, for example, to the reluctance of the public, despite the penetrating reports and the excellent recommendations of previous presidential commissions, to take the comprehensive actions needed to curb crime, eliminate racial discrimination, and
alleviate the problems of the ghetto poor. They will point especially to
middle-class America—to the "forgotten American"—and his concern

[9] Daniel P. Moynihan, *Maximum Feasible Misunderstanding* (New York: MacMillan, 1968), pp. 190–203.

over some consequences of racial integration, his rebellion against rising taxes, his distrust of dissent on the campus and protest movements in the capital. How realistic is it, they will ask, to think that the majority of Americans will support a reallocation of our national resources to deal with social problems?

Skepticism is understandable. But the majority of Americans have always responded constructively to national crises when they have been fully informed and responsibly led. The "silent majority," like most other Americans, do not wish to surrender any of the most important freedoms of our open society—freedom of movement, freedom from harm, freedom from fear. They stand to benefit from the programs necessary to retain these freedoms just as much as any disadvantaged minority. All Americans—the majority and our various minorities—must come to grips with the basic causes of violence in our society and do what must be done to achieve liberty and justice for all.

Some, with little faith in our nation, predict that majority indifference will result in a violent revolution of some kind. Indeed, nihilists and anarchists openly espouse this course. We see signs, however, that a peaceful revolution is already under way: a spirit of needed reform is rising steadily among the people and in the ranks of local and national leaders. We see a growing readiness to formulate new values, to set new priorities, and to make firm commitments now, to be honored as soon as resources are available.

Some ordinary citizens feel they can do nothing to influence the direction and the destiny of their nation. But more and more Americans are proving this to be a myth. A growing number of our citizens have found they need not stand idle while our cities rot, people live in fear, householders build individual fortresses, and human and financial resources flow to less urgent endeavors. A new generation of Americans is emerging, with the energy and the talent and the determination to fulfill the promise of the nation. As it ever was, the young—idealistic but earnest, inexperienced but dedicated—are the spearheads of the drive toward change, and increasing numbers of adult Americans are joining their ranks.

When in man's long history other great civilizations fell, it was less often from external assault than from internal decay. Our own civilization has shown a remarkable capacity for responding to crises and for emerging to higher pinnacles of power and achievement. But our most serious challenges to date have been external—the kind this strong and resourceful country could unite against. While serious external dangers remain, the graver threats today are internal: haphazard urbanization, racial discrimination, disfiguring of the environment, unprecedented interdependence, the dislocation of human identity and motivation created by an affluent society —all resulting in a rising tide of individual and group violence.

The greatness and durability of most civilizations has been finally determined by how they have responded to these challenges from within. Ours
will be no exception.

5. Youth Revolt: The Future Is Now

Margaret Mead

Our present crisis has been variously attributed to the overwhelming rapidity of change, the collapse of the family, the decay of capitalism, the
triumph of a soulless technology, and, in wholesale repudiation, to the
final breakdown of the Establishment. Behind these attributions there is a
more basic conflict between those for whom the present represents no
more than an intensification of our existing cofigurative culture, in which
peers are more than ever replacing parents as the significant models of behavior, and those who contend that we are in fact entering a totally new
phase of cultural evolution.

Most commentators, in spite of their differences in viewpoint, still see
the future essentially as an extension of the past. Edward Teller can still
speak of the outcome of a nuclear war as a state of destruction relatively
no more drastic than the ravages wrought by Genghis Khan, and historians
can point out that time and again civilization has survived the crumbling
of empires. Similarly, many authorities treat as no more than an extreme
form of adolescent rebellion the repudiation of present and past by the dissident youth of every persuasion in every kind of society in the world.

Theorists who emphasize the parallels between past and present in their
interpretations of the generation gap ignore the irreversibility of the
changes that have taken place since the beginning of the Industrial Revolu-

SOURCE: *Saturday Review* (January 10, 1970), 23–26, 113. Adapted from the chapter
entitled "The Future Prefigurative Cultures and Unknown Children," from Margaret Mead, *Culture and Commitment*, (New York: Doubleday, 1970). Copyright
© 1970 by Margaret Mead. Reprinted by permission of Doubleday & Company,
Inc.

tion. This is especially striking in their handling of modern technological development, which they treat as comparable in its effects to the changes that occurred as one civilization in the past took over from another such techniques as agriculture, script, navigation, or the organization of labor and law.

One urgent priority, I believe, is to examine the nature of change in the modern world, including its speed and dimensions, so that we can better understand the distinctions that must be made between change in the past and that which is now ongoing. To do so, I make distinctions among three different kinds of culture: *post-figurative,* in which children learn primarily from their forebears; *cofigurative,* in which both children and adults learn from their peers; and *prefigurative,* in which adults learn also from their children.

Although it is possible to discuss both post-figurative and cofigurative cultures in terms of slow or rapid change without specifying the nature of the process and to compare past and present situations when the focus is kept on generation relationships and on the type of modeling through which a culture is transmitted, it is only when one specifies the nature of the process that the contrast between past and present change becomes clear.

The primary evidence that our present situation is unique, without any parallel in the past, is that the generation gap is worldwide. The particular events taking place in England, Pakistan, the United States, New Guinea, or elsewhere are not enough to explain the unrest that is stirring modern youth everywhere. Recent technological change or the handicaps imposed by its absence, revolution or the suppression of revolutionary activities, the crumbling of faith in ancient creeds or the attraction of new creeds—all these serve only as partial explanations of the particular forms taken by youth revolt in different countries.

Concentration on particularities can only hinder the search for an explanatory principle. Instead, it is necessary to strip the occurrences in each country of their superficial, national, and immediately temporal aspects. The desire for a liberated form of communism in Czechoslovakia, the search for "racial" equality in the United States, the desire to liberate Japan from American military influence—these are particularistic forms. Youthful activism is common to them all. The key question is this: What are the new conditions that have brought about the revolt of youth around the world?

The first of these is the emergence of a world community. For the first time human beings throughout the world, in their information about and responses to one another, have become a community that is united by shared knowledge and danger. As far as we know, no such single, interacting community has existed within archaeological time. The largest clusters of interacting human groups have always been fragments of a still larger unknown whole, and the idea that all men are, in the same sense, human beings always has been either unreal or a mystical belief.

The events of the past twenty-five years changed this drastically. Exploration has been complete enough to convince us that there are no humanoid types on the planet except our own species. Worldwide air travel and globe-encircling TV satellites have turned us into one community, in which events taking place on one side of the earth become immediately and simultaneously available to peoples everywhere else. No artist or political censor has time to intervene and edit as a leader is shot or a flag is planted on the moon. The world is a community, though it still lacks the forms of organization and the sanctions by which a political community can be governed.

Men who are the carriers of vastly different cultural traditions are entering the present at the same point in time. It is as if, all around the world, men were converging on identical immigration posts, each with its identifying sign: YOU ARE NOW ABOUT TO ENTER THE POST-WORLD-WAR-II WORLD AT GATE I (GATE 23, etc.). Whoever they are and wherever their particular points of entry may be, all men are equally immigrants into the new era. They are like the immigrants who came as pioneers to a new land, lacking all knowledge of what demands new conditions of life would make upon them. Those who came later could take their peer groups as models. But among the first comers, the young adults had as models only their own tentative adaptations and innovations.

Today, everyone born and bred before World War II is such an immigrant in time as his forebears were in space—a pioneer struggling to grapple with the unfamiliar conditions of life in a new era. Like all immigrants and pioneers, these immigrants in time are the bearers of older cultures, but today they represent all the cultures of the world. And all of them, whether they are sophisticated French intellectuals or members of a remote New Guinea tribe, land-bound peasants in Haiti or nuclear physicists, have certain characteristics in common.

Whoever they are, these immigrants grew up under skies across which no satellite had ever flashed. Their perception of the past was an edited version of what had happened. Their perception of the immediate present was limited to what they could take in through their own eyes and ears and to the edited versions of other men's sensory experience and memories. Their conception of the future was essentially one in which change was incorporated into a deeper changelessness. The industrialist or military planner, envisaging what a computer, not yet constructed, might make possible, treated it as another addition to the repertoire of inventions that have enhanced man's skills. It expanded what men could do, but did not change the future.

When the first atom bomb was exploded at the end of World War II, only a few individuals realized that all humanity was entering a new age. And to this day the majority of those over twenty-five have failed to grasp emotionally, however well they may grasp intellectually, the difference between any war in which, no matter how terrible the casualties, mankind will survive, and one in which there will be no survivors. They continue to think that a war, fought with more lethal weapons, would just be a worse war. Our thinking still binds us to the past—to the world as it existed in our childhood and youth.

We still hold the seats of power and command the resources and the skills necessary to keep order and organize the kinds of societies we know about. We control the educational systems, the apprenticeship systems, the career ladders up which the young must climb. Nevertheless, we have passed the point of no return. We are committed to life in an unfamiliar setting; we are making do with what we know.

The young generation, however—the articulate young rebels all around the world who are lashing out against the controls to which they are subjected—are like the first generation born into a new country. They are at home in this time. Satellites are familiar in their skies. They have never known a time when war did not threaten annihilation. When they are given the facts, they can understand immediately that continued pollution of the air and water and soil will soon make the planet uninhabitable and that it will be impossible to feed an indefinitely expanding world population. As members of one species in an underdeveloped world community they recognize that invidious distinctions based on race and caste are anachronisms. They insist on the vital necessity of some form of world order.

No longer bound by the simplified linear sequences dictated by the printed word, they live in a world in which events are presented to them in all their complex immediacy. In their eyes the killing of an enemy is not qualitatively different from the murder of a neighbor. They cannot reconcile our efforts to save our own children by every known means with our readiness to destroy the children of others with napalm. They know that the people of one nation alone cannot save their own children; each holds the responsibility for all others' children.

Although I have said they *know* these things, perhaps I should say that this is how they *feel*. Like the first generation born in a new country, they listen only half-comprehendingly to their parents' talk about the past. For as the children of pioneers had no access to the landscapes whose memories could still move their parents to tears, the young today cannot share their parents' responses to events that deeply moved them in the past. But this is not all that separates the young from their elders. Watching, they can see that their elders are groping, that they are managing clumsily and often unsuccessfully the tasks imposed on them by the new conditions. The young do not know what must be done, but they feel that there must be a better way and that they must find it.

Today, nowhere in the world are there elders who know what the children know, no matter how remote and simple the societies are in which the children live. In the past there were always some elders who knew more than any children in terms of their experience of having grown up within a cultural system. Today there are none. It is not only that parents are no longer guides, but that there are no guides, whether one seeks them in one's own country or abroad. There are no elders who know what those who have been reared within the last twenty years know about the world into which they were born.

True, in many parts of the world the parental generation still lives by a post-figurative set of values. From parents in such cultures children may learn that there have been unquestioned absolutes, and this learning may carry over into later experience as an expectation that absolute values can and should be re-established.

There are still parents who answer such child's questions as why he must go to bed, or eat his vegetables, or learn to read with simple assertions: Because it is *right* to do so, because *God* says so, or because *I* say so. These parents are preparing the way for the re-establishment of post-figurative elements in the culture. But these elements will be far more rigid and intractable than in the past because they must be defended in a world in which conflicting points of view, rather than orthodoxies, are prevalent.

Most parents, however, are too uncertain to assert old dogmatisms. They do not know how to teach these children who are so different from what they themselves once were, and most children are unable to learn from parents and elders they will never resemble. In the past, in the United States, children of immigrant parents pleaded with them not to speak their foreign language in public and not to wear their outlandish foreign clothes. They knew the burning shame of being, at the same time, unable to repudiate their parents and unable to accept simply and naturally their way of speaking and doing things. But in time they learned to find new teachers as guides, to model their behavior on that of more adapted age mates, and to slip in, unnoticed, among a group whose parents were more bearable.

Today, the dissident young discover very rapidly that this solution is no longer possible. The breach between themselves and their parents also exists between their friends and their friends' parents and between their friends and their teachers.

These young dissidents realize the critical need for immediate world action on problems that affect the whole world. What they want is, in some way, to begin all over again. They are ready to make way for something new by a kind of social bulldozing—like the bulldozing in which every tree and feature of the landscape is destroyed to make way for a new community. Awareness of the reality of the crisis (which is, in fact, perceived most accurately not by the young, but by their discerning and prophetic elders) and the sense the young have that their elders do not understand the modern world, because they do not understand their children, has produced a kind of rebellion in which planned reformation of the present system is almost inconceivable.

Nevertheless, those who have no power also have no routes to power except through those against whom they are rebelling. In the end, it was men who gave the vote to women; and it will be the House of Lords that votes to abolish the House of Lords—as also, in the final analysis, nations will act to limit national sovereignty. Effective, rapid evolutionary change, in which no one is guillotined or forced into exile, depends on the cooperation of a large number of those in power with the dispossessed who are seeking power.

These, in brief, are the conditions of our time. These are the two generations—pioneers in a new era and their children—who have as yet to find a way of communicating about the world in which both live, though their perceptions of it are so different. No one knows what the next steps should be. Recognizing that this is so is, I submit, the beginning of an answer.

I believe we are on the verge of developing a new kind of culture, one that is as much a departure in style from cofigurative cultures as the institutionalization of cofiguration in orderly—and disorderly—change was a departure from the post-figurative style. I call this new style "prefigurative," because in this new culture it will be the unborn child, already conceived but still in the womb—not the parent and grandparent—that represents what is to come. This is a child whose sex and appearance and capabilities are unknown, but who will need imaginative, innovative, and dedicated adult care far beyond any we give today.

No one can know in advance what the child will become—how swift his limbs will be, what will delight his eye, whether his tempo will be fast or slow. No one can know how his mind will work—whether he will learn best from sight or sound or touch or movement. But knowing what we do not know and cannot predict, we can construct an environment in which a child, still unknown, can be safe and can grow and discover himself and the world.

Love and trust, based on dependency and answering care, made it possible for the individual who had been reared in one culture to move into another, transforming, without destroying, his earlier learning. It is seldom the first generation of voluntary immigrants and pioneers who cannot meet the demands of a new environment. Their previous learning carries them through. But unless they embody what is new post-figuratively, they cannot pass on to their children what they had acquired through their own early training—the ability to learn from others the things their parents could not teach them.

Parents, in a world where there are no more knowledgeable others to whom they can commit the children they themselves cannot teach, feel uncertain and helpless. Still believing that there should be answers, parents ask how they can tell their children what is right. So some try to solve the problem by advising their children, very vaguely, that they will have to figure it out for themselves. And some parents ask what the others are doing. But this resource of a cofigurative culture is becoming meaningless to parents who feel that the "others"—their children's age mates—are moving in ways that are unsafe for their own children to emulate, and who find that they do not understand what their children figure out for themselves.

It is the adults who still believe that there is a safe and socially approved road to a kind of life they have not experienced who react with the greatest anger and bitterness to the discovery that what they had hoped for no longer exists for their children. These are the parents, the trustees, the legislators, the columnists and commentators who denounce most vocally what is happening in schools and colleges and universities in which they had placed their hopes for their children.

Today, as we gain a better understanding of the circular processes through which culture is developed and transmitted, we recognize that man's most human characteristic is not his ability to learn, which he shares with many other species, but his ability to teach and store what others have developed and taught him. In the past men relied on the least elaborate part of the circular system—the dependent learning by children—for continuity of transmission and for the embodiment of the new. Now, with our greater understanding of the process, we must cultivate the most flexible and complex part of the system: the behavior of adults. We must, in fact, teach ourselves how to alter adult behavior; we must create new models for adults who can teach their children not what to learn, but how to learn, and not what they should be committed to, but the value of commitment.

In doing this we must recognize explicitly that the paths by which we came into the present can never be traversed again. The past is the road by which we have arrived where we are. Older forms of culture have provided us with the knowledge, techniques, and tools necessary for our contemporary civilization.

The freeing of men's imagination from the past depends on the development of a new kind of communication with those who are most deeply involved with the future—the young who were born in the new world. In the past, in cofigurational cultures, the elders were gradually cut off from limiting the future of their children. Now the development of prefigurational cultures will depend on the existence of a continuing dialogue in which the young, free to act on their own initiative, can lead their elders in the direction of the unknown. Then the older generation will have access to the new experiential knowledge, without which no meaningful plans can be made. It is only with the direct participation of the young, who have that knowledge, that we can build a viable future.

Instead of directing their rebellion toward the retrieval of a grandparental utopian dream, as the Maoists seem to be doing with the young activists in China, we must learn together with the young how to take the next steps. Out of their new knowledge—new to the world and new to us—must come the questions to those who are already equipped by education and experience to search for answers. The children, the young, must ask these questions that we would never think to ask, but enough trust must be re-established so that the elders will be permitted to work with them on the answers.

I feel that we can change into a prefigurative culture, consciously, delightedly, and industriously, rearing unknown children for an unknown world. But to do it we must relocate the future.

Here we can take a cue from the young who seem to want instant utopias. They say the future is now. This seems unreasonable and impetuous, and in some of the demands they make it is unrealizable in concrete detail; but here again, I think, they give us the way to reshape our thinking. We must place the future, like the unborn child in the womb of a woman, within a community of men, women, and children, among us, already here, already to be nourished and succored and protected, already in need of things for which, if they are not prepared before it is born, it will be too late. So, as the young say, the future is now.

6. Should the Teacher Always Be Neutral?

George S. Counts

I

It is impossible to discuss the question under consideration without an understanding of the role of culture in the life of man. First of all, we must realize that every human being is born helpless, but with infinite potentials in all directions. If left alone, he would quickly perish. But being born in a society with its cultural heritage he may rise above the angels or sink below the level of the brute. We can see this demonstrated throughout the ages and obviously in this twentieth century. Although every individual is unique, he is molded by his culture and thus becomes a human being.[1] Quotations from two very distinguished anthropologists are most appropriate here. Graham Wallas in his *Our Social Heritage,* published in 1921, wrote that "we have become, one may say, biologically parasitic upon our social heritage." Bronislaw Malinowski in the last of his great works, *Freedom and Civilization,* published after his death in 1944, said approximately the same thing in these words: "This brief outline of the cultural background of our problem in evolutionary perspective was given to show first and foremost that not a single human act, relevant to the science of man, occurs outside the context of culture." A distinguished British mathematician, H. Levy, in his *The Universe of Science* (1932) places the capstone on the argument: *"It* [our culture] *has inherited us."* Consequently, the nature of the human being is dependent on the culture which inherits him. Here is the supreme imposition.

Since the origin of *homo sapiens,* education, in both its informal and its formal aspects, has embraced the total process of inducting the young into

[1] We must realize, however, that no two individuals are identical and that every individual responds to his culture in terms of his own unique character.

SOURCE: *Phi Delta Kappan,* LI, 4 (December 1969), 186–89. Reprinted by permission of the publisher and author.

a given society with its culture, its ways of acting, feeling, and thinking, its language, its tools, its institutions, its ethical and aesthetic values, its basic ideas, religious doctrines, and philosophical presuppositions. It is therefore not an autonomous process governed by its own laws and everywhere the same. This process begins at birth and continues on through the years. And we are beginning to realize that the preschool years, the period of infancy and early childhood, are by far the most important years in the development of the talents and the molding of the character of the individual. During my first trip to the Soviet Union in 1927 I became acquainted with the Commissar of Education, Anatole Lunacharsky. One day when we were discussing the Soviet program of preschool education he repeated an old Russian proverb: "We can mold a child of 5–6 years into anything we wish; at the age of 8–9 we have to bend him; at the age of 16–17 we must break him; and thereafter, one may well say, 'only the grave can correct a hunchback!' "

Without this imposition of the cultural, as all of this makes clear, man would not be man, except in a biological sense—if he could survive. But the fact should be emphasized that cultures are extremely diverse. Consequently, a human being born and reared in one culture may differ greatly from one born and reared in another culture. I have often told my students that a person doesn't see with his eyes or hear with his ears, but with what is behind his eyes or behind his ears. And this depends on his native culture and his experience therein. This principle applies even to physical objects, such as the sun, the moon, and the stars. Obviously, the moon will never again be what it was before the flight of Apollo 11.

The language which is imposed on the child from the moment of his birth may well be regarded as symbolic of the culture. Lewis Mumford in his *The Myth of the Machine* (1968) demonstrates very clearly that in the evolution of man language has played a much greater role than the machine. Indeed, without language man would not be man. And, of course, we all know that there are many different languages. But the truth is not sufficiently emphasized that languages differ, not only in forms and sounds, but also in values. One may well say that every language, in a sense, constitutes a world apart from others. The translation of one language into another is often difficult because the "same" word will differ in meaning from one language to another. A dictionary will be of some assistance, but it will not solve all the problems. The basic idea in these observations is well documented in a great book entitled *The Poetry of Freedom* (1945), edited by William Rose Benét and Norman Cousins, which is a collection of poems from the major languages of the world. More than two-thirds of the volume, 554 of the 806 pages, are given to poems from the English-speaking peoples. And I know that the editors did everything they could to find appropriate poems from other languages. If they had chosen some other theme, such as worship of nature or military valor or romantic love, I am certain that the proportions would have been different. It is clear therefore that language constitutes a tremendous imposition on the individual. I have often told my students that, if we do not want to impose anything on the individual, we should not allow him to learn a language until he becomes 21 years of age and then let him choose the language he prefers.

II

A given society is always a bearer of a particular culture, and societies vary as their cultures vary. Consequently, an education that would be appropriate for one society might destroy another. After the first Sputnik soared into outer space in October, 1957, the question was asked over and over again: Is Soviet education superior to ours? The answer, of course, is that the question makes no sense because the two societies are so profoundly different. However, if the question were presented in this form the answer would be different: "Does Soviet education serve the purposes of Soviet society better than our education serves the purposes of our society?" In this case the answer might be in the affirmative, since education for a democracy is far more difficult than education for a dictatorship.

This truth has been recognized through the ages. More than two centuries ago Montesquieu in his great classic, *On the Spirit of the Laws,* wrote that "it is in a republican [democratic] government that the whole power of education is required." The reason for this resides in the fact that such a government must rest on "virtue," which involves "self-renunciation" and is "ever arduous and painful." Also, it "requires a constant preference of public to private interest," and "to inspire such love ought to be the principal business of education." Thomas Jefferson, the father of our democracy, agreed with Montesquieu. In 1824, the year before he died, he wrote in a letter to a friend: "The qualifications for self-government are not innate. They are the result of habit and long training." Horace Mann, father of our common school, saw clearly the relation of education to social and political systems. In his Ninth Annual Report (1845), he warned the citizens of Massachusetts: "If there are not two things wider asunder than freedom and slavery, then must the course of training which fits children for these opposite conditions of life be as diverse as the points to which they lead." Finally, Herbert Spencer, in his *The Americans* (1892), issued the following challenge to our education: "The republican form of government is the highest form of government; but because of this it requires the highest form of human nature—a type nowhere at present existing." In spite of the unprecedented expansion of our schools in this century, we have obviously failed to develop the "form of human nature required." To have done so would have required a revolutionary form of imposition. Political liberty, with all of its demands on human nature, if it is to endure, is certainly one of the most extraordinary impositions on the mind and character of man in the entire history of *homo sapiens*.

We must realize also that we are living not only in a very special kind of society but also in an age of revolution as wide as the planet. Henry Steele Commager, in his *The American Mind* (1950), warned us that "the decade of the nineties [was] the watershed of American history"—a watershed between an "America predominantly agricultural" and an "America predominantly urban and industrial." And Carl Bridenbaugh, in his inaugural address as president of the American Historical Association in 1963 stated without equivocation: "It is my conviction that the greatest turning point in all human history, of which we have any record, has occurred within the twentieth century." Thus, in view of the swiftness of social change, we may say that an education which may be appropriate for one generation may not be appropriate for another. We are consequently confronted today with William F. Ogburn's "cultural lag" and Alfred North Whitehead's generation gap. The fact is that since crossing the great watershed we have never sat down and considered seriously how our children and youth should spend their years in our urbanized and industrialized society. Also, with the reduction of the earth to the dimensions of a neighborhood we have failed to sense that the age of tribalism and nationalism is closing and that a new age of internationalism is well over the horizon. The nature of the imposition must be radically altered.

III

A few words in closing about the school. We must realize that whenever choices are made in the launching of a program values are involved. This is obviously true in the shaping of the curriculum, the selection of textbooks, the giving of grades, the organization of social activities, the construction of a school building, the hanging of pictures and paintings on the walls of a schoolroom, and in the selection of a teacher. I have often told my students that, if we want to avoid imposing anything on our children, we should alter the architectural style of the building every day. Also I call their attention to the fact that our arithmetic textbooks transmit to the younger generation countless social, political, and moral ideas—for the most part a white middle-class culture. And we know that our history textbooks, until very recently, practically excluded the Negro.

The need for developing the independent and critical mind in the members of the younger generation is implicit in much that I have written and is clearly a form of imposition. However, something more must be said. The student should not be encouraged to engage in criticism just for the sake of criticism. The truly critical mind is one of the most precious resources of a free society. At the same time such a mind should be highly disciplined. We should never disregard the basic thesis of Carl Becker in his *Freedom and Responsibility in the American Way of Life* (1945), one of the most insightful books in the literature of our democracy. That thesis is that with every right or freedom there goes a responsibility. The alternative is chaos and anarchy. The critical mind should be armed with knowledge and understanding, and perhaps with a modicum of humility and wisdom. Even a scientist must undergo and practice a severe discipline. He must practice the intellectual virtues of accuracy, precision, truthfulness, open-mindedness, and absolute integrity. The limits of freedom in the rearing of the child are thus expressed by Bronislaw Malinowski in his *Freedom and Civilization:* "We see quite clearly why the freedom of the child, in the sense of letting him do what he wishes and as he likes, is unreal. In the interest of his own organism he has constantly to be trammeled in education from acts which are biologically dangerous or are culturally useless." And Judge Learned Hand, one of our foremost students of jurisprudence, warned us: "A society in which men recognize no check upon their freedom soon becomes a society where freedom is a possession of only a savage few."

The big question therefore is not whether we should impose anything on the child in the process of education but *what* we should impose. In the swiftly changing world of the twentieth century we must certainly examine our cultural heritage critically in the light of the great and inescapable realities of the present age and the trends toward tomorrow. What this means, in my opinion, is to present to the younger generation a vision of the possibility of finally fulfilling the great promise of America expressed in the Declaration of Independence: "We hold these truths to be self-evident, that all men are created equal, that they are endowed by their Creator with certain unalienable Rights, that among these are Life, Liberty, and the pursuit of Happiness." Clearly, if science and technology can show us how to fly to the moon and circumnavigate the planets, we should be able to employ these powerful forces for bringing our practices into harmony with our historic professions.

A final illustration of the critical importance of the question of imposition in the rearing of the young in our democracy is clearly revealed in our treatment of the Negro down through the generations. Gunnar Myrdal, a renowned Swedish social scientist, in his great two-volume work, *An American Dilemma* (1944), issues a challenge that we can disregard only at our peril. In his first chapter, entitled "American Ideals and the American Conscience," he states: "America, compared to every other country in Western civilization, large or small, has the *most explicitly expressed* system of general ideals in reference to human interrelations." These ideals embrace "the essential dignity of the individual human being, of the fundamental equality of all men, and of certain inalienable rights to freedom, justice, and a fair opportunity." Our dilemma is the consequence of the great gap between our professed ideals and our practices. He adds, therefore, that "the treatment of the Negro is America's greatest and most conspicuous scandal, . . . America's greatest failure." And then he relates this condition to the subject of my article in the following generalization: "The simple fact is that an educational offensive against racial intolerance, going deeper than the reiteration of the 'glittering generalities' in the nation's political creed, has never seriously been attempted in America." Certainly a major problem confronting our program of education is the resolution of this *dilemma* in the shortest possible period of time. But to achieve this goal the teacher cannot be neutral and the essence of the traditional pattern of imposition in our culture must be reversed.

II. The Goals

In the early 1960s, the "in" word in educational circles was "excellence." The quest for quality in education was to be the primary purpose of the schools. Before "excellence" the slogan was "subject matter." In the thirties and forties, the "felt needs" of the child and "life adjustment" were the primary goals of education. Thus has the emphasis in the purposes of education changed from decade to decade as changing social conditions have engendered new priorities.

Yet, despite the shifts in priorities, teachers have been at work in the classroom, day by day, year by year, inculcating the three r's and exposing their students to the essentials of the social studies, language and literature, science and mathematics. And occasionally they have introduced their students to the rudiments of the fine arts—music, painting and sculpture, and drama—physical education, and, to a lesser extent, the practical arts of homemaking and vocational training.

Now, in the early 1970s, the "in" word in education is "relevance." Relevance is the "now" priority, stemming from our feelings of guilt over the poverty and racism that are eroding the foundation of American life. What is relevant? What, in addition to relevance, are being cited as the goals education must emphasize in the seventies? Is the purpose of education to prepare for life? For a job? For citizenship? For college? Has development of the intellect been neglected in favor of life adjustment or the whole child? Is intellect any more important on a scale of values than good citizenship? Getting along with others? Loyalty to democratic traditions? The ability to get and keep a job?

Are we still running schools as though our prime business was illiteracy rather than injustice, inhumanity, and irresponsibility?

Should everyone receive the same education or should some children be provided with a special educational diet designed to compensate for the inadequate background provided by their heritage, race, home, and neighborhood? Should we assume that all of our students are college-bound?

As teachers mold each succeeding generation, these questions, and the issue of priorities, will continue to challenge us. Each priority represents a philosophy about the ends of education and each has its separate defender.

To start with, we offer a good overview in Ralph Tyler's "Purposes of Our Schools." An educator of long experience and keen insight, Tyler provides a contemporary and broad perspective on which the subsequent articles in this part build. Those that follow Tyler's were selected to emphasize or expand on each of the purposes he discusses.

Defenders of the conservative view of education are represented here by James Koerner of the Council for Basic Education, in "Theory and Experience in the Education of Teachers" and Max Rafferty, California's ubiquitous former State Superintendent of Public Instruction, in "Today's Challenge to Education."

Defenders of the liberal position are represented by four writers, thus revealing the bias of editors Stone and Schneider. "Intelligence Without Morality" by Joseph Junell, a college supervisor of teacher education, pleads for the teaching of moral values in our schools—"the report card for mankind reads: A in Physics. B or B — in genetics. C or D in psychology. F in morality, ethics and the humanities."

In "Dropouts and the School," Thomas L. Millard points out the results achieved with a significant portion of our youth by pursuing the goals of the educational conservatives. To these one million students who quit the classroom annually, the conservative's goals are "phony." Millard calls for a "searching reappraisal of previously defined educational goals. . . ."

"After John Dewey, What?" by Jerome Bruner, the well-known Harvard psychologist, stresses process as a goal of education while still pointing to the primary purpose of intellectual training—"the process and the goal of education are one and the same thing."

"Learning to be Free" by Carl Rogers, best known for his contributions to counseling theory, and "Freedom and Learning: The Need for Choice" by Paul Goodman, are philosophically reminiscent of what was called progressive education in the twenties and thirties. As modern-day trumpeters of a new kind of functional education, they point out the direction we believe our schools should take in the seventies and eighties.

7. Purposes for Our Schools

Ralph W. Tyler

From their beginning the schools of our country have been sensitive to the needs and opportunities of our changing society. In the debates that took place in the early days of our nation over the establishment of free public education, two primary purposes were emphasized. For the individual child, education was to provide the opportunity to realize his potential and to become a constructive and happy person in the station of life which he would occupy because of his birth and ability. For the nation, the education of each child was essential to provide a literate citizenry. Since the new nation was ruled by its people, ignorance among the people would threaten the survival of the country.

Individual Self-Realization

Today, these remain two of the educational functions of our schools, recognized by the public generally and firmly imbedded in our thinking in the light of changed social conditions, new knowledge, and prevailing attitudes of the times. The goal of individual self-realization is even more necessary for the schools to stress in our mass society where economic, political, and social demands are frequently heard more distinctly than demands of the individual for education that will enable him to use the rich resources of an industrial society for his own fuller life. Kenneth Boulding, speaking in June, 1966, at the Eight-State Conference on "Prospective Changes in Society by 1980," eloquently expressed the contemporary problem in achieving this purpose:

"The final problem is subtle and hard to put one's finger on: nevertheless, it may be the most important problem of all. This is the problem of the role of the educational system in creating what might be called a moral identity. The obsolescence of older moral identities in the face of enormous technological

Source: National Association of Secondary School Principals, *Bulletin*, LII, 332 (December 1968), 1–12. Reprinted by permission of the publisher.

changes is a problem which underlies almost all others in the social system. . . . In its solution, the educational system would play an absolutely crucial role. It would be precisely indeed in the things which our conservatives despise as "frills" that the development of satisfying human identities may have to be found. It must never be forgotten that the ultimate thing which any society is producing is people. . . . If this principle is stamped firmly in the minds of those who guide and operate our educational system, we can afford to make a great many mistakes, we can afford to be surprised by the future, we can afford to make some bad educational investments, because we will be protected against the ultimate mistake, which would be to make the educational system a means, not an end, serving purposes other than man himself."

One test of our success in educating the individual for self-realization is whether at the end of each year of education he has a wider range of realistic choices in life available to him. If he is being narrowly specialized to fit into a niche in life with a real possibility of very limited choices, he has been miseducated. Each year should open new doors for him and develop new abilities to enable him to go through these doors as he chooses.

Literate Citizens

The reinterpretation of the development of literate citizens is profoundly important today when both the political problems and the functioning of the political system have increased enormously in scope and complexity. When the activities of government were largely restricted to maintaining law and order, providing schools, roads, and postal services, and protecting property from fire, the issues were easily grasped, and the agents and officers of government were generally known to a majority of the community. Now, the preservation of the nation, the health of the economy, the welfare of those in need, as well as education, have become mammoth operations with national and international implications. The agents and officers of government are known personally to only a small fraction of the people. Moreover, effective citizenship requires participation in a much more complex social system. A few years of schooling are not sufficient to prepare an intelligent and effective citizen, nor are the simple myths, which pass for American history in many places, adequate background for reasoned understanding. Educating a literate citizenry is in itself a major educational task.

Social Mobility

A third purpose of our schools has been recognized ever since the immigrating tide from Europe reached massive proportions in the latter part of the last century. As the children of recent immigrants became a considerable proportion of the school population in several of the states, many of the new citizens began to perceive the American schools as a means by which their children could have a chance through education to get better jobs and to enjoy the benefits of American life which they had been unable to do. Hence, in addition to providing opportunities for individual self-realization and educating for intelligent citizenship, the American schools have become a major avenue for social mobility—the means by which the American dream has been made a reality by many thousands of families and by which new streams of vigorous leadership have been injected into our maturing society.

But educating for social mobility has also required new interpretations with each generation. In the '90's, the prevailing notion among educators was that there were a few children among the many immigrant families whose moral character and native intelligence were equal to those of pupils from the middle class, old-American stock. They could make superior records in school if certain handicaps were eliminated. The handicaps recognized then were: limited knowledge of English, little time for study because of the need for their wages or help at home, and lack of supporting encouragement. Equality of educational opportunity meant, in that day, to furnish special help in acquiring the English language, raising money to reduce the time the child had to work, and for teacher and principal to give him friendly encouragement.

Now, we have learned that most children have capabilities in one or more areas and that, in place of estimating educational potential by a single scale of scholastic aptitude, we need to use various means of finding the strengths of each child on which further educational development can be based. Not only do we now expect to find many more children with potential social mobility than did our predecessors, but we have also learned about a broader range of handicaps that we need to eliminate in order that children and youth may move ahead. These include limited experience with standard English, limited access to the influence of educated people, nutritional and other health problems, lack of experience in successful learning, lack of disciplined work experience, and lack of confidence in ability to learn. The particular learning objectives and the kinds of educational programs that can enhance social mobility, we now know, must be designed in terms of the particular strengths and limitations of the pupils concerned.

Preparation for the World of Work

The expectation that the public elementary and secondary schools would prepare the workers needed in our expanding economy was not commonly held until the close of World War I. Farm laborers, construction workers for railroads and highways, domestic servants, and unskilled "helpers" comprised the majority of the labor force. Skilled tradesmen came from Europe or were trained through apprenticeship in this country. But the rapid rate of industrialization and business development after 1910 required many workers with higher levels of skills and understanding such as mechanics, stenographers, clerks, and sales people. The level of education required came to be expressed increasingly in terms of a high school diploma. Furthermore, specific vocational education was introduced in many high schools with grants-in-aid provided by the federal government. By 1925, the public generally, and the schools as well, were including as one of the purposes of American education the preparation of young people for the world of work.

Since 1925, and particularly since World War II, the rapid rate of technological development in agriculture, industry, commerce, defense, and the health services has so changed the occupational distribution of the total labor force that the chance for a youth or young adult without high school education to obtain employment is less and less. Farmers and farm laborers, who made up 38 percent of the labor force at the turn of the century, now comprise only 7 percent. Similarly, opportunities for employment in unskilled occupations have almost disappeared. Last year, only 5 percent of the labor force was unskilled. The proportion employed in skilled trades is not likely to increase. But there are large increases in the percentage of people employed in engineering, science, the recreational fields, accounting, and administration. Now, not only is high school education essential for most employment, but the percentage of jobs requiring college education is increasing at a rapid rate. Education as preparation for employment is more important than ever before.

But this function also requires continuing reinterpretation. Recent reports, such as the one by President Kennedy's Commission on Vocational Education, chaired by Benjamin Willis, and that of the National Association of Secondary School Principals, have documented the failures of our schools to maintain continuing contact with the needs, problems, and opportunities in educating youth for the world of work.

Mention was made earlier of the sharp shifts taking place in the composition of the labor force. In 1960, only 45 percent of the U.S. labor force was engaged in the production and distribution of material goods, while 55 percent was employed in providing non-material services in areas like the health services, education, recreation, social services, science and engineering, accounting, and administration. In 1967, it was estimated that only 40 percent of our labor force was required to produce and distribute material goods, and this is predicted to shrink to 25 percent by 1980. In spite of these great changes, high school vocational programs are still predominantly focused on production jobs, including farming, although only 7 percent of the labor force is engaged in agriculture.

The shift in demand to persons who provide non-material services poses a particular problem for males. A majority of boys from working-class homes have a self-image of being strong and manually dexterous. This is their notion of a "real man." But the opportunities for employment where physical strength and manual dexterity are important are becoming more and more limited. Instead, the new jobs that are increasingly available require primarily intellectual competence and social skills. Education that helps boys to prepare for employment really begins in the early grades, aiding them to develop a more realistic picture of the world of work and to perceive more clearly what characteristics are required for employment. In these early years, children can develop habits of responsibility, of thoroughness in work, of punctuality, as well as intellectual and social skills. In the junior high school period, career exploration and planning are important phases of the program. One of the most significant changes in occupational education is based on the recognition that every child needs to learn things that will prepare him for the world of work, that what is to be learned is much more than certain specific vocational skills, and that appropriate educational experiences will need to extend throughout the school years. Furthermore, the continuing transformation taking place in the nature and distribution of jobs requires not only the use of current projections of employment demands but also emphasis upon the development of generally useful abilities and skills, rather than confining the training to skills limited to specific jobs. This shift of emphasis will insure that re-education and training, when needed, will be more easily accomplished.

Wise Choices of Non-Material Services

To maintain and to increase the productivity of the American economy requires not only an ample supply of workers at higher levels of competence but also consumers who want and are willing to pay for the wide range of consumer goods and services which the economy can produce. If the American people wanted only food, clothing, and shelter, a major fraction would be unemployed because these goods can be produced by a small part of our labor force. The desire and the willingness to pay for health, education, recreation, including art, music, literature, sports, and the like, create the demand which enables the economy to shift its patterns of production to take advantage of the greater efficiency of technology, without stagnation. This sets a fifth major function of American education, namely, to develop in students understanding and appreciation of the wide range of experiences, services, and goods that can contribute much to their health and satisfaction. Only through education can people learn to make wise economic choices as well as wise choices in the personal, social, and political fields.

The consumer education courses that were constructed in the '20's and

'30's emphasized the development of the abilities required to make choices among material products, using information about the serviceable qualities and relative costs of these goods. The chief consumer problem of that period was believed to be to obtain useful products at lowest prices commensurate with necessary quality. Few of these courses dealt with the problems involved in making wise choices of goods and services that furnish non-material values, like the aesthetic values in music, art, and drama; the recreational values of sports; the personal and social values in various educational opportunities; the health values in different forms of health and medical programs. Frequently, English courses sought to develop an appreciation for literature that could afford continuing meaning and satisfaction to the reader, and a small number of courses were devoted to motion picture appreciation aimed to help students make wise choices of the movies they viewed.

Now that a majority of the labor force is engaged in the production of non-material services, the range of possible choices for the consumer is increasing greatly. Hence, the reinterpretation of this purpose in our age opens up a whole new area of consumer education and requires the development of relevant objectives and learning experiences. The wise choice of these services is profoundly important, in the development both of individuals and of our culture. Choices of literature, art, music, recreation, leisure time, educational opportunities, health services, and contributing social services have more to do with the quality of life than most of our material choices.

However, the relatively simple calculations involved in comparing the value of steak at one price with that of chicken at another is not the kind of decision process involved in choosing among non-material alternatives. The educational program will need to extend the opportunities for students to seriously explore experiences and services in ways that help them to perceive values, to find meaning in them, to discover how far they afford satisfaction. Furthermore, to help in making rational decisions, students will need opportunities to review their experiences, to reflect on their impact, to assess the probable future consequences, and to develop the habit of appraising the values of non-material experiences. This is a new area for many schools.

Learning to Learn

Teaching students how to learn has, in the last ten years, been accepted as another function of our schools. With the rapid acquisition of new knowledge, it is no longer possible to give the student in school an adequate command of the facts in each major subject which will serve him throughout the balance of his life. The school can only start him on a lifelong career of continued learning. Hence, an important educational aim today is to teach students to learn and to develop in them a strong interest in continued study together with the skills required to keep on with their learning after graduation.

At educational gatherings, the comment can be heard that this has always been a major purpose of our schools. It has certainly been stated as a desirable aim by educational leaders for centuries; but not only have the particular sources of learning and procedures for study changed with the times but for generations the pattern of school performance has been in sharp contrast to what is involved in learning outside of the formal school situation. In life outside the school, one encounters problems that are not clearly formulated, and he must analyze the situation sufficiently to identify particular problems or to see what questions are involved. He needs to know where he can get relevant information; he needs to be able to attack the particular problems appropriately in terms of the fields in which they can be placed—that is, science, literature, economics, politics, and the like. He needs to be able to verify or validate the procedures he follows and/or the answers or solutions he proposes.

These abilities can be acquired through experience which requires their use. But most schools do not provide much opportunity for this. Typically, the teacher poses the problems or questions rather than the student finding them as he works. The textbook or the teacher is most likely to furnish the answers rather than to require the student to work them out or to find dependable sources. If this new purpose is to be attained, the contrast between traditional study in school and the procedures of life-long learning must be eliminated by making the school experiences examples of continued learning. This requires teachers and students to take on new roles.

The increase in the number of functions which the American schools are expected to serve is the natural result of the changes in our whole society. In the nearly 200 years since this country was founded, society has increased enormously in complexity. Yet, today, the human individual at birth does not differ appreciably from the babies born at the time of the American Revolution. All of the knowledge, skills, and attitudes required to live in modern society must be acquired by each individual after birth. Since society is continuing to increase in complexity and scope, the development of youth for effective modern life increases in difficulty and in magnitude with each generation.

Critical New Tasks

The aforementioned six still remain the major functions of American schools, but from time to time special tasks take on immediate urgency. Two of them are stressed today.

We have seen that with the increasing use of technology the demand for unskilled labor has diminished to about 5 percent of the labor force. Yet, in the United States and in other advanced nations, between 15 percent and 20 percent of the population have not acquired sufficient skill and general literacy to qualify for skilled or higher levels of employment. The fact that more than 80 percent of our children have achieved an educational level above the minimum requirements for modern literacy and employment is a tribute to the determination of our people and the efforts of our schools. But this is not enough. Today, 19 out of every 20 of our children can and must be effectively reached by education. We know how to stimulate and guide the learning of children who come from homes where education is valued and where the basis for it has been laid in the home experiences. However, we do not have widely accepted means for reaching children whose backgrounds have given them little or no basis for school work. To reach all or nearly all of these children is a critical task of the present period.

A second urgent task of today is also partly a result of modern technology. As automation has sharply reduced the demand for unskilled labor, the occupations in which there are increasing demands as noted earlier, are those requiring a fairly high level of education. However, to provide employment opportunities for all our people and to keep our economy fully productive requires a much larger proportion of our youth to complete high school—many more than in the past—to gain professional, semi-professional, or technical competence. To provide these educational opportunities and to insure effective learning for youth from varied backgrounds of training, experience, and outlook is another new and important educational task which we now face. Neither the U.S. nor any other country has previously attempted it.

Mention is made of these two new tasks that the schools are being urgently asked to undertake, not because they involve additions to the basic functions or purposes of the schools but because they should be viewed as important tasks with purposes of their own.

Both of them—reaching the disadvantaged and making the high school effective for a large proportion of the population—must be undertaken with the six basic purposes in mind: to help each individual achieve his highest potential, to develop a broader base of intelligent and active citizens, to make possible social mobility, to prepare each person for the world of work, to help him choose non-material services that will furnish the greatest meaning and satisfaction, and to become a life-long learner.

In making education effective for a larger number of students, consideration must be given to the criticism made by students themselves of the high school program.

The most common complaint they make is its "irrelevance." In many cases, what is being taught could be highly relevant to the activities, interests, and problems of the students, and they fail to perceive the connection. Much of this is due to the separation of the school from the rest of life. For example, the separation of the school from the world of work and the world of community service results in several unfortunate consequences. Many students see the school as something apart from the adult world into which they will be going. This is one of the factors in dropping out of school; and for many students who do not drop out, the apparent lack of connection between the school work and their future lives results in low interest and effort in their studies. From the standpoint of the society, the separation of the school makes more difficult the transition from school to work and from school to constructive community membership. What is needed is the development of bridges to the rest of the community and greater openness in the school to outside persons and activities. We need to be providing cooperative education (work-study programs), community service programs, and other means by which school youth can be actively involved in work experiences, in community services, in joint civic participation with adults, and the like. Students are not likely to use what they learn unless they have practice in identifying problems and difficulties. Dealing with these requires learning—and practice in using what is learned—in situations outside of school.

Response of the Schools to Change

Although the American schools, when compared to those of Western Europe, have not rigidly adhered to obsolete programs but have been responsive to the changing needs and opportunities of the times, these educational changes have lagged some years behind the initiating forces, and the adaptation or transformations required in the schools have not always been largely effective. The lag appears to have been due both to the lack of continuing attention within the school to developments in the society and to the common failure of school leaders to translate needed changes into educational purposes and operations that guide the actual conduct of school work.

It has become modern business practice for the corporation to make continuing projections of environmental factors, such as population shifts, new technologies becoming available, and changing patterns of consumer preferences, that importantly affect its work. From these assessments and reassessments of changing conditions, the corporation commonly plans its production and distribution programs, adjusting the future plans each year in the light of facts of the past year. In this way, the company is able to respond quickly to changing conditions and frequently anticipates the changes before they actually take place. Educational systems and organizations could benefit from similar practices. A rationale for such planning procedures exists, and modifications to fit a particular system can be worked out. With such studies and with the attitude that change is the natural characteristic of our society and its institutions, our schools in the future can anticipate new educational needs as well as respond to present conditions more promptly.

Our failure to translate changing needs into guiding purposes and operational plans seems to be largely due to our following the pattern of leadership characteristic of a slowly changing society. Under conditions of very gradual shift, the operational modifications in the system are commonly made by the operators before they are recognized by the leaders. Then, the role of leadership is to explain these changes in terms of accepted principles so that the new practices now in operation are legitimized. Many statements of educational policy have been justifications of changes already under way rather than pointing the direction for new efforts.

Because our society is changing more rapidly with each decade, we must develop educational procedures that can reduce the lag between changing needs and educational programs that meet the needs. The American schools have shown their flexibility in responding to needs in the past. By developing procedures to scan the social horizon, we can anticipate impending changes and understand their probable impact. By employing task forces of scholars, scientists, curriculum makers, and teachers to translate needs into educational objectives and operational plans, we can expect to respond more promptly and more effectively in the future than we have in the past. Over the years, the purposes for our schools have been expanding, and in each generation older purposes require reinterpretation. This is necessary for schools to serve adequately the individual and the society of the times.

8. Theory and Experience in the Education of Teachers

James D. Koerner

Discussion of the theories by which American education is or ought to be carried on—whether concerned with the education of children, children's teachers, or teachers' teachers—has always been a highly imprecise and often meaningless exercise. And perhaps a tiresome one for the listeners. "A treatise on education," as Emerson put it a century ago, "a convention for education, a lecture, a system, affects us with a slight paralysis and a certain yawning of the jaws."

Yet the question of defining purpose and establishing priority in the enormous enterprise of American education remains paramount and inescapable. Susanne Langer, perhaps our most interesting woman philosopher, put the matter this way recently:

To determine the aims of education is probably the most urgent philosophical problem in the whole pedagogical field today; and it cannot but draw in vast further questions of the aims of human societies, the ultimate values that set up these aims, our basic ideas of society and individual life.

Unfortunately these basic ideas and ultimate values can be but poorly adumbrated through a general discussion of educational theory, and such discussions rarely produce concrete results, except perhaps to drive conventioneering educators to the nearest bar.

Nevertheless the crisis of American education is at bottom a philosophical one. It is a crisis of purpose, of the definition of goals, and we should not avoid this fact in any talk about contemporary teacher training. Much is said today of the importance of philosophy in education. But little that

SOURCE: *Strength through Reappraisal,* Sixteenth Yearbook of the American Association of Colleges for Teacher Education. Copyright © 1963 by the National Education Association (Washington, D.C.: the Association, 1963), pp. 13–18, 23. Used by permission of the American Association of Colleges for Teacher Education.

passes as educational philosophy, whether courses in the subject, arguments by individuals, or statements of purpose from educational agencies, has much resemblance to genuine philosophical exploration, and it never seems to relate to a developed theory of cognition, truth, or reality. Probably no one active in teacher education today, with the possible exception of the Jesuit educators, has developed anything that could properly bear the name of a philosophy of education or of teacher education. Most persons involved in training teachers operate on a less elevated plane in designing and carrying out their programs (even though the programs necessarily imply, wittingly or not, some philosophical position).

So I was pleased to see President Maucker . . . employ the modest term, "rationale," to indicate the focus of the discussion. We would be well advised to regard most statements about the purposes of teacher education as being neither theory nor philosophy, but at best as constituting a more or less reasonable rationale that must ultimately rely on persuasion or faith, but not on logic or demonstrable fact, for acceptance.

Presumably, we would all agree that the purposes we have in mind for public education dictate the purposes we pursue in teacher education; that is, that the education of Americans and the education of American teachers must grow out of the same rationale. That being true, we might look again at the few fundamental positions that have been taken in America about universal education.

There is, for example, the Jeffersonian view: the view that all children should be supplied with the rudiments of learning in order to enable them to become politically literate and perhaps continue to educate themselves. Beyond that, Jefferson thought that a very few "of the best geniuses [might be] raked from the rubbish annually" to create what he, the great democrat, called "a natural aristocracy of talents and virtue" and thereby furnish society with the kind of enlightened leadership essential to social progress. This is a position that frankly advocates the training of "an intellectual elite" (one of our current scare phrases) while recognizing the educational potential of the masses. One hears echoes of this view today in the writings of James Bryant Conant and of many academicians.

Then there is the Deweyan view in which purpose becomes so interlaced with method as to be nearly indistinguishable. So far as one can distill purpose from the ambiguities and contradictions of Dewey, who was much clearer and more provocative in his philosophical than in his educational writings, it seems to apotheosize the temporary, whether in the passing whim of the student or in the final outcome of school activity, and to denigrate the permanent. "Growth" is the key, but the word is always undefined. Growth leads only to more growth, never to immutable values, unless those values be growth and change themselves; and those values can be fostered, not by a few fixed and fundamental subjects, but by an almost limitless array of school activities based primarily on the changing and evolving interests of the students. Therefore school activity for its own sake, adaptation to changing conditions, a highly diversified and fragmented curriculum, and an uncritical, Jacksonian egalitarianism become the ends of education in a Deweyan classroom. This view of education as "process" and indiscriminate "growth" is still strongly held, I believe, by very large numbers, perhaps the majority, of professional educators.

At the other end of the spectrum is the view best represented and most eloquently set forth by Albert Jay Nock. It was Nock's conviction that the great majority of mankind was not educable in any serious way and that all of our vexing, insoluble educational problems in America arose from our failure to recognize this simple fact and in our useless attempts to educate everybody. Surveying our educational history, he found

. . . three most serious errors in the theory upon which the mechanics of our educational system were designed. This theory contemplates a fantastic and impracticable idea of equality, a fantastic and impracticable idea of democracy, and a fantastically exaggerated idea of the importance of literacy in assuring the support of a sound and enlightened public order.

He advocated universal training in vocational skills but not universal education, because "suitable material," as he put it, "for education is extremely scarce; suitable material for training abounds everywhere." He strongly urged the education of an aristocracy of talents and virtue similar to the Jeffersonian idea, though he obviously did not share Jefferson's optimistic estimate of the body politic. The heart of his position was that most men are condemned by nature to a non-intellectual life and that we had better take cognizance of this fact if we are ever to stop the appalling waste of our resources in education and begin to solve our biggest problems.

Finally, there is the view, best represented perhaps by Robert Maynard Hutchins, that almost all children are capable of sustained academic study and that it is the proper business of a public school system to give this study to them through the medium of what Matthew Arnold called "the best that has been thought and said in the world." In this system all students run on the same track but at their own best speeds; and all concentrate their education in a relatively few areas that encompass the most significant of man's knowledge. It is a competitive system, authoritarian if you like in about the same degree as those of Jefferson and Nock, and built on strong assumptions about the importance of priorities in education and on a highly optimistic assessment of the intellectual possibilities of most men.

Obviously, these four positions, those of Jefferson, Dewey, Nock, and Hutchins, do not exhaust the field, but they do represent the fundamental positions with which most others that influence modern education—

Maritain, Whitehead, or Kilpatrick—have a clear affinity. It is important
to remind ourselves that all such views are statements of position, not of
fact. They tend to be hortatory, histrionic, and proselytic. Each of them
must appeal for support to the collective experience of the race and each is
at heart an act of faith not closely related to observable, measurable phenomena. As Dewey commented in one of his best books, *Reconstruction in
Philosophy:*

> The material out of which philosophy finally emerges is irrelevant to science
> and to explanation. It is figurative, symbolic of fears and hopes, made of imagi-
> nations and suggestions, not significant of a world of objective fact intellectually
> confronted. It is poetry and drama, rather than science, and is apart from sci-
> entific truth and falsity, rationality or absurdity of fact in the same way in which
> poetry is independent of these things.

All of which is only to emphasize the idea that philosophical considerations, while they do indeed constitute education's first concern, are abstruse by nature and lend themselves more to persuasion than proof.

Let me, then, turn to the question of what rationale seems to me the
most valid today for the education of Americans and by extension the education of American teachers. I would not dignify my argument as a "philosophy of education" or even a theory, but I would defend it as a reasonable analysis and a practical program. Let me begin, not with first
principles about the nature of man, but with a commonplace observation
about the nature of the life man has created for himself. Whether we believe man to be a divinely inspired creature or merely a cosmic accident,
we have little choice, since most of us are not and do not wish to become
Rousseaus or Thoreaus, but to accept civilization as a good thing, and as
educators, to work for its advancement. But one cannot work intelligently
for the future, not to say the present, oblivious of the past. Whatever
man's origins or ultimate destiny, the life we know today is the product of
a long and painful process of taming, training, and refining the human animal, a process made possible by two characteristics that distinguish man
from all other animals: intelligence and compassion. These unique and
complementary virtues have enabled man to raise himself from savagery:
his intelligence, by which he has been able to investigate and in some measure understand and control both himself and his environment; his compassion, by which he has muted his natural selfishness and his continuing
capacity for barbarism and by which he has introduced some measure of
dignity and nobility into his own affairs.

It follows, I believe, that man's best hope for his future lies in the maximum cultivation within each person of these uniquely human endowments,
for only in this way do we have much chance of narrowing the gap between the real and the ideal. If it is true, as Santayana once suggested, that

"perhaps the only true dignity of man is his capacity to despise himself," it is true only because of man's peculiar capacity to see how far short he still falls of his possibilities, how wide the gulf still is between his achievements and his potential, between what is and what might be. The job of education, I believe, is to bridge this gulf.

Thus far most people would perhaps agree. They agree less readily about the educational implications involved. In the process of his own intellectual development—as he uncovered great knowledge, mostly through trial and error over eons of time—man finally was able to refine particular techniques for investigating phenomena, techniques that over long periods were found to produce results that were more fruitful than those produced in other ways. Through man's passion for classifying and codifying his knowledge, in order to continue improving it, some few fields have attained pre-eminence because they are generative, because they form the nucleus of other, secondary fields, because they represent pinnacles of human achievement, and because they now constitute bodies of knowledge of proven power and research techniques of proven effectiveness.

These basic fields include the major languages of mankind, the instrument without which all of us would still live like pre-Neolithic sub-men; they also include that other indispensable language, the language of mathematics, without which all of us would likewise still be primitives; they include history, which in its largest sense encompasses all the records of all the ages, without which the race would be as intellectually impotent as a man without a memory; and they include the natural sciences, which by becoming highly quantified and capable of extremely reliable predictions about the major phenomena of nature, have radically transformed the modern world. These fields, I suggest, are clearly the chief ones in which man has recorded his experience on earth and his understanding of life. One might justly argue that other fields are nearly as basic, or that what is basic in one age is not so in another, and that the pattern of educational programs must change accordingly. My only point is that the foregoing fields have been the chief means by which man has become what he now is and that they remain paramount at this particular point in his history. As such they have earned a pre-eminent place in the education of each new generation. In the common schools of our society, the question of priorities is compelling, for there is time only for those subjects which best serve the needs of all men, as citizens and human beings.

It may well be that this view of human abilities is ill-founded, and that the majority of men are condemned to slobbism and ignorance. It may be that Nock was right. But I don't see how this can be determined until some nation, hopefully the United States, gives universal education, not universal vocationalism, a serious trial. I submit that we have never really tried to educate our citizenry in the basic fields of human knowledge and achievement and that neither we nor any other nation knows from solid experience just how far the intellectual limits of the so-called common people extend. If Jerome Bruner is right in asserting that any subject can be taught to any schoolchild in some intellectually respectable manner, then what possible excuse remains for our failure to establish a clear system of priorities in public schools and finding out just how much genuine education the majority of the human race can absorb?

All politics, so they say, presuppose an idea of man. Surely all educational systems do also. And all educational theories, as I have said, have corollary implications for teacher training. Programs to train teachers for a school system built on the assumptions of Hutchins, for example, must be rather different from programs to train teachers for a Kilpatrick system. They must indeed differ as night from day. And it is precisely because of our persistent disagreements about fundamental educational purpose that teacher training continues to be as controversial, and I may say, as haphazard as it is. If we could achieve a consensus about the aims of universal education—and I for one feel that we as a nation are at least on the road, however long and rocky it may prove to be, toward a working consensus —a system of teacher training consistent with it would follow as a matter of course.

Clearly then, the first and most important dimension of a rationale for teacher preparation is a statement of belief about the aims of public, not of teacher, education. In my view, such a statement should recognize the primacy of basic education for all students: the systematic and sequential exposure of the mind of each person to those subjects that have contributed the most to the advance of civilization, and the simultaneous training of each person's habits of thought and expression. . . .

On the philosophical side, we can only hope that some agreement about fundamental aims and purposes will come out of the prolonged public discussion in which the nation is now engaged. I'm sure it remains as difficult as ever to persuade others through argument to one's educational point of view, and in fact it may not be possible. Every once in a while I think Rousseau may have had a point when he observed in his *Confessions* that "dogmatic belief is one of the fruits of education," from which it would seem to follow that the more education a man has the more dogmatic he becomes. But most of the time I would far rather put my faith at the other end of the line, where one day the majority of laymen and educators alike become convinced that basic education for all, made possible by liberally educated teachers of unquestioned ability, is the chief means, indeed, the only means, by which we have any chance of reaching the goal that has always lain at the heart of our republic: an enlightened, cultivated, rational community of free men.

9. Today's Challenge in Education: The Public School in Our American Heritage

Max Rafferty

I want to talk to you about the public school in our American Heritage and share with you some of my findings and views in regard to this topic. Public education, you know, is not only full of paradoxes, but is a paradox in itself, and in speaking about public education to people in a private institution such as this, I'm doing it deliberately because of two reasons: first, public education is really my specialty and the only thing in which I have any scope or competence. Secondly, public education should be the vital concern of all of us wherever we are engaged; whether we have our children in public or private schools; whether we ourselves are employed by public or private schools, or support those schools with our contribution or our tax money.

But public education is certainly a paradox today. Education has been hedged about by charms and incantation, ever since the shaven-headed priests of Isis and Osiris taught their awestruck neophytes how to create and preserve the magic hieroglyphics on leaves of the papyrus plants so many centuries ago in ancient lands ruled by god-emperors and their priestly hierarchies. Education was simply an extension of the sacred mysteries. It was confined to the initiated servants of the Nile god and the sun diety. By its very nature, how could it possibly be *public* education? Could the unwashed, uninitiated of old Egypt mouth the sacred phrases which made the great river rise and fall with supernatural regularity? Could the masses with their mud-caked hair and sun-baked bodies carve into imperishable granite the mystic symbols which alone could summon the departed soul to inhabit once again the mummified body? Obviously not, decided old Pharaoh. Education must be for the very few—the delvers into the unknown. Public education was a contradiction in terms.

SOURCE: *Vital Speeches of the Day*, XXIX, 15 (May 15, 1963), 450–54. Reprinted by permission of the publisher.

To the Greeks, who followed a few centuries later, education was an intellectual pastime—a sort of game. To the eminently practical Romans, education carried with it the ability on the part of orators to sway large audiences composed largely of illiterates. In either case, you see, education belonged only to the upper classes, to the patricians. Societies such as these, built upon mass slavery, regarded public education only as an instrument of subversion, which could only end as a form of state suicide.

Things were turned topsy-turvy in the Middle Ages. During this turbulent period, the aristocracy, for a change, was largely illiterate, preferring the sword to the pen, and the lowly clerks and monks were in charge of what little education then existed. Despite this apparent reversal of the usual order of things, education was still very much a minority commodity. It became the exclusive property of a universal church; the officers and servants of which alone possessed learning and the unique ability to impart it to others. But with the Protestant Reformation of the 16th century, *public* education became almost a necessity if the new faith were to survive at all. The Bible was translated into the countless vernaculars of Europe and the followers of Luther and Calvin were expected to read and to interpret the Scriptures for themselves.

This was the attitude of the Pilgrim fathers and they taught their children to read from the hornbook primers during those first bleak winters in New England. It was the attitude of their grandchildren, grown to manhood, who first set up a system of public-supported elementary schools in Massachusetts Bay Colony. And herein lies the first of the paradoxes of which I spoke. Public education, which was originally founded in our land to bulwark and to interpret religion, is today forbidden to do anything of the sort. After centuries of existence as a quasi-divine secret in one civilization, as an intellectual toy in another, as an instrument of power and control in still a third, education for the first time saw itself set free and commanded to teach not one group or one caste or one race, but all. And since that *all* included children of non-Christian, and indeed non-religious, parents, the use of the schools for sectarian, religious purposes entered upon a sharp and precipitated decline which has continued to this day, which has brought us recently to the point where the singing of Christmas carols in the schools came under attack and where graduation baccalaureate services, in many cases, have to be held off the high school campus altogether.

Reaction, in my opinion, has over-compensated. While public school teachers like me are usually not qualified to interpret the Scriptures, nor to distinguish among the myriad theological niceties, there is still a definite, positive place for non-sectarian spiritual emphasis in our nation's schools.

The history of religion, the immeasurable, cultural contributions to our heritage made by the Judeo-Christian tradition, the moral and ethical values of western civilization, all these things *can* and *should* be taught to the children of America. Our children should be told, among other things, that this nation was first settled by persons with devoutly religious convictions; that our people were among the very first to solve the age-old problem of permitting many different religious groups to live peaceably together side by side, and they should be told that no religious wars, uniquely enough, have ever sullied our American countryside.

By means of such instruction, we can make sure that a vital part of our American Heritage will no longer be neglected, and that a highly important but often ignored dimension of our national story will be added to our teaching of history. The concept of the individual as a child of God—that concept so important to our ancestors—is the basis of both the United States Constitution and the Declaration of Independence. If we expect to preserve inviolate the lasting truths of these great documents for our children to enjoy after we are gone, then we must make very certain that these same children are made aware of this essential underlying concept.

But the question of spiritual and ethical instruction in the schools is not the only paradox of modern education. Another great issue on which the battle lines have quite recently been drawn is that of education for our national survival. Only recently for instance, I was rather sharply criticized in certain educational circles for advocating that elementary school children be taught to love their country. Let me hasten to say here that I've no reason to suspect these critics of any disloyalty or lukewarmness toward America; their point was simply this: the schools should teach a logical, dispassionate understanding of our nation's past; its shortcomings as well as its virtues. The children should approach our history as they approach a science experiment, with no preconceptions, no bias, no emotions whatsoever. After they thoroughly understand the intricacies and complexities of our political, social, and economic evolutions, then the children will be in position to decide for themselves whether or not they should love their country, and if so, how much.

Well, I guess I respect this viewpoint. I think I understand it. I disagree with it one hundred per cent. After all, what other things, what other people do we learn to love, you and I, as a result of this logical process of thesis, antithesis, and synthesis? Do you love your mother, because at an early age you balanced her strengths against her weaknesses, and discovered to your satisfaction that the former outnumbered the latter? Do you love your father because in childhood you counted up the times that he was right as against the number of times that he was wrong?

I imagine that many of you here are married—we'll call for a show of hands; let's just stick the men with this. I always hate to ask ladies questions—I usually get unexpected answers. How many of you, before you got married, thoroughly understood your wives? Nobody. I'm sure this is true in my case. I've been married for 18 years and I don't understand my wife yet. She says she understands me, but women are smarter than we are. No, for most of us, love came first, didn't it? And only later some sort of approach to understanding because we had to have sufficient motivation in the form of love to attempt to reach an understanding.

If any of us had been so foolish as to abide this cold-blooded, counting-house method which I have described to the objects of our affection, we would never have been able to generate lasting regard for anybody or anything. There is nothing logical or analytical about love, thank heaven. It springs unbidden from the deepest wellsprings of the human spirit. It is an attribute unknown and unknowable of God himself, and patriotism is nothing whatever but love, that's all it is. I'm not at all sure how to teach it. Perhaps children can be led along the path to love of country by reminding them from time to time of what we receive from the country every day of our lives; by telling the children over and over again the wonderful tales from American History which are their proper birthright; by familiarizing them so completely with the lives and the personalities of our great heroes; that Washington and Lincoln, Franklin and Jefferson, and all the rest become names as friendly and familiar to them as are the names of their own classmates.

We can show the children by word and by example that we, their instructors, believe profoundly in the mighty truths which these men and their contemporaries forged for us in the flaming crucible of suffering and self-sacrifice; we can help the children observe the sacred national holidays, and explain to them exactly why they are in the calendar, and lastly, we can lead them to the flag and tell them of its symbolism and its meaning to whole generations of American patriots.

But while I may not be exactly sure how to teach patriotism, I'm positive how *not* to teach it: tell the children that our national heroes were just not very heroic after all; keep dwelling on Washington's temper—he had one, you know; on Lincoln's poor table manners, and they were; on Ben Franklin's popularity with the ladies, and he certainly was. Stress the countless weaknesses to which all flesh is heir. Emphasize our labor strikes and racial problems, and child labor 40 years ago, and the trusts 40 years before that. Tell the children all about the Teapot Dome scandal, about the mink coats and the deep freezers in more recent times; soft pedal things like Bunker Hill and Gettysburg, the Emancipation Proclamation and the Bill of Rights; make a fetish of balancing every virtue with a vice, no matter how deeply you may have to dig in order to dredge one up. In this way, you will produce in the minds of the children a balanced, planned, tasteless, lifeless image of their country, all in the sacred name of objectivity.

Such an image is not good enough. These boys and girls now listening to our words are after all the very ones who must defend, within a few years, all that Americans have held sacred for generations. Without love for a wonderful country, will they have the nerve and the sinew and the dedication to keep our ship of state afloat and breasting triumphfully the angry torrent which is the last half of this twentieth century? It seems to me that the first duty of the nation's schools is to preserve that nation. After all, if the nation goes under, so do the schools; so does the realization of the maximum potential of each child, so does the concept of the whole child, the struggle to restore standards, theory of adjustment to the peer group, and all the other hundred and one things which we educators and the lay public get periodically so excited about. Everything goes if Uncle Sam goes.

So, I say that we'd better make as certain as need be that Uncle Sam stays around awhile longer. And I'm sure that this will involve bringing home to the children in a very real and vital way the truths embodied in our American Heritage. Whatever we may have to do to achieve love of country in the hearts and minds of the generations now growing up all around us, we'd better do it and not fool around about it.

Of course, we've only begun to talk about the paradoxes in modern education. For instance, this whole controversy about teaching the *subject* versus teaching the *child* would seem side-splittingly funny to every educator who ever lived prior to 1900. They took for granted that you taught the subject *to* the child and they went ahead and did it—they didn't argue about it. Our often violent tantrums over this ludicrous, semantic will-of-the-wisp do us little credit as a profession. They are painfully reminiscent of the arguments back in the 12th century over how many angels could stand simultaneously on the point of a pin. No matter how many educators from Columbia University or elsewhere stand around shouting that subject matter must take a back seat to important concepts like "togetherness" and "in-groupness" and "life-adjustment," the facts of life remain. Subject matter is becoming increasingly, not decreasingly important, to whole nations as well as individuals.

Excellence in mastering specific, organized and disciplined subject matter is the only thing right now which stands between the United States of America on the one hand and atomized destruction on the other. So, since we educators pride ourselves that we are educating for life, let's get busy and do it by teaching subject matter better than we have ever done it before and for our lives' sake.

Still another paradox is the image of the educator in modern America. We're going to have to decide, we teachers, whether we want to be skilled technicians or learned scholars. A former high school pupil of mine came back to see me shortly after the close of World War II. He had served four years in the paratroops and had seen service in Italy, France, and Germany. His observations across my dinner table back in 1946 may be pertinent today. "When I was in training in Ft. Benning, Georgia," he told me, "I used to travel around quite a bit on my leaves. I got into the habit of asking one single question in every new town I visited in the state of

Georgia—'who are your three most successful citizens'?" The answer nearly always was, "The bank president, the Cadillac dealer, and the Coca Cola distributor."

"Coke" is real big in Georgia. The dollar sign, you see, was invariably the mark of success.

Then my former pupil went on: "When I got into Europe, as soon as I could find someone in the many little towns my outfit liberated who could speak English, I always asked the same question 'who are your three most successful citizens?' But there the response was quite different; 'the mayor or burgomaster, the curé or priest, and believe it or not, the schoolmaster'!" The mayor because he embodied the civic conscience. The priest because he embodied religious truths, and the schoolmaster because he embodied the learning and the culture of the community.

If my old school district over in La Canada had had a superintendent 50 or 60 years ago (and I don't think it did), the odds are that he could have boasted a full beard, an impressive bay window called in those days "the corporation," and a big gold watch and chain with an elk's tooth hanging from it. He would have been superintendent for life, or its professional equivalent. Today, a school administrator like me is lucky if he lasts out a four year contract. My, perhaps imaginary, predecessor would have known little about behavioristic psychology or acoustic tiles or standard deviations or dry wall construction in school buses. In a dozen ways, he was less competent than the fast-talking, fast-moving, fast-changing school superintendent of today. Why, then, was the old-time administrator an object of such universal respect? Perhaps because, although he was not very much on public relations, he could read the Aeneid in Latin, the Iliad in the original Greek, and discuss Miltonic blank verse without batting an eye; the educator in those days was respected precisely because he *was* educated. He retained his position for decades on end because he symbolized supremely well the cultural ambitions of the community which he served.

When a stranger entered the community of that day and asked to be taken to the most learned citizen in residence, he was led proudly and unquestioningly to the leading schoolman. It is our misfortune as a profession and as a nation that today this is no longer so. Now, don't misunderstand me, it's not necessary in this day and age to be a classicist in order to be cultured, but it is necessary for the schoolman to know how to write and speak English in a manner at least relatively free from gross errors. It's advisable for him to know enough about American history to be able to distinguish between Andrew Johnson and Andrew Jackson, and enough about European history to explain the difference between Napoleon I and Napleon III. And it's certainly expedient for him to be able to react with some show of recognition when someone in the course of the conversation mentions Cyrano de Bergerac, or the Wife of Bath or Uriah Heep. If the schoolman is unable to display this sort of minimum, cultured competence, then, who in heaven's name can we expect to do so?

But too many educators currently are at their weakest in this highly sensitive area. It cannot be attributed to any drop-off in the intellectual caliber of our school people during the past generation. Our teachers and administrators are just as talented and just as intelligent as they ever were, probably more so, but since the takeover of my profession about 35 years ago by the burning-eyed, thin-lipped disciples of one Dr. John Dewey, these men and women with their maddening and unshakeable assurance that they alone were right, they alone among all mortals somehow had divine certainty unveiled to them, and those of us who dared disagree with them in any particular were not only absolutely and blindly wrong, but also more than slightly stupid. Since the take-over of my profession by this clique, school people all over California and all over the country, working out in the field and in the firing line, have been told over and over and over and over again with all the persistence of a Chinese water torturer, that culture was of no consequence whatever in education. The education major in this state doesn't require any of it. No test is administered to the California applicant for the teaching credential to see if he can even spell or knows the multiplication tables.

An administrator like me has to know psychology, curriculum, finance, school law, but nobody could care less whether I've ever heard of the Platonic Absolutes or the Nicomachean Ethics. And any schoolman can get a doctoral degree from virtually any institution in the land without having anyone even asking him if he can distinguish between Bizet and Puccini; between Galileo and Copernicus, or between the Wars of the Roses and the Flowering of New England. In such a Philistine environment, under superiors on the highest state and national level who consistently sneer and deride the importance of cultural content, exposed solely to a philosophy which holds that there are no lasting values of any kind, no eternal truths, no positive standards; it's a living wonder to me that such a large number of our teachers and school administrators are as literate and as cultured as they are.

What is needed to restore the public school to its proper place in our American Heritage then, is a complete and total change in our national and state educational philosophy, an altering of our intellectual climate. We are going to need people increasingly in high professional places who will stand up and say for all to hear that certain things in this life, this world, this universe, are important in themselves just because they exist; not just for what they can do for us personally, or for how much money they are worth. We need to be told once again that the real purpose of education is, always has been and always will be, to pursue the truth—just that, but in order to do this, we must supply our children with the intellectual tools which the race over the centuries make indispensable. We will need to know that adjustment to one's environment, that fetish and shibboleth of my profession for a generation and more is not the soul, nor even a defensible goal of education, but rather an outworn and exploded relic of past thinking and antiquated practice.

If our ancestors, those brave men and noble women who came across a thousand leagues of stormy seas and founded this country had adopted this as their philosophy, passed it on to their children, we, their remote descendants, would today still be living along a narrow strip of the Atlantic Seaboard in log cabins and fighting off Indians. This would have represented a perfect adaptation and adjustment to the environment which they found. What they preferred to do, and what I hope that we and our descendants after us do, is to adjust our environment to ourselves, or rather to that which we would like ourselves to become. It will be in this way that we will continue to make this country at once the envy and wonder of the remainder of the world. When these new ideas have taken hold—and it seems strange to call these "new" doesn't it—because they are as old as the human race. But to the leaders of education, they are new because they have never heard of them before.

When these new ideas have taken hold, when spiritual non-sectarian values have been readmitted to our schools, when love of country is taught by word and by example, when subject matter is restored to its proper place as the cornerstone of our instructional program, then and only then, will the public school assume its proper role as the perpetrator, the enricher of our American Heritage, and that role does not belong to teachers and other school people alone. Just as war is said to be too important to be solely left to the generals, so also is American education far too important to be left only to the educators.

Over the years, our country has embarked upon a unique and far-reaching experiment called "Education for All," and all of us who make up that country in this the greatest of states, must now see to it that this experiment does not become, as it is in the greatest danger of becoming, politics for all, indoctrination for all, propaganda for all, or perhaps most dangerous here in California, pablum for all. This is a job for everyone of us, for every American citizen. Unless we tackle it without delay and without flinching, the golden moments of opportunity may be lost forever. If we will take the time and the interest, which education in the 20th century deserves and requires, we may yet establish this ancient and wonderful art of ours—greatest of them all—the art of teaching in its rightful place as the great supplier of the motive power in the modern race between civilization and catastrophe.

Thank you.

10. Intelligence Without Morality

Joseph S. Junell

There is a scene in *David Copperfield* (one of the few books I have read several times) that fills me with a sense of pathos I would ordinarily admit to only with considerable embarrassment. It is the scene in which David, after a series of cruel experiences, escapes from London and confronts his aunt, Betsey Trotwood, who has not seen him since the day of his birth. Standing before her, a dirty, ragged, underfed and shockingly misused child of ten, he pleads that he be accepted into her household. The scene is filled with all the outrageous sentimentality of which Dickens is master. Yet I cannot return to David's words without that familiar rush of absurd feelings.

"I am David Copperfield of Blunderstone, in Suffolk—where you came on the night when I was born and saw my dear mama. I have been unhappy since she died. I have been slighted and taught nothing, and thrown upon myself, and put to work not fit for me. It has made me run away to you. I was robbed at first setting out, and have walked all the way, and have never slept in a bed since I began the journey." Here my self-support gave way all at once, and, with a movement of my hands, intended to show my ragged state, and call it to witness that I suffered something, I broke into a passion of crying, which I suppose had been pent up within me all the week.

During the while, I experience all of David's tensions and emotions. His tears are my tears, for I, too, have suffered the calculated horror of the Murdstones, the educational process at Salem House that was next to sheer brutality, and the grim evils of the child's workhouse in London.

I do not pretend that this reaction to Dickens has shaped all my thinking about education, child labor, or the forces of evil and good; other impressions have long since helped round out the picture. But I should be dishonest if I did not confess that these emotional journeys with David, along with several others, have done much to forge the attitudes and feel-

Source: *Phi Delta Kappan*, XLIX, 1 (September 1967), 42–45. Reprinted by permission of the author and publisher.

ings which are primary to my system of values, and that they influence many of my thoughts and decisions with the force of conviction. While there are other significant functions claimed for the literary arts, this is surely among the more important.

It is this vital process, often called vicarious experience, which has been systematically deleted from elementary social studies, at a stage in the child's development when he is most susceptible to its influence. My complaint is not that school people engaged in teaching, writing, and editing of social studies refuse to juggle facts dishonestly for the sake of dramatizing them, but that they fail to dramatize facts or events even when to do so is historically legitimate. History abounds in rivalries, danger, and conflict containing strong moral issues charged with emotional content. These make fertile soil for the development of primary social values, so terribly important to the survival of the race. Unfortunately for elementary children, they seldom see the light of day. Too often they are suppressed or omitted because of opinionated ideas about emotional readiness or because of current fetishes regarding concept building, problem solving, and other panaceas.

As an example of how emasculation is achieved, I should like to cite from my own experience. Several years ago, while engaged in writing a textbook for elementary-grade children, I conceived the notion of telling the Northwest Indian story in terms of ruthless exploitation by the whites and the Indian's reaction to the swift destruction of his culture. To do this I described him briefly as he appeared at the coming of the white man— generous, cunning, childishly naive, yet cleverly resourceful—a being filled with purpose and the deep pride of his ways. As his time began to run out, however, he was presented through the eyes of several pioneer historians who had observed him at first hand—a human derelict cast away in small groups on some desolate stretch of beach, embittered by broken promises, sick and debauched by the white man's disease and bad whiskey. Landless and spiritually corrupted, he had lost all purpose and dignity.

Needless to say, my efforts were gently though firmly rebuffed. Such an approach, I was told, was not in good taste. For one thing it was too brutal for children of this tender age. For another, it was overly pessimistic.

Well, I had never supposed that it wasn't. But history, I knew, was on my side; the facts were there for anyone who wanted to examine them. Besides, I have always felt that a certain amount of guilt is salutary. I wondered if the unvarnished truth might not help instill in our children some sense of outrage at the enormous moral wrongs for which every white being on earth must assume a measure of responsibility. I was not unaware of our moments of greatness—of those noble acts of sacrifice and generosity which are also part of the record. But it seemed to me the fine things have always found ways of getting themselves publicized, while the ugly ones are more often swept under the rug. I wondered if it were not more fitting that our children walk in the shadow of humility than in the glare of overweening pride. I felt that the record was in need of better balancing.

But if this avenue was barred, I was encouraged to find others. Indeed, a sympathetic treatment of the Indian was not only desirable but imperative, and I had only to find a more acceptable way of showing what a fine fellow he was. The solution finally pointed out to me was through the development of "concepts," a theme familiar to most every writer of elementary text materials. In this instance the Indian is observed in close harmony with nature as he plays out his role as hunter, artisan, family man, and, occasionally, warrior. Out of the materials emerge the conceptual relationships between Indian art and religion, climate and culture, man and nature's resources, and so on. Except for patches of artificial dialogue intended to stimulate human interest, the style is expository, with great stress placed on organization and vocabulary control. It is, as one might suspect, a style which lends itself exceedingly well to dullness, rising occasionally to power, but limited for the most part by the nature of the materials.

I sighed in resignation and went to work. My own examination of sample elementary texts preparatory to writing, together with my teaching experience, should have taught me that social studies at this level are strongly materialistic in bias and that social ideas, except as they are treated innocuously on the community-helper level, are practically nonexistent. The feeling, generally, is that ideas of this caliber must await greater development of reflective powers before much can be done with them.

The notion raises some provocative questions. Among others, it implies that solutions to such problems are largely intellectual and underestimates the role of primary attitudes in critical thinking. By doing so it denies the interesting possibility that the giant step in solving social problems may not be intellectual at all and that if children do not learn to take this step in the elementary school, the chances are excellent that they never will.

Since the first systematic approach to the teaching of value structure is in fact reserved mainly for secondary students, it is helpful to explore the claims which professional educators make for this method and to report on one or two of its deficiencies. Reflective thinking, or problem solving, as the method is often called, grew directly out of John Dewey's book, *How We Think,* published in 1933. In it Dewey described several kinds of thinking, but he attached greatest importance to reflective thought, which he believed most nearly resembled the nature of scientific inquiry. The theory includes a careful analysis of such elements as the recognition of a problem, the collection of data, and the formulation and testing of a hypothesis. In spite of its numerous adherents and the promise it held for the social studies, the theory languished for a number of years for want of implementation. Only recently is it being revived under the aegis of one of its able and leading spokesman, Lawrence E. Metcalf.

Through his books, co-authored by Maurice P. Hunt, and his extensive survey of research in the field, Metcalf has perhaps given us the clearest conception of Dewey's meaning of reflective thinking and its application within the classroom. Most important to this writing is his essentially pragmatic view of how teachers should deal with conflicting values that pervade so many public issues. To illustrate this view, I quote from one of his articles:

Perhaps . . . a reinterpretation of problem solving . . . will help teachers to entertain the hypothesis that teaching people to be good is not their province. Teaching an understanding of how values affect and even distort perception is within their province. Teaching that certain values are inconsistent with other values is within their province as logicians. It is even their job to teach that some values are democratic. . . . But no one, least of all our teachers, can tell the American people what their values are to be.

To demonstrate how this might work in practice, Metcalf sets up a classroom model in which students investigate the problem of socialized medicine. "If students are to decide whether they are in favor of socialized medicine, they will find it helpful to learn what socialized medicine is, and what results from it." During the learning process the teacher is discouraged of any temptation to "purvey" his own private biases. His job is to "help them find data, if it is available, on the achievements and other effects of socialized medicine" and to assist individuals in coping "with the logic of those who are opponents or proponents of this institution." He would have students speculate on what would be the effects of socialized medicine in this country and even ask them to rate these effects according to their "desirability" or "undesirability." By pursuing this method of nonintervention, teachers would no longer be teaching "values" but "valuing," by which I think Metcalf means that things are given value only when evidence uncovered by reflective techniques has proven them worthy of it.

I do not argue with the general excellence of this approach. What I do object to is the implication that truly meaningful solutions to problems which involve conflicting values can be reached without reference to some preestablished framework of commonly held moral absolutes. We are led to believe that reflective techniques alone will enable us not only to make the wiser of alternate decisions but to achieve a responsible morality.

But wherever conflicting values are present, especially strongly held ones, whose interpretation of what is wise do we accept? Some of the most crucial issues are often most difficult to resolve on the basis of purely nonmoral data. Besides, it is no great trick for the clever protagonist to arm himself with a great mass of evidence in defense of any position he wishes to assume. Indeed, I watched the classic example of this truth a number of years ago when I chanced to see Dr. William Teller and Lord Bertrand Russell debate before a television audience on the merits and shortcomings of nuclear armament. Seldom is one privileged to witness a display of such incisive rebuttal, pinpoint documentation, and prodigious range of knowledge. Yet even more fascinating than the brilliance of their arguments was the fact that both men, having spent lifetimes employing reflective techniques in the pursuit of new scientific knowledge, could arrive at positions so diametrically opposed. One of these postures—which, only God knows —might well lead us to world holocaust. When men like these fall out over an issue embracing the fate of mankind, one is tempted to ask, somewhat cynically perhaps, if a bad decision is any less bad because it was made with full knowledge of the facts.

The need to teach reflective techniques is not in question here. Critical thinking should inform every proposed solution to the human predicament. But the solution itself must be the direct reflection of some fixed moral principle pinpointed somewhere on a scale of primary values. For example, if the value regarding human worth (which is largely internalized during childhood or not at all) were truly operative—approaching, let us say, the intensity of Schweitzer's concept of reverence—the idea of modern warfare as a solution to anything simply could not be countenanced. The immediate reaction to it would be one of such repugnance as to become virtually ego-destroying. Reflective thinking might well be employed to examine alternate courses of action, but rarely if ever one in direct conflict with the fundamental value itself.

If this sounds like some vastly artless oversimplification of a terribly complex problem, may I remind the reader that I am interested only in the elementary school child. A nodding acquaintance with the psychiatric view regarding the development of conscience, plus several years spent in personal observations, have convinced me that he is the main hope of the world. "Much of the most significant establishment of values and attitudes has occurred before school age," writes analyst Brock Chisolm, former world health director for the United Nations. ". . . As very many people accept the judgment of their consciences without question throughout their lives, and as the basic conscience can only repeat back whatever was learned in childhood, and as conscience presumes to deal with all matters of right and wrong, it is clear that the attitudes to which small children are exposed have tremendous importance for their future, and for the future of the community and the race."

It may not be within the province of teachers, as Metcalf suggests, to teach children how to be good, but we had better start telling them what social goodness means and what are some of its great motivating forces. I have briefly discussed one of them—human worth. To this I would add such others as dignity, equality, compassion, and a few of the democratic freedoms. I mention these for a simple reason. I believe they are universal among the peoples of the earth in having been embraced at some time, in some form, and to some degree by humans everywhere. I submit that they have reappeared time and time again throughout the long and troubled course of human history.

The techniques by which such values may be established in young school children are matters of grave concern. Frankly, they lie more within the province of the literary arts than in that of social studies, and it is perhaps time the social studies began to borrow seriously from them. I am not talking about the trappings and papier-mâché models of literature with which so much elementary social studies writing is now invested. This is the world of "synthetic plots" so ably criticized by R. J. Margolis for the *Teacher's College Record,* in which classroom children "take tours to museums and department stores, chatter about what they see, and on occasion get solid bits of information from a textbook (of all things) on the teacher's desk." (I blush in reading these lines, recalling some of my own efforts.) I speak of genuine literary talent, which includes a sense of drama, a sharp eye for significant detail, some insight into human behavior, and the ability to turn little words into big ideas. These are the qualities needed to breathe life into human events in which powerful moral values are at stake.

In this view of how social conscience may be developed in young children, I have tried perhaps too hard to tip the scale on the side of emotion. So be it. The world of pure intelligence has no answers to the irrefutable logic of Swift's *Modest Proposal.* It too easily condones the Auschwitz horror chambers and the charnel house at Hiroshima.

Besides, I can think of no other way of doing what so desperately needs to be done. During my years as a teacher, and in my daily visits to elementary and secondary classrooms, I have seen little to convince me that scholarly examinations of the great moral issues * have resulted in anything more than intellectual exercises. I cannot believe that you teach the values most deeply rooted in social experience by the construction of hypotheses, by field trips, or by the innocent mimicry of democratic processes. To the degree that such values can be taught at all, you teach them by involving children emotionally in the lives of individuals and groups locked in struggles of significant moral consequence. When a child has felt something of the degradation of the Negro slave through empathy, when vicarious experience has set the iron barb of subjection deep into his own flesh—then—and only then—does he begin to internalize the attitudes which give flesh and blood to the value we call equality. This is the work of the teacher or writer who is first a dramatist and second a historian— definitely in that order.

The primacy of literary truth still applies. Where children are concerned our priorities are crystal clear. We must set the stage for them at an earlier age than we ever thought necessary before. Moreover, the drama to be en-

---

* Our enslavement of the Negro, for example.

acted, borrowing equally from the vast record of man's inhumanity to man, must engage the heart even more than the mind. Its basic appeal, in short, must be emotional.

The advantage to this is as plain today as it was nearly two thousand years ago when the Father sent his only begotten child into the world, saying: "Remember, my Son, your adversary is a formidable logician with a breadth of knowledge next only to mine."

"I will play his game of chance," the Son of Man replied. He smiled cunningly as He spoke, fingering in the secret compartment of His robe a pair of loaded dice.

11. Dropouts and the School

Thomas L. Millard

When a youngster elects to quit school before formal completion, he is in effect removing himself from a potential lifetime income officially estimated at $165,000 for the high school graduate. A 16- or 17-year-old youngster simply may not comprehend the enormity of such a decision, or he may not possess the maturity of judgment to understand fully his own life situation, enabling him to arrive at such a decision intelligently. Such a youngster needs intensive guidance and counseling. The dropout may be a person with serious personality and environmental conflicts rather than an immature person who simply decides to walk away from his responsibilities.

We live in a fast-tempo, ever-changing, ever-demanding society characterized by a high success-value orientation. With this in mind, educators must not simply write off as failures the young people who follow sudden whims to "go it alone" in a job market, which, unknown to them, is rapidly closing its doors to individuals like themselves. Such youngsters need

SOURCE: *Educational Leadership,* XXII, 4 (January 1965), 247–50, 261. Reprinted by permission of the author and the Association for Supervision and Curriculum Development. Copyright © 1965 by the Association for Supervision and Curriculum Development.

adult attention, understanding, sympathy and expert guidance that enable them to appreciate fully the serious consequences of their "decision," which, in all probability, guarantees them permanent retirement from work, before they even begin.

Even a cursory review of the statistics bears this out: The unemployment rate among dropouts is double that of the general population; they are also out of work for longer periods; dropouts are identified as that hard core of uneducated young people who perform the most menial and routine work tasks.

Taking this further, in terms of upward strivings, some writers have suggested that social mobility is becoming less and less possible in America. When one considers the growing unemployment rate, especially among youthful workers, in the ranks of a diminishing unskilled labor class, it almost suggests that as class affiliation goes, we are probably witnessing the emergence of an "economically disaffiliated class" in the economic structure of a super-scientific America.

Reversing this possibility must begin in adequate school programs. Such programs incorporate the best that we know in educational principles and practices, including experimentally tested concepts and procedures in learning, resulting from present-day technological requirements and social demands found in an automated society.

A Challenge to the Schools

To be sure, there is no easy solution toward arresting these statistics. However, enough is known about the social, emotional and educational syndrome for dropouts and the myriad problems facing the dropout to permit parents, employment counselors, social agencies, business and industry and, more especially, the public schools to do something meaningful and lasting about the situation.

But present-day school programs dealing with the dropout crises are, but for a few exceptions, grossly unrealistic, inadequate, unimaginative and unsympathetic.[1] Too often, interested and willing teachers are frustrated by indifferent school administrators, jerry-built curricula that favor the "middle-class child" and a superfluity of hurried and aimless "crash programs" that collide with each other with incredible clumsiness. One example: The nationwide campaign in the summer of 1963 to induce dropouts to return to school, which to date has met with indifferent success.

An alarming percentage of those who came back are dropping out again —and rightly so—for what else was there to expect, reexposing them to

[1] For a capsule review of some of the projects now being conducted in various school districts, see Monica Bayley, "A Renewed Effort to Solve the Problem of Dropouts," *School Life,* Vol. 46, No. 3 (December 1963), pp. 11–16.

the same learning situation and frustration that caused the initial withdrawal.

The concern is that this is taking place within the school. Historically, the school has been the major social institution capable of influencing the child.

As an agent representative of the larger, more comprehensive and more complex organization we call "society," the school fittingly may provide that specialized assistance and all that socializes the individual into a useful and productive citizen.

Education is one of the two major influences in the life-preparatory experience of the child in terms of meaningful training for lifetime labor productivity. Thus, education can be an effective agency in developing the child's life goals and adequacy in meeting the labor requirements of an expanding, technological society.

Even such eminent investigators as Jersild,[2] Sullivan,[3] and Warner [4] view the school as second only to the home in its influence to shape the self-concept and self-esteem of the child. Yet in dealing with the dropout problem, it is a waste of time to point our fingers toward the home. The modern nuclear-age home simply does not have the preventive or "holding power" in regard to dropouts. If one must look for an institution that is big enough, with power and resources, the public schools are the answer. Within this framework, the central problem for public education is one of developing an imaginative and far-reaching curriculum with bold new concepts in teaching and with new techniques and devices for the prevention and/or holding of dropouts. Such an instructional program promises the highest potential for modifying the reactions of those students who find school an unrelated life experience in terms of the meaning which they invest in school.

For the almost one million youths who yearly quit the classroom, leaving school is nearly always a symptom indicative of overwhelming academic and social frustrations. To a great extent, they see themselves as "misfits" in the currently prescribed curricula in social and life-preparatory experiences. They mask their feelings of insecurity, inadequacy and loneliness by withdrawing from basic social learning.[5] That there is a sig-

[2] Arthur T. Jersild, *In Search of Self* (New York: Bureau of Publications, Teachers College, Columbia University, 1952).

[3] Harry Stack Sullivan, *Conceptions of Modern Psychiatry* (New York: W. W. Norton and Co., 1953).

[4] W. Lloyd Warner, Robert J. Havighurst and Martin B. Loeb, *Who Shall Be Educated?* (New York: Harper and Brothers, 1944).

[5] The reader's attention is directed to *School Failures and Dropouts,* a new Public Affairs pamphlet in which Edith G. Neisser summarizes what is known about the course and treatment of this serious personal and social problem. Also see Edgar Friedenberg, "An Ideology of School Withdrawal," a chapter in the NEA publication, *School Dropouts,* Daniel Schreiber, editor, 1963.

nificant relationship between the way a person views himself and the way he looks upon others has been shown by Berger,[6] Sheerer,[7] and Raskin.[8]

Thus there appears to be general agreement that how a child views himself is his most important belief. This is actually the psychic foundation for his very being. Snygg and Combs [9] suggest that the child not only values his self identity, but that he will engage in certain activities designed to protect and/or enhance it. Thus, the person derives meaning from his social situation only as he brings meaning to it.

This, in effect, means that the individual comes into a social situation prepared to learn certain things and also ready to resist or ignore those social situations which seem unrelated to his needs. Each individual has formulated these goals from his own unique life experience, no matter how enriched or deficient this may be.

In terms of the learning situation, Robert Bills [10] suggests that learning is a self-actualizing process and that the self-concept of the child influences his ability to function effectively.

Education Must Commit Itself

Study of the available data suggests we will not be able to eliminate the dropout problem at any time in the foreseeable future. Nevertheless, some inroads on the problem are possible, though only when public education realizes the commitment it must make and is aware of its own cumulative impact potential.

The focal point of any commitment must insure for the individual maximum learning opportunity to grasp the interlocking nature of social institutions that comprise our social and economic system,[11] to understand the

---

[6] E. M. Berger, "The Relation Between Expressed Acceptance of Self and Expressed Acceptance of Others," *Journal of Abnormal Social Psychology* (1953), 47:778–82.

[7] Elizabeth T. Sheerer, "An Analysis of the Relationship Between Acceptance of Self and Acceptance and Respect for Others in Ten Counseling Cases, *Journal of Consulting Psychology* (1949), 13:169–75.

[8] Nathaniel Raskin, "An Analysis of Six Parallel Studies of the Therapeutic Process," *Journal of Consulting Psychology* (1949), 13:206–20.

[9] Donald Snygg and Arthur W. Combs, *Individualized Behavior* (New York: Harper and Brothers, 1949).

[10] Robert Bills, "Believing and Behaving: Perception and Learning," *Learning More About Learning* (Washington, D.C.: Association for Supervision and Curriculum Development, 1959), pp. 55–73.

[11] This is a vital point, for the school is the only tax-supported institution devoted exclusively to the training of the young. Commenting on American education, Hofstadter suggests that our society has been "passionately intent upon education," but the results of our educational system have been "a constant disappointment." For more on this, see Richard Hofstadter, *Anti-Intellectualism in American Life* (New York: Alfred A. Knopf, 1963).

emerging requirements for economic participation and to think in a more meaningful way about his productive talents and their ultimate contribution to the economic system. Above and beyond this, what we really need is a sweeping and exacting program of self-criticism and analysis that will enable us to understand the "whole person" in the total context of his sociocultural life; but to date, no one has thought through just how this ought to be done. Apparently this is only a sociologist's pipe dream, for there is little evidence such a possibility is forthcoming to deal with the dropout problem.

Lacking this approach, the socio-pathological conditions that spawn dropouts will continue to be a blight upon a nation whose chief characteristic is human betterment and social improvement. It is precisely this aspect of an affluent society, the impossibility of achieving material well-being and adequate comfort, that is proving to be a cultural eyesore in an age of plenty and in a still expanding economy.

The need for such a program is clear enough, but the lack of interest is at least matched by the widespread and glaring deficiencies in imagination concerning it. This much, however, is true: It will only be through the long-term labor of genuine collective action of school, community and social agency, with the resourceful help of government and industry, that the roots of the dropout problem will be unearthed and the disease destroyed.

The Negro Dropout Problem

The dropout problem is particularly severe among Negro youngsters, who comprise a large percentage of today's unemployed youths. Negro youths, even when they are high school graduates, may experience even greater frustration in job finding than do their white contemporaries. In 1962, for example, about one out of every four Negro youngsters in the labor force was out of work, compared with about one out of every eight white youngsters. Since 1955, the jobless rate among Negro youngsters, according to official reports, has risen faster than among white boys and girls —up about 60 percent among Negroes compared with 30 percent among whites.[12]

From the Negro point of view, the greatest domestic challenge facing American society is making manifest and real equal opportunity for all so that we may live constructively and independently in modern society. As the Educational Policies Commission has pointed out: [13] "If the problems

[12] *Welfare in Review, 1963.* Vol. 1, No. 4 (Washington, D.C.: U.S. Department of Health, Education, and Welfare), p. 19.

[13] *Education and the Disadvantaged American* (Washington, D.C.: Educational Policies Commission, NEA, 1962).

of the disadvantaged are to be solved, the society as a whole must give evidence of its undifferentiated respect for all persons."

Understanding the Dropout

A random sampling of the life histories of most dropouts would seem to suggest the etiology of the dropout syndrome as falling into two groups:

(a) Those syndromes which develop slowly out of social and academic failures on the part of the individual to incorporate in his life-scheme orientation those attitudes and values which are in harmony with the larger society.

(b) Those syndromes which develop relatively rapidly, due to sudden deleterious influences in the person's social or academic milieu, precipitated either by the socio-physical difficulties of marginal living or the inadequacy of mutually reinforcing social interaction.

The influence on human personality of these social and psychological agents lies in the fact that it stirs up easily aroused feelings of envy toward the self-adjusted, goal-directed school child, contempt for the adult figure and distrust and/or perhaps hostility toward everyone in comfortable identity with the cultural values and their expectant goals.

In consequence, all the satisfaction and experiential background which the school experience can offer the individual meets with only limited success and subsequent failure as the individual becomes more or less socially and emotionally isolated from the mainstream of socialization.

To the disinterested, unattached school child (as with most dropouts) the school experience becomes an abstraction in which he plays an uncreative role in the discovery of ideas and meaning (whatever they are). While he does not know it, his unresponsiveness or anti-learning behavior, is, in part, external dramatization of powerful instinctual urges, unhampered by self-regulating experiences.

Obviously, it is the school's responsibility to ascertain the cause or causes for the child's unproductivity and, once the reason is found, the school program must be adjusted to meet the child's needs, or the child must be helped to adjust to the program. This must bring into play the full resources of the school—the psychologist, vocational counselor, the classroom teacher, the guidance personnel, the psychiatrist and the social worker in one collective and concerted act.

To find the root cause for disinterest in learning is a critical point, for learning to find satisfaction and pleasure in the immediate personal-social situation of school is the basis of the maintenance of educational interest.

In terms of the individual's need to acquire an understanding of the harmony and workings of his social environment and its varied parts, one looks to education, for it is education that bestows comprehension.

This must lead us to a searching reappraisal of previously defined educational goals, of methods and content and of our present ability to impart the message to children in the earliest grades.

Only so can they understand that school is the place where they belong and that taking advantage of its preparatory experiences is prerequisite for any meaningful relationship in an automated, nuclear society which calls for abilities of the mind as contrasted with previous needs of brute strength.

Seldom, if ever, has education been the instigator of important social change. It has, in fact, reflected more closely the basic social, political and economic changes going on around it and, in this sense, it lends itself beautifully to the requirements of pedagogical change.

12. After John Dewey, What?

Jerome S. Bruner

In 1897, at the age of thirty-eight, John Dewey published a stirring and prophetic work entitled "My Pedagogic Creed." Much of his later writing on education is foreshadowed in this document.

Five articles of faith are set forth. The first defines the educational process: "All education proceeds by the participation of the individual in the social consciousness of the race. This process begins unconsciously almost at birth, and is continually shaping the individual's powers, saturating his consciousness, forming his habits, training his ideas, and arousing his feelings and emotions." A second article of faith embodies Dewey's concept of the school: "Education being a social process, the school is simply that form of community life in which all those agencies are concentrated that will be most effective in bringing the child to share in the inherited resources of the race, and to use his own powers for social ends. Education, therefore, is a process of living and not a preparation for future living." In

SOURCE: *Saturday Review*, XLIV, 24 (June 17, 1961), 58–59, 76–78.
Copyright © 1961 Saturday Review, Inc. Reprinted by permission of the author and publisher.

a third credo Dewey speaks of the subject matter of education: "The social
life of the child is the basis of concentration or correlation in all his training or growth. The social life gives the unconscious unity and the background of all his efforts and all his attainments. . . . The true center . . .
is not science, nor literature, nor history, nor geography, but the child's
own social activities." A view of educational method gives form to Dewey's fourth faith: "The law for presenting and treating material is the law
implicit in the child's own nature." For Dewey, the law was that of action:
"The active side precedes the passive in the development of the child-na-
ture. I believe that consciousness is essentially motor or impulsive; that
conscious states tend to project themselves in action." And finally, Dewey's fifth thesis: "Education is the fundamental method of social progress
and reform."

One reads the document today with mixed feelings. Its optimism is
classically American in its rejection of the tragic view of life. It defines
truth in the pragmatic spirit: truth as the fruit of inquiry into the consequences of action. It expresses a firm faith not only in the individual's capacity to grow but in society's capacity to shape man in its own best
image. The final lines of the creed are these: "Every teacher should realize
the dignity of his calling; that he is a social servant set apart for the maintenance of proper social order and the securing of the right social growth.
In this way the teacher always is the prophet of the true God and the ush-
erer in of the true kingdom of heaven."

Yet, the very wholesomeness—the optimism, the pragmatism, the acceptance of man's harmonious continuity with society—leaves one uneasy.
For in the two-thirds of a century between 1897 and today, there has been
not only a profound change in our conception of nature, but also of society
and the world of social institutions. Perhaps more important, we have
lived through a revolution in our understanding of the nature of man, his
intelligence, his capabilities, his passions, and the forms of his growth.

Dewey's thinking reflected the changes, though he was limited by the
premises of his philosophical position. But between Dewey's first premises
and our day, there bristles a series of revolutionary doctrines and cataclys-
mic events that change the very character of the inquiry. Two world wars,
the dark episode of Hitler and genocide, the Russian Revolution, the rela-
tivistic revolution in physics and psychology, the Age of Energy with its
new technology, the sardonic reign of skeptical philosophy—all of these
have forced a reappraisal of the underlying premises in terms of which we
construct a philosophy of education.

Let us, then, re-examine the premises, being guided by what we know
today of the world and of the nature of human nature. But there is matter
that is liable to some misinterpretation in an enterprise such as this, and
we do well to clear it up at the outset. One writes against the background
of one's day. Dewey was writing with an eye to the sterility and rigidity of

school instruction in the 1890s—its failure to appreciate particularly the nature of the child. His emphasis upon the importance of direct experience and social action was an implied critique of the empty formalism of education that did little to relate learning to the child's world of experience. Dewey did mighty service in inspiring a correction. But an excess of virtue is vice. We, in our day, are reconsidering education against the background of such an excess. Misunderstanding often converted Dewey's ideas into sentimental practice that he deplored: "Next to deadness and dullness, formalism and routine," he wrote in his Creed, "our education is threatened by no greater evil than sentimentalism." The sentimental cult of "the class project," of "life adjustment" courses, of fearfulness in exposing the child to the startling sweep of man and nature lest it violate the comfortable domain of his direct experience, the cloying concept of "readiness"— these are conceptions about children often divorced from experiment on the educational process, justified in the name of Dewey. His was a noble yet tender view in his time. But what of our times? In what form shall we speak our beliefs?

Education seeks to develop the power and sensibility of mind. The task of education is twofold. On the one hand, the educational process transmits to the individual some part of the accumulation of knowledge, style, and values that constitute the culture of a people. In doing so, it shapes the impulses, the consciousness, and the way of life of the individual. But education must also seek to develop the processes of intelligence so that the individual is capable of going beyond the cultural ways of his social world, able to innovate, in however modest a way, so that he can create an interior culture of his own. For whatever the art, the science, the literature, the history, and the geography of a culture, each man must be his own artist, his own scientist, his own historian, his own navigator. No person is master of the whole culture; indeed, this is almost a defining characteristic of that form of social memory that we speak of as culture. Each man lives a fragment of it. To be whole, he must create his own version of the world, using that part of his cultural heritage that he has made his own through education.

In our time, the requirements of technology press heavily upon the freedom of the individual to create images of the world that are satisfying in the deepest sense. Our era has also witnessed the rise of ideologies that subordinate the individual to the defined aims of a society, a form of subordination that is without compassion for idiosyncrasy and that respects only the instrumental contribution of the individual to the progress of the society. At the same time, and in spite of ideologies, man's understanding of himself and of his world—both the natural and social world—has deepened to a degree that warrants calling our age an intellectually golden one. The challenge of the times ahead is to employ our deeper understanding not only to the enrichment of society but to the enrichment of the individual.

It is true, as Dewey said many years ago, that all education proceeds by the participation of the individual in the social consciousness of the race, but it is a truth with a double edge. For all education, good and bad alike, is of that order. We know now to what degree, to take but one example, the very language one speaks conditions and shapes the style and structure of thought and experience. Indeed, there is reason to believe that thought processes themselves are internalizations of social intercourse, an inner colloquy patterned by early external dialogues. It is this that makes education possible. But education, by giving shape and expression to our experience can also be the principal instrument for setting limits on the enterprise of mind. The guarantee against limits is the sense of alternatives. Education must, then, be not only a transmission of culture but also a provider of alternative views of the world and a strengthener of the will to explore them.

After a half-century of startling progress in the psychological sciences, we know that mental health is only a minimum condition for the growth of mind. The tragedy of mental illness is that it so preoccupies the person with the need to fend off realities with which he cannot cope that it leaves him without either the nerve or the zest to learn. But mental health is a minimum condition. The powers of mind grow with their exercise. Adjustment is too modest an ideal, if it is an ideal at all. Competence in the use of one's powers for the development of individually defined and socially relevant excellence is much more to the point. After a half-century of Freud, we know that the freeing of instinct and inclination is not an end in itself but a way station along the road to competence. What is most prophetic for us about Freud in this second half of the century is not his battle against the fetters of rigid moralism, but his formula: "Where there was id, let there be ego."

Education must begin, as Dewey concluded his first article of belief, "with a psychological insight into the child's capacities, interests, and habits," but a point of departure is not an itinerary. It is equally a mistake to sacrifice the adult to the child as to sacrifice the child to the adult. It is sentimentalism to assume that the teaching of life can always be fitted to the child's interests, just as it is empty formalism to force the child to parrot the formulas of adult society. Interests can be created and stimulated. In this sphere it is not far from the truth to say that supply creates demand, that the challenge of what is available creates response. One seeks to equip the child with deeper, more gripping, and subtler ways of knowing the world and himself.

The school is entry into the life of the mind. It is, to be sure, life itself and not merely a preparation for living. But it is a special form of living, one carefully devised for making the most of those plastic years that characterize the development of *homo sapiens* and distinguish our species from all others. School should provide not simply a continuity with the broader community or with everyday experience. It is the special community where one experiences discovery by the use of intelligence, where one leaps into new and unimagined realms of experience, experience that is discontinuous with what went before, as when one first understands what a poem is or what beauty and power and simplicity inheres in the idea of the conservation-of-energy theorems—that nothing is lost, only converted, and that measure is universally applicable. If there is one continuity to be singled out, it is to convert the autistic sense of the omnipotence of thought of the young child into that realistic confidence in the use of thought that characterizes the effective man.

In insisting upon the continuity of the school with the community on the one side and the family on the other, John Dewey overlooked the special function of education as an opener of new perspectives. If the school were merely a transition zone from the intimacy of the family to the life of the community, it would be a way of life easily enough arranged. It is interesting to examine the educational systems of primitive societies. It is almost universal that there comes a point, usually at puberty, where there is a sharp change in the life of the boy, marked by a *rite de passage* that has as its effect the establishment of a sharp boundary between childhood ways and the ways of the adolescent.

It would be romantic nonsense to pattern our practices upon those found in preliterate societies. I would only ask that we attend to one parallel: that education not confuse the child with the adult and recognize that the transition to adulthood involves an introduction to new realms of experience, the discovery and exploration of new mysteries, the gaining of new powers. This is the heady stuff of education and it is its own reward.

In the *shtetl* of Eastern Europe, the traditional Jewish ghetto, the wise scholar was a particularly important figure—the *talmud khokhem*. In his mien, his mode of conversation so rich in allusion, his form of poise, the wise man was the image not of a competent but, rather, of a beautiful person. Traditional Chinese society also had its image of the beautiful person, one who blended knowledge and sentiment and action in a beautiful way of life. The ideal of the gentleman served perhaps the same function in Europe of the seventeenth and eighteenth centuries. It is perhaps in this spirit that Alfred North Whitehead urged that education must involve an exposure to greatness if it is to make its mark. I would urge that the yeast of education is the idea of excellence, and the idea of excellence comprises as many forms as there are individuals, each of whom develops his own image of excellence. The school must have as one of its principal functions the nurturing of images of excellence.

A detached conception of idealized excellence is not enough. A doctrine of excellence, to be effective, must be translatable into the individual lives of those who encounter it. What is compelling about the *talmud khokhem,* the Chinese scholar-administrator, the eighteenth-century gentleman, is that they embody ways of life to which each can aspire in his own way and from which each can borrow in his own style. I believe, then, that the school must also contain men and women who, in their own way, seek and embody excellence. This does not mean that we shall have to staff our schools with men and women of great genius, but that the teacher must embody in his or her own approach to learning a pursuit of excellence. And, indeed, with the technical resources opened by television and the like, one can also present the student and his teacher with the working version of excellence in its highest sense. In the years ahead, we shall learn that the great scholar, scientist, or artist can speak as easily and honestly to the beginner as to the graduate student.

The issue of subject matter in education can only be resolved by reference to one's view of the nature of knowledge. Knowledge is a model we construct to give meaning and structure to regularities in experience. The organizing ideas of any body of knowledge are inventions for rendering experience economical and connected. We invent concepts such as force in physics, the bond in chemistry, motives in psychology, style in literature, as means to the end of comprehension. The history of culture is the history of the development of great organizing ideas, ideas that inevitably stem from deeper values and points of view about man and nature. The power of great organizing concepts is not only that they permit us to understand and sometimes to predict or change the world in which we live; it lies also in the fact that ideas provide instruments for experience. Having grown up in a culture dominated now by the ideas of Newton with a conception of time flowing equably, we experience time moving with an inexorable and steady one-way arrow. Indeed, we know now, after a quarter of a century of research on perception, that experience is not had direct and neat, but filtered through the programmed readiness of our senses. The program is constructed of our expectations and these are derived from our models or ideas about what exists and what follows what.

From this, two convictions follow. The first is that the structure of knowledge—its connectedness and the derivations that make one idea follow from another—is the proper emphasis in education. For it is structure, the great conceptual inventions that bring order to the congeries of disconnected observation, that gives meaning to what we may learn, and makes possible the opening up of new realms of experience.

The second conviction is that the unity of knowledge is to be found within knowledge itself, if the knowledge is worth mastering. To attempt a justification of subject matter, as Dewey did, in terms of its relation to the child's social activities is to misunderstand what knowledge is and how it may be mastered. The significance of the concept of commutativity in mathematics does not derive from the social insight that two houses with fourteen people in each is not the same as fourteen houses with two people in each. Rather, it inheres in the power of the idea to generate a way of thinking about number that is lithe and beautiful and immensely generative—an idea at least as powerful as, say, the future conditional tense in formal grammar. Without the idea of commutativity, algebra would be impossible. If set theory—now often the introductory section in newer curricula in mathematics—had to be justified in terms of its relation to immediate experience and social life, it would not be worth teaching. Yet set theory lays a foundation for the understanding of order and number that could never be achieved with the social arithmetic of interest rates and bales of hay at so much per bale. Mathematics, like any other subject, must begin with experience, but progress toward abstraction requires precisely that there be a weaning away from the obviousness of superficial experience.

There is one consideration of economy that is paramount. One cannot "cover" any subject in full—not even in a lifetime, if coverage means visiting all the facts and events and morsels. Subject matter presented so as to emphasize its structure will perforce be of that generative kind that permits reconstruction of the details or, at very least, prepares a place where the details, when encountered, can be fitted.

What, then, of subject matter in the conventional sense? The answer to the question "What shall be taught?" turns out to be the answer one gets to the question "What is nontrivial?" If one can once answer the question "What is worth knowing about?" then it is not difficult to distinguish between what about it is worth teaching and learning and what is not. Surely, knowledge of the natural world, knowledge of the human condition, knowledge of the nature and dynamics of society, knowledge of the past so that one may use it in experiencing the present and aspiring to the future —all of these, it would seem reasonable to suppose, are essential to an educated man. To these must be added another—knowledge of the products of our artistic heritage that mark the history of our esthetic wonder and delight.

A problem immediately arises concerning the symbolism in terms of which knowledge is understood and talked about.

There is language in its natural sense and language in its mathematical sense. I cannot imagine an educated man a century from now who will not be somewhat bilingual in this special sense—concise and adept in a natural language and mathematics. For these are the tools essential to the unlocking of new experience and the gaining of new powers. As such, they must have a central place in any curriculum.

Finally, it is as true today as it was when Dewey wrote that one cannot foresee the world in which the child we educate will live. Informed powers of mind and a sense of potency about coping are then the only instruments we can give the child that will be invariant across the transformations of time and circumstance. The succession of studies that we give the child in the ideal school need not be fixed in any but one way: whatever is introduced, let it be pursued continuously enough to give the student a sense of the power of mind that comes from a deepening of understanding. It is this, rather than any form of coverage over time, that matters most.

The process and the goal of education are one and the same thing. The goal of education is disciplined understanding. That is the process as well.

Let us recognize first that the opposite of understanding is not ignorance or simply "not knowing." To understand something is, first, to give up some other way of conceiving of it. Between one way of conceiving and a better way, there often lies confusion. It is one of our biological inheritances that confusion produces emergency anxiety, and with anxiety there come the defensive measures—flight, fright, or freezing—that are antithetical to the free and zestful use of mind. The limiting fact of mental life in child and adult alike is that there is a limited capacity for processing information—our span, as it is called, can encompass six or seven unrelated items simultaneously. Go beyond that and there is overload, confusion, forgetting. As George Miller has put it, the principle of economy is to fill our seven mental input slots with gold rather than dross. The degree to which material to be learned is put into structures by the learner will determine whether he is working with gold or dross. For this reason, as well as for reasons already stated, it is essential that before being exposed to a wide range of material on a topic, the child first have a general idea of how and where things fit. It is often the case that the development of the general idea comes from a first round of experience with concrete embodiments of an idea that are close to the child's life. The cycle of learning begins, then, with the particular and immediate, moves toward abstraction, and comes to a temporary goal when the abstraction can then be used in grasping new particulars in the deeper way that abstraction permits.

Insofar as possible, a method of instruction should have the objective of leading the child to discover for himself. Telling children and then testing them on what they have been told inevitably has the effect of producing bench-bound learners whose motivation for learning is likely to be extrinsic to the task at hand—pleasing the teacher, getting into college, artificially maintaining self-esteem. The virtues of encouraging discovery are of two kinds. In the first place, the child will make what he learns his own, will fit his discovery into the interior world of culture that he creates for himself. Equally important, discovery and the sense of confidence it provides are the proper rewards for learning. They are rewards that, moreover, strengthen the very process that is at the heart of education—disciplined inquiry.

The child must be encouraged to get the full benefit from what he learns. This is not to say that he should be required to put it to immediate use in his daily life, though so much the better if he has the happy opportunity to do so. Rather, it is a way of honoring the connectedness of knowledge. Two facts and a relation joining them are and should be an invitation to generalize, to extrapolate, to make a tentative intuitive leap, indeed even to build a tentative theory. The leap from mere learning to using what one has learned in thinking is an essential step in the use of mind. Indeed, plausible guessing, the use of the heuristic hunch, the best employment of necessarily insufficient evidence—these are activities in which the child needs practice and guidance. They are among the great antidotes to passivity.

Most important of all, the educational process must be free of intellectual dishonesty and those forms of cheating that explain without providing understanding. I have expressed the conviction elsewhere that any subject can be taught to anybody at any age in some form that is honest. It is not honest to present a fifth-grade social studies class with an image of Christopher Columbus as a typical American teen-ager musing after school with his brother, Bart, about what lies across the seas—even if the image set forth does happen to mesh with the child's immediate sense of social experience. A lie is still a lie—even if it sounds like familiar truth. Nor is it honest to present a sixth-grade science class with a garbled but concrete picture of the atom that is, in its way, as sweeteningly false as the suburban image of Columbus given them the year before. A dishonest image can only discourage the self-generating intellectual inquiry out of which real understanding grows.

I believe that education is the fundamental method of social change. Even revolutions are no better than the ideas they embody and the invented means for their application.

Change is swifter in our times than ever before in human history and news of it is almost instantaneous. If we are to be serious in the belief that school must be life itself and not merely preparation for life, then school must reflect the changes through which we are living.

The first implication of this belief is that means must be found to feed back into our schools the ever deepening insights that are developed on the frontiers of knowledge. This is an obvious point in science and mathematics, and continuing efforts are now being instituted to assure that new, more powerful, and often simpler ways of understanding find their way back into the classrooms of our primary and secondary schools. But it is equally important to have this constant refreshment in fields other than the sciences—where the frontiers of knowledge are not always the universities and the research laboratories but political and social life, the arts, literary endeavor, and the rapidly changing business and industrial community. Everywhere there is change and with change, we are learning.

I see the need for a new type of institution, a new conception in curriculum. What we have not had and what we are beginning to recognize as needed is something that is perhaps best called an "institute for curriculum studies"—not one of them, but many. Let it be the place where scholars, scientists, men of affairs, artists, come together with talented teachers constantly to revise and refresh our curricula. It is an activity that transcends the limits of any of our particular university faculties—be they faculties of education, of arts and science, of medicine or engineering. We have been negligent in coming to a sense of the quickening change of life in our time and its implications for the educational process. We have not shared with our teachers the benefits of new discovery, new insight, new artistic triumph. Not only have we operated with the notion of the self-contained classroom, but also with the idea of the self-contained school—and even the self-contained educational system.

Let me consider again what I said about the images of excellence and the role of constant curricular refreshment in helping produce those images. The Nobel laureate or the Ambassador to the United Nations, the brilliant cellist or the perceptive playwright, the historian making use of the past, or the sociologist seeking a pattern in the present—these are men who, like the student, are seeking understanding and mastery of new problems. They represent excellence at the frontiers of endeavor. If a sense of progress and change toward greater excellence is to illuminate our schools, there must be a constant flowing back of their wisdom and effort to enliven and inform teacher and student alike. There is not a difference in kind between the man at the frontier and the young student at his own frontier, each attempting to understand.

How put the matter in summary? Perhaps it is best to parallel John Dewey's "Credo": That education is not only the transmission of culture, but that it also gives shape to the power and sensibility of mind so that each person may learn how to inquire for himself and build an interior culture of his own. That the school is entry into the life of mind, with all this implies about confidence in the use of mind to push to the limit and test the implications of what each has come to know. That the subject matter of education is knowledge about the world and its connectedness, knowledge that has a structure and a history that permits us to find order and predictability in experience and delight in surprise. That the method of education is the method involved in any understanding—a disciplined and responsible effort to know on one's own and to convert what one has understood into an ordered representation of the world that respects the particular but recognizes the intellectual indispensability of the abstract.

That the school continues to be the principal instrument of social progress in an era of swift change and that, as such, it finds means of constantly refreshing and altering its instruction by feeding back the new insights of our times into its curriculum. All of these things depend in the end upon cultivating and giving expression to the forms of excellence that emerge in our varied society. Any aims less ambitious than these are surely unworthy of the challenges we face.

13. Learning to Be Free

Carl R. Rogers

To some, it must seem strangely out of tune with the modern world to speak of learning to be free. The growing opinion today is that man is essentially unfree. He is unfree in a cultural sense. He is all too often a pawn of government. He is molded by mass propaganda into being a creature with certain opinions and beliefs, desired and preplanned by the powers that be. He is the product of his class—lower, middle, or upper—and his values and his behavior are shaped to a large extent by the class to which he belongs.

He is unfree in a scientific sense. The behavioral sciences have made great strides in showing that all his actions and thoughts are determined, being simply the result of previous conditioning. Hence it seems increasingly clear that the individual is formed and moved by forces—cultural forces without, and unconscious forces within—which are beyond his control. He is in all these ways unfree.

However, the freedom I want to discuss is essentially an inner thing, something which exists in the living person, quite aside from any of the outward choice of alternatives which we so often think of as constituting freedom. It is the quality of courage which enables a person to step into the uncertainty of the unknown as he chooses himself. It is the burden of being responsible for the self one chooses to be. It is the recognition by the person that he is an emerging process, not a static end product.

SOURCE: *NEA Journal*, LII, 3 (March 1963), 28–30. Reprinted by permission of the author and publisher.

The individual who is thus deeply and courageously thinking his own thoughts, becoming his own uniqueness, responsibly choosing himself, may be fortunate in having hundreds of objective outer alternatives from which to choose, or he may be unfortunate in having none, but his freedom exists regardless.

Further, this experience of freedom exists not as a contradiction to the picture of the psychological universe as a sequence of cause and effect but as a complement to such a universe. Freedom, rightly understood, is a fulfillment, by the person, of the ordered sequence of his life.

It is a freedom in which the individual chooses to fulfill himself by playing a responsible and voluntary part in bringing about the destined events of the world he lives in.

It seems at least a possibility that in our schools and colleges, in our professional schools and universities, individuals could learn to be free in this sense. I say this in full recognition of the fact that the current trend in education is away from freedom. There are tremendous pressures today—cultural and political—for conformity, docility, and rigidity. The demand is for technically trained students who can beat the Russians—and none of this nonsense about education which might improve our interpersonal relationships! The demand is for hardheadedness, for training of the intellect only, for scientific proficiency.

For the general public and for many educators, the goal of learning to be free is not an aim they would select. Yet if a civilized culture is to survive and if the individuals in that culture are to be worth saving, it appears to be an essential goal of education.

So I would like to abstract, from various educational experiments and from pertinent research in psychotherapy, those conditions which appear to be essential if we are to inculcate in students this quality of inward freedom. I should like to describe these conditions as I see them.

In the first place, if self-initiated learning is to occur, it seems essential that the individual be faced by a real problem. Success in facilitating such learning often seems directly related to this factor. Professional persons who come together in a workshop because of a concern with common problems are a good example. Almost invariably, when they are given the facilitating climate I will describe, they at first resist the notion of being responsible for their own learning, but then they seize upon this as an opportunity and use it far beyond their expectations.

On the other hand, students in a required course expect to remain passive and may find themselves extremely perplexed and frustrated at being given freedom. "Freedom to do what?" is their quite understandable question.

It is thus necessary for self-initiated learning that the student, of whatever level, be confronted by issues which have meaning and relevance for him. In our culture we tend to try to insulate the student from too many of the actual problems of life, and this constitutes a difficulty. If we desire to have students learn to be free and responsible individuals, we must be willing for them to confront life, to face problems. Whether we are speaking of the inability of the small child to make change or the problem of his older brother in constructing a hi-fi set or the problem of the college student in formulating his views on international policy, some real confrontation by a problem seems necessary for this type of learning.

Thus far I have spoken of the essential conditions which involve the student. I come now to those conditions which only the teacher can provide. Experience indicates that the teacher who would facilitate this type of learning needs, first of all, a profound trust in the human organism. If we distrust the human being, then we *must* cram him with information of our own choosing lest he go his own mistaken way. On the other hand, if we trust the capacity of the human individual for developing his own potentiality, then we can permit him the opportunity to choose his own way in his learning.

Another requisite for the teacher is sincerity—realness, absence of a facade. He is a real person in his relations with his students. Because he accepts his feelings as his own, he has no need to impose them on his students. The teacher can dislike a student product without implying that it is objectively bad or that the student is bad. It is simply true that he, as a person, dislikes the product. Thus he is a *person* to his students, not a faceless embodiment of a curricular requirement or a sterile tube through which knowledge is pressed from one generation to the next.

Teachers who have been successful in promoting this type of learning value their students, prize them, feel acceptant of the feelings and opinions of their students. Such a teacher can accept the fear and hesitation the student feels as he approaches a new problem as well as the satisfaction he experiences in resolving it. Such a teacher can accept the student's occasional apathy and his desire to explore byroads of knowledge as well as his disciplined efforts to achieve major goals. He can also accept personal feelings which both disturb and promote learning—rivalry with a sibling, hatred of authority, concern about personal adequacy.

In other words, the teacher is able to accept the whole student—to prize him as an imperfect human being with many feelings, many potentialities. This prizing or acceptance is an operational expression of the teacher's genuine confidence in the capacity of the human organism.

Another essential teacher attribute is the ability to understand the student's reactions from the inside, an empathic awareness of the way the process of education and learning seems to the student. This is a kind of understanding too seldom exhibited in the classroom; yet when the teacher *is* empathic, it adds an extremely potent aspect to the classroom climate.

When a child says, in a discouraged voice, "I can't do this," that teacher is most helpful who naturally and spontaneously responds, "You're afraid that you can never learn it, aren't you?" The usual denial of the child's feeling by the teacher who says, "Oh, but I'm *sure* you can do it" is not nearly so helpful.

In addition to having the essential attitudes described above, the teacher who facilitates learning to be free provides many resources. Instead of organizing lesson plans and lectures, such a teacher concentrates on providing all kinds of relevant raw material for use by the students, together with clearly indicated channels by which students can avail themselves of these resources. I am thinking not only of books, workspace, tools, maps, movies, recordings, and the like but also of human resources—persons who might contribute to the students' knowledge.

Most important of these human resources is the teacher himself. He makes himself and his special knowledge and experience clearly available to the students, but he does not impose himself on them.

The teacher thus concentrates on creating a facilitative climate and on providing resources. He may also help to put students in contact with meaningful problems. But he does not set lesson tasks or assign readings. He does not lecture or expound (unless requested to). He does not evaluate and criticize unless the student wishes his judgment on a product. He does not give examinations. He does not set grades.

Such a teacher is not simply giving lip service to a different approach to learning; he is giving his students the opportunity to learn to be responsibly free.

When the teacher establishes an attitudinal climate of the sort I have described, when he makes available resources which are relevant to problems which confront the student, then a typical process ensues.

First, for students who have been taught by more conventional means, there is a period of tension, frustration, disappointment, disbelief. Students turn in such statements as "I felt completely frustrated by the class procedure," "I felt totally inadequate to take part in this kind of thing," "The class seems to be lacking in planning and direction," "I keep wishing the *course* would start."

One mature participant-observer, Samuel Tenenbaum, in my book, *On Becoming a Person* (Houghton Mifflin, 1961), describes the way one group struggled with the prospect of freedom after an initial session in which opportunities and resources had been set forth:

Thereafter followed four hard, frustrating sessions. During this period, the class didn't seem to get anywhere. Students spoke at random, saying whatever came into their heads. It all seemed chaotic, aimless, a waste of time. A student would bring up some aspect of the subject; and the next student, completely disregarding the first, would take the group away in another direction; and a third, disregarding the first two, would start fresh on something else.

At times there were faint efforts at a cohesive discussion, but for the most part the classroom proceedings seemed to lack continuity and direction. The instructor received every contribution with attention and regard. He did not find any student's contribution in order or out of order.

The class was not prepared for such a totally unstructured approach. They did not know how to proceed. In their perplexity and frustration, they demanded that the teacher play the role assigned to him by custom and tradition; that he set forth for us in authoritative language what was right and wrong, what was good and bad.

The statement above is a good description of the bafflement and chaos which is an almost inevitable initial phase of learning to be free.

Gradually, students come to various realizations. It dawns on them that this is not a gimmick; that they are really unfettered; that there is little point in impressing the teacher, since the student will evaluate his own work; that they can learn what they please; that they can express, in class, the way they really feel; that issues can be discussed in class which are real to them, not simply the issues set forth in a text. When these elements are recognized, there is a vital and almost awe-inspiring release of energy.

As the learning continues, personal changes take place in the direction of greater freedom and spontaneity. Here is a report given by a student at the end of a course conducted in this way:

Your way of being with us is a revelation to me. In your class I feel important, mature, and capable of doing things on my own. I want to think for myself and this need cannot be accomplished through textbooks and lectures alone, but through living. I think you see me as a person with real feelings and needs, an individual. What I say and do are significant expressions from me, and you recognize this. You follow no plan, yet I'm learning. Since the term began, I seem to feel more alive, more real to myself. I enjoy being alone as well as with other people. . . .

I believe the story of this kind of classroom experience is incomplete without some mention of the effect upon the instructor when he has been the agent for the release of such self-initiated learning. One such teacher says:

To say that I am overwhelmed by what happened only faintly reflects my feelings. I have taught for many years but I . . . never have found in the classroom so much of the whole person coming forth, so deeply involved, so deeply stirred. . . . I can only . . . say that I am grateful and I am also humbled by the experience.

Although empirical investigations of the sort of teaching I have described are neither large in number nor noteworthy for their research sophistication, they do indicate that improvement in personal psychological maturity is significantly greater in student-centered classes than in conventional ones. There is also evidence of a greater amount of self-initiated extracurricular learning and of greater creativity and self-responsibility.

As to the factual and curricular learning, this seems roughly equal to that achieved in conventional classes. Some studies report slightly more, others slightly less. The fairest summary seems to be that if we are solely concerned with the teaching of teacher-selected content material, this approach is probably no better or worse than the ordinary class. If we are concerned with the development of the person—with initiative, originality, and responsibility—such an approach produces greater changes.

In closing, I would like to say that it is my opinion that for the most part modern culture—in its two main streams, Western and communist— does not, operationally, want persons to be free, and is extremely fearful and ambivalent of any process which leads to inner freedom. Nevertheless, it is my personal conviction that individual rigidity and constricted learning are the surest roads to world catastrophe.

It seems clear that if we prefer to develop flexible, adaptive, creative individuals, we have a beginning knowledge as to how this may be done. We know how to establish, in an educational situation, the conditions and the psychological climate which initiate a process of learning to be free.

14. Freedom and Learning: The Need for Choice

Paul Goodman

The belief that a highly industrialized society requires twelve to twenty years of prior processing of the young is an illusion or a hoax. The evidence is strong that there is no correlation between school performance and life achievement in any of the professions, whether medicine, law, en-

SOURCE: *Saturday Review*, LI, 20 (May 18, 1968), 73–75. Copyright © 1968 Saturday Review, Inc. Reprinted by permission of the author and publisher.

gineering, journalism, or business. Moreover, recent research shows that for more modest clerical, technological, or semiskilled factory jobs there is no advantage in years of schooling or the possession of diplomas. We were not exactly savages in 1900 when only 6 per cent of adolescents graduated from high school.

Whatever the deliberate intention, schooling today serves mainly for policing and for taking up the slack in youth unemployment. It is not surprising that the young are finally rebelling against it, especially since they cannot identify with the goals of so much social engineering—for instance, that 86 per cent of the federal budget for research and development is for military purposes.

We can, I believe, educate the young entirely in terms of their free choice, with no processing whatever. Nothing can be efficiently learned, or, indeed, learned at all—other than through parroting or brute training, when acquired knowledge is promptly forgotten after the examination—unless it meets need, desire, curiosity, or fantasy. Unless there is a reaching from within, the learning cannot become "second nature," as Aristotle called true learning. It seems stupid to decide a priori what the young ought to know and then to try to motivate them, instead of letting the initiative come from them and putting information and relevant equipment at their service. It is false to assert that this kind of freedom will not serve society's needs—at least those needs that should humanly be served; freedom is the only way toward authentic citizenship and real, rather than verbal, philosophy. Free choice is not random but responsive to real situations; both youth and adults live in a nature of things, a polity, an ongoing society, and it is these, in fact, that attract interest and channel need. If the young, as they mature, can follow their bent and choose their topics, times, and teachers, and if teachers teach what they themselves consider important—which is all they can skillfully teach anyway—the needs of society will be adequately met; there will be more lively, independent, and inventive people; and in the fairly short run there will be a more sensible and efficient society.

It is not necessary to argue for free choice as a metaphysical proposition; it is what is indicated by present conditions. Increasingly, the best young people resolutely resist authority, and we will let them have a say or lose them. And more important, since the conditions of modern social and technological organization are so pervasively and rigidly conforming, it is necessary, in order to maintain human initiative, to put our emphasis on protecting the young from top-down direction. The monkish and academic methods which were civilizing for wild shepherds create robots in a period of high technology. The public schools which did a good job of socializing immigrants in an open society now regiment individuals and rigidify class stratification.

Up to age twelve, there is no point to formal subjects or a prearranged curriculum. With guidance, whatever a child experiences is educational. Dewey's idea is a good one: It makes no difference *what* is learned at this age, so long as the child goes on wanting to learn something further. Teachers for this age are those who like children, pay attention to them, answer their questions, enjoy taking them around the city and helping them explore, imitate, try out, and who sing songs with them and teach them games. Any benevolent grownup—literate or illiterate—has plenty to teach an eight-year-old; the only profitable training for teachers is group therapy and, perhaps, a course in child development.

We see that infants learn to speak in their own way in an environment where there is speaking and where they are addressed and take part. If we tried to teach children to speak according to our own theories and methods and schedules, as we try to teach reading, there would be as many stammerers as there are bad readers. Besides, it has been shown that whatever is useful in the present eight-year elementary curriculum can be learned in four months by a normal child of twelve. If let alone, in fact, he will have learned most of it by himself.

Since we have communities where people do not attend to the children as a matter of course, and since children must be rescued from their homes, for most of these children there should be some kind of school. In a proposal for mini-schools in New York City, I suggested an elementary group of twenty-eight children with four grownups: a licensed teacher, a housewife who can cook, a college senior, and a teen-age school dropout. Such a group can meet in any store front, church basement, settlement house, or housing project; more important, it can often go about the city, as is possible when the student-teacher ratio is 7 to 1. Experience at the First Street School in New York has shown that the cost for such a little school is less than for the public school with a student-teacher ratio of 30 to 1. (In the public system, most of the money goes for administration and for specialists to remedy the lack of contact in the classroom.) As A. S. Neill has shown, attendance need not be compulsory. The school should be located near home so the children can escape from it to home, and from home to it. The school should be supported by public money but administered entirely by its own children, teachers, and parents.

In the adolescent and college years, the present mania is to keep students at their lessons for another four to ten years as the only way of their growing up in the world. The correct policy would be to open as many diverse paths as possible, with plenty of opportunity to backtrack and change. It is said by James Conant that about 15 per cent learn well by books and study in an academic setting, and these can opt for high school. Most, including most of the bright students, do better either on their own or as apprentices in activities that are for keeps, rather than through lessons. If their previous eight years had been spent in exploring their own bents and interests, rather than being continually interrupted to do others' assignments on others' schedules, most adolescents would have a clearer notion of what they are after, and many would have found their vocations.

For the 15 per cent of adolescents who learn well in schools and are interested in subjects that are essentially academic, the present catch-all high schools are wasteful. We would do better to return to the small preparatory academy, with perhaps sixty students and three teachers—one in physical sciences, one in social sciences, one in humanities—to prepare for college board examinations. An academy could be located in, and administered by, a university and staffed by graduate students who like to teach and in this way might earn stipends while they write their theses. In such a setting, without dilution by nonacademic subjects and a mass of uninterested fellow students, an academic adolescent can, by spending three hours a day in the classroom, easily be prepared in three or four years for college.

Forcing the nonacademic to attend school breaks the spirit of most and foments alienation in the best. Kept in tutelage, young people, who are necessarily economically dependent, cannot pursue the sexual, adventurous, and political activities congenial to them. Since lively youngsters insist on these anyway, the effect of what we do is to create a gap between them and the oppressive adult world, with a youth subculture and an arrested development.

School methods are simply not competent to teach all the arts, sciences, professions, and skills the school establishment pretends to teach. For some professions—e.g., social work, architecture, pedagogy—trying to earn academic credits is probably harmful because it is an irrelevant and discouraging obstacle course. Most technological know-how has to be learned in actual practice in offices and factories, and this often involves unlearning what has been laboriously crammed for exams. The technical competence required by skilled and semiskilled workmen and average technicians can be acquired in three weeks to a year on the job, with no previous schooling. The importance of even "functional literacy" is much exaggerated; it is the attitude, and not the reading ability, that counts. Those who are creative in the arts and sciences almost invariably go their own course and are usually hampered by schools. Modern languages are best learned by travel. It is pointless to teach social sciences, literary criticism, and philosophy to youngsters who have had no responsible experience in life and society.

Most of the money now spent for high schools and colleges should be devoted to the support of apprenticeships; travel; subsidized browsing in libraries and self-directed study and research; programs such as VISTA, the Peace Corps, Students for a Democratic Society, or the Student Nonviolent Coordinating Committee; rural reconstruction; and work camps for projects in conservation and urban renewal. It is a vast sum of money—

but it costs almost $1,500 a year to keep a youth in a blackboard jungle in New York; the schools have become one of our major industries. Consider one kind of opportunity. Since it is important for the very existence of the republic to countervail the now overwhelming national corporate style of information, entertainment, and research, we need scores of thousands of small independent television stations, community radio stations, local newspapers that are more than gossip notes and ads, community theaters, high-brow or dissenting magazines, small design offices for neighborhood renewal that is not bureaucratized, small laboratories for science and invention that are not centrally directed. Such enterprises could present admirable opportunities for bright but unacademic young people to serve as apprentices.

Ideally, the polis itself is the educational environment; a good community consists of worthwhile, attractive, and fulfilling callings and things to do, to grow up into. The policy I am proposing tends in this direction rather than away from it. By multiplying options, it should be possible to find an interesting course for each individual youth, as we now do for only some of the emotionally disturbed and the troublemakers. Voluntary adolescent choices are often random and foolish and usually transitory; but they are the likeliest ways of growing up reasonably. What is most essential is for the youth to see that he is taken seriously as a person, rather than fitted into an institutional system. I don't know if this tailor-made approach would be harder or easier to administer than standardization that in fact fits nobody and results in an increasing number of recalcitrants. On the other hand, as the Civilian Conservation Corps showed in the Thirties, the products of willing youth labor can be valuable even economically, whereas accumulating Regents blue-books is worth nothing except to the school itself.

(By and large, it is not in the adolescent years but in later years that, in all walks of life, there is need for academic withdrawal, periods of study and reflection, synoptic review of the texts. The Greeks understood this and [would have] regarded most of our present college curricula as appropriate for only those over the age of thirty or thirty-five. To some extent, the churches used to provide a studious environment. We do these things miserably in hurried conferences.)

We have similar problems in the universities. We cram the young with what they do not want at the time and what most of them will never use; but by requiring graded diplomas we make it hard for older people to get what they want and can use. Now, paradoxically, when so many are going to school, the training of authentic learned professionals is proving to be a failure, with dire effects on our ecology, urbanism, polity, communications, and even the direction of science. Doing others' lessons under compulsion for twenty years does not tend to produce professionals who are autonomous, principled, and ethically responsible to client and community. Broken by processing, professionals degenerate to mere professional-personnel. Professional peer groups have become economic lobbies. The licensing and maintenance of standards have been increasingly relinquished to the state, which has no competence.

In licensing professionals, we have to look more realistically at functions, drop mandarin requirements of academic diplomas that are irrelevant, and rid ourselves of the ridiculous fad of awarding diplomas for every skill and trade whatever. In most professions and arts there are important abstract parts that can best be learned academically. The natural procedure is for those actually engaged in a professional activity to go to school to learn what they now know they need; re-entry into the academic track, therefore, should be made easy for those with a strong motive.

Universities are primarily schools of learned professions, and the faculty should be composed primarily not of academics but of working professionals who feel duty-bound and attracted to pass on their tradition to apprentices of a new generation. Being combined in a community of scholars, such professionals teach a noble apprenticeship, humane and with vision toward a more ideal future. It is humane because the disciplines communicate with one another; it is ideal because the young are free and questioning. A good professional school can be tiny. In *The Community of Scholars* I suggest that 150 students and ten professionals—the size of the usual medieval university—are enough. At current faculty salaries, the cost per student would be a fourth of that of our huge administrative machines. And, of course, on such a small scale contact between faculty and students is sought for and easy.

Today, because of the proved incompetence of our adult institutions and the hypocrisy of most professionals, university students have a right to a large say in what goes on. (But this, too, is medieval.) Professors will, of course, teach what they please. My advice to students is that given by Prince Kropotkin, in "A Letter to the Young": "Ask what kind of world do you want to live in? What are you good at and want to work at to build that world? What do you need to know? Demand that your teachers teach you that." Serious teachers would be delighted by this approach.

The idea of the liberal arts college is a beautiful one: to teach the common culture and refine character and citizenship. But it does not happen; the evidence is that the college curriculum has little effect on underlying attitudes, and most cultivated folk do not become so by this route. School friendships and the community of youth do have lasting effects, but these do not require ivied clubhouses. Young men learn more about the theory and practice of government by resisting the draft than they ever learned in Political Science 412.

Much of the present university expansion, needless to say, consists in federal- and corporation-contracted research and other research and has nothing to do with teaching. Surely such expansion can be better carried on in the Government's and corporations' own institutes, which would be unencumbered by the young, except those who are hired or attach themselves as apprentices.

Every part of education can be open to need, desire, choice, and trying out. Nothing needs to be compelled or extrinsically motivated by prizes and threats. I do not know if the procedure here outlined would cost more than our present system—though it is hard to conceive of a need for more money than the school establishment now spends. What would be saved is the pitiful waste of youthful years—caged, daydreaming, sabotaging, and cheating—and the degrading and insulting misuse of teachers.

It has been estimated by James Coleman that the average youth in high school is really "there" about ten minutes a day. Since the growing-up of the young into society to be useful to themselves and others, and to do God's work, is one of the three or four most important functions of any society, no doubt we ought to spend even more on the education of the young than we do; but I would not give a penny to the present administrators, and I would largely dismantle the present school machinery.

III. Teaching

Teaching has always been an important occupation; today it is one of national concern. The American public recognizes that no system of education, no curriculum, no school building can be better than the teachers who guide the learning experiences of the nation's boys and girls. The nation today faces no problem greater than that of securing and keeping teachers with intelligence, character, and training sufficient to educate citizens to the knowledge and will to continue, and improve upon, the society that is sacred to Americans and their way of life. Teaching that motivates creativity in young people and that challenges and develops thinking power on the part of the nation's youth will play a large part in keeping America free and safe from encroachment by influences undesirable to our democratic culture.

To do an effective job, a teacher must meet many demands: he must know about himself, his strengths and his weaknesses; he must know other people, what makes them behave as they do; he must have a vast fund of knowledge in his fields of specialization as well as in other subject areas; he must have a solid foundation in methodology—"how to teach"; he should be well grounded in the history, philosophy, sociology, and psychology of his profession. In addition, an effective teacher will be aware of the importance of education; he will have a keen sensitivity to the needs, interests, and welfare of children; he will have and maintain a philanthropic bent with a sincere desire to be of service to people, considering salary secondary to the other recompenses of teaching. Finally, he will have an eternal thirst for knowledge and will be willing to continue study in professional education and subject fields.

The teaching-learning process is of utmost importance because it is through this process that most of the objectives of education in America are achieved. It is through this process that the principles of child growth and development and the laws of learning are applied in classrooms; it is through this process that teachers best assist learners to reach their goals. It is in this process that teachers enable pupils to acquire skills that are needed for reflective thinking and the solving of problems, processes in which learners will be involved throughout their lives.

The articles in this part deal with teaching and teachers, emphasizing the changes in both that are coming about or that need to come about in order to keep up with a constantly changing culture. Some of the ideas expressed in the articles are not complimentary to practitioners in the schools, implying that teachers have not changed with the times. All of the articles do suggest, however, that teachers and teaching are in the process of changing and that the schools are struggling, against increasing odds, to stay abreast of and provide for the needs of pupils of today—and tomorrow.

In "Why Teachers Fail," Myrton A. Packer explores the paradox of teachers succeeding increasingly in achieving goals for which they are striving while at the same time they are, in his opinion, failing more and more seriously in the proper goals of education. However, Packer does absolve teachers from blame for what he terms "this sad state of education in our country today" and points to teachers' preservice education— particularly the general education courses taken prior to professional education offerings—as one possible culprit.

John I. Goodlad explains in "The Schools vs. Education" that frequently-recommended and frequently-discussed educational practices— such as attention to pupil's individual needs, attainments or problems as a basis for beginning instruction, and provision for individual opportunities to learn—did not exist in the schools that were involved in his recent study of primary classrooms in 100 schools in or near the major cities of thirteen states. Goodlad pinpoints many activities that teachers are or should be involved in, and points up some of the reasons why many of them are not.

As a capstone to the discussion of the teacher as an agent of change in a climate of change, Sandford Reichart presents a dissertation on the teacher and the ever-present reality of change. He states that some teachers consider change as a break in their routine to be viewed with suspicion or rejected outright, while others accept it as a challenge. He admonishes all teachers not to view change as a threat, but to use it as a dynamic alternative, and to facilitate it.

Sensitivity training is the "in" thing today in many businesses, professions, colleges and churches in America. To show that such training can take place in a high school class and in school faculty groups, the editors include in this chapter an article by Dan Simon and Diane Sarkotich entitled "Sensitivity Training in the Classroom." The authors of the article feel that success was achieved in several areas of interpersonal relationships as a result of such training.

Donald H. DeLay and David Nyberg, in "If Your School Stinks, CRAM It," present a model whereby teachers can individualize instruction—and perhaps more importantly, education. The authors of the article stress the importance of every good teacher's aim—to become un-necessary.

If the teacher conceives of his role in the classroom as that of a dis-penser of knowledge, a slave to the textbooks or a strict disciplinarian, then the inquiry-centered classroom is not for him, as indicated in "The Role of the Teacher in an Inquiry-Centered Classroom," by Dorothy J. Skeel and Joseph G. Decaroli. The writers present a number of classroom procedures which should prove effective in such a schoolroom; consider-able emphasis is presently being placed on the inquiry methodology as a means of helping youngsters learn how to learn.

15. Why Teachers Fail

Myrton A. Packer

It is indicative of the confused state of educational thinking in our country today that an eminent psychologist, who recently published an article entitled "Why Teachers Fail," could find the answer in the lack of a real technology of teaching. Yet colleges today, hard pressed to find room for all the qualified high school graduates who apply, constantly raise their standards for admission; professors find that they must upgrade their courses in order merely to keep ahead of the students now in their classes; and year after year, college presidents and deans announce that the present freshmen class is the best prepared they have ever had. Many institutions have found it possible to abandon the "bonehead" remedial courses once thought necessary to close the gap between secondary and higher education. Even after the admissions office has worked its mumbo jumbo with the computer and the only partly-understood statistical charts, many entering students bypass the beginning courses by the simple device of taking advanced placement examinations. Thousands of high school teachers are now successfully teaching courses that only a decade ago were offered in college or even graduate school. Rather than failing, teachers today, when measured by the accepted standards currently in vogue, are succeeding far better than they ever succeeded before.

Yet, in a deeper and much more serious sense, teachers *are* failing today. Paradoxically, as they succeed more and more in achieving the goals for which they are striving, the degree of their failure, in terms of proper goals of education, becomes more acute. Harried by historians, mathematicians, scientists, and colleges, they have abdicated their proper function and become recruiters for the graduate schools. In a time when college professors have been granted a disproportionate voice in the determination of educational goals, teachers have sought to become as much like them as possible and are succeeding so well that Dr. Robert Maynard Hutchins is willing to concede they have taken over the function of the first two years of college.

SOURCE: *The Journal of Teacher Education,* XIX, 3 (Fall 1968), 331–37. Reprinted by permission of the publisher.

Of all the developments in the past two decades in American society, this is probably the most dangerous, in that it has turned high school education away from its proper goal of aiding adolescents in the difficult task of becoming adults, a task that becomes ever more difficult as our culture becomes more complex. The door has been closed on meaningful education for a greater and greater proportion of our youth, for which our society has made no other provision except the street corner, the pool room, and the drive-in movie. Even the armed services, formerly a refuge for such youth, now reject them; sociologists refer to them as "superfluous people." Confused, hurt, resentful, they have responded to society's rejection of them by rejecting society and its values. Having nowhere else to turn for meaningful standards and satisfying activities, they have formed an adolescent subculture—usually covertly, but sometimes overtly—at war with the adult world.

Even the youth who manage to stay in school find little that is meaningful to them. They learn a host of strategies, including some highly sophisticated cheating, in order to give the appearance of knowing a great deal more than they really do. They adopt the ethics of the jungle, realizing that in the fiercely competitive world in which they live, it doesn't really matter how you have played the game, but whether you have won or lost. The teachers, realizing that their own security and advancement depend upon how well their students do on the various standardized tests, cooperate discreetly in the cheating, and by so doing, not only set an unfortunate example but even give tacit adult approval to the system. Unfortunately, so much emphasis is placed on test scores that there is little or no time for learning anything meaningful.

Because many teachers will challenge the above paragraph, let us look for a moment at what happens when a test is announced. (Very few teachers would dare to give a test unannounced!) Immediately, the students will set to work in a highly anxious manner to establish the ground rules, i.e., to get as much advance information out of the teacher as possible. How many questions will there be? Will they be true-false, multiple-choice, essay, or completion? How much of the book will the test cover? Are we responsible for any outside reading? How much will the test count toward our grade? Shall we be penalized for guessing?

Having limited the extent and uncertainty of the test as much as possible, the students will then go into an intensive training period, trying to memorize everything in the portion of the book to be covered. They will fight against having more than one test on the same day, because this contributes to possible confusion of the memory tracks they are seeking to establish. Many will stay up all night just before the test or rise at four o'clock in the morning to get one last fact or bit of data crammed into their memory banks.

When the time for the test comes, they enter the room with faces strained with anxiety (unless they have loaded up on tranquillizers, a more and more common procedure) and wait restlessly for the papers to be handed out so that they can begin feverishly writing down the answers before they forget them. A minority will complete the test quickly and hand it in, glad to be able to escape from the torture chamber; others will hang on until the last possible moment, frequently consulting the teacher in the hope of obtaining clues to the all-important "right" answer.

As soon as the papers have been handed in, students will begin to bombard the teacher as to when the grades will be announced. And when the results are finally known, there begins the endless, often acrimonious, struggle to try to get a few more percentage points, to raise the grade from a C to a B or from a B to an A. (Students who do not do this are often seen by teachers as not caring how they do!) Threats, sulking, tears, protracted attempts to wear the teacher down are all considered as legitimate tactics in getting the last jot and tittle of reward for the anxious hours spent in preparing for the test. Yet one cannot blame the students. This is the kind of world in which they live, and the stakes are high. Getting into the college of one's choice depends as much upon knowing the teacher as upon knowing the subject.

But what does all this have to do with learning? Or rather, what does it have to do with the kind of learning that, in Pater's words, would teach how to "burn always with this hard gemlike flame," to experience life richly and intensely, to know what Jersild refers to as "the pleasures of the mind," to have the fruits of an education? How does it help the eager adolescent grow into a thoughtful, sensitive, loyal, secure, adult? In the memorizing of dates, treaties, and other facts (which are often really only opinions), where is the sense of "history writ large"? In writing the character sketches, the memorizing of details about the lives of authors, or the fussing over the difference between a comma and a semicolon, where is the grasp of language as a vehicle for experiencing and expressing man's noblest and most down-to-earth experiences? In the endless memorizing, problem working, and experimenting, where is the vision of science as a tool with which to push back the boundaries of ignorance in every field, to approach nearer to the most satisfying understanding, not only of the universe but of man himself?

Many teachers will take refuge in the elitist argument—the claim that not all students are capable of absorbing an education. The implication is that those (including the teachers, of course) who can survive the insane process that we now honor with the name of education are the elite, and those who cannot survive are rightfully consigned to the scrap pile. Yet nobody really knows whether all students are capable of being truly educated, *because we have never really tried.* We have shaken all the students over a highly irrelevant screen, and pronounced "educated" those who did not fall out. No one really knows if what we have been doing is the best way, or even if it is *a* way, to educate anyone. There is, in fact, a great deal of evidence to the contrary.

Why do teachers continue to subject students to this process, which is not only meaningless but actually destructive? Increasingly, it is becoming apparent that even the successful students, those who survive after a fashion, have lost all creativeness, all curiosity, all capacity to do anything but to continue the nit picking that we call "scholarship." The really creative people in our culture, as often as not, are those who escaped from our educational system before it could blight their spontaneous sense of the essential and the worthwhile.

Why do teachers continue in their role of Lord High Executioner of real learning, creativity, curiosity? Chiefly because, being themselves products of the scholarship game, they do not realize what they are doing, they are not aware of the futility of what they are trying to do, and they have no notion of what education could be other than what they have made of it. They have accepted the standards and banalities of the scholarly world: the unimaginative piece-by-piece dissection of what they have been told is literature; the accumulation of meaningless, unrelated facts in history; the abstruse schoolroom tricks of the new math and the new linguistics; the drudgery of parallel reading, measured by the hundreds of pages and testified to by the glib report gleaned from the fraternity files. They have oriented themselves to the ubiquitous standardized test that rewards superficiality and penalizes the nonconformist who stops to think before pencilling in his signal to the grading machine. So devoted is their obeisance to the standardized test that they waste endless class hours drilling their students on the answers to old test items, in order (hopefully) to increase the appearance of their knowing what they do not really know.

However, teachers, who have been blamed for almost everything bad that has happened since 1940 or earlier, are not to blame for this sad state of education in our country today. Considering the circumstances in which they must work if they want to be teachers and the preparation they receive for their chosen work, they do marvelously well—much better than our society deserves in view of the rewards it offers them.

It has been nearly half a century since anyone did any serious, informed thinking about the goals and purposes of education. Most of the advances in educational theory since then have been a matter of tinkering with the machinery—developing standardized tests for the pupils and rating scales for the teachers; seeking administrative arrangements that would spread the meager funds as far as possible; fussing with weighty statistics like pupil-teacher ratios and how many books per pupil should be in the library. The cult of efficiency has replaced the search for values in the educational enterprise, and the cost of offering a course in Greek has become more interesting than the question as to whether or not a course in Greek should be offered. Very few policy decisions in the field of education today are made solely on the basis of educational considerations; very few of the policy makers are capable of making decisions on such a basis.

Beginning sometime after 1940, and especially since Sputnik, teachers have been assailed by a veritable flood of criticism from all sorts of critics, cranks, and crackpots. Curriculum, teaching methods, amount of homework, frills, some nebulous thing called progressive education, all these and anything else that came to mind, became the target of hysterical, uninformed, and often plain axe-grinding attacks upon schools and teachers. Left without leadership by their administrators, who often acceded to ridiculous demands in order to keep their jobs, the teachers could do little but sweat it out or leave the profession. Many, of course, did leave. Those who remained did so at the price of being forced into roles that they knew were futile. The happy ones were those who did not realize how little they were accomplishing or did not care; so long as the pupils were quiet and the pay checks regular, they were content.

But the basic source of our teachers' failure—the poison that pollutes the whole stream of our educational enterprise—is the kind of training that has been prescribed for teachers before they can enter the classroom. Many critics have poured out their vitriol on "those awful education courses," which, it must be admitted, are often dreary; *but the real failure has been in the general and special education that precedes the professional courses.* This general education, in theory at least, is made up of courses that are thought to comprise a necessary foundation or basis for all college students. In practice, it is often the result of a series of compromises between deans and department heads more bent on empire building or on making use of existing facilities and justifying new ones than on any systematic consideration of the needs of students. Often it largely repeats the content of the high school courses, presumably at a deeper level, although this is questionable.

This is the part of the curriculum most often staffed with graduate assistants or instructors without terminal degrees, where experimentation with large classes, TV, departmental tests, and other bargain-basement devices is most likely to be carried on. If any of the established, fully trained professors teach in these courses, they are likely to do so with ill grace and a minimum of interest and only because some department head has bribed them with the privilege of teaching upperclassmen and graduate students.

Scattered throughout these two years of general education are a number of not too carefully hidden trap doors, through which the unwary can be suddenly and finally delivered back to the outside world, *sans* degree, if they have not mastered the school tricks sufficiently well to survive in the intense and ruthless competition.

A predictable number of freshmen will drop out, but what of those who skillfully thread their way past the hidden traps and survive to become juniors? Will they be "educated"? Hardly. Just as in high school, they will have survived largely on the basis of their ability to outmaneuver, out-guess, and outlast the opposition (their fellow-students and the faculty). They will have memorized the irreducible minimum of facts, will have learned which are the "crip" courses and the easy professors, will have sought out the fraternity that has the most complete file of old tests and term papers; in short, they will have continued to refine the skills learned in high school, or even in grade school, in how to get through school without really learning anything. Only a fortunate few will have seen any meaning in the mishmash of courses, and fewer still will have been able to assimilate the meaning into their own need to grow and develop as thoughtful, sensitive, inner-directed persons.

Once past the general education hurdle, the student embarks upon his specialized education—his major—where he finds himself a member of a small and exclusive club. The competition is not quite so bloody now (after all, the department does not want to lose its majors), but the work is quite definitely pointed toward the Ph.D. and *not* toward the person who plans to teach the subject in high school. If anyone persists in such a notion, he will find himself under more or less subtle pressures: it will be harder for him to make the top grades, and he will be reminded pointedly of the greater rewards and prestige available if he will but set his feet on the Ph.D. path. In any event, whether he is going on for a Ph.D. or not, the courses will be taught as if he were: there will be great emphasis upon scholarship, lengthy bibliographies, reports, term papers, and research; he will be admitted to the heady heights of the seminar.

Once he has mastered the new set of tricks, the way ahead is smooth. He may still wonder occasionally when he is going to begin to experience the richer, fuller life that education is supposed to bring with it; but after a while, he may even begin to delude himself into thinking that what he is doing *is* the richer, fuller life. What basis does he have for thinking otherwise? Like the religious novice, he is slowly adapting himself to the almost monastic life of the college campus and simultaneously forgetting that there is any other kind of life.

Sometime during these last two years of college, our student will embark upon his professional training—those courses and experiences designed to help him take his place in the classroom as a teacher. If he is fortunate, at least some of his professional training will come at the hands of veterans of the profession—men and women who have been in the schoolroom and have mastered its multifarious duties—but the odds are increasingly against this. Driven by the need to become academically respectable, his education professors will seek to make their courses as much as possible like the dry tedious exercises in scholarship that he has already experienced. Having fled from the realities of the school room as quickly as possible, they have plunged back into the academic womb of graduate study.

Whether in education or in any of the older, more respectable disciplines, it is almost impossible to imagine anything more stultifying than graduate study. Here the scholarship game is played for blood. More courses, more seminars, more bibliographies, more research, which for the present at least must be scientific (meaning that it must be done on the computer), lead finally to the hectic search for a dissertation topic pleasing to the major professor and acceptable to the graduate dean. Having spied his grain of sand, the graduate student must shape and polish it to the satisfaction of all concerned, deleting a comma here, recasting a table there, changing a word somewhere else, until he becomes a stranger to what was supposed to be his own personal endeavor. As a crowning irony, he must defend the finished product before those who actually wrote it for him!

In the process, as a result of years of anxiety, and of seeing his own creation kidnapped and made over into another image by the faculty, whatever progress he may have made toward becoming a person is wiped out. When this process is adjudged by the faculty to be complete, he is allowed to take his degree and enter the professorial world to practice the same initiatory rites upon the next generation. By now he has decided that the richer fuller life does not exist and has only contempt for those naïve underclassmen who still seek it. He has been trained to believe that research is the be-all and end-all of existence. He very soon learns that in his chosen field of college teaching not to teach is safe but not to publish is fatal. He learns further that if he can publish sufficiently he may look forward to being relieved of the necessity of teaching; this is the ultimate status symbol in his circumscribed world.

These triple-distilled products of the scholarship game are the source of the training our teachers get before entering the classroom. They are the materials out of which teachers are supposed to derive an educational experience that will help them to become thoughtful, sensitive, loyal, courageous persons capable of aiding the coming generations to be the same. The odds against this happening are almost astronomical; having survived four years of meaningless high school subject matter and four more years of the same in college, without any experience of the richness and fullness of true education, teachers have nothing but subject matter to offer their students.

It is truly tragic that so many millions of dollars and man-hours of time are being currently wasted in educational research into the wrong things. The emphasis presently is on the development of technologies by which still more of the meaningless subject matter can be taught to an ever-increasing number of students. But this will produce only the same meaningless results we are now getting. We already have more technology than anyone knows how to use, and anyway there is no technology that can substitute for a teacher who is really a person—one who has developed an adequate self-concept and has an internalized system of values to bring to the complex life of the twentieth century.

It is no wonder that teaching machines can do most things that teachers do, and often do them better; of course, there is no personal contact with a teaching machine, but neither is there any with many teachers. If the teacher is nothing but a textbook wired for sound, why should he not make way for a tape recorder or a TV receiver? If human beings are to be made into obedient robots, then they can be taught by robots. But if we ever hope to see our children become mature persons, they must meet with mature persons in their educational experience. Until then, teachers will fail.

16. The Schools vs. Education

John I. Goodlad

The years from 1957 to 1967 constituted the Education Decade for the United States. It began with Sputnik and the charge to education to win the cold war; it ended with a hot war and the growing realization that education is a long-term answer to mankind's problems and must not be confused with short-term social engineering. The danger now is that we are becoming disillusioned with education, without realizing that we are only beginning to try it.

During the Education Decade, the school years were extended upward and downward, the school curriculum was revised from top to bottom, the Elementary and Secondary Education Act of 1965 brought the federal government into education as never before, the schools became both a focal point for social protest and a vehicle for social reform, and schooling joined politics and world affairs as leading topics of social discourse. "Innovation" and "revolution" were used interchangeably in discussing the changes taking place in the schools.

But the education scene today remains confusing. Put on one pair of glasses and the schools appear to be moving posthaste toward becoming centers of intense, exciting learning, marked by concern for the individual.

SOURCE: *Saturday Review*, LII, 16 (April 19, 1969), 59–61, 80–82. Copyright © 1969 Saturday Review, Inc. Reprinted by permission of the author and publisher.

Put on another, and they appear to be mired in tradition, insensitive to pressing social problems, and inadequate to the demands of learning.

Where are the schools today? How widespread have been the changes during the decade since Sputnik? What kind of changes are needed in the 1970s, and what lies ahead for the balance of the century?

While conducting studies of new approaches to school curricula during the early 1960s, I visited many schools and classrooms. Although the Education Decade was well underway, the reforms it espoused were not conspicuously present. Was the sample of schools visited inadequate, or were proposed changes losing their momentum before reaching their target? Several colleagues joined me in an effort to probe more deeply as we visited some 260 kindergarten through third-grade classrooms in 100 schools clustered in or around the major cities of thirteen states.

If the most frequently discussed and recommended educational practices of the Education Decade were already implemented, what would constitute a checklist of expectations? The following would seem reasonable. First, teaching would be characterized by efforts to determine where the student is at the *outset* of instruction, to diagnose his attainments and problems, and to base subsequent instruction on the results of this diagnosis. Second, learning would be directed toward "learning how to learn," toward self-sustaining inquiry rather than the memorization and regurgitation of facts. Third, this inquiry would carry the student out of confining classrooms and into direct observation of physical and human phenomena. Fourth, classrooms would be characterized by a wide variety of learning materials— records, tapes, models, programed materials, film strips, pamphlets, and television—and would not be dominated by textbooks. Fifth, attention to and concern for the individual and individual differences would show through clearly in assignments, class discussions, use of materials, grouping practices, and evaluation. Sixth, teachers would understand and use such learning principles as reinforcement, motivation, and transfer of training. Seventh, visitors would see vigorous, often heated, small and large group discussions, with the teacher in the background rather than the forefront. Eighth, one would find rather flexible school environments— marked by little attention to grade levels—and extensive use of team-teaching activities involving groups of teachers, older pupils, parents, and other persons in the teaching-learning process. And, certainly, it would be reasonable to expect to find innovative ways of dealing with special educational problems such as those presented by environmentally handicapped children.

Although these expectations seemed reasonable at the outset of our visits to schools, they did not constitute an accurate description of what we found. We were unable to discern much attention to pupil needs, attainments, or problems as a basis for beginning instruction, nor widespread provision for individual opportunities to learn. Most classes were taught as a group, covering essentially the same ground for all students at approximately the same rate of speed. Teaching was predominantly telling and questioning by the teacher, with children responding one by one or occasionally in chorus. In all of this, the textbook was the most highly visible instrument of learning and teaching. If records, tapes, films, film strips, supplementary materials, and other aids to learning were in the schools we visited, we rarely saw them. When small groups of students worked together, the activities engaged in by each group member were similar, and bore the mark of the teacher's assignment and expectations. Rarely did we find small groups intensely in pursuit of knowledge; rarely did we find individual pupils at work in self-sustaining inquiry. Popular innovations of the decade—non-grading, team teaching, "discovery" learning, and programed instruction—were talked about by teachers and principals alike but were rarely in evidence.

On a more general and impressionistic level, teachers and students did not appear to be intensely involved in their work. Only occasionally did we encounter a classroom aura of excitement, anticipation, and spontaneity; when we did, it was almost invariably a kindergarten class. This is not to say that classroom inhabitants were uninvolved but rather to suggest that it may be erroneous to assume that teaching and learning in the schools, more than other human enterprises, are characterized by excitement and enthusiasm. On the positive side, however, the teachers we observed were warm and supportive, and not sadistic as some polemicists have pictured them to be.

From the data, we were unable to differentiate practices in schools enrolling a high proportion of disadvantaged or minority group children from practices in other schools. Our descriptions of classrooms enrolling predominantly Mexican-American children, for example, were not distinguishable from our descriptions in general. Nor were there marked differences in our respective descriptions of classrooms in the inner city, on the fringe of the urban environment, and in suburbia.

It is dangerous to generalize about something as large, complex, and presumably diverse as schooling in the United States, or even about the first four years of it. As far as our sample of schools is concerned, however, we are forced to conclude that much of the so-called educational reform movement has been blunted on the classroom door.

Yet, the responsibility for this situation does not rest entirely with schoolteachers and principals. The elementary schools were anything but the "palaces" of an affluent society. In fact, they looked more like the artifacts of a society that did not really care about its schools, a society that expressed its disregard by creating schools less suited to human habitation than its prisons. These artifacts reflect the strange notion that learning proceeds best in groups of thirty, that teachers are not to converse with each other, that learning should be conducted under rather uncomfortable circumstances, and that schools proceed best with their tasks when there is little or no traffic with the outside world.

We had hoped to conduct sustained interviews with the teachers we observed, but there were rarely quiet, attractive places to confer. We held our interviews on the run or, more favorably, when we were able to have breakfast or dinner together. These teachers wanted to talk about education: what "good" things we had observed elsewhere; what we thought about current innovations; whether we had any suggestions for improving the teaching we had just observed; and on and on. Interestingly, those with whom we talked had a rather favorable image of what they were doing in the classroom; they thought they were individualizing instruction, teaching inductively, and encouraging self-propelled learning. Neither principals nor teachers were able to articulate clearly just what they thought to be most important for their schools to accomplish. And neither group was very clear on changes that should be effected in the near future.

Both our observations alone and those with teachers lead to several disquieting conclusions. Public schooling probably is the only large-scale enterprise in this country that does not provide for systematic updating of the skills and abilities of its employees and for payment of the costs involved. Teachers are on their own as far as their in-service education is concerned, in an environment designed for "telling" others, yet one that is grossly ill-suited to intellectual pursuits with peers. Teachers, we presume, can readily cast aside their old, inappropriate ways and acquire markedly different ones through some process of osmosis.

Sixteen or more years of schooling should educate teachers and others for self-renewal—and this frequently is the case. But general failure to do so for large numbers of people constitutes the greatest failure of our educational system. In the colleges as well as in the lower schools, the processes and fruits of human experience are so cut up in the curriculum and so obfuscated by detail that cohesiveness, relationships, and relevance are obscured.

Another aspect of our educational malaise is that an enormous amount of energy goes into merely maintaining the system. Studies have shown that administrators favor teachers who maintain orderly classrooms, keep accurate records, and maintain stable relations with parents and the community. Other studies reveal that middle managers in the educational system, such as principals and supervisors, tend to be recruited from among teachers who demonstrate these orderly qualities. Because they are rewarded for maintaining the system, administrators are not likely either to challenge it or to reward subordinates who do.

Just as teachers and principals appear to be uncertain as to what their schools are for, the communities they serve provide no clear sense of direction or guidelines. There is evidence to suggest that parents are somewhat more favorably disposed toward educational change than are teachers or school administrators, but legions of educators who push at the forefront of innovative practice stand ready to show their community-inflicted scars. Many parents are more interested in changes in the abstract or for someone else than in changes involving their own children. Social change is a formidable enterprise under the best of circumstances; schooling too often presents only the worst of circumstances, with resistance being built into both the setting and the internal structure.

It should come as no surprise, then, that comprehensive experiments in schooling are the rarest of all educational phenomena. Small wonder that teachers practice so little individualizing instruction, inductive teaching, non-grading, team teaching, or other recently recommended practices. They have not seen them. If teachers are to change, they must see models of what they are to change to; they must practice under guidance the new behaviors called for in the exemplary models. If teachers are to change, the occupation itself must have built into it the necessary provisions for self-renewal. The creation of these conditions is an important agenda item for the decade ahead.

Seers of bygone decades occasionally asked whether our schools had outlived their usefulness—and we laughed. The question is no longer funny. The schools are conspicuously ill-suited to the needs of at least 30 per cent of their present clientele: the large numbers of children from minority groups who live in harsh environments; the tens of thousands who suffer from crippling mental, physical, and emotional handicaps; and a few whose rare gifts separate them sharply from their peers. But the lack of "fit" between school and client extends into other realms until one is forced to ask whether our educational system serves even 50 per cent of its clientele in reasonably satisfying ways. Learning disabilities evidenced in the primary grades often go undiagnosed, persisting throughout life and seriously limiting human relations participation. Talents in music, art, and creative writing lie largely outside the school's scope and are usually brought to fruition in the home where parents can afford to, or not at all where parents cannot. The human models in these fields, so necessary to refinement of childhood talent, are inaccessible to the school because of teacher certification restrictions or sheer failure to recognize their powerful role in educating the young.

It is also questionable whether those students who appear to be adjusting well are acquiring desirable traits and repressing undesirable ones. Success in school seems to assure further success in school; good grades predict good grades. But academic success neither assures nor predicts good work habits, good citizenship, happiness, compassion, or other human virtues. The incidences of dropouts, non-promotion, alienation, and minimal learning reinforce our apprehension that schools have become or are fast becoming obsolete. They appear to have been designed for a different culture, a different conception of learning and teaching, and a different clientele.

The task of rehabilitating the schools, then, is indeed formidable. We dare not ask whether we *should* rehabilitate our schools, although this is a good question. Impotent and irrelevant though much schooling may be, the schools are at present the only educational institution deliberately created and maintained for inculcating something of man's heritage, for developing the basic tools of literacy, and for instilling some powers of rational thought and criticism. Although our civilization abounds in educational institutions and media, from scuba-diving school to television, none is centrally committed to this basic, cultural role. By seeking to rehabilitate the *educational* role of the school, rather than its various ancillary functions (baby-sitting, social stratification, economic investment, etc.), perhaps we will keep the meaning of education before us, experiment with improved means, and ultimately transfer the process to new and better institutions should the schools fail us and we them.

A brief analysis of television serves both to illustrate what I mean by rehabilitating the *educational* role of the school and to project us into the varied possibilities of an electronic educational future. Some of us still remember those wonderful evenings of intellectual discourse with friends, before that glass-faced monster took over. At first, exposure to the glass face meant only a few hours' diversion each week, watching the favorite programs we had only heard before. But now there are "hot" and "cool" stimuli, Marshall McLuhan's non-linear communication, and a television generation. From birth to high school graduation, today's young man or woman spends an average of 15,000 hours before television sets and just over 12,000 hours (1,000 hours each year) in school. I do not believe that these hours of schooling provide anything like an antidote for the formidable array of violence, cruelty, dishonesty, prejudice, and inhumanity to man provided by newspapers, magazines, movies, and television.

Our schools have not adopted television; nor has television adopted the schools. An occasional educational television program becomes a "tack-on" to the curriculum. During the Education Decade, a national network occasionally found it mildly profitable to feature a "special" on the schools. Meanwhile, however, television has gone about its business and the schools have gone about theirs. Television has not yet taken on the essentially educational function of humanizing the content of experience for teaching and learning. It seeks only to entertain, to hold the viewer. But neither have the schools been markedly successful in producing an intensely human environment in which children are caught up in man's adventure, whether in the arts, politics, the sea, or outer space.

Herein lies our dilemma. On one hand, a powerful medium has caught the attention—indeed, the very lives—of our children. But it lacks significant substance to nurture a civilization and appears to care not, despite its protestations, whether it uplifts or debases. On the other hand, the only institution charged specifically with the performance of educational functions fails to grip a significant portion of its clientele. Unfulfilled educational promise lies between.

In schools run by humans, we have not succeeded in developing intensely humanistic learning environments—not in process, not in content, and not in perspective. The schools do not, in general, foster man's most creative traits, nor grapple with his great ideas, nor relate these ideas and talents to the contemporary environment where man's dramas are continuously re-enacted. The schools are bogged down with routine, trivialities, and the lesser literacies. In the rat race to cover what is in the textbook, schooling has lost sight of education as an end in itself and has become instrumental to the next textbook, the next grade, higher education, and the Gross National Product. And now—at a critical time in the history of schools, education, and man—an electronic teacher of great power, the computer, comes into this human-based environment. The instructional era now on the horizon is one of man-machine interaction. Will the computer dehumanize learning and teaching even more? The choice is ours.

On an experimental basis, computers are demonstrating their usefulness in teaching spelling, mathematics, reading, and a host of cognitive skills. Tapes, video-screens, records, and other devices are combined with computer memory to produce a unique instructional system of sight, sound, and touch. Current writings on computer-aided instruction present a picture of instructional efficiency and the freeing of human teachers to do those truly *human* educational things. But what are these things? And have teachers been prepared to engage in them?

Already it is clear that computers, unlike television, are more efficient by far than humans in performing routine instructional tasks and in assuring error-free performance on the part of learners in those basic skills to which teachers devote so much time. It is clear, then, that computers have a viable, albeit threatening, role in the schools. The critical problem is how computers and people are to live together productively in the school environment. If educators continue to confuse instruction in the basic skills with education, then teachers will merely monitor the computer and, in time, become its servant. Under such circumstances, in due time, there would be no need for schools as other than custodial agencies, since computer terminals might more readily and profitably be placed in homes. State and local budgets, together with some transportation problems, would be substantially relieved.

A happier alternative, however, is that there will be a separation of those instructional tasks most appropriate for electronic teachers from those educational activities most appropriate for human teachers. Efficiently taught in the basic tools of their culture, young people would have much more time than is now the case to pursue education as a way of life. With the processes of providing these tools freed from the restraints of the human time and energy for teaching them, they would become readily accessible to all. But this alternative, too, destroys or drastically changes the school as we have known it.

The tireless computer is fully capable of working twenty-four hours a day every day. It can recall the same material and teach the same lesson over and over, and it can provide subject matters singly or in various combinations and sequences. No need, then, to confine teaching to the hours between 9 in the morning and 3 in the afternoon; nor to delay certain subjects until high school or college; nor to complete sixteen units of work in four years. Suddenly, we come to realize that schools as we know them are largely the product of limitations and conventions in the use of human energy. Introduce a new source of instructional energy and learning is unshackled.

But still to be accounted for in schooling are "those educational activities most appropriate for *human* teachers." Their human character demands libraries, seminar rooms, museums, studios, art galleries, courts of law, government offices, airports, housing developments, fields, ponds, counseling centers, hospitals, quiet study corners, work experiences, visits with exemplary models of accomplishment, and on and on. Take the educational environment beyond school and classroom and learning can be humanized.

With fundamental learning effectively taken care of, perhaps we can then correct our myopic perspective that equates education with schooling, and go beyond the utilitarian boundaries we have set for both ideas. We can then tend to the urgent need to value education for its own sake, to grapple with education's first question: What kinds of human beings do we seek? But even before looking toward where we want to be, perhaps we should ask fundamental questions about where we are. To what extent is each individual being provided with opportunities to develop his unique potentialities? To what extent is each individual developing a deep sense of personal worth—the kind of selfhood that is prerequisite to self-transcendence? To what extent are our young people coming into critical possession of their culture? And to what extent are our people developing a mankind identity—an identity that transcends all men in all times and in all places?

17. About the Teacher and Change

Sandford Reichart

In the aftermath of birth and death, the quality that is change seems almost an entity unto itself. It is as though we can taste it, touch it, hold it. The change we experience in our professional world is not always so apparent. Nevertheless, it is an ever-present reality. Whether it comes abruptly or gradually, harshly or gently, we must face it, accept it, and understand it if we are to use it.

Where Does Change Originate?

St. Augustine wrote that we must "Trust the Past to the Mercy of God, the Present to His Love, the Future to His Providence." In a sense he was telling us that the three major change periods we know as past, present and future are within the management province of God. Whether or not we accept this is a personal matter, but what is not personal is our acceptance of the fact that change itself is a natural phenomenon. Nothing is static. All things and all events have their moment of beginning, their antecedents, their evolution into other levels of development and expression, into other dimensions as they move on to other forms of energy, other uses. Even death may be viewed as another form of energy, not an ending but a change of condition, a change of form with a change of meaning.

In a professional sense, the teacher has too often replaced the God of St. Augustine with the ritualistic observance of tradition, has too often founded the actions of today only upon what was done yesterday, and thus has been detached from a futuristic attitude. Certainly the past should be a bedrock—but to stand upon to extend the grasp, not to sleep upon.

When a group of parents knocks at the classroom door and asks why some new technique for prenatally teaching the child to read has not been investigated, the teacher is apt to become defensively protective of status

SOURCE: Sandford Reichart, *Change and the Teacher* (New York: Thomas Y. Crowell, 1969), chap. I. Reprinted by permission of the author and the publisher.

quo. "I am the educator," she may say. "And I have done this for
hundreds of children all during the twenty-two years I have loved children
and taught children," she may continue amidst the quivering of her upper
lip. Or the teacher may be politely unmoved. "How terribly exciting that
must be," she will say. "I hadn't heard about it. You say you read about it
in the *Reader's Digest?* Well, I must get hold of that issue." Other teachers
may do nothing but hope that this ugly specter will vanish as though it had
never really appeared. Still other teachers may find the notion exciting and
even rational yet limit their enthusiasm and exhaust their energies with,
"Well, they may get that over there in the Weeping Lagoon School System,
but we'll never get it here. That's the trouble with us. We don't get paid
enough, we have too many children to teach, we have too much homework
to correct. How can they expect us to take this on too?" And suddenly the
issue of teaching the child to read prenatally is lost in the clouds of excuses and rationalizations that confuse so many educational discussions.

Change is a part of living. It makes for the birth of the new. It promises
the renaissance of the old. It furrows the way with memories, leaving shadows of what has been and may appear to be no more. It is tradition moving toward innovation. Change is life. Change is death. It is being born. It
is living. It is dying. In between it is sex and the expression of sex—and
reproduction. It is adolescence—and menopause—and old age. It is here
and now.

Change comes out of the interaction of people with the events they
make, out of their desire to create with events even as they are occurring.
We live within events, some being external to us, others being more immediate.

The teacher interacts with events on two main levels. There is the personal interaction with the many people and events that make up a private
world. There is the public interaction with authority figures, peer colleagues, parents, and the students. On each of these levels and with each of
the people involved, the teacher faces a kind of perpetual motion wherein
the people make an event. A child urinates on the floor, a teacher sternly
reprimands the child, a parent scolds the teacher for having made the child
nervous, a principal supports the teacher in her disciplinary actions, a colleague tells the teacher that she had difficulty with the same parent, and
the teacher's maiden Aunt Maude hearing the story reminds the teacher
that she herself as a girl had to be defended for wetting her panties. And
because of this event a response has to be made in the form of an action,
and as a result of this action an interaction takes place and out of this interaction the creative process develops.

So John's misplaced urine does not remain as remote to the teacher as
does perhaps the capture of the U.S.S. *Pueblo.* Instead, it becomes quite
immediate and an immediate chain of responses is released in the form of
actions, some of which are very creative. John cannot go on using the

floor, so he is given psychological referral for testing. The teacher cannot go on being too stern so the principal promises that she will ask her to be a bit more subtle in her approach. The parent does go right on being upset and organizes a group of mothers into a work-study organization with a school psychologist as their major consultant, and dedicated to the problems of toilet training and its role in education. Aunt Maude who has successfully faced wet panties decides to take adult education courses that might one day lead to emergency teaching certification: she has plain common good sense and you just don't learn that out of any book.

So any one happening can lead to changes of all sorts and try as we will we cannot stop these happenings. Our lives are made up of such situations, conditions, events. We do not live in a vacuum with abstractions filling in the void. We live within events that happened, that are happening, that will happen. Living means that we interact with these events because they affect us and we respond. We accept some, we reject others. To some we are dispassionate, to others we are aroused. At times the events make us tranquil, at times they make us frenetic. Now we love, now we hate, and all is a part of our being, of what we are and of what we would like to be. Sometimes these events bore us with their routine— how dull that the parent-teacher meeting must always be on Thursday night! Sometimes they fill us with fear because they are unknown—are we really capable of supervising a student teacher? They are the events of our work world, our private world, the world of our dreams, the world of our despairs. But we do not sit back and allow them to overwhelm us when we are prepared to be an active part of the world. Rather we try to change them even while they are taking shape. For these events and our interaction with them are the inner core of existence leading to war, to chaos, to the civil rights revolution; leading to the Renaissance, the Reformation, the ecumenical movement in religion, the exploration of space; leading to all that is to come.

The Negative Response to Change

Unfortunately, teachers as a group appear to most observers to lack the perspectives of long-range thinking. They do not look ahead to 1980 and probe those corridors of awesome mystery. They appear more here-and-now-oriented, more concerned with the immediacies of their present routines, present scheduling problems, present details of course study. However practical these concerns are, they should occupy but one part of the teacher's being. Another, larger part should place these matters in appropriate position relative to the effects the actions and activities of today will have upon the events of tomorrow. How many teachers ask "What relevancy does this lesson have to the days ahead?" How many see such relevancies? Or are they not apt to be more concerned with the apparent needs of the particular lesson at hand? The teachers who do not come by it naturally need to learn the posture of looking ahead for themselves and their students, of seeing long-range goals, of planning today with projections into the future. For example, not just how well is the student reading, but equally important, is he stimulated by comprehending the exciting and awesome reality that reading is a primary key to all knowledge? Are his motives, as well as his ability, directed toward the promise of the future?

Lacking this interest or ability, as the case may be, the teacher becomes an organism in danger of living in a cocoon, unaware or, worse yet, afraid of the metamorphosis that transforms it into another state of being. Teachers have been caught with their courses of study down more than once. On one occasion the ogre of programmed learning sprang out at them. At another time the computer breathed forth its electronic fires before the embers of educational television had cooled. In the wake of such "monsters" all too many teachers perceive change as a foreboding interlocutor who poses a threat, who casts a doubt over what is being done and attempts to modulate what ought to be done. Rather than welcoming the possibility of the unknown as a likely alternative able to present a positive yield or shield of support, the teacher is apt to reject the unknown because it is unknown and by doing so leave unexplored many exciting avenues of curriculum and instruction, leave themselves instead of one step forward, two steps behind when the next area of change unfolds. Why learn the principles and uses of the program, the computer, or the television? "It will never *replace* us," the innovation-breakers say. "They'll see we are better. Besides," they rationalize, "others will learn what to do with it, test its so-called importance, show up its weaknesses. I'll just wait until it's proved."

The teachers are too apt to perceive change as a break in their routine. And that which does not conform to the pattern of their habituated activity is all too apt to be viewed with suspicion or rejected outright. Only recently I had a teacher tell me, "No one will ever change my algebra periods from forty minutes of time every day of every week. Less time is too little—more is too much. And they need it every day." When I asked what if everyone does not need to take algebra someday, the teacher shouted back, "Never! *Everyone* needs algebra. It has always been that way and always will! That is, *here* it will. I don't know what they do in Russia."

The Challenge and the Inspiration of Change

Not all teachers view change this way. Some are able to see it as a challenge, for that is what it is. It allows an inquiry into the new—an exploration seeking new meanings and new relationships. It may be viewed as a search or a quest. Man has not shirked this possibility: whether as the

German critic Lessing devoted to the search, or as the Man of La Mancha pursuing the impossible dream, the quest has been a beacon lighting untraveled byways for many a journeyer throughout many an age.

You cannot become the traveler along the unknown road and remain as you were before. Along the way a metamorphosis occurs—you learn to use yourself differently and become different. You learn that as the signposts change, you change to capture their meanings. As the panorama shifts before your eyes, your attitudes adjust to take it in. You learn that we do not ourselves remain static in a world that moves. You discover that we meet the challenge through an expansion of our physical and mental capacities within the potential given us. And you learn that unused potential withers.

The use of this potential to greater fulfillment is our challenge. The use of ourselves in relating to all the changing patterns about us is our challenge. The making of a friend within the uncertainty of the unfamiliar is our challenge.

While working with a religious community, I experienced how exciting the untraveled byways can be. The Sisters of this order had been faced with the problem of a decreasing enrollment and had come to realize that some drastic educational program would have to be designed if their school was not to close. Faced with so grave a possibility, their initial modest attempts at change came to be viewed by them as not dynamic enough to meet so overpowering a confrontation. Their plan had been to add some more time to some of the class periods of seniors by combining certain subjects: the plan they ended up with involved all the classes, all the class periods, and all the students.

Whereas in their initial approach to a strange path they had been filled with fear of the unknown roads, they now stood fast and stilled their pounding hearts with the energy of thinking. As one Sister said, "Big. Stupendous." And it came as a revelation to them that they had to take the step of admitting that problems would exist but that nothing would be too formidable if they meant to resolve the obstacles. When their educational content faced challenge because of the schedule, they said, "Let's commit ourselves to the education we want and then work out the details." As they moved deeper and deeper into their commitment, they came more and more to work together, and their schedule rather than being a separator resulted in a type of cooperation rarely seen.

At the end of just one day of work, after nine hours of straight deliberation, the Sisters felt that their strangeness with the challenge had vanished. They had become campaign companions and been changed, even as their educational program was changed, by commiting a dying school to plans for renewal.

Life is filled with such changes and it is the change that challenges us.

The wonder of it all is that the change and the challenge become the inspiration that fills us with awe, that catapults us into action. Out of such inspiration man has risen to his finest moments.

What Changes Face the Teacher?

Since the teacher is a part of the world, he becomes part of all the changes within that world. These may be viewed as twofold, the macrocosmic conditions of living and those situational to being a teacher. Although they are related, the teacher is more apt to be concerned with those that are situational. Yet the macrocosmic conditions are generic to the human state. Whether conscious of them or not, the teacher is the recipient of the impact of all the forces surrounding the School. If there is a change in the life expectancy of man, the teacher is affected. A new wave of public concern over the population explosion affects the teacher as does an emergent change in attitude over morality, or an experiment that achieves the growth of a living cell in a test tube. Man's need to create within his environment, to interpret it differently, to modify its course, to control its dynamics, to probe its mysteries—all of this adds up to an influence upon the teacher. Why? Because for every question that is asked and every answer that is formulated, something more comes to be known about the world, something more comes to be known about life, something more comes to be added to the evidence that explains who we are, why we are, where we are going, and how we will get there. Every time man learns more, every time he analyzes more deeply, with every changing nuance he brings to his understanding of his world, the teacher is affected.

The pioneer attempts at heart transplant are certainly not immediate to the teacher. They are happening in South Africa or at Stanford to someone unknown. But such attempts must become part of the teacher's knowledge, part of his philosophical tone. To the science teacher certainly—but what if one is not a science teacher? Surely there are implications in heart transplants to man's understanding of himself and the world in which he lives, challenges to our emotions and ability to express empathy, to communicate with our dimensions of spirituality, our search for greater humanity through learning. Most certainly, whether or not a part of the subject field of the teacher, such attempts bring something new into the world and because of this something has changed. There will be no turning back for the researchers of heart transplant and teachers cannot turn back either. They have to be aware and have to translate that awareness into experience for the learners under their influence.

There is no place for the kind of teacher I observed saying to her English class of eighth graders, "Don't bring into this classroom those awful pictures of the blood and gore of that heart operation. There is a time and place for everything. This is English, not science." On the other hand, what of the General Science teacher who said to his class while I listened in, "I don't know about the transplant business. Haven't had time to read it yet. Why don't you do some extra credit reports on it? Make them two pages long and remember you get corrected on spelling in this class." If we don't know the answers, then, let's say so. There is no irrevocable sin in not being always on top of the moment, but we must not expect our students to compensate for our shortcomings. Even as we send them searching, we must go searching ourselves in the areas where change finds us wanting. And if our students, in their eager pursuit of knowledge, prod us beyond our self-imposed limits, we should not punish them with a grade at all in this area of their exploration—let alone mark them down for spelling! What creative mind caught up in the spirit of inspiration allows itself to be bogged down by such technicalities as spelling, grammar, and margins. These have their place, but not in the white heat of creative exploration, and never as an anchor to keep an inquiring spirit in tow behind us.

If the macrocosmic aspect of change often eludes the teacher, the situational changes seldom do, for these become part of the environment of the School and whatever the teacher's reaction, react he must. As society changes its style, as adjustments to problems are made, as new conventions are formulated, the School often responds by offering its interpretation through curriculum, through instruction, and through modifications in administrative apparatus. These become the changes that the teacher deals with by choice or through pressure. Whether it be a new approach to the teaching of mathematics or the use of television as a teaching aid, whether it be new content in social studies to deal with the war in Vietnam or the grouping of several teachers together to instruct as a team, the teacher feels these as changes in the situation that concerns him most. A different schedule, a different number of periods per week, the scheduling of training sessions: large or small, the teacher is attuned to such changes in the sensitive situation that is the School.

The teacher has to become quite accustomed to numerous operational changes, many of which relate to the personality of the principal. It is not uncommon to hear a weary teacher say at home something like, "Good grief, the new principal sure has changed a hell of a lot of stuff. He has us sending kids to the office *only* if they need counseling. Says it's our job if they need discipline. That wasn't old Thornton's way. He knew every kid in the school and they knew who was boss."

But then that is just one type of aggravating detail to which teachers grow accustomed but never resigned, and are seldom reluctant to bewail. There are changes in class schedules that sometimes occur the last minute, a new series of staff meetings that must be attended by all, a flock of transfer students dumped into the school without warning, a new textbook for World Geography, a change in the permanent record folder, and a brand

new office of Special Services at the Board of Education—to name a few.
Teachers do grow accustomed to such irritations as part of the liability of
being a teacher. They learn how to gripe when they are the recipients of
all kinds of assaults, and they learn how to develop that good stiff upper
lip that is prerequisite equipment for any martyr.

The problem with such pained resignation to situational innovations is
that the teacher does not develop positive attitudes about change. Seeing it
as something that upsets the applecart, as something to endure, something
that is part of the hazards of the profession does not nurture healthy perceptions. *Seen as a villain, change cannot be used as a champion.* True,
not all change is good, but all change is a possibility. Here is where the
teacher needs help. If, in fact, change is part of the eternal order of things
and if, in fact, the teacher is likewise a part of the eternal order, then these
two parts just have to get together, have to work together as members of a
team.

But teachers do not always work well together in any team sense. They
often like the roost of the prima donna and find cooperative roundelays
very hard to sing. As one of many examples, the dental profession is studying the adhesive properties of the barnacle and how the barnacle, which
seems to be impervious to water, may have properties with implications
for preventative dentistry. This is one of numerous cooperative ventures
underway and countless dentists await the results and follow the course
while waiting. It is difficult to find a comparable example of a group of
teachers researching their profession in such a fashion. If they are practitioners they seem to be content with letting those who are remote from the
classroom do the research for them. Then when the researchers to whom
they have defaulted present proposals for change, these same teachers hide
behind all the cliché excuses beginning and very often ending with, "It's all
right for *them* to talk—they don't have to do it!"

We don't know whether or not barnacle research will come up with anything and whether or not it will ever become the kind of adhesive we
might one day get in a dentist's chair—or want. But we do know one
thing; in spite of the fact that there will always be some who will resist
whatever is new, when the majority within a profession dedicated to serving mankind see some value in something new, they start taking the necessary steps to become a part of it or make it a part of them. This may be
the answer for teachers. Perhaps we must come to see that we are part of a
profession just as dedicated to serving mankind as, let's say dentistry, and
perhaps we need to study change as a way of giving more service to mankind. Why not? The human being who comes under our guidance in the
learning-growing process is certainly in a service relationship to us and
perhaps we need to perceive change as something that might benefit him
and therefore be mandatory to our teaching pattern. Whether or not we are
comfortable becomes irrelevant—after all, teaching should not be our
therapy.

The Teacher's Responsibility

More and more teachers will have to become less threatened by change. They will have to become so aware of change that it becomes second nature for them to analyze it as one fixed alternative among many. They will have to accept or reject change on the basis of rational behavior rather than upon emotional bias. Such an approach could result in teachers becoming leaders as they rightly should be by using change as something to create upon rather than having change control them through external pressures. Teachers should direct the course of change through the use of their trained minds and the development of abilities necessary to expose issues to dissection before plotting their direction.

Let us look, for example, at the time preceding the meteoric appearance of the new math. The classrooms were going along as usual while the nation's foreign affairs were going along less well. Thus, it was determined outside in that distant arena far from the School, called the seat of national government, that there was a shortage of math and science brains to carry us through the decades of the space age ahead, and the outside turned to look at the inside—the inside of those classrooms. Whether or not the classrooms looked back was unimportant (to everyone except the teachers perhaps) because the outside pressure decided that what was being taught in those classrooms was not good enough: they decided that crash programs had to be initiated to make an educational breakthrough which would produce the manpower needed. Teachers did not lead nor attempt to lead the way in changing the math curriculum: they did not control the events that were to follow, as they might have, by creating to fill the need. Even though they had not identified the need from the first, even though they had not been aware that what they were doing was inadequate, they could have emerged as directors of the process of the math revolution. Their training in the field, their professional abilities could have plotted the direction, could have communicated the issues to their colleagues. But no —the university professor of mathematics came down from his tower and brought the gospel of change. The practicing mathematician squeezed past the educational guardians and made his way out of the fields of the intellect where mathematics was a philosophy, a language, and an art into the wastelands where it had become but a required subject suffocated between the pages of yellowed outlines and mildewed textbooks. So it was then, uninvolved teachers saw crash training programs designed, small research groups formed by "outsiders," textbook companies dashing to the source of need where everyone ran to pick up the cash customer.

Teachers may or may not have known that the old math would not stand the light of the new day, but whatever they knew they were not involved enough in the changing scene that was their home base to be ahead of the changing math curricula. Reading, 'riting or 'rithmetic, we must not be caught like that again! *Teachers must see change as their responsibility.* For them there can be no basic morality in closing their minds to the real world of real people and real events. Teachers just have to know that the real world is filled with change and that they have to be prepared to deal with it. They have to understand it. They have to expand because of it.

How can teachers accept the responsibility of shaping the minds of the young if they do not see their own relationship to the changing order, the place of knowledge in this order, and the evolving nature of the order? Knowledge is no more static than are the tides. As the shore is washed by the tides, knowledge is washed by all the movements of the cycles that form the universe. Teachers cannot be responsible teachers or responsible citizens either unless they choose to accept the inevitability of Ovid's observation that "All things are in a state of flux, and everything is brought into being with a changing nature."

As the child before them changes, the ideas in the book he holds have changing applicability. Even as the applicability changes, new texts are being written, new presentations are being planned, new techniques of expression proposed. The teacher is responsible for putting all of this in perspective, responsible for dealing with it, responsible for contributing to it.

The teacher has a responsibility to accept change as an alternative, to use its dynamics and to become a leader through this use. The teacher has a responsibility to contribute to change. Apathy or neglect become ingredients of immorality.

The alternatives seem to be to wallow in the mire of fear and self-pity because change is threatening the safe little pigeonholes of our existence, or to see change as an opportunity that can lift us to fantastic heights of leadership at the peak of anticipation and can help us mold tomorrow's leaders.

The choice is ours to make now while there is still time. Soon, very soon, the choice will have been made and the need for those who resist change will be no more.

A Case Study

Scene: Teachers' Lounge. Elementary School Building. Suburban district. Pay good. Working conditions just fine.

Actors: Principal and crew: twenty-one teachers. Eight have been in this same building for over thirty years; six have over twenty-five years in the school district; three have had upward of five years of experience before joining the staff here; two are first-year teachers; one has been transferred into the building because her principal had a nervous breakdown and she could not get along with the replacement: the remaining two had between five and ten years of teaching experience before their own families came along when they left teaching to which they have just returned. One of these was once the PTA president in this very school.

Subject: Teacher training for the new math program.

Principal: "Well girls, we've been told at headquarters that we're going to have a new math course of study, new textbooks—the whole thing. And they are bringing in a Dr. Bronstein from some Eastern school to train us in all the new theory. We'll meet every Wednesday afternoon from 3:30 to 4:30. School will be dismissed on those days at 3:00 to allow us time to get to Toneville Junior High where the meetings will be held. There will be no absences. The superintendent is very anxious to have this go and we are spending a lot of money on this together with the Toneville School Board and the Liberty School Board."

Miss Ellsworth (an old-timer): "Gracious, June (they have known each other since they were really girls), how much do they expect us to do? Is there no end to their demands? Next thing we know they'll want this sort of thing in all the subjects. I say we're starting something that we'll all rue."

Miss Hendricks (another old-timer): "I agree with that. It's a fine day when some college professor has to tell us what to do. Some of us have probably been at it since before he was in diapers. Now everyone's telling us."

Principal: "I don't think that's in back of anyone's mind. It's just that so many new ways of doing everything have come about that we have to keep up. They told us, someone from some research group—I forget the name of either the man or the group—but they were telling us at this meeting with the superintendent that since Sputnik we just don't have enough good mathematicians to keep the country going and it's all very dangerous. I even think the government is in on it. So we have little choice."

Mrs. Lucas (the former PTA president): "You are so right. Why Jimmie (her son, and his mother's favorite) was telling me that at college no one does math the way I did or do it. He says I'm not quite with it but that it's all right for the little kids because no one expects them to learn anything down in these grades anyway, but that when you get to the upper grades everything is different. I can't even make heads or tails out of his simplest assignments. I remember when I used to be able to help him— but no more. Seems like everything he learns is just Greek to me. If only Jim, Sr., were alive. I still think that the kids would be better students. You need a man around for that certain touch I think. I'm all for going to these meetings. They'll help me with Jim, Jr."

Miss Kerry (the one whose former principal had the nervous breakdown): "Well, I just don't know how I'll be able to manage. It takes me forty minutes to drive home and with the winter weather and all if I have to go to another meeting I'll get home so late it'll be time to turn around again to come back to work. As it is I'm exhausted having changed from third to fourth grade this year."

Mrs. Bernaby (another one with a family): "That's just the sort of thing that bothers me. I have a longish drive and you know how I have to pick up Mercy (her nineteen-year-old daughter) on my way home, and as it is she has to wait for me twenty minutes or so, and then I've started going to the doctor for allergy shots and those appointments are on Wednesdays. I don't know how I'd ever change the appointment."

Principal: "Now look, this is all out of my hands. I tried to tell the superintendent that there would be sacrifices and hardships involved in this but he never asked any of us principals. We weren't consulted. This is just the way it goes. We were told and now you'll have to cooperate. As it is I expect I'll have a lot of trouble with some parents who will want to know what's going on that we have to have an early dismissal on Wednesdays. I haven't figured out how all of that will work yet with getting the youngsters out of here and the bus schedules changed and all sorts of other complications I'm sure we haven't even thought about."

Miss Swanson (twenty-four years in the system): "Well, that's my point exactly. It's come to a pretty state when we're treated like so much baggage and not even asked our feelings. That would never have happened when Mr. Riley was here (the former superintendent who was with the schools for thirty-nine years and who discovered many of these girls when they were still in normal school and brought them along with him into the system. He retired last year). He thought about us as people and he would have asked our advice. We never would be told after a decision had been made and embarrassed in this way in front of the parents. And who gets the idea that we need new math anyway? It was good enough the way we've been doing it all these years. Why isn't it good enough for someone Sputniking around? Maybe we'd all be better off if we didn't have such things anyway."

Teachers (a chorus of mixed voices from a variety of types): "She's right. Leave it to Swansie to tell them off. She's not afraid and she's right. Can't we protest or something? We need to have a voice in what's going on."

Principal: "I know how you feel, girls, and I don't think there's a thing we can do. The Board of Ed. is behind this whole thing and I bet that Mr. Arnold (an assistant professor at a local college specializing in engineering and a critic of the schools because his son is gifted in science and he has not been challenged. Mr. Arnold thinks that the school is holding his son back and that the boy won't get into Yale because of it) has had a big voice in all of this. You know what trouble we've had with that family and the way they think they can run the schools."

Miss Seldom (in the building for twenty-eight years): "Well, let's demand a formal statement of what we've been charged with doing so wrong that we need to be trained during our free time. No one really knows what a teacher's life is like. I'd like to see the average person be able to put up with all we do: the papers, the children, the parents, and all the pressures and uncertainties."

Teachers (*two simultaneous echoes*): "Why don't they pay us for going to the meetings?"

Principal: "There has been some talk of that. I guess they consider they're giving us something because we have some release time for this since school is dismissed early and since legally I guess we're actually supposed to be in the building after school until four o'clock anyway. So all that they're taking is an extra half-hour. And I guess they're talking about applying some of this toward salary increment, but it hasn't been worked out."

Miss Dwinder (*one of the new ones*): "I'd like to volunteer to be the building representative to the Board if they decide to have a committee to look this whole problem over, what with the questions of getting paid, getting credit and having time off. I bet there'd be some hot arguments and I'd sure like to get in on it. They told us at school that if you wanted a career in education you had to get involved and I guess I've always been good at shooting off my mouth."

Principal: "That's fine, dear. If they ask for such a committee we'll take a vote on the representative."

Miss Ellsworth (*the first old-timer who spoke*): "Leave it to the young to come up with good ideas. I think we should press for such a committee and refuse to go along with these meetings until a committee has studied the problem in more detail. We can't rush into every new cock-and-bull idea that comes along."

Teachers (*lots of voices chirping in unison*): "Right. Exactly. Yes. That's it. Sure. Exactly. Every new idea. Committee. Demand it. Right."

Mrs. Underwood (*the other new teacher*): "My husband tells me every night that what teachers need is a more active pressure group. This is what the Teacher's Union is good for. It's an active pressure group. We should use them in this whole matter."

Principal: "Now, dear, our building has gotten along without the Union which is really quite new in our system and as far as I know all of our teachers support our Teachers Organization which for over forty years has done so much for our system. And in our building we have had two presidents of the Teachers Organization and I once was Vice President."

Mrs. Lucas (*the former PTA president*): "I still have very good relations with the parents and still keep contact and quite active in the PTA and I'm certain that we could get mothers to help us. Lots of them come to me and tell me how they are really concerned that we have so much to do and have asked how they can help."

Miss Belle, the school secretary, interrupts the meeting. She leans over Miss Hendricks to whisper to the Principal.

Miss Hendricks: "Why, Joannie Belle, your hair looks wonderful. You've had it done. I hadn't noticed before. Oh I do like it."

Principal: "Excuse me, girls. I'll be right back. Telephone."

A lot of buzzing and chittering follows with occasional words breaking through like, "Joannie's hair." "Everyone does it nowadays." "Too blonde for school." "Youthful though." "Some of the sixth graders do it." "What do you expect with the mothers around here in their tight pants going to the supermarket?" "Times changing."

Principal (returning): "Well, girls, that was Miss Burns the principal over at Toneville Elementary. We've been friends for a long time. Her nephew is married to a distant cousin of mine. She tells me that her teachers are in the same sort of state we are and that she is going to talk to the principal's group tomorrow at Toneville and compare notes. I think I'll do the same. I'll get on the phone tonight and check with a couple of the girls."

Teachers (spontaneous approval from all sources, all sizes, shapes and ages): "Good!"

Principal: "Just sit tight and keep all of this under your hat. I'll get back to you tomorrow. Don't forget that Albert Avenue is blocked off due to that broken sewer so watch it going home. Your class registers are due in the office tomorrow. Miss Belle has to check them all over. It's a big job and some of you will insist on making mistakes in adding up the columns. We have that new adding machine in the office and you can use it but you'll have to check off the time you want it on the sheet on the wall. Too many traffic jams and we just have to know where it is."

Miss Swanson (this is Swansie whom the group thought was so right): "Well I haven't been able to use it yet. I've never been able to find it when I've gone into the office. Why does it have to leave? It'd be much better if it stayed on the counter and we could just dash in at some free time. As it is I just give up if I have to track it down like a hunter and who wants to pull it away from someone?"

Principal: "Well, girls, I'll have Miss Belle work out a system for the adding machine and she'll tell you about it individually. We do have to help her out with the registers and add them correctly. It makes quite a mess, you'd be surprised, when even two columns are wrong. That's all for now. Oh, Mrs. Underwood (the one with the husband and the business about pressure groups and the Union), could I see you for just a minute please? I have something to tell you."

Two days pass and on the morning of the third day the principal has had Miss Belle, the school secretary, place a mimeographed sheet in each teacher's mail box. It reads:

TO: All Teachers.
FROM: H. June Hamp, Principal.
RE: Math Meetings.

The math meetings are going to be studied by the superintendent. They're post-poned for now anyway. A committee is to be appointed representing the build-ings. We'll meet next Monday at noon for election of our representative. Our nominees are: Miss Ellsworth and Miss Hendricks.

Good news department: Shower for Elaine Dwinder at my place. Saturday at 1:00. She's engaged! Shower for Gert Underwood at my place, same Saturday at 1:00. She's expecting! Details to follow.

Sit tight, girls, and keep everything under your hats.

Analysis

The foregoing case study is based upon an actual series of events, experi-enced by the author. In the name of human decency, locations and person-ages are disguised. Yet the case study points up a chain of responses that might be said to characterize teacher mentality in relation to change.

These responses begin with the role of the principal and the teachers' interaction with her. Notice that H. June Hamp acts like a mother hen holding court over her brood. When a male teacher moves into this scene he is seldom, if ever, cock of the walk. The pecking order neuters his sex and he too becomes one of the principal's brood. She is on a girls-will-be-girls level of operation except where she is threatened by such dangerous ideas as Mrs. Underwood's injection of the Union notion and Miss Dwin-der's self-propelled notion about her qualifications to serve on the commit-tee. In the main, however, Miss Hamp has things under control and is not without her resources including those of an informal underground over at the Toneville school. The principals cultivate a broad field of this sort whereby the weeds that grow in their own back yard may be eradicated by the pesticides used in another yard. Miss Hamp needs to assert herself as principal from time to time and does so by inventing new routines such as the adding machine ritual.

The teachers show that those who have been around long enough get to feel quite nested in with the system and deal with Miss Hamp as they would any girl friend. Those who are less experienced try to inject into the proceedings the glad tidings of comfort and joy they have taken with them out of their college classrooms. Before those college notes get imple-mented, however, many a book will be yellowed with age. The teachers do not demonstrate any real educational leadership. They appear to be the re-cipients of decisions that have been made around them, almost in spite of them. They do not show any dynamic educational convictions but rather, they base their arguments upon self-centered needs completely irrelevant to the issues. Such things as after-school appointments and a break in their own routine seem of greater concern than the larger argument. They did not themselves anticipate the change and act unaware that there is a changed need in mathematics, but they nevertheless become defensive and protective. Their themes become melodies of what they have always done, how good it all was way back then, and "Why do things have to be as they are? Where are the good old days of yore when teachers were left alone?" The college appears as an alien world to them, not identified as being in partnership. Thus, they do not see themselves as educators on a par but as creatures put upon by outsiders. They admit to their inadequacies in mathematics but appear not to care. After all, there are other grades coming up for their students where all deficiencies can be remedied. They operate in an emotional whirlpool and the waters are easily agitated. Anything more is just too much. After all, the requirements of the job are terribly, terribly difficult. Nobody knows the suffering they see.

The projected mathematics changes are not the only kind that annoy. All changes do. Even the change in the bus schedule would be very difficult and the new plan around the adding machine will take a formal system to insure its operation. There will be everything to help except a lock and key and a Brink's truck. But then, Miss Belle, the secretary, will be custodial and keep the thing moving along.

They evoke the memories of the past, the days of Riley the retired superintendent, when men were men and the girls were loved and wanted and protected. Tradition is their sweet recollection of twilights of tenderness. Today is not tradition and so it cannot be good. It must be treated with suspicion. There are all kinds of people to watch out for and all kinds of places to put the blame. The parents like Mr. Arnold may be acting up, or right within their midst colleagues may do suspicious things like provoking sentiment for the Union.

And yet, in the presence of a teacher like Mrs. Underwood who is aware of the value of pressure, we see one kind of force for change that has come to be a part of today's style. Witness the effects of teacher strikes such as in New York City and the results of teachers' protests through their active union sanctions. There seems to be a growing energy focusing upon the use of labor tactics to bring about the kinds of internal changes teachers want. Also, witness the new look of a Miss Dwinder who volunteers and tries to push forward into a position for contributing to policy making. The administration did not involve the teachers nor, for that matter, the principals, but went ahead and made decisions about mathematics. Yet, did the teachers and principals evaluate what they were doing with mathematics in the light of the new technological need for mathematics and the new world events that contributed urgency to the problem? Was there time for involvement? It appears as though time must be taken for involvement if change is to be brought about. Without involvement the issues get confused, as in this principal's meeting, and because of the confusion progress is stopped.

Notice how teachers demand inducements if they are to change. Hence, they come around to the triad of salary increment, release time, and experience increment. Teachers show themselves to be human first and teachers next. They will do anything to protect their comfort in a situation. After all, they will even think of getting the parents involved in helping them forestall something which would in the long run be a help to the very children to whom they are committed. Notice how important the informal level of interaction is with teachers like Mrs. Lucas using the parents and her PTA contacts and Miss Hamp using her contact with other principals in other systems.

The teachers get all tied down to the small details of the small world that they choose to make theirs. So, the adding machine becomes just as important as the new math and details for resolving its dilemma take precedence. The minutiae become the major concerns of a life that shrivels into a web of insignificance rather than being challenged by the larger concerns of a larger world.

Out of all this some positive things do happen. Although the math training sessions are postponed, the pressure to have a committee of building representatives goes through. This is a change in the right direction. Whereas the teachers did not exert leadership to demand changes in math and did not organize study groups themselves, when pressed to change they united in defense of their rights and demanded representation. This is the way the administration should have proceeded in the first place. The issue should have been identified, supportive evidence should have been presented, then representatives appointed to study the problem and recommend directions for action. The teachers should have been asked to advise antecedent to the decision. But then you can see that change itself is thus slowed down and that the course is delayed by actions that are of less importance to the ultimate goal. But without those actions the goal itself will not be reached. Teachers do not move easily and are not above sabotaging anything that they do not perceive as comfortable to them.

18. Sensitivity Training in the Classroom

Dan Simon and Diane Sarkotich

I. Mr. Simon

In the past twenty years, thousands of educators, businessmen, and professional people have received "sensitivity training." Most of these people—including myself—received this training through one of the various programs offered by the NEA-sponsored National Training Laboratories.

Having received the training, I wanted to share what I had learned with the teachers in East Chicago (where I was superintendent) and perhaps with the students as well.

Informal talks with faculty members led to the decision to hold a series of meetings at which I would try to pass on my newfound insights and techniques by applying them in faculty meetings.

At the first session, each person told what he expected from the meetings. Following this, we grouped topics that seemed similar and arranged them by priorities. All participated in this process of agenda building. The first meeting concluded by each of us responding to such questions as "What did you do that was helpful to our meeting?" and "What could you have done to be more helpful?"

High on the list of priorities was a desire to be skillful in counseling. Specifically, we believed the skill we needed was the ability to listen well. To gain the skill, we discussed different meanings of listening and followed our discussion with exercises to improve listening. For one exercise, for example, we carried on a discussion guided by this rule: No one could introduce a new thought until he had accurately rephrased what the previous speaker had said.

How to stop being preoccupied by our own thoughts? How to attend to what others were saying and to avoid misinterpreting? The task was not

SOURCE: *NEA Journal*, LVI, 1 (January 1967), 12–13. Reprinted by permission of the authors and the publisher.

easy, but quickly in some cases, and more reluctantly in others, we stopped engaging in a series of monologues. Finally we realized that we were linking thought and feeling with one another, that we were helping one another, that we were making it clear to one another that we had heard what was said. We came to realize, too, that words do not always need to fill the air—that thoughtful silence can be productive.

At least once during each meeting, we paused to look at the process going on among us. We told each other, as objectively as we could, how we were reacting and feeling. An intangible benefit came from this: We grew accustomed to being nonjudgmental with one another's ideas, attitudes, and feelings. It became easier for us to speak about how people's behavior made us feel as we found that our words would be listened to in a nondefensive way.

We gained skill in techniques of asking and answering questions: to listen for clues in responses, to use the question to expand the response or to turn our attention in a new direction. Cooperatively, members of the group reported, diagnosed, and evaluated classroom problems, and planned ways to transfer learnings to classroom teaching and to counseling activities.

II. Miss Sarkotich

As an English teacher, I decided that a summer course I was about to teach provided an optimum situation in which to use what I had learned in our sensitivity-training meetings. It was an eight-week course in English literature; the class would be small and would meet two hours daily.

At first, the students fenced around, trying to "psych out" what I expected of them. For the first two weeks I told them in great detail: I drilled; I tested in quizzes; I monitored panel debates; I assigned compositions; I lectured and questioned.

By the end of the second week, the students were tired of being taught at. They began to ask, "Where do we go from here?" With my blessing, they shifted over to self-education and began setting their own rules for learning. They accepted the curriculum, saying that intelligent, successful people had designed it with care. Then they assured each other (and sought my reassurance) that the prescribed anthology would not restrict them.

Reading at their own volition, they used me as a resource person—to give them pertinent facts and make known the experts' opinions and interpretations.

Their ground rules required labeling opinions as such, not palming them off as facts. One student was asked to watch for and call attention to unproductive class activity, such as bogging down in a rut or wandering off the road completely.

The group soon realized that making decisions would be its toughest task: How much to read? What to talk about beyond the facts? Again and again, they asked themselves, "Where do we go from here?" The literature seemed the easiest part.

After much group discussion, a satisfactory pattern evolved: I would indicate the factual matter to be covered at the next session, and members of the group would read as much as they could of the material that would be discussed. Each day, following the exposition of factual matter, I would supply classic interpretation and report the opinions of experts about the literature under discussion. This was always labeled as opinion and accepted as such. Time was allowed for comments by any student. To initiate the task of interchanging ideas, open-ended questions were asked: What are your feelings about this? Is there anything to add?

Silence proved an effective technique. Sometimes it was a comfortable communication of appreciation for a jeweled experience just shared. Sometimes it was a stress device that made the group aware of its commitment and obligation to exploration.

Some of the most difficult class decisions were made after long periods of silence. One such period promised to be interminable until two students offered to be responsible for making a decision for the group and the rest, relieved and willing, accepted the offer.

Acceptance and silence became two great tools. After the class had heard opinions of experts in the field, any student's comment got a hearing, no matter how wild the thought.

Nonjudgmental acceptance, the class discovered, leaves room for modification. When told, "That's wrong," the immediate human response is, "I'm right," which restricts the learner to defense of an opinion that is usually half-formed. On the other hand, giving several views a hearing; finding parallels; borrowing from the communal wealth of ideas to build a composite—this approach allows movement of thought.

To transfer accurately a thought that is being formed in one mind to other minds is hard work, the class found. A speaker chooses words that mean the thought *to him*. The persons hearing him add their own interpretations, values, and prejudices.

Each member of the class learned the technique of checking his own understanding of what a speaker meant by restating the point: "Did I understand you to say that . . . ?" If confusion has occurred, the speaker can then reply, "No, I intended to say. . . ." This kind of interchange clarifies the point for the whole group.

If it has been established in a group that it is acceptable to present an opinion, then there is no stress at changing an opinion after hearing feedback, the class discovered. The person feeding back the thought isn't seeking to catch an error but merely to help clarify understanding—his own, the speaker's, or the group's.

At the end of the course, I asked students to comment on the methods used.

Hilario, a boy with a language problem, said, "This class has given me an idea of a new style of getting education, different from any in the past. I learned."

Kathy, a sophisticated, socially mature girl, said, "I don't remember learning as much in any class as I did in this one. I've participated quite a bit and made an honest effort to solve some of the problems the class ran into. I have never enjoyed a class as much as I enjoyed this one. I'd like to go on for about four more weeks, throw our books away, and turn this class inside out."

A straight-A student reported that "the things said in this class always worked me up. The quantity of my contribution to the discussion was very scant. You could say I was selfish. The real reason was lack of courage. I really dreaded those days when we were in a deadlock; I even tried to get my mom to let me stay home a few times. But now I feel that I've learned an awful lot especially about myself."

The approach of looking at process by observation, participation, and feedback had significant meanings for me as well as for my students. The approach helped all of us feel free to try—not always to succeed splendidly—but to try, to learn by our mistakes, and to try again. To us, this was the value of sensitivity training.

19. If Your School Stinks, CRAM It*

Donald H. De Lay and David Nyberg

One needs no special agility in perception to notice two characteristics of contemporary American education: Most people involved in it don't like it much, and everybody wants to "individualize" it. These attitudes are real enough but vague. One thing is clear, though; in the classroom a genuine

* Comprehensive Random Achievement Monitor CRAM was developed at Stanford University under a grant from the Charles F. Kettering Foundation.

SOURCE: *Phi Delta Kappan*, LI, 6 (February 1970), 310–12. Reprinted by permission of the authors and the publisher.

rift exists between teachers and students. Education is supposed to be facilitated by the relation between teachers and students—that is what teachers are for—but what transpires when there is a breach between teachers and students? Mistrust, resentment, misunderstanding, fear, gamesmanship, one-upmanship, failure, mutual avoidance, and precious little education. Students see school as unpleasant and irrelevant because, in general, that is what it is; teachers thus see students as stubborn, immature, and cheeky. When the bell rings everybody splits to find someone pleasant to be with and something worthwhile to do.

The real pathos of this situation is that the overwhelming majority of teachers and students are good people who want to do better, but somehow they have been forced into hiding. This, ironically, is caused by a need to "look good," a concept that can usually be traced to administrative public relations festoonery. If you've got to *try* to "look good," then chances are you are not looking "natural," the implication of which is that looking natural is not good.

This perhaps is the most insidious predicament of our public schools. To attend school *in propria persona* is asking to be ambushed, to be shot down by those who conceal themselves behind stone faces deep in the gullies of the customary.

There are many who share our distaste for ambush, and among these are some who talk of "individualizing" education as a means for protecting against ambush. Two of the most notorious procedures for "individualizing" instruction have been flexible scheduling and computer-assisted instruction (CAI). In too many cases, the former has become a flexible flub —we find the same people doing the same high-gloss nothing on a different time schedule. Substituting "module" for "class" simply won't do the trick; neither will lecturing to 15 instead of 45. As for CAI, the only significant "individualizing" that it provides is a flexible rate for each student to learn the same thing. CAI programs are, in the main, electronic textbooks still operating on a Yes-No paradigm covertly teaching that people can be wrong but machines cannot. We are not suggesting that these inventions are bad; they are just immature and at the moment tangential to what we feel is the significant problem.

We, too, want to "individualize" education, but even more we want to *personalize* it. We refuse to deal with "the learning organism" or "human material"; we deal with little people and big people who care about each other and about learning. We trust that people will learn unless they are prevented from doing so. A child with a normally healthy body cannot keep himself from learning to walk if the adults around have sense enough not to hobble him. We go on from this point and assume that a child will learn other new things naturally, by himself, asking the questions he needs to, and that adults should help show him the way and then get out of it.

The aim of a good teacher is to become unnecessary. Not many of us can stand that kind of ego torpedo, and that's one reason why not many of us are good teachers.

To become unnecessary is not to abandon a young person who is yet without self-confidence, an understanding of personal responsibility, a sense of trust in others, or a secure willingness to risk and explore. It is rather to help create these qualities, to replace coercion and control with consent, to replace fear and dependence with trust and cooperation. Everybody with even tepid blood knows this, but surprisingly few know that such things cannot be taught. They must be *experienced* to be understood. This means that a teacher must provide the opportunity and the environment for such experiencing if he wants to be a good teacher—i.e., eventually unnecessary. It takes a person who is secure and open about himself and his job as a teacher to do this. That's why it is not done by many nor often even by a few. It is a risky thing to do and we are conditioned cowards. It might be well to remember that cowardice is contagious—and so is openness, security, and the willingness to risk.

We are talking here of personal meaning, a level of knowing that is deeper than information acquisition. These days, the transmission of information can be done in a variety of more efficient ways than the traditional lecture-by-mouth method. The discovering and sharing of personal meaning, however, is a matter of individual confrontation and communication. I cannot tell you what your personal meanings are; you must tell me if I am to know. The best I can do is listen, not just hear, but *listen* and respond to you if I can, as honestly as I can. This means that we have to spend time together, discovering and sharing how we feel about what we know and don't know. We feel that this is not only a legitimate enterprise for the classroom but a necessary one if school, new information, and others are to have any relevance or personal significance to those who are in the classroom.

If we are to apply ourselves to the personal meaning level of knowing, we are faced with two problems immediately. The first is the resentment of school psychologists, counselors, and guidance personnel, who will say that we are not trained for such personal confrontations. If this accusation is valid, then parents should not be allowed to talk with their children around the supper table, for they are not trained to do so. Lovers should seek a third party, preferably a Ph.D. in one of the social sciences, to oversee and mediate their confidences in each other, and no one should admit anything or show any true feelings without permission from a licensed dealer in used feelings.

The second problem is a bit more serious. It has to do with time and numbers and state laws and college entrance requirements. We have too little time to present too much material to too many students to satisfy too many laws and meet too many mandates from too many institutions to do much talking about anything else. There are units to cover, tests to give and correct, achievement records to be kept, etc. And since the students don't want to do any of this, there are the problems of motivation and discipline, which take up most of the time between tests. No one has time to talk about personal meaning; everybody wants to, but nobody has time.

It is to this problem that we have addressed ourselves in developing the CRAM model for use as a teaching method. Teachers have a need (some say duty) to monitor achievement, to let the student know how he is doing. We agree. This function, however, should not become a prime issue either in time or classroom focus, and it should never act as a deterrent to motivation. It should be handled efficiently, it should provide comprehensive feedback for each student and the teacher, and it should be a valuable resource in itself.

CRAM is a very simple model based on two basic ideas: 1) continuous random sampling, and 2) continuous feedback in terms of *final* performance criteria. These ideas serve as means for implementing a new plan of learning built around the presentation to students of a final exam at several intervals and in several forms during the course. Not all students take the test at the same time; in fact, they never know when they are going to take it or what form of it they are going to take. During the course, however, all students take several forms of the test. Each form covers the entire concept range being dealt with, but each form includes different items from each of the concept subgroupings.

The first idea is almost self-explanatory. There is no good reason to go on counting on our fingers when we have at our disposal several very sophisticated sampling procedures which can provide accurate information about a population while eliminating most of the demeaning task of compilation. In our model, continuous random sampling techniques are applied both to the learners and to the final objectives of the course being taught. Instead of testing everybody every week on the same items of a segmented unit of a serial-step design, we propose that a sample of students be tested at randomized intervals on a randomized selection of the final list of performance criteria, or course goals. The data provided by this method are much easier to handle, take less of the teacher's time, less of the students' time, and can be used to establish individual learning curves for each student, teacher, course, and teaching method over as long a time period as desired.

The second idea, continuous feedback in terms of final performance criteria, requires a bit more explanation. The first point to be made is that the final performance criteria (PC) must be established at the beginning of the course. This can be done by department, by individual teachers, or, preferably, by the teacher and the students cooperatively. It amounts to sitting down beforehand and figuring out precisely what is to be accomplished over the course of a week, a term, or a year. PC must be specific and precise if they are to be effective. They must be stated in such a way as to be clearly understood by the students in terms of objectively defined terminal behaviors marking the achievement of the PC. In other words, the teacher should prepare a list of specified behaviors which students must be able to perform by the end of the course. This list should be given to the students and be subject to revision, modification, and final acceptance by them. When everyone knows precisely what is expected of him, much time and frustration will be saved—the teacher won't have to "hide" test items until the given hour, and students won't have to "psych out" the teacher to discover what they are supposed to know. Also, the final exam, the list of PC, can be given to students in the first week so the teacher and the students can discover how much they already know about the course material, thus avoiding a great deal of redundancy and enabling the students to share with each other their varied stores of knowledge.

The second important point to be made is that "feedback" is not the same as "evaluation." We have found that evaluation tends to separate the judge and the judged; it drives them away from each other and makes meaningful communication much more difficult than it would be otherwise. Evaluation also tends to be manifested in the form of extrinsic reward, which serves more of a failure-avoidance function than a positive motivating function. Feedback, on the other hand—merely letting the student know how he is progressing toward the goals he has selected—is a nonevaluative process because it does not involve a grade. It is just information about where the student is now in relation to where he wants to be.*

Now, when these two concepts—continuous random sampling and continuous feedback in terms of final performance criteria—are put together, several things happen. Testing, or information transmission, need no longer constitute a prime issue either in class time or class focus. Not everyone takes the tests at the same time and not everyone takes the same tests, so there is no reason to prime the whole class through the week for the climax on Friday. Everybody is at a different stage in terms of the final PC; hence there are varied foci of interest among the students. There is no point in lecturing to these students, but it is very important to answer their questions and respond to their need for resource help. There is no anxiety-provoking test anticipation to create a need for frantic study on Thursday

* While using CRAM in his class, one of the authors (Don De Lay) suffered his students' hostile onslaughts after the first few "surprise tests." As the course progressed, however, the students began to realize that they were not being evaluated, although they did have a clear notion of where they were in the course work. They began to *request* the test. They no longer saw it as a threat that Don held over them; they saw it as a tool to use on their own work and on Don's potential as a resource.

night because no one knows when he will be given a test (better called a feedback monitor). The random sampling of students and PC items provides a comprehensive and highly efficient feedback system for the teacher and the students in a very efficient way. Less time is spent taking and marking tests; the results can be used by other students as resource material for their own progress. (In this way the feedback monitor becomes a learning experience in itself and thus a valuable resource.) Since there are no grades attached to the feedback, there is no need to covet correct answers. Cooperation replaces competition. The point is for *everyone* to reach the minimum PC level, to "succeed" in the course. If a student arrives at the required minimum level of achievement during the second week, he has passed the course and is essentially free to go on with whatever interests him further, or, if he wishes, to share his knowledge with others in the class. He needn't just sit around waiting for the months to pass.

We believe, as John Dewey did, that there should be no lesser goal for an educator than to help a person grow and learn to continue to grow on his own.

This model is designed to meet the informational and material requirements in the public school. When these requirements are laid bare and organized into a list of specifics, they become less overwhelming in terms of time and content than we have generally assumed. It has been our experience that if a teacher gives a list of performance criteria to his students at the outset, he may not have to do much more except answer questions about resource material. When entrusted with the responsibility for their own progress and relieved of the constant threat of judgment, students in effect take over the information-gathering tasks that the teacher has traditionally assumed. Class time is liberated for other things; namely, exploring personal meaning.

How the area of personal meaning is addressed is a matter of personal style and a function of who is there. The class can meet as a large group or in small groups, every day or on another agreed-upon schedule. Out-of-class days can be spent in resource centers, conferences with the teacher or other students, etc. The main point is that now there is time to talk about what is going on in the class, how you feel about what is going on, how the class could be improved, why the class is important or not important to other personal interests, and any number of other topics that might emerge out of the group.

A good deal of talking goes on in schools as it is, but most of it is done by teachers and not by students, who are there, after all, to learn how to talk, too. There is also, as we mentioned earlier, an obvious press to "look good"; that is, to be right, to say things well or shut up. The problem with this is that things which are deeply felt, personally meaningful, are never easy to say well; hence genuinely important things don't get said. It is too risky.

We think that schools should be a place where it is safe to say things badly if that's the only way to say them, where it is not threatening to "look bad," where people can deal with what they feel is important. Not only would people come to understand each other better, have more to say to each other, and learn to trust each other, but the likelihood of creative behavior would increase almost inevitably. Being "creative" is being unafraid to "look bad" at first and to gamble on "looking good" later. It's hunching an idea, a whim, an impulse; saying things badly because they have not been said before; not being afraid to expose what one does *not* know.

This situation, if it were to exist, sounds dangerously close to a meaningful learning environment, and many schools are simply not ready for it. They "look too good" as they are: monuments to mortifying monologue.

20. The Role of the Teacher in an Inquiry-Centered Classroom

Dorothy J. Skeel and Joseph G. Decaroli

As you enter an inquiry-centered classroom, you will find small groups of children clustering about their desks to converse more readily, some groups moving to the table by the library center, other children remaining at their desks to peruse books and materials independently, and several children using tape recorders or films and filmstrips at the audio-visual center. A social-emotional climate permitting freedom of expression and movement is quite noticeable. There is an atmosphere of mutual respect and trust that is revealed as the children move from one area of the room

SOURCE: *Social Education*, XXXIII, 5 (May 1969), 547–50. Reprinted by permission of the authors, Dorothy J. Skeel, Associate Professor of Education, Indiana University, and Joseph Decaroli, Teaching Assistant, Tri-University Project in Elementary Education, University of Washington, and the publisher.

to another without seeking permission or disturbing others in their self-directed search for materials. As you listen to a discussion, you notice that information and ideas are contributed by both the teacher and the pupils. The role of the teacher is that of a motivator and diagnostician. As he moves from group to group, he encourages the pupils for their efforts, refocuses the search for information if necessary, notes areas of apparent strengths and weaknesses among the pupils, or prods the thinking of a stymied inquirer.

Teacher's Concept of His Role

How does a teacher successfully assume his role in an inquiry-centered classroom? Primary to this achievement is the teacher's concept of his role, hence, his philosophy of teaching. Inquiry falters if a teacher views his position as that of a central figure from which knowledge, ideas, value judgments, and conclusions spew forth to be absorbed by young minds. A teacher abdicates this position in an inquiry-centered classroom to accept the less prominent but equally important role of guide. He points the way to resources of knowledge, different interpretations of ideas, and establishes the necessary intellectual framework from which children learn to draw their own conclusions and to develop value systems. This role requires the teacher's willingness to listen to and accept from children a variety of possible answers instead of seeking the one "right" answer. The most difficult habit for the teacher to "kick" is that of being ready with the right answers. A time factor is frequently offered as an excuse, because it is less time-consuming to give an answer than to wait for children to arrive at their answers through a process of guided inquiry.

If "covering the textbook" is perceived by the teacher as a major instructional goal, he will not be comfortable using inquiry strategies. The inquiry process does indeed use the textbook as a source of knowledge, but the process does not assume consistent adoption of the textbook's conclusions without further investigation of other interpretations. The teacher, therefore, must provide materials that present different points of view and be objective in assessing their value.

Certainly the teacher who considers his role as disciplinarian with the task of quieting any disturber of the peace—any individual unwilling to fit into the neat pattern of a pupil who speaks when spoken to and remains in his seat—will experience difficulty with the inquiry method. In other words, the establishment of a climate within the classroom conducive to good human relations is a most vital factor in enhancing inquiry.

Essential to establishing and maintaining this suitable atmosphere is mutual respect between the pupils and between teacher and pupils. Are the children open-minded and willing to listen to the opinions of others? Are each person's ideas treated with respect and equality? The teacher should observe the children's behavior in the classroom for the answers to these questions. If the response is negative, procedures can be instituted to provide practice in establishing more effective human relationships.

Children are keen observers of the behavior of the teacher with respect to human relations. Is the teacher willing to listen to varying points of view? Does the teacher by the tone of his voice and facial expression encourage diverse answers and show enthusiasm for the inquiry? Children quickly shy away from class participation when a teacher is unwilling to listen to their ideas or snaps them off in the middle of a statement. The teacher's display of enthusiasm stimulates interest and often provides motivation for study.

Providing Motivational Activity

However, in providing motivation and direction in an inquiry-centered classroom, the teacher is attempting to do considerably more than expose children to a new approach to learning. Regardless of the motivational method or devices used, the teacher's central purpose should be the arousing of the pupil's curiosity and interest to the point where he begins to identify problems or raise questions about a situation. The teacher should therefore be aware of the individual and group interests in order to capitalize on them. As pupils use their past experiences or present situations to identify problems or raise questions, the inquiry process becomes more relevant to them.

The motivational activity should provide enough information to promote inquiry or discussion, but not so much that questions and discussions are stifled by the purely expository nature of the activity.[1] Those activities dealing with topics close to the pupils are likely to produce the best results —*e.g.* a film or filmstrip that presents selected data about the pupil's own city or country. Perhaps the local area is experiencing an economic problem. Information can be provided that is sufficient to suggest causes of economic difficulty but does not specifically state these causes. The teacher through questions and discussion guides the pupils to the identification of the problem. Throughout the motivational activity, the primary role of the teacher is directing pupil interest, while remaining flexible enough to deal with unanticipated questions and interests that might be pertinent to the study. The teacher directs pupils to see discrepancies in information, significant problems to be solved, and to raise questions that will guide their inquiry.

[1] Maxine Dunfee and Helen Sagl, *Social Studies Through Problem Solving.* New York: Holt, Rinehart and Winston, Inc., 1966. p. 36.

A major goal in an inquiry-centered classroom is providing pupils with an organized, improved method of thinking about and dealing with information. A characteristic of effective thinking is that it should be independent or autonomous.[2] To achieve this independent or autonomous thinking, activities must be provided that allow self-direction and the development of self-confidence. If the pupils are to value inquiry as a learning process and incorporate it into their repertoire of intellectual skills, they must have confidence in their ability to use the process successfully. The teacher must provide activities for each pupil that have goals within his reach. Not only will the achievement of these goals enhance the pupil's self-confidence but will motivate him in succeeding activities. This is not to say that pupils should produce a *right* answer. It merely means that pupils will gain confidence in their ability to arrive at *an* answer and that they are willing to modify that answer when confronted with new or more extensive information.

Furthermore, if pupils are to become independent, autonomous thinkers, they must demonstrate self-direction in their thinking and learning. Hence, the pupils pose their own problems to be solved, questions to be asked, and hypotheses to be tested. In providing activities promoting pupil self-direction, it is likely that the pupil will internalize the inquiry process and be able to apply it in varied instances.

Preparation and Planning

The greatest change for a teacher in an inquiry-centered classroom will be in his preparation and planning. This planning includes the preparation of behavioral objectives, questioning strategies, acquisition of materials, planning of activities, and evaluation. In addition to having more worthy goals for pupils than covering the textbook, the objectives for inquiry activities take on a new dimension for the acquisition of knowledge and understanding. This new dimension focuses on the pupil's ability to readily identify problems, to use previous knowledge to suggest hypotheses, to interpret data to test the hypotheses, and his ability to generalize from the conclusions of the inquiry. An objective that exemplifies this stated in behavioral terms is: The child demonstrates his ability to interpret data by comparing and contrasting the economic problems of his own city to those of the country under study. This objective would be achieved through a series of activities, each one involving the acquisition of skills such as analyzing, classifying, contrasting, and comparing data. The teacher, however,

[2] Kenneth D. Benne, "The Major Tasks of Contemporary Thinking." *Effective Thinking in the Social Studies. Thirty-Seventh Yearbook of the National Council for the Social Studies.* Washington, D.C., 1967. p. 2.

needs to be aware of the danger in attempting to achieve too many objectives in one activity.

One of the crucial areas of preparation and planning is that of questioning techniques and strategies. Inquiry begins with a question. It is imperative that the teacher ask appropriate questions. In doing this, the teacher also demonstrates an inquiring mind himself and serves as a model for the pupils. The teacher needs to know that there are several levels of questions, and he should be aware of the manner in which he employs them. The first level of questions seeks information: What did you see? What belongs together? The second level of questions interprets data: What does this mean? What would you conclude? The highest level of questions is one that applies data: What would happen if . . . ? Why do you think this would happen? [3]

There is still a place in inquiry strategies for the information question such as: In what parts of the world did civilized man first appear? The important thing for the teacher to know is when to leave this level of questioning for information and to move to the next level of questioning that requires reasoning: Why did civilization first appear here instead of in other parts of the world? This transition requires that the teacher be well prepared in the content of the topic under study as well as versed in the thinking and learning processes through which the pupils are proceeding. The teacher should not, however, be limited to the prepared questions to the extent that he cannot adjust to pupil responses or fail to realize that he is forcing a line of questioning when responses indicate that it should be discontinued.

Does the use of the inquiry process require special materials? Those designed specifically to aid the inquiry process are helpful, but they are not prerequisites or essentials to the use of the inquiry method. As much as possible materials should give information but not offer inferences, generalizations, or conclusions. These materials—textbooks, tradebooks, references, and audiovisuals—should be screened to determine whether they stimulate questions and discussion or terminate them. The inquiry method is best suited to in-depth studies of limited topics rather than extensive studies that cover a wide range. [4] Therefore, sufficient materials for in-depth studies must be available, and in addition, these materials should be varied enough to take into account pupils pursuing different aspects of a study.

The learning activities for a particular topic should be open-ended— *i.e.* activities leading to divergent thinking by pupils. These activities allow

[3] Hilda Taba, *Teachers' Handbook for Elementary Social Studies*. Palo Alto, California: Addison-Wesley Publishing Company, Inc., 1967. pp. 91–109.

[4] Bruce R. Joyce, *Strategies for Elementary Social Science Education*. Chicago: Science Research Associates, 1965. p. 168.

the pupils to offer creative or innovative answers rather than to lead all pupils to the same answer. Posing such problems as: "If you had been a pioneer in the early days of our country, how would you have solved the problems with the Indians?" will lead to alternative solutions. Certainly the teacher must require that these alternatives be supported by evidence.

Evaluation in an inquiry-centered classroom will require more than testing of factual information. There should be testing of the pupils' abilities to make inferences, produce generalizations, identify concepts, and to apply learnings to new situations.

Evaluating Teacher and Pupil Behavior

The evaluation of the process of inquiry and pupil behavior should be continuous and not reserved for the culmination of a unit of study. If the teacher observes how the pupils go about their tasks as well as the end-products of their work, he will have a balanced basis for evaluation.[5] Much of this can be done through joint pupil-teacher evaluation of both the process of inquiry and its product.

Pupil behaviors that can be evaluated include the type of questions children ask, how well they identify problems, how they handle information, how well they carry out their plans, and the extent to which they use inquiry methods outside of the social studies.[6] These behaviors can be evaluated by recording the lessons and analyzing the verbal participation. The teacher can define categories of skills necessary in the inquiry process such as explanation, description, questioning, hypothesizing, comparing, and testing. From the tapes of the lesson, he can measure the types of responses made by the children during the inquiry sessions. Thus the areas of strengths and weaknesses can be identified—e.g. pupils may have difficulty asking questions to secure information but have less difficulty hypothesizing.

Teacher behavior can be evaluated by reference to the pupil behavior. If few or none of the desired behaviors are produced, the teacher should look to his methods as a potential cause. Audio or video tape recordings are also helpful to the teacher in his evaluation. An analysis of classroom interaction—either by a fellow teacher or supervisor—as well as self-evaluation is another method that can be employed to evaluate the teaching process.

What behaviors will pupils demonstrate as a result of being involved in an inquiry-centered classroom? There will be purposeful activity as pupils

---

[5] Frank J. Estvan, *Social Studies in a Changing World: Curriculum and Instruction.* New York: Harcourt, Brace and World, Inc., 1968. p. 357.

[6] Maxine Dunfee and Helen Sagl, *op. cit.,* p. 305.

move about the room seeking materials to answer their questions. The attitude toward these sources of information will be more critical and analyzing. There will be less uncritical acceptance of anything written or spoken. An open-mindedness, or openness, toward one another will be displayed in the conversations among pupils. A successful inquirer has gained confidence in his ability to grasp a problem situation and stay with it until a conclusion can be reached. The social-emotional climate of the classroom has produced a lessening of the fear that an idea will be summarily rejected, and this climate also promotes the secure feeling that ideas will be scrutinized and judged on their merits.

The pupils will be less likely to make hasty judgments or leap to conclusions about their work or, of special importance, about each other. A greater self-direction or independence will be demonstrated in their investigation of problem situations. Does it seem that there is little for a teacher to do in such a classroom? Hardly, because it is the skilled teacher who must nurture the pupils through an inquiry process to bring about such behaviors.

IV. Pressures and Problems of Teaching

There are times when people in any field of endeavor feel that their choice of vocation presents more pressures, pitfalls, and problems than any other occupation they could have chosen. Teaching is no exception. Those who are guiding the learning activities of children and youth must realize that all occupations or professions present frustrations; teaching is not unique in this respect.

The profession does, indeed, have its share of deterrents and mettle-testing challenges. A number of studies reported in the literature, such as that made by Petersen,[1] list several important problems that are real and constant, such as discipline; lack of home-school cooperation; overcrowded classrooms; providing for individual differences in children and youth; excessive noninstructional duties; lack of teaching supplies, resources, and equipment. Without attempting to minimize the deterring effect of such problems which do, in fact, exist in schools all over the nation, the editors would admonish teachers to-be and teachers-in-service to analyze and evaluate the problems, the school-community situation, and *themselves* to see that the problems are genuine and not apparitions existing only in the minds and attitudes of individuals who are not happy in their profession.

There is, in fact, a large number of pressures and problems in the profession of teaching. One is hard put, as a matter of fact, to know just which pressures and problems to include in a discussion of them. The articles that follow, however, discuss most of the more apparent factors that result in teacher frustrations; some of the writers go into considerable depth in their discussions of them, while others barely mention them.

In the first selection, Helaine Dawson, in "The New Breed of Students," describes how she got "in" with pupils in her classroom in the Hunters Point area of San Francisco—how she applied human relations in working with young people in her inner city school as they prepared to take jobs. Mrs. Dawson also describes a number of the ways she overcame the stu-

[1] Dorothy G. Petersen, *The Elementary School Teacher* (New York: Meredith Publishing Company, 1964), p. 538.

dents' inadequate environment and attitudes in trying to make her classroom as much unlike a typical classroom as possible.

Many policy mistakes by state and national educational authorities are made when planners at those levels ignore the resources of classroom teachers. This is the theme of the article entitled "Teachers Tell It Like It Is." The writer of this selection also maintains that teachers perform too many nonprofessional chores and that more time is needed for research and for learning about better methods and materials. Other pressures and problems are also discussed.

Full-blown student aggression is an inevitable part of today's classroom, whether it is in kindergarten or in college, according to the next article, "Classroom Aggression Seen As Inevitable." Since the teacher is charged with handling aggressive behavior, it behooves him to learn about the causes and, if possible, about some of the possible cures for such unacceptable social behavior.

The increase in leisure time looms large on the horizons of people everywhere in the world as new time- and labor-saving technological advances are made. J. A. Simpson, in "Education for Leisure," discusses the problems involved in increased leisure time and the need for education and the teacher's part in getting students ready for it.

Mary Yeazell, in "Phads and Phantoms in American Education," speaks about the prospects for teaching machines, the curriculum reform movement, and the search for talent in special education programs. She discusses their implications for practitioners and pupils in the school classrooms.

The teacher's satisfaction in his work is subject to conditioning by factors inside and outside the profession, according to Alexander M. Feldvebel in the final selection in this part, "Teacher Satisfaction As a Function of Conditioning Factors in the School and Profession." Mr. Feldvebel is concerned with such factors as sex, status, and job satisfaction; role expectation, socialization and depersonalization of teacher-pupil relationships; and the stereotype syndrome.

21. The New Breed of Students: Implications for Teacher Education in the Public Schools and in Schools of Education

Helaine Dawson

It was the hopelessness that I saw when I first went to work at Hunters Point that disturbed me so deeply. But I have been able to communicate with the young people there; and the reason I have been able to do this, I think, is that I have done so many different types of things, been to so many places, and gone through an unimaginable number of crises. In fact, my whole life has been one crisis after another.

The only crisis that I will not object to is the fact that I was born in New York City. I'm glad I was born there because my having lived in that city has given me the kind of outlook on life that I have needed. Certainly, having survived in New York, I'm sure one can survive anywhere.

I have never lost the New York accent, and some people have been quite upset by it. I had never realized that I had one quite as strong as it is until I arrived in Chicago and was living at the University of Chicago Settlement House. The head worker there had been on the All-American Football Team; I learned this amazing fact because that's all he talked about. He also resented New Yorkers—especially female—and I was the only New Yorker living in the Settlement House at that time. His resentment, of course, included the accent. Naturally, I had to talk with him sometimes, and he *heard* the accent. But I was happy in the things I was doing and experiencing there because I was a volunteer worker with Mexican-American youth.

SOURCE: *Minutes and Proceedings of the Yosemite Conference, California Council on the Education of Teachers,* October 31, 1968, Yosemite, California (Sacramento: California State Department of Education, 1968), pp. 25–38.

A strong point I would like to make here is that the different kinds of experiences I have had in life have really prepared me for the kind of work I'm doing now. I'm sorry to say that it wasn't the pedagogy I learned at Hunter College that prepared me. When I was in my junior year at Hunter, we practiced in a model training school, which was across the street from the main building at that time in New York. As many people have said at this conference, the situation hasn't changed too much in teacher education. Now this wasn't a century ago—I still feel very useful and my arteries are still in good condition—but it was quite a while ago all the same. I remember that in this model school we saw sweet little students who sat with their hands folded. If the supervisor in charge of the training looked in, she said, "Oh, there is a marvelous teacher! Look how all the children sit there so quietly." This is the same kind of thing that relates to the whole question of discipline. If the youngsters are "sitting there quietly," everything is "wonderful." But what I am interested in is what is really going on there. I'm interested in what's happening in that room during that period. Are those young people really learning anything? My room at Hunters Point is not a very quiet one because I try to make it function as much unlike a classroom as possible—the actual physical walls don't stop us from anything. We work, we live, we try to understand. Things *happen*.

When I was a substitute teacher in New York City after having passed the teacher examination, I worried about how sensitive you must be as a human being and the ability you must have to relate to other people. But I found out that what was most important at that time—and still is important, unfortunately—is that you do not say "earl" for "oil" or "berl" for "boil" or "ideer" for "idea." Teacher education was—and still is—more concerned with words than with reality.

My first assignment was in an A82. Now at that time "2" meant "dull-normal," but nobody knows what "normal" means; so what does "dull-normal" mean? Well, they said "That's where you *are.*" Fortunately (or unfortunately) there was a lesson plan (which I never follow any more). Yes, a lesson plan was provided, and as a substitute teacher in my first assignment, I had to look at it. I looked at it and we followed it and nothing happened. I taught by the plan and the students followed it and nothing happened.

One day, after going through a grammar session and getting nowhere, I said, "We have finished grammar. Now we are ready for French." (I had studied French in high school, and three years of a language would come in handy.) I thought: well, I'll use the modern method, conversational French. So I began a conversation with two students in the front row. Just as we were getting involved—I thought the dialogue was going beautifully because two young people were really paying attention—the door opened and the assistant principal, a little man, made his appearance. At the moment he came through the door, an eraser hit him on the head. He roared, "Did you see where that came from?" I had been so busy with my conversational French that I hadn't been aware of an eraser, let alone a thrower of one. I looked at him in amazement and said, "No." The man was very scientific. He said, "Let's see, that was a 45-degree angle." And he went down the line. "Did *you* do it?" "Did *you* do it?" Of course, each one said "No." He spent all of forty minutes, and then the bell rang. Because he couldn't nab the culprit, he took two hostages out of the class. Well! That was my initiation in this kind of thing, which has happened and still happens in all too many schools.

I want to tell you about my first day at Hunters Point. Maybe you will understand some of the things I have learned. We were going along very nicely because I wasn't yelling. (I heard teachers shouting all along the hall. Any student who didn't act properly according to what the teacher thought was proper was sent to the principal's office. We didn't have a large enough office to accommodate all these "violators," so the shouting went on and on.)

But somehow that first day the students and I were beginning to "click." All of a sudden, as we were about to go on to another subject, one little fellow got up and started to do a tap dance. Everybody was watching— you know how you are tested, and as a new teacher you are certainly tested. The whole class was watching me very closely, and I, in turn was watching this boy, Jimmy Green, while he was doing his dance. Every time I raised my eyes to look around, I caught the eyes of the students. They were wondering what's the matter—when am I going to yell—when am I going to do something? And they were clapping to get the rhythm. I watched and watched; I knew he was going to get tired eventually. Finally he stopped, and I asked, "Have you finished, Jimmy?" He said "Ya." Then I asked, "Do you plan to go on the stage when you grow older? Have you figured that out yet, or do you want to do a nightclub act?" He said "Ya." I said, "Well, what?" He muttered, "A nightclub act." (He was only about fourteen or fifteen years old.) I said "Well, I'll tell you what— do you mind if I give you a suggestion or a little criticism, do you mind?" He blurted, "No, go ahead." I said, "Well, it seems to me that the left leg —the left leg is not going with the right. Something's wrong there. Maybe a little more practice will help. Now, I could put on a little imitation for you, but I only know it to 'Rosie O'Grady,' and that won't do for the kind of thing you want to do." Well, I was in. A little Italian fellow hopped up and said, "Hey, Teach! What'll we getcha? Need a little refreshment? Getcha some jellybeans?" I knew I was "in." It's this kind of thing I've been working with, and these are the kinds of things that happen.

I don't always figure them out. Sometimes they just happen. Maybe it's the fact that I'm not afraid as a person. I think that when we say the teacher is the key, we need to say that it isn't only the teacher; it's the person. Do you know who you are as a person? Have you strength within yourself? Can you laugh at yourself? Can you accept criticism before you can give it to somebody else? What about you? Can you accept it? Actually, very few people can do this. I don't want to attack anybody here. I don't think teachers deserve any attack. But I do believe that we all want to learn—not just stand still, but learn more and become more compassionate. Today a revolution is taking place—really a revolution, and that we know. It is happening not only in the teaching profession, but in every profession. Lawyers are talking about the same kind of thing, and certainly the medical profession and the paramedical profession. No professional— not even the politician—can escape the changes that are coming about. We are living in a kind of age in which change is part of life; but change, we hope, that will not fail to respond to the deep hunger of the human spirit.

Now, what has all this got to do with Hunters Point? It is simply that all these kinds of experiences are enormously valuable to the educator. I think that when a teacher or lawyer or doctor just goes through his schooling and through his practice without having humbling experiences, without working with people at various levels, without learning how to relate to people in a humane, sensitive way, then he is not truly alive. Not to bother about what people are going to think about us, not to worry about approval of what we do, but to get involved and to listen "to the other guy" and to learn in the process—these things are much more important.

When involvement and compassion enter the picture, you get an effective teacher. By the same token, you get an effective doctor who can relate to people, who doesn't think merely that there is a liver in Room 14, but that the liver belongs to a person and the person belongs to a family. It is so necessary to see things in their wholeness. When I was working for the Dental Association, the people thought of the mouth as a hole in the head. I couldn't get some people to understand that dental health and dental education are as important in health education as some of the other kinds of public education that we talk about. When I was trying to sell this idea to a man who was then head of one of the departments in San Francisco Unified School District, he said, "We have a Red Cross. Why, if we let you in here with dental health, we would have all kinds of people waiting to get in." He made the whole idea sound subversive.

That's the kind of reaction you get so often—this lack of understanding on the part of many people at high levels of operation who don't seem to know what the real needs are and don't seem to understand what's happening at the "grass roots" level or why the approaches are not exactly what they should be. I have definite convictions that I have developed over my years of experiences, plus my schooling, my teaching, and everything else; but I'm willing to change some of them, and I try to keep an open mind. I think the approach to problems is terribly important. No amount of money that is given to teacher education or to anything else will be able to bring about the kind of understanding we are striving for. The polarization that we see happening won't bring it about. But humane approaches will.

I want to tell you how I got "in" with my students and how I was able to apply some of my convictions. I don't talk about training as much as I do about education because training to me has almost the connotation of "imposing teaching." This is my personal feeling. You may not agree with me at all, and that is your privilege. When you say "to teach somebody something," I always get the impression that you come in as the authority, that you have the word, and that now you're going to pass the word on to your students. I feel, on the other hand, that education in its literal sense is helping students to develop their potentialities, helping them to bring forth from themselves what they don't even realize they have. This is what I try to apply when I work with the young people out at Hunters Point.

Now, how did I get out there and what did I learn that needs to be reinforced? I was very much involved in working with youth in the early and middle 1960s—before the Anti-Poverty Act, before Operation Breadbasket, Operation Grapefruit, and Operation Bootstrap—all of these operations that are now in existence. I learned a great deal—learned every day. And I learned from my students, *especially* from my students. I tried to help them—not just to impart information but to act as a guide and a resource person at different periods during these programs.

In 1963 I had been working in the Mission Adult School at night in adult education and developmental reading. I teach reading my own way. I don't like to work according to what someone else tells me to do. That doesn't mean I'm obnoxiously aggressive. It is simply my own way, which I have found workable. At this school I was getting along well. It was a three-hour class. The people attending it worked very hard in the daytime, and in order to keep their attention at night, I almost had to click my fingers and stamp my feet on the floor. But I managed to change the activities often, and I allowed no one to sleep. Things happened; progress happened.

Well, there was sleeping during my first two days at Hunters Point, and I'll tell you why. There was no problem; there was no challenge. I like things with a lot of challenge. It was just too easy. But I am getting ahead of myself. I had heard that out at Hunters Point there was going to be a new program. This was in 1963, prior to the militancy that exists today. This was the youth opportunity program, which was the first of its kind in the country at that time. I was going to be a part of the program, and it was slated to start at Hunters Point. It was to be a job training program, and the Manpower Development Training Act was to provide the funds for the faculty. There were six teachers, including myself, in this program. And there was going to be a youth opportunity center.

You may not be familiar with the geographical layout of Hunters Point. It's near Candlestick Park, and it has one of the most beautiful views in

San Francisco. The area has changed a great deal, as nearly all urban areas have changed since World War II. There has been great mobility. Whereas the population there was 50 percent black and 50 percent white prior to World War II, it is now about 99 percent black. The education has changed there, too. This is what I have heard directly from the parents at a meeting very recently when we were discussing this kind of thing. The young people in 1963, from the ages of sixteen to twenty-four, had dropped out of school or had been dropped. (And this is still going on.) According to newspaper reports, they were "causing problems" in the neighborhood, and so it was proposed that a training program to prepare these young people for jobs might be one way of cutting down on juvenile delinquency. This is what was thought.

A Ford Foundation grant was given to the Youth Opportunity Center. We all belonged to one program, but we were separated. There were psychologists and statistical analysts and representatives from the United Bay Area Crusade, the Department of Public Welfare, and many other agencies. It was the first time that at least seven or eight established agencies were going to try to work together. The six teachers I mentioned were under the supervision of the Board of Education Division of the San Francisco Unified School District.

We had no control over job selection or job training. According to the State Department of Employment, there were supposedly openings for general office clerks and for office boys. So the first group of fifty young men and women from the ages of sixteen to twenty-four were going to be trained for general office clerks and office boys. How little was understood by the people who were responsible for setting up this program! How little was understood about the feelings of the young people, about their culture, about their poverty! We have been learning much since then, but we knew so little at that time. I found entirely different kinds of things there from what I had learned in Chicago and even in New York City. Nevertheless, the Ford Foundation had granted the funds for the program, and we had to "get with it."

The people were really not ready for it. There was supposed to have been in-depth psychological interviews with the first fifty, but we found out later that no one had had the time to go into this part of the program at all.

In this group I was to teach personal development. The other five teachers were to teach business English, business mathematics, general office principles and practices, and typing. The typing teacher had to teach typing without typewriters for six weeks until the requisition had been made. This is the way things would go. The only place—the only facility—(I'm not anti-church when I say this) that could be found in the area was a beautiful church of Byzantine architecture; but alas, the inside, the interior, the facilities, were far from the modern era. In the front of the church I had a large room. There were four gas heaters in the church: one on either side in the front and one on either side in the rear, and there were two toilets. Now, this is important and I must tell you about it because it played an important role in the very early days of this program. There was only one toilet on either side of the church; each would accommodate just one person. The fumes from the gas heaters were horribly noxious. So these young people, who had been out of school, who had suffered or had been involved in most unsatisfactory experiences before they left school or before they dropped out, were now back in school with fumes bad enough to asphyxiate them. There was hardly any ventilation, except when the wind blew the door open. The other teachers taught in the usual way—a textbook, a workbook in which information was regurgitated—and that was it. No one was getting anywhere.

What is my method? I have no plans—I use a textbook only when it relates to something and then I adapt it. I haven't found materials that seem to be suitable for the groups I have been working with. I like to bring in newspapers; I like to be where the young people are, wherever they are. I have learned how they think, how they feel, what their attitudes are. I am interested not so much in changing their attitudes as in developing my own and also in helping to change the attitudes of other teachers. I'm sorry that many administrators and district superintendents have not had the opportunity to change their outlooks, and I believe, too, that better administrative control is needed.

To backtrack: Before the program opened, the principal of this school called me and asked, "How would you like to teach personal development? You are creative." "Oh, I'd love it!" I replied. "What am I suppose to do?" He said, "I don't know." I said, "That's marvelous." This is what I always like to do—something nobody else knows how to do so that I can work out the ways I feel are needed, and we work together, these students and I. We learn about one another in the process.

The opening day of this program was December 16, 1963. Just the date in itself showed the utter stupidity of the people who were responsible for the opening. These young people had been out of school for a long time; they couldn't stand school; they couldn't stand teachers or any authority symbol—and then just before Christmas, they open a school? That is stupid. The students started at 8:00 in the morning. As an incentive, they were being paid by the Manpower Development Training Act to come to school—from $20 a week to $55—which did not include transportation cost at first. They didn't even have basic education in the beginning. They've improved. There is much room for improvement. There have been many, many changes for the best.

Our orientation was the day before the opening. We met—the six faculty members—with this principal "who was a working principal." He let us know that. He took his jacket off; he rolled up his sleeves; he had a cigar hanging out the side of his mouth. But after that, he was very seldom around. We never knew what was happening except that at least he allowed you to "sort of work out things"; but he was never there, or hardly ever. When the day began, he came out there in his working uniform, with his sleeves rolled up, and rang a cowbell. Now this was 1963, not 1870. We were preparing people who were to be general office clerks in a technological era. I felt that these young people were being shortchanged again. Everything was wrong.

I had an afternoon session. I went into my room and waited until 1:00. The young people were out on the patio leading into the church; they had their transistor radios on and they were dancing. They were totally oblivious to the fact that the little cowbell had been rung. Finally, about 1:15, two young women came down and looked at me. They had never seen me before; I hadn't even opened my mouth, but they gave me such a look of hostility! They went in, sat down in the front row, and put their heads on the desks as though they were going to fall asleep at once. All right, I said nothing. I watched and I worried. I took all this in. About three minutes later they got up and went to the toilet. Ten minutes later, two more young women walked in with similar expressions; they sat down for a few minutes; they took out their mascara, compared lipstick shades, and so on, totally oblivious to me, and then they got up and went to the toilet. Now there were four in the one toilet.

Finally, some of the young men began walking in. They gave me a vacant look and ambled toward the back of the room. Two of them lay down on the floor and kept talking to each other in this supine position for quite some time, and then they got up and went to the men's toilet. It was now 1:25. The twenty-five students finally all arrived, and all twenty-five wound up in the toilets. It was now 1:40, and I was hoping that they would all come back and sit down before the bell rang so that I could introduce myself. It was the first day, and at least I wanted to get started. At twenty minutes to 2:00 o'clock, they all began to straggle back, and I smiled and said, "Everybody here?"

The principal had ordered us to make general office clerks out of these young people in thirty-nine weeks. He made me think of myself as a circus horse or something—not a person with understanding. Why? I'm always interested in behavior, in behavioral science. Why were these young individuals acting this way? They didn't know me. What were the reasons for their hostility?

I always think about this when I go home each night—what am I doing? I believe in evaluation and feedback and interaction, because without interaction in a classroom or any place—even in your own home with your husband—if there's no interaction, no communication, then something is definitely wrong. I feel that there has to be interaction and that learning takes place where there is interaction. Learning isn't just acquiring or accumulating facts.

Anyway, I said, "Everybody here? Well, let me introduce myself. I'm Mrs. Dawson." I wrote my name on the board. They assumed their positions. You know, sleeping in the back and slouching in the seats. One fellow opened his jacket and took out a half-pint of vodka. They had this all planned. One went to the cooler and got paper cups; they passed the cups around and filled them with vodka, and everybody got a sample, including the girls. I knew they were testing me. Everything seemed to be against me. The situation appeared to be hopeless, but it wasn't.

I don't worry about discipline problems because I feel that it is my responsibility as a teacher to reach the students, and if I can tune in and reach them, the "discipline problems" go by the board. Now, there may be a few young persons who are emotionally disturbed, and these I may not be able to reach; but eventually I'm going to find this out, and I'm going to try and get some kind of professional help for them if necessary.

To backtrack again: Confronting my class, I said, "The name of this course is 'Personal Development.' By the way, what does personal development mean to you?" One fellow who was lying down in back raised his head. I thought to myself: now that is interaction; the fact that he is raising his head is a sign of interest, or something. "What ya mean?" he blurted out. "You some kind of nut? Don't you know what it means?" I answered him in a calm, direct way: "Well, maybe I am a nut, but I hope you change your opinion after thirty-nine weeks."

That was simply my reaction. That's the way it was. But they didn't expect that kind of reaction. They expected me to send them to the principal's office—the whole pack of them. So many young people expect that if they don't conform to our standards of discipline, they will be dropped.

At a meeting later, some of the teachers said to me: "How do you take that lack of respect? How can you put up with it?" My answer was something like this: "You know what? I think there is a terribly important matter that all of us have got to learn. We must earn respect. I know that I'm going to have to earn it because these young people have been turned off; they have been rejected for so many years by society and by the school that they have no respect for a teacher, for the police, for anyone who symbolizes authority. They only know from their own experiences what has happened. That's the way they judge, and they are only reacting to what white society has done to them. I believe that the point I'm trying to get across is that this reaction on their part, because of the way they have been maltreated is enormously important." What I said then I say again. This is underlying very much of what is happening on our high school campuses today.

The fact that I admitted that I might be "a nut" and the way I approached the discipline problem on the very first day set the tone and helped to establish a relationship that grew between my students and me as each day went by. And of course I am learning in the process.

On that memorable first day, I said: "You know, we are going to do something different in this class. I'm not going to use a textbook. We will evolve our own text." And suddenly I heard myself using that word "evolve." I feel that this is something that very few teachers do: we don't listen to our own language. It's a middle-class language. It is not the language of the people in the ghettos and the poverty areas, or in any of the places where you find minority groups like the Negroes, the Mexican-Americans, the American Indians. It's not their language.

I put the word "evolve" on the board, and I asked, "Does anyone here know what 'evolve' means?" A young fellow said, "Ya, it means turn around." His buddy sitting next to him pounded him on the back and shouted, "Ahh, stupid, that's revolve!" So there was more interaction. We were beginning to work with language.

Dr. Stone and his group brought out this point this afternoon as a research finding. I try to experiment with various kinds of methods. I use role playing, of course. But something that works with one group may not work with another. I have found that each group, like each individual, is unique and that certain techniques work more effectively with one class than with another class.

You have to risk the chance of trying. Sometimes my colleagues ask, "How do you know it's going to be successful?" Well, that is what research is all about. No one knows what's going to happen, what the findings will be. When you finally "hit" something, it may be quite accidental; but you do get a response. The really big thing is that when you are working with people, you are at once and deeply involved in human relations; or you should be. I learned so much in the beginning! I saw so much hopelessness in those young people during those first days. I saw such sadness in their faces. Their so-called "insolent" behavior, their braggadocio type of thing, was simply a defense mechanism they used to protect themselves.

It has been several years now that I haven't been at Hunters Point on a daily basis. But in my working relations there, I am very close to the students, to their parents, and to other members of the community. I didn't remain there just for my hours of teaching. I worked afterward, without getting paid, because I was interested. It's this whole question of commitment that's immensely important in teacher education. The teacher has to become so involved that every pore is active and he is not thinking, "I've got to run home now," or rush out when the bell rings. He stays.

I think there are certain trends. I know that California State College at Hayward is considering the kind of education in the future when schooling will last seven days a week, or at least six days a week, and will be continuous, not just as adult education in the evening, but continuous beyond 3:30 in the afternoon. The teacher might even live in the area so that there would be a close working relationship and real understanding in the manner that some experiments are being conducted today during the summer months. But this arrangement would be on a regular basis.

That first day gave me clues as to how to operate. The fact that I didn't yell, the fact that I listened, the fact that I said, "Look I'm no authority, but I'm going to talk more today than I will ever talk. I think teachers talk too much, but I want to tell you how I'm going to operate. I don't operate like any of the teachers that you've had experience with. We're going to work in a semicircle." And I discussed what "semi" means. One kid said, "Oh, what we gonna have, family style?" I said, "Well, if you want to call it family style. We want to look at each other when we talk; we don't want to look at backs. We want to get to know each other. We're going to talk in this group about anything that is important to you. I'm not coming in here to tell you what's important to you. You have had too many outsiders coming in and telling you what's good for you. You know better than anybody else what's good for you. I have to learn what's good for you, and we are going to work together on this." They asked, "Are we all going to be pioneers?" I said, "Well, in a way, yes, we will be pioneers."

So whatever happened, I couldn't use a lesson plan as such, because this is a formula type of instructional aid. You can't work that way. This is an unorthodox approach when you look at it from the point of view of traditional methods of teaching or working. But it is the human relations way of operating. It's sensitivity training. I believe that the fact we even have to be made aware of this is an indictment of the educational system. You squelch children at a very early age in school, and then when they become young adults and they are afraid to be themselves, you have to institute sensitivity training to put back what you took out. This is what is happening today.

Now, one thing about working with young people in poverty areas and ghettos, at least from my own experiences, is that you know what they think because they let you know. There is no hypocrisy, especially if you are trusted. They'll play the game in the beginning the way anybody does. They'll put you on, but you have to know when you are being put on. Many teachers who are starting out don't know when they are being tested. These are all the things that you learn from experiences with various groups of people. We must begin to develop working relationships on a humane basis.

In the poverty areas, people hustle just in order to survive. The teacher who is going into that kind of area has to understand what hustling involves. The fact that business is best at night and that it goes into the early morning hours has an effect on these young persons when they come into a classroom. Even young children at the age of six or seven start hustling at night.

When teachers speak a middle-class language and the material in the textbook has absolutely no relevance to their life experiences, these young people are continually being turned off, and you can add the fact that they have already been told that they are failures. So naturally the failure syndrome is working; there is negativism and defeatism. This situation is beginning to be changed, because now with the black militants coming into the picture, there is a cry on their part to become better educated. To be black and beautiful is good; but to be black, beautiful and stupid is not good.

We are going to have a new program in Marin City—Operation Breakthrough. This is intended to involve young people in a genuine desire to learn. I found that there is a terrific interest on their part in learning.

When my students and I talk together, it's *we*. We're in this together. It's we this and we that. There is a great deal to be said about this kind of rapport. It's real. Teachers and administrators may not be aware of the disturbing fact that there is a condescending attitude on the part of many individuals who are working with people in the poverty areas and in the ghettos.

At lunch today I discussed a number of things with my colleagues. I talked about ways I have found and tried. Some methods did not turn out successfully, and others I found to be very successful. I was trying to share my experiences with the other teachers. I said, "No matter what subject you teach, it can be made exciting; but what happens most of the time is that it's dull, dull, dull."

Today, we have all kinds of competition. As someone said, "Media is the method." We have TV, rock and roll, and all these other things outside the school that have their special appeal. So if what happens in the classroom is exciting—and it can be—then learning can be an adventure.

George Leonard, who was the senior editor of *Look* magazine, has published a book called *Education and Ecstasy,* some excerpts of which appeared in *Look*. He's not an educator, but he has been very close to education. He has said some of the things I have said tonight. I can't stand dullness. Wherever you are, you've got to make your materials and your methods come alive. As a teacher, I have found that aliveness and understanding and empathy have helped me in my relationships with these young people and their community, with whom I am still in contact three, four, and five years later. The biggest reward is knowing that they know that you care.

There are many young people who are interested in working in these areas. But in looking at the whole fabric, I think that in the education of teachers, teacher candidates shouldn't be trained to work just with so-called disadvantaged ones. In my opinion, we are all disadvantaged. We are all disadvantaged because we have all been oriented to a dominant white race philosophy. This is it. It comes out in sudden ways all the time. The more I work with black youth or Mexican-American youth, the more I find this out. Their reaction is very plain. We don't pay enough attention to, or show enough respect for, their cultures and their needs.

We were talking about employers and preparing these young people for jobs. The whole approach, the whole understanding of how to prepare young people who are hustling at night, who are not used to the 9-to-5 kind of schedule, is unrealistic. Putting them on a job and saying, "Here we are. We're going to train you," isn't going to work. I think that the vocational education teacher and the employer are beginning slowly to understand that the way in which they have been operating has not been successful. The issue is not just working with culturally or economically disadvantaged youngsters; it also relates to the problems that exist, and they are every bit as crucial. Working in the white suburbs, how do we get the parents in these suburbs to understand that their children are being shortchanged because they are being isolated from many segments of society? When they become adults, what kind of outlook toward people from different cultures will they have? So these are some of the problems. I don't want to disregard or overlook anything or anybody. I want to look squarely at all human issues, because they are all tied together; they are all part of the same coin.

Among the many things I learned was how to introduce vocabulary. I'm very much interested in developing communicative skills because these young people do communicate. They have a wonderful language of their own; but in order to get into the mainstream of society, they still have to be conversant with the language of the middle class, or whatever you want to call it. You say they use four letter words. This is their language. At the beginning they'll use four letter words all the time. They'll punctuate whatever they say with four letter words; but this I say again, is their language. So instead of getting shocked and saying "don't say this" or "don't say that," instead of throwing negatives at them all the time, I say, "Look, it's all right to use that language when you're with your own group, but now we are going to learn another language. We're going to learn English as though it were a second language, as though it were French or German."

If you teach Swahili because this is what the young people want, then you have to learn Swahili. In the early 1960s, there wasn't this kind of interest. But I was able to use French with youngsters from Africa who spoke only French and came to our State Department to visit some of our American groups. This was the first contact that our young people had had with youths from any other country, especially a republic in Africa. They were amazed. They didn't know what language we were speaking. Later, when these young Africans left, they asked me, "What were you talking?"

I answered, "Do you want to take a guess?" One fellow said, "German." I said, "No, it was French." Then another boy spoke up. "Why don't ya teach us French? We like that." Then I said, "I'll tell you what, I'll give you a bonus. If we can work together learning English, we will throw in some French or some Spanish. You have some Spanish girl friends; we can learn a little Spanish that will help you in that direction."

What is so important in listening to language, learning to develop an ear for language—just listening. This is such an essential part of the whole question of communication, which is always a two-way process, needless to say—listening as well as talking. This fact is usually forgotten or passed over. My young people were not listening in the beginning. They were not listening to each other. They all thought and talked in the same way. What I found was that there is so much happening, so much to be done on all levels of thinking, that in education one has to learn how to become critical and not just "swallow" what he reads or what the teacher says or what any authority says. I question, and therefore dissent is important. Some of these things that I am saying may run counter to what we see happening in this whole focus in our country at the moment.

These matters are extremely important. If you are educated, you are able to read and to evaluate what you do. You don't jump to conclusions and make assumptions until you have as much information as you can find. This is what I was trying to work out with these young persons. We worked hard; we discussed everything that came up that was important to them. I taped almost all that was said, and I didn't edit a word. The next day they would listen to their tapes. In this way I got the young people interested in listening, and they began to become self-critical. At the same time, I was trying in every way to give them the support they needed—any little thing.

They were very sharp in learning. Vocabulary they loved—the word "chaos," for example, because everything was so chaotic at the beginning. There's no sleeping in the class anymore. After the third day, some young man came up to me and said, "You notice, Mrs. Dawson, I'm not sleeping anymore?" I responded, "Yeah, what happened?" He said, "Gee! this class is interesting, you're off on a trip all the time!" And this was before LSD. I asked him, "Is that good or bad?" I was learning their language. He said, "Well, it can be good or it can be bad, and I'll tell you when it's bad. But right now it's good."

We brought everything into that classroom. We didn't talk about just one thing. We discussed genetics, the DNA Code, what genealogy means, what genetics means—the roots of these words and terms. We went back to the origin—was the word from Greek or from Latin?—and they were interested, very much interested. I said, "You don't learn until you're able to use some of this vocabulary, until it has meaning." I explained the word experiences that would relate to their working in gangs or hustling, and then the words they would use when they went into other and better kinds of situations. It's this kind of thing—I don't want to bore you, and I have had so much to say here—but it's this kind of thing that means so much: listening and learning and then constantly trying to put yourself in the place of a student who may be one of eleven children, all of whom are on welfare.

Contrary to what the newspapers say, there is a substandard way of living. The hustling happens because of so much deprivation. What does that do to police records? Why the attitudes toward the police? Why arrest records? I was thinking about these matters when we were listening to the findings this afternoon. Along with the subject matter that teachers should have, there should be something on the law. I mean factual information regarding arrest records, reasonable cause, convictions, the difference between arrest and detention, and so on. These things are happening every day, and the teacher certainly must be conversant with what they mean and why there is a preponderance of arrest records. Why? Nothing that one has to condemn outright. This is one of the results of the white racist society, too. This is what has to be understood. Contrary to what many people think, these young people want to stop hustling as soon as they can. Out of 200 I've been working with since 1963, 85 percent are employed, although getting jobs is not the sole reason for my method of teaching. I think the job part is only secondary. The primary objective is to help young people, especially young people from ghettos and poverty areas who have never been told they could succeed—to make them feel that they can succeed. Remember, they have never been told this. To make them feel that they have potentials, that they can do things, that they can achieve, and to give them the tools so that they will be able to leave the area and not forget about where they came from, but help to improve conditions for their people. These are the goals that mean so much! This kind of effort is what the black militant groups are interested in doing, and this is a good thing. The fact is, many teachers and many white people from other professions are very much afraid. They feel threatened by the militancy, and they equate militancy with violence. Well, I don't.

Finally, I find that many of these young people are now working with younger sisters and brothers in their respective areas, and I'm thinking of two in particular who are in the Mission Rebels. There was some controversy recently about this group because a contract was signed with the superintendent of schools and with the Mission Rebels in regard to counseling. The counselors are going to be some of the Mission Rebels themselves. I don't know at this point what the status is. At first the Federation of Teachers approved, and now I understand it doesn't approve; but it may change again by Monday.

There is no formula. There is no one answer that one can give. What you have to do is to have some basic principles, and you have to be strong within yourself. You also must have the kind of leadership in the school, on the administrative level, that is not afraid of some of the public pressures. Also, there has to be truly a public education going along simultaneously so that the community can be brought into the picture. I have heard so many of you people saying these things about community understanding and participation, that we must all have a new way of looking at life because time is running out. I'm encouraged by what I've heard. For the future, at least, teacher education is going to take into consideration the community by bringing the community in—I don't mean on a one-shot basis, but from the very beginning—to plan and share, to evaluate and learn. This will be an education for all the members of the community, not only the children but also the parents and everyone else. The Chamber of Commerce could learn, too, and the industrial executives could learn, and the people on the draft board could learn. People on all levels must come to know and to understand. This is what has to happen! One must have an open mind. One must learn and keep on learning. And we don't learn just by getting degrees. We learn also by looking at life with open eyes and with an open heart. We have to "learn the language" wherever we are. Above all, we must learn to have compassion.

22. Teachers Tell It Like It Is

Teachers have too many answers and not enough questions. We all sit in little lounges and talk about how horrible the administrators are. How stupid the board of education is. How we don't know anything about the Office of Education. Yet when it comes right down to it, let a kid tell you that *you* are irrelevant and you will begin to defend every aspect of the system you criticize.

"What we need most is a national philosophy of education to tell us what our goals ought to be."

"You people in the Federal Government are always bringing in outside committees to rubber stamp what you have already decided. We teachers are tired of being manipulated."

SOURCE: *American Education,* IV, 9 (October 1968), 26. Reprinted by permission of the publisher.

Pointed words touched off three days of discussion between U.S. Office of Education officials and 30 teachers who were selected by a committee of classroom teachers and invited to Washington last summer. The conference gave policymaking people in the Office of Education the chance—for the first time—to meet directly with classroom teachers from various parts of the country. The discussion reflected the growing demand among American teachers to be included in policymaking at the local, State, and national levels. The teachers feel their trip to Washington was long overdue. They believe Federal and State planners have ignored for too long the potential resources of first-hand knowledge and know-how possessed by classroom teachers. The teachers blame many policy mistakes on a lack of discussion between those who make the policies and the classroom teachers who translate them into action. The result, said one, is that "teachers feel helpless in the system in which they work."

Another complaint was that, with hundreds of thousands of dollars being spent on remote, university-based educational research, more attention should be paid to the humbler experimentation which can and should take place right in the classroom. A Chicago teacher told the conference that the lack of attention paid to classroom teachers encourages professional laziness: "It's unfortunate that teachers rely on some guy in some university who has never seen the inside of a classroom to tell them what's wrong with their teaching. They ought to be doing their own research, conducting their own experiments."

The teachers emphasized that, once they are treated as professionals, they will be able to fill a professional role. "Too many non-professional school chores—clerical work, patrol duty, and the like—are assigned to teachers. A non-teaching staff should take over these jobs," an Oregon teacher said. "We must have more time to plan, time for research and investigation, time to learn more about better materials and improved methods. We need the opportunity to experiment in our classrooms with new ways of doing things. Just think what we could do if we had even one day a month for these purposes." Innovation must be encouraged —teachers must be freed from the uneasy feeling that their new ideas will be considered a threat.

The conferees urged the establishment of programs that will enable teachers to make direct application for developmental grants "without going through all the red tape and then being told 'No.' "

Amid talk of teacher power, student power, parent power, and related political conflicts which now characterize educational discourse, it was evident that the participants were more concerned with improving the quality of education than with power as such. "We must find a way to free the creative abilities of our teachers," was the common viewpoint.

The conference participants came from public and private schools, from urban, suburban, and rural areas. They were eager to learn about one another's problems. A teacher from a wealthy suburban school in Oregon suggested that—in the midst of so much current concern for the plight of the underprivileged child—we take a look at the job our educational system is doing with his more privileged peers. She described the upper-middle-class youngsters she teaches as culturally deprived, because they associate only with themselves. "These kids have the feeling that money buys everything—and the school is not telling them any different," she said, and added that overly permissive parents make it impossible for the school to teach students the concept of responsibility. "All the student has to do if he has forgotten an assignment or if he hasn't finished it is to call Mom and she brings it to him." Ambitious parents apply such pressure for top grades that their children have nervous breakdowns—or feel forced to cheat. "Grades are worth a great deal of money," she said. "Twenty-five dollars for an 'A' is not uncommon." Though this teacher blames the materialism pervading our society for the attitudes of these children and their parents, she faults the schools for not making it more difficult for such attitudes to flourish.

An Alabama teacher from a poor rural district was concerned with problems of a different nature. The limited funds in her school district mean low teacher salaries and inadequate facilities, equipment, and materials. The rural community's local government simply lacks the revenue to supplement funds received from the State and Federal Government. "In some of our schools you will find classes and such activities as band rehearsal, senior play practice, and the serving of lunches all going on simultaneously in one all-purpose room. The situation is one of total pandemonium."

A participant from a Chicago ghetto school stressed the importance of teachers' becoming full-fledged members of the community. "They must begin to relate to the total community they serve as human beings, not as experts. If you go out into the community you'll find a really interesting thing—everybody is teaching somebody, and they don't all have Ph.D.s." Our educational system, he emphasized, must try to bring all members of the community into some aspect of education decisionmaking. "When the people of a community can assist in developing the programs their community wants and needs and then can operate them, it will be a very important day in this country." He hopes that teachers will help bring about such a revolution in education policymaking.

Reaction to the conference by Office of Education personnel was enthusiastic. One high official commented that the meeting was one of the most lively and productive he had attended in months.

Associate Commissioner Don Davies, who heads the Bureau of Educational Personnel Development, said: "The meeting was exciting. Those who took part were honest with one another and with us. They had good ideas and made important suggestions. We need to find many ways to hear the voices from the classroom. A continuing connection between OE staff and classroom teachers will help both groups."

23. Classroom Aggression Seen As Inevitable

Student aggression—full blown and grown in schools today—is an inevitable part of the classroom, and a teacher is professionally responsible for learning how to handle it. This is the conclusion of an all-day institute "on handling aggression in the classroom" sponsored by the American Orthopsychiatric Association. More than 300 teachers and mental health workers talked candidly about the problem which is common to both the kindergarten teacher and the college professor.

Aggression, they concluded, does not have a simple cause or a single remedy. At the final session, the participants aptly redefined their title to "institute on struggling to handle desirable and undesirable aggression in the classroom in a mad, mad world." Educators at the sessions faced a range of problems—from the Harlem teacher whose children came to school angry because they were hungry to the elementary school principal from a wealthy Massachusetts suburb whose students were "emotionally starved."

Research should be directed at helping teachers know the sources of aggression, emphasized Fritz Redl of Wayne State University, formerly chief of the child research branch of the National Institutes of Health. Causes of aggression most frequently mentioned: home life; individual hang-ups of the students; "tribal rites," where students act out a pattern that is directed at pleasing their peers, rather than the teacher; and the teachers. Some teachers "lose their cool" over mere mumbling by the students; others completely ignore the signals that lead to aggressive behavior. Redl pointed out that many teachers have trouble handling aggression because they care too much—"they get desperate, make mistakes, and then feel totally helpless." One teacher with a fifth grade of forty children said she can

SOURCE: *Education U.S.A.* (April 7, 1969), 175. Copyright © 1969, National School Public Relations Association. Reprinted by permission of the publisher.

see the frustration grow in her students because she is unable to give them work at their level.

Sending the aggressive child out of the classroom was at the bottom of the list of cures. Many big city teachers said there would be no classes left to teach. At the top of the list was self-understanding by the teachers. If they are aware of their own limits they will be able to "act rather than react to aggression." Strongly stressed was sensitivity training for teachers. The burden is on the teacher to establish a rapport with students so that they can accept criticism without feeling rejected. The conferees said the teacher also must know the right moment to get children off the hook— "to stop a chain reaction without making too much of a mess."

The school administration must reexaminine its support of the teachers, the conferees said. Herman P. Schuchman of the University of Illinois, chairman of the institute, asked these questions: "How much pressure is there to have classrooms quiet, recess and hallways quiet? How much flexibility is there in the curriculum and in daily programs? How much pressure and punitive threat exists between the teacher and administration?" Lastly, the speakers and participants agreed that the community must support the teacher with smaller class loads, special personnel, e.g., psychologists and psychiatrists, who are available immediately when teachers need them, and with an understanding that "the aggressive elements in the community touch the teacher and it is likely that they will spill over her onto the students."

24. Education for Leisure

J. A. Simpson

Dangers and difficulties beset the concept education for leisure. In the first place, it may be translated into an emotive blur-phrase with which we can simply repackage any existing curriculum so that the same basic medicine, as with prescriptions like "education for life," or "for citizenship" or "for

SOURCE: *Trends in Education*, V (January 1967), 16–23. Reprinted by permission of the Controller of Her Britannic Majesty's Stationery Office.

democracy," can persist without much consideration of its effectiveness. A new rationale is found—a change in the vocabulary of educationists without, necessarily, much change in the practice of educators. As such it has serious contemporary rivals in "education for maturity" or "adjustment."

The second danger is a little harder to define and arises from that curious kitchen-sink *narodnichestvo* which nowadays prompts many of us to suspect our own predilections as prim and bourgeois, and induces us to ascribe almost moral force to mass behavior-patterns as revealed by sociological surveys, grounding an educational philosophy, almost, on consumer research. This has many merits and is a salutary check on such assumptions as that *paella* belongs to an ethically higher order of things than fishfingers. If pushed too far, however, it can abolish any real dialogue in education for leisure, reducing it to the facilitation of mass trends which are often dictated by irresponsible interests.

Surely educationists ought to be able to assert personal values based on the notion of more and less fulfilling activities, or on that of enlarging people's range of experience and choice. They can still be alive to the limitations, for mass application in 1966, of leisure patterns that have prevailed among elite classes—of the sort portrayed with considerable continuity from Jane Austen or Charlotte Yonge to Alison Utley. It may not be without significance that so many of these pictures are by women or that a woman—the late Dr. Macalister Brew—was among the foremost apologists of an education for mass leisure based largely on the assumption that elite mores should be diffused.

The third danger lies in an oversimplification whereby education is called upon to solve a "problem of leisure" which consists in the appearance or threat of large quantities of nonwork time created by automation and hanging heavy on the recipients. There may not be such a problem, and if there is, it is by no means so easily defined. It is true that since 1860 the average industrial worker has gained 1,500 hours a year of nonwork time, and at each stage of this increase some public concern has been expressed about the social and moral consequences.

Shortly after the 1914 war, for example, the International Labor Office studied the "problem" set up by the eight-hour day type of legislation and expressed concern at the possibilities of mass drunkenness, debauchery and ennui. These dire results do not seem to have followed, and none of the contemporary surveys today gives us a picture of people complaining that they have nothing to do—except for certain small categories of teenagers and pensioners. Overtime, the second job, the great increase in the married woman labor force, and the time necessarily given to academic and vocational education, may, in fact, have reduced the national annual quantity of leisure. And to fill it there is a vastly multiplied range of leisure activities brought by technology and affluence within the reach of the average citizen.

Educationists who plead the new problem of leisure as an urgent reason for the development of this or that in the curriculum cannot point to the horrors of blank time. Rather they are expressing, whether they are frank about it or not, their disappointment with the way ("trivial," "escapist," "stultifying," "unconstructive") that people use their time. Anyone, of course, is entitled to make such judgements, but if he is pressing for anything which involves the expenditure of our effort and resources he must convince us that some improvement in the use of leisure is necessary for specific aspects of the welfare and happiness of people individually and as a community. And he must indicate means whereby, in a free society, this improvement can be made—the sort of water from which, and the sort of setting in which, the horse will in fact drink. Otherwise we shall be no further ahead.

Widening Horizons

The present position seems to be that the schools and various establishments of further and higher education devote a considerable amount of their time to education which, whatever other purposes it also serves, should enrich leisure by widening horizons of interest and enjoyment, sharpening perception and discrimination, and leading toward that thing —is it a quality of mind or an accumulation of knowledge and skills?— which is known as "cultivation." The effects on mass leisure are, however, in the opinion of well-placed observers, disappointing. Some time ago, for example, Jack Longland suggested, at a NUT conference on popular culture, that the influence of thousands of hours in the schools given to the arts and crafts and to physical and cultural development was only very partially discernible in postschool leisure interests. It would, on the other hand, be a pity to be discouraged too soon. It is a matter of experience that there has been a small but steady increase in those who have been permanently won over to "higher values" by the work of the schools, and this will have a cumulative effect if we are patient, although the Newsom Report has identified a substantial section of pupils among whom this kind of development is rare and unlikely. Is it possible to do more? If so how? On what social and ethical grounds is there any special urgency at present for making the attempt? It is not suggested that the following considerations provide answers but that they may help toward a clearer definition of the questions.

Studies of the nature of leisure do not offer unmixed encouragement to educators. In less industrialized and specialized societies no very clear line is drawn between work and play or relaxation, and much of work is enveloped in ritual or in domestic informality. Until quite recently in our own type of society leisure, except as a period of recuperation from work, was the preserve of a minority. To think of training for mass leisure would have been pointless, although the lack of such training became painfully clear during the unexpected period of enforced mass leisure at the time of the great industrial depression, when the sense of aimlessness was more noticeable perhaps than malnutrition. Leisure for most people, as a separate block of time of significant dimension, is a product of the tertiary stage of industrialization. It seems to have led to some widespread change of attitude toward work—from a view of work as a desirable chief life-interest and as a moral end in itself to seeing it primarily as a means to personal life—the unavoidable substructure of leisure. A number of thinkers from the Greeks to Piaget have expressed the view, put concisely by Schiller, that "only in play is man fully human" and they have recommended an educational strategy based on this. Until recently, however, the inescapable economic condition of mankind has provided a soil that is refractory for the germination of such an idea, except for a privileged leisured class. A more protestant ethic has, accordingly, prevailed in education. Has technological advance altered all this? If so it might seem that golden vistas of personal development for millions were opening up before the educators' eyes. Some of the early diagnosticians of the ultimate effects of industrialization thought so. Marx, Engels and Proudhon envisaged a future in which emancipated workers would devote themselves to public affairs, astronomy and general cultivation. Only in limited measure has this type of expectation been fulfilled and, in so far as we are able to judge, even in countries where there is encouragement to the point of pressure, response to the sort of provision made in palaces and parks of culture and recreation has been far from reassuring. The very nature of leisure (the word is derived from "licere") implies that much of it will be self-organized or, by extension, satisfied through customer-purveyor relationships.

Social Change

It is perhaps only realistic to try and identify some of the needs of *homo conurbanus* which he seeks to assuage in leisure, particularly those which emerge from high-density living in the mid-sixties, and particularly those with which it might be thought, *prima facie,* education could help. Many of these needs have been so documented by academic studies, reputable surveys or reports like Albemarle and Newsom, that it is sufficient only to recall them briefly. Perhaps the most frequently mentioned is loneliness— the sense of isolation and lack of identity. It is odd that, as we become more densely populated, there is so much reference to the need for meaningful human contact, as opposed to the lonely togetherness of the crowded tube train or cinema. A good deal has been written about it, notably Riesman's *Lonely Crowd.* A study made here states flatly that "Loneliness among all age groups is the disease at the heart of our honeycomb society. The number of lonely people in Britain has been rising over the past twenty years and is an alarming iceberg of social malaise in a country which becomes more impersonal as mobility grows." Shifts in population, the breakup of the extended family, new housing, the resiting of industry, mass and passive entertainment, are among factors that have steadily diminished that group life which is the soil of mental health, where people can be persons and not merely faceless consumers, producers, viewers, passengers—units in somebody else's social engineering. Some indication of this may be given by the enhanced prestige of marriage and the nuclear family as the sole reality, the front door providing the only gateway from the anonymity of outside relationships into life as a real person. Yet we are assured that there are in-built psychological reasons why family life is bound to be an insufficient substitute for less emotionally charged groups. Allied to this and also to the increasing complexity, specialism, and professionalism, of modern life is a sense of impotence—often manifested as apathy—in influencing let alone controlling social environment, in finding a place for giving any significant service to individuals to the community.

New processes have tended to reduce, for many workers, including domestic workers, the demands which their job makes on personal skill, strength, technical mastery, initiative and creativity. This is true whatever classification—skilled, semiskilled or unskilled, or even professional—is allocated to the job.

Leisure pursuits and interests have acquired much greater importance in the lives of many, and it is in these often, rather than in their work nowadays, that they seek to find status and identity. Technical progress has opened up to a broad mass of people the chance of a personal life in non-work time, and it has made available to them a profusion of desirable possessions and activities the mastery of which often demands considerable skill which they wish to learn. Few, however, translate their wish into fact and one clearly emerging problem of affluence is underusage—the fact that so many people continue to mill round a restricted orbit in pursuits that make minimal demands on their personalities.

The sheer volume and intensity of advertisement—which seems to reflect some in-built need in our type of economy for demand to run somewhat ahead of expanding production—and, indeed, the rich profusion of entirely new materials and apparatus for personal life, constitute a formidable problem for many. Already consumer education has been identified as a valuable element in the schools and further education establishments. It is not entirely a matter of choosing between products. Admass pressures can lead to dependence on an endless and widening stream of things to buy as a solvent of all the needs, difficulties and frustrations of life, so that new-won leisure has to be lost again in an attempt to gain extra money—

by extra paid work—a process which is likely to be self-defeating and can lead to uneasy industrial relations. For this reason the cultivation of inner or independent sources of satisfaction might be seen as having social importance.

Our society is increasingly ordered. A larger and larger area of our lives is removed from chance, from hazard, or capricious individualism. It is subjected to an order which is manifestly just, well-planned and benevolent —an order which, we cannot deny, we have ourselves democratically created. It shepherds us into our proper traffic lanes and places us in clearly appropriate categories in various types of school or job, mental hospitals, or university, from the municipal maternity ward to the municipal crematorium. It is all sensible and just and leaves little room for causes that could hallow any expressions of human aggressiveness in embattled solidarity against oppressors within or foes without. The international scene too, is increasingly subjected to the rule of law, or the balance of terror. It may not be without significance that the World Health Organization has noted that countries with a high crime rate have a low mental illness rate. Undoubtedly, one of the real success stories of our Youth Service has been the type of adventurous activity associated loosely with the name "Outward Bound"; but it has a minority appeal and, indeed, it seems difficult to relate to the kind of life that most of us lead in this strange world of orienteering, slalom, tods, cliff rescue, mountain rescue, sea rescue, cave rescue, sheep rescue, and so on.

A feature of our epoch to which it might be supposed education has a contribution to make is the intensified difficulty in communication between the elder and the young. Some of the factors at work have been sufficiently stressed—affluent emancipated youth, courted by the labor market, wooed by salesmen who build up teenage pursuits, fashions and language to something splendid and separate, the high point of life—salesmen who are irresponsibly indifferent to the fate of exteenagers. Less attention has been paid to another side of the picture—that among adults there is increased health, wealth and longevity. There is indeed a good deal of jealousy between the generations.

Educational Contribution

Whether or not it is susceptible of any educational alleviation there is undoubtedly some malaise arising from widespread changes that are taking place in people's scales of values, and there is much confusion about which forms of conduct and what personal qualities are worth while. It has been observed that in many sections of the community, at all levels, a certain moral and social giddiness has arisen from the disappearance of those

clear standards and signposts which were, not so long ago, provided by religious faith or the behavior ideals set by higher social classes. It is a question of course how far education can be the creator of an ideology or how
far it must work within a datum in this report. The prevailing view seems
to be that education should put people in the position of "forging out their
own values." Much of the nature of personal life, of leisure, will depend
upon the type of standards and values which predominate at any given
time—upon the patterns of ideal behavior, and this includes recreation
and relaxation, that are considered to be desirable, whether the label is
"more refined," "nobler," "more with-it," or "more fun."

If this is the sort of area of social and educational leisure-need that we
must consider, what prospects are there of making a serious contribution
through the work of the schools and colleges, and later through voluntarily
undertaken further education? The pabulum that we have provided for
many years now—the liberal and social studies (humanities and sciences),
the arts and crafts, the physical skills—represents a distilled tradition of
wisdom and it has been constantly increased and refreshed as a result of
recent thinking and discovery. The techniques for its presentation and assimilation have themselves become a science. The diet has in the past few
decades been enlarged by the addition of means whereby suitable attitudes
and dispositions may be fostered in the young—means which are inherent
in the curriculum and not merely its by-product of social training and corporate life. In so far as there has been a failure to provide the answer to
leisure problems one may reasonably ask why this wisdom and these attitudes have proved inadequate.

Undoubtedly beneath all the prize-day tributes paid to education for
"life," "maturity," and so on, those elements in education predominate
which assist in replenishing and increasing the nation's stock of knowledge
and skill for self-maintenance in a competitive world, and while one may
question the relevance today of some of the elements of this knowledge
and skill that are still highly regarded, it could scarcely be said that the
time seems ripe for making education for leisure central rather than peripheral. But even in the fringe—and it is by no means a negligible fringe
—a certain mixture of austerity, academicism and high culture tends to
prevail—a legacy perhaps of Calvinism and a public educational system
which for much of its history was inspired by the conception of civilizing
the masses *de haut en bas*. As a result a certain hierarchy of priority appears to operate with considerable force in educational circles, whereby esteem is given in descending order to vocational education (and this includes academic and liberal subjects leading to examinations), other work
which could conceivably pay a career dividend (e.g. Spanish or economics
voluntarily taken by an adult student), high culture (which presupposes
some initial intellectual equipment), the creative arts, physical fitness, and
lastly education for sheer diversions of an innocuous kind, those which are

active and rural being placed higher than those which are passive and urban.

Leisure Surveys

The resulting mixture in education that bears on leisure often contrasts sharply with what most surveys of mass leisure patterns indicate to be the facts in a mainly urban society. These surveys vary, but if one allows for some noticeable difference between those dealing with adults and those with youth, it would not be unjust to find some consensus along the following lines. Heading the list by far comes casual, informal, human intercourse—domestic and outside the home, and including all the ascents, plateaux and declines of courtship, love, friendship and family affections. After this obvious element, pride of place goes to the mass media (mainly television and radio). Surprisingly, however, this place is almost shared by a group of active and creative utilitarian interests that center round the home—adaptation, extension, decoration, embellishment, purchasing, planning, gardening, dress, cookery.

These interests are heavily governed by commercial advertisement, have a strong note of social advancement—although the keynote is modernity rather than gentility—and depend largely upon the use of commercially produced materials, kits and tools that are rarely seen in the schools (foam, rubber, fiberglass, small power-tools). Close behind comes active outdoor interests. These increasingly center round the car and include car maintenance—but also the expeditions, trips, picnics, travels, and holidays whether by car or public transport and also active participation in sports, games, coursing, fishing, camping, skating, swimming, bowling, water pursuits—again very much affected by the latest forms of commercially advertised gear and dress. Recreational and social activities of a more structured kind follow—the dances, parties, meetings in clubs and pubs, visits to cinemas, spectatorship at games and other events. Reading books invariably occupies a surprisingly high place, but almost none of the surveys gives any clue as to the content of reading, and it must be remembered that nowadays, for a majority of people, the word "book" covers magazines and comics. These are the chief categories and they occupy at least twice as large a percentage as the next in order—hobbies such as collecting, crosswords, pets—and gambling. After that we have only fragmentary distribution and it is somewhere here that we find, variously placed, some reflection of our educational striving—the interest in nature, the less utilitarian crafts, amateur drama and music-making, the theatre, concerts, and other forms of high culture including a maintained interest in liberal or social studies, or the active exercise of democratic citizen responsibilities. In general, as one of the surveyors, Brian Groombridge, points out "Popu-

lar culture in Britain is a domestic culture centering on the home and garden and linked to the world outside by the car and TV."

One might add that it is a culture dependent in large measure upon the
commercial provision of commodities and facilities, and it is here too that
one may discern in much educational thinking and practice a traditional
suspicion or contempt which leaves these goods and facilities out of account. There are of course notable exceptions but there is often little disposition in educational practice to take cognizance of noneducational television programs, of the significance in children's lives of pop discs, of the
admass-induced conspicuous spending which is one of the notable mass
pressures of our time and has been called "the wall-to-wall dynamic," although among the young clothes predominate as the concrete symbol. Educational provision is slow to recognize the new rhythms of living that have
appeared in the two-income family with its effect on the timing, tempo and
content of leisure. The nourishing soup or pudding that needs careful
preparation, the stitchcraft that lends itself to endurance and repair are,
for many, as irrelevant as the concept of thrift in an age when the economy thrives on rapid, throwaway consumption and confident credit-buying.
Nor is enough note taken of what appear to be, in the case of many people, something like in-built limitations. In one study of life on a council
estate there was noted an almost universal aversion from serious music, to
the point, apparently, of genuine physical pain. A similar sense of nausea
in the presence of large arrays of books, as in a library, was noted by another. Most teachers of history have encountered a certain number of pupils for whom the past, in itself and in any shape or form, is nauseous.

The central difficulty about a program of leisure education seems to be
that as educationists we have not all in our hearts resolved a dilemma
which is thrust upon us with increasing clarity as we try harder. We cling
to the notion that everyone is capable of the highest (a highest about the
nature of which we have little doubt), or at least capable of some stage on
the road toward it, and that, at heart, they long for these heights and will
be the better for their progress upward, however painfully it has been
made. It is as if mankind were strung out along the trail toward some
golden west of attainment, some toiling manfully, some in breakdown postures, but all yearning onward—"Culture or bust." It is this sort of thinking which underlies many of the attempts to use popular culture, as the
surveys show it to us, as a "starting point"—something to educate *from*
and not *for*. Education through the popular arts is not infrequently a disguised form of changing the popular arts by critical analysis—a process,
in film, for example, of weaning away from *Goldfinger* to the works of
Fellini. It is not surprising that the intrinsic difficulties of doing this restrict its effectiveness to a minority. And yet, as educators, are we not dedicated to some such process in respect of all our pupils, not merely some?
Could we be content to educate a minority away from popular culture and

the rest for the enjoyment of it? Is not any dualism of aim and standard repugnant to us? It is by no means a new problem. Years ago Matthew Arnold, as an educator, joined issue with Tolstoy when he wrote, "At present I can contribute to nothing which raises me externally above others, which separates me from them. I cannot any longer recognize any quality beyond the quality of man. I cannot seek a culture which separates me from men." Tolstoy's words are surely moving, but can we take them less critically now than Arnold did?

But is this dilemma fundamental? Is it not being dissolved by the passage of time. Many readers of this article, like the writer, may admit that in their leisure they habitually enjoy some of the elements listed high in the surveys mentioned earlier. Enjoyment of some parts of both popular and high culture commonly coexist today. We can surely educate for both if we are so minded, and the process will be effective in so far as we take popular culture seriously in all its facets.

Acquisition of Skills

There may be room, too, in educational establishments for greater awareness of the increasing wish of adults to use their leisure to better their situation in life in a new way—not through further vocational or academic learning that leads to advancement in, or change of career, but through the acquisition of skills and mores and possessions that confer social prestige. It would, perhaps, be a useful exercise for those who frame curricula in the schools to consider the change, in the last twenty years, in the program of adult education classes provided by LEAs, and the increasing part played in it by classes in flower-arrangement, skiing, subaqua interests, stock market operations, fly-fishing, antique-buying, party-giving, the use of light in interior decoration, gastronomy and so on. The "graceful living" motif is, also, increasingly represented in the Youth Service. Yet, although there are many exceptions, the leisure interests opened up by the schools are not usually presented in ways that associate them with this powerful tendency. Recently a subsection of the Cultural Committee of the Council of Europe has identified a general trend in member countries as policies of *Education permanente*—life-long education based on the need, in a time of high-tempo social change, for regular refresher courses throughout life, as much in matters of personal and social, as in vocational life. Involved in this, explicitly, is the need in the schools for a basic education in these personal and social matters which takes cognizance of, and works in liaison with, what is being done in the postschool years.

Perhaps, in the long-run, one of the most fertile fields for developing education for leisure is indicated by the supreme place occupied in leisure-usage as we know it by human relationships and intercourse. Much can be done, and is done, as a preparation for effective personal life in this respect through well-established subjects of the curriculum, particularly English. In addition, the increasing use of group work in learning situations is likely to convey some knowledge of the mechanics and inherent benefits of group-life and of the attitudes and techniques which enable people to join, form and be valued and useful in groups in various ways and roles. On the other hand, to include this vast field in the curriculum in a more formal or direct way presents a formidable difficulty—one more of those difficulties in which the whole topic of leisure education abounds. Some of them have been sketchily outlined in this paper. Around them all lies a question which is not one for educationists as such. How far are we at present wise to place a particular stress in education upon preparation for leisure? It is a question that would lead us into economics.

25. Phads and Phantoms in American Education

Mary Yeazell

In Lewis Carroll's classic, *Alice in Wonderland,* the Queen of Hearts explains to Alice the difference in their two countries by saying, "Now, here, you see, it takes all the running you can do to keep in the same place. If you want to get somewhere else, you must run at least twice as fast as that." This seems to be a very apt description of American public education today in the space age. One of the reasons for the educator's constant running has been to keep up with developments in his field directly resulting from the changes in our society brought about by the revolution in knowledge, in population, and in technology. Americans have been characterized by sociologists as possessing an unwavering faith in progress. We have been described by psychologists as creatures having innate activity and curiosity drives so that we are easily stimulated by new things and by

SOURCE: *Peabody Journal of Education,* XLIV (May 1967), 333–40. Reprinted by permission of the publisher.

the need for change and relief from monotony. We have been criticized, however, and deservedly so, because all too frequently we mistakenly embrace the new and the change as being better than the tried and the old; or to put it succinctly, we assume that something new and different is inherently good, and hasten to put it into effect. We are a nation devoted to fads—from hula hoops to skate boards, from sweat shirts with cut-off sleeves worn inside out to mini skirts—we are a people who latch on to new things with vigor and pursue them relentlessly, often without thought or consideration as to their long-range consequences. And as the nation goes, so goes education, which leads to the first fad I would like to consider—that of technology in the classroom.

The September, 1966, issue of *Phi Delta Kappan* contained the statement that the educational technology market in this country had already reached the $500 million mark with a potential of $5 to $10 billion within a decade. The USOE reported that in the first year of operation of President Johnson's education bill, $200 million in federal funds were spent by local schools on educational hardware. This machine craze extends from the now old-fashioned movie projector through teaching machines to the Edison Responsive Learning Environment, an elaborate talking typewriter costing $30,000 which teaches children to read and write in thirty hours. Recently a demonstration was given in Miami University's audio-visual department of a classroom gadget which could direct stimuli from five sources—slide projectors, video tape recorders, movie projectors, overhead projectors and audio tape recorders—and receive multiple-choice responses from thirty or more stations, all operated by one person. I can visualize it now—a brave new classroom composed of a computeach, a computer programmed to automatically give illustrated lectures with instantaneous flexibility based on compustude feedback coming from 150 miniature tape recorders equipped with stop and go switches utilizing red and green lights to alert the computeach. Wouldn't it be wonderful? And how much would you care to bet that some sophisticated salesman couldn't sell it to a gullible educator.

Now most of us shudder at the possibility and pat ourselves on the back because of its improbability. However, the use of machines in the classroom is not a laughing matter as you well know. Recently, I met a young teacher friend who is currently expending her effort in a nearby slum school so economically impoverished that it receives almost 100% of its funds from federal allocations. She said that there were so many funds available to her for the wrong things that she could have five movie projectors but couldn't get a pencil or a book for love or money. And so, educators have entered into the technology business with full energy and the best of intentions.

To those of us who have labored grading drill sheets of spelling words or the 100 addition facts, or the parts of speech, or decided not to teach a particular topic in science because of a shortage of equipment, or have wished for a visiting expert on Pago Pago, the machine age has looked like the answer to a teacher's prayer, and there may be good reasons for our wholehearted acceptance of such hardware. The film, the slide, and the record player have allowed us to give our children vicarious experiences which we could never provide with our own limited community resources. The teaching machine can and should free us from directing the practice sessions that are a necessary part of the learning of every new skill; and the television monitor brings the world of living things and the laboratory demonstration within the vision of each child whether on the front row or back and further, with tours and experiments conducted by the finest teachers and experts in many fields. With such a wealth of materials and the free time which they provide for the teacher, one would surely expect to get in return a superior education such as has never before been conceived, let alone realized.

But before we sit down to relax and let the machine do it, let us pause to think through some other possible consequences. It was a little-known and seldom quoted President, Millard Fillmore, who said in his third annual state of the union message "Let us remember that revolutions do not always establish freedom." I am inclined to think that this may be the case with the technological revolution in education. The teaching machine, which so ably relieves the teacher from boring drill work, also gives each student the same subject matter, even with so-called branching programs. Thus, freedom from routine brings with it the ugly phantom of differential instruction for each individual. Do the machine makers and the teachers who use them really believe that bright children learn in precisely the same way as dull children? Is it possible to teach reflective thinking and inquiry skills by programmed learning? And just how creative can your responses be when you are given only a certain number of buttons to push? So, while the teaching machine obviously frees the teacher, what does this educational revolution do to the student? Or, consider another possible consequence resulting from the use of educational hardware. Most of us consider it not only desirable, but an essential part of every learning experience that there be some kind of personal interaction in a people-to-people situation. Consider the plight of the students and his machine. When Rex Harrison was questioned about his reaction to playing opposite a silent parrot in his new movie, "Dr. Doolittle," he said, "How do you establish a warm relationship with a bird?" And we might ask ourselves as teachers, while it may be possible for a student to be actively engaged with a teaching machine, how can he interact with a television set? Or, how much affection can a tape recorder give him?

Now, it has been shown without much doubt, that certain types of learning occur just as well if not better when accomplished via the machine or the television set, but is this rather impersonal kind of relationship in keeping with some of the desirable objectives of education? Is it possible that the devotees of the machine who are racing madly about inventing new ways to use it are merely repeating their own machinelike patterns of teaching?

James S. Coleman's recent report, *Equality of Educational Opportunity,* a USOE venture involving half a million students, 60,000 teachers, and 4,000 schools, reiterates on a large scale what most of us in education have long suspected; and that is, to the extent that schools do influence what students learn, their facilities and programs are the least important factors in the equation. If the quality of teachers and capability of students are held constant, luxurious physical facilities contribute little to the development of intellectual skills, and inadequate facilities do nothing to retard them. In a nutshell, while the report does not prove that as yet untried improvements in school facilities and programs would have no significant effect on learning, it does provide a good deal of evidence to indicate that this kind of innovation has made very little difference in the past.

Not the least of the consequences of machine age education rears its ugly head when we consider what the effect of eliminating the personal touch in education will be in an age in which man is already finding himself overwhelmed by the machine, when he seems to be fighting a losing battle to recover his identity as a self in a society without personal responsibility, personal satisfaction, or personal dignity.

The Greeks were full-time citizens of the world because of their slaves. We have the promise of being full-time citizens because of our technology. But the teaching machine, the television set, the slide projector, and even the Edison learning environment are only as good as the program itself, which leads me to a second fad in education, the curriculum.

Ever since the debate between Socrates and the Sophists, the curriculum has been under fire both for what it does and for what it does not do for the education of children. Nowadays, a school administrator cannot be respectable at school meetings unless he can say that his school, too, has BSCS, PSSC, SMSG, UICSM, FLES, modern math, structural linguistics plus team teaching, and an ungraded primary, all very recent and terribly expensive new curricula. Indeed, on first glance, it seems that alphabet soup would be a good title for today's curriculum theory. Of course, there must always be a scapegoat, and the Russians are as good as any, so we could attribute it all to Sputnik and the space race. Undoubtedly, 1956 was a banner year for critics of the curriculum because only then—in spite of the fact that public education had been in existence for hundreds of years —did scientists and mathematicians, artists and literary figures discover that students were still learning the same old things in the same old ways. Add to the cries of alarmists statements such as that of Jerome Bruner, who says in *The Process of Education,* ". . . any subject can be taught effectively in some intellectually honest form to any child at any stage of development," and you have ample ammunition for starting a full-scale war upon the content of education.

Armed with new knowledge, the scholars in science set about to right all the ills of American public education, and you know the result. It was reported at the 1965 Columbia University seminar on Technology and Social Change that the two-semester high school physics course, commonly known as PSSC, cost $5 million and several months, if not years, of work by a group of top-flight physicists. Since this was the first of many such new curricula, and figures are not available for the cost of the others, we can only speculate on the expense involved in just writing the curricula, let alone implementing them in all the schools which are now using them. Thanks to the National Science Foundation, money seems not to be a deterrent; so let us leave that problem for the moment and examine the basis for the new curricula.

Most of the new programs, with the possible exception of the creative expression movement in the fine arts, rest upon the notion of the structure of a discipline. Structure is defined in Bruner's work and in others as the fundamental ideas of a discipline; and Bruner points out that to know the structure of a thing is to know how it is related to other things; so that the revolution has come about in the content of subject matter which is taught to the child—that is, he is given exercises and experiments to help him learn the structure of matter, of energy, of the human body, the number system, and his language, rather than learning about how the refrigerator works, or how to diagram a complex sentence or the names of the phyla. It comes as a shock to some of us to hear third graders talking about the commutative and associative properties of numbers, base 5 systems, and pattern drills, and then someone tells us that they are learning structure. In art class, a child makes a four-legged animal with a mane and tail and is disappointed in us because we can't guess that it's a bug; and we are told by his art teacher that it doesn't matter what it looks like, if it represents his encounter with a motivator and the expression of that experience. And so, we have children learning the structure of mathematics, science, English, and perhaps art, but who seem unable to do simple addition and subtraction, whose handwriting is unreadable, who cannot distinguish a Picasso from a Rembrandt, and who freely use "ain't" and "he don't" because they communicate more effectively than standard grammatical forms. In other words, we have children who know the processes but have unrecognizable products.

The real question about curriculum reform seems to me to be, are we willing to accept mediocrity in practical performance as long as we have understanding at the levels of the theoretical and the abstract? Or, to put the question another way, what kind of society demands absolute perfection from its machines, but settles for inferiority from its citizen.

Curriculum reforms become even more alarming when we consider what seems to be, at least in recent times, their sources, or the programmers. While it is true that PSSC and BSCS were the products of the efforts of many top scholars, dedicated classroom teachers, and interested students, it appears that such will not always be the case in the future. Peter Schrag, in reviewing Francis Keppel's new book, *The Necessary Revolution in American Education,* points out that for the first time in history, curriculum development is being taken over by well-financed, well-organized private professionals such as General Learning Corporation, of which Keppel has recently become head. Who are these well-organized, well-financed private professionals? They are the computer technicians, the media specialists, and the learning theorists—many of whom have not sat in a public school classroom since they were enrolled in the twelfth grade. Doesn't it seem a bit odd to you that educators are acting much like the little boy on a bicycle who says, "Look, Ma—No Hands!"? Are we willing to let go the reins completely, or to quote a recent television series, isn't it time somebody tried to "ride the wild horses"?

But, many will say, surely this represents an improvement because it puts the child literally on the "frontier" of knowledge; and furthermore, the programs are designed so that the child feels like a scientist or mathematician or artist—he is discovering for himself. Again, ask yourself— with all that is to be learned, does it make sense for a child to spend a week discovering something which you could tell him in thirty minutes? And, really, just how many students in your third grade are going to grow up to be mathematicians, scientists, or artists? Ah—you will reply—but it makes them appreciate knowledge and the fields other than their own. And this brings me to the real paradox of our new curricula—the more we approach an understanding of the structure of a discipline, the more abstract it becomes; the more abstract an idea, the more difficult the understanding of it becomes. So again, we find ourselves teaching high level abstract terms—commutative, associative—to children in slum schools who cannot read simple words like "the ball is red" with comprehension and expression—in the hope that it will improve their appreciation of the world around them!

G. W. Ford and Lawrence Pugno, editors of *The Structure of Knowledge and the Curriculum,* point out that knowledge of the structure of an object provides little information about the relation of that object to other objects. Thus, the physicist understands the structure of the atom, but this knowledge does not tell him how atoms are related to chemistry. Both the chemist and the physicist use the mathematician's number system, but his knowledge of the structure of numbers does not explain to him how numbers are related to either of his colleague's disciplines. So, we may be educating a whole generation of youngsters who know all about the structure of various subjects, but little of how to integrate this knowledge for a better world. Thus, it is imperative that we examine the curriculum for its relation to education objectives and to the characteristics and needs of individuals. President James A. Garfield once defined education as himself on one end of a log and Mark Hopkins on the other. Would President Garfield have been willing to substitute for Mark Hopkins an electronic gadget which systematically presented to him a canned set of questions? I sincerely doubt that he would. I believe that Garfield was describing the personal encounter of a child with a great teacher who had something pertinent to say. It seems to me that we must let neither the machine nor the curriculum get in the way of the most essential ingredient in the educational process, and that is the child. All of which leads to a third and final fad in education, the search for talent.

Hardly a school system exists today which doesn't like to brag about its provisions for special education, which may mean nothing more than six ninth grade books in the seventh grade classroom; or it may mean an elaborate program for identifying the gifted and the handicapped with special provisions for each group. If I could single out two catch phrases in today's educational jargon, they would be the "gifted child," and "creativity." Education is currently engaged in a massive manhunt for the innocent child with the special talents—hopefully scientific and mathematical—who persists in lingering at the level of passing while his gifts are hotly pursued by the nation. If nothing else has been spectacular about the sixties, educationally speaking, one cannot say that teachers, school administrators, and public officials have neglected the area of special abilities. These have been the years of criticism of test makers, guidance directors, autocratic teachers—all of whom are engaged in a dark plot to undermine the nation's brightest and most creative youth. Yes, the search is on in a big way, largely financed by federal and foundation funds. The new frontier to be conquered is not economic or political—rather, it is intellectual. The search has taken many forms. Only this summer in an enterprising project called Upward Bound, 20,000 teenage students believed to possess college potential were selected from the ranks of the poverty stricken and given a taste of honey on some 200 college campuses, hopefully to increase the possibility of their acceptance into colleges. Add to this the thousands of students given remedial tutoring and "enrichment" under Title II programs, plus the hundreds of pre-schoolers who have been given a "Head Start," and it is not hard to see the passion with which this search has been undertaken.

And now that this mass of students have been returned to their same inadequate classrooms, poorly trained teachers, and the impoverished environments which have kept them stifled for years, what will happen next? How many can we expect to join the ranks of the specially talented and to enter college and succeed? Dr. Richard T. Frost, the Director of Upward

Bound, hopes that at least half the participants will be stimulated to realize their full potential. A more realistic estimate is that of Dr. Kenneth B. Clark who feels that only a small minority will succeed.

And the quest for giftedness goes on while our cities face a mass exodus of white, educated middle-class, public school-minded citizens from its gates. The flight to the suburbs is increasing daily—anyone can move out of the city except the poor who are stuck with the inferior buildings, the beginning teachers, and the segregated groups. It is no accident that many of our major cities now have a public school population which is more than 50 percent Negro, making racially integrated neighborhood schools possible. The Supreme Court, in the case of Brown *versus* Board of Education, substantiated for all time the hard fact that segregated schools are inherently bad and have a detrimental effect upon the segregated child. So, we have the paradox of the public school's great talent hunt—to sort out the special from the run-of-the-mill to place them in segregated situations, while at the same time fighting a major legal and physical battle to end segregation of another kind—because it is inherently damaging to the child!

Meanwhile, the pressure-cooker atmosphere of many of our public schools is causing the potentially useful, normal child to feel inferior and useless—as if he were letting his parents and his country down—when he even considers something other than college. And because pressures are so great, the National Institute of Mental Health expected at least 1000 college students to die by suicide by the end of the year 1966. Isn't there something wrong when a society measures the worth of a man by the degree initials following his name?—When one cannot get his car repaired or his undies laundered because there is no help to be hired? What manner of man pushes his child to succeed at a task in which he is miserable? What kind of country spends millions of dollars to find one scientist and allows five potential barbers or hairdressers or cooks or trash collectors to drop out of school or fold under the pressure? Why are we unwilling to spend money on technical and vocational education; and furthermore, why are we reluctant to encourage children to enter it?

As John W. Gardner points out in his provocative book, *Excellence,* we must come to the realization that it takes more than an educated elite to run a complex technological society. We must understand that excellence can be reached in places other than the rarified atmosphere of the institution of higher learning. Gardner further says that we must learn to honor, even demand, excellence in all lines of endeavor for "The society which scorns excellence in plumbing because plumbing is a humble activity, will have neither good plumbing nor good philosophy. Neither its pipes nor its theories will hold water."

Tomorrow's teachers have been educated in the era of the Rickovers and the Raffertys, the Koerners and the Conants. When they go out to teach next year or the year after, there will probably be more money, more fads, and more phantoms. Hopefully, they and we will have learned that we must look beyond the gimmick; for the easy answer is rarely, if ever, the golden key to the good education. As Dr. Bester said to Miss Barrett, in that delightful novel *Up the Down Staircase,* "Let it be a challenge!"

26. Teacher Satisfaction As a Function of Conditioning Factors in the School and Profession

Alexander M. Feldvebel

Job satisfaction is a rather global concept involving attitudes which people hold toward their work or toward factors associated with their work. The concept is not precise, and although it carries a lot of identical freight with such expressions as morale and esprit, we are not clear about the differences between these terms. The task of differentiating and explicating these concepts is outside of the scope of this paper. In spite of this objection, we will use these terms interchangeably and treat them as symbols of positive attitudes which individuals hold toward their work.

What is more, we must also be cautious about our assumptions concerning the sources of attitudes contributing to what we shall describe as job satisfaction. In a study conducted in industry, Brayfield and Crockett have warned against treating worker satisfaction as a global concept.[1] They have pointed out that most workers function in a number of social systems within and outside of the job situation. They also point out that conditions of the work performance on the job are seldom a means to satisfying relationships in all of these social systems. Differences in the orientation toward these various social systems and differences in the motivational struc-

---

[1] Arthur H. Brayfield and Walter H. Crockett, "Employee Attitudes and Employee Performance," *Psychological Bulletin.* Vol. 52, 1955, pp. 396–424.

Source: *The Clearing House,* XLIII, 1 (September 1968), 44–48. Reprinted by permission of the publisher.

tures of individuals accounts for a great deal of variability in job performance and job satisfaction within a work system that extends comparable, if not identical, work conditions to all its members.

It is one of our purposes here to examine a few of these conditioning factors in the school and teaching profession and to point out that motivational systems outside of, or ancillary to this job can be as potent in influencing individual attitudes as those inside of the system.

In addition to factors causing variability, there are those factors accounting for a commonality in experiences and the consequent common conditioning effect on attitudes. Some of these negative conditioning factors are so prevalent in the circumstances associated with teaching that one is inclined to consider them as almost indigenous to the profession. It is the position of this paper that although these pervasive factors are potent, their effects can be minimized and offset by imaginative personnel practices and policies.

Sex, Status, and Job Satisfaction in Teaching

Historically, the teaching profession in the United States has been a low status occupation. Josh Billings' nineteenth-century portrayal of "The Distrikt Skoolmaster" has been an image that has persisted throughout much of the history of education in the United States and has been softened only somewhat in recent times. As Billings relates, the "skoolmaster" is a man looked upon "with mixt pheelings of pitty and respekt." Josh also points out, "pitty and respekt, as a general mixtur, don't mix well." The present surge of teacher militancy is undoubtedly having a marked effect upon the remnants of the Billings' image of the schoolteacher.

Nevertheless, this heritage of low status has a marked conditioning effect upon those entering the profession and especially upon male teachers. The traditional male role as breadwinner has been embroidered with additional motives growing out of our middle-class orientation to the achievement and success ethic. Status and success are closely identified with a number of job characteristics, but pre-eminent among them is the factor of monetary remuneration. Low salary standards are, as a rule, related to low status. In our society the successful man is the man who earns a high income. Another low-status factor in teaching is the preoccupation with children, which has been traditionally viewed as the work of women.

A study of school climate in a large midwest suburban high school [2] supports the hypothesis that differences in levels of esprit among faculty members are associated with differences in sex. Esprit was here defined as

[2] "Articulation Study," Unpublished Report of a Study of School Climates Conducted in 1965–66 at Bloom Township High School, Chicago Heights, Illinois.

satisfaction derived from social and personal interactions in the school and was one subtest of an instrument intended to measure social climate in a school.

Lower male percepts of esprit in the school are probably further encouraged by the special control function which men are required to play in most school settings. Extra supervisory assignments in the school cafeteria, detention room, hall corridors, school bus, etc., are usually the domain of the male faculty member.

This finding leads to further speculation about differences between sexes in the profession. The greater need of the male for status in the occupation appears to be reflected, in part, in the distribution of sexes at the various grade levels of the school. Lowest status is associated with the youngest children at the lowest grade levels. This maldistribution is most evident at the primary school level for one extreme and at the college or university level at the other extreme. Here the ultimate in status is achieved when a professor has opted himself out of virtually all necessity to be associated with students and spends his time instead in the euphoria of research.

The content of instruction appears to be another factor associated with status. The more esoteric the content of instruction, the more prestige associated with the position. Once again, differences in the grade level of instruction are associated with prestige and the consequent maldistribution of sexes.

What are the implications of these observations? Social attitudes can be offset in part by internal motivational systems. Administrators have an obligation to devise other avenues for the achievement of status within the school and for providing means of achieving intrinsic satisfaction from teaching. A school climate which recognizes and rewards innovativeness and experimentation, a milieu which encourages the development of the teacher's personal characteristics as opposed to the standardization of the teaching role, and the encouragement of profession-wide interests and activities on the part of teachers are examples of interventions which can maximize internal satisfaction within the teaching profession.

Role Expectation, Socialization, and Depersonalization of Teacher-Pupil Relationships

In research reported by Dan Lortie [3] there is a hypothesis that teachers pass through three distinct stages. Stage one is characterized as a struggle to survive in coping with the day-to-day demands. Stage two is described as a period of experimentation in which the teacher is most likely to inno-

[3] Dan C. Lortie, "Teacher Socialization—The Robinson Crusoe Model," *The Real World of the Beginning Teacher,* Report of the Nineteenth National TEPS Conference, Hotel Commodore, New York City, 1965.

vate and exercise creative energies in his work. The third and final stage is seen as a period of crystallization in which the teacher settles into a stable pattern of routines and practices. Resistance to change is a hallmark of this last stage.

Once again, the school study reported earlier has provided additional evidence to support a finding arrived at independently by another author. In this study, pupils perceive significantly greater supportiveness among those teachers who differ from their colleagues primarily on the basis of amount of teaching experience.

We are inclined to agree that the beginning teacher in any school system must fight a battle for survival. A particularly important skirmish is the matter of coming to terms with the pupils over the respective roles of dominance and subordination.[4] This is a very unstable relationship, particularly for the new teacher, and it depends more upon the amount of prestige and personal ascendency that the teacher is able to establish than upon school sanctions and authority that may be brought to bear. This is a period of experimentation in which the teacher is developing his self-image and testing out any models that he may strive to emulate. At this stage the teacher is most concerned about teacher-pupil rapport and makes unusual efforts to be "liked" by his pupils.

The new teacher fights this battle between authority and rapport and over a period of time develops personal adaptations and a style to assure his ascendency. An important factor in this development is the process of socialization experienced through colleague relationships. Sanctions for the ascendency of the teacher in his classroom relationships come not only from the administration but also from fellow teachers to the extent that his status with fellow teachers and the administration frequently hinges upon his capacity to establish this ascendency over his pupils. More often than not, the advice and council received urges a relationship with pupils that is formal, impersonal, and marked by social distance. It is no wonder that the pupil sees such a teacher as restrictive rather than supportive.

A teacher in responding to administrative and community requirements for discipline and control tends to see this as a primary function of the teacher. His role, in *loco parentis*, is even sanctioned by the courts. The teacher who has mastered this role tends to place his relationship with students on a depersonalized level. Along with this, there may come a certain depersonalization of the teacher. The teacher learns from his colleagues that he must maintain this social distance and depersonalization in order to carry out his control role as expected.

The teacher spends the vast majority of his time in interaction with students; it is highly unlikely that the kind of relationship described here will

[4] Arthur L. Stinchcombe, *Rebellion in a High School.* Chicago: Quadrangle Books, Inc., 1964. Stinchcombe's study points up very poignantly the extent of the current rebellion against the traditional doctrine of adolescent inferiority.

produce many satisfying personal experiences and it will minimize the personal influence that teachers may have upon pupils. It is suggested that precisely here is where the potential for satisfaction from pupil relationships is greatest.

One of the obvious implications is that programs of instructional supervision must take into much greater account the complexity and subtlety of the authority-rapport problem of the classroom teachers. There must be more satisfying ways of managing and directing pupil behavior than through a rigid formalization of relationships. It is suspected that a great many matters which are treated as behavior problems are in fact instructional problems. To treat these issues as behavior problems may resolve them in the short run, but they will reoccur for continual confrontation in the long run. Perceptive supervision must lay emphasis upon those instructional shortcomings which may be the source of behavior problems.

It must also be stressed that, although the teacher's role in the classroom is one which requires direction and control of pupil behavior, there is a wide choice of modes of control open to the teacher. The modes of command and punishment are styles which, if used to the exclusion of other forms of more personal influence, are sterile and self-defeating techniques in pupil relationships.

The Stereotype Syndrome

In Lortie's research [5] it is reported that after five years of teaching experience the teacher tends to become more conservative and resistant to change. He attributes this to the "moss of psychological investment" that the teacher has in the particular style or mode of teaching which he has developed. In the study of school climates there is an indication that pupils perceive instruction by the more experienced teacher as more "task oriented" and more "routine" whereas the younger teacher is seen as more "stimulating." These perceptions are supported by the teacher's own perceptions of the classroom climate.

As we have already suggested, the teacher in his early years of experience has not yet established a firm professional self-concept. The whole experience of teaching must be described as experimental at this stage. The teacher is experimenting with subject matter, with his teaching methods, and in his relationships with pupils. In addition, he is closer in age and outlook to his students. All of this introduces variability into his job and his outlook toward the job.

There is, however, the risk in teaching, as in any other profession requiring a habitual response to recurring social situations, to respond in

[5] *Op. cit.*

stereotyped ways. The development of specialization and a proficiency along a particular line may be responsible for a loss in general adaptability and a deepening of certain grooves. As we have indicated, the experienced teacher sooner or later develops his self-concept as a teacher and more likely than not he resolves the problems of student relationships on the side of authority, dignity, and social distance. Intercourse with students is limited to "business" and relationships tend to be characterized by a shutting off of any student behavior which threatens this equilibrium.

In addition, the experienced teacher may come to look upon his task as a continuously recurring demand to "drill" his students. The zest of exploration and experimentation may have lost its glow and the teacher may become cynical by what is sometimes described as the "drag of the adolescent mind."

It is clear that these kinds of attitudes do not develop in all experienced teachers nor are we prepared to say what proportion of them can be described by this process. The answer to this problem lies perhaps in a closer look at the experienced teacher for whom teaching is a continuous experiment requiring continuous adaptation and renewal of outlook.

We are inclined to believe that the process of team teaching, at its best, carries with it an inherent tendency to bring out the dynamic and self-renewing aspect of teaching. There is a built-in requirement of continuous professional dialogue with colleagues and an incentive to teach well not only for the sake of students but almost as much for the fellow teachers who are also observers. Once again, an incentive or a motivational system ancillary to the classroom can have a significant bearing on job performance and job satisfaction.

In summary, we can see that teacher satisfaction is subject to conditioning by factors inside and outside of the profession. To understand these various motivational systems and the effect that they have upon teacher attitudes is a first step in devising policies and in developing an organizational climate which will minimize negative effects and maximize positive tendencies.

The whole question of how job satisfaction may be related to job performance is another problem. We will not attempt to explore this question, although there exists an unexamined assumption that higher teacher satisfaction will be reflected in improved job performance. Whether or not this is true, it would seem that the encouragement of positive work attitudes and the feeling of personal well-being associated with this is an end worthwhile in itself. The school administrator must recognize that the ideographic goals and purposes of individuals in the organization are his legitimate concern even though they cannot be demonstrably related to the furtherance of organization goals.

V. The Pupils

The school exists for pupils who come in all sizes, colors, and creeds, and with widely varying abilities and capacities. Teachers need always to keep in mind that their responsibility is to help each youngster meet his own unique needs, whatever these may be, and that each youngster needs to take on increasing responsibility for his own education.

This part is concerned with the pupils in the school and the responsibilities of teachers to pupils in their classrooms. The emphasis is on the pupils as learners.

"How Children Learn" by John Blackie, an educational leader in England, is the title of the article that leads off this part. Advocating the pursuit of all promising inquiry techniques in discovering how learning is accomplished, Mr. Blackie points up the importance of the learning theories of Jean Piaget, the importance of play activity for young children, the place of language in a child's learning, and, finally, the role of teachers in the process of putting into practice the knowledge gained from research and experience.

Next Jerome S. Bruner, in "Man: A Course of Study," emphasizes the importance of pupils learning that man is distinctive in his adaptation to the world and that there is discernible continuity between man and his animal forebears. Bruner then lists and discusses the five great humanizing forces, each of which defines the distinctiveness of man and his potentiality for further evolution.

If we are to develop effective educational systems and practitioners such as farmers and physicians, we will need to develop and use more practices based on a scientific understanding of how learning takes place. So believes James L. McGaugh, who states these beliefs in "Some Changing Concepts about Learning and Memory." McGaugh discusses current theories and implications emerging from recent scientific findings, and suggests, among other ideas, the discarding of intelligence tests as we know them today.

In "Why Inquiry?" Owen A. Hagen and Steve T. Stansberry restate the strong case that already exists in favor of the problem-solving and other investigation-oriented teaching methods. They hold that such methods develop a more responsible, self-directed, and active pupil.

Finally, David Elkind, in "Giant in the Nursery—Jean Piaget," brings into focus the long and distinguished career of the famous Swiss psychologist whose theories on learning developed more than thirty years ago are now becoming "late" educational research in the United States. The article describes the three phases of Piaget's learning theory and illustrates a number of his studies on how children learn. Appropriately, Elkind concludes that teachers, after becoming acquainted with Piaget's work, can never again see children in the same way.

27. How Children Learn

John Blackie

The human race learned and achieved an enormous amount long before anyone began to think about the learning process. Man developed social institutions; discovered fire; and learned to feed, clothe, and protect his family without worrying very much about how he did it. One might conclude from the fact of man's survival that concern with the theory of learning is unnecessary and a waste of time, that experience and intuition will equip a teacher to teach.

Of course, knowledge of the latest theory of learning does not guarantee good teaching. Also, the urge to learn is so powerful in young children that they will survive quite a lot of mismanagement and discouragement, though by no means unscathed. And certainly educational thinkers are not all of one mind about the learning process—a great deal still is not known about it.

These might be good arguments for leaving the matter to the researchers until they can tell us more, while parents and teachers continue to work intuitively and pragmatically. But the validity of such arguments is questionable. No one really believes that all children make the most of themselves. The school is not equally successful with all, one of the reasons being the fact that not enough is known about the learning needs of children and therefore some of them receive the wrong treatment in school.

If we can discover anything about this process that will help us to help children to learn more, better, and more easily, we would be very wrong to neglect to do so simply because we cannot discover *everything*.

Basic, scientifically conducted research is essential, but it needs to be fed by the observation and trials and errors of countless teachers and parents. Intuition and experience have not found all the answers for all the children all of the time, but it would be a bad day for education if they came into disrepute. The only sensible course is to pursue all promising lines of inquiry.

SOURCE: *NEA Journal*, LVII, 2 (February 1968), 40–42. Reprinted by permission of the Controller of Her Britannic Majesty's Stationery Office.

A theory of learning that has received wide acceptance is Jean Piaget's. Piaget conducted an immense number of investigations into the ways in which children learn. He describes learning as being composed of two processes—assimilation and accommodation. Assimilation is what is done to what has to be learned so that it can be learned, and accommodation is what the learner has to do within himself in order to learn.

A very simple example may make this clearer. To learn to open a door, a child has to manipulate the handle, find out whether the door needs pushing or pulling, and what the weight of the door is. This is assimilation. But he must also do the right things, turn the handle the right way, push or pull with appropriate force, and thus accommodate himself to the experience of door opening. Through this process, the child establishes a pattern of behavior that Piaget calls a *schema* (pl. *schemata*)—something that can be repeated and generalized. Each time the child encounters the door, the *schema* is repeated.

But not all doors are the same. They have different kinds of handles. Some have latches. Some open out, some inward. Some are heavy; some are light. Each of these unfamiliar features will require assimilation and accommodation. The original simple *schema* will have to be modified.

Modifications will always be needed whenever a new experience is encountered. An elderly man who thinks he knows all about opening doors will have to assimilate and accommodate when he first meets one that opens automatically by means of a photoelectric cell, as he approaches it. His experience with this new kind of door will be momentarily disconcerting.

The process of assimilation and accommodation begins at birth, increases in intensity in early childhood, and continues throughout life, though the ability to assimilate and accommodate in most people declines as they grow older. The *schemata* increase in number, grow more and more complex, and interact with each other. In the early stages, learning takes place in the sensory-motor field. Children must see, hear, feel, smell, or taste things in order to learn what they are. They cannot yet learn by being told. They cannot form abstract or imaginary concepts.

They learn, too, by their own movement. They find that they cannot touch everything they see. They must stretch out or crawl in order to reach a desired object. Only later can they judge distance, and, much later still, understand what is meant when they are told of a distance. ("It is five miles from here.") As they grow older, they can assimilate abstractions and accommodate themselves to them. A mathematical process, a discussion of a seventeenth-century political issue, a debate on the existence of God—the process remains essentially the same.

But by the time this stage of learning is reached, the individual has undergone an immensely complex change. Each new experience, however slight, has had to be assimilated, and the resultant accommodation has slightly modified the whole system of the *schemata* that add up to the individual as he is.

Two points about *schemata* must be mentioned here. First, they need exercising. Everyone is familiar with this truth at the adult stage. "I used to play tennis a lot, but now I can hardly hit a ball." "I haven't read any Latin for years; I wouldn't understand a word now." Remarks like these are often heard, but they generally refer to matters of marginal importance or to activities which need the strength and vigor of youth for their performance.

If they had been of major importance they would not have been forgotten. But with young children *everything* is important. They are learning about the world they live in, and they must be allowed to do things over and over again and thus reassure themselves that what they have learned is true; that patterns do repeat themselves; that things, if not people, are constant.

The other point about *schemata* is that exercising them is pleasurable. Piaget has collected a great deal of evidence to this effect, and common observation confirms it. Anyone who has watched a two-year-old trying to fit two things together has noticed his smile and his delight when the task is accomplished. But many parents do not regard that sort of activity as learning. They think of it as play, and as the child grows older and goes to school, they contrast it with something different called work.

This business of play, and its contrast with work, now needs our attention. Presumably, children have played since the earliest days of man, but it was not until the appearance of Froebel's *The Education of Man* (in 1826 that the importance of play as a means of learning was first realized. Although all educators now recognize the value of play in the learning process, it is still little understood by many parents. If parents were to observe their children's play closely and systematically, they would soon realize that play is much more than the release of surplus energy. It is something undertaken with great seriousness and concentration and is unmistakably important to the child.

What is he doing as we watch him? For much of the time, he is finding out about materials. He is pouring water from one vessel to another, squeezing it out of a sponge, running it through a sieve, splashing it, using it to wet other things. He is running sand or earth through his fingers, building it into heaps, digging holes in it. He is piling blocks on top of each other, knocking them down again. He is trying to lift or drag heavy things; throwing light things into the air and watching them float or fall to the ground again.

These and countless similar kinds of play are the ways in which children discover the nature of materials and begin to form concepts of weight, size, texture, softness, hardness, plasticity, impermeability, transparency, and so on. In playing with materials, children begin also to discover the possibilities and limitations of their own powers. They can reach some things and not others. They can hold wet sand, but dry sand runs away. They can hold clay but not water. They can destroy what they have made. They can break a stick but not a log.

Through this kind of play, they unconsciously explore the physical world and discover how that world is related to their own inner feelings. Anyone who grew up without this ability to relate the physical world to himself would not survive for long. A knowledge of the properties of materials, of how they behave in particular circumstances, is vital in both primitive and advanced societies.

It is equally important for children to understand adults. Children are surrounded by adults who control the greater part of their day and who themselves are occupied in all sorts of ways that the child sees and wants to understand.

Once again, the child gains his knowledge through his play. He imitates the adults. He plays at being father or mother. Dolls and teddy bears become children whom he feeds, clothes, teaches, and punishes. By means of this fantasy or pretending, he begins to discover what it is like to be father or mother and thus he begins to understand their behavior.

All the adults who impinge on his life tend to be imitated—not only parents, but the milkman, the truck driver, the doctor, the mailman. And not only people: He will be a dog or a horse or a tiger he has seen at the zoo. His play serves a further purpose: It helps him to understand his own role, and at the same time enables him to escape from that role, to try other possibilities.

The situations that turn up in the child's life will also be dealt with by play. He will repeat a painful situation in play—an accident, a death, a parting—in order to make it more tolerable, to "live with it." Sometimes he reenacts the situation many times, and usually adds to it. Features that were suppressed in the first enactment are brought in until the whole experience comes into focus and control. This particular characteristic of play is often most clearly seen in child guidance clinics; a child who is deeply disturbed will, over a period of time, play out the situation that is causing the trouble and, to that extent, cure himself.

Around the end of the first year of life, the child begins to develop language. This is an exciting moment for young parents. Their baby is at last going to be able to communicate with them, to *tell* them what he has been feeling and thinking all this time. They give him every encouragement. They talk to him and listen to him. They do no systematic teaching, and yet by the time the child starts school, he has performed the most difficult learning feat of his whole life. He knows two or three thousand words, and he can speak fluently and clearly. How has this come about?

Various influences have been at work. A vital condition of learning has been supplied by his parents, who have encouraged, joined in, answered questions, read aloud, corrected. When they have *not* done this, the consequences are painfully obvious.

The influence of play is equally vital. The meanings of a great many words can only be learned through play. If we watch the play of children from age 2 or 3 right on through the early elementary grades, we notice how much language enters into it.

The meaning of a word is not usually an exact and limited thing which, once learned, is fixed and complete. "Daddy," for instance, is the man who lives in the house, who goes out in the morning and comes back in the evening, who shares a bedroom with Mommy, who fixes things, who sometimes gets very cross and irritable, who comes home drunk, and the like. The child at play mimes these and other appropriate characteristics, and uses and learns the words that stand for them.

He goes through the same process with materials. He learns the word *water* quite early, but its full range of suggestion can only be learned through play, through his having discovered all the things that water can and cannot do as well as the words (run, soak, drip, boil, freeze, gurgle, splash, etc.) that stand for those things.

All this continues to be true of children when they reach school age. It is not made less true by the fact that school represents a new phase of life and that most children expect to learn new things there. But the shock of separation from home and of finding oneself in a crowd of others is, for many children, quite considerable, and the experience requires its own period of assimilation and accommodation before the new demands become insistent.

What is more to the point, however, is that the process of learning develops gradually, and play continues to be of the greatest importance as a means of understanding and learning. If play is eliminated too soon, the delight and pleasure of learning may go with it and drudgery may take their place. Indeed, play is valuable in all work throughout life.

Watch a man cultivating a garden and, whether he is doing it for a living or as a hobby, do you not detect an element in the work that can be properly called play? When that element is absent, work becomes dull, repetitive, uninspiring, and worth doing only because you make money by it.

We have been talking so far almost as if teachers did not exist, as if all that was necessary for the education of children were intelligent parents and the right materials. It is perfectly true that the work of a teacher is much easier and much more productive if he has intelligent cooperation from parents and that, given suitable material, children will learn a great deal without further help from adults. Take a three-year-old down to the seashore, and you will not have to tell him what to do with sand, and stones, and shells.

I have intentionally emphasized this early stage of learning, because what goes on in the modern elementary school cannot be understood without some knowledge of it. This emphasis, however, must not lead anyone to believe that the role of the teacher is any the less important. Far from it! To apply the knowledge gained from research and experience makes very heavy demands on the patience, good humor, energy, ability, and skill of the teacher.

28. Man: A Course of Study

Jerome S. Bruner

There is a dilemma in describing a course of study. One must begin by setting forth the intellectual substance of what is to be taught, else there can be no sense of what challenges and shapes the curiosity of the student. Yet the moment one succumbs to the temptation to "get across" the subject, at that moment the ingredient of pedagogy is in jeopardy. For it is only in a trivial sense that one gives a course to "get something across," merely to impart information. There are better means to that end than teaching. Unless the learner also masters himself, disciplines his taste, deepens his view of the world, the "something" that is got across is hardly worth the effort of transmission.

The more "elementary" a course and the younger its students, the more serious must be its pedagogical aim of forming the intellectual powers of those whom it serves. It is as important to justify a good mathematics course by the intellectual discipline it provides or the honesty it promotes as by the mathematics it transmits. Indeed, neither can be accomplished without the other.

Structure of the Course

The content of the course is man: his nature as a species, the forces that shaped and continue to shape his humanity. Three questions recur throughout:

SOURCE: *Social Studies Curriculum Project* (Watertown, Mass.: Educational Services, Summer–Fall 1965), pp. 3–11. Reprinted by permission of the Education Development Center, Inc., Cambridge, Mass.

What is human about human beings?
How did they get that way?
How can they be made more so?

We seek exercises and materials through which our pupils can learn wherein man is distinctive in his adaptation to the world, and wherein there is discernible continuity between him and his animal forebears. For man represents that crucial point in evolution where adaptation is achieved by the vehicle of culture and only in a minor way by further changes in his morphology. Yet there are chemical tides that run in his blood that are as ancient as the reptiles. We make every effort at the outset to *tell* the children where we hope to travel with them. Yet little of such recounting gets through. It is much more useful, we have found, to pose the three questions directly to the children so that their own views can be brought into the open and so that they can establish some points of view of their own.

In pursuit of our questions we shall explore five matters, each closely associated with the evolution of man as a species, each defining at once the distinctiveness of man and his potentiality for further evolution. The five great humanizing forces are, of course, tool-making, language, social organization, the management of man's prolonged childhood, and man's urge to explain. It has been our first lesson in teaching that no pupil, however eager, can appreciate the relevance of, say, tool-making in human evolution without first grasping the fundamental concept of a tool or what a language is or a myth or social organization. These are not obvious matters. So we are involved in teaching not only the role of tools or language in the emergence of man, but as a necessary precondition for doing so, setting forth the fundamentals of linguistics or the theory of tools. And it is as often the case as not that (as in the case of the "theory of tools") we must solve a formidable intellectual problem ourselves in order to be able to help our pupils do the same.

While one readily singles out these five massive contributors to man's humanization, under no circumstances can they be put into airtight compartments. Human kinship is distinctively different from primate mating patterns precisely because it is classificatory and rests on man's ability to use language. Or, if you will, tool-use enhances the division of labor in a society which in turn affects kinship. And language itself is more clearly appreciated by reference to its acquisition in the uniquely human interaction between child and parent. Obviously, the nature of man's world view, whether formulated in myth or in science, depends upon and is constrained by the nature of human language. So while each domain can be treated as a separate set of ideas, as we shall see, success in teaching depends upon making it possible for children to have a sense of their interaction.

Language

Teaching the essentials of linguistics to children in the elementary grades has limits, but they are wider than we had expected. There are certain pedagogic precautions to be respected if ten-year-olds are to be captivated by the subject. It must not, to begin with, be presented as a normative subject—as an exercise in how things *should* be written or said. It must, moreover, be disassociated from such traditional "grammar" as the child has encountered. There is nothing so deadening as to have a child handle the "type-and-order" problem by "recognizing" one category of words as "nouns" and parroting, upon being asked what he means by a noun, that it is a "person, place, or thing." It is not that he is either "right" or "wrong," but rather that he is as remote from the issue as he would be if he attempted to account for grief over the assassination of a President by citing the Constitution on the division of powers. And finally, the discussion needs to remain close to the nature of language in use, its likely origin, and the functions to which it is put.

Whether it is true or not that a ten-year-old has a complete grammatical repertory, he is certainly capable of, and delighted in, recognizing all linguistic features when confronted with instances of them. The chief aid to such recognition is contrast—the opportunity to observe the oppositional features that are so much a feature of human language. What comes hard is to formulate these features conceptually; to go beyond the intuitive grasp of the native speaker to the more self-conscious understanding of the linguist. It is this task—getting children to look at and to ponder the things they can notice in their language long enough to understand them —that is most difficult and it should not be pushed to the point of tedium.

Our section on language includes a consideration of what communication is—by contrasting how humans and animals manage to send and receive messages. The early sessions have proved lively and in the course of them nearly every major issue of linguistics is raised and allowed to go begging. This preliminary exercise has the great virtue that it can be repeated on later occasions, when students have achieved varying levels of sophistication, with the result that they readily recognize how much progress they have made.

The opening session (or sessions, for students often want to continue the arguments over animals and humans) usually indicates which among several openings can be best pursued in later units. The instance which follows is influenced by far too little experience to be considered the general rule, but it is at least one example.

The discussion led naturally to the design features of a language. We designed a language game based on bee language, requiring the children to find hidden objects by using messages in this bee-like language. The children are encouraged to design similar languages and to improve on the design of the language used. They take to this readily and are eager to discuss and make clearer such design features as semanticity, voice-ear link, displacement, and cultural transmission. The game, of course, is a lead into the demonstration of bee language as presented in the von Frisch film (which is not altogether satisfactory). We were struck, however, at how much more interested the children were in talking about their own language than in discussing bee language or von Frisch's analysis of it. It is as if the bee linguistics were interesting as an introduction into the closer analysis of their own language.

Our next objective is to present the powerful ideas of arbitrariness, of productivity, and of duality of patterning, the latter the exclusive property of human language. We have approached arbitrariness by the conventional route of comparing how pictures, diagrams, charades, and words refer to things. There are nice jokes to be used, as in the example given by Hockett of the tiny word *whale* referring to a big thing, while the large word *microorganism* refers to a tiny one. With respect to productivity, we have had considerable initial success with two exercises. The first is with a language containing four types (how, what, when, where) with a limited number of tokens of each type (e.g., by hand, by weapon, by trap, as tokens of the "how" type) and with a highly constrained set of orders each referring to a different kind of food-related activity. By this means we readily establish the idea of *type* and *order* as two basic ideas. They readily grasp the idea of substitutivity of tokens within a type. (Indeed, given the interest in secret codes based on substitution of words or letters for code breaking, they need little instruction on this score.)

Once the ideas of type and order are established, we begin the following amusing exercises to illustrate the interchangeability of language frames. We present:

1	2	3	4	5
The	man	ate	his	lunch
A	lady	wore	my	hat
This	doctor	broke	a	bottle
My	son	drove	our	car

and the children are now asked to provide "matching" examples. They can do so readily. They soon discover that so long as they pick words in the order 1 2 3 4 5, from any place in each column, something "sensible" can be got—even if it is silly or not true, like "My doctor wore a car," or "A lady ate a bottle," it is at least not "crazy" like "Man the lunch his ate."

The students need no urging to construct new frames and to insert additional types into frames already set up (like a new first column the tokens of which include *did, can, has,* etc.). Interesting discoveries are made—

such as the relative openness of some positions and the closed nature of others. We hope to devise methods to help the children discover some of the deeper features of grammar, better to grasp what a language is—for example, that one can start with relatively simple sentence frames, "kernel sentences," and transform them progressively into negatives, queries, and passives, or any two or even three of these, and that more complex forms can be returned to simpler forms by applying the transformations in reverse.

Finally, a game has been devised (a game involving signaling at sea) to illustrate duality of patterning, that most difficult feature of human language. It involves developing a language initially with a very limited set of building blocks (as with human languages, each of which combines intrinsically meaningless sound elements, phones, into a unique system that renders them into meaningful phonemes, a change in one of which will alter the meaning of a word so that, in English, *rob* and *lob* are different words, but not so in Japanese where /r/ and /l/ are allophones of the same phoneme just as plosive /p/ (*pin*) and non-plosive /p/ (*spin*) are "the same" for us but not for others). Three kinds of word blocks can be arranged in a frame, making twenty-seven possible "words" or lexemes. But there must be rules as to which combinations mean things and which do not. It is very quickly apparent to the children that the blocks as such "mean" nothing, but the frames do—or some do and some do not. We are in progress of going from this point toward other aspects of duality at this time.

It is a natural transition to go from syntax to the question of how language is acquired by young humans and other primates. We shall use the considerable resources provided by recent studies of language acquisition to show the manner in which syntax emerges from certain very elementary forms such as the pivot-plus-open-class and the head-plus-attribute. The idea of "writing a grammar" for any form of speech encountered will also be presented. In addition, the child-adult "expansion-idealization" cycle will be explored as an example of a powerful form of social grouping that is crucial for transmitting the language. For contrast, we hope to examine the problems of language development of Vicki, a chimpanzee raised by a family along with their own child of like age. The subtle problem of "traditional" and "hereditary" transmission is bound to emerge.

Finally, and with the benefit of their newly gained insight into the nature of language, we shall return to the question of the origins of human language and its role in shaping human characteristics. We hope first to cover the newly available materials on the universal characteristics of all human languages—first getting the children to make some informed guesses on the subject. Then we shall consider the role of language in the organization of the early human group and the effectiveness it might add to such group activities as hunting, given its design features and its universals. To go from this point to a consideration of myth and its nature is not a difficult step.

Tool-Making

One starts with several truths about children and "tools." They have usually not used many of them, and in general, tools will not be of much interest. This may derive from the deeper truth that, in general, children (like their urban parents) think of tools as set pieces that are to be bought in hardware stores. And finally, children in our technologically mature society usually have little notion of the relation between tools and our way of life. Production takes place in factories where they have never been, its products are packaged to disguise the production process that brought them into being.

The tool unit is still under discussion. What follows are some of the leading ideas that animate the design of the unit.

We begin with a philosophical approach to the nature of tool-using. What is most characteristic of any kind of tool-using is not the tools themselves, but rather the program that guides their use. It is in this broader sense that tools take on their proper meaning as amplifiers of human capacities and implementers of human activity.

Seen as amplifiers, tools can fall into three general classes—amplifiers of sensory capacities, of motor capacities, and of ratiocinative capacities. Within each type there are many subspecies. There are sensory amplifiers like microscopes and ear horns that are "magnifiers," others, like spirit levels and bobs, that are "reference markers," etc. Some implement systems "stretch out" time (slow motion cinematography) and others condense it (time-lapse registration). In the realm of motor amplifiers, some tools provide a basis for binding, some for penetrating, some even for steadying —as when one of our pupils described a draughtman's compass as a "steadying tool." And, of course, there are the "soft tools" of ratiocination such as mathematics and logic and the "hard tools" they make possible, ranging from the abacus to the high speed digital computer and the automaton.

Once we think of tools as imbedded in a program of use—as implementers of human activity—then it becomes possible to deal with the basic idea of substitutability, an idea as crucial to language as it is to tools. If one cannot find a certain word or phrase, a near-equivalent can be substituted in its place. So too with tools: if a skilled carpenter happens not to have brought his chisel to the job, he can usually substitute something else in its place—the edge of a plane blade, a pocket knife, etc. In short, tools are not fixed, and the "functional fixedness" found by so many psychologists studying problem-solving comes finally because so much thinking about tools fixes them to convention—a hammer is for nails and nothing but nails.

Our ultimate object in teaching about tools is, as noted before, not so much to explicate tools and their significance, but to explore how tools affected man's evolution. The evidence points very strongly to the central part in evolution played by natural selection favoring the user of spontaneous pebble tools over those proto-hominids who depended upon their formidable jaws and dentition. In time, survival depended increasingly on the capacities of the tool-user and tool-maker—not only his opposable forefinger and thumb, but the nervous system to go with them. Within a few hundred thousand years after the first primitive tool-using appears, man's brain size more than doubles. Evolution (or more simply, survival) favored the larger brained creatures capable of adapting by the use of tools, and brain size seems to have been roughly correlated with that capacity. There are many fascinating concomitants to this story. Better weapons meant a shift to carnivorousness. This in turn led to leisure—or at least less food-gathering—which in turn makes possible permanent or semipermanent settlement. Throughout, the changes produced lead to changes in way of life, changes in culture and social organization, changes in what it is possible to do.

A few of the exercises being planned to the "tool section" give some flavor of the pedagogy. One unit calls for the taking of a "census of skills" —the tasks that children know how to perform, along with some effort to examine how they were learned (including tool skills). Another unit consists of trying to design an "all-purpose" tool so that the children can have some notion of the programmatic questions one asks in designing a tool and why specialized use has a role.

There will also be an opportunity (of which more in a later section) for the children to compare "tool play" of an Eskimo boy and Danai boy of New Guinea with the play of immature free-ranging baboons, macaques, and chimpanzees. We are also in process of obtaining films on the technique of manufacture of flint implements and hope also to obtain inexpensive enough materials to have our pupils try their hand at flint knapping and other modes of instrument making, guided possibly by films on the subject by the distinguished French archeologist, Dr. Bordes.

There will be some treatment of tools to make tools as well as of tools that control various forms of natural power. A possible route into this discussion is an overview of the evolution of tool-making generally—from the first "spontaneous" or picked-up tools, to the shaped ones, to those shaped to a pattern, to modern conceptions of man-machine relations as in contemporary systems research. Indeed, if we do follow this approach we shall also explore the design of a game of tool design involving variables such as cost, time, gain, specificity of function, and skill required, with the object of making clear the programmatic nature of tools and the manner in which tools represent a selective extension of human powers.

Social Organization

The section on social organization is still in preliminary planning, save in one respect where work is quite well advanced. The unit has as its objective to make children aware that there is a structure in a society and that this structure is not fixed once and for all. It is an integrated pattern and you cannot change one part of the pattern without other parts of the society changing with it. The way a society arranges itself for carrying out its affairs depends upon a variety of factors ranging from its ecology at one end to the irreversible course of its history and world view at the other.

A first task is to lead children to recognize explicitly certain basic patterns in the society around them, patterns they know well in an implicit, intuitive way—the distinction between kin and others, between face-to-face groups and secondary groups, between reference groups and ones that have corporate being. These, we believe, are distinctions that children easily discover. We should also like the children to grasp the rather abstract fact that within most human groups beyond the immediate family, continuity depends not so much upon specific people, but upon "roles" filled by people—again, as with language and tool-use, there are structures with substitutability.

Such social organization is marked by reciprocity and exchange—cooperation is compensated by protection, service by fee, and so on. There is always giving and getting. There are, moreover, forms of legitimacy and sanction that define the limits of possible behavior in any given role. They are the bounds set by a society and do not depend upon the individual's choice. Law is the classic case, but not the only one. One cannot commit theft legally, but then too one cannot ignore friends with impunity and law has nothing to do with it.

A society, moreover, has a certain world view, a way of defining what is "real," what is "good," what is "possible." To this matter we turn in a later section, mentioning it here only to complete our catalogue of aspirations of ideas we hope to introduce in this part of the course.

We believe that these matters can be presented to children in a fashion that is gripping, close to life, and intellectually honest. The pedagogy is scarcely clear, but we are on the track of some interesting ways of operating. One difficulty with social organization is its ubiquity. Contrast may be our best way of saving social organization from obviousness—by comparing our own forms of social organization with those of baboon troops, of

Eskimo, of Bushmen, of prehistoric man as inferred from exacavated living floors in Europe and East Africa. But beyond this we are now developing a "family" of games designed to bring social organization into the personal consciousness of the children.

The first of these games, "Hunting," is designed to simulate conditions in an early human group engaged in hunting and is patterned on the life and ecology of the Bushmen of the Kalahari desert. The elements of the game are Hunters, Prey, Weapons, Habitats, Messages, Predators, and Food. Without going into detail, the game simulates (in the manner of so-called Pentagon games used for increasing the sensitivities of generals) the problem of planning how far one wishes to go in search of various kinds of game, how resources need to be shared by a group to go beyond "varmint" hunting to larger game, how differentiation of labor can come about in weapon-making and weapon-using, how one must decide among different odds in hunting in one terrain or another. Given the form of the game (for which we are principally grateful to Dr. Clark Abt), its content can be readily varied to fit the conditions of life of other hunting groups, such as the Eskimo, again with the object of contrast.

What has proved particularly interesting in our early work with the game is that it permits the grouping of a considerable amount of "real" material around it—accounts of the life of the Kalahari Bushmen (of which there is an extraordinarily rich record on film and in both literary and monographic form), their myths and art, the "forbiddingly" desert ecology that is their environment. And so too with the Eskimo, should we go ahead to construct an analogue game for them, for we are in possession of an equally rich documentation on the Netsilik Eskimo of Pelly Bay. . . .

Child Rearing

This unit has just begun to take shape at the time of writing. It is proceeding on three general themes in the hope of clarifying them by reference to particular materials in the areas of language, of social organization, of tool-making, and of childhood generally. The first general theme is the extent to which and the manner in which the long human childhood (assisted as it is by language) leads to the dominance of sentiment in human life, in contrast to instinctual patterns of gratification and response found to predominate at levels below man. That is to say, affect can now be aroused and controlled by symbols—human beings have an attitude about anger rather than just anger or not anger. The long process of sentiment formation requires both an extended childhood and access to a symbolized culture through language. Without sentiment (or values or the "second signal system" or whatever term one prefers) it is highly unlikely that human society or anything like it would be possible.

A second theme is organized around the human (perhaps primate) tendency toward mastery of skill for its own sake—the tendency of the human being, in his learning of the environment, to go beyond immediate adaptive necessity toward innovation. Recent work on human development has underlined this "push toward effectance," as it has been called. It is present in human play, in the increased variability of human behavior when things get under control. Just as William James commented three-quarters of a century ago that habit was the fly-wheel of society, we can now say that the innovative urge is the accelerator.

The third theme concerns the shaping of the man by the patterning of childhood—that while all humans are intrinsically human, the expression of their humanity is affected by what manner of childhood they have experienced.

The working out of these themes has only begun. One exercise now being tried out is to get children to describe differences between infancy, childhood, and adulthood for different species—using live specimens brought to class (in the case of non-human species) or siblings for humans. For later distribution, of course, the live specimens (and siblings) will be rendered on film. Yet the success of a session, say, with a ten-day-old, stud-tailed macaque suggests that the real thing should be used whenever possible.

World View

The fifth unit in preparation concerns itself with man's drive to explicate and represent his world. While it concerns itself with myth, with art, with primitive legend, it is only incidentally designed to provide the stories, the images, the religious impulses, and the mythic romance of man's being. It would be more accurate to describe the unit as "beginning philosophy" in both senses of that expression—philosophy at the beginning and, perhaps, philosophy for young beginners.

Central to the unit is the idea that men everywhere are humans, however advanced or "primitive" their civilization. The difference is not one of more or less than human, but of how particular human societies express their human capacities. A remark by the French anthropologist, Levi-Strauss, puts it well.

Prevalent attempts to explain alleged differences between the so-called primitive mind and scientific thought have resorted to qualitative differences between the working processes of the mind in both cases, while assuming that the entities which they were studying remained very much the same. If our interpretation is correct, we are led toward a completely different view—namely, that the kind of logic in mythical thought is as rigorous as that of modern science, and that the difference lies, not in the quality of the intellectual process, but in the nature of things to which it is applied. This is well in agreement with the situation known to prevail in the field of technology: What makes a steel ax superior to a stone ax is not that the first one is better made than the second. They are equally well made, but steel is quite different from stone. In the same way we may be able to show that the same logical processes operate in myth as in science, and that man has always been thinking equally well; the improvement lies, not in the alleged progress of man's mind, but in the discovery of new areas to which it may apply its unchanged and unchanging powers.

All cultures are created equal. One society—say, that of Eskimos—may have only a few tools, but they are used in a versatile way. The woman's knife does what our scissors do, but it also serves to scrape hides, and to clean and thin them. The man's knife is used for killing and skinning animals, carving wood and bone, cutting snow for building blocks for the igloo, chopping meat into bites. Such simple weapons are "the mother of tools," and by specialization a number of tools derive from them. What is "lost" in variety of tools is won in the versatility of uses; in brief, an Eskimo man and wife have tools for all their tasks and can carry most of these tools about with them at all times.

So too with symbolic systems. The very essence of being human is in the use of symbols. We do not know what the hierarchy of primacy is between speech, song, dance, and drawing; but, whichever came first, as soon as it stood for something else other than the act itself, man was born; as soon as it caught on with another man, culture was born, and as soon as there were two symbols, a system was born. A dance, a song, a painting, and a narrative can all symbolize the same thing. They do so differently. One way of searching for the structure of a world view is to take an important narrative and to see what it ultimately tells. A narrative, or at least a corpus of narratives, may be what philosophy used to be. It may reflect what is believed about the celestial bodies and their relation to man, it may tell how man came into being, how social life was founded, what is believed about death and about life after death, it may codify law and morals. In short, it may give expression to the group's basic tenets on astronomy, theology, sociology, law, education, even esthetics.

In studying symbolic systems, we want the students to understand myths rather than to learn them. We will give them examples from simple cultures for the same reason for which the anthropologist travels into an isolated society. Our hope is to lead the children to understand how man goes about explaining his world, making sense of it, and that one kind of explanation is no more human than another.

We have selected for our starting point some hunting societies. An Eskimo society, a Bushman society, an Australian aboriginal society will certainly suffice to show what the life experience of hunting peoples is. From the scrutiny of the myths of these groups, it is immediately clear that you can tell a society by the narratives it keeps. The ecology, the economy, the social structure, the tasks of men and women, and the fears and anxieties are reflected in the stories, and in a way which the children can handle. One good example of Eskimo narrative or Eskimo poetry, if skillfully handled in class, can show the child that the problems of an Eskimo are like our problems: to cope with his environment, to cope with his fellow men, and to cope with himself. We hope to show that wherever man lives, he manages not only to survive and to breed, but also to think and to express his thoughts. But we can also let the children enjoy the particulars of a given culture—the sense of an alien ecology, the bush, or ice and snow, and a participant understanding for alien styles.

We introduce an origin myth, things taking their present order, the sun shining over the paths of the Bushmen, and the Bushmen starting to hunt. But we should equip the children with some possible theories to make the discussion profitable, theories not in words, but in ways of reading and understanding a myth. If the narrative is to be called a myth, it should portray conditions radically different from the way things are now. It is possible to devise ways for children to analyze a plot. If done with one story variant only, such an analysis may yield something akin to a phrase-structure grammar; if done with a group of myths, something comparable to a transformational grammar may result. It is intriguing to see how stories change. Children know such things intuitively and can be helped to appreciate them more powerfully.

One last thing: why should such things be taught so early? Why not postpone them until the student can handle the "theory" itself, not only the examples? There is a reason: if such things are new to a twenty-year-old, there is not only a new view to learn, but an old established view to unlearn. We want the children to recognize that man is constantly seeking to bring reason into his world, that he does so with a variety of symbolic tools, and that he does so with a striking and fully rational humanity. . . .

Pedagogy

The most persistent problem in social studies is to rescue the phenomena of social life from familiarity without, at the same time, making it all seem "primitive" and bizarre. Three techniques are particularly useful to us in achieving this end. The first is contrast, of which much has already been said. The second is through the use of "games" that incorporate the formal properties of the phenomena for which the game is an analogue. In this sense, a game is like a mathematical model—an artificialized but often powerful representation of reality. Finally, we use the ancient approach of stimulating self-consciousness about assumptions—going beyond mere admonition to think. We believe there is a learnable strategy for discovering one's unspoken assumptions.

Before considering each of these, a word is in order about a point of view quite different from ours. It holds that one should begin teaching social studies by presenting the familiar world of home, the street, and the neighborhood. It is a thoroughly commendable ideal; its only fault is its failure to recognize how difficult it is for human beings to see generality in what has become familiar. The "friendly postman" is indeed the vicar of federal powers, but to lead the child to the recognition of such powers requires many detours into the realm of what constitutes power, federal or otherwise, and how, for example, constituted power and willfully exercised force differ. We would rather find a way of stirring the curiosity of our children with particulars whose intrinsic drama and human significance are plain—whether close at hand or at a far remove. If we can evoke a feeling for bringing order into what has been studied, the task is well started.

A word first about contrast. We hope to use four principal sources of contrast: man *versus* higher primates, man *versus* prehistoric man, contemporary technological man *versus* "primitive" man, and man *versus* child. We have been gathering materials relevant to each of the contrasts—films, stories, artifacts, readings, pictures, and above all, ideas for pointing up contrasts in the interest of achieving clarity.

Indeed, we often hope to achieve for our pupils a sense of continuity by presenting them first with what seems like contrast and letting them live with it long enough to sense that what before seemed different is, in fact, closely akin to things they understand from their own lives. So it is particularly with our most extensive collection of material, a film record taken through the full cycle of the year of a family of Netsilik Eskimo. The ecology and the externals are full of contrast to daily life in an American or European setting. But there is enough material available to go into depth, to work into the year's cycle of a single family so that our pupils can get a sense of the integrity not only of a family, but of a culture. It is characteristic of Netsilik Eskimo, for example, that they make a few beautifully specialized tools and weapons, such as their fishing lester or spear. But it is also apparent that each man can make do with the stones he finds around him, that the Eskimo is a superbly gifted *bricoleur*. Whenever he needs to do something, improvised tools come from nowhere. A flat stone, a little fish oil, a touch of arctic cotton and he has a lamp. So while the Eskimo film puts modern technological man in sharp contrast, it also serves, perhaps even better, to present the inherent, internal logic of any society. Each society has its own approach to technology, to the use of intelligence.

Games go a long way toward getting children involved in understanding language and social organization; they also introduce, as we have already noted, the idea of a theory of these phenomena. We do not know to what extent these games will be successful, but we shall give them a careful tryout. The alleged success of these rather sophisticated games in business management and military affairs is worth extrapolating!

As for stimulating self-consciousness about thinking, we feel that the best approach is through stimulating the art of getting and using information—what is involved in going beyond the information given and what makes it possible to take such leaps. Crutchfield has produced results in this sphere by using nothing more complicated than a series of comic books in which the adventures of a detective, aided by his nephew and niece, are recounted. The theme is using clues cleverly. As children explore the implications of clues encountered, their general reasoning ability increases, and they formulate more and better hypotheses. We plan to design materials in which children have an opportunity to do this sort of thinking with questions related to the course—possibly in connection with prehistoric materials where it will be most relevant. If it turns out to be the case that the clothing that people wore was made from the skins of the ibex, what can they "postdict" about the size of a hunting party and how would they look for data? Professor Leaky informs us that he has some useful material on this subject.

Children should be at least as self-conscious about their strategies of thought as they are about their attempts to commit things to memory. So too the "tools" of thought—what is explanation and "cause." One of those tools is language—perhaps the principal one. We shall try to encourage children to have a look at language in this light.

The most urgent need of all is to give our pupils the experience of what it is to use a theoretical model, with some sense of what is involved in being aware that one is trying out a theory. We shall be using a fair number of rather sophisticated theoretical notions, in intuitively rather than formally stated form, to be sure, but we should like to give children the experience of using alternative models. This is perhaps easiest to do in the study of language, but it can also be done elsewhere.

We shall, of course, try to encourage students to discover on their own. Children surely need to discover generalizations on their own. Yet we want to give them enough opportunity to do so to develop a decent competence at it and a proper confidence in their ability to operate on their own. There is also some need for the children to pause and review in order to recognize the connections within the structure they have learned—the kind of internal discovery that is probably of highest value. The cultivation of such a sense of connectedness is surely the hub of our curriculum effort.

If we are successful, we would hope to achieve five ideals:

1. To give our pupils respect for and confidence in the powers of their own minds.

2. To give them respect, moreover, for the powers of thought concerning the human condition, man's plight and his social life.
3. To provide them with a set of workable models that make it simpler to analyze the nature of the social world in which they live and the condition in which man finds himself.
4. To impart a sense of respect for the capacities and plight of man as a species, for his origins, for his potential, for his humanity.
5. To leave the student with a sense of the unfinished business of man's evolution.

29. Some Changing Concepts about Learning and Memory

James L. McGaugh

Those who study man generally agree that it is our mental capacity that sets us apart from the other animals. Countless centuries ago, we domesticated plants and animals and began other technological achievements which surpass those of all other species. We also developed elaborate forms of communication, including language, which enabled us to transmit acquired knowledge to our offspring. All of these achievements are based, of course, upon our ability to learn: to record experiences and to utilize records of the past in dealing with the present. In adapting to our environment, we have relied upon learning ability to a greater extent than have any other animals. Learning ability is central to the biological and social evolution of man.

In most areas of human enterprise, technological achievements long preceded scientific understanding. Animal husbandry, agriculture, and even medicine antedated recorded history. In each of these areas, however, scientific discoveries of recent decades, in disciplines such as genetics, microbiology, and biochemistry, have so profoundly influenced technological developments and practices that the techniques of the farmer and the

SOURCE: *NEA Journal*, LVII (April 1968), 8–9, 51–52, 54. Reprinted by permission of the author and the publisher.

physician today bear little resemblance to those used even a few years ago. In areas essential for our survival, we have come to expect our technology to be continuously modified by scientific knowledge.

Although education is clearly essential for survival, the practices of education have been less significantly influenced by basic research findings than have those of agriculture and medicine. Understanding of the nature and biological bases of learning and memory has not, as yet, significantly affected the educational technology. Most of the significant innovations have been concerned either with the *content* of education or with procedures for automating traditional teaching methods; few innovations and varied practices have grown out of basic research concerning the nature of learning and memory.

There are several possible reasons for this state of affairs. First, we simply may not yet know enough about the processes of learning and memory. Second, inadequate traditional views of the nature of learning and memory may have been misleading. Third, we may not have made sufficient effort to examine the implications of recent findings for educational practices. Whatever the reasons for the present situation, it seems clear that if we are to develop effective educational systems, teachers, like farmers and physicians, will need to develop and use more practices which are based on scientific understanding. Society cannot afford the luxury of ignoring this important problem.

The problem is complicated by the fact that at one time educators made a valiant attempt to understand and use principles of learning theory, but the theory they worked with was neither very good nor very helpful. From the time of Thorndike to the present, the dominant theories have emphasized the learning of stimulus-response connections and have stressed the value of rewards.

It has been difficult to reconcile these emphases with the obvious fact that much, if not most, learning consists of acquiring information or knowledge as a consequence of some sensory impact (watching, listening, reading). Learning may occur *prior to* responding and *prior to* rewards. While overt responding undoubtedly influences learning, it does not do so simply by strengthening stimulus-response connections. Responding provides a repetition or rehearsal of acquired information and, in addition, provides an opportunity for correcting errors if what was remembered was incorrect. But the response cannot occur unless some learning has already occurred.

Understanding of the nature and bases of learning and memory has increased steadily if not dramatically over the past several decades. Unfortunately, we have not yet reached the stage where such information is as relevant for the teacher as the findings of genetics, biochemistry, and microbiology are for the farmer and physician. Nonetheless, the theories and implications emerging from recent findings should not be ignored. In this brief essay, I will discuss a few of them, emphasizing three points—the increasing tendency to view learning and memory from a biological perspective, the considerable emphasis being placed on learning and memory as complex processes involved in the storage and utilization of information, and a cautious but increasing interest in considering the educational implications of these emerging facts and theories.

Learning and Memory from a Biological Perspective. Theories of learning have, to a considerable extent, ignored biological factors. The psychologist, John B. Watson, once proposed to take any one of a dozen well-formed, healthy infants and train them to become ". . . any type of specialist . . . doctor, lawyer, artist, merchant, chief . . . even beggar man and thief, regardless of his talents, penchants, tendencies, abilities, vocations. . . ." Beggar man and thief aside, this is, of course, the American Dream—an educational bill of rights that every one of us would like to accept as true.

In evaluating Watson's proposal, much depends upon the meaning of the words *healthy* and *well-formed.* Unfortunately, as far as ability is concerned, all men are not created equal. Because of inborn errors of metabolism, many infants will, regardless of training, never have the ability to become doctors and lawyers. They will be fortunate to learn to speak, feed themselves, and to tie their shoes.

"Normal" variations in intelligence also appear to be at least in part biologically based. Studies of the IQ's of twins have shown that in sets of identical twins the correlation of IQ scores is typically greater than $+.80$, while that for fraternal twins is usually approximately $+.50$. The similarity in IQ between pairs of fraternal twins is no greater than that of ordinary brothers and sisters. Numerous studies of this type show that, in general, similarity in IQ varies directly with the genetic similarity. Undoubtedly, heredity influences IQ scores.

Unfortunately, IQ tests were not developed to provide a measure of a psychological process or set of processes. They were developed simply on an empirical basis to provide a score which can be used to predict academic success. As such, IQ tests are used to predict—not to diagnose. They are, of course, not simply tests of learning and memory. They do, however, include subtests which provide measures of learning and memory.

Experimental studies using laboratory rats have shown that it is possible to develop, by selective breeding, strains of rats that are bright and strains that are dull on specific learning tests. Further, numerous different strains of mice specially developed for tumor incidence have been found to differ in learning ability on various tasks. In mice and men, learning ability is genetically influenced.

Learning ability is not, however, completely determined by genetic factors. David Krech and his colleagues at the University of California at Berkeley have found that environmental stimulation influences the learning ability of rats.

Rats reared in an enriched laboratory environment are better learners than rats reared in less stimulating surroundings. Again, however, biological factors appear to play a role; the rats who were better learners differed from the other rats in several morphological and biochemical measures.

We do not yet know in detail how genes and environmental stimulation act to produce normal variations in intelligence and learning ability. The learning tests used with rats and mice provide rather crude measures of learning ability—much in the same way that IQ tests provide crude measures of children's mental capacities. In spite of this crudeness, the tests are able to provide indirect measures of processes which are biologically based.

Learning and Memory as Complex Processes. The processes underlying learning and memory are undoubtedly extremely complicated. Consider what is involved in learning a telephone number. First, the information has to be attended to and received; second, the information must be registered or stored in some way; third, the information must be retained for a period of time; and fourth, it must be retrieved when needed. Learning ability depends upon the efficiency of each of these processes. Since deficiencies in one or more of the systems could cause poor learning, we need to know the nature of the brain processes underlying these systems.

Studies of memory in humans with memory defects have provided some leads. Dr. Brenda Milner at Montreal Neurological Institute has conducted studies of memory in patients with brain lesions in the temporal lobes of both hemispheres of the brain. In some ways, the memory processes of such patients are fairly efficient. Immediate or short-term memory may be normal, and there may be no impairment of the patient's ability to remember events which occurred some time prior to the brain damage. IQ scores are usually unaffected. However, although the patients may appear to be quite normal, they are not. They have completely (or almost completely) lost the ability to acquire and retain new information. The case of one such patient, who received brain damage 10 years ago, illustrates the nature of the defect:

"Ten months after [the occurrence of the brain damage] the family moved to a new house . . . situated a few blocks away . . . on the same street. . . . A year later the man had not yet learned the new address, nor could he be trusted to find his way home alone because he would go to the old house. . . . Moreover, he is unable to learn where objects constantly in use are kept. . . . He will do the same jigsaw puzzles day after day without showing any practice effects and reads the same magazines over and over again without ever finding the contents familiar."

Research in my laboratory and in numerous other laboratories has shown that it is possible to produce amnesia in animals experimentally, by administering treatments including electroshock stimulation and various drugs, after animals are trained on a task. Amnesia results only if the treatments are given within a few minutes or hours after the training. The magnitude of the amnesia decreases as the interval between training and treatment is increased.

Findings such as these suggest that information can be retrieved from at least two memory systems: a short-term system and one for long-term storage. Both brain damage and the treatments such as drugs and electroshock stimulation appear to block storage processes in the long-term memory system.

It seems possible that at least some "normal occurring" deficiencies in learning and memory might be due to impaired functions of the two memory systems. Studies of memory disorders in geriatric patients and retarded children provide some support for this view. For example, W. K. Caird at the University of British Columbia reported results suggesting that, at least in some cases, the memory disorder in elderly patients may be due to a loss of efficiency in the long-term memory storage system.

Millard C. Madsen at UCLA has found that, in comparison with children with high IQ's (an average of approximately 120), children with low IQ's (an average of approximately 60) appear to have poorer short-term memory. Further, the lower-IQ children required longer intervals between training trials for optimal learning. This suggests that mental retardation may be due in part to deficiencies of short-term and long-term memory storage systems. In one study Madsen found that children with low IQ's could learn almost as efficiently as children with high IQ's when a relatively long interval lapsed between repetitions of the material.

Additional evidence that memory storage involves several systems has come from our studies of drug effects on memory storage. We have found in our laboratory that it is possible to enhance learning of laboratory animals by administering certain stimulant drugs shortly after training. These findings indicate that the drugs facilitate learning by enhancing long-term memory storage processes. The effects, like those obtained with memory impairing treatments, are time-dependent. Facilitation is obtained only if the drugs are administered within an hour or two following the training.

A large number of drugs are now known to enhance memory. Many appear to facilitate long-term memory storage in the manner just described. Others appear to act on short-term memory and retrieval systems. Unfortunately, not much is known about the specific ways in which the drugs influence neural functioning to produce memory effects, and we do not yet know whether comparable effects can be obtained with humans.

Implications. Although much has been learned in recent years about the nature and biological bases of learning and memory, we have probably not yet reached the point where such knowledge is of immediate significance for educational technology. All indications are that this point is rapidly being approached, however. Even at the present state of knowledge there are some important implications.

First, it is probably time to discard intelligence tests as we know them now—and time to develop tests designed to assess specific processes of learning and memory. Such tests could be used to diagnose individual differences in learning efficiency and might even prove useful (as IQ tests have not) in helping to develop teaching practices designed to deal with individual differences in learning and memory.

Second, it may be time to anticipate the possibility that, in the future, drugs might be used to correct learning and memory deficiencies in the same way that corrective lenses are now used to correct visual defects. Drug treatment of memory defects could become as common as drug treatment of allergies and emotional disorders. It may be that some day, by these means, educators will be able to fulfill John B. Watson's dream. Perhaps it will be the right of every child to have the opportunity to become a doctor, lawyer, merchant, or chief. The social and economic implications of this possibility are enormous. Perhaps we should begin to give them some thought.

30. Why Inquiry?

Owen A. Hagen and Steve T. Stansberry

On all the questions that can be asked about investigation-oriented teaching methods, whether they are called inquiry, problem solving, reflective thinking, or discovery, the most fundamental one is "Why?" This deceptively simple question has concerned educators for many years, and nu-

SOURCE: *Social Education*, XXXIII, 5 (May 1969), 534–37. Reprinted by permission of the authors, Owen A. Hagen, Chairman, Department of Elementary Education, State College, St. Cloud, Minnesota, and Steve T. Stansberry, and the publisher.

merous individuals [1] in their own styles and from their own vantage points have advocated such investigation-oriented approaches through their writings and have pressed for refinement of responses to the question "Why inquiry?" The focus of this analysis is also centered on this fundamental question, and although the temptation is great to frame a case for inquiry around the respected and eloquent words of recognized authorities, the authors have chosen to use words of the less-heard-from authorities—children. Before calling for their assistance, a few words of introduction are needed to clarify the general dimensions of the inquiry approach.

Although it is impossible to offer here a set of refined and adequately researched dimensions of inquiry approaches agreed on by all educators, it is becoming increasingly clear that for many of our educational purposes such approaches are superior to the expository mode of classroom instruction. These approaches seem to share the common goal of having the pupil assume the central role in the educative process and become an active inquirer in his own education as opposed to the passive role of the learner, which is often, but not always, characteristic of expository teaching. In the latter the pupil generally assumes the role of the respondent to questions posed by the classroom teacher and rarely raises questions himself. He tends to spend most of his time listening to what the teacher has to say about a topic rather than engaging in classroom dialogue with his peers and with the teacher. In short, he is teacher dependent. Inquiry strategies more frequently engage the pupil in decision making regarding his own instruction. The pupil in this approach assumes an active role in activities relating to his own learning and generally interacts with his peers and his teacher to a larger degree. The inquiry approach is a student-centered mode of instruction rather than teacher-centered.

John Dewey [2] made one of the earliest and most significant protests against a curriculum based on the teaching of specific facts and generalizations. He maintained that true education is not only the transmission of accumulated knowledge but also a process of assisting the development of certain natural tendencies of the child. One such tendency is to inquire;

[1] Ernest E. Bayles, *Theory and Practice of Teaching.* New York: Harper and Bros., 1950; Jerome S. Bruner, *On Knowing: Essays for the Left Hand.* Cambridge: Harvard University Press, 1962; John Dewey, *Logic: The Theory of Inquiry.* New York: Henry Holt and Co., 1938; Jean Fair and Fannie R. Shaftel, editors, *Effective Thinking in the Social Studies. Thirty-Seventh Yearbook of the National Council for the Social Studies.* Washington, D.C., 1967; Bernice Goldmark, *Social Studies: A Method of Inquiry.* Belmont, California: Wadsworth Publishing Company, Inc., 1968; Gordon H. Hullfish and Philip A. Smith. *Reflective Thinking: The Method of Education.* New York: Dodd, Mead, and Co., 1961; Byron Massialas and Benjamin Cox, *Inquiry in Social Studies.* New York: McGraw-Hill Book Company, 1966.

[2] John Dewey, *Democracy and Education.* New York: The Macmillan Company, 1916.

i.e. wanting and trying to find out. He also believed that such inquiry, together with learning how to search effectively for answers to questions raised, is more important than learning particular information. The development of such inquiry and procedures for seeking answers is useful to the pupil in any situation that might confront him. Dewey viewed facts as meanings that have already been established and that should be used as resources for conducting new inquiries, which lead to new information, concepts, and generalizations.

Although there are numerous contemporary vantage points from which to view the inquiry approach, Carpenter provides a firm operating foundation when she suggests that: "Inquiry is considered to be the process by which a child, more or less independently, comes to perceive relationships among factors in his environment or between ideas that previously had no meaningful connection." [3] She sees new understandings evolving through application and reorganization of past experiences on the part of the pupils and further relates that insight and self-confidence grow as the child successfully meets situations of increasing abstractness and complexity—*i.e.* as he moves up the ladder from observation, classification, and application to generalization. Perhaps the following well-chosen words best reflect the "pulse" of the inquiry approach:

Thus the inquiry approach views the learner as an active thinker—seeking, probing, processing data from his environment toward a variety of destinations along paths best suited to his own mental characteristics. It rejects passiveness as an ingredient of effective learning and the concept of the mind as a reservoir for the storage of knowledge presented through expository instruction directed toward a predetermined, closed end. The inquiry method seeks to avoid the dangers of rote memorization and verbalization as well as the hazard of fostering dependency in citizens as learners and thinkers. . . . The measure of ultimate success in education through inquiry lies in the degree to which the teacher becomes unnecessary as a guide. [4]

In short, the pupil assumes the central role, or at least works from a more cooperative position with the teacher than is generally the case in the expository mode of classroom instruction. He becomes more of a questioner himself and less of a respondent to the questions of the teacher, facilitating to a larger degree self-discovery of certain basic concepts and principles.

Despite the strong philosophical case for the inquiry approach, one is somewhat alarmed by what appears to be a very strong verbal commitment without much evidence of inquiry approaches in actual practice. In short,

[3] Helen McCracken Carpenter, "The Role of Skills in Elementary Social Studies." *Social Education* 31:219–221, March, 1967.

[4] *Ibid.* p. 220.

we do not seem to be practicing what we believe to the extent that would be desirable in our classrooms.

Even though we are experiencing this instructional lag, there is still the need for continued discussion of the value and desirability of inquiry approaches in the literature. As previously noted, various champions of inquiry seem to have followed through with this responsibility. There is, however, one sound to these recurring messages that is noticeably absent. This is the sound of children, and it is this "new sound" that we draw upon in offering a case for the inquiry approach.

The "Sound of Children"

The "new sound of children" incorporated within the following discussion is taken from actual statements of pupils. These personal perceptions were solicited by the authors in interviews with a single group of thirty, sixth-grade pupils engaged in an inquiry-oriented unit of study reflecting much of the spirit of the inquiry approach and philosophy expressed by Carpenter. No claim is made for having solicited the true perceptions of children, and the responses have been treated only as "reported perceptions." No claim is made that these reported perceptions are reflective of all children everywhere. On the contrary, we are simply using the language of a handful of pupils to assist us in communicating to the reader elements of a strong case for the inquiry approach.

In building or restating such a case one is immediately drawn to the possibilities within the inquiry process for developing a more responsible, self-directed, and active pupil in the learning process. Indeed, the literature abounds with statements that frame the importance of developing pupil characteristics, leading to active involvement as well as statements that encourage and endorse inquiry. Children also sense the value of active involvement, and, although the words they have available to express their feelings might not be the same as those found in the literature, this in no way detracts from the importance of the message they have to share. For example, one sixth-grade girl in commenting on her experiences in an inquiry-based unit of study states: "It gets kinda boring to just sit and listen to someone who is always talking. It's kinda fun to make decisions for yourself and think about it instead of having someone tell you all the time." Another girl, after having made essentially the same statement, adds an important reason for her position when she relates: "It would help a lot if they [teachers] just wouldn't talk so much and give us something to do, because more gets through to you if you are working yourself and making decisions."

One boy, in sharing feelings about his involvement in the inquiry-based unit, seems to touch at the very quick of the development of pupil independence when he says: "We have to be able to be independent. We can't always be asking the teacher what everything is—like I have developed a way of just trying not to ask the teacher everything. But sometimes that's hard too, so you have to ask some things." Once again, although the words at times may tumble over one another, the message is clear.

The inquiry process would also appear to contribute to a positive desire to learn on the part of the pupil. This is because primarily the inquiry process facilitates and encourages a personal identification with areas of study within the school program. It is an ego-directed process by which the individual "consciously defines his problem and his terms, marshals his data, tests and verifies his hunches, judges the evidence, and systematizes the knowledge he has obtained." [5] Indeed, he is dealing with problems from his frame of reference, and in so doing it would seem that he is not just conducting an indiscriminate search for facts. On the contrary, he is pursuing meanings and understandings that are real and important to him and at the same time making decisions about their significance. This personal involvement would appear to be a prerequisite for stimulated inquiry into any field of knowledge because what the material will mean to the pupil cannot be predetermined by the instructor. All he can do is to create, to the best of his ability, a working environment conducive to stimulating inquiry. Because motivation is essentially a personal matter, whether a pupil is motivated to learn can only be determined by the pupil himself.

The teacher who in one way or another *compels* students to learn certain things at a particular time and in a particular way complicates an already confused situation, *viz.*, the struggle of the student to find himself. He unwittingly projects his own will-struggle into the learning-teaching activity, not skillfully and professionally, but as one who, personally, has something at stake. This robs the student of the chance to discover himself.[6]

It would be somewhat of an oversimplification to state that we cannot afford to allow these "robberies" to occur. Take it from the pupil who says: "I think you learn more than the book gives you. You work in the book and, well, you mostly just forget it. If you do it yourself, you are more interested and you remember it longer." Or another pupil commented: "You're planning everything—you're really doing it." Sometimes the reasons were not always clear to the pupil, but again the message comes through: "I really don't know why—it just makes you want to do it

---

[5] Charlotte Crabtree, "Supporting Reflective Thinking in the Classroom." *Effective Thinking in the Social Studies. Thirty-Seventh Yearbook of the National Council for the Social Studies.* Washington, D.C., 1967. p. 87.

[6] Nathaniel Cantor, *The Dynamics of Learning.* Buffalo: Foster and Stewart, 1950. p. 275.

more. The books aren't as much fun when you just copy down a couple of sentences and answer the questions and stuff."

The key to how successful we will be in providing for this high level of motivation lies in the extent to which intrinsic, rather than continually directed extrinsic, rewards guide the thoughts and actions of pupils. Learning is personal and only takes place within the learner; therefore, teachers, at best, serve as mediators with the basic task of creating situations where pupils are brought into meaningful confrontation with important areas of concern within the social studies program. Do pupils view the teacher's role in this way? We will let you be the judge: "There is teaching where the teacher tells you what to do, and one where the teacher just talks and talks, and then there's the kind where we help decide what to do. That's what we are doing in social studies, and it's really fun."

A further advantage of the inquiry approach is that it should contribute to "learning how to learn," or what Bruner refers to as learning the heuristics of discovery.[7] What do the pupils say? "We get a lot of new ideas from working in groups. I learn more than reading a book. When I read a book, I can be thinking about something else—here I have to be thinking about it all the time." Another pupil puts it this way: "Well, I like it because we can do it ourselves, and you don't always have to have the teacher looking right over you to make sure you're doing it. You just feel more relaxed about it, and everything, and you are learning how to find answers to questions." In short, as one sixth-grade philosopher so eloquently expresses it: "You couldn't learn anything if the teacher told you everything." The authors would agree and add that you can't learn how to learn unless you are given practice in inquiry and the opportunity to figure out things for yourself. As Bruner states it: "Of only one thing am I convinced: I have never seen anybody improve in the art and technique of inquiry by any means other than engaging in inquiry." [8]

The possibility that the process of inquiry effectively facilitates important thinking operations such as comparing, summarizing, observing, interpreting, and criticizing is also discussed at length in the literature. Although the reported perceptions of children understandably do not reflect in great detail on these thinking operations, there were numerous reactions that appeared on the fringe of what they had to say about other matters. For example, one boy, in commenting on the dynamics of group discussion and debate, related that: "We can give our own ideas and if someone thinks up an idea we don't always have to go along with it—we can do it another way." It would seem that such freedom to openly debate and critically analyze issues contributes to the refinement of important thinking op-

[7] Jerome S. Bruner, *On Knowing: Essays for the Left Hand.* Cambridge: Harvard University Press, 1962. p. 92.

[8] *Ibid.* p. 94.

erations. The beauty of reaching certain destinations in harmony after a period of group debate and refinement comes through in one girl's deceptively simple statement when she relates: "Yes, we have a lot of disagreements—like sometimes we make suggestions when we discuss something and sometimes we have little arguments, but we turn out all right."

The inquiry approach does not guarantee, however, that such debate and analysis of issues is automatically inherent in the learning process. The following statement offered by a girl might serve as a caution in this respect: "The other girl in my group made all of the decisions, and all I did was write them down."

The importance of recognizing and comparing various viewpoints as an important thinking operation comes alive in the following remark regarding references: "You need to be able to look for lots of references and find out what they say. You can't just look at one book and say that's what it is, because I have seen lots of books that have different stories but are based on the same thing." Such opportunities that relate to a variety of thinking operations would appear to be more easily facilitated and realized through inquiry than through an expository approach to classroom instruction.

An additional advantage realized through the inquiry process is that this approach should provide a natural springboard for the transfer of learning. Indeed, if learning is to broaden the individual's potential for effective behavior in and out of school, the learner must see the relation of the current learning to his life and must be able to recognize situations where the new understanding or skill is appropriate and apply it.

The pupils interviewed had very limited experience with inquiry procedures. Perhaps even more limiting was the lack of ability of the interviewers to ask truly appropriate questions of these children to determine meaningful transfer. A few comments made by the children seemed to indicate, however, that they were indeed transferring learnings from other subjects and previous experiences to solve their immediate problems. As one boy stated: "You can really tell who has learned from last year. You know who has really gotten something out of what you have studied before. He is the guy that can correct things and know what to do."

Another pupil remarked about his experiences in creating new laws for an imaginary state the class was developing: "It's not easy to make up laws. You've got to find a certain one that everybody likes. If nobody likes it, like if one man like a dictator makes up a law—say he made up a law nobody liked—they wouldn't follow it." Here we see an attempt to express a point that the pupil has not clearly thought out, but certainly there is an attempt to relate previous learnings to a problem at hand.

There are, undoubtedly, numerous other potential advantages of investigation-oriented approaches such as their contribution to greater self-confi-

dence on the part of the pupils, greater retention, and a more positive attitude toward social studies in general. To be all-inclusive, however, was
never our purpose in this analysis, and although the sounds of children
could go on, perhaps the setting should change from this article to your
classroom. The sounds are there if we would listen.

In conclusion, it might be well to reiterate that it has not been our purpose in this article to create a new case for the process of inquiry; rather it
has been to restate with a new sound the strong case that already exists.
Continued experimentation and refinement is called for as many questions
remain unanswered and are in need of attention. Among them: Are all pupils suited for the inquiry approach? Do some pupils learn more effectively via another approach? Does the inquiry process accommodate all
learning styles? How much of the program should be devoted to inquiry?
Is there a danger of the inquiry process becoming a ritual? These are only
a sampling of issues that demand our attention as we press for refinement
of inquiry strategies. It is a challenging and difficult task, but as one pupil
expressed it: "Sure it's a little harder—but it's funner too!"

31. Giant in the Nursery — Jean Piaget

David Elkind

In February, 1967, Jean Piaget, the Swiss psychologist, arrived at Clark
University in Worcester, Mass., to deliver the Heinz Werner Memorial
Lectures. The lectures were to be given in the evening, and before the first
one a small dinner party was arranged in honor of Piaget and was attended
by colleagues, former students and friends. I was invited because of my
long advocacy of Piaget's work and because I had spent a year (1964–65)
at his Institute for Educational Science in Geneva. Piaget had changed

SOURCE: *The New York Times Magazine,* CXVII (May 26, 1968), 25–27, 71–80. Copyright © 1968 by The New York Times Company. Reprinted by permission of
the publisher.

very little since I had last seen him, but he did appear tired and mildly apprehensive.

Although Piaget has lectured all over the world, this particular occasion had special significance. Almost sixty years before, in 1909, another famous European, Sigmund Freud, also lectured at Clark University. Piaget was certainly aware of the historical parallel. He was, moreover, going to speak to a huge American audience in French and, despite the offices of his remarkable translator, Eleanor Duckworth, he must have had some reservations about how it would go.

Piaget's apprehension was apparent during the dinner. For one who is usually a lively and charming dinner companion, he was surprisingly quiet and unresponsive. About half way through the meal there was a small disturbance. The room in which the dinner was held was at a garden level and two boys suddenly appeared at the windows and began tapping at them. The inclination of most of us, I think, was to shoo them away. Before we had a chance to do that, however, Piaget had turned to face the children. He smiled up at the lads, hunched his shoulders and gave them a slight wave with his hand. They hunched their shoulders and smiled in return, gave a slight wave and disappeared. After a moment, Piaget turned back to the table and began telling stories and entering into animated conversation.

It is Piaget's genius for empathy with children, together with true intellectual genius, that has made him the outstanding child psychologist in the world today and one destined to stand beside Freud with respect to his contributions to psychology, education and related disciplines. Just as Freud's discoveries of unconscious motivation, infantile sexuality and the stages of psychosexual growth changed our ways of thinking about human personality, so Piaget's discoveries of children's implicit philosophies, the construction of reality by the infant and the stages of mental development have altered our ways of thinking about human intelligence.

Piaget's is a superbly disciplined life. He arises early each morning, sometimes as early as 4 A.M., and writes four or more publishable pages on square sheets of white paper in an even, small hand. Later in the morning he may teach classes and attend meetings. His afternoons include long walks during which he thinks about the problems he is currently confronting. He says, "I always like to think on a problem before reading about it." In the evenings, he reads and retires early. Even on his international trips, Piaget keeps to this schedule.

Each summer, as soon as classes are over, Piaget gathers up the research findings that have been collected by his assistants during the year and departs for the Alps, where he takes up solitary residence in a room in an abandoned farmhouse. The whereabouts of this retreat is as closely guarded as the names of depositors in numbered Swiss bank accounts; only Piaget's family, his long-time colleague Bärbel Inhelder and a trusted secretary know where he is. During the summer Piaget takes walks, meditates, writes *and* writes. Then, when the leaves begin to turn, he descends from the mountains with the several books and articles he has written on his "vacation."

Although Piaget, now in his seventy-second year, has been carrying his works down from the mountains for almost 50 summers (he has published more than 30 books and hundreds of articles), it is only within the past decade that his writings have come to be fully appreciated in America. This was due, in part, to the fact that until fairly recently only a few of his books had been translated into English. In addition, American psychology and education were simply not ready for Piaget until the fifties. Now the ideas that Piaget has been advocating for more than thirty years are regarded as exceedingly innovative and even as avant-garde.

His work falls into three more or less distinct periods within each of which he covered an enormous amount of psychological territory and developed a multitude of insights. (Like most creative men, Piaget is hard put to it to say when a particular idea came to him. If he ever came suddenly upon an idea which sent him shouting through the halls, he has never admitted to it.)

During the first period (roughly 1922–29), Piaget explored the extent and depth of children's spontaneous ideas about the physical world and about their own mental processes. He happened upon this line of inquiry while working in Alfred Binet's laboratory school in Paris where he arrived, still seeking a direction for his talents, a year after receiving his doctorate in biological science at the University of Lausanne. It was in the course of some routine intelligence testing that Piaget became interested in what lay behind children's correct, and particularly their incorrect, answers. To clarify the origins of these answers he began to interview the children in the open-ended manner he had learned while serving a brief internship at Bleuler's psychiatric clinic in Zurich. This semiclinical interview procedure, aimed at revealing the processes by which a child arrives at a particular reply to a test question, has become a trademark of Piagetian research investigation.

What Piaget found with this method of inquiry was that children not only reasoned differently from adults but also that they had quite different world-views, literally different philosophies. This led Piaget to attend to those childish remarks and questions which most adults find amusing or nonsensical. Just as Freud used seemingly accidental slips of the tongue and pen as evidence for unconscious motivations, so Piaget has employed the "cute" sayings of children to demonstrate the existence of ideas quite foreign to the adult mind.

Piaget had read in the recollections of a deaf mute (recorded by William James) that as a child he had regarded the sun and moon as gods and believed they followed him about. Piaget sought to verify this recollection by interviewing children on the subject, and he found that many youngsters do believe that the sun and moon follow them when they are out for a walk. Similar remarks Piaget either overheard or was told about led to a large number of investigations which revealed, among many similar findings, that young children believe that anything which moves is alive, that the names of objects reside in the objects themselves and that dreams come in through the window at night.

Such beliefs, Piaget pointed out in an early article entitled "Children's Philosophies," are not unrelated to but rather derive from an implicit animism and artificialism with many parallels to primitive and Greek philosophies. In the child's view, objects like stones and clouds are imbued with motives, intentions and feelings, while mental events such as dreams and thoughts are endowed with corporality and force. Children also believe that everything has a purpose and that everything in the world is made by and for man. (My 5-year-old son asked me why we have snow and answered his own question by saying, "It is for children to play in.")

The child's animism and artificialism help to explain his famous and often unanswerable "why" questions. It is because children believe that everything has a purpose that they ask, "Why is grass green?" and "Why do the stars shine?" The parent who attempts to answer such questions with a physical explanation has missed the point.

In addition to disclosing the existence of children's philosophies during this first period, Piaget also found the clue to the egocentrism of childhood. In observing young children at play at the *Maison des Petits,* the modified Montessori school associated with the Institute of Educational Science in Geneva, Piaget noted a peculiar lack of social orientation which was also present in their conversation and in their approaches to certain intellectual tasks. A child would make up a new word ("stocks" for socks and stockings) and just assume that everyone knew what he was talking about as if this were the conventional name for the objects he had in mind. Likewise, Piaget noted that when two nursery school children were at play they often spoke *at* rather than *to* one another and were frequently chattering on about two quite different and unrelated topics. Piaget observed, moreover, that when he stood a child of 5 years opposite him, the child who could tell his own right and left nevertheless insisted that Piaget's right and left hands were directly opposite his own.

In Piaget's view, all of these behaviors can be explained by the young child's inability to put himself in another person's position and to take that person's point of view. Unlike the egocentric adult, who can take another person's point of view but does not, the egocentric child does not take another person's viewpoint because he cannot. This conception of childish egocentrism has produced a fundamental alteration in our evaluation of the preschool child's behavior. We now appreciate that it is intellectual immaturity and not moral perversity which makes, for example, a young child continue to pester his mother after she has told him she has a headache and wishes to be left alone. The preschool child is simply unable to put himself in his mother's position and see things from her point of view.

The second period of Piaget's investigations began when, in 1929, he sought to trace the origins of the child's spontaneous mental growth to the behavior of infants; in this case, his own three children, Jaqueline, Lucienne and Laurent. Piaget kept very detailed records of their behavior and of their performance on a series of ingenious tasks which he invented and presented to them. The books resulting from these investigations, "The Origins of Intelligence in Children," "Play, Dreams and Imitation in Children" and "The Construction of Reality in the Child" are now generally regarded as classics in the field and have been one of the major forces behind the scurry of research activity in the area of infant behavior now current both in America and abroad. The publication of these books in the middle and late nineteen-thirties marked the end of the second phase of Piaget's work.

Some of the most telling observations Piaget made during this period had to do with what he called the *conservation of the object* (using the word conservation to convey the idea of permanence). To the older child and to the adult, the existence of objects and persons who are not immediately present is taken as self-evident. The child at school knows that while he is working at his desk his mother is simultaneously at home and his father is at work. This is not the case for the young infant playing in his crib, for whom out of sight is literally out of mind. Piaget observed that when an infant 4 or 5 months old is playing with a toy which subsequently rolls out of sight (behind another toy) but is still within reach, the infant ceases to look for it. The infant behaves as if the toy had not only disappeared but as if it had gone entirely out of existence.

This helps to explain the pleasure infants take in the game of peek-a-boo. If the infant believed that the object existed when it was not seen, he would not be surprised and delighted at its re-emergence and there would be no point to the game. It is only during the second year of life, when children begin to represent objects mentally, that they seek after toys that have disappeared from view. Only then do they attribute an independent existence to objects which are not present to their senses.

The third and major phase of Piaget's endeavors began about 1940 and continues until the present day. During this period Piaget has studied the development in children and adolescents of those mental abilities which gradually enable the child to construct a world-view which is in conformance with reality as seen by adults. He has, at the same time, been concerned with how children acquire the adult versions of various concepts such as number, quantity and speed. Piaget and his colleagues have amassed, in the last twenty-eight years, an astounding amount of information about the thinking of children and adolescents which is only now beginning to be used by psychologists and educators.

Two discoveries made during this last period are of particular importance both because they were so unexpected and because of their relevance for education. It is perhaps fair to say that education tends to focus upon the static aspects of reality rather than upon its dynamic transformations. The child is taught how and what things are but not the conditions under which they change or remain the same. And yet the child is constantly confronted with change and alteration. His view of the world alters as he grows in height and perceptual acuity. And the world changes. Seasons come and go, trees gain and lose their foliage, snow falls and melts. People change, too. They may change over brief time periods in mood and over long periods in weight and hair coloration or fullness. The child receives a static education while living amidst a world in transition.

Piaget's investigations since 1940 have focused upon how the child copes with change, how he comes to distinguish between the permanent and the transient and between appearance and reality. An incident that probably played a part in initiating this line of investigation occurred during Piaget's short-lived flirtation with the automobile. (When his children were young, Piaget learned to drive and bought a car, but he gave it up for his beloved bicycle after a couple of years.) He took his son for a drive and Laurent asked the name of the mountain they were passing. The mountain was the Saleve, the crocodile-shaped mass that dominates the city of Geneva. Laurent was in fact familiar with the mountain and its name because he could see it from his garden, although from a different perspective. Laurent's question brought home to Piaget the fact that a child has difficulty in dealing with the results of transformations whether they are brought about by an alteration in the object itself or by the child's movement with respect to the object.

The methods Piaget used to study how the child comes to deal with transformations are ingenuously simple and can be used by any interested parent or teacher. These methods all have to do with testing the child's abilities to discover that a quantity remains the same across a change in its appearance. In other words, that the quantity is conserved.

To give just one illustration from among hundreds, a child is shown two identical drinking glasses filled equally full with orangeade and he is asked to say whether there is the "same to drink" in the two glasses. After the child says that this is the case, the orangeade from one glass is poured into another which is taller and thinner so that the orangeade now reaches a higher level. Then the child is asked to say whether there is the same amount to drink in the two differently shaped glasses. Before the age of 6 or 7, most children say that the tall, narrow glass has more orangeade. The young child cannot deal with the transformation and bases his judgment on the static features of the orangeade, namely the levels.

How does the older child arrive at the notion that the amounts of orangeade in the two differently shaped glasses is the same? The answer according to Piaget, is that he discovers the equality with the aid of reason. If the child judges only on the basis of appearances he cannot solve the problem. When he compares the two glasses with respect to width he must conclude that the wide glass has more while if he compares them with respect to the level of the orangeade he must conclude that the tall glass has more. There is then no way, on the basis of appearance, that he can solve the problem. If, on the other hand, the child reasons that there was the same in the two glasses before and that nothing was added or taken away during the pouring, he concludes that both glasses still have the same drink although this does not appear to be true.

On the basis of this and many similar findings, Piaget argues that much of our knowledge about reality comes to us not from without like the wail of a siren but rather from within by the force of our own logic.

It is hard to overemphasize the importance of this fact, because it is so often forgotten, particularly in education. For those who are not philosophically inclined, it appears that our knowledge of things comes about rather directly as if our mind simply copied the forms, colors and textures of things. From this point of view the mind acts as a sort of mirror which is limited to reflecting the reality which is presented to it. As Piaget's research has demonstrated, however, the mind operates not as a passive mirror but rather as an active artist.

The portrait painter does not merely copy what he sees, he interprets his subject. Before even commencing the portrait, the artist learns a great deal about the individual subject and does not limit himself to studying the face alone. Into the portrait goes not only what the artist sees but also what he knows about his subject. A good portrait is larger than life because it carries much more information than could ever be conveyed by a mirror image.

In forming his spontaneous conception of the world, therefore, the child does more than reflect what is presented to his senses. His image of reality is in fact a portrait or reconstruction of the world and not a simple copy of it. It is only by reasoning about the information which the child receives from the external world that he is able to overcome the transient nature of sense experience and arrive at that awareness of permanence within apparent change that is the mark of adult thought. The importance of reason in the child's spontaneous construction of his world is thus one of the major discoveries of Piaget's third period.

The second major discovery of this time has to do with the nature of the elementary school child's reasoning ability. Long before there was anything like a discipline of child psychology, the age of 6 to 7 was recognized as *the age of reason*. It was also assumed, however, that once the child attained the age of reason, there were no longer any substantial differences between his reasoning abilities and those of adolescents and adults. What Piaget discovered is that this is in fact not the case. While the elementary school child is indeed able to reason, his reasoning ability is limited in a very important respect—he can reason about things but not about verbal propositions.

If a child of 8 or 9 is shown a series of three blocks, ABC, which differ in size, then he can tell by looking at them and without comparing them directly, that if A is greater than B and B greater than C, then A is greater than C. When the same child is given this problem, "Helen is taller than Mary and Mary is taller than Jane, who is the tallest of the three?" the result is quite different. He cannot solve it despite the fact that it repeats in words the problem with the blocks. Adolescents and adults, however, encounter no difficulty with this problem because they can reason about verbal propositions as well as about things.

This discovery that children think differently from adults even after attaining the age of reason has educational implications which are only now beginning to be applied. Robert Karplus, the physicist who heads the Science Curriculum Improvement Study at Berkeley has pointed out that most teachers use verbal propositions in teaching elementary school children. At least some of their instruction is thus destined to go over the heads of their pupils. Karplus and his co-workers are now attempting to train teachers to instruct children at a verbal level which is appropriate to their level of mental ability.

An example of the effects of the failure to take into account the difference between the reasoning abilities of children and adults comes from the New Math experiment. In building materials for the New Math, it was hoped that the construction of a new language would facilitate instruction of set concepts. This new language has been less than successful and the originators of the New Math are currently attempting to devise a physical model to convey the New Math concepts. It is likely that the new language created to teach the set concepts failed because it was geared to the logic of adults rather than to the reasoning of children. Attention to the research on children's thinking carried out during Piaget's third period might have helped to avoid some of the difficulties of the "New Math" program.

In the course of these many years of research into children's thinking, Piaget has elaborated a general theory of intellectual development which, in its scope and comprehensiveness, rivals Freud's theory of personality development. Piaget proposes that intelligence—adaptive thinking and action—develops in a sequence of stages that is related to age. Each stage sees the elaboration of new mental abilities which set the limits and determine the character of what can be learned during that period. (Piaget finds incomprehensible Harvard psychologist Jerome Bruner's famous hypothesis to the effect that "any subject can be taught effectively in some intellectually honest form to any child at any stage of development.") Although Piaget believes that the order in which the stages appear holds true for all children, he also believes that the ages at which the stages evolve will depend upon the native endowment of the child and upon the quality of the physical and social environment in which he is reared. In a very real sense, then, Piaget's is both a nature *and* a nurture theory.

The first stage in the development of intelligence (usually 0–2 years) Piaget calls the sensory-motor period and it is concerned with the evolution of those abilities necessary to construct and reconstruct objects. To illustrate, Piaget observed that when he held a cigarette case in front of his daughter Jaqueline (who was 8 months old at the time) and then dropped it, she did not follow the trajectory of the case but continued looking at his hand. Even at 8 months (Lucienne and Laurent succeeded in following the object at about 5 months but had been exposed to more experiments than Jaqueline) she was not able to reconstruct the path of the object which she had seen dropped in front of her.

Toward the end of this period, however, Jaqueline was even able to reconstruct the position of objects which had undergone hidden displacement. When she was 19 months old, Piaget placed a coin in his hand and then placed his hand under a coverlet where he dropped the coin before removing his hand. Jacqueline first looked in his hand and then immediately lifted the coverlet and found the coin. This reconstruction was accomplished with the aid of an elementary form of reasoning. The coin was in the hand, the hand was under the coverlet, the coin was not in the hand so the coin is under the coverlet. Such reasoning, it must be said, is accomplished without the aid of language and by means of mental images.

The second stage (usually 2–7 years), which Piaget calls the preoperational stage, bears witness to the elaboration of the symbolic function, those abilities which have to do with representing things. The presence of these new abilities is shown by the gradual acquisition of language, the first indications of dreams and night terrors, the advent of symbolic play (two sticks at right angles are an airplane) and the first attempts at drawing and graphic representation.

At the beginning of this stage the child tends to identify words and symbols with the objects they are intended to represent. He is upset if someone tramps on a stone which he has designated as a turtle. And he believes that names are as much a part of objects as their color and form. (The child at this point is like the old gentleman who, when asked why noodles are called noodles, replied that "they are white like noodles, soft like noodles and taste like noodles so we call them noodles.")

By the end of this period the child can clearly distinguish between words and symbols and what they represent. He now recognizes that names are arbitrary designations. The child's discovery of the arbitrariness of names is often manifested in the "name calling" so prevalent during the early school years.

At the next stage (usually 7–11 years) the child acquires what Piaget calls concrete operations, internalized actions that permit the child to do "in his head" what before he would have had to accomplish through real actions. Concrete operations enable the child to think about things. To illustrate, in one study Piaget presented 5-, 6- and 7-year-old children with six sticks in a row and asked them to take the same number of sticks from a pile on the table. The young children solved the problem by placing their sticks beneath the sample and matching the sticks one by one. The older children merely picked up the six sticks and held them in their hands. The older children had counted the sticks mentally and hence felt no need to actually match them with the sticks in the row. It should be said that even the youngest children were able to count to six, so that this was not a factor in their performance.

Concrete operations also enable children to deal with the relations among classes of things. In another study Piaget presented 5-, 6- and 7-year-old children with a box containing twenty white and seven brown wooden beads. Each child was first asked if there were more white or more brown beads and all were able to say that there were more white than brown beads. Then Piaget asked, "Are there more white or more wooden beads?" The young children could not fathom the question and replied that "there are more white than brown beads." For such children classes are not regarded as abstractions but are thought of as concrete places. (I once asked a pre-operational child if he could be a Protestant and an American at the same time, to which he replied, "No," and then as an afterthought, "only if you move.")

When a child thought of a bead in the white "place" he could not think of it as being in the wooden "place" since objects cannot be in two places at once. He could only compare the white with the brown "places." The older children, who had attained concrete operations, encountered no difficulty with the task and readily replied that "there are more wooden than white beads because all of the beads are wooden and only some are white." By the end of the concrete operational period, children are remarkably adept at doing thought problems and at combining and dividing class concepts.

During the last stage (usually 12–15 years) there gradually emerge what Piaget calls formal operations and which, in effect, permit adolescents to think about their thoughts, to construct ideals and to reason realistically about the future. Formal operations also enable young people to reason about contrary-to-fact propositions. If, for example, a child is asked to assume that coal is white he is likely to reply, "But coal is black," whereas the adolescent can accept the contrary-to-fact assumption and reason from it.

Formal operational thought also makes possible the understanding of metaphor. It is for this reason that political and other satirical cartoons are not understood until adolescence. The child's inability to understand metaphor helps to explain why books such as "Alice in Wonderland" and "Gulliver's Travels" are enjoyed at different levels during childhood than in adolescence and adulthood, when their social significance can be understood.

No new mental systems emerge after the formal operations, which are the common coin of adult thought. After adolescence, mental growth takes the form—it is hoped—of a gradual increase in wisdom.

This capsule summary of Piaget's theory of intellectual development would not be complete without some words about Piaget's position with respect to language and thought. Piaget regards thought and language as different but closely related systems. Language, to a much greater extent than thought, is determined by particular forms of environmental stimulation. Inner-city Negro children, who tend to be retarded in language development, are much less retarded with respect to the ages at which they attain concrete operations. Indeed, not only inner-city children but children in bush Africa, Hong Kong and Appalachia all attain concrete operations at about the same age as middle-class children in Geneva and Boston.

Likewise, attempts to teach children concrete operations have been almost uniformly unsuccessful. This does not mean that these operations are independent of the environment but only that their development takes time and can be nourished by a much wider variety of environmental nutriments than is true for the growth of language, which is dependent upon much more specific forms of stimulation.

Language is, then, deceptive with respect to thought. Teachers of middle-class children are often misled, by the verbal facility of these youngsters, into believing that they understand more than they actually comprehend. (My 5-year-old asked me what my true identity was and as I tried to recover my composure he explained that Clark Kent was Superman's true identity.) At the other end, the teachers of inner-city children are often fooled by the language handicaps of these children into thinking that they have much lower mental ability than they actually possess. It is appropriate, therefore, that pre-school programs for the disadvantaged should focus upon training these children in language and perception rather than upon trying to teach them concrete operations.

The impact which the foregoing Piagetian discoveries and conceptions is having upon education and child psychology has come as something of a shock to a good many educators and psychological research in America, which relies heavily on statistics, electronics and computers. Piaget's studies of children's thinking seem hardly a step beyond the prescientific baby biographies kept by such men as Charles Darwin and Bronson Alcott. Indeed, in many of Piaget's research papers he supports his conclusions simply with illustrative examples of how children at different age levels respond to his tasks.

Many of Piaget's critics have focused upon his apparently casual methodology and have argued that while Piaget has arrived at some original ideas about children's thinking, his research lacks scientific rigor. It is likely that few, if any, of Piaget's research reports would have been accepted for publication in American psychological journals.

Other critics have taken somewhat the opposite tack. Jerome Bruner, who has done so much to bring Piaget to the attention of American social scientists, acknowledges the fruitfulness of Piaget's methods, modifications of which he has employed in his own investigations. But he argues against Piaget's theoretical interpretations. Bruner believes that Piaget has "missed the heart" of the problem of change and permanence or conservation in children's thinking. In the case of the orangeade poured into a different-sized container, Bruner argues that it is not reason, or mental operations, but some "internalized verbal formula that shields him [the child] from the overpowering appearance of the visual displays." Bruner seems to believe that the syntactical rules of language rather than logic can account for the child's discovery that a quantity remains unchanged despite alterations in its appearance.

Piaget is willing to answer his critics but only when he feels that the criticism is responsible and informed. With respect to his methods, their casualness is only apparent. Before they set out collecting data, his students are given a year of training in the art of interviewing children. They learn to ask questions without suggesting the answers and to test, by counter-suggestion, the strength of the child's conviction. Many of Piaget's studies have now been repeated with more rigorous procedures by other investigators all over the world and the results have been remarkably consistent with Piaget's findings. Attempts are currently under way to build a new intelligence scale on the basis of the Piaget tests, many of which are already in widespread use as evaluative procedures in education.

When it comes to criticisms of his theoretical views, Piaget is remarkably open and does not claim to be infallible. He frequently invites scholars who are in genuine disagreement with him to come to Geneva for a year so that the differences can be discussed and studied in depth. He has no desire to form a cult and says, in fact, "To the extent that there are Piagetians, to that extent have I failed." Piaget's lack of dogmatism is illustrated in his response to Bruner:

"Bruner does say that I 'missed the heart' of the conservation problem, a problem I have been working on for the last 30 years. He is right, of course, but that does not mean that he himself has understood it in a much shorter time. . . . Adults, just like children, need time to reach the right ideas. . . . This is the great mystery of development, which is irreducible to an accumulation of isolated learning acquisitions. Even psychology cannot be learned or constructed in a short time." (Despite his disclaimer, Piaget has offered a comprehensive theory of how the child arrives at conservation and this theory has received much research support.)

Piaget would probably agree with those who are critical about premature applications of his work to education. He finds particularly disturbing the efforts by some American educators to accelerate children intellectually. When he was giving his other 1967 lectures, in New York, he remarked:

"If we accept the fact that there are stages of development, another question arises which I call 'the American question,' and I am asked it every time I come here. If there are stages that children reach at given norms of ages can we accelerate the stages? Do we have to go through each one of these stages, or can't we speed it up a bit? Well, surely, the answer is yes . . . but how far can we speed them up? . . . I have a hypothesis which I am so far incapable of proving: probably the organization of operations has an optimal time. . . . For example, we know that it takes 9 to 12 months before babies develop the notion that an object is still there even when a screen is placed in front of it. Now kittens go through the same sub-stages but they do it in three months—so they're six months ahead of the babies. Is this an advantage or isn't it?

"We can certainly see our answer in one sense. The kitten is not going to go much further. The child has taken longer, but he is capable of going further so it seems to me that the nine months were not for nothing . . . It is probably possible to accelerate, but maximal acceleration is not desirable. There seems to be an optimal time. What this optimal time is will surely depend upon each individual and on the subject matter. We still need a great deal of research to know what the optimal time would be."

Piaget's stance against using his findings as a justification for accelerating children intellectually recalls a remark made by Freud when he was asked whatever became of those bright, aggressive shoeshine boys one encounters in city streets. Freud's reply was, "They become cobblers." In Piaget's terms they get to a certain point earlier but they don't go as far. And the New York educator Eliot Shapiro has pointed out that one of the Negro child's problems is that he is forced to grow up and take responsibility too soon and doesn't have time to be a child.

Despite some premature and erroneous applications of his thinking to

education, Piaget has had an over-all effect much more positive than negative. His findings about children's understanding of scientific and mathematical concepts are being used as guidelines for new curricula in these
subjects. And his tests are being more and more widely used to evaluate
educational outcomes. Perhaps the most significant and widespread positive effect that Piaget has had upon education is in the changed attitudes
on the part of teachers who have been exposed to his thinking. After becoming acquainted with Piaget's work, teachers can never again see children in quite the same way as they had before. Once teachers begin to
look at children from the Piagetian perspective they can also appreciate
his views with regard to the aims of education.

"The principal goal of education," he once said, "is to create men who
are capable of doing new things, not simply of repeating what other generations have done—men who are creative, inventive and discoverers. The
second goal of education is to form minds which can be critical, can verify, and not accept everything they are offered. The great danger today is
of slogans, collective opinions, ready-made trends of thought. We have to
be able to resist individually, to criticize, to distinguish between what is
proven and what is not. So we need pupils who are active, who learn early
to find out by themselves, partly by their own spontaneous activity and
partly through materials we set up for them; who learn early to tell what is
verifiable and what is simply the first idea to come to them."

At the beginning of his eighth decade, Jean Piaget is as busy as ever. A
new book of his on memory will be published soon and another on the
mental functions in the preschool child is in preparation. The International
Center for Genetic Epistemology, which Piaget founded in 1955 with a
grant from the Rockefeller Foundation, continues to draw scholars from
around the world who wish to explore with Piaget the origin of scientific
concepts. As Professor of Experimental Psychology at the University of
Geneva, Piaget also continues to teach courses and conduct seminars.

And his students still continue to collect the data which at the end of
the school year Piaget will take with him up to the mountains. The methods employed by his students today are not markedly different from those
which were used by their predecessors decades ago. While there are occasional statistics, there are still no electronics or computers. In an age of
moon shots and automation, the remarkable discoveries of Jean Piaget are
evidence that in the realm of scientific achievement, technological sophistication is still no substitute for creative genius.

VI. The Pupils: Color Caste and Social Class

What are rich hilltop kids made of?
  Sugar and spice and——
What are poor street kids made of?
  Rats and snails and——
What are the ghetto, the *barrio,* the reservation, made of?
  Joblessness, hopelessness, kids who steal and knife,
  Broken homes, broken windows, bad food, bad self-images,
  Disillusioned middle-class teachers—tired and cross;
  Dilapidated houses, boarded-up stores, run-down schools,
    Crumbling brick and old mortar,
    Smells and odors and cracked mirrors.

Yes, mirrors reflecting poverty and hopelessness, revealing the power of a white, affluent, upper-middle-class society that pays for the schools, propagates its own values in them, and preserves the ghetto, the *barrio,* and the reservation. Thus, as the schools are designed, they foster and perpetuate the socioeconomic system of the white middle class.

So, in order to really "see" education as it is experienced by lower-class migrant children and racially mixed, inner-city-bound youth, middle- and upper-class teachers need perspective—the kind of objective insight that can come from a cool analysis of the nature of the social-class—color-caste problem. If we want to know what ghetto schools are like, and why, we must look to the social milieu that surrounds those schools and at the disparity between the ghetto world and the dominant middle-class world. From each social environment, the school takes its essential characteristics—the hilltop school is new, clean, its students college-bound; the ghetto school is old, run down, its students work-bound. Understanding the ghetto school is further complicated because it is caught up in the conflict between the teacher's WASP values (derived from the middle and upper classes) and the values (derived from the culture of poverty) of those who are there to be taught.

Our schools are failing. In particular, they are failing the poor street kids. More particularly they are failing poor blacks, poor *latinos,* poor Indians, poor Asians, and poor *chicanos.* The questions the selections in this part attempt to answer are:

1. How and why are our schools failing those learners who wear a badge that says, "I am poor"?

2. Why and how are they failing those who wear a badge that says "I am poor" and "My skin is black, brown, copper, red, yellow"?
3. What is to be done?

Jonathan Kozol's article "Where Ghetto Schools Fail" shows vividly what is wrong with our slum schools. That the blacks are not alone and that the school system must accept the blame for the failure of its students are documented in Rosalie H. Wax's "The Warrior Droputs," a study of Sioux Indians in elementary schools on Indian reservations and in town high schools. "*La Raza* Brings Much to School" describes the educational advantages that bilingual and bicultural Mexican-Americans bring to the classroom and the frustration, alienation, and degradation they suffer when teachers ignore the advantages of *la raza*. In his study of Puerto Ricans in New York and Puerto Rico, Oscar Lewis states that "The Culture of Poverty" constitutes a truly separate culture that transcends national borders and racial types. The application of social-class theory to a specific racial group is presented in a scholarly manner by Andrew Billingsley, himself a black, in "Social Status in the Black Community."

Our schools are failing not only our minority students; they are also failing all of our young people in that they do not develop all human potential more fully. In "No School?" George Leonard describes how the schools limit human potential through boredom. Victor Eisner, in "Alienation of Youth," analyzes the suburban community to show how such segregation alienates middle-class youth. Robert J. Havighurst, in "Social Class and Education," demonstrates how the typical school discriminates against the lower social classes and favors the middle and upper social classes.

James Baldwin's "A Talk to Teachers" tells what it is like to be black and gives prophetic insight into the pent-up anger and hostility characteristic of black youth in the inner city. Where America's black people stand in their fight for freedom and equality and how the prejudices of American society are reflected in its schools are discussed in "The Black Revolution in Education" by Price Cobbs.

Many people blame our status quo administrators for blocking needed changes in our schools. However, one school administrator, Neil V. Sullivan, points out how we can reconstruct education, even without additional funding, in his "Hope for the Half-Democracy."

Finally, if we are to reverse the decaying condition of our schools, especially our slum schools, we must train teachers who are truly equipped to serve the residents of our ghettos. James C. Stone proposes a new model for teacher education—a separate institution planned and directed by the local community, the schools therein, and the adjacent social and educational agencies—in "Training Teachers of the Disadvantaged: Blueprint for a Breakthrough."

32. Where Ghetto Schools Fail

Jonathan Kozol

There has been so much recent talk of progress in the areas of curriculum innovation and textbook revision that few people outside the field of teaching understand how bad most of our elementary school materials still are. In isolated suburban school districts children play ingenious Monopoly games revised to impart an immediate and first-person understanding of economic problems in the colonial period. In private schools, kindergarten children begin to learn about numbers with brightly colored sticks known as cuisenaire rods, and second-grade children are introduced to mathematics through the ingenuity of a package of odd-shaped figures known as Attribute Games. But in the majority of schools in Roxbury and Harlem and dozens of other slum districts stretching west across the country, teaching techniques, textbooks, and other teaching aids are hopelessly antique, largely obsolete, and often insulting or psychologically oppressive for many thousands of Negro and other minority schoolchildren.

I once made a check of all books in my fourth-grade classroom. Of the slightly more than six hundred books, almost one quarter had been published prior to the bombing of Hiroshima; 60 percent were either ten years old or older. Of thirty-two different book series standing in rows within the cupboard, only six were published as recently as five years ago, and seven series were twenty to thirty-five years old. These figures put into perspective some of the lofty considerations and expensive research projects sponsored by even the best of the curriculum development organizations, for they suggest that educational progress and innovation are reaching chiefly the children of rich people rather than the children of the urban poor.

Obsolescence, however, was not the only problem in our textbooks. Direct and indirect forms of discrimination were another. The geography book given to my pupils, first published eighteen years ago and only modestly updated since, traced a cross-country journey in which there was not

SOURCE: *The Atlantic Monthly*, CCXX, 4 (October 1967), 107–10. Copyright © 1967 by Jonathan Kozol. Reprinted by permission of the Houghton Mifflin Company.

one mention, hint, or image of a dark-skinned face. The chapter on the South described an idyllic landscape in the heart of Dixie: pastoral home of hardworking white citizens, contented white children, and untroubled white adults.

While the history book mentioned Negroes—in its discussion of slavery and the Civil War—the tone of these sections was ambiguous. "Men treasure freedom above all else," the narrative conceded at one point, but it also pointed out that slavery was not an altogether dreadful institution: "Most Southern people treated their slaves kindly," it related, and then quoted a stereotyped plantation owner as saying: "Our slaves have good homes and plenty to eat. When they are sick, we take care of them. . . ."

While the author favored emancipation, he found it necessary to grant to arguments on the other side a patriotic legitimacy: "No one can truly say, 'The North was right' or 'The Southern cause was better.' Remember, each side fought for the ideals it believed in. For in Our America all of us have the right to our beliefs."

When my class had progressed to the cotton chapter in our geography book, I decided to alter the scheduled reading. Since I was required to make use of the textbook, and since its use, I believed, was certain to be damaging, I decided to supply the class with extra material in the form of a mimeographed sheet. I did not propose to tell the children any tales about lynchings, beatings, or the Ku Klux Klan. I merely wanted to add to the study of cotton-growing some information about the connection between the discovery of Eli Whitney's cotton gin and the greater growth of slavery.

I had to submit this material to my immediate superior in the school, a lady whom I will call the Reading Teacher. The Reading Teacher was a well-intentioned woman who had spent several years in ghetto classrooms, but who, like many other teachers, had some curiously ambivalent attitudes toward the children she was teaching. I recall the moment after I had handed her that sheet of paper. Looking over the page, she agreed with me immediately that it was accurate. Nobody, she said, was going to quibble with the idea that cotton, the cotton gin, and slavery were all intertwined. But it was the question of the "advisability of any mention of slavery to the children at this time," which, she said, she was presently turning over in her mind. "Would it," she asked me frankly, "truly serve the advantage of the children at this stage to confuse and complicate the study of simple geography with socioeconomic factors?" Why expose the children, she was asking essentially, to unpleasant facts about their heritage?

Then, with an expression of the most honest and intense affection for the children in the class, she added: "I don't want these children to have to think back on this year later on and to remember that we were the ones who told them they were Negro." This remark seemed to take one step further the attitude of the textbook writers. Behind the statement lay the unspoken assumption that to be Negro was a shameful condition. The longer this knowledge could be kept from the innocent young, the better off they would be.

After the journey across America, the class was to study the life of the desert Arab. Before we began, the Reading Teacher urged upon me a book which she said she had used with her own classes for a great many years. It was not the same book the children had. She told me she preferred it, but that it was too old to be in regular use.

I took the book home that night and opened it up to a section on the Arabs:

The Bedouin father is tall and straight. He wears a robe that falls to his ankles and his bare feet are shod in sandals of camel's leather. . . . Behind the Bedouin father walk his wife and his children. . . .

These people are fine looking. Their black eyes are bright and intelligent. Their features are much like our own, and, although their skin is brown, they belong to the white race, as we do. It is scorching desert sun that has tanned the skin of the Arabs to such a dark brown color.

Turning to a section on Europe, I read the following description:

Two Swiss children live in a farmhouse on the edge of town. . . . These children are handsome. Their eyes are blue. Their hair is golden yellow. Their white skins are clear, and their cheeks are as red as ripe, red apples.

Curious after this to see how the African Negroes would be treated, I turned to a section on the Congo Valley:

The black people who live on this great continent of Africa were afraid of the first white men who came to explore their land. They ran and hid from them in the dark jungle. They shot poisoned arrows from behind the thick bushes. They were savage and uncivilized. . . .

Yumbo and Minko are a black boy and a black girl who live in this jungle village. Their skins are of so dark a color that they look almost black. Their noses are large and flat. Their lips are thick. Their eyes are black and shining, and their hair is so curly that it seems like wool. They are Negroes and belong to the black race.

Perhaps without being conscious of it, the Reading Teacher had her own way of telling the children what it meant to be Negro.

Not all books used in a school system, merely by the law of averages, are going to be consistently and blatantly poor. A large number of the books we had in Boston were only mildly distorted or else devastatingly bad only in one part. One such book, not used in my school but at the junior high level, was entitled *Our World Today*. Right and wrong, good and bad, alternate in this book from sentence to sentence and from page to page:

> The people of the British Isles are, like our own, a mixed people. Their ancestors were the sturdy races of northern Europe, such as Celts, Angles, Saxons, Danes and Normans, whose energy and abilities still appear in their descendants. With such a splendid inheritance what could be more natural than that the British should explore and settle many parts of the world and in time build up the world's greatest colonial empire? . . .
>
> The people of South Africa have one of the most democratic governments now in existence in any country. . . .
>
> Africa needs more capitalists. . . . White managers are needed . . . to show the Negroes how to work and to manage their plantations. . . .
>
> In our study of the nations of the world, we should try to understand the people and their problems from their point of view. We ought to have a sympathetic attitude towards them, rather than condemn them through ignorance because they do not happen always to have our ways. . . .
>
> The Negro is very quick to imitate and follow the white man's way of living and dressing. . . .
>
> The white man may remain for short periods and direct the work, but he cannot . . . do the work himself. He must depend on the natives to do the work. . . .
>
> The white men who have entered Africa are teaching the natives how to live. . . .

Sooner or later, books like these will be put to pasture. Either that, or they will be carefully doctored and rewritten. But the problem they represent is not going to be resolved in any important way by their removal or revision. Too many teachers admire and depend on such textbooks, and prefer to teach from them. The attitudes of these teachers are likely to remain long after the books have been replaced.

Plenty of good books are available, of course, that give an honest picture of the lives of black Americans. The tutorial programs in Boston have been using them, and so have many of the more enlightened private schools. In the public schools of this city, however, it is difficult to make use of books that depart from the prescribed curriculum. When I made a tentative effort to introduce such materials into my classroom, I encountered firm resistance.

Earlier in the year I had brought to school a book of poetry by the Negro author Langston Hughes. I had not used it in the classroom, but it did at least make its way onto a display board in the auditorium as part of an exhibit on important American Negroes, set up to pay lip service to "Negro History Week."

To put a book by a Negro poet on display is one thing. To open the book and attempt to read something from it is quite another. In the last weeks of the spring I discovered the difference when I began to read a few of the poems to the children in my class. It was during a period in which I also was reading them some poems of John Crowe Ransom, Robert Frost, and W. B. Yeats.

Hughes, I have come to learn, holds an extraordinary appeal for many children. I knew this from some earlier experiences in other classes, and I remembered, in particular, the reaction of a group of young teen-agers in a junior high the first time I ever had brought his work into a public school. On the book's cover, the children could see the picture of the dark-skinned author, and they did not fail to comment. Their comments concentrated on that single, obvious, overriding fact:

"Look—that man's colored."

The same reaction was evident here, too, among my fourth-grade students: the same gratification and the same very vivid sense of recognition. It seemed a revelation to them that a man could have black skin and be a famous author.

Of all the poems of Langston Hughes that we read, the one the children liked the best was a poem entitled "Ballad of the Landlord." The reason, I think, that this piece of writing had so much meaning for them was not only that it seemed moving in an obvious and immediate human way, but also that it *found* its emotion in something ordinary. It is a poem which allows both heroism and pathos to poor people, sees strength in awkwardness, and attributes to a poor person standing on the stoop of his slum house every bit as much significance as William Wordsworth saw in daffodils, waterfalls, and clouds. At the request of the children, I mimeographed some copies of that poem, and although nobody in the classroom was asked to do this, several of the children took it home and memorized it on their own. I did not assign it for memory, because I do not think that memorizing a poem has any special value. Some of the children just came in and asked if they could recite it. Before long, almost every child in the room had asked to have a turn.

One day a week later, shortly before lunchtime, I was standing in front of my class playing a record of French children's songs I had brought in. A message-signal on the wall began to buzz. I left the room and hurried to the principal's office. A white man whom I had never seen before was sitting by her desk. This man, bristling and clearly hostile to me, as was the principal, instantly attacked me for having read to my class and distributed at their wish the poem entitled "Ballad of the Landlord." It turned out that he was the father of one of the few white boys in the class. He was also a police officer.

The mimeograph of the poem, in my handwriting, was waved before my eyes. The principal demanded to know what right I had to allow such a poem—not in the official course of study—to be read and memorized by children. I said I had not asked anyone to memorize it, but that I would defend the poem and its use on the basis that it was a good poem. The principal became incensed with my answer and blurted out that she did not consider it a work of art.

The parent was angry as well, it turned out, about a book having to do with the United Nations. I had brought a book to class, one of sixty or more volumes, that told about the UN and its Human Rights Commission. The man, I believe, had mistaken "human rights" for "civil rights" and was consequently in a patriotic rage. The principal, in fairness, made the point that she did not think there was anything wrong with the United Nations, although in the report later filed on the matter, she denied this, and said, instead, "I then spoke and said that I felt there was no need for this material in the classroom." The principal's report went on to say that she assured the parent, after I had left the room, that "there was not another teacher in the district who would have used this poem or any material like it. I assured him that his children would be very safe from such incidents."

I returned to my class, as requested, and a little before two o'clock the principal called me back to tell me I was fired. She forbade me to say good-bye to the children in the class or to indicate in any way that I was leaving. She said that I was to close up my records, leave the school, and report to School Department headquarters the next morning.

The next day an official who had charge of my case at the School Department took a much harder line on curriculum innovation than I had ever heard before. No literature, she said, which is not in the course of study could *ever* be read by a Boston teacher without permission of someone higher up. She said further that no poem by any Negro author could be considered permissible if it involved suffering. I asked her whether there would be many good poems left to read by such a standard. Wouldn't it rule out almost all great Negro literature? Her answer evaded the issue. No poetry that described suffering was felt to be suitable. The only Negro poetry that could be read in the Boston schools, she indicated, must fit a certain kind of standard. The kind of poem she meant, she said by way of example, might be a poem that "accentuates the positive" or "describes nature" or "tells of something hopeful."

The same official went on a few minutes later to tell me that any complaint from a parent meant automatic dismissal. "You're out," she said. "You cannot teach in the Boston schools again. If you want to teach, why don't you try a private school someday?"

Other Boston officials backed up these assertions in statements released during the following hectic days. The deputy superintendent, who wielded considerable authority over these matters, pointed out that although Langston Hughes "has written much beautiful poetry, we cannot give directives to the teacher to use literature written in native dialects." She explained: "We are trying to break the speech patterns of these children, trying to get them to speak properly. This poem does not present correct grammatical expression and would just entrench the speech patterns we want to break."

A couple of weeks later, winding up an investigation into the matter, School Committee member Thomas Eisenstadt concluded that school officials had handled things correctly. Explaining in his statement that teachers are dismissed frequently when found lacking in either "training, personality or character," he went on to say that "Mr. Kozol, or anyone else who lacks the personal discipline to abide by rules and regulations, as we all must in our civilized society, is obviously unsuited for the highly responsible profession of teaching."

In thinking back upon my year within the Boston system, I am often reminded of a kind of sad-keyed epilogue that the Reading Teacher used to bring forward sometimes at the end of a discussion: "Things are changing," she used to say with feeling; "I am changing too—but everything cannot happen just like that."

Perhaps by the time another generation comes around a certain modest number of these things will have begun to be corrected. But if I were the parent of a Negro child, I know that I would not willingly accept a calendar of improvements scaled so slowly. The anger of the mother whose child's years in elementary school have been squandered may seem inexplicable to a person like the Reading Teacher. To that mother, it is the complacency and hypocrisy of a society that could sustain and foster so many thousands of people like the Reading Teacher that seem extraordinary. The comfortable people who don't know and don't see the ghettos deliberate in their committee rooms. Meanwhile, the children whose lives their decisions are either going to save or ruin are expected to sit quietly, fold their hands patiently, recite their lessons, draw their margins, bite their tongues, swallow their dignities, and smile and wait.

33. The Warrior Dropouts

Rosalie H. Wax

Scattered over the prairie on the Pine Ridge reservation of South Dakota, loosely grouped into bands along the creeks and roads, live thousands of Sioux Indians. Most live in cabins, some in tents, a few in houses; most lack the conventional utilities—running water, electricity, telephone, and gas. None has a street address. They are called "country Indians" and most speak the Dakota language. They are very poor, the most impoverished people on the reservation.

For four years I have been studying the problems of the high school dropouts among these Oglala Sioux. In many ways these Indian youths ate very different from slum school dropouts—Negro, Mexican-American, rural white—just as in each group individuals differ widely one from another. Yet no one who has any familiarity with their problems can avoid being struck by certain parallels, both between groups and individuals.

In slum schools and Pine Ridge schools, scholastic achievement is low, and the dropout rate is high; the children's primary loyalties go to friends and peers, not schools or educators; and all of them are confronted by teachers who see them as inadequately prepared, uncultured offspring of alien and ignorant folk. They are classified as "culturally deprived." All such schools serve as the custodial, constabulary, and reformative arm of one element of society directed against another.

Otherwise well-informed people, including educators themselves, assume on the basis of spurious evidence that dropouts dislike and voluntarily reject school, that they all leave it for much the same reasons, and that they are really much alike. But dropouts leave high school under strikingly different situations and for quite different reasons.

Many explicitly state that they do not wish to leave and are really "pushouts" or "kickouts" rather than "dropouts." As a Sioux youth in our sample put it, "I quit, but I never did *want* to quit!" Perhaps the fact that educators consider all dropouts to be similar tells us more about educators and their schools than about dropouts.

Source: TRANS-*action* (May 1967) 40–46. Copyright©May 1967 by TRANS-action, Inc., New Brunswick, New Jersey.

On the Reservation

The process that alienates many country Indian boys from the high schools they are obliged to attend begins early in childhood and reflects the basic Sioux social structure. Sioux boys are reared to be physically reckless and impetuous. One that does not perform an occasional brash act may be accepted as "quiet" or "bashful," but he is not considered a desirable son, brother, or sweetheart. Sioux boys are reared to be proud and feisty and are expected to resent public censure. They have some obligations to relatives but the major social controls after infancy are exerted by their fellows—their "peer group."

From about the age of seven or eight, they spend almost the entire day without adult supervision, running or riding about with friends of their age and returning home only for food and sleep. Even we (my husband, Dr. Murray L. Wax, and I), who had lived with Indian families from other tribal groups, were startled when we heard a responsible and respected Sioux matron dismiss a lad of six or seven for the entire day with the statement "Go play with Larry and John." Similarly, at a ceremonial gathering in a strange community with hundreds of people, boys of nine or ten often take off and stay away until late at night as a matter of course. Elders pay little attention. There is much prairie and many creeks for roaming and playing in ways that bother nobody. The only delinquencies we have heard Sioux elders complain about are chasing stock, teasing bulls, or occasionally some petty theft.

Among Sioux males this kind of peer-group raising lends to a highly efficient yet unverbalized system of intra-group discipline and powerful intra-group loyalties and dependencies. During our seven-month stay in a reservation community, we were impressed by how rarely the children quarreled with one another. This behavior was not imposed by elders but by the children themselves.

For example, our office contained some items very attractive to them, especially a typewriter. We were astonished to see how quietly they handled this prize that only one could enjoy at a time. A well-defined status system existed so that a child using the typewriter at once gave way and left the machine if one higher in the hierarchy appeared. A half-dozen of these shifts might take place within an hour; yet, all this occurred without a blow or often even a word.

Sioux boys have intense loyalties and dependencies. They almost never tattle on each other. But when forced to live with strangers, they tend to become inarticulate, psychologically disorganized, or withdrawn.

With most children the peer group reaches the zenith of its power in school. In middle-class neighborhoods, independent children can usually seek and secure support from parents, teachers, or adult society as a whole. But when, as in an urban slum or Indian reservation, the teachers stay aloof from parents, and parents feel that teachers are a breed apart, the peer group may become so powerful that the children literally take over the school. Then group activities are carried on in class—jokes, notes, intrigues, teasing, mock-combat, comic book reading, courtship—all without the teacher's knowledge and often without grossly interfering with the learning process.

Competent and experienced teachers can come to terms with the peer group and manage to teach a fair amount of reading, writing, and arithmetic. But teachers who are incompetent, overwhelmed by large classes, or sometimes merely inexperienced may be faced with groups of children who refuse even to listen.

We marveled at the variety and efficiency of the devices developed by Indian children to frustrate formal learning—unanimous inattention, refusal to go to the board, writing on the board in letters less than an inch high, inarticulate responses, and whispered or pantomime teasing of victims called on to recite. In some seventh- and eighth-grade classes there was a withdrawal so uncompromising that no voice could be heard for hours except the teacher's, plaintively asking questions or giving instructions.

Most Sioux children insist they like school, and most Sioux parents corroborate this. Once the power and depth of their social life within the school is appreciated, it is not difficult to see why they like it. Indeed, the only unpleasant aspects of school for them are the disciplinary regulations (which they soon learn to tolerate or evade), an occasional "mean" teacher, bullies, or feuds with members of other groups. Significantly, we found that notorious truants had usually been rejected by classmates and also had no older relatives in school to protect them from bullies. But the child who has a few friends or an older brother or sister to stand by him, or who "really likes to play basketball," almost always finds school agreeable.

Day School Graduates

By the time he has finished the eighth grade, the country Indian boy has many fine qualities: zest for life, curiosity, pride, physical courage, sensibility to human relationships, experience with the elemental facts of life, and intense group loyalty and integrity. His experiences in day school have done nothing to diminish or tarnish his ideal—the physically reckless and impetuous youth, who is admired by all.

But, on the other hand, the country Indian boy is almost completely lacking in the traits most highly valued by the school authorities: a narrow and absolute respect for "regulations," "government property," routine, discipline, and diligence. He is also deficient in other skills apparently essential to rapid and easy passage through high school and boarding school —especially the abilities to make short-term superficial social adjustments with strangers. Nor can he easily adjust to a system which demands, on the one hand, that he study competitively as an individual, and, on the other, that he live in barrack-type dormitories where this kind of study is impossible.

Finally, his English is inadequate for high school work. Despite eight or more years of formal training in reading and writing, many day school graduates cannot converse fluently in English even among themselves. In contrast, most of the students with whom they will compete in higher schools have spoken English since childhood.

To leave home and the familiar and pleasant day school for boarding life at the distant and formidable high school is a prospect both fascinating and frightening. To many young country Indians the agency town of Pine Ridge is a center of sophistication. It has blocks of Indian Bureau homes with lawns and fences, a barber shop, big grocery stores, churches, gas stations, a drive-in confectionary, and even a restaurant with a juke box. While older siblings or cousins may have reported that at high school "they make you study harder," that "they just make you move every minute," or that the "mixed-bloods" or "children of bureau employees" are "mean" or "snotty," there are the compensatory highlights of movies, basketball games, and the social (white man's) dances.

For the young men there is the chance to play high school basketball, baseball, or football; for the young women there is the increased distance from over-watchful, conservative parents. For both, there is the freedom, taken or not, to hitchhike to White Clay, with its beer joints, bowling hall, and archaic aura of Western wickedness. If, then, a young man's close friends or relatives decide to go to high school, he will usually want to go too rather than remain at home, circumscribed, "living off his folks." Also, every year, more elders coax, tease, bribe, or otherwise pressure the young men into "making a try" because "nowadays only high school graduates get the good jobs."

The Student Body: Town Indians, Country Indians

The student body of the Oglala Community High School is very varied. First, there are the children of the town dwellers, who range from well-paid white and Indian government employees who live in neat government housing developments to desperately poor people who live in the paper shacks. Second, there is the large number of institutionalized children who have been attending the Oglala Community School as boarders for the greater part of their lives. Some are orphans, others come from isolated sections of the reservation where there are no day schools, others come from different tribal areas.

But these town dwellers and boarders share an advantage—for them entry into high school is little more than a shift from eighth to ninth grade. They possess an intimate knowledge of their classmates and a great deal of local know-how. In marked contrast, the country Indian freshman enters an alien environment. Not only is he ignorant of how to buck the rules, he doesn't even know the rules. Nor does he know anybody to put him wise.

Many country Indians drop out of high school before they have any clear idea what high school is all about. In our sample, 35 percent dropped out before the end of the ninth grade and many of these left during the first semester. Our first interviews with them were tantalizingly contradictory—about half the young men seemed to have found high school so painful they could scarcely talk about it; the other half were also laconic, but insisted that they had liked school. In time, those who had found school unbearable confided that they had left school because they were lonely or because they were abused by more experienced boarders. Only rarely did they mention that they had trouble with their studies.

The following statement, made by a mild and pleasant boy, conveys some idea of the agony of loneliness, embarrassment, and inadequacy that a country Indian newcomer may suffer when he enters high school:

At day school it was kind of easy for me. But high school was really hard, and I can't figure out even simple questions that they ask me. . . . Besides I'm so quiet [modest and unaggressive] that the boys really took advantage of me. They borrow money from me every Sunday night and they don't even care to pay it back. . . . I can't talk English very good, and I'm really bashful and shy, and I get scared when I talk to white people. I usually just stay quiet in the [day school] classroom, and the teachers will leave me alone. But at boarding school they wanted me to get up and talk or say something. . . . I quit and I never went back. . . . I can't seem to get along with different people, and I'm so shy I can't even make friends. . . . [Translated from Lakota by interviewer.]

Most of the newcomers seem to have a difficult time getting along with the experienced boarders and claim that the latter not only strip them of essentials like soap, paper, and underwear, but also take the treasured gifts of proud and encouraging relatives, wrist watches and transistor radios.

Some of the kids—especially the boarders—are really mean. All they want to do is steal—and they don't want to study. They'll steal your school work off you and they'll copy it. . . . Sometimes they'll break into our suitcase. Or if we have money in our pockets they'll take off our overalls and search our pockets and get our money. . . . So finally I just came home. If I could be a day scholar I think I'll stay in. But if they want me to board I don't want to go back. I think I'll just quit.

Interviews with the dropouts who asserted that school is "all right"—and that they had not wished to quit—suggest that many had been almost as wretched during their first weeks at high school as the bashful young men who quit because they "couldn't make friends." But they managed to find some friends and, with this peer support and protection, they were able to cope with and (probably) strike back at other boarders. In any case, the painful and degrading aspects of school became endurable. As one lad put it: "Once you *learn* to be a boarder, it's not so bad."

But for these young men, an essential part of having friends was "raising Cain"—that is, engaging in daring and defiant deeds forbidden by the school authorities. The spirit of these escapades is difficult to portray to members of a society where most people no longer seem capable of thinking about the modern equivalents of Tom Sawyer, Huckleberry Finn, or Kim, except as juvenile delinquents. We ourselves, burdened by sober professional interest in dropouts, at first found it hard to recognize that these able and engaging young men were taking pride and joy in doing exactly what the school authorities thought most reprehensible; and they were not confessing, but boasting, although their stunts had propelled them out of school.

For instance, this story from one bright lad of 15 who had run away from high school. Shortly after entering ninth grade he and his friends had appropriated a government car. (The usual pattern in such adventures is to drive off the reservation until the gas gives out.) For this offense (according to the respondent) they were restricted for the rest of the term—they were forbidden to leave the high school campus or attend any of the school recreational events, games, dances, or movies. (In effect, this meant doing nothing but going to class, performing work chores, and sitting in the dormitory.) Even then our respondent seems to have kept up with his class work and did not play hookey except in reading class:

It was after we stole that car Mrs. Bluger [pseudonym for reading teacher] would keep asking who stole the car in class. So I just quit going there. . . . One night we were the only ones up in the older boys' dorm. We said, "Hell with this noise. We're not going to be the only ones here." So we snuck out and went over to the dining hall. I pried this one window open about this far and then it started to crack, so I let it go. . . . We heard someone so we took off. It was show that night I think. [Motion picture was being shown in school auditorium.] . . . All the rest of the guys was sneaking in and getting something. So I said I was going to get my share too. We had a case of apples and a case of oranges. Then I think it was the night watchman was coming, so we run around and hid behind those steps. He shined that light on us. So I thought right then I was going to keep on going. That was around Christmas time. We walked back to Oglala [about 15 miles] and we were eating this stuff all the way back.

This young man implied that after this escapade he simply did not have the nerve to try to return to the high school. He insisted, however, that he would like to try another high school:

I'd like to finish [high school] and get a good job some place. If I don't I'll probably just be a bum around here or something.

Young Men Who Stay in School

Roughly half the young Sioux who leave high school very early claim they left because they were unable to conform to school regulations. What happens to the country boys who remain? Do they "shape up" and obey the regulations? Do they, even, come to "believe" in them? We found that most of these older and more experienced youths were, if anything, even *more* inclined to boast of triumphs over the rules than the younger fellows who had left. Indeed, all but one assured us that they were adept at hookey, and food and car stealing, and that they had frequent surreptitious beer parties and other outlaw enjoyments. We do not know whether they (especially the star athletes) actually disobey the school regulations as frequently and flagrantly as they claim. But there can be no doubt that most Sioux young men above 12 wish to be regarded as hellions in school. For them, it would be as manly to have any other attitude.

An eleventh grader in good standing explained his private technique for playing hookey and added proudly "They never caught me yet." A twelfth grader and first string basketball player told how he and some other students "stole" a jeep from the high school machine shop and drove it all over town. When asked why, he patiently explained: "To see if we can get away with it. It's for the enjoyment . . . to see if we can take the car without getting caught." Another senior told our male staff worker: "You can always get out and booze it up."

The impulse to boast of the virile achievements of youth seems to maintain itself into middle and even into old age. Country Indians with college training zestfully told how they and a group of proctors had stolen large amounts of food from the high school kitchen and were never apprehended, or how they and their friends drank three fifths of whiskey in one night and did not pass out.

Clearly, the activities school administrators and teachers denounce as immature and delinquent are regarded as part of youthful daring, excitement, manly honor, and contests of skill and wits by the Sioux young men and many of their elders.

They are also, we suspect, an integral part of the world of competitive sports. "I like to play basketball" was one of the most frequent responses of young men to the question "What do you like most about school?" Indeed, several ninth and tenth graders stated that the opportunity to play basketball was the main reason they kept going to school. One eighth grader who had run away several times stated:

When I was in the seventh grade I made the B team on the basketball squad. And I made the A team when I was in the eighth grade. So I stayed and finished school without running away anymore.

The unselfconscious devotion and ardor with which many of these young men participate in sports must be witnessed to be appreciated even mildly. They cannot communicate their joy and pride in words, though one 17-year-old member of the team that won the state championship tried, by telling how a team member wearing a war bonnet "led us onto the playing floor and this really gave them a cheer."

Unfortunately, we have seen little evidence that school administrators and teachers recognize the opportunity to use sports as a bridge to school.

By the eleventh and twelfth grades many country Indians have left the reservation or gone into the armed services, and it is not always easy to tell which are actual dropouts. However, we did reach some. Their reasons for dropping out varied. One pled boredom: "I was just sitting there doing anything to pass the time." Another said he didn't know what made him quit: "I just didn't fit in anymore. . . . I just wasn't like the other guys anymore." Another refused to attend a class in which he felt the teacher had insulted Indians. When the principal told him that he must attend this class or be "restricted," he left. Significantly, his best friend dropped out with him, even though he was on the way to becoming a first-class basketball player.

Different as they appear at first, these statements have a common undertone: They are the expressions not of immature delinquents, but of relatively mature young men who find the atmosphere of the high school stultifying and childish.

The Dilemma of Sioux Youth

Any intense cross-cultural study is likely to reveal as many tragi-comic situations as social scientific insights. Thus, on the Pine Ridge reservation, a majority of the young men arrive at adolescence valuing *élan,* bravery, generosity, passion, and luck, and admiring outstanding talent in athletics, singing, and dancing. While capable of wider relations and reciprocities, they function at their social best as members of small groups of peers or relatives. Yet to obtain even modest employment in the greater society, they must graduate from high school. And in order to graduate from high school, they are told that they must develop exactly opposite qualities to those they possess: a respect for humdrum diligence and routine, for "discipline" (in the sense of not smoking in toilets, not cutting classes, and not getting drunk), and for government property. In addition, they are expected to compete scholastically on a highly privatized and individualistic level, while living in large dormitories, surrounded by strangers who make privacy of any type impossible.

If we were dealing with the schools of a generation or two ago, then the situation might be bettered by democratization—involving the Sioux parents in control of the schools. This system of local control was not perfect, but it worked pretty well. Today the problem is more complicated and tricky; educators have become professionalized, and educational systems have become complex bureaucracies, inextricably involved with universities, education associations, foundations, and federal crash programs. Even suburban middle-class parents, some of whom are highly educated and sophisticated, find it difficult to cope with the bureaucratic barriers and mazes of the schools their children attend. It is difficult to see how Sioux parents could accomplish much unless, in some way, their own school system were kept artificially small and isolated and accessible to their understanding and control.

Working-Class Youth

How does our study of the Sioux relate to the problems of city dropouts? A specific comparison of the Sioux dropouts with dropouts from the urban working class—Negroes, Puerto Ricans, or whites—would, no doubt, reveal many salient differences in cultural background and world view. Nevertheless, investigations so far undertaken suggest that the attitudes held by these peoples *toward education and the schools* are startlingly similar.

Both Sioux and working-class parents wish their children to continue in school because they believe that graduating from high school is a guarantee of employment. Though some teachers would not believe it, many working-class dropouts, like the Sioux dropouts, express a generally favorable attitude toward school, stating that teachers are generally fair and that the worst thing about dropping out of school is missing one's friends. Most important, many working-class dropouts assert that they were pushed out of school and frequently add that the push was fairly direct. The Sioux boys put the matter more delicately, implying that the school authorities would not really welcome them back.

These similarities should not be seized on as evidence that all disprivileged children are alike and that they will respond as one to the single, ideal, educational policy. What it does mean is that the schools and their administrators are so monotonously alike that the boy brought up in a minority social or ethnic community can only look at and react to them in the same way. Despite their differences, they are all in much the same boat as they face the great monolith of middle-class society and its one-track education escalator.

An even more important—if often unrecognized—point is that not only does the school pose a dilemma for the working-class or Sioux, Negro, or Puerto Rican boy—he also poses one for the school. In many traditional or ethnic cultures boys are encouraged to be virile adolescents and become "real men." But our schools try to deprive youth of adolescence—and they demand that high school students behave like "mature people"—which, in our culture often seems to mean in a pretty dull, conformist fashion.

Those who submit and succeed in school can often fit into the bureaucratic requirements of employers, but they are also likely to lack independence of thought and creativity. The dropouts are failures—they have failed to become what the school demands. But the school has also failed to offer what the boys from even the most "deprived" and "under-developed" peoples take as a matter of course—the opportunity to become whole men.

S. M. Miller and Ira E. Harrison, studying working-class youth, assert that individuals who do poorly in school are handicapped or disfavored for the remainder of their lives, because "the schools have become the occupational gatekeepers" and "the level of education affects the kind and level of job that can be attained." On the other hand, the investigations of Edgar Z. Friedenberg and Jules Henry suggest that the youths who perform creditably in high school according to the views of the authorities are disfavored in that they emerge from this experience as permanently crippled persons or human beings.

In a curious way our researches among the Sioux may be viewed as supporting both of these contentions, and they suggest that some young people leave high school because they are too vital and independent to submit to the dehumanizing situation.

34. *La Raza* Brings Much
to the School

Jack Forbes

For far too long many teachers have looked upon culturally different children as being "culturally deprived." Such pedagogues have conceived of their duty as being one of filling this "cultural vacuum" with Anglo-American traits. Unfortunately, this negative (and narrow) attitude has led to the ignoring of the rich legacy which many non-Anglo pupils either bring to school or acquire outside of school through the educational processes of the folk community.

Mexican-American youth often bring to the school a varied background of experiences and skills which can be utilized as mediums for both the development of the Mexican-American pupil's potential and for the enrichment of the school experiences of non-Mexican scholastics.

The ability to speak more than one language has, in most societies, been regarded as an essential characteristic of the fully educated man. The European educated classes have for centuries spoken French, English, German, and sometimes other languages in addition to their native idiom. American Indian groups commonly grew up speaking three or more divergent idioms, in addition to possessing some familiarity with other languages. People in the United States are today coming once again to the realization that, as in the days of Thomas Jefferson and Benjamin Franklin, a knowledge of several languages is indeed essential.

The Mexican-American child usually has a head start over the Anglo-American because of his familiarity with two languages (and a few Mexican-Americans speak or understand an Indian language as well). It is true that often the knowledge of both Spanish and English is imperfect, but nonetheless the most precious linguistic skills, the ability to switch back and forth from one language to another and the "feel" for being comfortable in two or more languages, is present as either a fully or partially devel-

SOURCE: *CTA Journal*, LXV, 4 (October 1969), 15–17. Reprinted by permission of the publisher.

oped resource. It is also true that most Mexican-Americans speak a dialect of American Spanish while teachers are often acquainted with European Spanish or a standardized international Spanish. American Spanish is, nonetheless, as "correct" and legitimate as any modern idiom and has the asset of being far more "American" than standard American English, incorporating as it does thousands of words of native American origin. What is fundamental is that Mexican-American pupils possess an entrée into two viable languages, both of which (American Spanish and American English) can be utilized as vehicles for sound linguistic development.

Those educators who recognize the value of linguistic training can certainly enrich the total program of their classroom or school by making full use of the Mexican-American child's language advantage. A truly bilingual learning experience can be produced that will not only allow the Mexican child to develop both of his languages but which will make it easier for monolingual English-speaking children to *master* a second tongue.

Bicultural Experience Enriches Program

Mexican-American children also bring to the school a variety of bicultural experiences which can enrich almost every facet of the school's program. Their knowledge of folk arts, cooking, music, literature, and dances can be utilized as vehicles for cross-cultural education and for acquainting children who are new to the region with the rich heritage of the Southwest. Additionally, Mexican-Americans, in sharing their skills with fellow pupils (being teachers, as it were), can help develop in themselves that degree of pride and self-confidence which is so necessary for successful learning generally,

Those Mexican-American pupils who come from folk-level or low-income homes will also possess valuable experiences denied to many affluent children, such as a direct knowledge of domestic arts (taking care of baby brother, et cetera) and practical work (harvesting crops, repairing tractors, et cetera). Such children often have had to assume *important* responsibilities at an early age and their relatively more mature outlook should prove of immense value to affluent children who never have had contact with life at its more fundamental level.

Needless to state, the adult Mexican-American community possesses valuable resources for school enrichment. It is not uncommon for a *colonia* (neighborhood) to possess some persons skilled in arts and crafts, folk music, folk dancing, piñata-making, costume-making, Mexican cooking, or in various commercial activities associated with Mexican arts or food. These persons can often be brought into the school as resource people and part-time instructors, thus expanding in a vast way the "bank of skills" possessed by any school district. Additionally, of course, close contacts between the school and the community can be developed or enhanced by this procedure. In a similar manner, professional-level persons of Mexican origin can be called upon to discuss Mexican history, literature, et cetera, and can suggest books, magazines, films, phonograph records, and newspapers which can be used in the school.

Insofar as is feasible a school serving substantial numbers of Mexican-American pupils should serve as a bridge between these students and the adult world which they will subsequently enter. This adult world will sometimes be Anglo in character, but more often it will be of mixed Anglo-Mexican culture. In any case, the school, if it is to be a bridge, must serve as a transitional experience and not as a sudden leap into a totally foreign set of values and practices.

The school environment should have some element of Mexican character, subject, of course, to the desires of the local Mexican-American community. Such character can be created by means of murals depicting aspects of the Mexican-American heritage, Hispano-Mexican architecture, the erection of statues depicting outstanding leaders of Mexican ancestry (such as governors of California), displays of Mexican arts and crafts, bulletin boards depicting Mexican persons and accomplishments, and by the adoption of a name for the school which is relevant to our Hispano-Mexican past. The expense involved in the above will not necessarily be great, as adults in the local Mexican-American community might well become involved in projects which would have the effect of making the school "their" school.

How Teachers Can Help

Teachers and administrators in such a school should be familiar with the Spanish language and should be encouraged to utilize this linguistic asset. At the very least, every such school must possess several professional employees capable of conversing with Spanish-speaking parents, since it is generally accepted that a successful school program demands adequate parent-school interaction and communication.

Communications intended for parents, such as announcements, bulletins, and report cards, should be prepared in both English and Spanish. Similarly, Parent-Teacher Association groups should be encouraged to follow a bilingual pattern. Where many parents cannot understand Spanish, consideration should be given to organizing an English-speaking sub-section for those parents who are not bilingual; or, more preferably, using the PTA as a vehicle for teaching Spanish and English to all parents.

Every effort should be made to encourage full development in both Spanish and English. Until truly bilingual schools become a reality, this may mean essentially that both Spanish and English are taught in the elementary grades. On the other hand, imaginative administrators and teachers may wish to further encourage a bilingual atmosphere by the use of signs and displays throughout the school featuring both languages.

Second Language Instruction

In schools composed primarily of Spanish-speaking pupils, and where permitted by law (California does), instruction should probably commence in Spanish, with English being taught as a second, or foreign, language. In a mixed school both languages will need to be taught as if they were new idioms.

Supplementary materials utilized in the classroom, as well as library resources, should include Spanish-language and/or Mexican-oriented items (magazines, newspapers, books, phonograph records, films, et cetera), in order to provide bilingual and bicultural experiences for all pupils.

Curricula in the school should possess a Mexican dimension wherever appropriate. In social science courses where the development of the Western United States is being discussed, attention should be given to the Hispano-Mexican pioneers of the Southwest, to Mexican governors and explorers, and to economic and political developments taking place under Mexican auspices. Courses in state history in the Southwest should devote considerable time to the total Mexican heritage, including that of modern-day Mexican-Americans.

Courses in literature should include readings in Mexican literature (in translation, if necessary) and works by and about Mexican-Americans.

Making Use of Music, Arts, and Crafts

Curricula in music and "music appreciation" should give attention to all classes of Mexican music, including folk-Indian, Hispano-Mexican, and neoclassical forms. In many schools, instruction in mariachi music, Aztec music and dance, or Mexican brass band might well replace or supplement the standard band and orchestra classes.

Art and craft courses should acquaint all pupils with Mexican art forms and should provide instruction in Mexican ceramics, mosaic work, weaving, et cetera, wherever feasible or appropriate.

Mexican cooking, folk-dancing, and costume-making should be available as a part of the school's programs in home economics and fine arts wherever sufficient interest exists.

Mexican-American adults and youth should be involved in the life of the school as resource people, supplementary teachers, teacher's aides, and special occasion speakers. One of the primary objectives of educators should be the linking of the school with the local adult community.

Our Mexican cultural heritage, whenever brought into the school, should be treated as an integral and valuable part of our common southwestern legacy, and not as a bit of "exotica" to be used solely for the benefit of Mexican-American pupils.

In a school composed of students from diverse cultural backgrounds every effort should be made to bring a little of each culture into the school. A part of this effort might involve incorporating each major ethnic celebration into the school routine (focusing on Chinese-Americans at Chinese New Year, Mexican-Americans during Cinco de Mayo, et cetera).

Counselors (and to a lesser degree, the entire staff) should receive special training in Mexican-American culture and history and should have a background in anthropology and/or sociology.

Tests Should Be Unbiased

School personnel who believe that it is important to examine pupils periodically in order to provide data on "ability" for future counseling or "tracking" should wish to obtain accurate information by the use of tests which are relatively unbiased. It is difficult to ascertain the potential of Spanish-speaking or dialect-speaking youth by means of standard English-language tests, nor can that of low-income students be predicted on the basis of tests oriented toward middle-class paraphernalia or concepts. On the other hand, biased tests will substantially predict the formal achievement level of culturally different pupils attending biased schools. Therefore, a change in tests will accomplish little unless accompanied by changes in the school, which serve to realize and enhance the potential revealed by the new test.

The above suggestions are basically designed to change the atmosphere of the school so as to provide greater motivation for all concerned, as well as to impart useful knowledge. In addition, many curricular and methodological innovations are available which are expected to improve learning for *all* students and these new programs should certainly be made available to Mexican-American youngsters. It is to be suspected, however, that a school which is basically indifferent or hostile toward the Mexican heritage will not succeed in stimulating greater learning merely by the use of methodological innovations unaccompanied by a change in the general orientation of the school.

35. The Culture of Poverty

Oscar Lewis

Poverty and the so-called war against it provide a principal theme for the domestic program of the present Administration. In the midst of a population that enjoys unexampled material well-being—with the average annual family income exceeding $7,000—it is officially acknowledged that some 18 million families, numbering more than 50 million individuals, live below the $3,000 "poverty line." Toward the improvement of the lot of these people some $1,600 million of Federal funds are directly allocated through the Office of Economic Opportunity, and many hundreds of millions of additional dollars flow indirectly through expanded Federal expenditures in the fields of health, education, welfare and urban affairs.

Along with the increase in activity on behalf of the poor indicated by these figures there has come a parallel expansion of publication in the social sciences on the subject of poverty. The new writings advance the same two opposed evaluations of the poor that are to be found in literature, in proverbs and in popular sayings throughout recorded history. Just as the poor have been pronounced blessed, virtuous, upright, serene, independent, honest, kind and happy, so contemporary students stress their great and neglected capacity for self-help, leadership and community organization. Conversely, as the poor have been characterized as shiftless, mean, sordid, violent, evil and criminal, so other students point to the irreversibly destructive effects of poverty on individual character and emphasize the corresponding need to keep guidance and control of poverty projects in the hands of duly constituted authorities. This clash of viewpoints reflects in part the infighting for political control of the program between Federal and local officials. The confusion results also from the tendency to focus study and attention on the personality of the individual victim of poverty rather than on the slum community and family and from the consequent failure to distinguish between poverty and what I have called the culture of poverty.

SOURCE: *Scientific American*, CCXV, 4 (October 1966), 19–25. Copyright © 1966 by Oscar Lewis. An expanded version of this essay appears in *La Vida*, by Oscar Lewis. Reprinted by permission of Random House, Inc.

The phrase is a catchy one and is used and misused with some frequency in the current literature. In my writings it is the label for a specific conceptual model that describes in positive terms a subculture of Western society with its own structure and rationale, a way of life handed on from generation to generation along family lines. The culture of poverty is not just a matter of deprivation or disorganization, a term signifying the absence of something. It is a culture in the traditional anthropological sense in that it provides human beings with a design for living, with a ready-made set of solutions for human problems, and so serves a significant adaptive function. This style of life transcends national boundaries and regional and rural-urban differences within nations. Wherever it occurs, its practitioners exhibit remarkable similarity in the structure of their families, in interpersonal relations, in spending habits, in their value systems and in their orientation in time.

Not nearly enough is known about this important complex of human behavior. My own concept of it has evolved as my work has progressed and remains subject to amendment by my own further work and that of others. The scarcity of literature on the culture of poverty is a measure of the gap in communication that exists between the very poor and the middle-class personnel—social scientists, social workers, teachers, physicians, priests and others—who bear the major responsibility for carrying out the anti-poverty programs. Much of the behavior accepted in the culture of poverty goes counter to cherished ideals of the larger society. In writing about "multiproblem" families social scientists thus often stress their instability, their lack of order, direction and organization. Yet, as I have observed them, their behavior seems clearly patterned and reasonably predictable. I am more often struck by the inexorable repetitiousness and the iron entrenchment of their lifeways.

The concept of the culture of poverty may help to correct misapprehensions that have ascribed some behavior patterns of ethnic, national or regional groups as distinctive characteristics. For example, a high incidence of common-law marriage and of households headed by women has been thought to be distinctive of Negro family life in this country and has been attributed to the Negro's historical experience of slavery. In actuality it turns out that such households express essential traits of the culture of poverty and are found among diverse peoples in many parts of the world and among peoples that have had no history of slavery. Although it is now possible to assert such generalizations, there is still much to be learned about this difficult and affecting subject. The absence of intensive anthropological studies of poor families in a wide variety of national contexts— particularly the lack of such studies in socialist countries—remains a serious handicap to the formulation of dependable cross-cultural constants of the culture of poverty.

My studies of poverty and family life have centered largely in Mexico.

On occasion some of my Mexican friends have suggested delicately that I turn to a study of poverty in my own country. As a first step in this direction I am currently engaged in a study of Puerto Rican families. Over the past three years my staff and I have been assembling data on 100 representative families in four slums of Greater San Juan and some 50 families of their relatives in New York City.

Our methods combine the traditional techniques of sociology, anthropology and psychology. This includes a battery of 19 questionnaires, the administration of which requires 12 hours per informant. They cover the residence and employment history of each adult; family relations; income and expenditure; complete inventory of household and personal possessions; friendship patterns, particularly the *compadrazgo,* or godparent, relationship that serves as a kind of informal social security for the children of these families and establishes special obligations among the adults; recreational patterns; health and medical history; politics; religion; world view and "cosmopolitanism." Open-end interviews and psychological tests (such as the thematic apperception test, the Rorschach test and the sentence-completion test) are administered to a sampling of this population.

All this work serves to establish the context for close-range study of a selected few families. Because the family is a small social system, it lends itself to the holistic approach of anthropology. Whole-family studies bridge the gap between the conceptual extremes of the culture at one pole and of the individual at the other, making possible observation of both culture and personality as they are interrelated in real life. In a large metropolis such as San Juan or New York the family is the natural unit of study.

Ideally our objective is the naturalistic observation of the life of "our" families, with a minimum of intervention. Such intensive study, however, necessarily involves the establishment of deep personal ties. My assistants include two Mexicans whose families I had studied; their "Mexican's-eye view" of the Puerto Rican slum has helped to point up the similarities and differences between the Mexican and Puerto Rican subcultures. We have spent many hours attending family parties, wakes and baptisms, responding to emergency calls, taking people to the hospital, getting them out of jail, filling out applications for them, hunting apartments with them, helping them to get jobs or to get on relief. With each member of these families we conduct tape-recorded interviews, taking down their life stories and their answers to questions on a wide variety of topics. For the ordering of our material we undertake to reconstruct, by close interrogation, the history of a week or more of consecutive days in the lives of each family, and we observe and record complete days as they unfold. The first volume to issue from this study is to be published next month under the title of *La Vida, a Puerto Rican Family in the Culture of Poverty—San Juan and New York* (Random House).

There are many poor people in the world. Indeed, the poverty of the two-thirds of the world's population who live in the underdeveloped countries has been rightly called "the problem of problems." But not all of them by any means live in the culture of poverty. For this way of life to come into being and flourish it seems clear that certain preconditions must be met.

The setting is a cash economy, with wage labor and production for profit and with a persistently high rate of unemployment and underemployment, at low wages, for unskilled labor. The society fails to provide social, political and economic organization, on either a voluntary basis or by government imposition, for the low-income population. There is a bilateral kinship system centered on the nuclear progenitive family, as distinguished from the unilateral extended kinship system of lineage and clan. The dominant class asserts a set of values that prizes thrift and the accumulation of wealth and property, stresses the possibility of upward mobility and explains low economic status as the result of individual personal inadequacy and inferiority.

Where these conditions prevail the way of life that develops among some of the poor is the culture of poverty. That is why I have described it as a subculture of the Western social order. It is both an adaptation and a reaction of the poor to their marginal position in a class-stratified, highly individuated, capitalistic society. It represents an effort to cope with feelings of hopelessness and despair that arise from the realization by the members of the marginal communities in these societies of the improbability of their achieving success in terms of the prevailing values and goals. Many of the traits of the culture of poverty can be viewed as local, spontaneous attempts to meet needs not served in the case of the poor by the institutions and agencies of the larger society because the poor are not eligible for such service, cannot afford it or are ignorant and suspicious.

Once the culture of poverty has come into existence it tends to perpetuate itself. By the time slum children are six or seven they have usually absorbed the basic attitudes and values of their subculture. Thereafter they are psychologically unready to take full advantage of changing conditions or improving opportunities that may develop in their lifetime.

My studies have identified some seventy traits that characterize the culture of poverty. The principal ones may be described in four dimensions of the system: the relationship between the subculture and the larger society; the nature of the slum community; the nature of the family; and the attitudes, values and character structure of the individual.

The disengagement, the nonintegration, of the poor with respect to the major institutions of society is a crucial element in the culture of poverty. It reflects the combined effect of a variety of factors including poverty, to begin with, but also segregation and discrimination, fear, suspicion and apathy and the development of alternative institutions and procedures in the slum community. The people do not belong to labor unions or political parties and make little use of banks, hospitals, department stores or museums. Such involvement as there is in the institutions of the larger society —in the jails, the army and the public welfare system—does little to suppress the traits of the culture of poverty. A relief system that barely keeps people alive perpetuates rather than eliminates poverty and the pervading sense of hopelessness.

People in a culture of poverty produce little wealth and receive little in return. Chronic unemployment and underemployment, low wages, lack of property, lack of savings, absence of food reserves in the home and chronic shortage of cash imprison the family and the individual in a vicious circle. Thus for lack of cash the slum householder makes frequent purchases of small quantities of food at higher prices. The slum economy turns inward; it shows a high incidence of pawning of personal goods, borrowing at usurious rates of interest, informal credit arrangements among neighbors, use of secondhand clothing and furniture.

There is awareness of middle-class values. People talk about them and even claim some of them as their own. On the whole, however, they do not live by them. They will declare that marriage by law, by the church or by both is the ideal form of marriage, but few will marry. For men who have no steady jobs, no property and no prospect of wealth to pass on to their children, who live in the present without expectations of the future, who want to avoid the expense and legal difficulties involved in marriage and divorce, a free union or consensual marriage makes good sense. The women, for their part, will turn down offers of marriage from men who are likely to be immature, punishing and generally unreliable. They feel that a consensual union gives them some of the freedom and flexibility men have. By not giving the fathers of their children legal status as husbands, the women have a stronger claim on the children. They also maintain exclusive rights to their own property.

Along with disengagement from the larger society, there is a hostility to the basic institutions of what are regarded as the dominant classes. There is hatred of the police, mistrust of government and of those in high positions and a cynicism that extends to the church. The culture of poverty thus holds a certain potential for protest and for entrainment in political movements aimed against the existing order.

With its poor housing and overcrowding, the community of the culture of poverty is high in gregariousness, but it has a minimum of organization beyond the nuclear and extended family. Occasionally slum dwellers come together in temporary informal groupings; neighborhood gangs that cut across slum settlements represent a considerable advance beyond the zero point of the continuum I have in mind. It is the low level of organization that gives the culture of poverty its marginal and anomalous quality in our highly organized society. Most primitive peoples have achieved a higher degree of sociocultural organization than contemporary urban slum dwellers. This is not to say that there may not be a sense of community and *esprit de corps* in a slum neighborhood. In fact, where slums are isolated from their surroundings by enclosing walls or other physical barriers, where rents are low and residence is stable and where the population constitutes a distinct ethnic, racial or language group, the sense of community may approach that of a village. In Mexico City and San Juan such territoriality is engendered by the scarcity of low-cost housing outside of established slum areas. In South Africa it is actively enforced by the *apartheid* that confines rural migrants to prescribed locations.

The family in the culture of poverty does not cherish childhood as a specially prolonged and protected stage in the life cycle. Initiation into sex comes early. With the instability of consensual marriage the family tends to be mother-centered and tied more closely to the mother's extended family. The female head of the house is given to authoritarian rule. In spite of much verbal emphasis on family solidarity, sibling rivalry for the limited supply of goods and maternal affection is intense. There is little privacy.

The individual who grows up in this culture has a strong feeling of fatalism, helplessness, dependence and inferiority. These traits, so often remarked in the current literature as characteristic of the American Negro, I found equally strong in slum dwellers of Mexico City and San Juan, who are not segregated or discriminated against as a distinct ethnic or racial group. Other traits include a high incidence of weak ego structure, orality and confusion of sexual identification, all reflecting maternal deprivation; a strong present-time orientation with relatively little disposition to defer gratification and plan for the future; and a high tolerance for psychological pathology of all kinds. There is widespread belief in male superiority and among the men a strong preoccupation with *machismo,* their masculinity.

Provincial and local in outlook, with little sense of history, these people know only their own neighborhood and their own way of life. Usually they do not have the knowledge, the vision or the ideology to see the similarities between their troubles and those of their counterparts elsewhere in the world. They are not class-conscious, although they are sensitive indeed to symbols of status.

The distinction between poverty and the culture of poverty is basic to the model described here. There are numerous examples of poor people whose way of life I would not characterize as belonging to this subculture. Many primitive and preliterate peoples that have been studied by anthropologists suffer dire poverty attributable to low technology or thin resources or both. Yet even the simplest of these peoples have a high degree of social organization and a relatively integrated, satisfying and self-sufficient culture.

In India the destitute lower-caste peoples—such as the Chamars, the leatherworkers, and the Bhangis, the sweepers—remain integrated in the larger society and have their own panchayat institutions of self-government. Their panchayats and their extended unilateral kinship systems, or clans, cut across village lines, giving them a strong sense of identity and continuity. In my studies of these peoples I found no culture of poverty to go with their poverty.

The Jews of eastern Europe were a poor urban people, often confined to ghettos. Yet they did not have many traits of the culture of poverty. They had a tradition of literacy that placed great value on learning; they formed many voluntary associations and adhered with devotion to the central community organization around the rabbi, and they had a religion that taught them they were the chosen people.

I would cite also a fourth, somewhat speculative example of poverty dissociated from the culture of poverty. On the basis of limited direct observation in one country—Cuba—and from indirect evidence, I am inclined to believe the culture of poverty does not exist in socialist countries. In 1947 I undertook a study of a slum in Havana. Recently I had an opportunity to revisit the same slum and some of the same families. The physical aspect of the place had changed little, except for a beautiful new nursery school. The people were as poor as before, but I was impressed to find much less of the feelings of despair and apathy, so symptomatic of the culture of poverty in the urban slums of the U.S. The slum was now highly organized, with block committees, educational committees, party committees. The people had found a new sense of power and importance in a doctrine that glorified the lower class as the hope of humanity, and they were armed. I was told by one Cuban official that the Castro government had practically eliminated delinquency by giving arms to the delinquents!

Evidently the Castro regime—revising Marx and Engels—did not write off the so-called *lumpenproletariat* as an inherently reactionary and antirevolutionary force but rather found in them a revolutionary potential and utilized it. Frantz Fanon, in his book *The Wretched of the Earth,* makes a similar evaluation of their role in the Algerian revolution: "It is within this mass of humanity, this people of the shantytowns, at the core of the *lumpenproletariat,* that the rebellion will find its urban spearhead. For the *lumpenproletariat,* that horde of starving men, uprooted from their tribe and from their clan, constitutes one of the most spontaneous and most radically revolutionary forces of a colonized people."

It is true that I have found little revolutionary spirit or radical ideology among low-income Puerto Ricans. Most of the families I studied were politically conservative, about half of them favoring the Statehood Republican Party, which provides opposition on the right to the Popular Democratic Party that dominates the politics of the commonwealth. It seems to me, therefore, that disposition for protest among people living in the culture of poverty will vary considerably according to the national context and historical circumstances. In contrast to Algeria, the independence movement in Puerto Rico has found little popular support. In Mexico, where the cause of independence carried long ago, there is no longer any such movement to stir the dwellers in the new and old slums of the capital city.

Yet it would seem that any movement—be it religious, pacifist or revolutionary—that organizes and gives hope to the poor and effectively promotes a sense of solidarity with larger groups must effectively destroy the psychological and social core of the culture of poverty. In this connection, I suspect that the civil rights movement among American Negroes has of itself done more to improve their self-image and self-respect than such economic gains as it has won although, without doubt, the two kinds of progress are mutually reinforcing. In the culture of poverty of the American Negro the additional disadvantage of racial discrimination has generated a potential for revolutionary protest and organization that is absent in the slums of San Juan and Mexico City and, for that matter, among the poor whites in the South.

If it is true, as I suspect, that the culture of poverty flourishes and is endemic to the free-enterprise, pre-welfare-state stage of capitalism, then it is also endemic in colonial societies. The most likely candidates for the culture of poverty would be the people who come from the lower strata of a rapidly changing society and who are already partially alienated from it. Accordingly the subculture is likely to be found where imperial conquest has smashed the native social and economic structure and held the natives, perhaps for generations, in servile status, or where feudalism is yielding to capitalism in the later evolution of a colonial economy. Landless rural workers who migrate to the cities, as in Latin America, can be expected to fall into this way of life more readily than migrants from stable peasant villages with a well-organized traditional culture, as in India. It remains to be seen, however, whether the culture of poverty has not already begun to develop in the slums of Bombay and Calcutta. Compared with Latin America also, the strong corporate nature of many African tribal societies may tend to inhibit or delay the formation of a full-blown culture of poverty in the new towns and cities of that continent. In South Africa the institutionalization of repression and discrimination under *apartheid* may also have begun to promote an immunizing sense of identity and group consciousness among the African Negroes.

One must therefore keep the dynamic aspects of human institutions forward in observing and assessing the evidence for the presence, the waxing or the waning of this subculture. Measured on the dimension of relationship to the larger society, some slum dwellers may have a warmer identification with their national tradition even though they suffer deeper poverty than members of a similar community in another country. In Mexico City a high percentage of our respondents, including those with little or no formal schooling, knew of Cuauhtémoc, Hidalgo, Father Morelos, Juárez,

Díaz, Zapata, Carranza and Cárdenas. In San Juan the names of Rámon Power, José de Diego, Baldorioty de Castro, Rámon Betances, Nemesio Canales, Lloréns Torres rang no bell; a few could tell about the late Albizu Campos. For the lower-income Puerto Rican, however, history begins with Muñoz Rivera and ends with his son Muñoz Marín.

The national context can make a big difference in the play of the crucial traits of fatalism and hopelessness. Given the advanced technology, the high level of literacy, the all-pervasive reach of the media of mass communications and the relatively high aspirations of all sectors of the population, even the poorest and most marginal communities of the U.S. must aspire to a larger future than the slum dwellers of Ecuador and Peru, where the actual possibilities are more limited and where an authoritarian social order persists in city and country. Among the 50 million U.S. citizens now more or less officially certified as poor, I would guess that about 20 percent live in a culture of poverty. The largest numbers in this group are made up of Negroes, Puerto Ricans, Mexicans, American Indians and Southern poor whites. In these figures there is some reassurance for those concerned, because it is much more difficult to undo the culture of poverty than to cure poverty itself.

Middle-class people—this would certainly include most social scientists —tend to concentrate on the negative aspects of the culture of poverty. They attach a minus sign to such traits as present-time orientation and readiness to indulge impulses. I do not intend to idealize or romanticize the culture of poverty—"it is easier to praise poverty than to live in it." Yet the positive aspects of these traits must not be overlooked. Living in the present may develop a capacity for spontaneity, for the enjoyment of the sensual, which is often blunted in the middle-class, future-oriented man. Indeed, I am often struck by the analogies that can be drawn between the mores of the very rich—of the "jet set" and "café society"—and the culture of the very poor. Yet it is, on the whole, a comparatively superficial culture. There is in it much pathos, suffering and emptiness. It does not provide much support or satisfaction; its pervading mistrust magnifies individual helplessness and isolation. Indeed, poverty of culture is one of the crucial traits of the culture of poverty.

The concept of the culture of poverty provides a generalization that may help to unify and explain a number of phenomena hitherto viewed as peculiar to certain racial, national or regional groups. Problems we think of as being distinctively our own or distinctively Negro (or as typifying any other ethnic group) prove to be endemic in countries where there are no segregated ethnic minority groups. If it follows that the elimination of physical poverty may not by itself eliminate the culture of poverty, then an understanding of the subculture may contribute to the design of measures specific to that purpose.

What is the future of the culture of poverty? In considering this question one must distinguish between those countries in which it represents a relatively small segment of the population and those in which it constitutes a large one. In the U.S. the major solution proposed by social workers dealing with the "hard core" poor has been slowly to raise their level of living and incorporate them in the middle class. Wherever possible psychiatric treatment is prescribed.

In underdeveloped countries where great masses of people live in the culture of poverty, such a social-work solution does not seem feasible. The local psychiatrists have all they can do to care for their own growing middle class. In those countries the people with a culture of poverty may seek a more revolutionary solution. By creating basic structural changes in society, by redistributing wealth, by organizing the poor and giving them a sense of belonging, of power and of leadership, revolutions frequently succeed in abolishing some of the basic characteristics of the culture of poverty even when they do not succeed in curing poverty itself.

36. Social Status in the Black Community

Andrew Billingsley

The various social forces described [in a previous chapter] have converged to form a pattern of social classes among Negro families not altogether unlike that in the general community, but with its own features reflecting the history and struggle for survival of the Negro people.

There are no exact figures on the Negro social class structure. Despite all the references to the Negro lower class, no studies have been done which would estimate the proportion of Negro families in each of the social classes. It has not been done for some of the reasons we have cited in

SOURCE: Andrew Billingsley, *Black Families in White America* (Englewood Cliffs, N.J.: Prentice-Hall, 1968), pp. 137–45. Copyright © 1968 by Andrew Billingsley. Reprinted by permission of Prentice-Hall, Inc., Englewood Cliffs, New Jersey.

the Appendix. Still, more limited studies have been done, and the census reports have generated comprehensive data on the education, income, and occupation of Negroes. It is thus possible to make some approximations of the shape of the Negro class structure. In the early 1940s, Drake and Cayton, using a combination of education, rental payments, and occupation as criteria, estimated that about 5 per cent of Negro families in Chicago could be considered upper class, 30 per cent middle class, and 65 per cent lower class.[1] Today we would estimate that in the urban areas of the country, where nearly 75 per cent of Negro families live, roughly 10 per cent would be considered upper class, 40 per cent middle class, and 50 per cent lower class in the Negro community. This social class structure is illustrated in Figure 1.

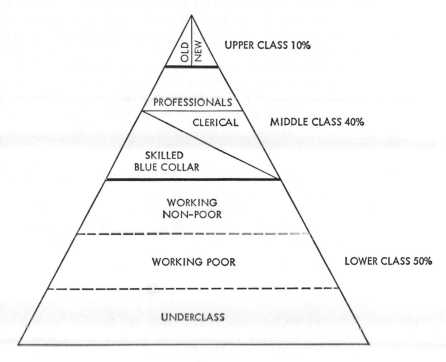

FIGURE 1
Social Classes in the Negro Community

The indices of social class which have been developed in social science research are relatively more reliable when used within white ethnic groups, where they were developed, than when used unmodified with Negro groups. For example, the family of a high school principal in a white community may be considered middle class. In a Negro community, however,

[1] St. Clair Drake and Horace Cayton (see footnote 9).

in all probability, the Negro high school principal's family will be considered upper class. Not only do absolute levels of education, income, and occupation take on somewhat different meanings in the Negro community, but factors other than these, including respectability and community activity, loom large in the attribution of social status.

The problems associated with the description of Negro families in social class terms are so great, particularly at the lower social status levels, that a number of students of the Negro experience are beginning to question its utility. To refer to the masses of Negro families as lower class obscures rather than clarifies much of the variety of status and behavior in that group. And to combine two concepts and refer to this stratum as lower class culture, which is often done, further confounds the reality.

In our view, there is still considerable utility in the concept of social class if it is used carefully. However, the current popularity of the term probably adds to its distortion. It is probably most usefully employed as an index of economic and social position, or of level in the community. In the Negro community, it does not provide a very accurate description of who associates with whom, although it still has relevance for who looks up to or down to whom. It is completely inadequate and inappropriate for describing behavior or values or preferences or styles of life or child rearing patterns in the Negro community. Its chief value is as a description of the basic life conditions of the subjects, and they, of course, have some, though not complete, correlation to attitudes and behavior. The importance of social class for our purposes is that the higher the social class status of a family, the greater access its members have to the resources of the wider community, and the greater the level of supports they receive from the wider community, and consequently, the greater will be the family's ability to meet the requirements of society and the needs of its members.

The Upper Classes

The more differentiated the social class concept, the more accurate it is as a description of social status. It therefore seems very useful to divide each of the three major social classes into further subdivisions. At the upper class level, for example, two subclasses may be distinguished: the "old" upper class families and the "new" upper class families in the Negro community. These distinctions are more parallel than hierarchical.

The old upper class includes those families headed by men and women whose parents before them were upper or middle class. The families of Negro judges, physicians, dentists, high government officials, educated ministers of large congregations, college presidents, and wealthy businessmen, particularly insurance company executives and bankers, are prominent among the old upper class. It often happens that they have built on the head start given them by their parents. Sometimes their grandparents were considerably more privileged than the mass of Negroes, and further back, their ancestors were often either free Negroes during slavery or privileged slaves (house slaves or artisans instead of field slaves), who often inherited money or property, or were given a modicum of education by their masters. Negro families in the old upper class, then, reach back several generations for the roots of their achievement and current status. They have added to this head start and acquitted themselves well in the world of affairs. They are our "Black Brahmins."

The new upper class may have as much or more money, education, and status, but they are likely to have reached the top in one generation, due in large measure to their own talent and good fortune. Prominent among the new upper class are celebrities such as entertainers and athletes, who may become wealthy, famous, influential, and highly prestigious in the community. Still another prominent group in the new upper class which got to the top by talent and good fortune is the "Shadies," those gamblers, racketeers, pimps, and other hustlers who often manage to become wealthy, to wield a considerable amount of influence, and to garner a great deal of prestige in the Negro community.

The old upper class is probably the predominant element in the highest Negro stratum, though the new upper class is growing fast. The hustlers are only a very small segment of the upper class.

Let us illustrate the distinction between old and new upper class families. The Negroes who are now at the very apex of the three branches of the federal government are all excellent representatives of "old families" among the Negro upper class. These are Secretary of Housing and Urban Development Robert Weaver, in the executive branch, Senator Edward W. Brooke in the legislative branch, and Justice Thurgood Marshall in the judiciary. Even before reaching his present government position, each had been at the top levels of his profession, and each could afford to support his family at a level of living distinctly superior to the overwhelming majority of American families. These men are distinctly upper class by any careful assessment of socioeconomic structure, though they are often mistakenly referred to as "middle class" by the general writing public. They are also sometimes referred to in romantic terms as men who "pulled themselves up by their own boot straps." They did nothing of the sort. They are truly remarkable men, but the point we are making is that they had a head start in life, the kind of head start rare in the experience of Negroes of their generation. They are members and products of the "old upper class." They reached the top in large measure because of their origins and upbringing in upper middle class families. They have been able to build upon the head start provided them by their own family orientation and the concomitant opportunities made available to them.

Each of these men had a distinctly upper middle class or upper class family background. Each had at least one parent who was a college graduate. Each had parents with professional occupations. Each had a measure of economic security denied 90 per cent of the Negro youth of his generation. Each had two parents who were prominent members of the community. Each has meaningful associations with extended families. Each has a light complexion reflecting both the exploitation and the privilege of the past. Each was able to spend long years in college and graduate school preparing himself for major professions. Two took their first degrees at Negro colleges, a characteristic source of achievement for Negro upper class families. Two took their advanced degrees at white universities, another characteristic pattern. Let us consider the family background of each of the men briefly.

Secretary Weaver's father was a postal clerk, a distinctly middle class occupation for Negroes even to this day. His mother was a schoolteacher, a distinctly upper middle class occupation among Negroes. It should be observed that status in Negro families derives as much from the mother's occupation and education as from the father's, unlike the situation among white families. Furthermore, Weaver's maternal grandfather was a graduate of Harvard and a dentist. Weaver grew up in the Brookland section of Washington, D.C., where his was one of nine Negro families among more than 3,000 white families. His distinctly upper middle class background is also reflected in the particular educational aspirations his parents held for the children. "Their one ambition," he has said, "was to send us to New England schools." They were eminently successful. Both Robert Weaver and his older brother graduated from Harvard with honors. Both Weaver and his wife are holders of the Ph.D. degree. Mrs. Robert Weaver is the only wife of a presidential cabinet member to attain such high academic achievement.

Senator Brooke is also the product of an upper class Negro family in Washington, D.C. His father was a U.S. government attorney and his family was among the prominent Negro families of the city. Despite the Senator's oft repeated statement that he did not grow up in hardship because of his race, there are indications that the racial barrier constrained the level of achievement his father might have attained. Referring to his father Brooke has said, "I thought of the frustrations he must have had because he had the ability but not the opportunity to do more." [2] It is also apparent that the Senator's grandmother played an important role in his upbringing. "I thought of what my grandmother used to say," he once observed, " 'stay in your place.' This advice was given to protect me from injury because if you didn't follow this advice, you knew what would happen. But this was a statement I never could accept." [3]

[2] *Ebony Magazine,* April 1967, p. 153.
[3] *Ibid.,* pp. 153–54.

Such an economically secure, educated, and cultured family background provided not only a head start in social achievement for the future Senator, but also a set of values and preferences and a style of life. He has described himself as a natural conservative. He exhibits a kind of quiet elegance which makes him prominent among both white and black Brahmins. It is quite in keeping with his style of life, then, that he is president of the Boston Opera Society and not the Boston Jazz Society. But despite all his ability, achievement, and acculturation, he still is not simply an upper class American, but an upper class Negro American. This is in part imposed on him by society and in part a reflection of preference. He is a product of a Negro college and has characterized himself as a "soul brother." It is said that after his inauguration as the first Negro senator since reconstruction, he "retired to his hotel quarters and feasted on his favorite gourmet delight—hog maws and greens." [4]

Perhaps one of the more perceptive comments on the upper class morality of Senator Brooke was a comment by Thomas Pettigrew, a professor of social psychology at Harvard: "I really believe he will have an upgrading effect on the private lives of some senators." [5]

The final member of this illustrious triumvirate, Supreme Court Justice Thurgood Marshall, owes much of his development to his upper middle class family background and the opportunities this made available to him. His father held the highly prestigious position of country club steward. His mother was a schoolteacher. His brother, who is a physician, has described the Justice as very much like his father: "very argumentative and aggressive." [6] One indication of the father's influence on his son, as well as of the conditions of life they experienced, is reflected in the father's oft repeated admonition to his sons: "If anyone calls you nigger, you not only got my permission to fight him—you got my orders." [7] Again the Negro college played a key role in the achievement of this family.

Thus life in the upper reaches of Negro privilege and economic security provided the basis and the support for a progressively high level achievement for these men and their families. Still, the racial barrier barred them from many opportunities, privileges, rights, and amenities which can be taken for granted by much less worthy white people.

New Negro Upper Class

Not all Negro families of outstanding achievement are products of these old established families with generations of privileges. Many whose

[4] *Ibid.*, p. 150.

[5] *Ibid.*, p. 152.

[6] *Ebony Magazine*, November 1965, p. 69.

[7] *Ibid.*

achievement is equally great rose in one generation from poverty and obscurity to the top. These families comprise the membership of the new upper class.

Prominent among the new upper class are two men who are also government officials. These are Mayor Carl B. Stokes of Cleveland and Mayor Richard Hatcher of Gary, Indiana. Before their recent election, both were distinguished attorneys who reached the top levels of society in one generation. Both were born into lower class families. Stokes was born in the slums of Cleveland. His father, a laundry worker, died when he was one year old. His mother alternated between working as a maid and receiving public welfare assistance, making Stokes the only mayor of a large city who was supported as a child by AFDC. While his mother worked, he and his brother were cared for by their grandmother. Both he and his brother became distinguished attorneys. The strong commitment his mother had to education, plus the opportunities provided by World War II and big city politics are among the screens of opportunity which enabled these very able young men to move from the lower class into the upper class within the span of a few years. Stokes has told how he had to hide books under his clothes as he brought them from the library, because in his neighborhood reading books was "against the mores."

Mayor Hatcher is also a man of humble origins. Born in the slums of Michigan City, Indiana, he was one of thirteen children. His father was a factory worker, but was often out of work. Richard worked his way through college and law school. The sources of his achievement are many and varied. They are not as predictable as those of the old upper class. They are, nevertheless, firmly grounded in the Negro family and community institutions. After his election as Mayor, a reporter asked him how he accounted for his rise "from a very humble beginning to a position of national stature in only thirty-two years." Hatcher pointed to his father and the church as specific influences.

The one person who has had a steady and solid influence on me has been my father. He is seventy-six now. He was a laborer in a foundry for thirty-six years and retired from there six or seven years ago and became a custodian in a county building. He was absolutely honest about everything. He also paid his bills on time. Even if it meant going without meals, the bills were paid on time. I was impressed by those two things. He also put a lot of faith in God. I picked that up too.[8]

What the literature on Negro families needs is several systematic studies of the past, current, and future families of these remarkable men and the hundreds of others like them, not only as a chronicle of achievement on the part of selected families, but as an index of some of the fluidities and rigidities of our American society.

These two pathways to high social status, family stability, and achieve-

8 *Ebony Magazine,* January 1968, p. 35.

ment are also reflected in the lives and careers of thousands of less public figures than these high government figures. In a recent analysis of *Current Biographies* between the years 1945 and 1967 we found 120 entries of Negroes of outstanding achievement. These may be classified along several dimensions. This analysis shows that professional men and women are more likely to represent Negro families of the old upper class, while celebrities, including entertainers and athletes, are more likely to represent the new upper class. Among the forty-four professional men, for example, thirty-five (roughly 80 per cent of them) have family origins in the middle or upper classes. Among the twenty-one professional women, eighteen (roughly 86 per cent) may be so described. Among celebrities, on the other hand, only ten of the seventeen male entertainers (59 per cent) were from old upper class families, while just half of the female entertainers and only two of the sixteen male athletes had such privileged family backgrounds. Athletics, which offers an excellent opportunity for many Negro boys from humble origins, is nevertheless conspicuously oriented to social class origins. For example, while it is by no means clear that professional football, basketball, and tennis require more ability or hard work than baseball or boxing, it is obvious that the outstanding professionals in the first category tend to have middle class origins, while baseball players and boxers tend to have lower class origins. This is because the structure of athletics is such that recruitment to the professional ranks in the first category of sports takes place primarily through college teams, and Negro men are more likely to get to college and stay long enough to demonstrate their ability if they come from middle class backgrounds.

The data also shows that representatives of old upper class families are much more likely to be highly educated for the professions, are likely to have reached the peak of their fame at older ages than the new upper classmen, are more likely to be light in complexion, and to have grown up in nuclear families with strong fathers. Thus, getting to the top is a bit more assured and orderly for those with social origins in the middle class. Their families are the more likely to have the education, economic security and social connections to facilitate achievement. It is possible to make it without that particular kind of head start, but considerably more precarious and more heavily dependent on a great deal of talent, a great deal of luck, and the favorable operation of opportunity screens from the several levels of society where this potential lies. If these new families are at the top of the Negro social class pyramid, they are often precariously so, for they have not completely escaped the shadows of the plantation that stalk the Negro people whatever their status. The description of this upper class group advanced by Drake and Cayton is still appropriate. "It is," they found,

an articulate social world of doctors, lawyers, schoolteachers, executives, successful business people, and the frugal and fortunate of other occupational groups, who have climbed with difficulty and now cling precariously to a social position consonant with what money, education, and power the city and the caste-like controls allow them. They are challenged at every point, however, by the same forces that condemn the vast majority of the people to poverty and restricted opportunities.[9]

The precariousness of upper class status is underscored by the facts that Negro professionals earn less in a lifetime than white professionals and that their wives often have to work to keep them in this status. Negro physicians, for example, who are at the top of the Negro upper class, can count on earning less than 60 per cent of what white physicians earn in their lifetimes. Of all Negro professionals, only engineers approach equity, with an income potential about 95 per cent of white engineers. Thus it is not surprising that engineers are prominent in the new upper class and are increasing much more rapidly than many other professional groups. Between 1950 and 1960, for example, there was a 400 per cent increase in the number of Negro engineers. Still, those 3,378 men represented only about four-tenths of 1 per cent of all engineers in the United States in 1960.[10]

The Negro upper class is an important and growing phenomenon. Andrew Brimmer has observed, for example, that "although the Negro community can claim only a handful of millionaires, it can boast of a fairly large number of prosperous families and individuals." He found that in 1963, 274,000 Negro families had incomes above $10,000 and over a quarter of these had incomes over $15,000. He also noted that "the $10,000 and over group rose by 50 per cent between 1959 and 1963."

With incomes in this level, such families not only can afford comfortable housing (when they manage to purchase it in an essentially segregated market) but they can also provide a college education for their children. They can entertain graciously and participate in a variety of cultural activities. They can travel widely at home and abroad.[11]

These upper class families are much better able to meet the needs of their members and to fulfill the functions required of families by the wider society than are other Negro families. We shall see below some of the specific ways in which they are able to meet both instrumental and expressive functions of family much better than families with less resources and so-

[9] St. Clair Drake and Horace Cayton, *Black Metropolis: A Study of Negro Life in a Northern City*, revised and enlarged ed. (New York: Harper & Row, Publishers, 1962), II, 522.

[10] We are indebted to Dr. Horace Mann Bond for this information.

[11] Andrew Brimmer, "The Negro in the National Economy," in *The American Negro Reference Book*, ed. John P. Davis (Englewood Cliffs, N.J.: Prentice-Hall, Inc., 1966), p. 266.

cietal supports. At the same time, however, we shall also see some of the respects in which these families have not solved all the problems associated with being black in a white society, nor that myriad of other problems more generally associated with the human condition. Let us turn now, however, to an outline of some of the major dimensions of the middle classes.

The Middle Classes

Among the Negro middle classes there is a similar historical dimension of old families, with traditions of achievement. In addition, however, somewhat of an hierarchical differentiation is reflected in the three subgroups of the middle class. The first subgroup is the *upper middle class,* composed of families headed by persons in the minor professions which require college education but do not rank in prestige and status with the major old line professions. Prominent in the upper middle class are families of teachers, social workers, accountants, technicians. Many attorneys who have not yet established themselves, ministers of small congregations, and celebrities who have not yet reached the top or who are on the way down may also fall into this group. The line between the Negro upper class and the Negro upper middle class is a rather fluid one. For many purposes the two groups may be viewed as one. Since the majority of Negro families are considerably lower in social status than these two groups, one tends sometimes to lump both of them together. Indeed, it is difficult for any college graduate with any degree of visibility in the community to escape the attribution of status much higher than he could command in the white community.

Public school teachers with bachelor's degrees from college account for the major share of upper middle class Negro professionals. These teachers, in fact, make up more than half of all Negro professional, technical, and kindred workers. Elementary school teachers account for 43 per cent and secondary teachers account for 10 per cent. For men, 13 per cent of all professional, technical, and kindred workers were secondary teachers and 12 per cent were elementary teachers. Moreover, while there is a slight increase in the proportion of Negro teachers to the over-all teaching profession during the past few years, even this large group of professionals, the most highly developed in the Negro community, is underdeveloped. Negro public school teachers accounted for only 7 per cent of all public school teachers in 1960. (By 1966 this proportion had increased to 10 per cent.) Furthermore, these teachers are highly concentrated in the South, where they have been the outstanding representatives of Negro family achievement. The paucity of Negro teachers in the urban ghettos where most Northern Negroes live is approaching a national disgrace as the country becomes more aware of the important contributions these professionals can make, not only to black and white pupils and teachers in the school, but to community leadership as well.

Another relatively large group of upper middle class families is headed by ministers, who accounted for about 12 per cent of all Negro professionals in 1960. Other upper middle class occupations that received relatively high preference as goals for male college students were junior management level jobs in business and in government, preferred by 17 per cent of the men but less than 5 per cent of women. Social work was the choice of nearly 10 per cent of the women but only about 5 per cent of the men. These are all respectable and responsible upper middle class occupations in the Negro community.

Families in this social class category often have incomes ranging between $6,000 and $10,000. Family income fluctuates widely, however, both above and below this range, depending on the part of the country and on whether one or two family members work. Incomes are higher in urban areas than in the country as a whole; they are higher in the North and West than in the South; and they are higher for the more highly educated families. Among Negro families in large urban areas where both husband and wife were college graduates, fully 76 per cent earned $6,000 or more in 1960.

It must be observed that being middle class for Negro families is not always as economically or socially secure as that status might seem to imply. It is often a precarious existence. Five case vignettes from families in a study of Negro families in a large Western city will illustrate this observation.[12]

1. By education, income, occupation, and residence, the Douglas family is distinctly upper middle class. Mr. Douglas is twenty-seven and his wife is twenty-five. They have been married for five years and have two children, Robert, Jr., who is four, and Sarah, who is 2½. Both parents are college graduates and both are schoolteachers. They have a combined income of $13,000 per year, an expensive house in a white neighborhood, and an expensive late-model car. They hire "help" to take care of the children. Both have parents who were college graduates. It may be said that they have no money problems, except during those periods when Mrs. Douglas is on maternity leave and their income drops to $7,500 per year. Mr. Douglas has only one job. His is distinctly head of the house. Mrs. Douglas attends church on Sunday, but her husband stays home and reads the Sunday papers and does schoolwork. She is an avid tennis player but he prefers bowling. They take turns reading to the children and putting them to bed. He, however, is a bit more firm with discipline, while she

[12] This study is being conducted by the author at the University of California under a grant from the Children's Bureau, U.S. Department of Health, Education and Welfare. All names are fictitious.

leans toward permissiveness. He spanks a bit more than she thinks is necessary. It is essentially an equalitarian, upper middle class family with a
slight tilt toward the patriarchal style. He would like it to be a bit more
patriarchal and she would like it to be more equalitarian. It is not in danger of becoming matriarchal. And if he can ever manage to finish his master's degree, for which she nags him a bit, he can teach in a junior college
and will, no doubt, fortify his status not only in the outside world but in
the family structure as well.

2. The Baldwin family is also middle class. Mr. Baldwin is thirty-seven
years old and Mrs. Baldwin is twenty-seven. They have been married for
ten years and have two children, Larry, age ten, and Sonny, age six. The
fact that Mrs. Baldwin was only seventeen and pregnant by another man
was not a barrier to their marriage. They have had a successful family life
for ten years, according to the social criteria of success. They are both
high school graduates. He is a postal employee. She is a secretary-typist.
Their combined annual income was $9,000 last year. Mr. Baldwin's sister
lives with the family and helps care for the children in exchange for her
room and board. They have a mortgage on a nice home in a Negro residential neighborhood. Mr. Baldwin is industrious. In order to help make
ends meet, he drives a taxi after his regular job. Although the neighborhood they live in might be characterized as "poor," the house is "nice"
and the furnishings are "expensive." The Baldwins are pillars of their
community. They have surmounted many obstacles and achieved stability
and success. Their status is heavily dependent, however, not only on the
wife's working and the husband's having two jobs, but on the services of
his sister. Between their jobs and community responsibilities, there is little
time left for the "frills" of family life. It is not an uncommon predicament
for the precarious Negro middle class.

3. Another striking example of the precariousness of Negro middle
class life is the Adams family. They are in many respects a model, middle
class American family. Mr. Adams is thirty-four and his wife is thirty-
two. They have been married for ten years and have three children, Michael, age six, Dennis, age four, and Denise, age two. An Army veteran
with two years of college, Mr. Adams is a professional photographer with
a steady income. Mrs. Adams also has two years of college. The family income was $10,600 last year. They have a heavy mortgage on their own
home on the edge of a black ghetto.

They have planned their family to suit their economic abilities. They
delayed having children for the first four years of their marriage, "in order
to get on our feet financially." During those first years she worked as an
office secretary while he worked at the Post Office.

In other ways, too, they are a model American couple. He is tall and
slender, weighs about 185 pounds; he is good looking, dresses well and
tastefully with a slight flair, and is in manner and bearing not exactly ag-

gressive, but, as he would describe himself, "somewhat forward." He is industrious, works hard, likes spectator sports, drives a late-model car, and drinks to be sociable. He does not go to church because he is tired on Sunday, likes to work around the house and watch television. Mrs. Adams is also an attractive, well groomed young woman, though perhaps a bit less sophisticated than her husband and not quite as forceful in manner. She pays the bills and takes the children to the Protestant church and Sunday School. She makes most of the decisions about the children. It is, on balance, an equalitarian family.

There are other aspects of their family life which support this middle class equalitarian mold. He gets out of bed first in the morning, for he is an "earlier riser." He dresses the three children and plays with them until she has breakfast ready. He kisses them all goodbye when he leaves the house. They even had a typical middle class family problem. She is often not ready for work on time, and he "cannot afford to be late." When they drive to work together in their one car, this causes friction.

But if this is in many respects a model American middle class, equalitarian family, it is only precariously so. Consider their education. While they are more highly educated than a majority of their fellow Americans, they do not have enough to fortify their middle class position. Their $10,600 last year put them in a distinctly upper middle income bracket but it was earned at a high price. As in 90 per cent of Negro middle income families, Mrs. Adams worked to help maintain that family income level. Besides, that income was for last year; this year, in keeping with their middle class style of life and their concern for the care and well-being of their children, particularly since the aunt who used to live there and care for them got married and moved to another city, Mrs. Adams decided to stop work and become a full-time housewife. She enjoys the role very much. But this year the family income from Mr. Adams' earnings alone will be $6,400. Now they will still be a middle class, educated, handsome American couple, but the precariousness of their status and the tenuous hold they have on their economic and social well-being are apparent. Mr. Adams has taken an extra job a few hours a night "so that the washing machine and dryer could be paid for without sacrificing the house payments."

Now Mr. Adams, though still keeping up a well dressed appearance in public, does not bathe quite as often as he used to. Now when he leaves his extra job at night he lingers a bit longer at the tavern than he used to. He even seems to drive his car faster and more recklessly than he did before.

4. Mr. and Mrs. Earley are both high school graduates. He is the owner and operator of his own janitorial service. Last year he earned $10,000. Mrs. Earley worked as a bookkeeper in a department store for three years, until the first baby was due. Now she stays home and cares for their four

children, three girls, ages nine, three, and two, and a boy, age one. They have a spacious, attractive two-bedroom apartment in a very nice, middle income Negro neighborhood in a fairly large city. Their apartment is attractively decorated with modern furniture. These surroundings reflect the willingness of Mr. Earley to "provide a decent standard of living" for his family. They are even more reflective of the "good taste and ingenuity" of his wife. The couple is saving money for a down payment on a home.

The Earleys are middle class, upwardly mobile, hard working—a model American family. He is thirty years old and she is twenty-eight. They have been married for ten years. They grew up in the same city and went through school together. After high school he served two years in the Army. Upon his discharge they got married. He took a job as a janitor by day and completed high school by night. He saved enough money to get a loan and open his own business. Now he works for himself. Like a typical small businessman, he works long hours, six days a week. He rests on Sunday. His habits are exemplary. He neither smokes nor drinks nor runs around with women. In spite of his long working hours, he spends at least two hours a day helping Mrs. Earley with the children.

In a number of respects, life has been good to the Earleys. Their education, income, residence, and style of life put them distinctly ahead of their less privileged kinsmen and countrymen. But their middle class status is more than a bit precarious. Mrs. Earley has recently become pregnant with her fifth child. This will be a second unwanted baby, just as she was beginning to look forward to returning to work. Neither the family budget nor the family home is adequate to take in one more member. Should they force themselves to buy a house before they have sufficient down payment and before Mr. Earley has paid off the mortage on his business, or should they try to rent a larger place? Renting a larger place on their present budget means returning to the ghetto. But the problems presented by the new baby are not all financial and social. Some are intensely personal. Mr. Earley is inclined to tighten his belt and make a place for the new one, but Mrs. Earley is not at all sure that she has "enough energy, strength, or desire to love and care for another baby."

5. Mr. and Mrs. Franklyn had a family income of $10,400 last year. They have one child, a ten-month-old girl. He has a high school education and works as a janitor. She has finished junior college and works as an office clerk. Both her parents are college graduates; his never went to high school. Her parents were distressed with her marriage, feeling that she was "selling herself short." Mr. Franklyn presently works at two jobs in order to earn $135 a week. Mrs. Franklyn wants him to find another job in "some kind of business or management." She also wants him to go back to school. He works at night, she works during the day. They have few mutual friends, partly because of their work schedules, but also and more importantly because of their different social class orientations. Most of their

contacts are with "his friends" because she is not sure her friends will accept him. Thus, even in the black middle class viable family life is ever threatened.

The Lower Classes

Most Negro families are composed of ordinary people. They do not get their names in the paper as outstanding representatives of the Negro race and they do not show up on the welfare rolls or in the crime statistics. They are headed by men and women who work and support their families, manage to keep their families together and out of trouble most of the time. They are not what might be generally conceived of as "achieving families." They are likely to be overlooked when the white community goes looking for a Negro to sit on an interracial committee, or take a job where Negroes have not been hired before. For they have not gone to college and they are not part of that middle and upper class group most likely to come into intimate, daily contact with the white world. At the same time, they are likely to be overlooked by the poverty program and other efforts to uplift the poor and disadvantaged. They often do not qualify to take part in these programs because they are not on welfare. They are, in a word, just folks. They are the great unknowns, typically left out of the literature on Negro family life. Once in a while they appear in fiction, but even then generally as oversimplified stereotypes rather than in all their ordinary, human complexity. And yet, these ordinary Negro families are often the backbone of the Negro community. They are virtually unknown to white people, particularly white people who depend on books and other mass media for their knowledge of life in the most important ethnic subsociety in America today.

Dr. Charlotte Dunmore has done a study of 173 families in a Negro ghetto of Hartford, Connecticut, which provides considerable support for the above description. She has described for us the "average" family in her study, as the picture was developed by IBM computers from responses of all her study families.

The family is Negro and Protestant. The mother was born and reared in the rural or semi-rural southern United States. She came to live in Hartford sometime after her eighteenth birthday. The family has two legally married parents and contains 4.7 members. Father is the chief breadwinner earning $4,800 per year from his employment as a skilled craftsman, steward, or machinist.

Mother, who stays home to take care of the children, perceives them as growing, developing human beings amenable to her control, if only to a limited degree.

The parents want their children to have at least some college education. They hope that their children will become skilled technicians, specialized clerical workers, or go into one of the minor professions—library science, teaching, the arts. The children are involved in at least two organized community activities (Scouts, the "Y," settlement house, etc.). Previous to the summer school project, they had been actively involved in some other type of voluntary educational opportunity program.

Mother has achieved a rather high degree of integration into her neighborhood and is involved in a meaningful (to her) give-and-take relationship with her neighbors. At the present time, she is participating in at least two community activities. She is a registered voter and voted in the last election. She listens to the radio, watches television, and reads one of the two Hartford newspapers every day.

The family is geared to obtaining a better life for its children, including more education and more materially rewarding, status-giving employment. Hartford is perceived as a racially prejudiced community and education appears to be considered the primary method for circumventing this prejudice.[13]

Families like these, despite their stability, achievement, and contributions within the Negro community, are often ignored by the wider society because of the general tendency to lump all "lower class" Negro families in the ghetto into a single category and to focus on the most dysfunctional patterns of family life there.

Half of all Negro families may be considered distinctly lower class. They view themselves that way and are viewed by their fellows as such. It should be added, however, that this large group of people is highly differentiated and is by no means a uniform mass. Three distinct groupings within this lower class may be identified, including (1) the working nonpoor, (2) the working poor, and (3) the nonworking poor.

At the very top of the lower class is a group of families headed by men in the semi-skilled, highly paid, unionized, steady industrial jobs. These are members of the *industrial working class*. Families of Negro men holding good steady jobs as truck drivers (in the Teamsters Union), construction workers, and semi-skilled factory workers are in the upper reaches of the lower class. If it were not for the color of their skins and the housing discrimination they face, many of these men would be able to join the ranks of the new majority of labor union members who, it is said, now drive from work to their homes in the suburbs, sit in the backyard drinking martinis, and complain about high taxes. But if this is an elite working class, it is indeed a small one. Less than 7 per cent of Negro working men

---

[13] Charlotte Dunmore, "Social-Psychological Factors Affecting the Use of an Educational Opportunity Program by Families Living in a Poverty Area" (unpublished Ph.D. dissertation, Brandeis University, October 1967), Chap. 3. Reprinted by permission of Charlotte Dunmore.

are truck drivers, constituting about 12 per cent of all truck drivers. But not all of them are members of the Teamsters Union. About 3 per cent are lumbermen, but many of these are in the south where wages are low. Less than 2 per cent are auto mechanics and semi-skilled factory workers. Less than 1 per cent are longshoremen, though they account for a third of the workers in this class, often earning $12,000 to $15,000 a year. When to the secure occupational base of these men and their wives are added the style of life they can afford and a degree of community activity in the church, or lodge, or other specifically Negro institution, their status can be considerably higher than that suggested by the term lower class. Dr. Dunmore's "average" family in the Hartford ghetto is among the working nonpoor. She found, in fact, that between half and two thirds of the families with school-age children in her study would meet none of the current official definitions of poverty.

A second category of lower class Negro families is the working poor. The fact is not generally appreciated in the wider society that the majority of poor Negros live in nuclear families headed by men who work hard every day, and are still unable to earn enough to pull their families out of poverty. Each point of this statement should be emphasized.

1. The majority of poor Negros live in nuclear families, and not in segmented families. Nearly 60 per cent of children in families with less than $2,000 annual income were living with both parents in 1959. If we consider families with earnings between $2,000 and $4,000, the proportion of children living with both parents rises to over 80 per cent. It increases, of course, as income does.[14]

2. The majority of poor Negroes live in nuclear families headed by men and not by women. Among families earning less than $3,000 in 1966, nearly 60 per cent were headed by husbands and fathers. Among those earning between $3,000 and $5,000, the proportion of male-headed families increased to nearly 75 per cent.[15] As income increases the proportion of male-headed families increases.

3. The majority of poor Negroes live in families which are self-supporting and are not supported by public welfare. While 41 per cent of all Negroes were living in poverty in 1966, only 14 per cent were supported by public welfare. Thus, nationally about a third of all poor Negroes (3.2 million out of 9.6 million) were supported by welfare. This proportion varies by communities. In her Hartford neighborhood, Dr. Dunmore estimated that nearly 60 per cent of her poor families were self-supporting. These are the working poor. It seems obvious, then, that the guaranteed family al-

---

[14] "Social and Economic Conditions of Negroes in the United States," Joint Report of Bureau of Census and Bureau of Labor Statistics, BLS Report No. 332, Current Population Reports, Series P-23, No. 24, October 1967, p. 76.

[15] *Ibid.*, p. 71.

lowance of $3,000 per year for a family of four, the most generous figure being considered in discussions of proposed family allowance systems, will in itself do little to alleviate the conditions faced by the overwhelming majority of poor black people, to say nothing of the social and economic hardships faced by that even larger number of black people who do not now qualify as "poor." Most poor black people live in poor black neighborhoods. The open housing provisions of the Civil Rights Act of 1968 are not likely to change that fact.

The working poor families are often headed by unskilled laborers, service workers, and domestics. More Negro men work as janitors or porters in this country than in any other specific occupation. In 1960, 7.3 per cent of all Negro male workers were janitors and porters. These 235,000 men comprise 37.2 per cent of all men in this job category. But Negro women, who are often heads of families in this group, are even more highly concentrated in low level, unskilled jobs than men. More than a third of all Negro women who were employed at all worked as private household domestics. These men and women support families in that dominant segment of the lower class which outnumbers every other class stratum and includes probably a third of all Negro families. It should be noted that these men and women work and support their families on very low wages. They are the *working poor*. They are an unorganized mass of workers, in whom labor unions are only now beginning to express an interest, as among the hospital workers of New York, and the hotel and restaurant workers in a number of large cities. They are engaged in a struggle for economic existence, and the vast majority of them is self-supporting. Even among female-headed families, the majority of the mothers work and support the family.

So far we have described in socioeconomic terms 80 to 85 per cent of Negro families. We come, finally, to that group on the bottom of the economic ladder who occupy the lowest status in both the general community and the Negro community. These are the *nonworking poor,* that 15 or 20 per cent of Negro families headed by members with less than eighth grade education, who are intermittently if at all employed, and who have very low levels of job skills. These are families often supported by relatives and by public welfare. In many respects, though we describe them as part of the lower class, they may be more appropriately referred to as the *under class,*[16] for like the majority of Negro families a hundred years earlier, they are outside and below the formal class structure. In this sector, the basic conditions of life are most abject. Many of these family heads have not gone beyond sixth grade, and their incomes are often below $2,000 per year, and sometimes below $1,000. Among them are families living in

[16] Joan Gordon, *The Poor of Harlem: Social Functioning in the Underclass* (New York: Office of the Mayor, 1965).

dilapidated housing or, if they are very fortunate, in public housing projects.

Even in the under class, however, there are some variations in life conditions. For example, there are geographic variations. Families in the under class are in the most dire straits if they live in the rural South, where nearly a quarter of Negro families still live, and especially if they live in one of the 135 counties in the South where Negroes constitute a majority, and more especially still, if they live in the black belt counties of Alabama, Mississippi, or Louisiana. The nation learned dramatically in the summer of 1967 that literally hundreds of families in these areas were not able to prevent their children from starving, while local and state authorities looked the other way. And even the federal government seemed helpless to prevent it, although it has several programs specifically designed to combat starvation in communities where authorities permit these programs to operate and among families with sufficient money income and foresight to purchase food stamps. But hundreds of families have no money income whatever.

Families in the under class are somewhat better off if they live in the urban South, where welfare payments, though pitifully low, are nevertheless available to a few Negro families provided they meet the standards of morality decreed by the local establishment. And still better off are those under class families living in the urban ghettos of the North, where the economic opportunity structure, including welfare policies, is likely to be more supportive. Even here, it should be observed, in most states it is not possible for families to qualify for federally supported welfare payments if there is a husband and father in the home. Opportunities for jobs that pay a minimum wage are better for men between the ages of thirty-five and forty-five than for youth or older men. Opportunities for just any job, including domestic work, are better for women than for men. Opportunities for welfare payments are similarly better for female-headed families than for male-headed families. But more important, regardless of whether these very poor families are a little better off in one community or another, because of the color barrier they are all considerably worse off than white families in similar circumstances. Both the treatment they receive when in this status, and the pathways out of it, are conditioned by the long, resilient shadows of the plantation.

Living Poor and Black

What does it mean, then, to be living poor and black in America more than a hundred years after emancipation? The meaning varies. But in many respects the conditions of life for Negro families in the ghetto are getting worse rather than better relative to the conditions of middle class white Americans.

As a society, we have not made an appreciable dent in the wall of discrimination which separates Negro people from other Americans. At the same time we have made no appreciable dent in the twin problem of poverty. Thus, the abolition of racial discrimination and poverty remain the nation's and the Negroes' chief cross and chief hope for viability. Low income Negro families in urban slums and rural conclaves are the chief victims of this double jeopardy. These are the most conspicuous residents of that other America which has been described so vividly by Michael Harrington.[17]

Thus, to be living poor and black in 1968 means severe restrictions in the most basic conditions, particularly focused in the areas of family income, education of parents, occupations of family heads, family housing, and health care. And, if the conditions of life in these five crucial areas are not met, the Negro family cannot be expected to assume the same structure as other, more achieving and affluent families. And, if they do not have the basic supports for their society in these areas and do not develop the most effective structures of family life, they cannot be expected to meet the functions of family life required of them by their members and their society. And yet, they are expected to do these things. And many are able to perform in a remarkably functional manner. Just as there is variety and range in the basic life conditions and societal supports available to Negro families, there is variety and range in both the structure and function of Negro family life. There is no single uniform style of Negro family life, not even in the most depressed sections of urban ghettos. But if there is not complete uniformity, there also is not random variety. There are patterns, and modalities of life which are immanently tied in to the basic conditions of life, both contemporary and historical.

There are several bases for the patterning of life among low income Negro families. First, there is geographic patterning. Some families live in the rural South, others in the urban South, and still others in the urban North and West. In the latter category some families live in the heart of the ghetto, others live on the fringes, and still others live outside the central cities. The conditions of life for low income Negro families are most abject in the rural South, less so in the urban South and less so still in the urban North and West. The ability of Negro families to meet the requirements of society, particularly for achievement, is highly associated with this geographic patterning.

A second basis for patterning is socioeconomic. Even among the lower class, there are at least three major groupings, the *working nonpoor,* the

[17] Michael Harrington, *The Other America: Poverty in the United States* (Baltimore, Md.: Penguin Books, Inc., 1963).

working poor, and the *nonworking poor.* Both family stability and family achievement, and thus viability, follow very closely variations in socioeconomic status.

Thirdly, there are patterns in the structure of Negro family life, based on household composition. Thus some families are *basic families* with only the two married adults present. Others are *nuclear families* with two married adults and children. Still others are *attenuated nuclear families* with one adult missing. And each of these three types of primary family groups may be further elaborated into *extended families, sub-families,* or *augmented families* with nonrelatives functioning as intimate members of the household.

Still a fourth type of patterning is related to size. There are small, medium, and large-sized families in the lower class. Size may serve as both an obstacle, and a facilitator of achievement depending on the age, sex, relationship, character, and contribution of the various family members.

A fifth type of patterning is associated with authority and decision making in the family. Here there are three distinct groups. There are the vanishing *patriarchies,* where men make most of the decisions in crucial areas of family life. They form a minority among low income Negro families, but they still exist to some extent. Then there are the resilient *matriarchies* in which the wife and mother exerts an inordinate amount of authority at the expense of or in the absence of the husband and father. This is the second most common authority pattern among low income Negro families, and not the most common as is often assumed. Then, finally, there are the expanding *equalitarians.* These are families in which both husband and wife participate actively and jointly in decision making in the major areas of family life. Their tribes are increasing at the expense of both the patriarchy and the matriarchy. This is the most common pattern of authority among lower class Negro families today.

A sixth type of patterning has to do with family division of labor. Some families have a more or less strict, traditional division of labor based on sex. The man earns the livelihood, and does little else of the household and family chores. The wife and mother has her work which she performs largely unaided. These are role-segmented families. In still other families, however, there is role flexibility and mutual cooperation between husband and wife in meeting the instrumental needs of the family in both the external world and within the family. Still other families have children or other relatives able and willing to participate jointly with husband and wife in these major functions of family life. Among low income Negro families, the segmented role relationships are probably most common, although, as the above discussion has shown, collaboration is probably more common than is generally thought. Also, when there are older children in the family, they are drafted into service with household tasks, including child rearing tasks at a much earlier age in these families, than among other ethnic subsocieties.

Seventh, and finally, there are patterns of Negro family life reflected in their attitudes and behavior toward the socialization of children. Some low income Negro families take very good care of their children and inspire and aid them on toward conformity and achievement in the major areas and institutions of life. These are families that are considered to function adequately. They are able to understand, intervene actively and manipulate to some extent the plethora of institutions on which they depend and which, often, in themselves, function most inadequately. A second category of families function less adequately. They function better in some areas of life than others; and better at some times than others; and always they function better under some (favorable) conditions than under others. These families may be on and off welfare. Their children may be in and out of trouble. They are engaged in a struggle for respectability, conformity and achievement. Then, at the bottom of life's resources, is a relatively large group of low income Negro families who have been most deserted by their society. They receive the least supports from the major institutions of society. They are the most victimized by discrimination and poverty and general lack of opportunity. They are, consequently, the most chronically unstable, dependent and deviant. Their children are most likely to get into trouble or to be neglected. These are the problem families and the long-term welfare recipients.

But it cannot be stressed too strongly that not all lower class Negro families are poor. Not all poor families are broken. Not all single parent families are on welfare. And not all welfare families are chronic problems. A more adequate income structure would remove many of them from the arena of social concern.

These are the major dimensions along which Negro family life is patterned in the other America. They interact with and overlap each other. Families move from one category to another as time and circumstances change. They do this in response to life conditions and in an effort to survive, to conform, and to achieve in a society which expects these ends, but often provides them with inadequate means to their attainment.

Summary

While this discussion of socioeconomic status and mobility has been confined to the social forces defining the basic conditions of life, particularly jobs, housing, education, and income, it is easy to anticipate the relationship between these basic conditions and the behavior of family members which will be considered in the following chapters. The ability of the

Negro family to meet the needs of its members and the functional requirements of society is intimately associated with its position on the socioeconomic pyramid.

We have observed that while a hundred years ago more than 90 per cent of Negro families subsisted in abject poverty, and as late as 1900 the overwhelming majority was still confined to the lower reaches of the lower class, there has been a transition, paralleling the rise in geographic mobility, which has resulted in a highly differentiated socioeconomic structure of Negro family life. A tenth of Negro families may be considered upper class, and another 40 per cent may be considered middle class, but half are still clustered in the lower classes. Each of these major class levels is further subdivided, however, into substrata of meaningful proportions. There are two upper classes, the old upper class of families whose status is built upon that of previous generations of privilege, and the new upper class built in one generation on the basis of talent and good fortune. The middle class is stratified into a comfortable upper middle class of educated professionals and businessmen, a middle middle class of white-collar clerks and salesmen, and a lower middle class of skilled artisans and small businessmen. The lower class is stratified into three components, including an upper lower class of steadily employed, relatively high earning tradesmen, a middle lower class of unskilled laborers, service workers, and domestics, and an under class composed of families headed by intermittently employed and unemployed persons largely assisted by other relatives and by a grossly inadequate welfare system. We are faced with a highly differentiated group of families, reflecting the differential availability of the basic perquisites of life which enable them to meet the needs of their members and the requirements of society. At every level, however, Negro families and their members are faced by obstacles associated with the color bar which restrict their resources, opportunities, and choices—and consequently their ability to survive, to conform, and to reach the level of social achievement of which they are capable.

37. No School?

George B. Leonard

The most obvious barrier between our children and the kind of education that can free their enormous potential seems to be the educational system itself: a vast, suffocating web of people, practices and presumptions, kindly in intent, ponderous in response. Now, when true educational alternatives are at last becoming clear, we may overlook the simplest: no school.

This means just what it says: the elimination of educational institutions housed in separate buildings with classrooms and teachers. At the least, it involves the end of all compulsory school attendance. The idea may seem entirely impractical. But the recent development of a technology of individualized learning has changed things. "No school" has now become feasible. Before going on to other alternatives, we might well give this one a fair hearing. The case may be stated as follows: Practically everything that is *presently* being accomplished in the schools can be accomplished more effectively and with less pain in the average child's home and neighborhood playground.

The man who first brought this proposal to my attention is Dr. M. W. Sullivan, the educational programmer whose work was covered briefly in the chapter on the human potential. Sullivan is an outspoken and passionate man, and he argues with the prejudice of one who has seen the power of well-designed, self-instructional materials. But I doubt if there is anyone who can state the case better.

Sullivan first began mulling over the "no school" idea in the late 1950s, when he and others at Hollins College in Virginia were developing some of the earliest programmed instruction. Why ship the bodies of our children through crowded streets to overstuffed schools, he wondered, when we can much more easily ship instructional materials to their homes?

SOURCE: George B. Leonard, *Education and Ecstasy* (New York: Delacorte Press, 1968), Chap. 6. Copyright © 1968 by George B. Leonard and used by permission of the publisher, Delacorte Press.

In the entire psychological literature [Sullivan says], you can find no evidence that the teacher *per se* helps learning. You can find much evidence that the teacher does harm to the learning process. The average school, in fact, is no fit place to learn in. It is basically a lock-up, a jail. Its most basic conditions create a build-up of resistance to learning. Physically, the child is worn down by the fatigue of sitting in one position for inordinate lengths of time. Mentally, he is stunned by the sameness of his surroundings and the monotony of the stimuli that bombard him. Can you imagine the amount of energy it takes just to sit still, waiting, against every impulse, for your turn to respond?

When *you* think, you want to get up, move, pace around. But most schoolrooms are set up to *prevent* thinking, learning, creativity—whatever you want to call it. You'd be surprised how many new teachers are told, "Classroom control must come first. The most important thing the child has to learn is how to take instructions, so if you spend the first two months, or two years, teaching them to take instructions, it will be well worth while."

The average kid gets few chances to respond during the school day. And when he does get a chance, it's generally an echoic response. He just gives the teacher back what the teacher wants to hear. And you end up with an organism that has no integrity at all. Too often, when the organism does break through and start responding, he gets slapped down. He learns to sit still, to line up in orderly rows, to take instructions, to feel guilt for his natural impulses—and perhaps to do a few simple things that he could learn to do one-fiftieth—yes, *one-fiftieth*—of the time it usually takes him.

Now what would happen if you shipped the learning materials to the child rather than shipping the child to the dungeon? Let's assume no technological advances—no computers or electronic consoles. All you'd have to have would be the present form of programmed textbooks plus tapes that could be played on $24.95 Japanese tape recorders equipped with foot pedals. We already have programs for teaching languages and other auditory subject matter; the child goes through a written program, turning on the recorder with a foot pedal wherever stars appear in the program. Thus we can combine all the needed written, visual, auditory stimuli. We can provide any learning of importance that goes on in most present classrooms.

So I would have to say that, even with the present rather primitive programs, even the worst ghetto home can be a better learning environment than most schools. At least in the ghetto home, the child can get up and run around when he wants to. If he can just be kept out of school, he won't be taught that learning is dull, unpleasant work. He'll just assume it's what it is: the greatest pleasure in human life. There'll be no guilt and fear. He'll play with his learning materials when he feels like it. And if it's only a half hour a day, he'll be *far* ahead of school learning in all the basic subjects.

But what of social contacts, I asked Sullivan? What of "learning to get along with others in the peer group?" Sullivan replied:

Is there any indication that such a thing takes place in school? What is this *getting along* or *making out* with others? Why can't children learn that much better in neighborhood playgrounds or on the sidewalks or even in the streets?

These bowling-alley places where you leave kids. They're good. Much better than schools where children are subjected to a totally false discipline and totally artificial relationships with each other.

In my own case, I was the only kid in my neighborhood who was sent to kindergarten. It was optional then in Connecticut. So for almost a year my peer group was out playing, learning, creating their own very exciting world while I was being tortured in school. They built a tree-house. They built a hut. And what did I do? I learned how to lie on a mat, how to listen to stories, how to line up, how to sit still. Finally, I figured how to escape. I wet my pants and they sent me home. *They sent me home.* The first time was an accident, but after that I made sure to do it every day. And I was free to learn again.

School is a terrible thing to do to kids. It's cruel, unnatural, unnecessary.

Many people would argue, I reminded Sullivan, that the school is a model of the world. Eventually, the child probably will have to face unpleasant working situations, narrow competition. There will be unreasonable deadlines, hasty instructions that will have to be understood and heeded—all sorts of hardships.

Yes, I know. The old idea was, if you want the kid to get along in life, you put him in that situation as soon as possible. If he's going to be in a lousy situation where he feels inadequate later, you put him in a lousy situation where he feels inadequate now. It just doesn't work that way. There was a very interesting study made on those Marines in World War II who went through the worst campaigns of the war, the ones who hit Guadalcanal and went through the whole thing—boredom, jungle rot, water up to the waist in foxholes, people dying all around them. As it turned out, the guy who stands up under all this is the one who would be considered to have had a very fortunate childhood, the good boy who has always told he was good. And who cracks wide open? The person who had been up against tough conditions in his childhood, with all sorts of hardships, the guy who had never had a chance at success.

You see, the whole argument falls apart however you look at it, even in the extreme case of the Marines in combat. But the world is generally not that extreme. The world isn't any damned way. It's what people make it. You can go a long way toward making your world. And that's just where the school steps in. It warps your expectations so that you'll see the outside world like the school and then you'll tend to make your world that way. You'll be trained to see learning as hard and painful. And you'll go out and perpetuate a world in which those conditions exist.

You know, you have to *teach* any organism how to be unhappy. And the human being is the only organism that has *learned* unhappiness—except maybe some of his has spilled over onto his dog. I must insist that schools as they now exist are well designed to produce unhappiness and little else.

At this point, I felt constrained to raise the most powerful objection of all. "Whatever you say," I told Sullivan, "the mothers won't buy it. They just don't want their kids around the house, under their feet all day."

You're probably right. It's strange. They're so anxious to have the kids, then they seem to want to get them out of sight as quickly as possible. We'd have to teach the mothers a different attitude toward their children, not so much goddess and slave as playmates. We'd have to relieve their nervousness about the whole area of book learning. We'd have to show them how to reinforce their children's exploratory behavior whenever possible. Most of all, we'd have to teach them to spend a lot more time just leaving them alone—and perhaps enjoying them.

The trouble is that the parents have been to school, too. If we could just get the kids *out* of school for one generation, we'd solve the whole problem.

Parents who would reject Sullivan's views as extreme have a simple way of checking them out. Arrange for a visit to your child's school—but not on the usual parents' visiting day. (Go then, too, if you wish, but don't expect to find out what really goes on; the teacher and class have probably spent several days or weeks preparing for this charade.) Arrive early in the morning, with your child. Chat for a few moments with the teacher to put him at ease, and allow him to introduce you to the class. Assure him that you plan to create no disturbance whatever but simply to melt into the woodwork. Then take a chair near the back of the room at a position where you have an oblique view of your child. Be natural, casual, friendly. When children turn to look at you, smile slightly in acknowledgment and reassurance, then turn away. If you are natural and at ease, you will probably be surprised at how quickly you are ignored. And, though the teacher may tend to be on guard, his basic style of teaching and relating with the children is generally too deeply ingrained to allow for very much dissembling. You will have the opportunity of experiencing what your child experiences.

Take the opportunity. Focus in on your child. Try to assume his viewpoint, feel what he feels, learn what he learns. Become sensitive to his body positions; see when he sits straight, when he hunches over, when he squirms, when he languishes. Balance the weight of the teacher's words against the pressure on your seat. Try not to daydream. Remember that time goes more slowly for a child than for an adult.

Now are you ready for a little walk? A cup of coffee? A visit to the restroom? A cigarette? Forget it. Stay with your child. Stand only when he stands. Leave the room only when he leaves the room. Concentrate on him. *Become* your child.

Bored beyond endurance? Let us hope not. Let us pray for our children and for all children that you have found one of those master magicians who, in spite of every obstacle, manages to pull each unlikely new moment out of a hat, wiggling and full of life. If not, be easy on yourself for a little while; steal a few moments from the day (though your child has no such opportunity) for a modest experiment. Take out a watch with a second hand. Mark the lines of a sheet of notebook paper with tiny cross-hatches, each representing ten seconds. An hour's worth will fit neatly on a single sheet of notebook paper. Select a typical period, say, arithmetic instruction. During this period, mark each ten-second interval during which your child is really *learning* something. Leave the other intervals blank. . . . Bear in mind that true learning is change (not needless repetition of something already known) and that the learning has to do with the response of the child, not with the presentation of the teacher.

This little exercise will take sensitivity; you will have to be, in a sense, inside your child's mind. It will be more easily accomplished in the lower grades than in high school (or college, for that matter), where the lecture system makes it virtually impossible to know if learning is taking place. It will involve some guessing and can under no circumstances be termed "scientific." Nonetheless, it will most likely prove a revelation to you. I have tried it with my own children and with scores of others in all sorts of schools. The results are discouraging. Even marking with a kind of desperate generosity, I have rarely been able to fill in more than a third of the intervals. Often I have found that "classroom control" plus waiting for other children to recite plus all the other unwieldy manipulations demanded by the usual classroom environment leave less than ten percent of any child's time for anything that can remotely be termed "learning."

When you have had enough of this exercise, *stay where you are*. No coffee, no cigarettes, no moving around to relax your body and stimulate your thoughts.

Playtime. *Freedom*. Not so fast. First (if you are in a typical classroom), the entire class must come to order. That means stillness, silence. Perhaps each row of children will be pitted against the others; the row achieving submissive nonactivity first gets to line up first at the door. After all the children, again, have come to order and after teacher, again, orders the class to walk, not run, down the stairs, the door is opened. The children explode onto the play yard.

Go with them. Sit down somewhere among them so that you can experience the child's world at the child's level. True learning can take place under the conditions of play. But are you observing *play?* Probably not, unfortunately. The children are likely to be merely letting off steam, with shrill yells and frenetic running about. It has been my experience that, wherever the classroom situation is repressive and antithetical to learning, the playground situation, in direct ratio, is hyperactive and equally antithetical to learning. In true play, the child is intent, responsive, unhurried, completely involved. There is a lovely seriousness about it. The child who explodes out of and in reaction to a static, nonlearning environment is hurried, unresponsive, indeed almost spastic. This is not delight; it is desperation. After experiencing the playground situation, ask yourself, "Is this the kind of social interaction for which I'm sending my child to school?"

Back in class again, then to lunch. And then the afternoon. Does the classroom seem stuffy? Watch the eyes of your child and all the others. Are they becoming heavy with incipient sleep? Are the tender half-moons of delicate skin just beneath them becoming puffy and discolored? Look closely. And how about your own eyes? Do you find yourself stifling yawns? Let us hope not. Let us hope the day has been an exhilarating one.

If not, however, don't hasten to blame the teacher. The environment in which he works, the expectations he tries to fulfill, the techniques generally offered him are woefully inadequate to the human potential. The teacher who prevails over such conditions is an artist, a hero of our times.

And yet do not let compassion for the teacher soften the sense of tragedy that you may feel. The world is filled with wrongs—war, disease, famine, racial degradations and all the slaveries man has invented for his own kind. But none is deeper or more poignant than the systematic, innocent destruction of the human spirit that, all too often, is the hidden function of every school. And do not think that your child can escape unscathed. There has been a lot of speculation lately about LSD's permanently altering the brain structure. This is a naïve way of putting it. First, as pointed out in Chapter II, the brain does not have a set "structure." Second, there is very little that is entirely "permanent" about the behavior of the central nervous system. Learned behavior is generally reversible, though reversing a behavior learned early in life takes a great deal more energy at a later stage than was originally needed to establish the behavior. Still, it might well be said that a number of LSD trips do alter the brain, if only because of the changes wrought through the behaviors engaged in during those trips. This being the case, it must be said that the typical first-grade experience probably alters the brain of your child even more than would many LSD trips, doing untold violence to his potential as a lifelong learner.

"Tragedy" is a strong word, but I can think of no other to describe what happens to most children during the early elementary years. Visiting schools around the country, I have shuttled again and again from a kindergarten room to, say, a fourth grade. (If you have the chance, you might try this for yourself.) And I have talked with hundreds of teachers about the seemingly mysterious human discrepancy revealed on that short journey. It is almost as if you are viewing specimens of two different species. Teachers are the first to agree that this is so. Nor did I receive a single letter of dissent when I described the trip in a *Look* magazine story called "What Your Child Can Teach His Teacher," in December of 1966:

> Go into a kindergarten room. By and large, the five-year-olds are spontaneous, unique. Tell them to dance, and they move naturally with a sort of unorganized grace. Read them a story, and their eyes give you back its suspense, fear, laughter. We like to say their faces light up (a particularly telling phrase), and when we look into this illumination, we are not ashamed to let our own faces glow in return. All of this, we assume, is a natural condition of the very young.

Walk down the hall to a fourth-grade classroom. Very quickly, you will notice that something has been lost. Not so many eyes are alight. Not so many responses surprise you. Too many bodies and minds seem locked in painful self-awareness. This, too, we carelessly attribute to the natural order. It's just part of growing up.

But is it really? Is it really necessary for the human animal to lose in spontaneity and imagination as it gains in knowledge and technique? Must we shed the brightness of childhood as we put on the armor plating of age?

Perhaps it is no coincidence that the growth rate of intelligence falls off so rapidly just at the point when the child enters school. Older concepts of how the brain works offered physiological explanations for the startling fact that most humans have achieved eighty percent of their intelligence growth by their eighth birthday. Each new fact, it was said many years ago, makes a little crease or rut in the gray matter. After so long, there is no space for any more ruts. In more recent times, the synapses were said to be somehow "filled up," or the brain cells were "committed." The best recent research, however, as was pointed out in Chapter II, suggests that the brain can never be "filled up." But it can be *taught* to stop learning—that is, changing. It can be *taught* to stop exploring, to reject the unfamiliar, to focus on a limited number of stimuli, to make repetitive, standard responses.

Indeed, the entire education process as it is usually constituted in our schools may best be viewed as a funnel through which every child is squeezed into an ever-narrowing circle; at the end there is room only for a single set of "right answers." The funnel does not stop constricting at the end of the lower grades, or even at high-school graduation. Educator Harold Taylor told me of what he called "four of the most depressing days of my life," with students from each of the four classes of a small, elite Eastern college—one day for each class, starting with freshmen. The experience had the quality of stop-action photography, in which the effects of four years of college were compressed into that many days. The freshmen, Dr. Taylor said, were still, to some extent, open and inquisitive, ready for new ideas. Each subsequent class was less so, with the seniors seeming bored, cynical and interested only in "How will this help me get a better grade?" or "What's in it for me?"

Professor William Arrowsmith goes another step, in writing of his preference for teaching the undergraduate in the humanities rather than the graduate student, whom he finds

already half-corrupted by the fate he has chosen, the fate which makes him a graduate student. He wants knowledge and information. He has examinations on his mind, and hence tends to conform to his professor's expectation of him —the fate they have jointly chosen and now jointly enforce. The resentment they both frequently feel is their resentment of this mutual fate. For the graduate student, the undergraduate's lucky integration is no longer possible—or if it is, God help him! The present is now less insistent for him. He has chosen to *know* rather than to *be*. For a man with a gift of life, that loss is like castration; the best leave rather than suffer it. Others grit their teeth and will their way through.

It is not that the "product" of our education system is not "capable." He comes out with "skills." He may be a usable component in the social machine. But he is just about finished as a learner.

Only the inefficiency of the present school system and the obdurance of certain individuals can account for the creativity, the learning ability that survives after age twenty-five. Dr. Harold G. McCurdy of the University of North Carolina has studied the childhood patterns of those historical geniuses about whose childhood most is known. Seeking factors common to the early life of the twenty geniuses he selected, Dr. McCurdy came up with three: "(1) a high degree of attention focused upon the child by parents and other adults, expressed in intensive educational measures and, usually, abundant love; (2) isolation from other children, especially outside the family; and (3) a rich efflorescence of phantasy, as a reaction to the two preceding conditions." McCurdy concludes that "the mass education of our public school system is, in its way, a vast experiment on the effect of reducing all three of the above factors to minimal values, and should, accordingly, tend to suppress the occurrence of genius."

When McCurdy refers to public education as an "experiment," he is, unwittingly, taking educators into dangerous territory. For if we *did* consider schooling as experimental in nature, educators might well stand indicted under at least five of the ten essential principles of the Nuremberg Code for research involving human subjects. Imagine your children as the subjects:

1. The voluntary consent of the human subject is absolutely essential.
2. The experiment should be such as to yield fruitful results for the good of society, unprocurable by other means of study, and not random and unnecessary in nature.
3. The experiment should be designed and based on the results of animal experimentation and a knowledge of the natural history of the disease or other problem under study, so that the anticipated results will justify the performance of the experiment.
4. The experiment should be so constructed as to avoid all unnecessary physical and mental suffering and injury.
5. During the course of the experiment, the human subject should be at liberty to bring the experiment to an end if he has reached the physical or mental state where continuation of the experiment seems to him impossible.

The first and last provisions cited here would seem to be the most grossly violated by the present system of compulsory mass education. That children should be forced by law to stay in school until late adolescence may someday be perceived as outrageous. The current series of public-service advertisements urging adolescents to remain even longer already reveals the crux of the matter:

EDUCATION IS FOR THE BIRDS
The birds that get ahead
or
BOY
Drop out of school now and that's what
they'll call you all your working life.

Behind the words, society's naked face—patronizing, insulting, ultimately utterly cynical.

But the slogans are true, aren't they? Yes. And there's the trouble. Jobs *are* withheld from those who don't possess a certain diploma. The diplomas, however, are screening devices. The job-dispensing agencies are not really interested in what the job seeker has learned in the school, but merely that, for whatever reason, he has survived it.

When you come right down to it, the amount of learning that goes on in high school, even in the simplest and most explicit techniques of our civilization, is minuscule. Look, for example, at the English textbooks from seventh grade through twelfth. They are basically the same book. And the student who writes and comprehends skillfully in the seventh grade will most likely be doing equally well at high-school graduation and forever after. To quote the recent president of the National Council of Teachers of English, Dr. Alfred H. Grommon: "Forty years of teaching traditional English grammar to American students of varying backgrounds has failed to improve their ability to speak or write it."

Perhaps we should be glad that schools do generally fail in their present task, which is, as I have said before and undoubtedly will say a few more times, to teach a few tricks and otherwise limit possibilities, narrow perceptions and bring the individual's career as a learner (changer) to an end. Such a task may have seemed necessary, if ignoble, in the precarious fragmented society of the past, when individuals, as components, had to prop up the great social machine.

It is the basic premise of this book, however, that the highly interactive, regenerative technological society now emerging will work best, indeed will *require* something akin to mass genius, mass creativity and lifelong learning. If this premise proves out, schools *as they now exist* are already obsolete. And, if someone like Sullivan can provide us with the wherewithal to do at home, easily, painlessly and quickly, what the schools attempt presently to do, in pain and failure, then perhaps we should consider ending the affliction, the tyranny that for so long has entrapped schoolchild and schoolmaster alike—and save billions of dollars in the process. (Linguistic note: The only two entries under the word "disciplinarian" in the index of Roget's *Thesaurus* are "tyrant" and "teacher.")

But let me hasten to stress again that what is usually being taught in school today makes up only a tiny fraction of man's education, present or potential. Nor does programmed instruction offer salvation; it will soon become outmoded. But this mode of learning—and others, such as the new speed-reading technique—provides hope and confidence to those who would expand education's domain and pursue ecstasy in learning. It proves that, *if need be,* we can even now remedy most educational ills that have plagued our children and confounded the "experts" over the years. Excepting the severely handicapped (possibly less than one percent of the population), *every* child can learn to read, to write, to spell, to manipulate quantities, to learn all the hard stuff of present-day schooling—in less than one-third the present time.

We might end schools rather than let them remain as they are today. Except for the legal difficulties, I would prefer having my own children learn at home; I have seen what schools, in spite of every good intention, have subtracted from their lives. But, instead of taking that alternative, we can move on into the unexplored lands of the human potential. We can take that extra two-thirds of present school time available to us right now (as a few experimental schools already are doing) and get on with the most exhilarating experiment in man's history: to help every child become, *in his own way,* an artist; to help every child become, *in his own way,* a genius; to see just how far toward ecstasy and accomplishment every human being can go.

About that day in class, your visit to school: I was not being hypothetical. I seriously recommend that you do it. Most teachers and administrators will probably welcome you. If, however, some administrator should bridle, remind him that you have every educational, moral and legal right to be there. The kind of visit outlined above, one parent a day, creates far less disruption than does a mass visitation on special days or weeks. And anyway (we keep forgetting) the schools belong to us. If they are failing to educate, it is, ultimately, because we don't care enough.

38. Alienation of Youth

Victor Eisner

In March of 1968 a Presidential Commission issued a report on the riots which many cities experienced in the summer of 1967. This report documented a deep-seated alienation among Negro dwellers in our central cities. Negroes have failed to share in what we like to call the American Way of Life, and they have in many cases ceased to believe that America can be, for them, a land of either opportunity or equality. One result of this was rioting. Other results include high crime rates, many social ills such as high illegitimacy and venereal disease rates, and high percentages of youths who drop out of school.

Among the factors which have led to the isolation of Negroes in central cities is the massive migration of white people to the suburbs. The proportion of middle class white families living in our cities is growing smaller every year, and every year sees more farm land dug up, paved, and converted to housing tracts. On the whole, these suburbs contain a white population. There are a few areas where suburban homes are occupied by black families, but these areas are exceptional. The metropolitan areas of the United States can be described, with very little inaccuracy, as black central cities with white suburbs.

One of the most important reasons why white families move to the suburbs is to find a suitable place to raise their children. Suburbs have a low population density. This results in large open areas where children can play. Suburban schools score better than city schools on such achievement tests as average reading ability of students or average arithmetic ability. The suburbs are said to be free of such urban evils as gang warfare, juvenile delinquency, dope peddlers, or prostitution. Most important, suburbs contain socially stratified populations, so that each family can be reasona-

SOURCE: *The Journal of School Health*, XXIX, 2 (February 1969), 81–90. Reprinted by permission of the author and publisher. Material in this paper is taken from *The Delinquency Label* by Victor Eisner. Copyright © 1969 by Random House, Inc. Reprinted by permission.

bly sure that neighboring families, and the neighboring children with whom their children will associate, are of similar backgrounds and similar value systems. The children do not get into "bad company."

Nevertheless, all is not well in the suburbs. Social problems *do* arise, and despite all of the advantages for which fathers are willing to spend hours each day on the highway, children do not always grow up free of problems in the suburb. It has become obvious even to the casual observer that many young people from middle class white families are showing signs of alienation from our society. It is commonplace to read of student unrest and disorder. Many young people, such as those in the Haight-Ashbury area of San Francisco, are denying the validity of our way of life, refusing to support our country's wars, openly disobeying narcotics laws, and paradoxically, raising the same cry of "police brutality" that is heard from the Negro ghetto.

Why is this? It is not difficult, once one becomes aware of the harsh facts of ghetto life, to find reasons for the alienation of Negroes. It is much harder to explain alienation among young people who can share in all of the rewards and opportunities which our society has to offer. The paradox is not lost upon ghetto Negroes, who say "all we want for our children is what these hippies are rejecting."

It is my thesis tonight that this situation is the result of major defects in the structure of our society. These defects are to be found in the ways we have developed for bringing up children and for educating them to become a part of society. Our methods for doing this have created a barrier between adults and adolescents which is so great that the director of the National Institute of Mental Health was recently able to report to a Senate subcommittee that "The current problem of alienation [of all youth] is wider, deeper, and more diffuse than at any previous time in our history" (1).

The barrier we have set up between adults and adolescents has three component parts: segregation by age, institutionalized social life, and a lack of alternate pathways to success.

The first of these, segregation by age, results from an attempt to meet a fundamental need of school-age children. In the years from six to twelve, when a child is in school, his psychological task (2) is to develop a so-called "sense of industry." This is analogous to the "sense of identity," which an adolescent develops. If he fails to develop a sense of industry, the alternative is called "inferiority": the sense of personal inadequacy which a child develops if he does not receive recognition for his efforts. The school-age child accomplishes this task by his successes in doing and making things. Usually he obtains these successes in competition with others of his own age. Basically, the reason for dividing school children into grades, or for dividing baseball teams into age groups, is to provide each child with appropriate competition so as to give him a chance for his due share of successes. For the same reason an age-graded school class may be divided into ability-graded sections.

But a school-age child needs more than competition with his peers. Like the adolescent, he needs role models. The six-year old needs to see how seven-year olds act so that he in turn will be a successful seven-year old. The seven-year old needs to observe eight-year olds, and so on. A child also needs an opportunity to react with adults. In infancy, a child needs one adult, his mother. Later he needs many adults. The adolescent needs *young* adults, as well as all of the other adults who make up a community.

With these psychological necessities in mind, let us look at the middle class suburb to see what opportunities a child has.

The most prominent feature of suburban life is the isolation of individual families. The ideal of the American middle class is for each nuclear family to own its own home, preferably containing large open areas both indoors and outdoors in which children can play. Each home is inhabited by a mother and her preschool children during the day, and by two parents and all of their children at night. Grandparents and other members of the extended family live elsewhere. The population consists essentially of two age groups: below 20, and 30 to 55. There are few inhabitants between 20 and 30, or above 55. Customarily, families of the same age are neighbors, so that a child finds children of the same age to play with when he is not engaged in a scheduled activity. The suburban home is reached by automobile, and nearly all excursions away from home require the car. Very few suburban children can be sent to the store for a loaf of bread.

A child living in such a home finds that his life away from that home is carefully scheduled, and supervised. His mornings and part of each afternoon are spent in school. After school he may have one of many types of additional education, such as music lessons, or he may join a group activity such as a supervised athletic session or a supervised recreation session. Occasionally he may engage in free play with his contemporaries. On weekends, he usually accompanies his parents in a family activity.

An important feature of this life is the extent to which activities are arranged so that the children who participate in them are all of the same age. Practically no organized activity except baby-sitting puts adolescents in contact with school-age or pre-school children. A child's contacts with adults are largely restricted to his parents, substitute parents, and teachers. As a child grows older, this age segregation continues. Adolescents find teen-age centers, teen-age clinics, teen-age dances, and teen-age conferences to discuss the problems of teen-agers. They rarely find an activity in which they can participate in the company of adults. One might imagine that our society hates children, since we have carefully arranged that only parents and people employed for the purpose have any contact with them. In many cultures, old people play an important role as the natural teachers

of children. In the typical suburb they are not present to do this, since segregation by age is not limited to children. We also have a variety of methods for segregating and isolating old people.

The necessary and meaningful *work* of our society is carried on by
young and middle-aged adults. Children and adolescents do not participate
in this work; they are restricted to activities designed to prepare them for
adult life. They carry on these activities in groups with an age spread of
only a few years.

The physical conditions of middle class housing also affect the child's
social life. The suburban life requires an institutionalized rather than a
spontaneous pattern of socialization. Children meet each other and engage
in social activities by pre-arrangement and on a rigid time schedule. If
David wants to visit Scott, he or his mother must first phone to see if Scott
will be home. Then David's mother drives him to Scott's house saying,
"I'll pick you up at quarter to five. Be ready to go when I ring the doorbell
because we have to pick up Marcia at her dancing class at five sharp and
then I have to get home and start supper." Scott lives too far away for
David to walk over, and the dancing class is several miles from Marcia's
home. Mother spends a large portion of her day on such errands, because
they must all be done in the automobile which only she can drive. She
must keep to a rigid schedule if she is to accomplish her tasks at all.

But few of a suburban child's activities are even as spontaneous as David's visit to Scott. Many activities for children in middle class communities
take place at certain times of certain days. Some of these, such as Cub
Scouts and Little League, are supervised by parents. Some, such as Park
Department recreation and athletic periods, are supervised by adults hired
for the purpose. The activities are entered into by prearrangement and
schedule, like attendance at school. The thoughts of youth are no longer
"long, long thoughts"—modern children have little time left for daydreaming. Until a child is old enough to command his own wheeled transportation, he is confined to the schedule imposed by Mother's automobile.
The independence which allows children spontaneous, unplanned meetings
may come with possession of bicycles at seven or eight years of age. In
many areas a bicycle is unsafe because of heavy automobile traffic, and independence arrives only with a driver's license.

The institutionalization of social life has the benefit that children are
kept safely away from many hazards. They do not play on the streets, nor
are they for long outside of the sight of adults. It has the corresponding
disadvantage that children are relentlessly guided into conformity to the
customs of our society. They have no choice concerning the portion of the
society they are expected to enter. They are being prepared to earn high
incomes, and to establish middle class homes in which they will repeat the
lives of their parents.

The main institution which enforces middle class conformity is the school, and other institutions perform a supporting role. It may well be said that the school is the most powerful influence except his parents to which the middle class child is exposed.

In recent years it has become fashionable to criticize schools. On the one hand, their failures to deal adequately with lower class children are deplored, and on the other, it is pointed out that middle class children are deficient in mathematics, reading or whatever the current popular concern may be. These criticisms neglect the undoubted fact that our schools are designed by middle class standards to educate middle class children. When they are able to confine themselves to this task they do a remarkably good job. They are to be criticized, I believe, for what is a consequence of this very success: schools have become so much a part of the socialization of middle class children that there is no longer any alternate route available.

For a middle class boy, success in school is absolutely essential. If he is not well-prepared in grammar school he will be unable to succeed in high school. If he does not finish high school he will be unemployable. His stakes in high school are even greater than a lower class boy's, for he needs not only a diploma, but high grades in order to get into college. Success in the middle class world depends more and more upon a college education.

There is no other choice for the middle class child who wishes to enter the world his parents live in. Admission requires him to have behind him the education that is now considered necessary for middle class employment, and this education is available only from high schools and colleges. He can no longer leave high school and go into a lower class occupation, for this too requires at least a high school education. There is no longer a system by which a boy who is unable or unwilling to do well in school can enter an apprenticeship or a beginner's level job from which he can rise according to his ability. Success in school is the only available route.

Middle class parents are well aware of this. They have made a world which gives their children the best possible chance to succeed in school. They have moved, at the cost of considerable commuting inconvenience, to the all-white suburbs whose schools contain only middle class children. They have organized car-pools, cooperative nursery schools, children's athletic leagues, youth centers, and all of the time-consuming activities which keep their children in the company of other children of similar background. Parents' efforts to organize children into age groups, to institutionalize their lives, and to motivate them into success in the educational system are designed to ensure that they will grow into adults who are well prepared to enter middle class occupations. Middle class adults have, in short, very efficiently and with the best of motives, excluded children and adolescents from all adult activities.

Friedenberg (3) has compared the social system we have for our youth to a colonial system. He states (p. 181): "Teenagers, prisoners, and mental hospital patients are helpless in the toils of their respective institutions. By definition they are there for their own good . . ." His analogies are apt. An adolescent is confined in a network of laws, regulations and customs based on the middle class patterns of preparation for life in a middle class world. This network is designed to ensure that he completes an adequate preparation for adult life, but its effect is, in many cases, alienation. To understand why, we must take our eyes off the long-range goals of parents and look at what this system does for the immediate needs of adolescents.

From this point of view, the entire social system might have been designed to keep adolescents out of the productive segment of society. As I pointed out, an adolescent has no opportunity to have a significant relationship with any adult besides his parents and teachers. He cannot work except at odd jobs that have no relation to his subsequent career, and in the suburbs he cannot even watch his commuter father work. Suburban children have very little concept of how their fathers actually earn money, but they learn early in life that this work is important and fascinating, like the apples which hang out of reach on a tree. A child who is developing a sense of industry can only do so by succeeding at children's tasks. He is not allowed to try his hand at any economically meaningful work.

Children learn that adults have other privileges besides that of employment: adults are mobile, for they can drive; they are allowed the privileges of sex; they are permitted drugs, such as tobacco and alcohol, which alter mood and state of consciousness; and they are able to go where they please at any hour. These, like work, are all privileges denied to adolescents while they are striving to become adults.

An adolescent has four options regarding these privileges. He can of course, wait and enjoy them later. Deferred gratification is an important middle class value. This is what he is expected to do, and on the whole this is what most young people do. For most of them this choice leads to a rewarding life. But an adolescent who cannot or will not wait has three other possible choices, all undesirable. He may assume adult status and privileges before he has completed his education, or he may rebel against the middle class social system. As a final choice he has suicide, which is appallingly frequent among adolescents (4, 5).

Our culture contains no *rites de passage*. There is no functional ceremony which marks the point at which a boy becomes a man: confirmation and Bar Mitzvah are anachronisms which entitle a boy to an adult status only in ceremonial functions. The only statuses a boy (or a girl) can voluntarily assume which carry adult privileges are those of marriage and parenthood. Thus, many adolescents in middle class communities marry before they complete their education and so acquire adult rights to sexual intercourse and a certain control over their own activities.

Instead of marriage, a non-conforming adolescent may choose rebellion. Typically this is aimed at what appear to be the dominant values in the suburb: money and education. The adult "rat race" for high income and status is condemned, and (at least at the present time) non-material, spiritual values are substituted. Within the past few years we have seen, for example, Zen Buddhism, a crusade for civil rights, and an attempt for "meaningful relationships." On the other hand, rebellions may be directed at the schools, as we are seeing now. Regardless of the current fashion, the rebellion includes a denial of the validity of the usual suburban ideals.

A rebellion of this type is highly functional for many young people, especially when it can be carried on with the support of a like-minded group. Rebellion in a group allows conformity to the standards of an alternate social system. This often can be described as a youth culture. An adolescent who conforms to the values of the current youth culture solves a number of problems at one stroke. His problems of success in school and obtaining a good job are solved by rejecting the necessity for either. The problem of sex is solved by rejecting society's sanctions—for example, sex may be seen as an expression of a meaningful relationship. A desire to experiment with drugs becomes a new "drug culture" (6) in which the alterations of consciousness produced by LSD, methedrine, or marijuana are seen as important self-fulfilling experiences.

I am not arguing that teenagers should marry, nor that the use of LSD should be encouraged. Early marriage (and illegitimate pregnancies and venereal disease) and the growing use of dangerous drugs seem to me to be results of refusing to allow adolescents to participate in adult activities, and restricting them to only one legitimate pathway to success. Even though this pathway is a good way, it is obvious from the reaction of adolescents that it cannot be perfect, nor is it one which fits the needs of all middle class youth. We must, in view of the results, admit that we do not, in many cases, really know what is best for our children.

This is why I say that our methods for raising children constitute a defect in the structure of our society. We have not developed these methods because we wanted this particular outcome. We have developed them in part by choosing the best paths for children to follow and then systematically closing all other paths. But we have also developed these methods as a result of our desires for privacy in our homes and door-to-door convenience in our transportation. To a great extent the pattern of child rearing I have described is the result of the geography of the suburb and the patterns of living necessitated by automobiles. Regardless of our reasons, we have decided to raise our children in isolation from the rest of our society.

It is instructive to compare the child growing up in the suburb with the child growing up in an urban ghetto. When this is done, the situation of the middle class adolescent suddenly shows many points of similarity with the situation of a Negro boy in the ghetto. The resemblances are psychological, rather than material. In both groups, the rich and the poor, the advantaged and the deprived, the privileged and the rejected, we find the same causes of alienation. Like Negroes, adolescents belong to a minority group which is prevented from sharing in all of the benefits of our society. The benefits sought by each group are different, but the fact of exclusion is the same. Like the lower class Negro adolescent, the middle class white adolescent is isolated from the adult role models whom our culture considers most appropriate. The Negro, who is allowed more freedom, finds his role models in the pool halls and streets. The suburban white boy may find his in literature, on television, in his school, or elsewhere, but (again like the Negro) his role model cannot be a man at work because the boy is not allowed to enter the world of work. Both Negro and white adolescents try out various roles among their contemporaries, but the suburban white boy's isolation from adults makes him especially prone to develop his own culture rather than to conform to the culture around him as the Negro can. Thus, both Negroes and suburban adolescents, excluded from a world they want to enter and isolated from appropriate role models, become alienated and eventually reject the very world they had tried to enter. The Negro rejects the white world, and the suburban adolescent rejects the adult world. The economic and social consequences differ, but the psychological situation is similar.

This analysis of factors leading to the alienation of youth implies that the youth themselves are of two minds about the adult world. Alienation is neither inevitable nor irreversible. For evidence of whether adolescents themselves want to participate in the adult world, and whether they believe they are allowed to do so, I would like to go back several years. Rather than use current examples, I shall quote a series of recommendations made in 1965 by several thousand high school age youths from all areas of Northern California, at a conference sponsored by the Governor. The delegates to this conference made a total of sixty-four recommendations, ten of which especially pertain to the issues I am discussing:

Education
> Students . . . be given more responsibility for student affairs
> Students be involved in setting school standards and rules through youth Councils

Participation in Community Action
> Schools and youth organizations be encouraged to involve students more actively in problems concerning the community
> A program be devised to give youth a voice in community government (perhaps an elected youth official)
> Youth be involved in civic projects for which they would receive recognition
> Youth serve on committees with adults
> Youth serve in youth-serving organizations to bridge the gap between

the adults in the agency and the recipients of the services of the agency

Jobs

School curriculum should be expanded to expose all students to the world of work, particularly college-bound students

Job opportunities be developed for all youth, not just drop-outs

Students be included as members of school or district committees working with the industrial community to develop youth employment opportunities

The fact that these recommendations could be made by a group of youth, many of whom are now burning draft cards and smoking marijuana, shows an essential ambivalence in our youth cultures. I conclude that just as Negroes tried for a century to attain equality in the white world and only now have begun to consider separatism, suburban youth choose the path of alienation from our society only after they have failed to enter it. And they have failed primarily because the structure of our society has no place for adolescents.

Before I discuss ideas for changing this situation, I would like to consider the place of punishment in preventing undesirable forms of behavior. These ideas come from a paper by K. T. Erikson (7). His thesis is that punishment can only serve as an effective measure of social control when it is applied to a small proportion of the population. If too many people are punished, the result can be rebellion. If only a few people who have committed the worst offenses are punished, others will be deterred from similar offenses. In an ideal situation, punishment by society should become a "boundary-maintaining mechanism." In his view, the interactions of members of a society with law enforcement officers serve as a visible reminder to other members of the society of the limits of permissable conduct in that society. These interactions serve to "mark the outside limits of the area within which the norm has jurisdiction, and in this way assert how much diversity and variability can be contained within the system before it begins to lose its distinct structure, its cultural integrity."

Our present gap between the generations stems from our cultural intolerance of diversity and variability. Our boundaries are far too restrictive. In our effort to maintain our ideal culture we have excluded from that culture most Negroes, and all adolescents who are not in school. Our culture, (which we like to believe consists of men and women who work, keep house, and raise their children) also has no room for the unemployed, for the immature, for the inefficient or for other deviants. To preserve our image of American life we have adopted a variety of methods for isolating those individuals who do not conform to our ideal. Thus, Negroes are isolated in ghettoes, adolescents are isolated in schools, and incompetents are isolated in mental hospitals or prisons. Even though these groups together probably comprise more than half of our population, once they have been isolated their plight can be ignored. It usually is.

We belong to a pluralistic culture which we persist in treating as uniform. Our laws are made by only one segment of this culture, but there are large groups of people for whom many of the laws are unnecessarily restrictive. As a result, we have alienated too many people. The situations which I have discussed are evidence that our boundary-maintaining mechanism has excluded too many adolescents. The solution is to integrate the diverse elements into our society rather than to punish them ever more severely for being outside.

Our present boundary-maintaining mechanism no longer protects the integrity of our culture; it has become one of the forces for disintegration of our society. Our narrow definition of acceptable behavior can hardly be satisfied by a normal teenage boy in a city. This can be illustrated by examples taken from the laws in force in San Francisco. A boy who was not in his home or at school could be arrested for playing ball in the street, exploding a firecracker, shooting a BB gun, lighting a fire, gambling, throwing paper in the street, writing on a wall, penciling a mustache on a billboard, engaging in a fight, bullying another boy, swearing, or possessing liquor. In addition, he could not loiter on a corner or be on the street late at night. In school, he could be arrested for a "behavior problem" and, at home, for refusing to obey his parents. Sexual relations (unless he were married) were illegal, and so was any other action which could be considered a "danger of immorality." It is hard to imagine just what he could do, besides go to school or engage in organized recreation.

The results of our restrictions on adolescents are seen not only in delinquency statistics, but in the development of "youth cultures." It is becoming increasingly difficult for young people to progress smoothly into adult society, and their response in many instances has been to form a society of their own. More and more our youth culture appears to be rejecting the entire value system of the middle class adult world. This is not due simply to the psychological necessity for a rebellion in adolescence. Normal developmental patterns require an adolescent rebellion directed at parents, but not one directed at our entire cultural pattern. Our adolescents are rejecting our society mainly because our society has already rejected the adolescents.

The best answer to the development of a youth culture is not to punish rebellious youth: It is to find a place for them in the conventional world where they can achieve a measure of self-fulfillment. This place should be in productive activity, and it should be in a place where they associate with adults.

In order to do this we can turn again to the voice of the adolescents themselves. The recommendations from the Governor's Conference which I read can be heard as a cry for help. Adolescents are asking to be allowed to join American society, not (to use Friedenberg's analogy) as colonial subjects, but as participants. They want to have an opportunity to influence their own lives. If we persist in denying this to them, we leave the independent spirits, the malcontents, and the incapable among them to find their own ways, outside of the system we have imposed. In our present system all options other than waiting for future gratification are defined as illegal or immoral: that is why I consider the barrier to participation in adult life to be the major cause of middle class alienation.

The solution to the problem of a separate culture of youth is to absorb it into the general culture of adults. This is what the youth at the Governor's Conference wanted, and I submit that most middle class adults would also prefer this. To do this, we must do as young people themselves suggest: that is, we must devise mechanisms whereby youth can make its opinions known to adults. But we must go even farther if we want to change youth cultures. We must allow adolescents the opportunity to make their own decisions in matters which affect them. We must even allow them the option of making decisions which we do not like. To protect our children from disastrous choices, we should provide a variety of pathways, all of which can lead to a worthwhile place in society. We badly need mechanisms for entering adult life (similar to an apprenticeship system) which can serve as alternatives to conventional education.

Alienation of middle class youth would not disappear if we allowed teenagers to participate in adult activities and if we provided an alternative pathway to a working life. But these steps would remove much of the pressure which is driving our children into non-conformity.

I can now return to the question with which I started: Why are children in the suburbs growing up alienated from the American Way of Life? The fault is not in the children, nor for the most part is it in their struggling and bewildered parents. The fault is in our intolerant society. The intolerance now centers in the all-white suburbs in which there is so homogeneous a population. I have shown that the intolerance is not only racial, but that it extends to almost any deviation from the norm. The boundaries of our American Way of Life have become so narrow that we have excluded our own children. We now must start the task of devising new patterns of life which will bring adolescents, as well as Negroes and other excluded groups, into the main stream of America's culture.

References

1. Yolles, S. F. Quoted in *The San Francisco Chronicle*, March 6, 1968.
2. Erikson, E. "Childhood and Society." New York, W. W. Norton & Co., 2nd ed., 1963.

3. Friedenberg, E. Z. "Coming of Age in America." New York, Random House, 1963.

4. Bruyn, H. B., and Seiden, R. H. "Student Suicide: Fact or Fancy." *J. Am. Coll. Health Assn. 14*: 69–77, 1965.

5. McNassor, D. "This Frantic Pace in Education." *J. Secondary Educ. 42:* 99–105, 1967.

6. Blumer, H., *et al.* "The World of Youthful Drug Use." Univ. of Calif. School of Criminology, Berkeley, Calif., 1967. Mimeo., 87 pp.

7. Erikson, K. T. "Notes on the Sociology of Deviance." In Becker, H. S. (ed.), "The Other Side: Perspectives on Deviance." Glencoe, The Free Press, 1964, pp. 9–21.

39. Social Class and Education

Robert J. Havighurst

Introduction

As a part of the process by which a social group brings up its children to become adults, education always takes place in and for a given society. The present state and structure of the society is mirrored in its schools and reflected through the schools into the lives of its children. At the same time a society which is undergoing internal changes uses education as a means of facilitating these changes.

These two contrasting functions of education—the perpetuating and the change-promoting functions—should always be kept in mind when studying social class and education. If only one function is seen at a time, education is likely to be grossly misunderstood. For instance, the fact that children from the higher classes get better grades on the average and go further in school than children from the lower classes may lead the hasty observer to the conclusion that education perpetuates the status quo and,

SOURCE: Robert J. Havighurst, "Social-Class Influences on American Education," *Sixtieth Yearbook of the National Society for the Study of Education,* Part II, 1960, 120–43. Copyright © 1960. Reprinted by permission of the publisher.

therefore, is "undemocratic." Yet another incautious observer may note that education is used by clever lower-class youth as a means of social climbing and, thus, is an important factor in the relatively high rate of social mobility in the United States; and he may leap to the conclusion that education contributes to instability in the social structure with a loss of the values that come from continuity and cultural tradition.

Both of these conclusions have a severely limited validity, as would be evident to an observer who saw the whole picture.

EDUCATION REFLECTS THE SOCIAL-CLASS SYSTEM

The American social-class system is now generally understood to consist of three classes with subdivisions. There is a large working class, consisting of some 60 percent of the population, most of whom work with their hands. Above this group in the social hierarchy is a substantial middle class of white-collar workers with almost 40 percent of the population. At the top, in terms of social status, is a small upper class of 2 or 3 percent, who have the highest social prestige and the greatest wealth.

When the middle and the working classes in the United States are subdivided, the result is the five-class system [1] which will be used in this chapter with the following percentage composition: upper, 2 percent; upper-middle, 8 percent; lower-middle, 30 percent; upper-lower, 40 percent; lower-lower, 20 percent. This composition varies from one section of the country to another and from one city to another, but it will serve the purposes of this chapter to use these average figures for the situation in 1960.

The kind of education an American child gets depends very much on the social-class position of his family. This fact was reported by Warner [2] in the early 1930's for "Yankee City" in New England, by Hollingshead [3] in the early 1940's for "Elmtown" in the midwest, by Davie [4] in 1950 for New Haven, Connecticut, and by Havighurst and his colleagues [5] in 1958 for the midwest community of "River City." These are a few of the many studies that have documented this now familiar fact.

There was in River City in the 1950's, as there has been throughout the United States, a close relation between progress through school and the so-

[1] W. Lloyd Warner, Marchia Meeker, and Kenneth Eells, *Social Class in America* (New York: Harper & Bros., Torchbook, 1960).

[2] W. Lloyd Warner, Robert J. Havighurst, and Martin B. Loeb, *Who Shall Be Educated?* (New York: Harper & Bros., 1944).

[3] August B. Hollingshead, *Elmtown's Youth* (New York: John Wiley & Sons, 1949).

[4] James S. Davie, "Social Class Factors and School Attendance," *Harvard Educational Review*, XXIII (1953), 175–185.

[5] Robert J. Havighurst, Paul H. Bowman, Gordon P. Liddle, Charles V. Matthews, and James V. Pierce, *Growing Up in River City* (New York: John Wiley & Sons, 1961).

cial class of a child's parents. However, there has also been a progressive increase in the amount of education obtained by children of working-class families. . . . Whereas in 1920 it was extremely rare for a student of working-class background to enter college, by 1960 the gross numbers of college students from working-class homes exceeded the numbers from upper- and upper-middle-class homes.

EDUCATION AS AN AGENT OF SOCIAL CHANGE

There are two types of social change. One is change within a society whose general pattern does not change. This is the type discussed in this chapter—changes within a social structure whose broad outlines are not changing. The second type is change which affects the society as a whole —its political institutions, its system of economic production, or the major elements of its social structure. The latter type of social change will not be treated in this chapter.

If even one boy from a working-class home graduates from high school and college and gets a middle-class job and salary, to this extent education has contributed to change in the society. . . . There is a large and growing amount of preparation for upward social mobility through education by youth from working-class and lower-middle-class homes.

Education also prepares people for upward group mobility by giving them knowledge and skills that make them more productive as a group of manual workers or white-collar workers, and thus giving them a higher standard of living even though they stay in the social classes of their fathers.

Social-Class Policies for Education

Since the several social classes have cultures of their own which are variations of the dominant American culture, it would be expected that they might differ in their notions about the purposes and functions of education and about the methods to achieve these purposes. They certainly do differ; but they also share a common set of educational ideals.

To take the common ideals first, there is a general belief in the value of education, at least up to the end of secondary school. There is a general belief that education will lead to better jobs and higher incomes. There is a less general belief that education is a good thing, in and of itself. There is a general belief that educational opportunity should be freely available to all people.

These beliefs provide the basis in public acceptance and support for a free educational system open to all through the secondary school and widely available through the university. There is a general, or "official," ideology that favors education as a quantitative good.

Where the social classes differ is not so much in broad educational ideals as in the *means* they devote to the realization of these ideals. The middle classes are most effective in making use of education because they are "future-oriented." That is, they believe that it is worthwhile to forego present satisfactions in order to gain greater ones later. Therefore, they save money, and they devote time and energy to secondary and higher education not so much for present satisfaction as for future gain.

The typical lower-class person is more "present-oriented" than "future-oriented." He has less desire and willingness than a middle-class person to sacrifice present gains for future ones. Furthermore, his resources in terms of income are smaller, and therefore he has less real possibility of saving for investment in the future. He is less likely to encourage and assist his child to go to college, for example. This is seen in the recent survey made by Elmo Roper for the Ford Foundation on the plans of parents for college education of their children. While there was a general tendency for parents to want their children to go to college, most of the low-income parents who wanted a college education for their children had done nothing to make this a possibility by saving money for this purpose.

Another distinction between classes which bears on their educational attitudes is their attitude toward social change. Middle-class people seem to be the leaders of social change, the lower class are most resistant to it, and the upper class are selective about it. David Riesman [6] sees the middle class of today as the group which "first perceives social change, of a non-cataclysmic sort: it constitutes the nervous system of society, vulnerable to news and to what is new. The middle class mans the communications and research industries including teaching, . . . it is the middle class that joins voluntary associations, such as the League of Woman Voters, which devote themselves interalia to calling attention to and disseminating the news."

Recently the middle class seems to have become more tolerant toward the lower-class attitudes and easy-going qualities with respect to child-rearing, in contrast to its former coldness and demand for early independence and achievement on the part of children. This at least is the interpretation placed by Bronfenbrenner [7] on the changes of the last thirty years in child-rearing practices, though the present writer sees the lower class as also moving toward the earlier middle-class norms in child-rearing. Perhaps there is a reduction in social-class differences in child-rearing, due to the spreading of a common culture in this area through the work of maternal and child health clinics and of pediatricians.

The middle class may be seen as the fluctuating class, open to influences

[6] David Riesman, "The Psychological Effects of Social Change," *Journal of Social Issues,* XVII, No. 1 (1961), pp. 78–92.

[7] Uric Bronfenbrenner, "Socialization and Social Class Through Time and Space," in *Readings in Social Psychology,* Maccoby, Newcomb, and Hartley (eds.) (New York: Henry Holt & Co., 1958), pp. 400–424.

from above and below in the social structure, and open also to influences from domestic and world economic conditions and from ideologies in other parts of the world. The upper class is idiosyncratic, combining a traditional conservatism with a high degree of individual variability which prevents this class from speaking with a common voice on matters of educational policy. The lower class is earthy, looking for immediate practical results from education and seeing its advantages in bread-and-butter terms.

LOWER-CLASS CHARACTERISTICS

Within the lower class there are variations in the extent to which a family can and will act in accord with the educational attitudes to which they give lip service. These are illustrated by the following account of the visit of a primary-grade teacher to two lower-class mothers. The first mother is trying to do her best to co-operate with the school, while the second is indifferent.

I visited Mrs. Smith, who is the mother of Joan Swanson. She has five children, the oldest is about 9 or 10 years old, and she is pregnant again. The house seems a lot neater and more attractive than the house they lived in previously. They have three rooms—two small bedrooms and a kitchen; the bath is in a kind of lean-to behind the kitchen and is probably shared with other families in the building. I asked the mother how she thought Joan got along this year and she said, "Well, Joan seems to like school very well, and I think that she's gotten along pretty well, as far as I can tell." I said that Joan had done good work in school, was reading at a pretty adequate level, and that her seat work was always neat and well done. I said that she seemed very shy and the mother said that she knew this was true, but we both agreed that she seemed reasonably happy. The mother said that her new husband, Mr. Smith, is a big improvement on Joan's father who was often extremely mean to the children and that she thought that this would help Joan.

The mother said that she hoped they would get over having lice in their hair and they wouldn't have to be bothered with that next year. She said that every child had it—it went through the family—and we talked a little bit about methods of getting rid of them. The house seemed quite neat throughout.

In contrast, Tony Shannon's house was about as dirty as anything I have ever seen. With the exception of the new 21-inch television set, the entire living room furniture would not bring two dollars at an auction. There is a small Benjamin Franklin type wood stove in the living room with broken isinglass windows in the front, and otherwise there are only chairs and a davenport— mostly without cushions—that haven't been cleaned for twenty years or more. In the bedroom in the next room I saw some extremely tumble-down davenports and beds. There are five or six children in the family, ranging in age from about two to thirteen. Mr. Blake, who is the present father, makes $52 a week according to the mother, but they don't have any money for book rental, she said. I said I would take up the book-rental matter with the principal and would communicate with the mother further. The mother seemed quite unable to see, this time, and had trouble finding the one bare light that is in the middle of the living room. Neither the mother nor any of the children seemed to have had a bath for weeks, if not months. I told the mother that Tony was supposed to be out at the Clinic tomorrow to get glasses since he had lost one of the lenses out of his and the other is badly scratched. I told the mother that Tony could do pretty well in school, but that he didn't seem very motivated and often drifted off when he was supposed to be doing his studies. She said that's the way he's always been at home too, and she didn't seem at all concerned about it; she said if I wanted to keep him another year that was perfectly all right.

Is There a Class War? American education reflects the fact that there is no class war in this society. That is, there is no explicit conflict between a militant, class-conscious labor group and an equally militant capitalist group. For this reason it is possible to have general acceptance on the verbal level, at least, of middle-class educational values and standards.

Still, it would be naïve to suppose that there is no class-consciousness in America. There certainly is such a consciousness, combined with a considerable degree of hostility toward the middle class by some of the lower class who are unsuccessful by middle-class standards. This is illustrated in the following interview with Bernice Hatfield, a girl from a lower-class family who dropped out of school before she was sixteen and was married shortly afterward. The interview was made as one of a routine series on school drop-outs.

Bernice is living with her mother-in-law. I scaled a fifteen-foot muddy embankment up to this little run-down house. Apparently, there is a more accessible route from the rear. Bernice required very little explanation. I asked her how long she had been out of school.

"I quit two weeks before the end of school a year ago. I was only fifteen at the time but I talked to Mr. McCoy (principal). He said that they wouldn't come get me because I would be sixteen before fall. I just didn't take the exams. I knew I wouldn't pass anyway because I didn't do any work except in typing. I really loved typing. It seems I didn't like all of my teachers. I got kicked out of English six times. Me and the teacher couldn't get along. I don't think half the kids liked her. She talked about the same thing for about a week and you didn't learn anything. Then she would spend the whole period with one kid. I took a dislike to her the first two days. I guess I could have gotten along with her but after that I didn't try. And then I just didn't understand general math, I suppose because I don't understand arithmetic. I love it, but I don't get it. I just love fractions, but those reading problems, I could never get those all the way through school. I was really going to go all the way through Home Ec because I liked it, but then my schedule was changed so I could be in a different gym class. They said they wanted to break up a gang of us girls because we were beating all the other teams and smarting off a lot. Then I got changed to a gym class with a lot of these high-class girls, as we call them. They think they are better than everyone else. They got a lot of money. They don't like us, and we don't like them. When my class was changed, I didn't even dress for gym. So I failed that too."

"Bernice, what seems to be the rub with those high-class kids?"

"Well, they seem to look down on us kids in this neighborhood. You know, they think we are scabs. You know, those kids always hung out on the east side of the building and us kids were always on the west side. Then in class, the rich kids always had their lessons. They never came without their lessons. Then if us kids didn't have ours, and we usually didn't, they would look at us. There were only two girls, Sally Clancy and Georgia Lane, that I could get along with out of that bunch. I guess it's a good thing I quit school because whenever there was any trouble, I was in the middle of it, street fights or anything else. It seems like it has been that way all my life. My temper gets me into trouble. I slap and ask questions later. That's the way my Mother and Dad were and I guess that's the way I am."

MIDDLE-CLASS POLICIES ON SPECIFIC EDUCATIONAL QUESTIONS

With this discussion of social-class orientations as a background, it can be expected that the dominant trends and styles in education will be sponsored by the middle class, with the lower class going along, in general, though occasionally resisting on some issue where lower-class opportunity appears to be threatened, while the upper class takes no active part in educational decisions for the public and counts on its prestige and power to guarantee satisfactory educational arrangements for its own purpose.

This hypothesis can be tested with respect to the principal educational emphasis of the 1950's. One of these has been the emphasis on "tough" education with more stress on science and mathematics in the secondary school and a heavier schedule of school and home study. The strongest proponents of this policy have been middle-class business and military men aided by a number of university and college educators. The most vocal opponents of this policy have also been middle-class people. There has been no explicit lower-class position on the matter. The great interest in education for gifted children during the present decade has been mainly a middle-class interest, focused on providing special facilities and special experiments for gifted children, including such things as foreign language in the elementary school and college-level courses in the high school. The great majority of the children of working-class homes do not participate in such programs.

Another emphasis is on expansion in higher education. This is to the direct advantage of working-class youth, who have the greatest difficulty getting into college, but the movement is led by the middle-class people who argue for it on the ground that the society needs more college-trained people. When the shortage of trained manpower is over, as it is likely to be by 1965, middle-class attitudes about expansion of higher education may change.

The issue of federal government support for education has not been resolved during the past decade, though a substantial increase in federal government support has taken place. On this issue, the working class seems to be fairly positive, through its spokesmen in organized labor. But the middle class is divided on this issue, and no basic resolution is likely to be achieved unless middle-class opinion becomes more solid in one direction or another.

Social Class and Decision-Making in Education

There are three decision-making groups with respect to education in the United States. Each of these broad groups may be examined with respect to its social-class status and the relation of its goals to its social-class composition.

OFFICIAL POLICY-MAKERS

Control of schools and colleges is legally vested in boards of education, boards of trustees, and boards of regents who appoint the administrators and the teachers and are responsible for the making of educational policy. There are two questions with regard to these people. What is their socioeconomic status, and do they favor their own social classes in conducting educational affairs?

With respect to the socioeconomic status of board members, the facts are established. Charters [8] reviewed the evidence for public school board members in 1953 and concluded, "that board members are recruited from among business and professional men (except in rural areas) or, in different language, from among persons in the upper-middle class of the community." There are a few apparent exceptions to this rule in communities where a "quota" of working-class men are appointed or elected to the school board.

In the field of higher education, the trustees or regents are generally upper-class or upper-middle-class men and women, the higher status people being on boards of the higher-status institutions.

The next question is whether board members favor their own social classes in their roles as educational policy-makers. On the whole, it appears that they do not favor their own social classes in an explicit way. Seldom is there an issue in which class lines can be clearly drawn. A hypothetical issue of this sort might deal with the establishment of a free public junior college in a community where there already was a good private college which served the middle-class youth adequately but was too

[8] W. W. Charters, Jr., "Social Class Analysis and the Control of Public Education," *Harvard Educational Review*, XXIII (1953), 268–283.

expensive for working-class youth. In situations of this sort the board generally favors the expansion of free education. Campbell [9] studied the records of 172 school board members in twelve western cities over the period of 1931–40 and found "little or no relationship between certain social and economic factors and school board competence," as judged by a panel of professional educators who studied the voting records on educational issues.

The few cases of clear favoritism along social-class lines are as likely as not to involve representatives of the working class on the school board who favor some such practice as higher wages for janitors rather than pay increases for teachers, and such issues are not issues of educational policy.

In general, it appears that trustees and board members attempt to represent the public interest in their administration of educational policy, and this is made easier by the fact that the dominant values of the society are middle-class values, which are generally thought to be valid for the entire society. There have been very few cases of explicit conflict of interest between the middle class and any other class in the field of educational policy. If there were more such cases, it would be easier to answer the question whether the policy-makers favor their own social classes.

There is currently a major controversy of public education in which group interests and values are heavily engaged. This is the issue of segregated schools in the South. In this case it is primarily a matter of conflict of racial groups rather than social-class groups. Thus, the white middle and lower classes are arrayed against the Negro middle and lower classes. This conflict may be resolved in a way which will suit white middle-class people better than it suits white lower-class people. If this happens, there may be some class conflict in the South, with school boards and school teachers taking the middle-class position.

THE EDUCATIONAL PROFESSION

The members of the educational profession have a major voice in the determination of educational policy, their position being strongest in the universities. They are mostly upper-middle- and lower-middle-class people, with a few in the upper class. Do they make class-biased decisions?

In a society dominated by middle-class values and working in an institution which transmits and strengthens these social values, it is clear that the educational profession must work for the values which are characteristic of the society. There is no problem here. The problem arises, if it does arise, when the educator has to make a choice or a decision within the area of his professional competence, but which bears some relation to the social structure. For instance, in giving school grades or in making recom-

[9] Roald F. Campbell, "Are School Boards Reactionary?" *Phi Delta Kappan*, XXVII (1945), 82–83, 93.

mendations for the award of a college scholarship, does he consciously or unconsciously favor students of one or another social class? Again, in deciding on the content and method of his teaching, does he favor a curriculum which will make his students stronger competitors in the race for higher economic status, or does he favor a curriculum which strengthens students in other ways?

The answers to questions such as these certainly depend to some extent upon the educator's own social-class position and also upon his social history, as well as upon his personality and what he conceives his mission to be as an educator. In a set of case studies of teachers with various social-class backgrounds, Wattenberg [10] illustrates a variety of approaches to students and to teaching which depend upon the teacher's personality as well as on his social-class background. One upward-mobile teacher may be a hard taskmaster for lower-class pupils because she wants them to develop the attitudes and skills that will enable them to climb, while another upward-mobile teacher may be a very permissive person with lower-class pupils because he knows their disadvantages and deprivations at home, and he hopes to encourage them by friendly treatment.

One social-class factor which plays a large part in educational policy today is the fact that a great many school and college teachers are upward mobile from urban lower-class and lower-middle-class families. Their own experience in the social system influences their work and attitudes as teachers. While this influence is a complex matter, depending upon personality factors in the individual as well as upon his social-class experience, there probably are some general statements about social-class background and educational policy that can be made with a fair degree of truth.

Teachers who have been upward mobile probably see education as most valuable for their students if it serves students as it has served them; that is, they are likely to favor a kind of education that has vocational-advancement value. This does not necessarily mean that such teachers will favor vocational education, as contrasted with liberal education, but they are likely to favor an approach to liberal education which has a maximal vocation-advancement value, as against a kind of "pure" liberal education that is not designed to help people get better jobs.

There is no doubt that higher education since World War II has moved away from "pure" liberal education toward greater emphasis on technology and specialization. There are several causes for this, one being rapid economic development with increasing numbers of middle-class positions requiring engineering or scientific training. But another cause may lie in the experience of so many new postwar faculty members with their own use of education as a means of social advancement.

[10] William Wattenberg, "Social Origin and Teaching Role: Some Typical Patterns," in *The Teacher's Role in American Society*, Lindley J. Stiles (ed.) (New York: Harper & Bros., 1957), Ch. 4.

Compared with the college and university faculty members of the period from 1900 to 1930, the new postwar faculty members consist of more children of immigrants and more children of urban working-class fathers. Their experience is quite in contrast with that of children of upper- and upper-middle-class native-born parents, who are more likely to regard education as good for its own sake and to discount the vocational emphases in the curriculum.

THE "PUBLIC INTEREST" GROUPS

Educational policies are formed by several groups who are officially or unofficially appointed to act in the public interest. Legislators are one such group, and state legislators have major responsibility for educational legislation. They generally vote so as to serve their own constituency, and if the constituency should be solidly middle class or solidly lower class, they might be expected to vote and work for middle- or for lower-class interests in education. However, there are relatively few such political constituencies, and, as has been pointed out, there is seldom a clear-cut distinction between the educational interests of one social class and those of another.

Another public interest group is the commission of laymen or educators which is appointed to study an educational problem and to make recommendations. Generally these commissions work earnestly to represent the interest of the entire society, as they conceive it. Nevertheless, their conclusions and recommendations cannot please everybody, and they often represent a particular economic or political point of view. For instance, there have been two Presidential Commissions on higher education since World War II. President Truman's Commission on Higher Education tended to take a liberal, expansionist position, while President Eisenhower's Committee on Education Beyond the High School was slightly more conservative. Both Commissions consisted of upper-middle- and upper-class people, who attempted to act in the public interest.

An example of a more definite class bias is noted in proceedings of the Commission on the Financing of Higher Education sponsored by the Association of American Universities and supported by the Rockefeller Foundation and the Carnegie Corporation. This Commission recommended against the use of federal government funds for the assistance of private universities and against a broad program of government-supported scholarships. This might be said to be an upper- or an upper-middle-class bias, but the Commission published as one of its staff studies a book by Byron S. Hollingshead entitled *Who Should Go to College?* which recommended a federal government scholarship program. Furthermore, the Commission set up the Council for Financial Aid to Education as a means of encouraging private business to increase its support of private higher education. Thus, the Commission acted with a sense of social responsibility within the area of its own convictions about the problem of government support to private education.

Then there are the trustees and officers of the great educational foundations, who inevitably exert an influence on educational decisions by their support or refusal to support various educational programs, experiments, and demonstrations. These people are practically always upper- or upper-middle-class persons, who attempt to act in what they regard as the interest of the entire society.

Finally there are the parent organizations and the laymen's organizations such as the National Association of Parents and Teachers, and the Citizens Committee on Public Schools. These have an upper-middle-class leadership and a middle-class membership, with rare exceptions, where working-class parents are active in local P.T.A. matters. Like the other policy-making groups, these are middle class in their educational attitudes, and they attempt to act in the general public interest, as they see it.

In general it appears that educational decisions and educational policies are made by people who intend to act in the interests of the society as a whole. They are predominantly middle- and upper-class people, and undoubtedly share the values and attitudes of those classes. They may be unaware of the existence of lower-class values and consequently fail to take them into account. But there is very little frank and conscious espousal of the interests of any one social class by the people who have the power to make decisions in education. They think of themselves as trustees for the entire society and try to serve the entire society.

Attempts to Influence Social Structure Through Education

Educational policy in the United States has as an explicit goal the maximization of economic and cultural opportunity. Insofar as this goal is achieved, the society becomes more fluid, artificial barriers to social mobility are reduced, and people at the lower end of the social hierarchy share more fully in the material and cultural goods of society. On the other hand, there is a counterbalancing purpose in education which is to pass on the advantages of the parents to their children. This leads to efforts at exclusiveness through private schools and to the maintenance of social stratification in the schools. Both of these purposes exist side by side without much overt conflict under present conditions.

MAXIMIZING ECONOMIC AND CULTURAL OPPORTUNITY

The broad expansion of free education results both in raising the average economic and cultural level of the society and in promoting fluidity within the social structure. Fifty years ago the general raising of the school-leaving age to sixteen was an example of this movement. During the past decade the program has been carried on through expansion of free higher education in state universities, state colleges, and community colleges. The reaffirmation of American faith in the comprehensive high school, as expressed in the Conant study,[11] is another indication of the liveliness of the ideal of maximizing opportunity through the equalizing of educational opportunity.

The recent federal government's student-loan program is another step in the direction of making higher education more available to lower-status youth. It is probably more effective than the expanded scholarship programs of the past decade, because the scholarship programs mainly aided the students with the best academic records (who were usually middle-class), and these students tended to use the scholarship funds to go to more expensive colleges. Meanwhile, the private colleges have increased their tuition rates so much that they have raised an economic barrier which dwarfs their scholarship funds. The gains in educational opportunity during the past decade have taken place largely in the publicly supported institutions.

Another means of increasing educational opportunity and thereby increasing individual social mobility is the use of guidance procedures at the eighth or ninth grade to discover and motivate able lower-class youth to go to college. This has been promoted by the National Defense Education Act.

INCREASING GROUP MOBILITY

Although there has been a great upward movement of the working class as a group during the present century, this has not been reflected in education that aims to promote working-class solidarity and working-class economic and cultural gains independent of the gains of other classes. Rather, education has provided both general and vocational training that has served to raise the earning power of working-class people, while the technological improvement in the arts of production has made possible a gain in real income from which the working class has profited along with the other classes.

There has been relatively little emphasis on teaching about labor unions, about working-class solidarity, about consumer economics, and consumer co-operatives. The consumer-education movement has been more a middle-class rather than a lower-class activity.

Education has not been used effectively to better the position of one social group in relation to the positions of other groups.

[11] James B. Conant, *The American High School Today* (New York: McGraw-Hill, 1959).

EFFORTS TO PRESERVE STRATIFICATION

Private schools with high tuition fees and selective, privately supported colleges are the traditional means through which upper-class and upper-middle-class parents have attempted to confer status advantages upon their children. In varying degrees they offer the same privileges to a few lower-middle- and lower-class youth through scholarships.

A more widely prevalent method of preserving social stratification is the creation and maintenance of upper- and upper-middle-class suburbs with public schools that are 90 per cent or more middle and upper class in composition. This practice has probably increased in scope since World War II, with the great growth of metropolitan-area population.

Trends in Social Structure and Their Effects on Education

On the whole, it seems that education is more *responsive* to social forces than *responsible for* them. There are vast socioeconomic movements under way, which work to change the social structure; and education is an instrument for effecting these changes.

GROWTH OF A TECHNOLOGY-BASED AND ORIENTED SOCIETY

American society has become urbanized and industrialized in harmony with the development of a working force which requires technological training. The number of unskilled labor jobs is decreasing rapidly, while the number of jobs requiring technical or professional training is increasing. In *The Affluent Society*, John Kenneth Galbraith writes of the "new class"—the class of people who man society's productive machinery in strategic places and who require higher education for these jobs. The "new class" includes upper-middle- and lower-middle-class people. Taking account of the growth of this group, the writer estimates that the upper-middle and lower-middle classes among the 25-34 age-group will increase from 38 per cent of the male working force in 1950 to 47 per cent in 1980.[12] At the same time, the working-class proportion will shrink comparably from 60 per cent to 52 per cent. Thus, the time is in sight when half of the population will be middle class, with corresponding middle-class educational expectations.

[12] Robert J. Havighurst, *American Higher Education in the 1960's* (Columbus: Ohio State University Press, 1960).

RISE OF THE COMMON-MAN CULTURE

The two largest social classes—lower-middle and upper-lower, make up 70 per cent of the population and will continue to do so. Although this group is a mixture of white-collar and blue-collar, it is becoming more homogeneous culturally, with the rising incomes of the blue-collar workers giving them approximately the same standard of living as that of the minor white-collar worker. Both groups are gaining in college entrants, and they dominate numerically both the high-school graduating class and the college-entrance group. They are in a minority in the selective colleges and universities and in the suburban high schools, but everywhere else in the field of education the "common-man" group has the weight of numbers.

The educational aspirations of the "common-man" group tend to be practical and work-oriented and will probably continue the present emphasis upon education for economic competence. However, this is a group with growing quantities of leisure and a good deal of interest in such "leisure arts" as music, travel, gardening, camping, and spectator sports. These interests are likely to be reflected in school education and also in adult education.

ELEMENTS INFLUENCING STRATIFICATION IN SOCIETY AND IN EDUCATION

A strong case can be made for the proposition that social forces are producing a converging society with more and more shared values, and that education is important in bringing about such convergence. On the other hand, there are some forces that tend toward greater rigidity of the social structure and a retention, if not an actual increase, of present social-class differences.

One of these rigidity-producing forces is the middle-class birth rate. During this century and until the close of World War II, the upper-middle and lower-middle classes fell far short of reproducing themselves, thus creating vacancies in the working force with each new generation, the vacancies being filled by upward-mobile youth of lower-status families. This has been an important source of upward mobility in the United States. But since World War II, the middle-class birth rate has risen and stayed at a level high enough to replenish its numbers.

If this higher middle-class birth rate stays up, there will be relatively more middle-class youth in the next generation to compete for entrance to college and for good places in the working force, and they will have many advantages in competition with working-class youth. In such a situation guidance practices in high school and college-admission practices may come under pressure of middle-class parents to favor their children. Moreover, the present attitude of educators, which favors the promotion of opportunities for working-class youth to go to college in a period of manpower scarcity, may shift to one of encouraging boys and girls of working-class background to seek lower-status jobs which pay well for people at the level of high-school graduation.

DEVELOPMENT OF HOMOGENEOUS COMMUNITIES

Another element making for rigidity in the social structure is the development of communities with a limited social-class range, especially in expanding metropolitan areas. It is well known that the areas of greatest population growth at present are metropolitan areas, many of which include an industrial center and its dependent suburbs. The older pattern of a population complex in a town or city, which was almost a replica of the social-class distribution of the entire society, is being replaced by communities of ten to fifty thousand which are tied loosely together into a metropolitan complex. Some of these communities are suburbs with their own local governments and school boards, while others are local community areas within large cities, with their own elementary schools feeding into a high school.

There are now three clearly marked types of homogeneous communities with corresponding school systems. One is an upper-middle- and upper-class suburb, with a very small number of lower-middle-class residents. Another is a working-class and lower-middle-class suburb, essentially of the "common-man" character, with very few lower-lower-class residents. A third is a city slum, almost solid lower class, and as much as half lower-lower. Wherever such communities exist, the school system reflects the fact, and teachers are acutely aware of it.

In the central areas of the big cities this causes acute problems, because the central city sees itself steadily becoming a grand slum as its middle- and upper-working-class residents flee to the edges of the city and beyond, to the suburbs. Thus, a great city which in 1920 was self-contained, with 20 to 25 per cent lower-lower-class residents, may in 1960 have 40 per cent lower-lower-class residents who cover great stretches of what were formerly middle-class neighborhoods.

In their efforts to halt this urban blight, the city-planners tear down old tenement buildings and erect public housing, or they spend public money on slum removal and sell the land to private developers, hoping that new middle-class residential areas will be built to restore the city to its earlier condition of balance among the social classes.

This process of urban renewal has involved the schools as a crucial factor. Middle-class parents insist upon sending their children to schools with a middle-class ethos or atmosphere, and this requires a pupil population which has more than a certain critical proportion of middle-class children.

The exact size of this critical proportion is not known, and in any case it depends upon other factors such as the relative proportion of upper-lower- and lower-lower-class children and their race and nationality backgrounds. Probably the critical proportion of middle-class children is in the neighborhood of 40 per cent, if the school is to maintain itself as an attractive place for middle-class families and their children. When a school drops below this critical figure, middle-class parents begin to move out of the neighborhood or to put their children into private schools.

Urban renewal generally occurs over large enough areas to maintain an elementary-school district with an atmosphere that is satisfactory to middle-class parents and children. But it is more difficult to maintain a secondary-school district with a satisfactory social-class distribution for middle-class people in the central sections of a great city. Then, if the secondary school is not satisfactory, middle-class families move out to the city's edge and to the suburbs, making the experiment in urban renewal a failure in the small renewal areas in spite of the excellent physical condition of these areas.

Thus, the nature of population distribution in a metropolitan area is interrelated with the nature of the secondary schools of the area. To explain this more clearly, three types of secondary-school population distribution are shown in Figure 1. In this figure the social-class distribution of the school enrollment is shown, against a background of the social-class distribution of the nation's youth. If a school had an enrollment representing a cross-section of the nation, this would be shown by a straight line across the top of the figure, indicating that the enrollment contained 10 per cent upper- and upper-middle-class youth, 30 per cent lower-middle, 40 per cent upper-lower, and 20 per cent lower-lower. This, however, would be a rare event, since many working-class youth drop out of school before high-school graduation, thus lowering the curve in these segments of the chart.

A typical comprehensive high school is shown in Figure 1A for a self-contained community of ten to fifty thousand, which has all social classes in it, and in roughly the same proportions as in the nation. The percentage of upper- and middle-class students in the graduating class is about 50, while in the ninth grade, before there is much dropping out, this percentage is about 40.

A high school in an upper-middle-class suburb has the distribution shown in Figure 1B, with very few students of working-class background. These are the schools which walk away with scholastic honors in national and state scholarship contests, while holding their own in athletics. Middle-class parents move to the suburbs to put their children in such schools.

Figure 1C shows the population distribution in the high school of a district of a big city which is subject to the encroachment of slums. More than half of the students are of upper-lower-class background, with lower-lower and lower-middle about evenly balanced and upper-middle-class stu-

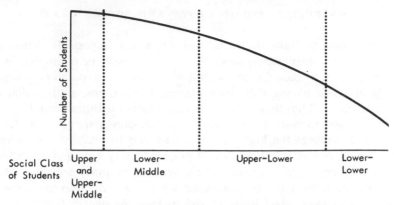

A. THE TYPICAL COMPREHENSIVE HIGH SCHOOL

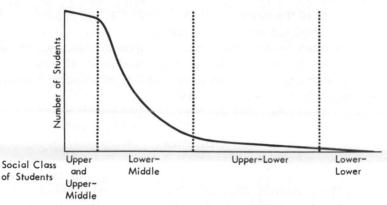

B. AN UPPER-MIDDLE-CLASS SUBURBAN HIGH SCHOOL

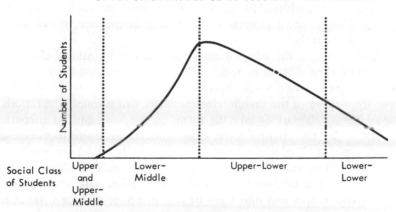

C. A CITY HIGH SCHOOL IN AN AREA WITH
ENCROACHING SLUMS

FIGURE 1

Social-Class Distribution of Students in Three Types of Secondary Schools

dents in a small minority. In this school it is almost impossible to maintain a college-preparatory atmosphere. However, this may be attempted by establishing a multi-track system, with a small college-preparatory group on the upper track having their own classes, homerooms, study halls, and even assemblies. Thus they tend to become a school within a school.

Another way to meet the problem for middle-class parents of the C-type school is to enlarge the high-school district and to establish two parallel high schools, one of academic or college-preparatory type and the other of a vocational type. The academic-type school can be made selective, admitting only students with above-average school records, thus reducing the proportion of lower-class students and making the distribution more like that of Figure 1A. Something like this is being done in the secondary schools of some of the eastern cities. New York City has accomplished this with its special high schools for abler students.

Thus, the trend toward development of subcommunities within metropolitan regions which are relatively homogeneous in social class is causing some acute problems for educators, and the fate of attempts at urban renewal is largely in the laps of educators.

Summary

The social structure of the United States is changing in the direction of increasing the proportion of middle-class people and decreasing the proportions in the lowest reaches of the social scale. At the same time there is an expansion of middle-class ideology throughout the society, with an expansion of high school graduates and college attendance, which are middle-class characteristics.

In this situation, the educational system is run by middle-class people with middle-class standards, tempered by some understanding of the fact that working-class values and aspirations as well as habits are enough different from those of the middle class to make educational adaptations desirable. These adaptations take the form, on the one hand, of encouraging and motivating the brighter lower-class students to aspire to middle-class status by means of education and, on the other hand, of recognizing that many lower-class students will not profit from such academic fare and should be treated differently in school, with more emphasis on getting them through school and into a job or into marriage with or without high-school graduation.

Thus the schools give educational and, thereby, economic and cultural opportunity to large numbers of pupils and play an essential part in keeping the social structure fluid.

However, there are some tendencies toward hardening of the social structure and toward more rigid stratification. These are seen most sharply in the metropolitan areas. Here there are some crucial problems for educational policy-makers. They can work against the forces that make for stratification and rigidity, or they can go along with these forces, often not aware that they are doing so.

Under present conditions of economic growth and population expansion, it appears likely that the class structure will remain open and fluid, and the tendencies toward stratification and rigidity can be successfully controlled, if educators understand the social forces which are influencing the society and act wisely with respect to them.

40. A Talk to Teachers

James Baldwin

Let's begin by saying that we are living through a very dangerous time. Everyone in this room is in one way or another aware of that. We are in a revolutionary situation, no matter how unpopular that word has become in this country. The society in which we live is desperately menaced, not by Khrushchev, but from within. So any citizen of this country who figures himself as responsible—and particularly those of you who deal with the minds and hearts of young people—must be prepared to "go for broke." Or to put it another way, you must understand that in the attempt to correct so many generations of bad faith and cruelty, when it is operating not only in the classroom but in society, you will meet the most fantastic, the most brutal, and the most determined resistance. There is no point in pretending that this won't happen.

Now, since I am talking to schoolteachers and I am not a teacher myself, and in some ways am fairly easily intimidated, I beg you to let me leave that and go back to what I think to be the entire purpose of education in the first place. It would seem to me that when a child is born, if I'm the child's parent, it is my obligation and my high duty to civilize that child. Man is a social animal. He cannot exist without a society. A society,

SOURCE: *Saturday Review*, XLVI, 51 (December 21, 1963), 42–44. Reprinted by permission of the author and the publisher.

in turn, depends on certain things which everyone within that society takes for granted. Now, the crucial paradox which confronts us here is that the whole process of education occurs within a social framework and is designed to perpetuate the aims of society. Thus, for example, the boys and girls who were born during the era of the Third Reich, when educated to the purposes of the Third Reich, became barbarians. The paradox of education is precisely this—that as one begins to become conscious one begins to examine the society in which he is being educated. The purpose of education, finally, is to create in a person the ability to look at the world for himself, to make his own decisions, to say to himself this is black or this is white, to decide for himself whether there is a God in heaven or not. To ask questions of the universe, and then learn to live with those questions, is the way he achieves his own identity. But no society is really anxious to have that kind of person around. What societies really, ideally, want is a citizenry which will simply obey the rules of society. If a society succeeds in this, that society is about to perish. The obligation of anyone who thinks of himself as responsible is to examine society and try to change it and to fight it—at no matter what risk. This is the only hope society has. This is the only way societies change.

Now, if what I have tried to sketch has any validity, it becomes thoroughly clear, at least to me, that any Negro who is born in this country and undergoes the American educational system runs the risk of becoming schizophrenic. On the one hand he is born in the shadow of the stars and stripes and he is assured it represents a nation which has never lost a war. He pledges allegiance to that flag which guarantees "liberty and justice for all." He is part of a country in which anyone can become President, and so forth. But on the other hand he is also assured by his country and his countrymen that he has never contributed anything to civilization—that his past is nothing more than a record of humiliations gladly endured. He is assured by the republic that he, his father, his mother, and his ancestors were happy, shiftless, watermelon-eating darkies who loved Mr. Charlie and Miss Ann, that the value he has as a black man is proven by one thing only—his devotion to white people. If you think I am exaggerating, examine the myths which proliferate in this country about Negroes.

Now all this enters the child's consciousness much sooner than we as adults would like to think it does. As adults, we are easily fooled because we are so anxious to be fooled. But children are very different. Children, not yet aware that it is dangerous to look too deeply at anything, look at everything, look at each other, and draw their own conclusions. They don't have the vocabulary to express what they see, and we, their elders, know how to intimidate them very easily and very soon. But a black child, looking at the world around him, though he cannot know quite what to make of it, is aware that there is a reason why his mother works so hard, why his father is always on edge. He is aware that there is some reason why, if he sits down in the front of the bus, his father or mother slaps him and drags him to the back of the bus. He is aware that there is some terrible weight on his parents' shoulders which menaces him. And it isn't long—in fact it begins when he is in school—before he discovers the shape of his oppression.

Let us say that the child is seven years old and I am his father, and I decide to take him to the zoo, or to Madison Square Garden, or to the U.N. Building, or to any of the tremendous monuments we find all over New York. We get into a bus and we go from where I live on 131st Street and Seventh Avenue downtown through the park and we get into New York City, which is not Harlem. Now, where the boy lives—even if it is a housing project—is in an undesirable neighborhood. If he lives in one of those housing projects of which everyone in New York is so proud, he has at the front door, if not closer, the pimps, the whores, the junkies—in a word, the danger of life in the ghetto. And the child knows this, though he doesn't know why.

I still remember my first sight of New York. It was really another city when I was born—where I was born. We looked down over the Park Avenue streetcar tracks. It was Park Avenue, but I didn't know what Park Avenue meant *downtown*. The Park Avenue I grew up on, which is still standing, is dark and dirty. No one would dream of opening a Tiffany's on that Park Avenue, and when you go downtown you discover that you are literally in the white world. It is rich—or at least it looks rich. It is clean —because they collect garbage downtown. There are doormen. People walk about as though they owned where they were—and indeed they do. And it's a great shock. It's very hard to relate yourself to this. You don't know what it means. You know—you know instinctively—that none of this is for you. You know this before you are told. And who is it for and who is paying for it? And why isn't it for you?

Later on when you become a grocery boy or messenger and you try to enter one of those buildings a man says, "Go to the back door." Still later, if you happen by some odd chance to have a friend in one of those buildings, the man says, "Where's your package?" Now this by no means is the core of the matter. What I'm trying to get at is that by this time the Negro child has had, effectively, almost all the doors of opportunity slammed in his face, and there are very few things he can do about it. He can more or less accept it with an absolutely inarticulate and dangerous rage inside— all the more dangerous because it is never expressed. It is precisely those silent people whom white people see every day of their lives—I mean your porter and your maid, who never say anything more than "Yes Sir" and "No Ma'am." They will tell you it's raining if that is what you want to hear, and they will tell you the sun is shining if *that* is what you want to hear. They really hate you—really hate you because in their eyes (and they're right) you stand between them and life. I want to come back to that in a moment. It is the most sinister of the facts, I think, which we now face.

There is something else the Negro child can do, too. Every street boy —and I was a street boy, so I know—looking at the society which has produced him, looking at the standards of that society which are not honored by anybody, looking at your churches and the government and the politicians, understands that this structure is operated for someone else's benefit—not for his. And there's no room in it for him. If he is really cunning, really ruthless, really strong—and many of us are—he becomes a kind of criminal. He becomes a kind of criminal because that's the only way he can live. Harlem and every ghetto in this city—every ghetto in this country—is full of people who live outside the law. They wouldn't dream of calling a policeman. They wouldn't, for a moment, listen to any of those professions of which we are so proud on the Fourth of July. They have turned away from this country forever and totally. They live by their wits and really long to see the day when the entire structure comes down.

The point of all this is that black men were brought here as a source of cheap labor. They were indispensable to the economy. In order to justify the fact that men were treated as though they were animals, the white republic had to brainwash itself into believing that they were, indeed, animals and *deserved* to be treated like animals. Therefore it is almost impossible for any Negro child to discover anything about his actual history. The reason is that this "animal," once he suspects his own worth, once he starts believing that he is a man, has begun to attack the entire power structure. This is why America has spent such a long time keeping the Negro in his place. What I am trying to suggest to you is that it was not an accident, it was not an act of God, it was not done by well-meaning people muddling into something which they didn't understand. It was a deliberate policy hammered into place in order to make money from black flesh. And now, in 1963, because we have never faced this fact, we are in intolerable trouble.

The Reconstruction, as I read the evidence, was a bargain between the North and South to this effect: "We've liberated them from the land—and delivered them to the bosses." When we left Mississippi to come North we did not come to freedom. We came to the bottom of the labor market, and we are still there. Even the Depression of the 1930s failed to make a dent in Negroes' relationship to white workers in the labor unions. Even today, so brainwashed is this republic that people seriously ask in what they suppose to be good faith, "What does the Negro want?" I've heard a great many asinine questions in my life, but that is perhaps the most asinine and perhaps the most insulting. But the point here is that people who ask that question, thinking that they ask it in good faith, are really the victims of this conspiracy to make Negroes believe they are less than human.

In order for me to live, I decided very early that some mistake had been made somewhere. I was not a "nigger" even though you called me one. But if I was a "nigger" in your eyes, there was something about *you*— there was something *you* needed. I had to realize when I was very young that I was none of those things I was told I was. I was not, for example, happy. I never touched a watermelon for all kinds of reasons. I had been invented by white people, and I knew enough about life by this time to understand that whatever you invent, whatever you project, is you! So where we are now is that a whole country of people believe I'm a "nigger," and I *don't,* and the battle's on! Because if I am not what I've been told I am, then it means that *you're* not what you thought *you* were *either!* And that is the crisis.

It is not really a "Negro revolution" that is upsetting this country. What is upsetting the country is a sense of its own identity. If, for example, one managed to change the curriculum in all the schools so that Negroes learned more about themselves and their real contributions to this culture, you would be liberating not only Negroes, you'd be liberating white people who know nothing about their own history. And the reason is that if you are compelled to lie about one aspect of anybody's history, you must lie about it all. If you have to lie about my real role here, if you have to pretend that I hoed all that cotton just because I loved you, then you have done something to yourself. You are mad.

Now let's go back a minute. I talked earlier about those silent people— the porter and the maid—who, as I said, don't look up at the sky if you ask them if it is raining, but look into your face. My ancestors and I were very well trained. We understood very early that this was not a Christian nation. It didn't matter what you said or how often you went to church. My father and my mother and my grandfather and my grandmother knew that Christians didn't act this way. It was as simple as that. And if that was so there was no point in dealing with white people in terms of their own moral professions, for they were not going to honor them. What one did was to turn away, smiling all the time, and tell white people what they wanted to hear. But people always accuse you of reckless talk when you say this.

All this means that there are in this country tremendous reservoirs of bitterness which have never been able to find an outlet, but may find an outlet soon. It means that well-meaning white liberals place themselves in great danger when they try to deal with Negroes as though they were missionaries. It means, in brief, that a great price is demanded to liberate all those silent people so that they can breathe for the first time and *tell* you what they think of you. And a price is demanded to liberate all those white children—some of them near forty—who have never grown up, and who never will grow up, because they have no sense of their identity.

What passes for identity in America is a series of myths about one's heroic ancestors. It's astounding to me, for example, that so many people really appear to believe that the country was founded by a band of heroes who wanted to be free. That happens not to be true. What happened was that some people left Europe because they couldn't stay there any longer and had to go someplace else to make it. That's all. They were hungry, they were poor, they were convicts. Those who were making it in England, for example, did not get on the *Mayflower*. That's how the country was settled. Not by Gary Cooper. Yet we have a whole race of people, a whole republic, who believe the myths to the point where even today they select political representatives, as far as I can tell, by how closely they resemble Gary Cooper. Now this is dangerously infantile, and it shows in every level of national life. When I was living in Europe, for example, one of the worst revelations to me was the way Americans walked around Europe buying this and buying that and insulting everybody—not even out of malice, just because they didn't know any better. Well, that is the way they have always treated me. They weren't cruel, they just didn't know you were alive. They didn't know you had any feelings.

What I am trying to suggest here is that in the doing of all this for 100 years or more, it is the American white man who has long since lost his grip on reality. In some peculiar way, having created this myth about Negroes, and the myth about his own history, he created myths about the world so that, for example he was astounded that some people could prefer Castro, astounded that there are people in the world who don't go into hiding when they hear the word "Communism," astounded that Communism is one of the realities of the twentieth century which we will not overcome by pretending that it does not exist. The political level in this country now, on the part of people who should know better, is abysmal.

The Bible says somewhere that where there is no vision the people perish. I don't think anyone can doubt that in this country today we are menaced—intolerably menaced—by a lack of vision.

It is inconceivable that a sovereign people should continue, as we do so abjectly, to say, "I can't do anything about it. It's the government." The government is the creation of the people. It is responsible to the people. And the people are responsible for it. No American has the right to allow the present government to say, when Negro children are being bombed and hosed and shot and beaten all over the deep South, that there is nothing we can do about it. There must have been a day in this country's life when the bombing of four children in Sunday School would have created a public uproar and endangered the life of a Governor Wallace. It happened here and there was no public uproar.

I began by saying that one of the paradoxes of education was that precisely at the point when you begin to develop a conscience, you must find yourself at war with your society. It is your responsibility to change society if you think of yourself as an educated person. And on the basis of the evidence—the moral and political evidence—one is compelled to say that this is a backward society. Now if I were a teacher in this school, or any Negro school, and I was dealing with Negro children, who were in my care only a few hours of every day and would then return to their homes and to the streets, children who have an apprehension of their future which with every hour grows grimmer and darker, I would try to teach them—I would try to make them know—that those streets, those houses, those dangers, those agonies by which they are surrounded, are criminal. I would try to make each child know that these things are the results of a criminal conspiracy to destroy him. I would teach him that if he intends to get to be a man, he must at once decide that he is stronger than this conspiracy and that he must never make his peace with it. And that one of his weapons for refusing to make his peace with it and for destroying it depends on what he decides he is worth. I would teach him that there are currently very few standards in this country which are worth a man's respect. That it is up to him to begin to change these standards for the sake of the life and the health of the country. I would suggest to him that the popular culture—as represented, for example, on television and in comic books and in movies—is based on fantasies created by very ill people, and he must be aware that these are fantasies that have nothing to do with reality. I would teach him that the press he reads is not as free as it says it is—and that he can do something about that, too. I would try to make him know that just as American history is longer, larger, more various, more beautiful, and more terrible than anything anyone has ever said about it, so is the world larger, more daring, more beautiful and more terrible, but principally larger—and that it belongs to him. I would teach him that he doesn't have to be bound by the expediencies of any given Administration, any given policy, any given time—that he has the right and the necessity to examine everything. I would try to show him that one has not learned anything about Castro when one says, "He is a Communist." This is a way of *not* learning something about Castro, something about Cuba, something, in fact, about the world. I would suggest to him that he is living, at the moment, in an enormous province. America is not the world and if America is going to become a nation, she must find a way—and this child must help her to find a way—to use the tremendous potential and tremendous energy which this child represents. If this country does not find a way to use that energy, it will be destroyed by that energy.

41. The Black Revolution and Education

Price Cobbs

Education used to be thought of as such a quiet and sedentary profession. Now in these turbulent times, it is almost impossible to believe that only a short while ago people were accused of going into a career in teaching so they could avoid the real world. In fact, the change has been so drastic that I did not know whether to come to this meeting wearing a bulletproof vest, or looking as if I was carrying a Molotov cocktail.

These are perilous times in which to speak. If a person speaks too passionately about the problems of his time, he is labeled as alienated from the society and, therefore, unqualified to speak critically about it. On the other hand, if he does not raise his voice in at least *some* anger, there is another voice saying that he is not involving himself in the struggle, that he has no moral integrity—that he has sold out.

With everyone, including educators, saying that they do not know why schools have become such a focus for the Black Revolution, I think it is time to spell out in some detail what has happened, as I understand it. I should like to analyze why the Black Movement has rushed into the halls of academia.

Why have groups of people who have heretofore been labeled friends now been labeled enemies? What has been the process by which the teacher and school administrator now find themselves in the eye of an increasingly mounting storm? As always, we must look to history, recent and remote, to better understand that which is happening around us.

Americans, including educators, are reluctant to look at the past. We are a nation of fast movers, of future seekers, and to look back, even under the cover of scholarships, is at times to invite charges that one is not forward-seeking.

The end of 1968 found me, along with countless other Americans, enveloped by melancholia. Americans demonstrated during that year that they

SOURCE: National Association of Secondary School Principals, *Bulletin,* LIII, 337 (May 1969), 3–18. Reprinted by permission of the publisher.

still were not ready to solve our pressing social problems. We saw the war in Viet Nam continue to go on, reminding the world of our immorality. During 1968, black people continued to press their demands and continued to feel that too little was being done. During 1968, we saw our noble black advocate, Martin Luther King, assassinated. He had counseled patience and faith and his voice was stilled by the very violence that he sought to prevent. We saw the assassination of Robert Kennedy, who, whatever his deficiencies, was attempting to align himself with the forces of change. During 1968, we saw black students from college to elementary school confronting teachers, administrators, and school boards and asking for an education that was relevant to their lives. And, with all of this, the majority of people kept talking about law and order and adhering to the status quo.

But if we are to truly understand 1968 and be ready for 1969, we must take a look back into our recent past. Black people have for over 100 years been asking for change. Now we see black people and their oppressed allies turning to the institutions of education and asking for change. And people look at each other and ask why they are doing this.

Education—A Fickle Mistress

Few bewildered and angry white Americans seem to know that education has long been a fickle mistress to black Americans. The institutions of education, from elementary school to graduate programs, have promised so terribly much and delivered so painfully little. Because of great promises, education has been spared when other institutions of this country have come under scrutiny. There was always the frequently acknowledged feeling that somehow an education, any kind of education, would help that painful transformation into full Americans.

Black people have always felt implicitly that getting an education could somehow make them a little less black. More than a little magical thinking has been behind the belief that to get an education was to be cleaner, more responsible, and less like the stereotype of a black person. Along with so many endeavors in the life of black Americans, getting an education became also the moral and virtuous thing to do. The black man thus needed an education so that he would be ready to prove his responsibility and thereby attain full citizenship.

Education for Slavery

Recently, however, many black people have come to the realization that education has been used to prevent them from attaining full citizenship.

The process began during slavery when the education of bondsmen quickly became yet another tool for dominating them. Early slavemasters quickly learned that to provide a slave with an education, however meager, was to stir a dormant curiosity which could lead to hopes and yearnings for freedom. In order to prevent this possibility, education became a very practical and utilitarian instrument in the institution of slavery, and the educating of slaves could no more be left to chance than any other aspect of their existence.

If a slave needed to read and write to carry out the business of his master, he was taught to read and write just to that extent. Book learning was parceled out to few slaves and only to the extent that it saved the master from an unpleasant or tedious chore. The same was true for other aspects of knowledge. If the job of a particular slave demanded the understanding of elementary addition and subtraction, then what could be taught was just *elementary* addition and subtraction. The rudiments of an education could be received, but only to the precise point that it had maximal value to an owner and not one step further. Beyond that precise point lay the danger that an education would have more value to the slave than to the master, and a mind might be unshackled only to begin plotting escape.

Those caught in the cruel institution of slavery evolved their own method of education. Information was passed on by a vast apprentice system which functioned from generation to generation. This system of apprenticeship began when the slave was born, and became crucial at the age of five or six when the child went out to the fields or into the master's home. The odious chores of slavery were learned by doing, and to survive physically and psychologically the young child had to learn a great deal in a very short time. To be a slave and not learn all the nuances of one's job at an early age was to invite death. That many young slaves lived and worked refutes the popularly held white idea that black kids can't learn.

The use of education as a tool to control black people continued as the prime model when slavery ceased. The Emancipation Proclamation purported to free the slaves, but it sharpened a dilemma for white Americans. Frantically waiting to take their places as citizens were several million ex-slaves who were like helpless pawns in a game of someone else's choosing. Whatever means the white man chose for deliverance and, hence, assimilation would surely indicate whether freeing the slaves was an act that had resulted from the outraged conscience of America or had occurred because slavery was outmoded and too expensive. To be apprenticed into the halls of business and finance would have demonstrated a much different commitment than being allowed to remain as sharecroppers and tenant farmers. The intermediate step of entering growing industries as skilled and unskilled workers would have revealed some intention of white Americans to truly share some of the fruits of this society with black Americans. But the solution to the dilemma was delayed to the present, and the white American betrayed the shallowness of his commitment by turning to the education of blacks not as a primary task but as the only task.

A Society Reflected in Its Schools

One needs no evidence to prove that the freed slaves were ignorant and in need of an education. Over 200 years of bondage had prepared them for survival in a cruel system but had hardly prepared them to flourish. There is no doubt that schools were among the basic needs of newly freed slaves. But if there is truth in the dictum that one sees a society, its magnificence and flaws, reflected in its schools, then the post-slavery schools established for blacks were harsh mirrors. The proliferation of segregated black schools introduced a jarring note of reality that white America was committed—if not dedicated—to a segregated society. The formation of Negro colleges and other educational institutions in the reconstruction period laid bare the fact that only the visible institution of slavery was dead. The thought processes and rationalizations which allowed slavery to endure were turned to new tasks.

Of all the jobs needing attention, why the focus on education and education alone? Few businesses were started and subsidized, and the little land that was apportioned was quickly retaken by force. Any pathways by which black Americans could ultimately join the rest of America were blocked. The sad truth is that the black schools of the nineteenth century taught millions of black Americans to read and write and, once beyond that, the educational effort became a means to try to make blacks somehow more respectable and serviceable to white Americans. The foundation of Negro education was reinforced by the belief—held to this day—that white people are inherently superior to black people. That there have been profoundly dedicated teachers, white and black, who have tried to alter this belief and could not only serves to remind us of the tenacity of this belief.

The history of this country demonstrates that no sizeable group of immigrants has risen to power, either economic or political, solely via the educational route. Since these are the two main constellations of power in this country, the decision to focus on education for the ex-slaves was, underneath, a decision to keep them powerless.

Washington and DuBois

Generations of Americans, black and white, have castigated Booker T. Washington as a hopeless Uncle Tom. But the hindsight of history teaches that the villains are few who do not exploit thoughts and feelings present in the majority of the population. Washington was truly a man of his time who had a finely tuned antenna, listening for what whites wanted to hear and then feeding it back. Whites wanted blacks to stay to themselves, teach themselves, and receive ample training to be of service to whites. What better way to insure this and have a minimum of agitation than by a control on the philosophy and direction of the education of blacks? Those few blacks who understood this and raised their voices to prevent it were in no position to effect a change, and there was scant white support from which they could draw allies. The virtues of a classical education may have been apparent to all, but these virtues have continued to be of little use to most black Americans. That Washington seemed to feel the same way about a classical education certainly demonstrated that he was shortsighted, but the negative labels might more appropriately be applied to his white supporters. He may have been guilty of too vigorously enforcing the mandates of white men, but he can hardly be accused of having misread the currents of his time. Many of those who now cry loudest that Booker T. Washington was a flagrant sellout to his race forget that white America was not at that time, nor at this, ready to truly educate its black citizens. The same educational establishment which later tried to disinherit him was previously only too glad to have him as a stalking horse.

W. E. B. DuBois will ultimately be rewarded well by history for his many scholarly contributions, but he remains for black Americans their most visible symbol of the failure of education. He took a route that white America had decreed the avenue by which all unfortunate blacks could attain equality. He possessed a superb mind, and he used it to secure an education. Starting from a poor background, he obtained a classical education with a doctorate from one of America's foremost universities. He possessed the qualities that black people were exhorted to strive for: He was respectable, urbane and responsible, and his skin color was light enough to make him almost acceptable to whites.

As if this were not enough, DuBois studied in Europe and became even more whitened. He became a connoisseur of good food and fine wines and a devotee of the theatre and opera. During all this time, he was honing his intellect and using it in serious and scholarly studies as did few of his contemporaries. Upon returning to his native land, he must have felt somewhere inside a personal triumph in breaking barriers and in the feeling that he would be personally accepted. What a shock this magnificently educated man must have felt when he was rejected by those very institutions of education that had previously encouraged him. He had done all they said to do and had done even more, but still they rejected him because he was black. That he continued to have a productive career after the trauma of such a primary rejection speaks probably of a mind that through the ages has had few equals.

During his career, DuBois continued to experience the occupational misfortune of the visionary by being ahead of his time. Just as he had secured an education and had exploded the myth that America would then accept him, he advanced ideas about his people that few were willing to accept. He drew from the infant discipline of sociology and showed how black Americans were the unfortunate victims of history and an oppressive society, and were not the lazy and indolent primitives so dear to the minds of racists. He made the mistake of proposing an intellectual aristocracy of black people when the country was scarcely prepared to tolerate an intellectual aristocracy of whites. But, ultimately, DuBois may have fallen victim to his own soaring intellect and scholarship. He must have known that the earliest schools taught the children of nobility to wage war and to govern, and the schools established to teach blacks did neither.

In whatever direction his inquisitive mind took him, he found blocks to himself personally and hypocrisy about professed American ideals. We can only speculate that his later disenchantment with the American system was in partial response to his disillusionment in ever being such an idealist as to think that American schools were truly interested in the education of black people.

Black Idealism and Disillusionment

Every perceptive study of education repeats in some manner the truism that schools are designed to train the children of a society to participate in the work of that society. *They serve less to impart knowledge about a nation than to impart attitudes about that nation.* Schools serve to teach some that they are perpetual followers and to teach others that they are ordained leaders. In postbellum America, they were ideally suited to help black Americans repeat idealistic slogans about democracy but never share its fruits.

The wrenching and constricting idealism so characteristic of black Americans has been reinforced by the school experience. Birthdays of American heroes who have borne no relationship to black people have been celebrated, while authentic black heroes have been forgotten. Black children have learned of the birth of this country, the early settlers, the magnificent currents of American history without even a footnote about the contributions of their forebears. They have been offered courses of instruction that, once moving beyond the rudiments of simple reading, writing and arithmetic, have borne not the slightest reference to anything in their lives or the lives of those around them.

Black people have suffered greatly in the schools of this country. They have suffered most in schools, because it has been in them that the greatest unkept promises have been made. Many times, an education has done little more than open yearnings which this country is not yet prepared to satisfy.

But American education for whites has not been static and has responded and changed as the needs of the country altered. As the nation became more industrial and immigrants poured to these shores, it fell to education to Americanize the new arrivals. This was no altruistic decision dictated by starry-eyed patriots, but a necessary response to an emergency situation. The rapidly growing industries of the country needed American workers with American attitudes and American skills for American profits. The educational directives may have been differently phrased, but this necessity underlay the cry that went out. Expanded schools, night hours, classes in English, apprentice programs in an endless variety of trades, all attest to the response to a challenge. And in studying this period in American education, we can see why education for black people has failed so miserably up to this time.

In this society, the demands of business and commerce have determined to a large extent the direction of education. Education in this country achieved its finest hour when called upon to fill the factories and plants of an expanding economy. For all his moralizing and pretense, every captain of industry has known that education in this country is an appendage which can be directed and controlled by outside forces. That blacks came so belatedly to this realization once again points out that they remain the most idealistic of Americans.

In the period of this country's greatest industrial expansion, white America demanded workers—white workers—and it got them. In contrast, the response of America to its uneducated blacks was at first to establish agricultural and mechanical schools and later to act as if the education offered by these schools was adequate. In the South of the reconstruction era, commercial interests demanded that blacks remain as docile and unobtrusive as possible so as not to hinder profits; the education of black throughout the nation today continues to reflect this policy.

Education—A Means of Deliverance

As the country has grown, blacks have continued to focus on education as a means of deliverance. As the population shifted from rural to urban and from southern to northern, the demand for an education remained unchecked. This demand would not seem so curious if the same amount of energy had been expended by both blacks and whites for better housing, black industries, and voting power. It was as if a great store of feeling had to be directed toward something innocuous, much as a priest or minister is called to talk to a man about to jump from a building. And always the black American continued with his idealism mixed with optimism, undergirded by cynicism and depression about his chances of ever making it into the mainstream.

In the face of a reality that pointed in a different direction, black people have been admonished always to continue seeking deliverance by getting educated. Whatever their problems, they have been told that an education would solve them. The two world wars should have convinced all with eyes to see that the black man's fixation on education was diversionary. Wars bring out the best and worst in the front line soldier and in the people on the homefront.

In the society at large, the excitement of an emergency has a way of stripping away much pretense. Jobs that blacks had been repeatedly told were not theirs because of educational inadequacies were suddenly available, and they were filled by blacks. Uneducated black men and women poured into major cities and began working on assembly lines in aircraft factories and in shipyards. And all of this happened without benefit of the very education that black people had been told was such a deficiency. In other instances, training programs were set up to prepare workers quickly for a particular task. Whereas black people had been told that to perform a certain job required years of preparation and training, they discovered that training could be finished in a matter of weeks. Whereas blacks had been rebuffed and told they needed years of preparation to perform a simple task, they were literally pulled off the streets and cajoled into performing. In the services, the same thing was happening. So-called white occupations were suddenly blackened when it was discovered that the only people around to fill them were black.

An old black woman recalled her years at a defense plant during World War II. She moved from the South to a large city, uneducated and looking for work. She quickly went to a defense plant, expecting to be placed in the cafeteria, and found herself in a training class for riveters. After a minimum of training, she found herself on the assembly line placing rivets in airplanes. Everytime she read or heard of a plane crash, there would be a curious mixture of feeling. She would first experience an intense personal guilt; then she would begin laughing and thinking, "Serves them white folks right for trying to make a riveter out of black-assed me."

Effect of World War II

The end of World War II may have finally begun the process of dissipating the fantasy of the black American that an education would make him free. Black soldiers returned home as eagerly as anyone else, and the G.I. bill allowed them to go to school in greater numbers. Then the message began to seep in, that few changes were going to be made. The endless rhetoric about democracy that was needed to prepare a people to wage war had been more for enemy consumption and was again ignored on the home front. At some point during this time, with many minds still freshly wrung by the horrors and trauma of war, a scrutiny of education was begun.

Previous generations of college-educated blacks had privately joked about a black person in college taking chemistry or business as a major; but after a war in which large numbers of blacks fought and died, the jokes became even more hollow. The safety valve of turning to teaching became increasingly useless as black college graduates attempted to find jobs outside the South. There was always a certain fatalism present when there was the knowledge of being the last hired and first fired, but the anger moved much closer to the surface when it became more evident that there were fewer jobs for which to be hired.

Black people have a sure wisdom nurtured by centuries of oppression: Whenever neighborhoods are ravaged, jobs are abolished, and when experiments in human engineering collapse, they know long before anyone else who the victims will be.

Empty Promises Recognized

During the decade following the Second World War, some of the empty promises of education began to lose their ability to placate even a patient people, and the anger nurtured by long-suppressed reality began to emerge. This anger began to rise with the long-denied realization that there had been a massive hoax. It was a hoax that began early in slavery and continued on to plague black Americans: the indoctrination of black people to believe that education would qualify them for full acceptance as Americans. Black Americans with an education finally began that painful process of looking at themselves and seeing that a cynical America had played a cruel trick on them. In their idealism and faith in this country, a certain blindness had been created which prevented them from observing that which was around them. For much of the life of this country, the schools of this country took European immigrants and called them imperfect Americans. They accepted this designation in the hope that the process of education would transform them into Americans. This worked for most, and after one or two generations of attending American schools and eliminating Old World customs and names, the process was complete.

But black people, including those with an education, continued to stand outside waiting to be invited in. A rage began to rise—increasingly directed at education—as blacks came to see the obscene discrepancy between America's treatment of the European immigrant and its treatment of them. Where the immigrant was viewed as an imperfect American, the black American was characteristically seen by the educational establishment as an imperfect white person. Going to school could Americanize, but it could not change pigmentation and did not change the thought that white is inherently superior to black. Once the veil began to be lifted, the black American started to see that a major aim of the educational process was to make him more white—an impossibility. At times, the frenzied search for an education became as suicidal as a moth's repeatedly crashing into an incandescent light. One could get an education and more education and more education, but to the majority of the population you were still a nigger.

Casualties on the Altar of Education

The lore of black life is filled with instances attesting to the numerous casualties on the altar of education. Post offices throughout the country are filled with educated black men and women with higher degrees than their white co-workers—many of them cynical and despondent after the long years of being unable to find the work they had spent years educating themselves for.

The boy recalled a peculiar incident. His physician father had many friends who would occasionally stop by. They would be in the city for a convention or vacation or just passing through. On one occasion, a man visited who was "running on the road." This meant that he was a dining car waiter, a high calling for depression-era blacks. The boy recalled that the man had a particularly reticent and distraught quality. As he sat and talked, the physician father kept referring to the man as a classmate—although this seemed strange, for the man clearly did not work at his chosen calling. After a rather hurried dinner, the man looked at his watch, gave thanks, and left. His leaving seemed to trigger a strange gloom in the boy's father. Years later when the boy had grown to manhood and had chosen the calling of his father, the incident became clear. The young physician was seeing a patient who kept muttering, "There but for the grace of God go I."

The time immediately after the war was a period of awakening for vast numbers of blacks. Deteriorated buildings, over-crowded classrooms, and inexperienced and underpaid teachers all pointed to the sad conclusion that white people had never been serious about the education of black children. Hand-me-down textbooks borrowed from white schools across town, if they did nothing more, pointed out a certain system of priorities. And as more and more Americans scrutinized school systems, they found that blindness and sterility had affected all schools—white and black alike. Looking at schools finally resulted in the discovery that they were often a joke for white students as well as black students. What at one time had at least been a place of refuge had never really educated, and now had ceased even to comfort.

Then on May 17, 1954, the Supreme Court of the United States ruled on "separate but equal" education. After close to a century of justifying the travesty of black education, the dam, it was thought, had been cracked. And if the speed of the needed changes did not satisfy the early ebullience, it was still a landmark decision which continues to affect American education. Black and white parents for the first time began to look at the schools attended by their children, and their vision became more clear.

Education Has Condoned Inhumanity

Now blacks are directing rage at school with the same intensity as that formerly reserved for bus stations in dusty southern towns. The startling and frightening realization has come that they are both the same. If society promises a man a job and then reneges, in his anger he turns to the streets to burn and loot and take what he feels is his. That innocent victims are in the way shows how we all share, however passively, in the inhumanity of society. And the institutions of education have been surpassed by none in condoning that inhumanity. Where the police department has been a repressive force for keeping blacks in line, the educational establishment has been a tranquilizer for lulling them into a foolish sense of security.

Just as the unemployed laborer eventually settles on his enemy, the school child and his parents are now settling on their enemy. The battlefield has shifted, but the underlying anger is the same. Many black parents are now saying *this school which has stood so imposing and remote, which has promised my kids that it would transform them, has lied to me. These teachers who have grinned at me and patronized me and insulted me have lied to me. And now, I will be lied to no more.*

First in college, and now even in elementary school, black students are also saying that they will be lied to no more. They at last realize the duplicity of the American educational system, and the intensity of their reaction can be likened to that of a scorned and discarded lover.

Yet, people in the educational establishment look up with bewilderment and protest their good faith and intentions. We are trying, they say. Give us time. But young black Americans are now repaying their eternal mistress education for all her past indiscretions and infidelities.

Now we have reached an historic moment in the life of this country. Education is being assaulted by those who are asking for change. For those of you who revere the American Revolution and, yet, incongruously feel that America is forever sealed off from change, I have a message: Right now, in the midst of modern-day America, we are experiencing a major social revolution. Black Americans are undergoing psychological changes of the most profound implications, and the wonder is that up till now it has been so peaceful.

If truth is the goal of any scholarly inquiry, we must honestly, though sadly, conclude that too few white Americans are really changing their fundamental attitudes and beliefs. Many of our leaders, including those in education, who are now talking about violence, are in reality causing the very violence they profess to deplore. To tell one portion of the population to remain static while the other part is changing is to invite a holocaust. The way to avoid violence is to appeal to the instincts for change—to facilitate change rather than to resist it. If there is a streak of violence insinuated into the national character, it is there because there have always been elements in this country which have set themselves in opposition to change. To resist necessary and healthy change in America today is to incite violence and riots, the blame for which will probably then be laid at the feet of black militants.

Powerful Forces Unleashed

Black Americans are now responding to their moment in history and can no more be stopped than can an overflowing stream. We have been bred with the words of freedom, but immersed in bigotry and oppression. The winds of change are adrift in the minds of black Americans, and they are as powerful as the forces at the Alamo which directed men to fight to the death. We, who have been rebuked and scorned, are now fighting our battles and they are not in Khe Sanh, but in the schools of America.

Black people and their oppressed allies have finally joined a revolution. When we ask for black studies, black curriculum, black faculty, more black students we are asking that this primary institution of our culture speak directly to the needs of the black community, as it has to other communities.

We must have a revolutionary change in the national character of this country if black people are to survive, and the educational establishment must participate in this. We must immediately change the way Americans perceive themselves and others. Black survival demands that, either willingly or unwillingly, institutions of education reflect *our* heritage, *our* contributions, *our* pride. Black survival, and perhaps the survival of this country, demands that black be exalted in this country—that white people and white institutions reflect that Black is Beautiful.

Finally, the American Revolution has been joined by black people. And we now intend to force America to make good its promise to be a melting pot where all are respected and honored. In resolving the issues of the day, we realize at long last that the piecemeal approach can no longer serve us.

I am asked to renounce black anti-semitism—and I do—fully and with no reservations, but the equation does not stop there. What about those of you who personally and professionally have never renounced white anti-semitism and white racism?

We Must Change the National Character

We must now ask that educators join the revolution and demand that the institution of education—the keeper of tradition—move on to the truly revolutionary task of a radical mutation of the American national character. We must ask that educators renounce curricula and teachers who follow too closely the racist traditions of this country, and that they renounce governors who get elected by exploiting educational and racial unrest and then talk of keeping schools open by bayonet. We now ask you to attack the super patriots who demand repression and, yet, have never responded to any demands, however mild, for change. And I ask that you listen carefully to college presidents who now advocate law and order, while referring to legitimate black voices as kooks and yahoos.

The lesson of Ocean Hill, Brownsville, San Francisco State College, Columbia, Berkeley, and Prince George's County is that we must change the national character of this country from its original White Anglo-Saxon Protestant outdated model to something that reflects all America. Anything less is to repeat the lessons of history's losers and not survive. We must radically alter the national character of this country so that when one thinks of an American he will no longer think just of a white American, but also of a black American, an oriental American, a Mexican-American. Educators at this very convention can start this process by asking that the birthdays of Martin Luther King and Malcolm X be national and school holidays.

I wish that there was some way I could offer a tranquilizer and say that change is not needed, but by doing so I would be untrue to my people and my profession. I wish that I could come to you as "a responsible Negro" and tell you that everything is going to be all right, but there are now few in our ranks who can honestly say to anyone that everything is going to be all right. There is an emergency in this land.

In this season of change, with a new administration in Washington, the institutions of education can side with oppressed people and ask for very specific things. We can ask that Brotherhood Week be changed to "Racial Confrontation Week." We must no longer dread the confrontation but push it, so that people can be transformed. The educational process must be shifted in school so that every class at every grade level will discuss feelings, starting with feelings about race. We must make this nation one vast encounter group, dedicated and committed to immediate change—to a radical transformation of the national character. All schools such as those where you work should devote an entire semester to discussing nothing but race. Business and commerce must show change by dropping all barriers and admitting black people into their ranks.

There are no more psychological tricks blacks can play upon themselves to make it possible to exist in dreadful circumstances—

> no more lies to tell themselves
> no more dreams to fix on
> no more opiates to dull the pain
> no more patience
> no more thought
> no more reason

—only a welling tide risen out of all those terrible years of grief, now a tidal wave of fury and rage, and it's all black, black as night.

> "For unless man puts an end to this damnable sin,
> He will put the world in a flame—
> What a shame."

42. Hope for the Half-Democracy

Neil V. Sullivan

The nation, including some educators, is well aware that the public schools are failing to prepare properly millions of young people—particularly minority students—for life, careers, jobs in business or industry, full citizenship, entrance as students into institutions of higher learning.

The people of this great half-democracy are waiting—but no longer patiently—for the educational establishment to begin immediately to put our house in order and develop a system that will make it possible for all students to achieve some measure of success upon completion of their training.

SOURCE: *The Journal of Industrial Arts Education*, XXVIII, 4 (March–April 1969), 14–17. Reprinted by permission of The American Industrial Arts Association.

Who can be optimistic at this point in history about the establishment's desire or ability to avoid disaster? There is small reason for optimism, but some reason for hope. Here are a few encouraging signs of the times.

For one thing, the Massachusetts Board of Education was willing to name an educational innovator—an avowed integrationist—as their new Commissioner of Education, the fourteenth successor to Horace Mann (Massachusetts' first Commissioner of Education).

Another equally pleasing sign was the action taken by the Berkeley Board of Education in naming the imaginative, creative Richard Foster as their new school superintendent.

Perhaps these two actions could set a trend in public education.

All too many of our leaders have been directed to one major ambition and goal—namely, to retain the *status quo*. That is one of the main reasons why today's world is in crisis and education is in the doldrums.

Many educators have constantly protected procedures which were successful in 1900 and never opened their eyes, or their minds, to a new vibrant society which grew up around them.

Yes, grew up despite them, but in such a sick way that millions have been relegated to second-class citizenship because of the kind of schooling these old-time educators so righteously, but so stupidly, defended.

All of this must change—and *NOW*—if public education is to continue.

Standardized tests for entrance into the armed services present but one of many evidences that an enormous proportion of minority high school graduates—the overwhelming majority in some states—are "functional illiterates." In other words, even though we "educationists" have "taught" these students for twelve years, we have failed to teach them to read.

This is indeed a national scandal. The scandal is compounded by the many instances in which failure is accepted as either right or unavoidable. It is, of course, neither. Minority youngsters, like their Caucasian counterparts, will learn successfully—*when* they are taught successfully.

The fact that schools simply cannot continue to fail so grossly to teach a large proportion of students raises these issues:

1. How can teacher attitudes toward students be altered so that each will be viewed with an advance expectancy of success?

2. How can schools fulfill their responsibilities in developing student motivation?

3. How can our schools be remolded—in structure and in curriculum—to promote both the academic and the attitudinal education of *all* students and prepare them for life in a multi-ethnic society?

Note that the first word in each of these issues is "How," not "if." These problems *must* be solved and time is running out!

A generation or two ago—when there was a greater demand for unskilled labor—the schools could bury their failures in the labor market. This is no longer true. There is an ever-shrinking demand for that kind of work. Within the next several years thousands of unskilled and semiskilled jobs will have vanished. Almost eight million unprepared youth with less than a high school education will hit the hot streets.

Furthermore, modern society is growing so complex that greater education is needed simply to function as a citizen.

The consequences of continued failure could destroy society itself, as millions of our school failures at last refuse to accept the role in society to which they are consigned. Instead of accepting the traditional failure, these citizens are demanding that we educate *all* children, rather than just those from middle class and privileged backgrounds.

This is a big order, but one which must be met if our schools are to do their part in preparing students of all ethnic backgrounds for college and for effective participation as citizens in a multi-racial society.

What is needed for success?

The single factor of teacher expectancy can itself stimulate success. Last year a research study was conducted at the Oak School in South San Francisco. The teachers in Oak School were told that about 20 percent of the children selected at random in each of the school's eighteen classrooms showed unusual potential for intellectual achievement based upon a new test called the "Harvard Test of Inflected Acquisition."

Eight months later, lo and behold!, the experimental group had made significantly higher gains than had the other students in the classes.

Teacher expectation was the key here, and it was built upon the "mis-premise" that a randomly selected group of students showed an unusual potential for intellectual achievement.

It is common knowledge that teachers all too frequently form advanced judgments about students on irrelevant criteria—then educate them accordingly. And who is it that suffers from low teacher expectations? Certainly not the well-groomed, well-clothed, polite, white, blue-eyed Anglo-Saxon child from a middle- or upper-class home.

Our brainwashed teachers, educated in a racist society, brought up in racist homes, really believe that they should not expect too much from their black students. In many quarters it was thought "cruel" to try to stimulate black boys and girls to a level of learning that was supposedly over their heads. Worse, in some sections of our country, its children have been deliberately undereducated as a matter of policy. Blacks were to be kept in an inferior position in the work world and in society in general. Therefore, their educational opportunities were deliberately scuttled.

These conditions must change immediately. The immorality of the policies and practices which consign certain children to the educational scrap heap must be exposed and condemned.

Our teachers must recognize the right of all children to the *a priori* assumption they can be educated and then must educate all children to their full potential.

Too often we hear this excuse for a student's failure—he simply lacked motivation and was not trying.

Of course, motivation is crucial. Who dares to shrug that fact off and accept the symptom as the disease? We must realize that motivation, although an inner force, can be stimulated from without.

Many middle-class homes have built-in motivation. We applaud when the baby utters his first syllable or takes his first halting step. We shower our children with fringe benefits when they behave properly or when they get good grades in school.

We let them know what kind of success is expected, and we reward them both tangibly and with subtle forms of recognition when they achieve it. Our own drives for success are passed on to our children. Incentive is always there.

This is not true with masses of our minority children in inner cities. Many homes do not provide the stimuli necessary to motivate children for success in school. There are many reasons for this—lack of material possessions, the lack of background in what constitutes academic success. It is not a lack of wanting what's best for the children or lack of love. Rather, it's lack of the means to provide the same reward stimulus found in many middle-class homes.

Up to now, our schools have largely abdicated their responsibility to motivate. They succeeded. The school felt no responsibility for those non-middle-class students who did not bring that motivation with them.

Schools can no longer use "lack of motivation" as an alibi for failure to educate all the children.

Schools have a two-pronged assignment—to supply the external incentive for success in school, to promote personal motivation to learn by making the material relevant, and the learning process itself a source of pleasure and satisfaction.

Outwardly our organization needs to be altered—to promote racial balance in the schools.

This is a multi-racial nation. It is a nation in which each ethnic group has major contributions to make to its own members and to members of other groups.

The future of the nation rests on how well these diverse groups relate to each other. We must help each child build feelings of genuine respect both for his own groups and for all others in our society. This cannot be done if racial groups are kept apart during their important school years.

Though academic achievement can take place in racially imbalanced settings—provided we are willing to spend the money necessary to achieve it—the attitudes necessary for a multi-racial democratic society cannot be achieved in that kind of setting. This we must know after 300 years' experience with separation. We must come to grips with the failure to educate millions of minority children, even as we struggle to integrate.

The content of curriculum must be made relevant to the needs of today's students now. Methods of teaching too, must be drastically altered.

To deprecate the contribution to American folklore of the "dedicated school marm" who carried the sole responsibility for all of the education of her twenty-five or thirty youngsters would serve no purpose. Nevertheless, the "Miss Dove" syndrome is clearly out of place in a school program which recognizes individual differences and stimulates each youngster to progress at his own maximum pace.

What is needed is a greater role for the kind of programmed learning developed by Dr. M. W. Sullivan of the Behavioral Research Laboratories. That program has been successfully introduced into Dr. Rhody McCoy's Ocean Hill-Brownsville District in New York City.

Far from undercutting the teacher, it makes her much more effective in dealing with the widely diverse needs of the youngsters.

Frequently the teaching establishment insists on more money for higher salaries and smaller classes. That is a fine hope except for one thing—the current sources of money have just about dried up.

The major cause for the dry-up is the high priority our country has placed on financing a war machine and the low priority the Federal government has placed on educating the nation's youth.

A total of 79 cents of each income tax dollar goes or is spent for defense purposes. Only one cent of the tax dollar is spent on education and welfare.

Until this nation establishes new and realistic goals for education, until we concentrate as a people on peace and not war, until we take the onus for the support of public education off the local property tax, our schools will have to operate with new approaches but with about the same amount of money.

It is for us the educators to reconstruct education in the image of all the students and within the framework of financial reality. Perhaps the future will be brighter. But at this writing, and as we face financial retrenchment, even as we challenge the old tired programs and practitioners, here is a minimal prescription.

If this means fewer high-paid administrators, so be it.

If this means a teaching role for many of our so-called "special teachers and supervisors," so be it.

If this means fewer classroom teachers deployed in different fashion, so be it.

If this means that some of our master teachers receive salaries comparable to some of our administrators, so be it.

If this means reducing teaching staff and adding paraprofessionals, so be it.

If this means we turn some of our programs, e.g., vocational education, over to private industry and concentrate on the humanities, so be it.

If this means we build large, educationally challenging and economically realistic new plants and end the day of the small neighborhood school, so be it.

If this means that we narrow the number of electives for some students in order to provide early childhood education for all children, so be it.

If this means keeping our schools open 12 months a year and asking those professionals in our schools to take a one-month vacation rather than three, so be it.

If this means having the young people in our schools decide on what in the curriculum is relevant and eliminate the irrelevant, so be it.

If this means a "take-over" of our schools by parents because of the procrastination and vacillation of some board of education, so be it.

We, the professionals, must be prepared to recommend that this nation take whatever steps are necessary in order to provide equal educational opportunities immediately for all of the nation's children.

The list of changes could go on and on. However, this brief discussion is sufficient to show that our schools must be reorganized if they are to accomplish their purpose.

There is the story of a poor Irish boy whose mother was so determined that he receive the kind of education needed to get ahead in this society that she maneuvered him out of a ghetto school and into a middle-class school within walking distance of the ghetto in which they lived.

There he was exposed to middle-class children. That exposure was challenging in certain ways, and his own self-image improved by the discovery that he could do some things better than they could. His attitude changed as conditions around him changed. He developed the skills of getting along with people across ethnic lines.

How come that poor Irishman—who was Superintendent of Schools in Berkeley and is now Commissioner of Education of Massachusetts—could achieve a measure of success when millions of minority children who have the same at-birth intelligence and achievement potential are failing in such large numbers?

It is because of his mother's encouragement and the attitude of his teachers. They were convinced that because he was white, despite an immigrant background, he could learn. They expected him to learn. They insisted that he learn. He therefore learned.

Our students will learn only if: (1) their teachers expect them to learn; (2) the schools fulfill their responsibility to develop motivation; and (3) the schools are reorganized to promote the academic and attitudinal education of *all* students.

We must recognize that failure of a child in school is failure of the school with the child. Schools are only as successful as their students. Yes, there is small room for optimism, but there is some hope.

43. Training Teachers of the Disadvantaged: Blueprint for a Breakthrough

James C. Stone

1. Disadvantaged Teachers of the Disadvantaged

We came to this conclusion: the teachers of the disadvantaged—are desperate. They are so desperate they welcome *any* training activity that seems likely to help them even a little bit in their struggle to cope with the problems of teaching disadvantaged students. In these circumstances, they do not seem to have very strong preferences for one type of training activity over another, they like them all for their purposes, if they are conducted well enough to serve their purposes at all.[1]

The teachers of the disadvantaged are disadvantaged themselves. This is a finding of a recent study of 2,000 teachers who participated in ESEA Titles I or III and NDEA Title XI projects which offered special training for teachers of the disadvantaged.

The results of the study suggest different curriculum models are appropriate for different purposes, regardless of the community setting in which

[1] James C. Stone, *Teachers for the Disadvantaged* (San Francisco: Jossey-Bass, 1969).

SOURCE: *Resources for Urban Schools: Better Use and Balance,* CED, Supplementary Paper, Number 33 (New York: Committee for Economic Development, forthcoming). Reprinted by permission of the publisher.

the training programs are conducted, just as long as the over-all training objectives are sufficiently comprehensive.

———it seems appropriate to assert that local school districts, in cooperation, and even collaboration, with colleges and universities, are the agencies most likely to be able to provide the experiences, activities, and facilities necessary (or at least desirable) for the comprehensive training programs we are proposing for teachers of the disadvantaged. At issue is the matter of how these two agencies—local school districts and colleges—can effectively combine their resources with those of the communities in which the disadvantaged live and "have their being." [2]

In the considered judgment of the research team that conducted the investigation, model curriculums for the training of teachers of the disadvantaged can be most efficiently and effectively initiated, organized and implemented by an educational agency which is:

(1) situated more advantageously in relation to the resources, opportunities, and problems of local communities and school districts than colleges and universities usually are, and (2) operated more independently from social, economic and political pressures for particular uses of resources and opportunities and for specific solutions to those problems than local school districts usually are. The institution which we regard as most appropriate for the professional education and training of teachers—not only teachers of the disadvantaged but all teachers—would have the following features: It would (1) provide training that was centered in the ghetto, the *barrio,* the reservation, (2) emphasize participation, encountering, confrontation of all persons involved as the basis for the teachers' (or prospective teachers') learning about theories, concepts, principles, (3) be governed by representatives of *all* of the groups providing the necessary resources—the local community, the local school district, the college or university, the trainees themselves, the profession, and (4) draw its staff from *all* of the agencies providing the resources, thus employing as teachers of teachers the students, parents, community agency workers, and civic leaders of the local community, as well as the public school teachers and supervisors in the local school districts, the faculty and graduate students of colleges and universities, and other professional specialists.

Assuming that there is merit in the researchers suggestions, the question remains: How and where can the model curriculums and programs best be mounted, and under what administrative arrangement would the best chance of immediate and effective implementation occur? The clue to a new institutional model is contained in a summary of the interview findings:

[2] *Ibid.*

These teachers were convinced that training activities must be planned and conducted *from* and *at* the grass roots level, rather than *by* or *at* the district office or the college, removed as they are from the local school and neighborhood.

A number of new administrative vehicles for training teachers come to mind which have similar, if not identical, features. Some public schools and colleges have organized a "special learning center" that offers remedial, developmental, and supplementary instruction for disadvantaged pupils; others have initiated a "curriculum and instructional materials center" that develops, field tests, and evaluates innovative instructional units for disadvantaged pupils; still others have tried a "demonstration-laboratory center" that is either a comprehensive school program or a program of special classes for disadvantaged pupils and their parents.

The organization and operation of a multipurpose center for teacher education is a cooperative and collaborative arrangement between a college or university and a local school district or school. The instructional and administrative staff of the center is drawn from both agencies. Rather than being conducted regularly and exclusively on a college campus, the principal activities of the center are conducted either in a public school or in a facility immediately adjacent to one. Among other activities, the program of the center includes workshops, seminars, extension courses, and similar training activities for the teachers of disadvantaged pupils. In sum, the multipurpose centers conduct comprehensive, coherently articulated, coordinated, cooperative and collaborative programs for the immediate and direct benefit of disadvantaged pupils and their teachers.

In almost every respect but one, the institutional model embodied by the multipurpose center seems to be worthy of being emulated. The one respect in which this model can and must be improved is in its *control* and *governance*. The governing authority of the center can be: (a) a local school district, (b) a college, (c) a consortium involving a district and a nearby college or university, (d) a trusteeship including representation from these groups and also local community agencies.[3] The joint-power authority formed to govern the model institution we have in mind can and should provide for more equitable delegation of responsibility and distribution of decision-making functions.

From what is known of the paradigm of change,[4] of the bureaucracy of the establishment, and the cement of tradition in which most schools and

---

[3] As one project director sized up the situation: "Either the public school or the college becomes the banker, calling the tune to which the others dance."

[4] As applied to school curriculum projects, see Mario D. Fantini and Gerald Weinstein, *The Disadvantaged: Challenge to Education* (New York: Harper and Row, 1968), pp. 298–300. As applied to the preparation of teachers and other higher education personnel, see James C. Stone, *Breakthrough in Teacher Education* (San Francisco: Jossey-Bass, 1968), pp. 178–180.

colleges are mired, it is difficult to see how the center can be the long-term answer for the radical reforms and dramatic changes needed in order to successfully recruit, train, retrain and retain teachers of the disadvantaged.

In several previous publications we have pointed out the failure of traditional teacher education,[5] a failure which is particularly alarming with respect to our total lack of accomplishment in recruiting, training, retraining and retaining ghetto teachers. This failure is that of the colleges, the schools, the state, and the profession.

THE COLLEGES

Most colleges—as institutions—have *not* taken seriously their responsibility to educate teachers. As institutions, their efforts have been incidental largely—tangential to other missions which they see as more important, such as preparing liberal arts graduates, or, at the professional level, doctors and lawyers. Certainly, in the present crucial need for teacher training—preparing teachers of the disadvantaged—colleges and universities are far removed from the problem. Since institutions of higher education have not taken seriously this social obligation of teacher training, since they cannot be forced into active social responsibility, and since the most significant aspect of this training must occur in the ghetto and in classrooms of disadvantaged children, why not move this unwanted stepchild from the colleges?

THE SCHOOLS

For years public and private schools merely accepted WASP* teachers trained by the colleges, however adequate or inadequate, and sent them back occasionally for refresher courses and advanced degrees. Similarly, the schools have passively accepted student and intern teachers and permissively provided them with whatever laboratory experiences the college or university requested. In more recent times, aided and abetted by federal grants, school systems have developed their own in-service education programs to which teachers have come in large numbers and generally applauded.

Building on this newly acquired know-how, it would be logical for the schools also to become the preservice educators of teachers, particularly those of the disadvantaged, thus replacing the institutions of higher education. For the increasing numbers of public schools involved in internship programs, this would be a logical and simple step. Assistant superinten-

---

[5] *Ibid.*, chap. 12, *passim*, and James C. Stone, "Reform or Rebirth?" *NEA Journal*, 57, 5 (May 1968), 23. Also James C. Stone, "Whither Reform in Teacher Education?" *Educational Leadership*, 25, 2 (November 1967), 127–131. Reprinted in *The Education Digest*, XXXIII, 5 (January 1968).

* White, Anglo-Saxon, Protestant.

dents in charge of staff development are appearing with greater frequency in the schools. Such persons are qualified individuals who might direct and organize preservice teacher education just as they now successfully organize and direct in-service training. An obvious benefit of such a step would be to close the gap that has existed so long between preservice and in-service education. Internship programs were expected to achieve this but, unfortunately, few have.

In publicly supported education, this shift of responsibility would involve a simple transfer of funds from higher to public education. Such a shift would create in every school system a division of teacher education—in-service and preservice. Such a division would be closer to the operational level than the present college education departments and university schools of education, bound up as they are in the bureaucracies, politics, and the distractions of higher education. As already indicated, the teacher education centers previously described are examples. Yet public education bound up as it is by inertia, unresponsive bureaucracy, middle-class traditions, overlegislation, and underfinancing, has already failed in the ghetto. To expect it to mount on a wide-scale basis and at high levels and sustain such centers is to expect what is not and what is not likely to be.

THE STATE

The education of teachers long has been recognized as a state responsibility. Originally states took this obligation seriously and provided special institutions—the normal school, the teachers college—as their prime vehicle for preservice and in-service education. The last decade has seen the demise of these single purpose institutions. Most have evolved into state colleges interested in the education of all other occupational groups, including teachers in general (but not teachers of the disadvantaged). The recent conversion of these institutions to state universities has thus continued and hastened the decline of interest in teacher education at the collegiate level.

Meanwhile, state departments of education have been content with confining their teacher education obligations to the certification of teachers and the accreditation of colleges and universities for teacher education. In most states, the accreditation function amounts to an approval system based primarily on whether the institutions offer the specific courses prescribed by the certification office. And, as a recent TEPS publication points out, state departments have failed to provide leadership.

> Thus a no-man's-land is created for the college—school function (of teacher training) which is typically characterized by dual administration, improper financing, and conflicting supervision.[6]

[6] *A New Order in Student Teaching* (Washington, D.C.: National Commission on Teacher Education and Professional Standards, NEA, 1967), p. 21.

THE PROFESSION

World War II created a critical shortage of teachers and was followed by an unprecedented increase in the birthrate which simply worsened the teacher shortage. Out of this crisis came the "professional standards movement" in which the NEA took the leadership through the formation of its Commission on Teacher Education and Professional Standards in 1946. While all of us connected with this movement over the past twenty-five years—at local, state, and national levels—can enthusiastically testify to its many accomplishments, the simple fact is that, despite these efforts, the average teacher still is uninterested in and uninformed about teacher education and the professional processes such as certification, accreditation, in-service training, personnel standards, and the like. If you doubt this statement, look around at the next school conference you attend. Check how few general sessions are given over to the topic of teacher training. Visit the section meetings on training, certification, accreditation, or ethics and note the paucity of teachers at these section meetings in contrast to the "Standing Room Only" signs on doors marked "Salary," "Negotiating Councils," "Collective Bargaining," and the like. Check on who goes to conferences on teacher education—a few public school "master" teachers and personnel directors, yes, but mostly college or university professors of education. We can't blame the teachers. We've never really opened the doors of teacher education to them. When it comes to preservice training, we college people have given a few public school supervising teachers a look inside, but we've not dared to go further than recommending the grade a student or intern teacher should receive. We, the college supervisors, who only visit the student teacher about two or three times a semester are empowered with the final judgment! And when it comes to in-service training, teachers are merely the recipients of our ideas and are seldom involved in the planning for what is needed by and desirable for them.

We could open the door wider and make supervising teachers in the public schools faculty members. We could give them preservice teaching responsibilities for the whole professional sequence instead of the student teaching problems seminars we typically toss to a few of them. We could set up procedures whereby teachers actually plan, organize, and conduct their own in-service training. Any such moves would be in the right direction, but there is scant hope that from these forms of tokenism, the profession will be moved to a concern for teacher education.

SOCIAL INSTITUTIONS

All attempts to reform teacher training [7] have failed to recognize that the social institutions in which teacher education is embedded—the

[7] There have been many reform efforts. Among the major attempts have been the Commission on Teacher Education of the American Council on Education

schools, the colleges, state departments of education—were created by society *not* for the purpose of bringing about change and innovation, but for preserving the status quo. As guardians of the establishment, the schools, institutions of higher education, and regulatory agencies of the state were specifically created to see that change does *not* take place. The primary functions of these educational agencies, like education has been since the days of primitive man, is to pass on the cultural heritage to the upcoming generation. Designed to preserve what is, they have been staffed largely by those who are wholly committed to this end. Few teachers, for example, see their role as agents of change. The result is that reform efforts have done little to break the patterns of traditional teacher education.

As long as education and its handmaiden, teacher education, remain fixed in the concrete of college, public school and state department traditions, both will remain substantially as they are now. Reform efforts will continue to come and go without making any appreciable impact on either higher education, public education, or state departments of public instruction where teacher education has its roots.

If ever we hope to break what George Counts, writing some twenty-five years ago, called "the lock-step in teacher training," we must create new organizational structures; we must be willing to go one step further than modifying the present establishment. We need to cut the ties, plough over the old college-school ruts in which teacher training is quagmired, and begin afresh.

This summation of the failures of general teacher education (of which the training of teachers of the disadvantaged is an unfortunately small appendage) and its traditional role in society brings to mind the statement by Felix Robb, the former, long-time president of George Peabody College for Teachers (one of the two remaining U.S. teachers' colleges still in existence):

"If the successors to teachers colleges become mediocre and abandon their concern for teachers, another generation will have to start teachers colleges all over again." [8]

While not wishing simply to go "back" as Robb suggests, we do propose a new model which takes something from the past—the idea of a separate social institution for teacher training. But this new institution would have several new dimensions I believe to be crucial for the education of the teachers of the disadvantaged: *training that is "planned and conducted from and at the grass roots level" and that intimately involves the local*

(1938–1946); the NEA TEPS Commission (1946–to date); the Fund for the Advancement of Education (1950–1959); the Ford Foundation's "Breakthrough Programs," (1960–1966); NDEA, ESEA, and other Federal Grants (1964 to date).

[8] Henry C. Hill, "Wanted: Professional Teachers," *The Atlantic* (May 1960), p. 39.

school and neighborhood; it would be an agency controlled by the client-groups that comprise the local community.

We have called this new social institution an EPI—Education Professions Institute. I offer it as a theoretical model of a breakthrough for training teachers of the disadvantaged, if not for all teachers. For those of us who have been in the teacher education business most of our professional lives, proposing an alternative and competing agency to the one that has nurtured us these many years is a difficult task. As Minnis has said:

"No one likes to point out that the king is naked. If you are the tailor, it is especially difficult." [9]

2. A Theoretical Model

The EPI (Education Professions Institute) would be a separate agency of higher education with a distinct, unique, and differentiated function.[10] The unique purpose of the EPI would be to provide professional training for teachers-to-be, teacher aides, associate teachers, intern teachers, regular teachers, master teachers, and teachers-of-teachers, through the bachelors and master degrees. It would recruit adults and high school dropouts of all ages from the community in which it is located as well as from the ranks of high school graduates, the junior colleges, four-year colleges, and universities. For example, those teachers and prospective teachers who had not themselves grown up in a ghetto would be expected to both live and work in the local community for a significant part of their training period.

[9] Douglas Minnis, "Rebellion in Teacher Education: Requiem for a Fossil in White Tie and Tails" (CASCD Conference address, November 21, 1968), p. 2 (mimeographed).

[10] In an address to the California Council on the Education of Teachers, Burns stated:

"It is no longer possible for colleges and universities, through the instrumentation of schools or departments of education, adequately to prepare teachers within the relative isolation of the campus—even when that preparation involves, as it usually does, some cooperative efforts between the colleges and the public schools. The coalition between colleges and schools should be expanded to include representatives from student and community groups and, since neither the college nor the public school is able by itself to provide for that kind of extension of the teacher education coalition, the creation of new institutions responsible for the training of educational personnel. Put simply, the creation of quasi-governmental or multi-institutional consortia or corporations for the preparation of education personnel. While such an institution must and would include schools and colleges it would also include other groups now excluded; and the full meaning of that, of course, is to suggest that the present school-college coalition surrender some of its present sovereignty over teacher education to a new quasi-governmental institution. . . ."

Hobert Burns, "The Public Schools As Trainers of Teachers: A (Modest) Proposal." (California, October 31, 1968), mimeographed.

Fiscal support for such Institutes might come from a variety of sources. Some might be funded entirely by the state or the federal government; others might be supported in whole or in part by private foundations, business or industrial groups, or professional associations. *Initially, the Institute would offer an alternative to present agencies of teacher training, and thus provide healthy competition to existing college, university, and school district operations. In time, the EPI might completely replace colleges and schools as the trainers of teachers.*

Regardless of source or sources of financial support, the EPI should be viewed as a natural extension of the state's responsibility for teacher education. Or better, it would be a case of the state's returning to itself the responsibility it always has had but has failed to exercise since the demise of the teachers college. The Institute would be accredited by the state for developmental and experimental purposes. Special and unique licensing provisions would need to be established in the states for those completing EPI training. This is not to suggest a lowering of standards, but rather different standards for a different group in order to accomplish a purpose not now adequately served by any existing social agency.

The EPI would draw its faculty from the communities in which it is located, the local schools, adjacent colleges and universities, and other social, governmental, business and industrial agencies. While strictly a professional institution, the EPI might admit prospective teachers and paraprofessionals at any point in their college career when they were deemed ready to begin professional training. During any semester of enrollment, the trainees would be paid by the Institute, the state, and/or local school for rendering teaching or community services of various kinds. This "paid to learn" feature is especially significant in terms of recruiting from the ghetto community itself. In-service teachers would enroll in the Institute for afternoon or evening workshops, seminars, or summer colloquiums, conferences, institutes, sabbaticals, and the like, using scholarships provided by local, state and federal governments, foundations, the business community, professional associations, and school district sabbatical leaves.

The single most distinguishing feature of the EPI would be that it is a *teaching* institution. Its educational style would be to "learn to teach by teaching," so all trainees would be involved in some form of teaching as the central focus of their learning activities—"everyone teaching something to someone."

The EPI is envisioned as a prestige agency, paying better salaries, for example, to its faculty than do traditional colleges, universities or school systems. This would be a truly professional school analogous to the medical school, the law school, the divinity school. Its program for the education of teachers of teachers would encompass research that is focused on professional problems in the teaching-learning process.

There would be equality of status and prestige for those faculty having differentiated responsibilities for the so-called theoretical and practical aspects of teacher training since any one individual would be expected to be equally involved in both. The heart of the EPI would be either a series of exemplary schools or a school system which it would adopt or organize. The Institute and the school would be housed together and professional education would grow out of the instructional problems of teaching children. Laboratory experiences in classrooms and neighborhoods of the disadvantaged would be the central focus of the in-service and preservice teacher training program. The professional curriculum would be tailored to each individual and would be so organized that every trainee, during his stay at the Institute, would be simultaneously involved in a stream of classroom or community experiences and a concurrent stream of theoretical seminars, both taught and supervised by a team of instructors working with a particular group of trainees. The EPI would have the advantage of being close to the schools, yet removed one step from the politics of local school systems. Though ultimately responsible to the state, it would be characterized by "home rule" from the local community and the trainees themselves. However funded, it would be administered by and for the local community and trainee clientele. The State Department of Education, the local school district, and adjacent institutions of higher education would have a cooperative and consultative relationship with the Institute.

The EPI would be chartered by the State under a "joint powers" agreement. This is a legal entity provided for in most states, but which, until now, seldom has been used in education circles except in connection with the federally sponsored Research and Development Laboratories. The powers brought together to organize the EPI and to formulate policy for it, within broad state guidelines, would be (1) a local community, (2) the trainees, (3) a college, or university, (4) a school system and (5) the organized profession. These powers would establish an independent local board of control which would have fiscal and administrative authority to operate the EPI. The five powers initially comprising the governing board might appoint additional representatives, including the public-at-large.

Within state departments of public instruction, there would be a specific unit of higher education with responsibility to provide leadership for the EPI and coordinate their efforts. The permanent staff would be a small cadre of higher education and urban education specialists. This nucleus would be augmented by yearly appointments of a much larger number of consultants and faculty drawn from the institutes, the schools, colleges, communities, and other educational social agencies.

The curriculum of the EPI would provide for a number of levels of training for a number of different roles. Thus, persons with roughly the equivalent of a high school education might enter the EPI to become teacher aides; those with junior college preparation might become associate teachers; those with an AB degree, intern teachers; and those with teaching credentials, master teachers or teachers-of-teachers. Each program would end in employment opportunities, but the possibility of movement from one program and role to another would also be provided. Everyone would be paid during their period of training for everyone would be serving in some educational capacity in the local school or community.

A school in the ghetto would be the "home" of the Institute, with the local district supplying a room for seminars and an office for the staff.

Academic preparation needed by trainees would be provided by nearby colleges on a contractual or cooperative arrangement.

In the vernacular of the times, the EPI would be "where the action is" —in the disadvantaged community. And it would stay there in the sense that it would be controlled, in part, by the local community. It would address itself solely to the problem that not only have our schools failed to help enough children from the lower classes to enter the mainstream of society, they actually have prevented many of them from doing so. Burns said,

"We are now educating students whose lives will be lived as much in the next century as this one, but our schools and colleges are . . . still based on structures, functions, and curricula more apropos of the last century than the next. . . . For many . . . the judgment has been made that the urban schools are failures because the present ends of the schools are not acceptable as the proper ends by . . . students and parents from impoverished or minority groups." [11]

And if our schools have failed, teacher training likewise has failed. Both are part and parcel of the present establishment. We teacher educators thus are admitted failures, but we can also be part of the solution through the EPI. And we can draw a lesson from a parallel problem that long has been prevalent in rural America. Like the present ghetto, rural teachers have been and are in short supply. An attempt to solve the rural problem was made by recruiting from the country young women who would be trained at colleges located in the towns and cities. Upon qualifying for teaching certificates, however, precious few returned to the country to teach. The EPI would draw from its area many of those who were local residents, but it would train them on the spot, with a greater likelihood of their remaining in the area after being trained to serve in the local schools.

Since the EPI is *the model* which emerged from my research findings,[12]

[11] *Ibid.,* p. 11, 12.

[12] The researches include the study of federal projects previously referred to as well as those funded by the Ford Foundation and analyzed in *Breakthrough in Teacher Education.*

I wish to underscore and reiterate that in an EPI the ghetto community and its trainees would be active participants in determining their own and their children's education. They clearly would have a stake in it—a piece perhaps *the* piece of the action. The growing belief by ghetto communities that schools and teacher education institutions no longer serve the ends they believe in is the cause of the increasing demands and increasingly intense confrontations by blacks, Mexican-Americans, Puerto Ricans and American Indians. In an EPI, the ghetto community and the trainees would not only have a *voice* but a *vehicle* for remaking their own education and the education of their children.

No one doubts the difficulty of establishing such a new social institution, especially those of us who have been "the tailors" (Minnis's term) for so many years of conventional training in traditional colleges and universities. Yet surely the times demand action, new approaches, radical departures, brave new worlds. Henry David Thoreau once wrote:

> Why should we be in such desperate haste to succeed, and in such desperate enterprises? If a man does not keep pace with his companions, perhaps it is because he hears a different drummer. Let him step to the music which he hears, however measured or far away.

Let those of us who are committed to training teachers for ghetto communities and retraining present staffs who teach the disadvantaged be given the opportunity to march to a different drummer whom we now hear in *crescendo*.

3. Blueprint for the Breakthrough

A specific blueprint for the needed complete and utter breakthrough in the education of teachers of the disadvantaged is presented now under the rubric of the Black Peoples Institute of Teacher Education. This blueprint has been developed during the past year by representatives of the black community of Hunters Point, San Francisco, California, the San Francisco Unified School District, and the University of California at Berkeley and Santa Cruz. This practical blueprint differs from the theoretical model of an EPI in the following respects:

1. It proposes a non-state-controlled private agency completely independent from and equal to other public educational agencies such as school districts and colleges or universities. This is a significant departure: The EPI would be wholly community and clientele controlled.
2. It proposes to offer extensive undergraduate as well as graduate training, and academic as well as professional education.

In other respects the blueprint is a black community's replica of the theoretical EPI model.

The blueprint offers evidence that the EPI is a viable and workable concept, sufficiently flexible to be adopted and adapted to various communities and clienteles. The next step is to make it operational so that we can test it for the breakthrough in training teachers of the disadvantaged which it purports to be.

The Black People's Institute of Teacher Education

ASSUMPTIONS

One overriding assumption on which the Black People's Institute of Teacher Education is based is that the community has within itself the ability and the power to make all decisions concerning the education of its children and its teachers.

Another assumption is that, while the Institute is essentially intended to be for black people and run by black people, it will be open to applicants of other races and from other communities.

A third assumption is that the theoretical notion of an EPI is a bold, new approach to training inner city teachers and this approach should be tested. [13]

PURPOSE

The purpose of the Black People's Institute of Teacher Education is to provide liberal and professional education needed for the training of people of minority backgrounds to become teachers. Special priority will be given to recruiting and preparing people from the Hunter's Point-Bayview Southeast San Francisco area. However, consideration also will be given to people from other communities.

The Institute will be established as a private, nonprofit educational agency, owned and operated by the residents of the greater Hunter's Point-Bayview Community. Because the Education Committee believes that the characteristics of the liberally educated man are basic to professional competence in teaching, the design of the teacher development program will include the integration of academic and professional studies, (along with whatever remedial work needs to be done), in a tailor-made curriculum for each student in the Institute. The program will be designed in a unique way to allow for continuous opportunities for trainees to relate

[13] *Ibid.*, p. 178–190.

theroy and practice through work experiences, participation, field assignments, and a wide variety of teaching and community service activities.

Administrative Organization

As the basic form of self-government, the Education Committee assumes responsibility for the formation of the Black People's Institute of Teacher Education. Authority for the organization and operation, educationally and budgetarily, will be vested in a Community Trustee Board, a body selected by the Coordinating Council. It is understood that the Board will include some representatives from the Hunter's Point Youth Council. The Board may also include one or more educational advisers appointed by it as exofficio members.

Administrative responsibilities will be conceived as service functions to the governing board, the faculty and the trainees. In order to meaningfully assure the necessary kind of community control, a unique advocacy approach to educational issues will become a part of the Institute. Thus, the community will have direct, on-going access to diverse points of view affecting the educational development of their children and their teachers. Operating as an administrative team, these officers will be appointed by the governing board to guide and supervise such functions as:

Over-all coordination of the Institute.
Coordination of ethnic relativity and educational advocacy, curriculum and instruction, student affairs, research, personnel services, and finance.

Coordinators may be assisted by consultants, associates, or administrative trainees, depending on their designated duties and responsibilities.

Students

All people from the community desiring an education will be admitted, irrespective of traditional academic deficiencies. A serious effort will be made to recruit and hold high school dropouts who wish to work in an educational agency, and also parents who reside in the area.

Students in professional education from other colleges and universities will be screened by an appropriate committee of the Institute to engage in its programs. The programs will involve teaching and tutoring on a regular and intensive basis. Each student will also have contact with a family (probably the family of his tutees) or with some group of young people and will be expected to live in the Southeast San Francisco area during the training period.

The goal of the program for students recruited from outside the community will focus both on the activity of teaching and tutoring as well as direct experiences with the people of the Southeast San Francisco area.

While the programs of the "inside" and "outside" students will differ in emphasis and concentration, the theoretical component for both groups will include such learning experiences as:

1. *Analyzing the learning process.* As future teachers, concern will center on the relationship between teacher, environment, and pupil, with both learning how to focus or cue in on each other and on the subject material being examined.
2. *Coping with the educational needs and potential of students, tutees, and their families.* While the focus will be on the young students, some facts will be gathered about their educational situation. Is the school adequate? How do school officials and teachers approach their pupils? What is a relevant education? What causes negative learning? What causes a dropout? These and other questions will concern the trainees.
3. *Understanding the culture.* What is cultural deprivation? Are the students and their families culturally deprived or just culturally different from the majority white middle-class culture? Indeed, to what should that culture be compared?
4. *Dealing with the emotions of pupils.* Problems of self-identity, aggressiveness that is inappropriate in the classroom, violence, and fear hinder learning if uncontrolled. Confidence, sense of self, hope for the future are desirable characteristics. How these emotions rise and fall will concern the trainees.

RECRUITMENT, ADMISSION, FEES, PAY

Appropriate Institute committees will be responsible for recruiting and admitting students to the Black People's Institute of Teacher Education. Consultants may be used from the community, and colleges and universities to aid in recruiting college students to the Institute so that a diversity of trainees—i.e., hard-core dropouts, parents, and college-age students may be drawn from the following groups:

Hard-core school dropouts
High school graduates
Parents from the community
Returning black Vietnam veterans
Students with one year of college education
Students with two years of college education
Students with three years of college education
Students with four years of college who qualify for internship training

Admissions policies will be established by the Community Trustee Board whose over-all responsibility will be to supervise the quality of the Institute.

No tuition will be charged or fees required of students recruited from Southeast San Francisco, the Institute's service area. The concept of students being "paid to learn" will be adhered to and the Institute's budget will provide the specific amounts to be paid students at the various levels of training, as follows:

First year	$2,000
Second year	2,500
Third year	3,000
Fourth year	4,000

Fifth-year intern teachers will be paid a regular beginning teachers salary by the employing school district. Applicants from outside the service area who can afford to pay tuition for the special training available at the Black People's Institute of Teacher Education, will pay a fee, to be determined by the governing board and used to augment the Institute's scholarship and fellowship fund.

THE CURRICULUM: PROGRAMS

The Institute will provide:

1. A two-year program in the academic as well as professional courses to prepare the two-year college candidate to achieve full academic and professional attainment for credentialing as a beginning teacher.
2. A three-year program to prepare the one-year college candidate to achieve full academic and professional attainment for credentialing as a beginning teacher.
3. A one-year program to prepare the three-year college candidate to achieve full academic and professional attainment for credentialing as a beginning teacher.
4. A post-baccalaureate internship program to prepare the four-year candidate, both practically and professionally, for achieving the skills, art and methodology of teaching minority community children.
5. A parent-community resource program to prepare parents and other community people in both the academic and professional education necessary to achieve the skills and methodology of teaching in modern classrooms as assistant, associate, and intern teachers and teacher aids.
6. A teacher-tutor program of academic studies using high school dropouts, to be organized as a Student Teaching Corps.
7. An in-service teacher education program to provide new experience for credentialed teachers who wish to teach in schools located in minority communities, and to train master teachers and teachers of teachers.
8. An in-service training program for school counselors and school administrators who may be assigned to schools in minority communities.

THE CURRICULUM: GENERAL CHARACTERISTICS

While the curriculum will be designed by an appropriate committee of staff and trainees, it should have these essential distinguishing characteristics. It should:

1. Focus on the black community—its history, culture, and ethnic relativity.
2. Center on "paid to learn," supervised field experiences—teaching, tutoring, and allied community service activities.
3. Integrate theory and practice—drawing from each to illuminate and explain the other.
4. Be organized, for teaching purposes, into large time-blocks of "experiences" (rather than "courses," "lectures," "credits," "examinations.")
5. Be taught by teams of instructors—each team working with a particular group of trainees over an extended period of time.
6. Be planned by committees of faculty and students, and based on trainees' needs and interests.
7. Be evaluated by performance criteria, on a satisfactory or unsatisfactory basis.
8. Be experimental and open-ended in its search for answers to the question: What is education?

LEARNING BY TEACHING

The single most distinguishing feature of the Institute will be its strict adherence to the values of learning by teaching. Learning by teaching will apply to faculty and students alike. Teaching will be understood as broadly as is conceivable—preschool and adult education as well as elementary, secondary and higher education, and will include such additional teaching activities as tutoring, home teaching, counseling, student and faculty recruitment, program evaluation, service in community agencies, and the like.

"Each one teach one," "start where they are," "paid to learn," "tailor the instruction to each student's individual needs and interests," "learn to teach by teaching," a "community of learners"—these are the phrases that embody the learning by teaching philosophy and will be the watchwords of the Institute.

Thus, the educational style of the Institute will be both professional and collegial. By this it is meant that faculty, students, and the community will regard themselves as professional colleagues jointly engaged in a search for better, more effective solutions to the problems and tasks confronting their profession, a search to which each of them can make a contribution. In this atmosphere, in which faculty, students and the community are joined together in work of common professional concerns, the search itself becomes the educational experience, in contrast to the I-teach-you-learn relationship that pervades traditional education. In this sense, the Institute should be thought of as a center for learning and discovery, as well as a teaching center. It will be difficult to establish this style, because it involves a departure from traditional patterns of instruction which are both attitudinal and structural.

The direct-experience activities conducted under the aegis of the Institute will be innovative and experimental—at the *leading* rather than the *trailing* edges of teacher education. This feature has important implications for the structure of the Institute. The barriers to innovation and experimentation in established colleges and universities are well known. To preserve a priority commitment to innovation, experimentation, and openness, the Institute will control its own policies and intake, although it obviously will need to establish working arrangements with other school, college, and community agencies. But while an autonomous structure is a necessary condition for preserving a priority on innovation, structure in itself is not sufficient to ensure that this priority will be realized. Equally important will be the involvement of the faculty and community representatives— organized into teaching-learning teams, with a particular group of trainees over a long enough period of time, to become known to each other on a first-name basis rather than as Dr. X (professor), Mrs. K (parent), Mr. John (student). The Institute will provide maximum flexibility for the creation, operation, and evaluation of the teams, their educational style, and their goal of learning by teaching.

For each instructional team, released time must be provided for planning, and adequate human, material and capital resources made available. Each team should be a truly cooperative endeavor concerned with the subject matter, the learner, the needs and requirements of the world of work, and it should be actively associated with other educational processes such as counseling, and selection and placement, to ensure against the premature shutting off of student aspirations.

Effective use of instructional teams will require meeting together during summer months and frequently during the school year, working together to evaluate existing conditions, operating as a teaching team for testing new curricula, and will further require freedom to experiment.

The focuses of such instructional teams will be (1) curriculum development, (2) teaching, (3) evaluation, (4) learning, (5) in-service education, and (6) research. The purpose of such activities as would develop from these focuses would be to develop curricula in the several academic areas that would be relevant to the real needs of these students for both continued education and the world of work. Additionally, scholarly participation in such activities would assure relevancy to current knowledge of the particular discipline.

A typical team might consist of (1) Institute instructors, (2) school-community supervisors, (3) students, (4) trainees from other curriculum models and ladders, and (5) consultants from the community, the world of work, and/or other colleges or universities or other disciplines. The use of such consultants should be an intrinsic part of this type of operation. Workshops, instructional clinics, university seminars should also be built into the model. Parents and other members of the community should be consulted and informed, and their ideas, suggestions, or criticisms given full and complete attention before any final decisions are made.

Operational procedures will need to be developed so that the instructional team could engage in activities such as these:

1. Testing of newly developed curricula against
   existing curricula
   research—e.g., learning, sociology, behavior, etc.
   the desires of students and community
   ideas from other areas of the total curriculum
   ideas from other scholars and teachers in the field
   the competencies of the teaching staff and the students.
2. Demonstrations of the curricula in actual classroom teaching-learning.
3. Retesting against both objective and subjective outcomes of the demonstrations.
4. Articulation of the new curricula with other subject matter areas, other levels of schooling, other types of education or training, other situations.
5. Continual reevaluation, revising, and reconstruction of the curricula as
   new research data becomes available
   new data from the use of the curricula becomes available
   the situation changes.

THE CURRICULUM: MODELS AND LADDERS

There will be a number of curriculum ladders and models—1-year models for training tutors and nonprofessionals, 2-year models for associate teachers, 4-year models for intern teachers, 5-year models for master teachers. A trainee may be graduated from a model and seek regular employment on the basis of his training or he may apply for admission to the next advanced model.

In each curriculum model there will be academic and technical training and each will encompass a wide range of different teaching-learning activities and seminars. In the 1-year model, for example, the technical component, will include but not be limited to the following:

1. Skill in tutoring procedures.
2. Understanding the programs of the school and various other community agencies—their goals, methods, timetable, underlying rationale and concepts.
3. Appreciation of low-income culture and sociological views regarding this stratum and its subgroups.
4. Information regarding service-giving procedures.
5. Knowledge regarding the goals of a community approach to service.
6. Interviewing and establishing contact procedures.
7. Reporting methods and record keeping.
8. Conducting meetings and conferences.

Exemplary Schools

Schools used by or developed for the Institute are to be planned and staffed as EXEMPLARY-schools teacher-training, demonstration centers of modern, experimental, open-ended education. Centers will be unique and concentrate on seeking answers to the question: What kind of education is most appropriate for the inner city? Examples of educational thrusts for the exemplary centers would include:

1. Preschools using Montessori approaches to teacher and development. Although educational alternatives including Montessori approaches will be generally available, special attention should be directed toward encounter-type learning and the Initial Teaching Alphabet as related to Montessori early childhood education.

2. Elementary schools geared to artistic creativity in the various art forms. This would be coupled with exposure to all aspects of the visual environment—the development of a sense of the beauty of nature and involving training in natural phenomena: geology, weather, seasons, plant and animal forms and their growth. Special classes in the program would concentrate on creativity, including but not limited to the music, art, dance, and poetry that exist in abundance in all children. Such an unfolding could lead naturally to an intrinsic interest in the "three R's." An artist-teacher resident program could be a part of an exemplary school whereby future art, music, dance, and creative writing teachers would live in and aid in the development of an after-school creative arts program—one that could eventually foster professional artist-in-residence projects whereby well-known artists will move into and become an integral part of the community.

3. Intermediate schools that would develop a multicultural, multimedia, multidimensional, seeing, feeling, "tactile quality," affective approach to learning, building upon the experience and experiments of Project EPOCH in the Berkeley Unified School District.

4. High schools and adult schools that are nongraded and interest based, and that provide work experience programs for *all* students; so organized that academic instruction goes hand-in-hand with practice. Such an occupational-interest-centered school might become completely noncoercive, with an individually-tailored, imaginative curriculum that achieves greater retention power than present nonvoluntary high schools do.

5. Any or all the exemplary schools might have a research-oriented educational laboratory for development and assessment of individualized, experimental learning programs. Among the questions researched might be: How do inner-city children and adults learn best?, What are the most effective curriculums and teaching strategies?, and, What are some paths to integration and assimilation as well as to employment?

DEGREES AND CERTIFICATES

Three degrees will be offered as follows:

A.T. (Assistant Teacher) 2 years
B.T.E. (Bachelor of Teacher Education) 4 years
M.T.E. (Master of Teacher Education) 5 + years

Five credentials will be awarded as follows:

Tutor Certificate (1 year)
Assistant Teacher Certificate (2 years)
Associate Teacher Certificate (3 years)
Intern Teacher Certificate (4 years)
Master Teacher Certificate (5 years and in-service training)

STAFF

The administrative and teaching staff will be selected by the governing board on the basis of their competence, interest, and commitment to teaching, and irrespective of such traditional concepts as degrees and credentials. Thus, the faculty will be drawn from such diverse groups as:

1. Community resource people and parents
2. Business and industry personnel
3. Public and private school administrators and teachers
4. College and university professors
5. Social agency and association personnel.

The ratio of full-time faculty to students will be 1-to-15. This full-time staff will be augmented by a corps of school and social agency personnel indigenous to the community itself, who will provide immediate supervision for the students' "paid to learn" activities on a ratio of one-per-three trainees. Initially, the Institute will enroll 300 trainees, distributed approximately as follows:

200 at levels 1 and 2
30 at level 3
20 at level 4
50 at level 5

LIBRARY AND OTHER INSTRUCTIONAL SERVICES

In each of the training centers to be established on the site of an exemplary school, there will be a professional library, an instructional materials center, and audio-visual and allied equipment.

EVALUATION AND RESEARCH

A major effort will be to rigorously evaluate the over-all project, and an evaluation design, involving both hard and soft data and longitudinal studies, will be developed. Students from nearby colleges and universities, teachers, and others in the community will be given stipends to serve as research fellows to assist in the evaluation and/or to initiate other studies of interest to the Institute.

In addition, it is expected that all direct-experience activities carried on by the Institute will be subject to continuous monitoring and evaluation. Each direct-experience activity will incorporate, as an integral part of its practices, evaluation and follow-up procedures in such a way that it will be possible to make reasonably definitive statements about the effectiveness of all direct-experience activities at the Institute. In this unique way, the Institute can make a continuous and useful contribution to knowledge, and trainees will perceive evaluation, follow-up, and performance criteria as integral components of professional practice, equal in importance and indispensability to study, involvement, and intervention.

PHYSICAL FACILITIES

Use of classrooms within the Hunter's Point-Bayview-Southeast San Francisco area will be mandatory in order to provide for the various forms of supervised teaching activities, seminars, and laboratories for the 300 teacher-candidates. The seminar plan of drawing theory from a core of practical experiences—the heart of the teacher training program—by its very nature, must be conducted in settings with children. This means that classrooms will be needed five days a week, evenings, and Saturdays. Contracts for these facilities will be negotiated with the school district and other community agencies. The headquarters of the Institute will be donated by the community, preferably at Hunter's Point.

HOUSING OF STUDENTS

Students, adults as well as younger people, who may need to live within the greater Hunter's Point-Bayview community may inquire of the Education Committee for a housing list prepared by that committee for such instances. The Education Committee will screen not only prospective applicants wishing to live with a black family, but also those families desiring such residents. After acceptable screening by the Committee, the family will enter into a contract by which that family will be reimbursed for room and board. Such room and board should not exceed $450 a quarter, and the student resident will be asked to contribute a few hours a day of tutoring the children in that family.

THE IN-SERVICE PROGRAM

A variety of in-service educational programs, comprised of meaningful seminars and laboratory experiences, will be created for teachers and administrators especially those employed in the Southeast San Francisco area. The program will be designed to provide them with an accurate, in-depth and comprehensive knowledge base pertaining to minority group cultures and will examine the dynamics underlying the involvement of teachers, parents, and the community power structure. The major emphasis would be to aid teachers in relating more effectively not only to the youngsters in their charge but to the inner city population as a whole. Such an in-service program might focus on such issues as:

1. Developing in teachers a greater sensitivity in terms of the multicultural reality of American life and history, including minority group viewpoints.
2. Aiding teachers in developing personal sets of strategies involving curricular and methodological innovations.
3. Providing them with a resource pool of community leaders for future reference and use in the education of the culturally different.

GRADUATE EDUCATION

A 1-year graduate training program will be offered leading to the M.T.E. degree. Two such programs might be initiated: the first program could be the graduate internship teacher preparation curriculum, the second program could be for teachers and administrators in service who wish to become teachers-of-teachers. The same essential characteristics governing the undergraduate curriculum will be features of the M.T.E. degree.

INNOVATIVE FEATURES

While the entire notion of an EPI is in itself innovative, other features in the presently-proposed blueprint include:

1. Control by the black community.
2. Advocacy approach to educational issues.
3. Recruitment of inner city parents and hard-core dropouts and training them "where they are."
4. Exclusive focus on inner city teacher preparation.
5. Full implementation of the learning by teaching philosophy.
6. A "paid to learn," theory-practice integrated, team-teaching curriculum.
7. Establishment of exemplary schools as the heart of the professional education training.
8. Development and use of performance criteria as the basis of student evaluation.
9. Rigorous, "hard data" assessment and evaluation of a 5-year experimental, open-ended educational experience.

VII. The Past

A merica's history is one of the most interesting stories in modern civilization; it is also an account of undeniable world import. In a relatively short time, events have catapulted the United States into a position of world leadership. Over the years, the American people have endured hardships and sacrificed a great deal in an effort to make their country the outstanding example of democracy. Battles have been waged and won in legislative halls; in courts; in classrooms; in the behavioral sciences, the natural and social sciences, and the humanities; and on the battlefields. Those struggles made American society one that all of its citizens can be proud. Yet, despite the fact that our scientific advancements have made this nation the first to land human beings on the moon, there remains much to do on planet Earth before some of the great social problems are solved. And education's role in man's efforts to solve these problems will undoubtedly be a prominent one.

The history of American education is one of the great epics of modern civilization. As the country has grown from the colonies on the eastern seaboard to the fifty-state nation extending from the Atlantic to the Pacific and beyond, public education has striven to keep pace with the expanding and increasingly complex culture. Education today, as it has done throughout the country's history, is not basking in reflected glory, but is doing its utmost, oftentimes under extremely adverse conditions, to keep abreast of a changing America.

This part focuses on the current American educational scene, touching only briefly on the forces and personalities in Europe that have affected its history and paying only scant attention to comparative education today. To begin the chronological survey of the history of education in this country, we present a portion of an extremely well-written but brief study by S. Samuel Shermis. The complete selection appears in the book *The Pursuit of Excellence: Introductory Readings in Education,* by Donald C. Orlich and Mr. Shermis. Stressing the history of American education since colonial times, this excerpt presents many of the problems educators have faced and, in some instances, solved since the nation's beginnings, and concludes that every social problem that arises in this country also becomes an educational problem with which the schools must wrestle.

All students of American educational history are acquainted with Noah Webster—at least they have heard of or read about his famous "Blue-Backed Speller." Besides promoting American literature and nationalism, Webster had other reasons for writing his *A Grammatical Institute of the English Language, Part I,* published in 1783. In the second article in this section, Michael V. Belok reveals some of the objectives of Webster and other early textbook writers that history of education students have probably not considered.

Leonard A. Wenz, in his selection on Horace Mann, presents some of the important events during the career of the man who was probably the most important figure in the field of education during the early years of the nation. The article describes many of Mann's contributions to education in the Commonwealth of Massachusetts which eventually were used to improve schools throughout the United States.

Carleton W. Washburne, one of the great innovators in American education, died late in 1968. The February, 1969, edition of *Phi Delta Kappan,* the journal of the professional fraternity for men in education, was dedicated to his memory; in that edition, Harold G. Shane, a professor of education at Indiana University who succeeded Washburne as Superintendent of Schools in Winnetka, Illinois, in 1946, wrote a dedication in which the educational milestones in Washburne's life are described. That article is included in this part.

In education, as in other professions, it is well to study the past so that practitioners may have a better understanding and appreciation of how the profession arrived at its present place in time. Perhaps they can avoid some of the errors of the past as they attempt to provide outstanding educational programs for future citizens. It is well, also, to project a bit into the future to see where the profession is headed. This is done in the final contribution by Robert A. Pittillo.

44. A Brief Study of American Education

S. Samuel Shermis

Colonial Education

On the West Gateway at Harvard University there is a tablet that contains the following poignant phrase:

> AFTER GOD HAD CARRIED VS SAFE TO NEW ENGLAND
> AND WEE HAD BVILDED OVR HOVSES
> PROVIDED NECESSARIES FOR OVR LIVELI HOOD
> REARD CONVENIENT PLACES FOR GODS WORSHIP
> AND SETLED THE CIVILL GOVERNMENT
> ONE OF THE NEXT THINGS WE LONGED FOR
> AND LOOKED AFTER WAS TO ADVANCE LEARNING
> AND PERPETVATE IT TO POSTERITY
> DREADING TO LEAVE AN ILLITERATE MINISTERY
> TO THE CHVRCHES WHEN OVR PRESENT MINISTERS
> SHALL LIE IN THE DVST.
> NEW ENGLANDS FIRST FRVITS

When the infant colony was on fairly solid footing—with some towns established, agricultural techniques learned, and most towns prosperous— the New Englanders turned their attention and energy to creating an educational system. Oddly enough, the first educational institution to be established was a college—Harvard College, later to become Harvard University. A "worthy man," John Harvard, left a bequest for the college of about 260 volumes and £850, to which the Massachusetts legislature added, in 1636, another £400. Two years later Harvard, the first institu-

SOURCE: Donald C. Orlich and S. Samuel Shermis, *The Pursuit of Excellence: Introductory Readings in Education* (New York: American Book Company, 1969), pp. 13–45. Copyright © 1965 by Litton Educational Publishers Inc., by permission of Van Nostrand Reinhold Company.

tion of higher learning in our country, was built. At first, as might be expected, Harvard (and later Yale, Columbia, and the other "Ivy League" colleges) specialized in producing ministers to supply the Christian faith with religious leaders.

In the decade of the 1640's, the New Englanders turned their attention to elementary education. The "Massachusetts Law of 1642" and the famous "Olde Deluder Satan Act" of 1647 were the first two pieces of legislation affecting education. Prefacing the Old Deluder Satan Act with the wish "that learning may not be buried in the grave of our fathers," the New England stewards created the beginnings of what was to become the American public-school system. The act required towns with a population of at least 50 families to establish a reading-and-writing, or elementary, school, and towns of at least 100 families to provide for grammar schools. Although the act was not always obeyed, as evidenced by the number of communities that had to be fined to require obedience, New England had a "public" school system. The early "public" schools, however, were essentially publicly supported parochial schools.

Although the very limited curriculum, the uncomfortable classrooms, and the frequently untrained schoolmasters were not impressive, this kind of educational apparatus did fulfill its major cultural imperative: it educated for godliness. New England colonists operated under the Calvinist assumption that man was inherently wicked: human nature was perverse, corrupt, and evil. This corruption, of course, was the result of the sin and casting out of Adam and Eve from the Garden of Eden. Because of Adam's primal sin, man was forever doomed to be a sin-ridden, perverted creature. And because of this, education was essential.

Education was an attempt to redirect man's wicked impulses. By being saturated with religion and godliness, by memorizing the cardinal rules of virtue (recall the ancient Hebrew child memorizing sections of the Torah), the young colonial child would at least have a chance to redirect his naturally wicked ways. Therefore the New England curriculum was basically religious, the discipline was religiously motivated, and the aim of education was religious.

The child, who may have attended a dame school, a nursery school conducted usually by an old widow, learned his ABC's. He then memorized a few hymns and learned some Biblical poetry and, of course, the basic postulates of Calvinism. Here, for example, are some rhymes by which children learn their alphabet:

> A   In *Adam's* fall
>   We Sinned all.
> Z   Zaccheus he
>   Did climb the tree
>   His Lord to see.

Below is a portion of Westminster Catechism, taken from the *New England Primer,* one of the most frequently used textbooks in colonial New England:

Q. What is the chief End of Man?
A. Man's chief End is to glorify God and enjoy Him forever.
Q. What Rule hath God given to direct us how we may glorify and enjoy Him?
A. The word of God which is contained in the Scriptures of the Old and New Testament, Is the only rule to direct us how we may glorify and enjoy Him.

These phrases, prayers, hymns, and catechetical texts were memorized, were used as examples of writing, and were the subjects for innumerable sermons. The aim of this type of education, combined with strict laws, stern discipline, and harsh punishment for transgressors, was to redirect the child's naturally bad human nature, with salvation as the ultimate goal. It meant that education, as an inseparable part of religion, became an absolutely necessary part of the culture. Although the twentieth century has moved rather far from the Puritan seventeenth century, education is still conceived to be something all men need.

It was only in New England that "public" education achieved great significance. By and large, education in the Middle Colonies was essentially parochial. Education was generally controlled by the dominant religion in the area, and since there were so many different religions in the Middle Colonies, there were many different patterns of education.

In the South the situation was somewhat different. Instead of either public education (and in the seventeenth and eighteenth centuries "public" meant education provided by and for the local township) or parochial education, the South provided either private education or pauper education. Of course, there was some public education and some parochial education, but neither was characteristic of the South as a whole. Those Southern families who could afford it tended to employ private tutors to teach their children the "Three R's" and those subjects appropriate for an elite class —art, dancing, music, and the like. There was pauper education provided by such organizations as the Society for the Propagation of the Gospel in Foreign Parts. A missionary would teach children of the poor their letters and some hymns and prayers. The schoolhouse was often an abandoned building on a worn-out piece of land; hence, you may find the pauper education of this era referred to as "old field schools."

There was almost no education provided for Negroes. Indeed, in the South it eventually became a serious crime to teach Negroes to read. In South Carolina in the eighteenth century a fine of 100 pounds could be levied against a person for teaching a Negro to read. In Massachusetts at the same time an entire city would be fined 5 pounds for not establishing a school!

After the founding of Harvard in 1636 by the Puritans, other religious sects soon founded their own colleges. Today the Ivy League (Harvard, Yale, University of Pennsylvania, Princeton, Columbia, Dartmouth, Brown, and Cornell) is composed mainly of these early American institutions. These are still in operation today and are still among the leaders in the field of higher education.

In the eighteenth and nineteenth centuries all American colleges were, in some sense, church-oriented—that is, church-affiliated or church-directed. Whether the colleges were founded solely for the purpose of perpetuating the faith or whether they had a wider aim, their orientation was toward a particular denomination. In a recent study of American colleges and universities, Frederick Rudolph points out that, although the direction of colonial American colleges was religious, there was still a good deal of diversity in the structure and curricula of higher education. The denominational rivalry encouraged "toleration," but this rivalry was detrimental to the higher-education movement in colonial America.[1]

The curriculum of the colonial American college was both religious and classical. It attempted first of all to inculcate the dogmas and religious beliefs of a particular denomination. Otherwise, the curriculum generally was restricted to a study of the Greek and Latin classics. As in its European counterpart of a few centuries earlier, much of the learning was verbal, centering around debate, rhetoric, and disputation.

Colonial colleges, unlike present-day colleges and universities, were aristocratic by tradition, and they were designed to serve the aristocratic elements of colonial society. However, this aristocracy was continuously being subjected to "American" conditions, which tended to modify it.[2]

The classical curriculum and the emphasis on verbal acquisition contributed to a sterility of the colonial and the eighteenth- and nineteenth-century college so marked that it has led both Messerli and Rudolph to attribute any effectiveness of the college to either extra-curricular or noncollege factors.[3]

Therefore, if we wish to understand the chief significance of colonial ed-

---

[1] *The American College and University* (New York: Knopf, 1962), p. 18.

[2] *Ibid.*, p. 19.

[3] In an account of the college life of Horace Mann, often called the "father of American public education," Jonathan C. Messerli says, "If one is to judge from Horace Mann's own account, the period of 1816 to 1819 which he spent at Brown University had little significance as preparation for his future educational work." See Jonathan C. Messerli, "Horace Mann at Brown," *Harvard Educational Review,* 33 (Summer, 1963): 285. Rudolph says, "In the extracurriculum the college student stated his case for the human mind, the human personality, and the human body, for all aspects of man that the colleges tended to ignore in their single-minded interest in the salvation of souls." See Rudolph, *American College,* p. 155.

ucation as a force in shaping the destiny of this country, we must concentrate on the embryonic public schools of New England.

The Period of Innovation and Consolidation

One cannot date precisely the period of American educational innovation. In a sense, the period began when colonists landed on our shores. As noted in the previous section, early American education was extremely restricted, guided by religious ideals, and not genuinely "democratic"; much change was necessary before American education could be characterized as "democratic."

The changes that came about during the nineteenth century were the result of a number of forces:

1. The increasingly democratic nature of other American political and social institutions, particularly those associated with Jacksonian democracy in the midnineteenth century.
2. The arrival of a torrent of European immigrants who needed to be rapidly enculturated
3. The increase in industrialism, which demanded a much higher level of literacy skills.
4. Related to the above, an increased urban population. City life is inherently more complex than rural and requires more skills to provide for the interdependence growing out of the need for sanitary facilities, judicial institutions, specialized occupations, and greater social interaction.
5. The growing sensitivity of the Americans. Eventually, education was viewed as something that went beyond individual or state concern. Education was considered a necessity that society should guarantee to everyone.
6. The importation of rather unique educational theories. The views of Jean Jacques Rousseau, an eighteenth-century French writer and philosopher, generated a great number of later educational philosophies, including those of Johann Heinrich Pestalozzi and Friedrich Froebel. The practical effect of their writings was to make education in general considerably more pleasant and effective.

Let us discuss each of these factors in some detail:

1. *The increasingly democratic nature of American political and social institutions.* "Democracy" means, in part, self-government. That is, the people as a collective body make those decisions that affect them. In a monarchy or an aristocracy an individual (the monarch) or a group of individuals (the aristocracy) makes the important decisions. In a democracy individuals rule themselves, either directly or through elected representa-

tives. Much of colonial America of the seventeenth century was a kind of theocracy [4] ruled by Puritans or patricians.

As democratic beliefs and institutions spread, the notion that the people were capable of ruling themselves also spread, as did awareness of the need for education. Decision-making on the part of the people meant that they would need the facts and information to make decisions; it also meant that the people would need to know how to obtain information. Thus a need for information created a simultaneous need for literacy, and the people realized that increased literacy was a prerequisite for democracy. Little by little the "common" school arose—that is, a school for the children of the common man. By the middle of the nineteenth century, most Americans believed that elementary-school education was a necessity.

2. *The arrival of immigrants.* The characteristics of the mass immigration from Europe changed considerably in the nineteenth century. Instead of drawing almost exclusively from England and Germany, America began to draw immigrants from southern and eastern Europe. Famines, repressive governments, the desire for religious freedom and, most important, a hunger for land vastly increased immigration to this country during the nineteenth and early part of the twentieth century. Italians, Russians, Lithuanians, Yugoslavs, Irish, Chinese, and people of many other nationalities arrived by the hundreds of thousands and, between the Civil War and 1920, by the millions!

As we already noted, it is essential for the young, immature person to develop and become a part of the society in which he lives. For the immigrant a similar process—acculturation—must take place. To become acculturated means to learn the ways of a culture that is not your native culture. The torrent of immigrants had to learn a new language, a new monetary system, a new set of attitudes toward government—in general, they had to remake their lives.

It was the task of our educational system to turn the newly arrived immigrants into Americans. Schools, principally in large cities, received the immigrant children,[5] although many immigrants settled in farm areas—as the Germans did in the Dakotas. By and large, the schools succeeded in their task of acculturation. They succeeded in providing the immigrant child with literacy skills, promoted certain democratic attitudes, inculcated the American ideal of upward social mobility and, in many cases, taught immigrants occupational skills. The last point is most important, for many

---

[4] A "theocracy" is a government in which an elect few, who claim to represent the divine will, rule in the name of God.

[5] And adults, too. Adult education played an extremely important part in the acculturation of the new immigrants. For a humorous and sympathetic portrayal of an immigrant striving to become Americanized, see Leonard Q. Ross (pseudonym for Leo C. Rosten), *The Education of H*Y*M*A*N K*A*P*L*A*N* (New York: Harcourt, Brace, 1937).

European immigrants came to this country with skills that were either inappropriate or unwanted in the United States. Manual-arts schools and polytechnical institutions, particularly in the East, imparted occupational skills that were more useful in a society becoming industrialized.

3. *Increase in industrialism.* By the third or fourth decade of the nineteenth century, New England had become industrialized, while the South relied on cotton as its economic mainstay. The Civil War provided a tremendous impetus to industry both in New England and in the Middle States. By the end of the nineteenth century and the beginning of the twentieth century, the United States had charted its course as an industrial nation. Our country experienced a need for trained financial experts, as well as for manufacturing experts. Banking, investments, merchandising, and import-export businesses also thrived in the industrial age.

An increased need for trained workers and highly educated professionals developed. Little by little the semiliterate factory worker and the uneducated ranch hand began to pass from the scene. Individuals needed to possess computational and literacy skills far in advance of what had been needed in, say, 1800. Therefore, both secondary schools and institutions of higher education were given the job of seeing to it that a growing, technological culture would have sufficient numbers of adequately trained workers. The character of both secondary schools and colleges changed drastically during the late nineteenth century. The academy and the liberal-arts college of the early nineteenth century, designed to develop a genteel, elite class, began to decline in relative importance, although there are still many such schools, especially in the East and South. The comprehensive high school, originating in 1821 in New England, became more important than the private academy. After 1863, land-grant colleges and universities sprang up by the dozen.[6] Their objective, in addition to the perpetuation of the liberal arts, was to create trained professionals—physicians, attorneys, and scientists. They also had to create scientific agriculturists, journalists, teachers, businessmen, and a host of needed professional specialists. Hence expanding American industrialism created a pressing need for a highly skilled and literate populace.

4. *Increase in urban life.* The nineteenth century saw the beginning of the flow toward the cities. Better jobs, a more comfortable way of life, and (less strongly) a higher level of culture (art, music, drama, and lectures) were some of the many attractions that lured people away from the farms and into the cities and suburbs. It has been estimated that during the Revolutionary War in 1776 about 90 percent of the population lived on farms. Present-day statistics indicate that about 70 percent of the American peo-

[6] See Oliver C. Carmichael, "A Hundred Years of the Land-Grant Movement," *Saturday Review,* 45 (April 21, 1962): 58–59, 71–72 (which is reprinted in this section), for an interesting account of land-grant colleges and their impact on American higher education.

ple live in either cities, towns, or suburbs. We are no longer basically an agrarian nation.

To accommodate itself to an inherently more complex way of life, education underwent both quantitative and qualitative changes. In place of only the "Three R's," schools began to offer a much wider curriculum. In place of insisting on education for a rather limited number of children, Americans began to take it for granted that any normal child should receive schooling. And in the twentieth century even subnormal children are expected to receive some kind of education or training. For a person to be able to work, vote intelligently, buy insurance, choose a home or a car, talk about national or international events, deal with questions of fire and police protection, understand something of the art, literature, and music that surround him—in other words, for all of the complex skills involved in city life—a more sophisticated and a wider level of education was needed. The twentieth century has seen constant debate as to just what *kind* of education this is to be, but most persons take it for granted that their children will be educated. The debate is now over means—how it is to be accomplished.

The impact of what is known as "mass media" has been huge. In the nineteenth century, books, magazines, journals, and newspapers created a considerable cultural need for increased literacy. The twentieth century has added radio, movies, and television. Communications media in both centuries have interacted with our culture: they have required increased literacy skills to be understood, and they have increased the desire for literacy.

5. *The growing sensitivity of the American people.* The nineteenth century saw a uniquely American phenomenon: the growth of a tremendous faith in education. No matter how he defines education, almost everyone agrees that education is desirable. Education makes "something" out of a person that he would not be without it. What that "something" is has not been completely clear. But as Americans have viewed their goals, education has been seen as that which fulfills a person and that which helps an individual develop his potentialities. Aside from the fact that a formal education opens up occupational vistas, many, if not most, Americans seem to feel that the more formal education a person has, the better he is.[7]

---

[7] Though this belief is widely held, the opposite belief is also entertained by many: education is often seen as a kind of frill that one does not need. Many people can be heard to say something like, "No, I didn't have much formal education, and perhaps I would have gone further with more. But I have not done badly as it is. I learned in the school of hard knocks; I learned by experience. In fact, I would say that the kinds of experiences I have had have done more for me than college has for many of the college-educated kids I hire." This position may well be the minority viewpoint, but it clearly exists as an alternative. It appears to reflect an older belief that if an individual is good, if he has the capacity, he will develop without an education. The extreme position is that formal education may well be a handicap to one's development. Remember that many preachers are "called" to

Americans have had a good deal of faith in education. The more widespread this faith became, the more it created a demand for elementary, secondary, and higher education.

6. *Importation of European educational theories of the eighteenth and nineteenth centuries.* In the eighteenth century, Rousseau devised a revolutionary educational theory. In brief, Rousseau believed that education ought to be pleasant and "natural." He assailed those schoolmasters who drove their lessons in with the cane, ruler, and switch. Disparaging memorization of unrelated and obscure concepts, Rousseau believed that the young child ought to be given an education that followed both his "real" human nature and natural laws. Rousseau's writings, especially his book *Émile,* had considerable influence on Europeans during his lifetime, but their real impact came after his death in 1778.

A somewhat eccentric Swiss schoolteacher named Heinrich Pestalozzi attempted to put Rousseau's theories into action. He opened several orphanage schools and attempted to teach young waifs to read and write, to learn a useful occupation, and to appreciate the wonders of nature. Of course, he had to modify Rousseau's ideas considerably, for Rousseau was not a schoolteacher; he was a theorist whose writings were imaginative and insightful but whose views were quite impossible to implement. Pestalozzi's theories came to this country in various ways.[8] They became known as "objective teaching," and soon enthusiastic disciples of Pestalozzi's methods were teaching his principles at normal schools and teacher-training institutions throughout the country.

Other European educational theorists included Joseph Lancaster and his so-called Lancasterian system, a monitorial method in which the brighter and more advanced child taught platoons of other children; Friedrich Froebel, a disciple of Rousseau and Pestalozzi who developed many theories and methods of childhood education; and Johann Friedrich Herbart, another German, who attempted to make a science of education.

By the end of the nineteenth century disciples of Pestalozzi, Rousseau, Froebel, Herbart, and other European educational theorists had brought their theories and methods to this country. The effect was to revolutionize American education. Teacher-training institutions began to teach educational sociology, psychology, and philosophy. Courses in methods, curriculum, and administration were added. In the twentieth century education courses have been combined with a liberal-arts curriculum. In essence, in America—and, of course, in Europe—there began to develop the idea

---

preach the word of God—without formal seminary training. And it is often held erroneously that a good teacher is "born," not "made," and really does not need formal training.

[8] For a recent excellent discussion of Pestalozzi, see Charles Brauner, *American Educational Theory* (Englewood Cliffs: Prentice-Hall, 1964), especially Ch. 3, "Feeling as a Basis for Thought: Object Teaching."

that education is a complex undertaking that requires specially educated and intelligent practitioners. The American people have very, very slowly realized that truly good education also requires libraries, laboratories, teaching materials, and adequate classrooms.

The higher the level of educational aspiration, the more essential education became. The more education was viewed as essential, the more widespread educational institutions became.

The Mold Is Formed—the Development and Growth of Institutions

By the beginning of the twentieth century, American educational institutions were established and formed. With two exceptions—the junior high school and the junior college—the major American educational institutions with which we are all familiar developed in the seventeenth, eighteenth, and nineteenth centuries. Let us review the kinds of educational institutions that have developed in the United States.

In the first place, common schools were created for all of the children of all the people.[9] In part, through the efforts of Horace Mann and Frederick Barnard, public schools became part of what is loosely but with great conviction called "the American way of life." In the first half of the nineteenth century, education passed from either private or parochial hands and became a more public institution. By the time of the Civil War, most Americans expected a "common school"—that is, an elementary-school—education for their children.

Secondary schools developed from the academies of the eighteenth century. Benjamin Franklin's educational dream of a secondary school that would meet the practical needs of the American people resulted in the academy, whose heyday was from 1750 to 1820. The academy was an improvement over the Latin grammar school in at least two respects: it expanded the curriculum to include modern languages, science, and commercial and vocational subjects; and it considered girls as being educable. (The last point is most significant, for Western civilization has not, by and large, considered girls to be the equal of boys.)

In 1821 a high school was opened in Boston, and during the next fifty years the high school grew rather slowly.[10] In 1872 an important legal decision arising out of the famous Kalamazoo case made it possible for cities

---

[9] This is the claim, and it is generally true. But we must not lose sight of the fact that the formal education of Negroes and girls is a fairly recent phenomenon.

[10] Why the name "high school" was chosen is not clear. There is a German word, *Hochschule,* which does not mean high school; it has the designation of "higher education." An ambitious graduate student might find a doctoral dissertation in research on the origin of the name "high school."

to levy taxes to support public secondary schools. After this decision by the Supreme Court in Michigan, the number of high schools began to increase rapidly. The comprehensive high school, which offers three types of curricula—college preparatory, terminal, and vocational—is considered by some to be the crowning glory of America. By the end of the nineteenth century, the high school was an important institution.

America has had colleges since 1636. These institutions were exclusively undergraduate, liberal-arts institutions. The midnineteenth century saw the creation of the university, a grouping of colleges and professional schools. A typical university has an undergraduate college of liberal arts, a graduate school, and various professional schools, including law, education, medicine, engineering, nursing, and religion. Some institutions of higher education are noted for their concentration on some particular subject. For example, in California, Fresno State College and the University of California at Davis offer intensive specialized training in agriculture; Eastman Conservatory at Rochester, New York, provides advanced training in music.

In 1875 Daniel Coit Gilman established what was to be the first true graduate school in the United States. His institution, Johns Hopkins, provided for education beyond the B.A. degree. Previously, Americans who wished an M.A. or Ph.D. degree had to attend a European university, frequently German. By the end of the nineteenth century, American graduate schools were attracting graduate students who otherwise would have gone to Europe for their advanced degrees.[11]

Specialized institutions of higher education and specialized secondary schools also arose in the nineteenth century. Secondary schools for future machinists, dressmakers, electricians, and so on developed in large Eastern cities. Colleges of agriculture, engineering, and forestry also arose at this time. The status of these schools remains somewhat ambiguous. While they fill a real need, many would question their classification as truly educational institutions. Be that as it may, they are a part of the entire system of American education and are likely to continue as such for a long time to come.

Night schools—college extension and adult schools—as previously indicated, increased greatly during the nineteenth century. Night schools and adult schools had a variety of purposes, ranging from basic literacy and citizenship training to training in hobbies, continuation school, vocational training, and even college course work. In the nineteenth century, colleges and universities began offering courses to people who could not go to the colleges. Instructors went to the villages and towns of rural America to

[11] For a good short summary of graduate schools, see the chapter entitled "Long-Range Forces That Have Shaped Doctoral Work," in Ernest V. Hollis, *Toward Improving Ph.D. Programs* (Washington, D.C.: American Council on Education, 1945).

teach the latest and most efficient methods of canning, planting, sewing, insect control, and the like. The twentieth century has seen a continuation and expansion of these activities. Many teachers drive long distances in an evening to teach extension classes in communities far from the home institution.

Negro education developed only after the Civil War. Although it was still a crime in several Southern states to educate a Negro, the ending of the Civil War saw a tremendous rush on the part of Negroes to learn to read and write. Many missionary-type educators from the North went to the South to open schools for Negro children and adults. Soon formal educational institutions for Negroes arose, such as the vocational institutes established by Booker T. Washington. By and large, Negro education centered around providing basic literacy and training in skilled occupations.[12] In part because of segregation and discrimination, few colleges and professional or graduate schools for Negroes arose in the nineteenth century. However, a few Negro colleges and universities, such as Howard, Tuft, and Dillard, did offer an opportunity for Negroes to obtain a higher education. In the 1950's and 1960's there has been a vigorous attempt on the part of Negroes to obtain integrated education, and elementary schools, high schools, and universities have very slowly opened their back gates to Negro students.

Education for women was another ideal promulgated during the nineteenth century in this country. As we noted, in Western civilization girls and women were long considered incapable of benefiting from formal education; their education was usually of the homemaking-vocational type. But institutions called "female academies" first opened their doors in the nineteenth century. In addition to the usual academic work, these academies attempted to provide upper-class polish for girls, who were instructed in foreign language, some art, music, fancy crocheting, and the other "polite arts."

Beginning with Oberlin College in Ohio in 1838, American colleges began to offer higher education to women. In both the nineteenth and twentieth centuries, colleges established exclusively for women provided an excellent education for the "bright, rich, and beautiful" girls of upper-middle- and upper-class American families. Some of the more famous women's colleges are Mt. Holyoke, Smith, Vassar, Radcliffe, Sarah Lawrence, and Bennington.

Eventually most colleges and universities and many professional schools

[12] For an interesting treatment of Negro education, see the *History of Education Journal,* 7 (Summer, 1957). There are two articles of considerable importance: "Forty Acres and a Mule and a Speller," by Edgar B. Wesley, discusses Negro education in general after the Civil War. "The Washington-DuBois Controversy and Its Effect on the Negro Problem," by C. Spencer Poxpey, deals with the long controversy between two Negro leaders, Booker T. Washington and W. E. B. DuBois.

opened their doors to young women, and soon the "co-ed" became accepted in higher education. However, a new set of problems has been created, centering around the question of what should be done by the college-educated woman who rears a family and makes no *use* of her formal training. One investigator has found a high incidence of emotional disorders among college-educated women and has suggested that the whole problem reflects a general cultural dilemma: How we can utilize the hard-won skills of the college-educated woman in a culture in which the dream-desire of woman is to be wives and mothers.[13]

To summarize: By 1900 the United States had developed most of the educational institutions we have today. Established and consolidated between 1870 and 1900 were elementary schools open to all, secondary schools, institutions of higher education, schools for Negroes and for women, specialized vocational educational facilities, graduate schools, teacher-education institutions, and a wide variety of adult-education facilities.

A Prelude and Two Revolutions

That tremendous educational progress took place in the nineteenth century is undeniable. That most or even many Americans were completely satisfied with the quantity and quality of schooling their children received, however, does not necessarily follow. As the nineteenth century closed, both the amount and the bitterness of criticism leveled at educational institutions increased.

Why were Americans critical of their schools? What did they find wrong? What kind of education did they want? In a recent book Lawrence Cremin discusses both the reasons for American dissatisfaction and the revolution that took place in the opening decades of the twentieth century.[14] The reader must remember that the decade of the 1890's and the first ten or fifteen years of the twentieth century were also periods of dissatisfaction with many other American institutions. The "muckrakers" wrote and lectured on every conceivable kind of evil, from the savage tactics used by the "robber barons" to build empires in the industrial and business world to impurities in food and drugs, from crime and poverty in the cities to the inadequacies of the medical profession.[15]

---

[13] For a sympathetic discussion of this problem, see Betty Friedan, *The Feminine Mystique* (New York: Norton, 1963).

[14] *The Transformation of the American School* (New York: Knopf, 1962).

[15] See Ida Tarbell's *History of Standard Oil Company,* Upton Sinclair's *The Jungle,* Lincoln Steffens' *The Shame of Our Cities,* Gustavus Myers' *History of Great American Fortunes,* Jacob Riis's *How the Other Half Lives,* John Spargo's *The Bitter Cry of the Children,* Frank Norris's *The Pit,* and George Kibbe Turner's

The period between the Civil War and the early twentieth century saw the rise of almost unrestricted capitalism. The cities were growing much faster than facilities could be devised to take care of the many immigrants and native Americans who wished to live there. One could go on at great length describing both the social problems and the critics and reformers of this era. Suffice it to say that in every aspect of our social life pressing social problems arose to demand attention, and there was no lack of editors, writers, lecturers, novelists, social workers, and other critics to expose these problems to the American people and to suggest solutions.

One of the first educational critics to attract considerable attention was a physician, Joseph Rice. Becoming interested in what went on in classrooms, Rice traveled and observed many schools. What he saw horrified him. Classes were tremendously overcrowded. Desks were bolted down in rows and students sat in them, woodenly repeating what they had memorized. Corrupt political influence sent the incompetent niece of the local politician to teach school. Administrators who ruled like autocratic tyrants over their cowed teachers were common. The teachers themselves were disorganized, poorly trained, and ineffective. The school buildings were frequently unsanitary and dilapidated. The curriculum, teaching methods, textbooks, and facilities were outdated and ineffective. A continuing problem was the constant use of corporal punishment. Students of both sexes were beaten, flogged, whipped, and switched. Some were made to stand in uncomfortable positions for hours. It seemed to Dr. Rice that sadism and cruelty were dominant elements in American schools.[16]

In both the country and the city these conditions resulted in a high mortality rate. Many students, finding nothing of value in their classes, simply dropped out of school and went to work. (The concern about "dropouts" is by no means of recent origin. American schools have always had a dropout problem. The recent publicity probably means that we are becoming more aware of it!) Most frequently it was the children of the poor, the immigrant, the racial minority who cut their education short. This made it painfully obvious to Rice and others that our schools were far from democratic and were actually being operated by and for a rather limited segment of our population. The charge (and documentation) that schools operate under this bias has been made so often since the 1890's that it is no longer capable of arousing shock. However, when Rice, Kilpat-

---

Daughters of the Poor. For a discussion of the "muckrakers" and other reform movements, see Samuel Eliot Morison and Henry Steele Commager, *The Growth of the American Republic* (5th ed.; New York: Oxford U. Press, 1962), II, Ch. 16, "The Progressive Movement, 1890–1917," pp. 440-475.

[16] See James P. Jewett, "The Fight Against Corporal Punishment in American Schools," *History of Education Journal*, 5 (Autumn, 1958): 1–10; and Paul Nash, "Corporal Punishment in an Age of Violence," *Educational Theory*, 13 (October, 1963): 295.

rick, Dewey, Lynd, and other educational critics brought this to the attention of the American people four, five, and six decades ago, it did arouse shock and resentment. How could schools, it was asked, which were supposed to be dedicated to the democratization of all the people, be so fundamentally undemocratic?

The undemocratic character of schools revealed itself in both the curriculum and the teaching methods. After "mastering" the basics, the "Three R's," students would presumably go on to more advanced learning. This learning, though it sometimes included geography, science, art, and music, most often tended to center around the classics, ancient history, mathematics, foreign languages, and literature. These subjects, hallowed by the years, were defended as excellent means of disciplining one's mind.[17] That subject matter could be intrinsically interesting or that it could have application in any practical sense was not widely believed. Without knowing basically what the classics meant, both teachers and those laymen who approved of the classics tended to see them as necessary.

The necessity of a secondary-school curriculum based on the classics seemed, to many, to be but a poor rationalization for an educational system designed exclusively for an elite, ruling class (held in disrepute in this nation). Historically such a curriculum had indeed been designed for a ruling class in Europe, and to many it was outmoded. Defenders of the classics replied that the very fact that a classical curriculum was ancient was sufficient reason to retain it: it must have had some value, or it would not have been kept for so many centuries.

Whatever the "ultimate" truth of either argument, the fact remained that the classical curriculum did indeed have little appeal to the sons and daughters of bricklayers, factory workers, farmers, and other members of the working class. Why, they asked frequently and with bitterness, could schools not teach something that was useful, helpful, and practical?[18] Thus little by little there arose an increased demand for vocational subjects and a curriculum that would, somehow, be useful to students.

In brief, American education (then as now) was under heavy attack for offering outdated curricula, employing obsolescent and often unreadable textbooks, being influenced by corrupt politicians, utilizing incompetent and poorly trained teachers, and making almost sadistic use of corporal

---

[17] See the essay "Influences on the Curriculum: Theories of Mind" in this text.

[18] The entire argument is difficult to assess, even a half century later. First, the same argument—should schools offer "practical" curricula or should studies be designed to "train the mind" for a later time—is by no means dead. Second, with few exceptions, no one had even the foggiest notion just what subjects could be considered "practical"; in fact, the term "practical" is extremely difficult to define. Third, the entire argument involves the traditional American distaste for theoretical, abstract, or intellectual subjects, and different people use the same argument with very different underlying assumptions or reasons.

punishment. The entire school, from the classical curriculum to the tyrannical administrator, seemed an island of antidemocratic practices in a land supposedly democratic. Finally, learning often was entirely a matter of rote memorization, with things repeated and completely misunderstood by or having little meaning for most students. These were the accusations; how accurate they were is difficult to say. That they were partially valid is undoubtedly true. That they represented a completely accurate picture of the schools might be doubted: those who are trying to reform a situation invariably both exaggerate the evil of the status quo and tend to overlook any virtues that exist.

No institution in this country, particularly one so close to the people as the schools, can long remain indifferent to widespread criticism. Almost immediately, reform elements began to attempt solutions.[19] The reform movement followed a variety of paths. Parents of school-age youngsters grouped together to find out just what was happening to their children's classrooms. States passed laws to establish at least minimal standards for teachers. Commissions of inquiry sought to discover more about education at all levels. But perhaps the most important reform was made by educators themselves—the creation of a kind of educative method known as "Progressive Education."

Though the battle over whether our schools should adopt the program proposed by those known as Progressive Educators has passed, the phrase "Progressive Education" is still a fighting word to many. To some, Progressive Education was a profoundly humanitarian experiment designed to democratize education by making it more "natural" and humane. To other extremely vocal groups, Progressive Education was the most damaging and the most unfortunate disaster that ever afflicted American education.

Progressive Education was neither a single idea nor the result of the contributions of a single person. As one might expect in our culture, it represented the pooled beliefs and philosophies of a variety of persons. The spiritual father of the Progressive movement in education was undoubtedly Jean Jacques Rousseau, the apostle of naturalism in education. Rousseau's theories, modified and put into practice by Heinrich Pestalozzi in Switzerland, formed a set of assumptions that were to guide Progressivism a century later. In the nineteenth century the pioneer in childhood education, Friedrich Froebel, a German philosopher and educational theo-

---

[19] In other areas as well as education. Laws to control abuses in our factories were passed—often to be struck down by the Supreme Court. Attempts were made to redress the grievances of farmers. In 1905 Congress passed a pure food and drug act. Citizens began to band together to fight political corruption in cities. The entire wave of criticism and reform culminated in Woodrow Wilson's first term in office. The reader is referred to Ch. XVIII, "The New Freedom, 1913–1917," in Morison and Commager, *The Growth of the American Republic*, II, 522–545, for a brief but excellent discussion of this era.

rist, further developed the Rousseauian and Pestalozzian philosophy. John Dewey, in the late-nineteenth and early-twentieth century, provided some important ideas for this movement.[20] Finally, William Heard Kilpatrick, the much-beloved professor of education at Columbia Teachers College, probably did more to shape Progressivism than any other single person. Other significant Progressive Education advocates were H. Gordon Hullfish, Carleton Washburne, Harold Rugg, George Counts, Jesse Newlon, and Bruce Raup. The Progressives wrote voluminously—books, journal articles, speeches, tracts, pamphlets, and essays. Those theorists referred to above are but a tiny fraction of the active Progressive Educational theorists. These persons, and many more, were heavily influenced by naturalism, romanticism, the scientific method, democracy, and humanism.

The second aspect of the revolution was created by a rather different group of theorists who, while they joined with the Progressives, nevertheless held views quite different from theirs. We are referring to the Science of Education group.

If the Progressives were interested in naturalism and democracy in education, the Science of Education movement, as its name implies, was heavily influenced by "science." The methods of science had spread from the physics and chemistry laboratories and were applied, in the late-nineteenth century, to the study of human behavior. Psychologists, sociologists, and certain professors of education felt that the methods of science could be applied both to human behavior and to education. One could formulate hypotheses, gather data, and treat them statistically and through the experimental method decide what should be taught and how it should be taught. To this end, the Science of Education advocates turned their attention to virtually every aspect of education. They measured the neatness of handwriting and the accuracy of spelling. They evaluated the reading speed and comprehension of students. They devised tests designed to measure aptitudes, achievement, and (much less successfully) personality characteristics. They attempted to find out precisely how much money was spent by schools and how this money could be spent more wisely. They investigated the rate at which children learn to divide by a two-digit number and the speed with which they forget what they learned. They measured children's manual dexterity and their ability to handle abstract concepts. A Stanford University professor, Lewis Terman, improved on the French intelligence tests and came up with one of his own, the Stanford-Binet Test (called frequently but incorrectly the "I.Q. Test").

Science of Education enthusiasts investigated the curriculum and de-

---

[20] Although John Dewey is often blamed as the evil genius of Progressivism, he in fact had comparatively little to do with it. He was not a particularly active participant in the Progressive Education Association and as early as the late 1920's criticized Progressivism severely for its shortcomings. The reader is cautioned to take all impassioned attacks on Dewey and Progressivism with a grain of salt.

cided that it could be made truly useful by carefully analyzing what people actually did in their daily lives. For instance, in the eighteenth and nineteenth centuries students learned to use such fractions as $19/37$, $5/19$, and $11/23$. The Science of Education curriculum devisers discovered that people in the business and industrial world rarely used these fractions; they more often used halves, thirds, fourths, and fifths. Therefore, the Science of Education people replaced the complex, rarely used fractions with those most typically employed by persons in their daily lives.

The most important name associated with the Science of Education movement was Edward Lee Thorndike. For almost forty years, during which time he was a professor at Columbia University, Thorndike was the acknowledged leader in educational research. Not only did he formulate the theory of stimulus-response psychology, but he conducted research in teaching methods, testing, curriculum construction, learning theory, and virtually anything else that touched on education. Thorndike's findings and theories had an enormous impact on education, probably every bit as great as that of Progressive Education.

The two movements that comprised the educational revolution, the Science of Education and Progressive Education, were radically different in orientation, approach, and consequences. Unfortunately, the differences between the two schools were not appreciated. Both schools were lumped into one movement, with neither the general public nor many professional educators discriminating between the two. In the textbook *Foundations of Method* William Heard Kilpatrick, who studied under both Dewey and Thorndike, attempted to combine the theories of both educational theorists without realizing that these theories were not harmonious.

Progressive Educators, such as Kilpatrick, assumed that people learn as they grow and develop—that is, there is a kind of built-in urge that enables persons to develop from stage to stage. The Science of Education advocates, such as Thorndike, believed that most learning is the result of outside influences. This is not simply a theoretical difference: these two theories result in two radically different conceptions of teaching!

If a child grows and develops in a predetermined fashion, much as a plant grows from seed to bud to full-grown plant, then education is a matter of teachers (1) finding out just how students grow and (2) allowing students to learn just what is in line with their natural development. Therefore, Kilpatrick and other Progressives believed that students ought to determine the major portion of what they are to learn and of how they are to learn. Students should study what *they* feel is important, and then *they* should plan their courses of study. Students ought to be responsible for executing these plans and, finally, they should play a major part in evaluating what they have studied. Progressive Education, therefore, placed heavy emphasis on student interests. Instead of the teacher giving assignments, hearing students recite, and testing them, the teacher should act as a guide.

He should assist students in the learning process but should not dominate it.

The Science of Education movement had quite different notions of what education should be. The teacher must first of all know what is to be taught. He must then present the material to students. Then he must test them to determine how much they learned. In practice, this meant that teachers introduced small units of work and drilled students in the work until they made the correct responses. Correct responses were evidence that the student truly had learned.

Progressive Education led to spontaneity, an interest in the arts, and emphasis on self-expression. It led to a curriculum in which student interests dominated and to teaching methods in which the teacher accepted the secondary role of a guide. The Science of Education led to the teacher-dominated classroom, in which teachers initiated, planned, presented, and judged. One can perhaps get an insight into both approaches by looking at a typical unit of work.

In a Progressive classroom the students might decide that they wanted to learn about animals, and therefore that a field trip to the zoo was in order. Before they went on the field trip, all students would probably read about the animals they would see. Some might give reports on certain animals, others might construct clay models of giraffes and elephants, and others might paint a mural of a zoo. All the students would then go to the zoo, with the teacher acting as guide. When they returned, there would likely be a class discussion of what they had seen. The class would cooperatively decide what testing procedures would enable the students to show what they had learned. That is, they would decide on the best method of evaluating the "experience"—a key term in Progressive Education—that they had "undergone." Perhaps the zoo unit would lead into the next unit, as students would build plans for future learning on present knowledge. Throughout the unit many skills would be utilized—reading, arithmetic, discussion, writing, research, oral reports, and the like.

In a classroom conducted by a disciple of the Science of Education the teacher would decide, for example, that it was important for students to learn about the exports of the United States, so that as adults they could make intelligent economic decisions in the light of their knowledge about geography, agriculture, industry, and the like. In all likelihood, the teacher would give students a pretest to see what they knew. Students would read a geography book, concentrating on the chapter entitled "The Exports of the United States." The teacher would then ask questions designed to elicit correct responses—that is, to indicate whether or not there was an accurate understanding of the subject matter. After the recitation students would take an objective test, with their answers being compared with those on the pretest.

Both the Progressive movement and the Science of Education influenced educational theory and practice. Not many people today are "pure" Science of Education or Progressive advocates. But it is this eclecticism, the indiscriminate mixing and joining of two different theories, that has provided some rather serious problems for teachers since the 1920's.

Teaching on the early elementary level tends to follow Progressive patterns. The children are given a good deal of freedom to initiate and perform. Their interests are frequently taken as the starting place for most activities. Art, music, and enjoyable subjects play an important part in the curriculum. As children reach the third or fourth grade, however, the picture changes: in place of freedom, interest, guided activities, and field trips, the emphasis switches to subject-matter-to-be-covered. Workbooks, "units" of study, drill, mastery of information, and other curricular concepts associated with the Science of Education dominate. Not many persons have asked, "How desirable is it for children to experience this abrupt change in the educative process?" Nor is it frequently asked whether one or the other of the learning theories *is better*. It is assumed, without awareness, that younger children have different education goals, learn differently, and require different teaching than intermediate-aged children.

Today the curricular and methodological contributions of both movements are so ingrained in American education that they appear to be natural. This is a typically American pattern: the combination of theoretically inconsistent beliefs without concern for the inconsistencies in either theory or practice—as long as it "works." But it is crucial to ask, "What does it mean for something to 'work'?"

The American Depression of the 1930's

In October of 1929, as most people know very well, the stock market fell apart. Financial chaos precipitated by the stock-market crash deepened into a depression in which the reduction of consumer demand led to the laying off of workers. Unemployment led to still further reduction in demand, and the vicious cycle continued, until in the early 1930's between 7 and 13 million workers—perhaps 6 percent to 11 percent of the population of this country—were out of work. This, however, is only an estimate, because no one is certain as to the precise number of unemployed. Savings were soon depleted; jobs became impossible to find; men and boys by the hundreds of thousands roamed the country, often riding the rails in a desperate and usually unsuccessful search for work—any kind of work.[21] Marriages were postponed, and couples deliberately reduced the number of children they would have. Breadlines and free soup canteens appeared in

[21] One estimate in a 1934 newspaper was that 1,000,000 men and boys were "bumming the rails."

major cities. Agricultural regions also experienced crises, for the reduced demand affected the raising of crops. Indeed, so low were the prices for agricultural products that it became "good economic sense" to pour milk into sewers, to plow oranges into the ground, and to slaughter immature animals so that agricultural products would not glut the market and reduce prices even further.

It became obvious to most Americans that something was basically wrong. There was no good reason that a nation of 123 million previously rich, proud, and comfortable people should suffer a catastrophic depression. Yet, unless one wished to believe that the depression was a punishment from heaven, it appeared obvious that it must have been man-made. For ten or more years, writers, economists, educators, and philosophers searched for an answer, or the answers that would help explain the depression. The answers that were given all involved the belief that our basic social philosophy was wrong and that education had failed to create desirable social attitudes in the young.

Many influential educational critics in this country, from John Dewey on down, offered analyses that went something like this: The economic and social philosophy of the eighteenth and nineteenth centuries is inadequate for today. The capitalistic philosophy of Adam Smith [22] emphasized that unrestricted economic activities of individuals would somehow create a desirable economic situation for all. That is, the fewer the controls and restrictions on individual entrepreneurs, the more prosperous any country would become. The trouble with this philosophy, said its critics, is that it tended to make the selfish desires of individuals the basis of all morality. In place of the cooperative member of society, this nineteenth-century capitalism set up the aggressive, profit-seeking, power-hungry businessman as the moral model for all Americans. It was further concluded by the critics that unrestricted competition and uninhibited profit-seeking as the supreme values were at the root of our troubles. The schools simply cooperated in passing on this selfish, antisocial morality. [23]

The answer: *Let the schools lead the nation in devising and passing on a new social philosophy!* Those who advocated this point of view were called Social Reconstructionists, for they wished to reconstruct our society and fervently believed that teachers should lead the American people to a

---

[22] Adam Smith, a Scottish economist and philosopher, wrote his *Wealth of Nations* in 1776. This book, which became the bible of nineteenth-century capitalism, expounded the basic beliefs and assumptions of capitalism, including the importance of private property, unrestricted economic activity, and profit.

[23] If this sounds like a left-wing argument, it is not surprising. Many American critics of the 1930's who were not themselves Marxists or Communists were heavily influenced by a Marxist position. To a historian of the depression, it may seem almost as if the Communists had a monopoly on social criticism, although they did not.

better tomorrow. Educational theorists such as George Counts, author of *Dare the Schools Build a New Social Order?* formed a new curricular movement. They published a journal, *The Social Frontier,* which reflected their beliefs. Soon other professors of education, speakers, and textbook writers adopted the viewpoint that the schools should lead society.

Instead of schools simply transmitting the cultural heritage, schools would *change* the cultural heritage. Teachers would see to it that students learned how to criticize social institutions and, in the act of criticism, would come to prefer a more rational, a more just, a more democratic, and a more equitable way of life. In place of the nineteenth-century capitalistic philosophy and the egocentric Protestant ethic,[24] the schools were to transmit a new cooperative ethic, one based on the scientific method of knowing, on democracy as a way of life, on equality, and on progressive amelioration of the socioeconomic scene.

The Social Reconstructionists did not go unchallenged. Boyd Bode, an associate of John Dewey who interpreted Dewey's pragmatism to teachers and professors, raised one major objection. He accused the Social Reconstructionists of attempting to indoctrinate children in liberal, left-wing philosophy. To Bode, indoctrination in education was to be avoided, whether it was left-wing or conservative indoctrination.

Bewildered as Americans were by the depression of the 1930's, they were not quite ready to turn schools over to what appeared to them to be left-wing Utopian dreamers.[25] The movement lost steam and slowly died out. On December 7, 1941, the entire question became academic, for Americans faced another challenge that completely eclipsed the problems and questions that arose during the depression years.

Despite the death of Social Reconstructionism as a meaningful movement in American education, the controversy surrounding it raised numerous issues that are still relevant. First, the controversy established the fact that, far from being morally neutral, schools are indeed in the business of passing on some kind of philosophy. Second, it highlighted the enormous importance of education. More and more people began to see the schools as a battleground on which was being fought a crucial war—or rather, a series of crucial wars. And more and more organized pressure groups began to want to take a part in this struggle for children's minds.

[24] The origin and meaning of the phrase "Protestant ethic" cannot be discussed here. However, the student is invited to do some research to understand the significance of an ethical principle that blended capitalism and seventeenth- and eighteenth-century ethical beliefs. See, for example, Vernon Parrington, *Main Currents in American Thought* (New York: Harcourt, Brace, 1927), I and II; and Crane Brinton, *The Shaping of the Modern Mind* (New York: Mentor, 1953).

[25] Most of the original Social Reconstructionists, such as Newlon and Rugg, have passed on. Counts is retired and is pursuing other interests. The only remaining forceful advocate of this position is Theodore Brameld. See his *Philosophies of Education in Cultural Perspective* (New York: Holt, 1955).

As far as making any real change in the social-studies curriculum went, the Social Reconstructionist movement was a failure. The course called "social studies," despite numerous formal changes (called "integration," "correlation," "fusion," and the "Core"), has remained essentially the same as it always was—a collection of frequently unrelated facts, taken from history, economics, and geography, which is concerned with the formal structure and function of our society and very little else.[26]

From 1945 to the Present

The end of the Second War in 1945 saw the beginning of a new set of questions for American education. In place of "What is wrong with American society and how can we improve?" the question became, "How under the existing democracy can we: (1) continue to lead the world as an industrialized, democratic society and (2) develop the talents of *all* our children?" One assumption behind these questions was that our democracy and economic system were quite adequate. All existing inequalities and weaknesses, it was widely believed, would soon be ironed out as appropriate legislation was passed to remedy the situations.

The other assumption was that America faced a new enemy. In place of the defeated fascist and nazi regimes of Germany, Italy, and Japan, a new movement—international communism—presented us with a new challenge. Communism, which combines some extremely appealing and humanitarian goals with oppressive measures to reach those goals, appeared to be a formidable opponent. It became obvious to most Americans in the days following World War II that America was destined to lead the Western world against an aggressive international communistic movement.

The conflict between America and other Western democracies and the Soviet Union and its allies became known as the Cold War. The Cold War has had an enormous impact on American education in a variety of ways. First, it can be claimed that much of the national wealth that might have been channeled into education has been spent and is being spent on building and maintaining a huge defense apparatus of men and machines. Second, much of our educational energy is spent on Cold War-related activities, such as the recent legislation (known as the National Defense Educational Act, or the NDEA, which was passed by the Congress in 1958) to create more trained personnel in science, foreign languages, and mathematics. This emphasis has created curricular distortions, for it has meant that the humanities—philosophy, art, literature, music—have had

---

[26] For a sharp criticism of the social studies, see Martin Mayer, *Where, When and Why* (New York: Harper and Row, 1963). For a more scholarly and balanced approach to the social studies, see Maurice Hunt and Lawrence Metcalf, *Teaching High School Social Studies* (New York: Harper, 1955).

to take a back seat to science and mathematics. Third, the Cold War has meant that the social studies are given over, to a rather large degree, to prodemocratic and anticommunist indoctrination. That is, in place of objective study, students are often exposed to a one-sided dose of propaganda in which "we" are the "good guys" and "they" are all bad.

In addition to the Cold War, other movements and events have had considerable consequences for the programs of American schools. Let us describe the educational scene briefly:

1. *Population expansion.* In 1930 our country had about 123 million people; in 1940 that figure was 132 million; in 1950 we had attained a population of 151 million. And in the 1960's our population will grow to 200 million. What this means is that schools are "bursting at the seams." At the elementary, secondary, and university levels, more and more students are in school. These huge numbers of students are taxing the facilities of schools—crowding lecture rooms, laboratories, and classrooms, exhausting the often meager stock of books in libraries, and requiring a wide variety of ingenious inventions, such as teaching machines, which we shall discuss in a moment. Education is not only big business, it may well be second in size only to national defense.

2. *Technology.* Technological advances have had a wide variety of effects on schools. The increasingly complex level of technology in our country has made education more and more important. In our recent past there was always some kind of job for the illiterate or semiliterate workers; they could pick cotton, run elevators, or dig ditches. Now we have cotton-picking machines, automatic elevators, and high-speed ditchdiggers. The term used to describe this increasingly complex technology in which ingeniously sophisticated machines do the work formerly done by human beings is "automation."

Though automation has displaced hundreds of thousands of workers, it has given work to many others. People have to design, produce, sell, and service these wonder machines, and these people must be rather well educated. Thus there is an enormous need for programmers, electronic technicians, repairmen, and the like. Our educational system, it must be noted, is responding rather slowly to the new needs of our society, for most high-school vocational classes are teaching skills that are either inappropriate (to the need) or are and have been obsolete for years. A startling evidence of educational lag is the fact that, despite the *decreasing* need for farmers, many states still offer vocational agriculture as the primary vocational course.

Another effect of automation on education has been an increase in the number of gadgets in classrooms. Educational television, programmed learning, including teaching machines, and a wide variety of other audiovisual materials are increasing at a rapid rate. Many universities and high schools are experimenting with language laboratories, and several states in the Midwest have experimented with an airborne educational television station that beams a televised lecture to many thousands of students.

The actual value of all of this experimentation is most debatable. That educational television and teaching machines save teacher time and are efficient is granted; that they actually result in the desired and desirable kinds of learning is not so certain. After all, as has been pointed out, one cannot talk back to a machine, and "talking back" may well be an indispensable element of education.

3. *Experimentation.* The tried and true arrangements in education are being questioned by almost everyone. The notion (found, incidentally, in the Old Testament) that the ideal classroom consists of one teacher and twenty-five students is now being challenged by proponents of variable-sized classrooms. It has been found that the size of a class can—and perhaps should—vary from small seminars to huge lecture audiences, with from a few students to several hundred.

Similarly, the *modes* of teaching are being debated. There is a rather ancient idea that a teaching situation is one in which a teacher, an expert in some branch of subject matter, transmits information to students, whose main job is to "get" that information. This idea has been challenged by a number of theoreticians. First, some say that teaching which follows exclusively the ancient pattern of transmitting information is simply poor teaching. It usually results in a low retention rate and in poor motivation. Second, most areas of knowledge have expanded so rapidly that it is quite impossible to know all there is to know in one field. Therefore, some educators talk about learning how to inquire—that is, learning how to formulate important questions and how to discover their solutions. Educators also discuss the structure of a field of knowledge and what it means to learn this structure.[27]

Experimentation to improve the teaching of mathematics and the natural sciences is now in full swing. New and rather radical curricula are proving effective. The BSCS (Biological Science Curriculum Study), a modern approach to high-school biology, has attempted to get away from the old practice of memorizing vast amounts of conceptually unrelated information—names of animals, species, parts of the body, and so on. The new approach emphasizes the process of scientific inquiry—the nature of a hypothesis and of data. It makes extensive use of laboratory-type situations, which replace the almost exclusive use of a textbook. Similarly, the SMSG, School Mathematics Study Group (to name one of the organizations interested in improving the teaching of mathematics), has attempted to introduce new teaching concepts. This approach emphasizes the nature of the deductive process in mathematics, stressing the logical progression

[27] One of the major exponents of this point of view is Jerome Bruner, *The Process of Education* (Cambridge: Harvard U. Press, 1961).

of propositions. Those of us who suffered through a geometry course in which we "proved" that something or other is congruent with angle X without understanding what we were about are especially happy to hear of this new approach.[28]

One could describe a good many other rather exciting experiments in education today. Suffice it to say that every aspect of education is undergoing scrutiny and that rather ancient, long-accepted practices are in process of being drastically overhauled. This is true from the elementary-school level to postgraduate education. It is affecting every subject-matter specialty and every method of teaching. Just where it is all leading is difficult to say now, for those in the midst of a revolution scarcely know its direction.

4. *Expanding humanitarianism.* The idea that our country ought to educate each person to the full limits of his capabilities is becoming stronger and more persuasive with each passing year. While there are many barriers in the way of this extremely humane goal, there is evidence that we are moving toward it successfully. For instance, the present concern with our rather high dropout rate means that we no longer feel quite so unconcerned about the waste inherent in a half-finished education. Thus many experiments are being attempted today to see what can be done to salvage dropouts, from before potential dropouts begin kindergarten to after they have officially quit school. Efforts ranging from nursery-school training for slum children to work-study programs for dropouts seem to hold promise for rehabilitating children who would otherwise become half-literate castoffs, unfit for anything but poorly paying, dead-end jobs.[29]

Another manifestation of growing American social sensitivity is our concern with special education. "Special education" refers to the teaching of children who deviate rather widely from some accepted norm. This group includes the blind, the deaf and dumb, the mentally retarded, the cerebral-palsied, the emotionally disturbed child, and the child with speech defects, on the one hand, and the extremely bright child, on the other. Special teachers are being trained to work with these children and, assisted by psychological, medical, neurological, and genetic research, they are accomplishing a great deal. It is becoming increasingly apparent that those children formerly considered too stupid or too deviant to be helped really can be helped.

The significance of our efforts to help the culturally deprived, the handicapped, and the brilliant child is this: The idea that education exists in part to develop the potentialities of *all* children to their limit has been extended to include those children who have many and apparently insur-

[28] See Allen F. Strehler, "What's New About the New Math?" *Saturday Review,* 47 (March 21, 1964): 68–69, 84.

[29] For an interesting and rather poignant treatment of these attempts, see "School for Poverty's Children," *Life,* 56 (April 3, 1964): 71–89.

mountable barriers to an adequate development of their potentialities and those who, because of superior intelligence, cannot benefit from the "standard" curriculum. What has historically been available to a comparative few is now being made available to the many.

5. *Changes in the profession.* As we shall point out in the essay on professionalism, teaching has been accorded somewhat too little respect. The notion of a teacher as a semieducated, not especially talented person—either man or woman—is slowly giving way to the idea of a teacher as thoroughly educated, intelligent, and effective. This ideal has by no means been attained, but there are signs that both the profession and its practitioners are improving.

For example, both the National Education Association and the American Federation of Teachers are attempting to improve salaries and conditions of work. This improvement is attracting more capable people to teaching. Those persons who have heretofore looked to the more settled professions for a career are beginning to be drawn to teaching as it carries with it higher salaries, desirable fringe benefits, a chance to improve one's skills constantly, and an opportunity for upward social mobility.

This improvement will not come about, however, without considerable friction, debate, and hard feeling. For teachers all over the country to make rather substantial improvements in their way of life, power necessarily will slowly drift from the local level to the professional association of teachers. That is, as teachers become more militant and better organized, they will make more and more decisions previously left to the superintendent and the board. What this amounts to is a weakening of representative democracy at the local level. It would appear, however, that either teachers will gain in power and improve their profession by establishing strong state and national organizations or most educational decisions will continue to be made at the local level. And what this latter alternative has meant historically is that the board and the superintendent, single-mindedly devoted to lowering educational costs, hire young, inexperienced teachers for low wages and provide them with inadequate facilities.

6. *Changes in teacher preparation.* Numerous improvements are reported in the area of teacher education. For years there has been debate and wrangling, often savage and acrimonious, over the question of the kind and extent of teacher education. Apparently there is a definite move on the part of college professors to talk to each other about just what kind of course preparation is essential for teachers.[30]

---

[30] The history of this problem is ably reported in G. K. Hodenfield and T. M. Stinnett, *The Education of Teachers* (Englewood Cliffs: Prentice-Hall, 1961). See also James B. Conant, *The Education of American Teachers* (New York: McGraw-Hill, 1963). Conant's ideas have drawn the wrath and scorn of a number of professors of education.

The result of this dialogue has been agreement on some basic issues: teachers need to know what to teach—that is, the subject matter—and they need to know something about teaching—that is, children's growth and learning patterns, teaching techniques, philosophy of education, and the organization and function of schools. It is also generally (although not by any means completely) agreed that the previous practice of allowing people with two or three years of college education to teach is no longer desirable—if it ever was. Most teacher-education institutions and many state departments of education are now thinking of certifying only those teachers who have a four-year degree. Some states are even talking about the necessity of either a five-year college program or a Master's degree.

7. *Higher education.* Higher education, too, has undergone a variety of important changes. In addition to the most obvious change—more and more students taking a greater variety of specialized course work—there are other important modifications.

Junior or community colleges have arisen by the hundreds during this century. Junior colleges have at least four functions: (1) continuing the high-school curriculum; (2) providing the first two years of college at a minimal cost; (3) providing terminal training; and (4) supplying adult or continuing education. The junior college may well be the solution to the vexing problem of how to provide further education for those who may not have the interest or intellectual ability to profit from a regular college experience.[31]

Graduate schools have increased in number and offer a greater quantity of course work. More and more people in a variety of fields are discovering that they need advanced study. Graduate schools in every field from physics to packaging are offering advanced study. Graduate study is quite unlike undergraduate work. The emphasis in graduate study is on individual study, research, small classes, and intense concentration on some limited aspect of a field.

Research is far more important to colleges and universities than it was a few years ago. Those in higher education, which both creates and disseminates knowledge, have discovered that the production of new information requires staff members and facilities that the institution usually does not have. Therefore wealthy foundations, private industry, and government have increasingly come to subsidize research in many fields.[32] The salaries of professors are augmented, buildings are constructed and expensive equipment acquired, and graduate students and secretarial help are se-

[31] See Clyde E. Blocker, "Comprehensive Community College," *NEA Journal,* 51 (September, 1962): 20–21.

[32] For a most interesting treatment of both higher education and graduate research, the reader is referred to Christian K. Arnold's "Higher Education: Fourth Branch of Government," *Saturday Review,* 47 (January 18, 1964): 60–61, 75–77.

cured; the result is a flood of articles, pamphlets, books, and monographs on every topic, from the sex life of the blue whale to the reasons for delinquents and delinquency.

The rapid increase in graduate research, however, has not been uncriticized. First, since there is more money and prestige in research than in teaching, many professors tend to emphasize research and publication at the expense of their students. Second, research can actually distort the program of an entire university. If a great deal of money and professors' energies are channeled toward research, fewer resources are expended on undergraduate teaching. In addition, questions have been raised about the ultimate value of this research. It is difficult to tell, at any given time, whether a particular bit of research is really useful and significant or mere academic boondoggling. Finally, the research itself is apparently one-sided; there is a heavy concentration on the physical sciences and much less on the humanities and the behavioral sciences.[33]

8. *Vocational education.* Since our culture, with its increasingly complex technology, requires special training for certain vocations, the problem of vocational education is increasingly becoming one for the public schools. Although we have had vocational education since the turn of the century, when the Smith-Hughes and Smith-Lever Acts subsidized vocational training in agriculture and home economics, vocational education has been something of a stepchild. Frequently the vocational school has been a dumping-ground for students who could not do well in an academic program, and frequently it has trained students in obsolescent skills on obsolescent machines.

However, it appears that there is a considerable awakening to the need for a modern, useful vocational education program in our secondary schools. Although only about 2 percent of federally reimbursed programs in six states sampled currently offered training in trade of industrial occupations,[34] there is reason to believe that the picture will change. We are beginning to realize that we can no longer turn masses of teenagers loose in the employment market with either no skills or obsolescent work skills. Therefore, there are studies presently in progress that are attempts to determine the types and curricula of vocational education. The next step is to design the kind of vocation education program that will keep abreast of the rapidly changing employment picture.

[33] Insofar as overemphasis on published research is concerned, in a case reported in *Time Magazine,* 83 (April 24, 1964): 86–87, a professor was fired for lack of research, even though he had written a rather famous book—out of his field. This subtle administrative "coercion" is known in the field as "publish or perish." For a scholarly discussion of this general issue, see Theodore Caplow and Reece J. McGee, *The Academic Marketplace* (New York: Basic Books, 1958).

[34] J. Chester Swanson, "Whither Vocational Education?" *NEA Journal,* 52 (October 1963): 59–60.

In Conclusion

This rather brief summary of the history of American education is only a bare outline. Many events and a great many significant figures who have affected education have not even been mentioned. However, the student should be cognizant of the following important ideas:

Education began as a rather humble, local, religiously-oriented project. It has turned into a complex, nationwide enterprise that—in one way or another—affects everyone in this country.

Education began as a privilege for a fairly small elite. It is now regarded as the birthright of all Americans.

Certain persistent problems have troubled this culture since the seventeenth century. Precisely who is to be educated? What are the students to learn? For what purpose are they to learn? The extent and intensity of educational controversies indicate that we are not very close to finding solutions.

Because of the pluralistic nature of our society, education will continue to be rather responsive to the wishes of different groups. This is both a value and a problem. It makes education a servant of our needs, but at the same time it makes it difficult for professional educators to know what to teach.

If the above conclusions are correct, there is a rather disturbing implication: every social problem is eventually an educational problem.

45. Noah Webster's Speller and the Way to Success

Michael V. Belok

When in 1783 Noah Webster published his *A Grammatical Institute of the English Language, Part 1,* one of his aims was to promote American literature and nationalism. But *The American Spelling Book,* the title Webster

SOURCE: *Phi Delta Kappan,* XLIX, 2 (October 1967), 85–87. Reprinted by permission of the author and publisher.

gave to later editions, or "The Blue-Backed Speller," the name the public gave it, also had another purpose. Too much attention to Webster's rhetoric tends to blind us to this other aim and the way the speller functioned. Webster did intend to promote uniformity of language, he did intend to promote patriotism, and he did write, "A national language is a bond of national union." But Webster said something more: The speller might facilitate the education of youth, enabling teachers ". . . to instill into their minds with the first rudiments of the language some just ideas of religion, morals, and domestic economy." What Webster proposed to do was provide a vehicle of self-advancement as well as an "engine for nationalism."

Noah Webster, architect of a national system of education, was also proposing to establish a national anti-poverty program. Answering charges that he was an enemy of the poor, Webster in a 1796 *Letter to the Public* wrote, "The author has, besides, been attentive in particular to the common laboring people in the more necessary and useful sciences by annexing in his *Institutes* or publishing in some cheap form the most general truths in agriculture, morals, and politics. By annexing abridgments of these useful subjects to a cheap schoolbook, he has thrown them in the way of *poor people,* and this was his express design."

Much later Webster reiterated his conviction that education was the most efficacious means of eliminating poverty. He said, "To form plans for diffusing literary and moral improvement among the poorer classes of citizens, in connection with religious instruction, will be no less our pleasure than it is our duty. To draw from the obscure retreats of poverty the miserable victims of ignorance and vice, to enlighten their minds and correct their evil habits, to raise them to the ranks of intelligent, industrious, and useful members of society will never cease to be the object of deep solicitude with a wise legislature. . . ."

The speller, then, was to be a book that prepared young Americans for "getting ahead," a sort of self-improvement book. It would teach the young person to speak and write correctly, how to behave; it would provide him with a body of useful knowledge and, hopefully, improve his sense of right and wrong.

Farfetched? Even though Webster, like so many other Americans, eulogized the agrarian life, commerce was never far away. Success, more often than not, was to be found in the city. And even though most of the boys were to remain on the farm, literary skills, manners, and general knowledge could be useful. At least they stamped one as being different from one's neighbors—different in a way that counted, not by birth but by earned merit. The man who got ahead in America might be lucky, but that was not always enough. Something else was needed, and that something was a specific type of character structure. To become one of the elect required discipline. One needed to school oneself and develop certain habits and virtues. Benjamin Franklin was the prime example. If opportunity opened up, a man had to be ready. In the meantime he ought to do something to help it open up.

Benjamin Franklin and Noah Webster. Why link the two? When Noah Webster published his speller, Franklin was already a living legend. He was an authentic American hero—a model for young Americans to emulate. Consciously or unconsciously, Webster probably emulated him. Franklin was amazingly versatile; so was Webster. Franklin was a politician, writer, journalist, and scientist, among other things. Webster was a politician, writer, journalist, and scientist. At least he considered himself a scientist. Witness his two-volume *History of Epidemics and Pestilential Diseases*. Much of Franklin's fame and influence came from the humble almanac. Much of Webster's fame was to come from a humble speller. Both used their specific vehicle to mold character—the type of character that would fit into the ideal society they envisaged, a society of hard-working, honest, thrifty men.

For all their genius, Franklin and Webster were indebted to others for much of their material. As Louis B. Wright has shown, the maxims of Benjamin Franklin had a long history. For more than two centuries, Englishmen had heard "the wise saws" of Franklin's Father Abraham. Moreover, books of advice on how to improve oneself had been coming off the presses in a veritable flood for about the same length of time. There were books for everything: how to write a letter, how to court, how to behave, how to educate a gentleman, or how to have a successful marriage. There were also conduct books for children, some of which were used in teaching children how to read. Two of these were F. Seager's *School of Vertue* and Eleazar Moody's *School of Manners*. *School of Vertue,* first published in 1557, contained a morning prayer and sections on "How to wash and dress yourself," "How to behave going to and at school," "How to wait at table," and "How to behave when conversing." Other sections told of "The fruits of gaming, vertue, and learning" and "The fruits of charity, love, and patience." Others admonished against "anger, boredom, and malice," "the horrible vice of swearing," "the vice of filthy talking," and "the vice of lying." It ended with a "Prayer to be said when thou goest to bed." Eleazar Moody's *School of Manners,* published in Boston during the eighteenth century, is a virtual copy of the *School of Vertue.*

Now let us look at Webster's speller. Although it does not contain either a morning prayer or an evening prayer, the speller is heavily laden with religious material and frequent quotations from the Bible. Practically every page of reading material (it was also an introductory reading book) has some reference to religion or religious ideas. At the very end is a "Moral Catechism." This section discusses moral virtue, humility, mercy, purity of heart, anger, justice, generosity, truth, charity, avarice, frugality and economy, industry, cheerfulness, and gratitude. If we compare this list with the contents of Seager's *School of Vertue,* we find more than a little resemblance.

Why so much religion? The speller is, as we have indicated, a form of self-improvement book. As such it shares many of the characteristics of the "courtesy" books of the time. These books were originally plans of education for gentlemen. Their utility for the man hoping to rise in the world was obvious. The key ideal of the courtesy tradition was virtue. As the courtesy books became more and more sought-after by middle-class citizens, and as England became more Puritan, the connection between virtue and religion was increasingly emphasized. Not that religion was absent from the older courtesy books; it was not. But more and more in the new books religion became an indispensable precondition of virtue. The virtuous man would be religious; and the religious man would, more than likely, be virtuous. Religion, accordingly, became the basis of good character, and manners were conceived of as "character in action." For Webster, as for John Locke and the various writers of self-improvement manuals, virtue and religion were inseparable. Habituation was also important in character formation and Webster followed the advice of Solomon quoted in the Speller, "Train up a child in the way he should go; and when he is old he will not depart from it."

If a man were to get ahead he needed to be virtuous. A cynic might guffaw at this, but the point was valid. To be virtuous was to possess certain characteristics which were much esteemed; it was also a practical necessity for the man who was to function successfully in the society of the time. In an earlier society, virtue meant courage, liberality, fortitude, justice, and magnanimity; in the developing middle-class culture of England and America these were still important but, in addition, industry, thrift, piety, and honesty were necessary.

Noah Webster knew this; it was part of his very makeup. The first reading lesson in his speller has 15 short exercises and the first 11 are religious. Number 12 is a lesson in manners: "Be a good child; mind your book; love your school; and strive to learn." The words are worth lingering over. These were the words of a new kind of man, not of an Englishman of the middle ages, not of a peasant. Why would a peasant need book-learning? Would it make him a better farmer? Not very likely at that time. Would it make him happier, more contented? Hardly. But for the rising middle-class Englishman and American, education was becoming the magic key to status and success. If the child minded his books, great rewards were open to him.

Lesson 12 continues: "Tell no tales; call no ill names; you must not lie, nor steal, nor cheat, nor swear." Subsequent lessons offer more advice on how to behave. Following the first law of pedagogy, Webster does not hesitate to repeat himself.

THE PAST

A good child will not lie, swear, nor steal. He will be good at home, and ask his book to read; and when he gets up he will wash his hands and face clean; he will comb his hair, and make haste to school; he will not play by the way, as bad boys do.

As for those boys and girls that mind not their books, and love not the church and school, but play with such as tell tales, tell lies, curse, swear and steal, they will come to some bad end, and must be whipt till they mend their ways.

A clown will not make a bow, nor thank you when you give him what he wants; but he that is well bred will do both.

If you want to be good, wise and strong, read with care such books as have been made by wise and good men; think of what you read in your spare hours; be brisk at play, but do not swear; and waste not too much of your time in bed.

The Speller is full of sections entitled "advice," "remarks," "observations," and "select sentences." Many of the maxims and adages found in these sections remind one of *Poor Richard's Almanac*.

We may as well expect that God will make us rich without industry, as that he will make us good and happy without our endeavors.
He seldom lives frugally, who lives by chance.
Without frugality, none can be rich, and with it few can be poor.
Most men are more willing to indulge in easy vices, than to practice laborious virtues.

It is this last observation that is the heart of Webster's advice and philosophy. In a lesson entitled "Domestic Economy, or, The History of Thrifty and Unthrifty," Webster illustrates the virtues which will lead to success and the opposite vices which will lead to failure and ruin. He prefaces the "history" with the comment that there is a great difference among men in their ability to gain property and use it to advantage. Two men may start out with the same amount of money but one will become rich while the other loses everything. "A chief and essential difference in the management of property," Webster wrote, "is, that one man spends only the *interest* of his money, while another spends the *principal*."

He tells of a farmer named Thrifty who practices the necessary virtues to achieve success. Thrifty gets up early, takes care of his stock, sees that all is in order for the workmen when they arrive, uses his time wisely, and retires at an early hour. "In this manner," wrote Webster, "he earns and gains money."

Now Webster comes to the heart of the management of money. Thrifty, when he acquires property, does not let it get away from him without gaining some benefit. He uses his property to increase his wealth or gain some other goal. In Webster's words, "He pays his taxes and debts when due or called for, so that he has no officer's fees to pay, nor expense of courts. He does not frequent the tavern, and drink up all his earnings in liquor that does him no good. He puts his money to use, that is, he buys more land or stock, or lends his money at interest—in short he makes his money produce some profit or income. These savings and profits, though small by themselves, amount in a year to a considerable sum, and in a few years they swell to an estate—Thrifty becomes a wealthy farmer, with several hundred acres of land, and a hundred head of cattle."

Unthrifty, who is contrasted to Thrifty, does not practice *laborious virtues*. Rather he practices the *easy vices*. Unthrifty gets up late, goes to the tavern for a drink of bitters, and eats his breakfast when he should be working. As a result of poor management and want of foresight, Unthrifty is ruined financially.

The moral is obvious: Though no one would maintain that God has treated all equally, what we do with what we have is dependent upon our own vices or virtues. We and we alone are responsible. The wise man will not cry or lament his lot. Rather he will be up and about his business, practicing the laborious virtues, and eschewing the easy vices. Poverty, in a bountiful country, need not be. Education, self-improvement, industry, thrift were the keys, and everyone of Adam's American sons might become almost anything—merchant, banker, lawyer, congressman, senator; and, who knew, even President.

46. Horace Mann: Founder of American Education

Leonard A. Wenz

One of the towering figures in the early history of our country of particular interest to Scottish Rite Masons was a famous educator of whom Henry Steele Commager wrote: "If a single name had to represent American education, it would be of necessity, Horace Mann. (1796–1859)" His dy-

SOURCE: *The New Age Magazine*, 76 (September 1968), 19–22. Reprinted by permission of the author and publisher.

namic personality, his intellectual achievements, his standing in the legal profession, his fame as an educator and civic leader all blended together to give him a capability in private life as far-reaching as his political activities as a member of the Massachusetts State Senate and a Member of the United States Congress.

In his day, Mann was considered a radical by many who could not understand the need for proposed educational and civic reforms. Indeed his generation from 1830 to the Civil War was known as the great reform period in American history. Mann found himself among a distinguished group of reformers of that period including Ralph Waldo Emerson, William Ellery Channing, William Lloyd Garrison, Theodore Parker, and others. Influenced by Emersonian idealism, these architects of a new enlightenment avowed that there was divinity in all men and that anything that interfered with or prevented the fullest, spiritual, moral, and intellectual development of men was a hindrance to human progress. Mann understood well the relationships between freedom, self-government, and free universal public education. He wrote in his Annual Report of 1846 that universal education could be the "great equalizer of human conditions," the "balance wheel of the social machinery," and the "creator of wealth undreamed of."

When Mann was first elected to the Massachusetts State Senate in 1837, rich and poor alike experienced the effects of one of the most far-reaching financial panics in history. It was in this same year that the state board of education was formed to bring order out of the chaos of a statewide delapidated school system. Mann was elected secretary of the state board with instructions to investigate, report, and recommend. The board was originally set up for service, not control; but under Mann control grew. He made his decision after giving up a lucrative law practice, and he served as secretary for twelve years in which education in the Commonwealth was transformed from a "hollow mockery into a secular and public system of highest order and dignity."

When Mann assumed his duties as secretary of the board, he found many existing school laws neglected or ignored, equipment and buildings broken down, scholastic standards so disabled that they were almost worthless, untrained teachers, thousands growing up illiterate, and a public largely unconcerned about education. It was under these deplorable conditions that he began his program of reform and enlightenment. He was especially fitted by temperament and innate ability for the task ahead. He was one of the great public speakers of his time, an accomplished organizer, and he had a knack of enlisting the good will of prominent citizens in the struggle. He traveled extensively up and down the State, year after year, preaching the gospel of the common school, urging the establishment of State-supported and controlled schools on the assumption that "in a Republic ignorance is a crime." He wrote articles for *The Common School*

Journal—a publication of the board—and other journals of the time. He summed up each year's accomplishments and made recommendations for the future in his annual reports which were often masterpieces of clarity and commonsense.

Mann, no doubt was influenced by Thomas Jefferson who, too, had a deep and unshaken belief in self-government. They both believed that a well-informed, educated public could be trusted to recognize and follow sound and enlightened leadership, and consequently both men advocated free, universal public school education. The idea itself was not new. It was born in the Massachusetts School Law of 1647, two centuries earlier. Mann was to further build on that foundation and erect a superstructure that was to stand for all time. He was well aware of the diversity of the American people, and very early he recognized that America could be hopelessly fragmented and powerless as a Nation unless there was developed a common value system. The common school was to be the instrument to bring unity out of diversity. It would be open to all, nonsectarian, supported by the State, and controlled by duly elected representatives of the local community.

The fight for free schools in Massachusetts was a bitter one against formidable opposition. Any chance for improvement was greatly handicapped by the system of supporting schools from local property taxes. Strict qualifications for voting were common. The people who were most apt to vote for an improved school system were excluded from voting. The well-to-do sent their children to private schools and so were not particularly interested. The ballot favored the people who were most strongly opposed to spending money to improve schools. Many church leaders, fearing secular schools, were in the first ranks of the opposition. Mann had no quarrel with nonsectarian religious instruction per se but opposed denominational propaganda in the public schools. He emphasized that free public school education in our democratic society must be secular and that the family, church or some other agency must assume responsibility for religious education. Mann knew how to influence people, how to make them more reflective, and how to appeal to what was noblest in them. In the end he broke down all barriers.

Commenting on the famous Act of 1647 formally providing for public schools in the Bay Colony, Horace Mann wrote in his Annual Report for 1846, "As a fact, it had no precedent in the world's history; and as a theory, it could have been refuted and silenced by a more formidable array of argument and experience than was ever marshalled against any other institution of human origin. But time has ratified its soundness. Two centuries of successful operation now proclaim it to be as wise as it was courageous, and as beneficent as it was disinterested." Now a century later, the issue of religious education has taken on some new aspects. Mann writing today would find much to commend, but he would be saddened to note that religious education in some States and communities is deviating from the time-honored principle he fought for. By providing sectarian religious instruction in public schools at public expense the separation of church and state is violated.

Horace Mann was one of those rare men whose good works and influence live on for decades and even for centuries. Truly he won a significant victory for mankind. One of Mann's biographers summed up well Mann's contribution to posterity when he wrote, "Not in the United States alone, but in many lands, children in free schools are Horace Mann's living memorial. Mann's words have been translated into many languages, and devoted teachers have taught rising generations 'to obey their own laws' or 'be held in bondage to the laws of tyrants.' It is a hard lesson, not always understood, but those who teach and those who listen are winning their victory for humanity. They are the living proof that Horace Mann's whole life was a victory."

Among the many utterances for which Horace Mann is remembered are the famous concluding words of a baccalaureate address to the Antioch College class, June 1859, shortly before his death: "I beseech you to treasure up in your hearts these my parting words: Be ashamed to die until you have won some victory for humanity."

Fittingly, these words were engraved on Horace Mann's tombstone.

47. Carleton W. Washburne: In Respectful Retrospect

Harold G. Shane

Carleton W. Washburne, who joined Phi Delta Kappa in 1925,* died late in 1968 while this issue of the KAPPAN was being prepared. It is with ap-

---

* It was completely in character that, in 1936, Washburne became one of the first of many liberal-minded educators to withdraw from Phi Delta Kappa because of the so-called white clause, which excluded Negroes and other non-whites. The white clause was removed from the fraternity constitution in 1942.

SOURCE: *Phi Delta Kappan*, LI (February 1969), 320–21. Reprinted by permission of the author and publisher.

preciation and respect that we dedicate the February issue of our journal to his memory.

Washburne was one of the great innovators in U.S. education. His record of creative leadership is all the more remarkable in that there was vigorous resistance to, rather than a well-funded quest for, socially desirable educational innovation during the era most influenced by his exceptional imagination, scholarship, and classroom know-how.

There are many ways in which we might phrase a tribute to Carleton Washburne, but no words are more effective than a summary of some of the innovations he made in the Winnetka Public Elementary Schools superintendency to which he gave a quarter-century of distinguished service. Here are some of the "firsts" he pioneered or helped to develop.

Early childhood education. Under public school auspices, a program for three- and four-year-olds began operating around 1927.

Programmed instruction. The so-called "Winnetka Plan" was based on self-instructional programmed materials and individualized rates of progress approximately 40 years before B. F. Skinner's ideas began to influence education.

The M.A.T. In the early 1930's Washburne and several associates chartered the Winnetka Graduate Teachers Colleges, an intern program for liberal arts graduates that many universities began to introduce as the M.A.T. after 1950.

Elementary school guidance. Guidance for young children began to become an offering in schools of education in the 1960's. Washburne developed the idea of a Department of Educational Counsel in the Twenties. As early as the Thirties school psychologists, a psychiatrist, a psychometrist, and secretarial workers were housed in Winnetka's specially built suit of counseling and testing rooms.

International education. Author of *New Schools in the Old World* in the 1920's, Washburne introduced education for international understanding of such quality that even today it has few peers.

School plant development. The N-6 Crow Island School in Winnetka was designed to fit the program of the school rather than to provide the egg-crate classroom popular in 1937, when it was built. Eero Saarinen, the imaginative designer, served as consultant, and Larry Perkins, a young architect, spent six months planning the building with the faculty—a rare procedure 30 years ago. The school they produced drew as many as 10,-000 visitors to Winnetka in its early years and greatly influenced school building design for two decades.

Scientific curriculum planning. A novel rationale for curriculum content in the social studies was produced by Washburne and his associates of the Twenties. They made a word-count of the persons, places, and events mentioned in popular periodicals such as *Time, Harper's,* the *Atlantic, Reader's Digest,* and *The New York Times* Sunday magazine section. The "cultural heritage" thus defined was phased into the curriculum for grades 1–8. One of the first sex education programs (c. 1926) and one of the early programs in science education were initiated in Winnetka. Mr. and Mrs. Washburne and Frederick Reed, a Winnetka principal, wrote the textbook used in the science program. Washburne's leadership was also preeminent in a major grade-placement study in mathematics.

The middle school. The idea of a uniquely developed middle school (grades 6–8) was brought into being under Washburne's direction in the late 1920's and 1930's. A remarkable approach to student participation in school living and school government was one of the middle school's special features.

In-service education. Unusual practices, for 30 years ago, were introduced in Winnetka's in-service program. Educational travel was an important feature. When travel was interrupted by World War II over 50 percent of the Winnetka faculty had worked or studied overseas for a year or longer—and received salary schedule credit for doing so. Sabbatical leaves and the opportunity to retire at 60 with a supplementary annuity were other personnel policies of note.

The Winnetka Education Press and Correspondence School. Because of the policy of creating instructional aids locally, Washburne introduced a publishing and distribution center in Winnetka. A children's correspondence school, second largest in the U.S. during the 1930's, was a novel by-product.

Space precludes reporting further details of Washburne's unique innovative powers. A clue to his inventiveness can be found, however, in a closing anecdote. He and the writer were walking toward the rocky beach near Washburne's cottage in Michigan. "Just what is the 'Winnetka Plan'?" I asked.

Washburne chuckled, then replied, "You know, there never was a 'Winnetka Plan,' despite the fact that you can read about it in 20 books. People came to Winnetka, saw what we were doing, and called it a plan."

We walked for a few minutes in silence. Then he spoke again. "Perhaps I should say that we had Winnetka *planning.* If so, the 'plan' was to apply human judgment and our values in an effort to meet school problems with as much intelligence as we could find among teachers, parents, and the community."

48. Our Future
in Public Education

Dr. Robert A. Pittillo, Jr.

The American public education system, with its absence of Federal control and its emphasis on local control, is a truly American invention and the foundation of our democracy. Like Jefferson, I believe in the ultimate wisdom of the decisions made by an informed, enlightened, and participating electorate.

Our public school system is our greatest working demonstration of democracy. The school system maintains the value of each individual and his right to a competitive education. Those in the public schools can and must provide a sound and competitive education for the children of all the people. The public schools of our country must bear the major responsibility for transmitting our culture, our ideals, and our American way of life to our children and youth.

What lies ahead?

First, there is a compelling sense of urgency. We are changing very rapidly—more so than ever before. Our times appear to be troubled as never before. Frank Jennings writing in the June 15, 1968 issue of the *Saturday Review* describes April 1968 as the wildest April since Paul Revere's ride in 1775. With respect for the urgency of our times and a firm belief that the American educational system can and must provide the substantial answers to our problems, the following five imperatives should guide our planning in the public schools:

1. Make education more relevant.
2. Give education a higher degree of permanency.
3. Make the learning process more efficient and more exciting for the learners.
4. Bring competitive education within the reach of the children and youth of all the people.
5. Make more effective the transmission of our culture, our heritage, and our ideals to our youth.

SOURCE: *The New Age Magazine*, LXXVII (April 1969), 42–46. Reprinted with permission of the author and publisher.

What do we mean by the relevancy of education?

It is through continuous examination of our society and attention to the changing needs of our children and our youths that we find a means to determine what is relevant. Little is to be gained by teaching a youngster to operate an obsolete machine or to recite insignificant and oftentimes incorrect facts. Our young people are with us so short a time that we can ill afford to squander their time in the pursuit of an inconsequential education. Our curriculum must be contemporary and significant. We must lead our students to understand the reason for the requirements of our classroom. There is little to be accomplished, for example, when a student is required to recite the names of the battles of the War Between the States and yet he does not understand the principal causes or the far-reaching results of that conflict.

The second imperative I have listed is a more permanent education.

In the past fifty years, man has more than doubled his store of knowledge, and the pace is accelerating. Research today is common to almost all organized endeavors. The truths of today represent changes of yesterday and are sometimes outmoded before they can be recorded on the pages of our textbooks. In the face of the magnitude of discovery and the incredible rapidity of change, how can we achieve a permanency in education? I see permanency through the development of intellectual power, not the accumulation of facts. By intellectual power we mean the ability of the individual to acquire new knowledge and skills unassisted, on his own, independently. Education, thus, might be more accurately defined as the ability of the individual to acquire new knowledge and subsequently to apply that knowledge to novel situations. Our need to refurbish our knowledge will intensify, not diminish.

Our next imperative is to make the learning process more effective and more exciting. This phase of our planning offers to educators a particularly wide latitude for experimentation and creativity. Industry is constantly examining its processes to find better and more efficient ways to accomplish a task. Workers in education are applying the same examinations to their "production lines"—our classrooms. We know now, for example, that there is nothing sacred about meeting a class in algebra one hour a day, five days a week.

In addition to the questionable time allocation for courses, general organization of the schools has come under severe attack. Now, at the present time, we are trying to personalize education, and in so doing we aim to give each child the opportunity for continuous progress. Thus, we are trying to develop continuous-progress schools where there is less of the preordained pattern of progress and more opportunity for unrestricted growth. If we can develop this kind of school, the bright and the dull child will each have a realistic opportunity to move at individualized speed, unrestricted by the program of the other. In addition, there is need for less spoon feeding and more opportunity for independent study. Many times a student can learn more on his own, faster and more thoroughly, if he is given proper, directed study and the tools, equipment, and environment in which to work. Under properly planned circumstances, a student can accomplish far more in independent study than would be possible for him to learn in a conventional classroom, listening to a lecture by a teacher.

Our classes are becoming laboratories with meaningful experiences of discovery. Much more is to be accomplished when a student discovers a scientific principle through the process of experimentation than by his learning the same scientific principle through the process of rote memorization.

Our students need the opportunity to debate their ideas and examine the positions of their peers. True seminar classes can offer the student the opportunity to present his ideas to his peers and to defend his position. Through this process of learning our students gain more confidence in themselves and they learn the value of disagreeing without being disagreeable. They can debate with respect for their opponent. They learn the excitement and the rich experience of the successful defense of a paper or a position.

Our fourth imperative is to bring education within the reach of the children of all the people.

In order to accomplish this goal, we must give each child a realistic opportunity for success in a competitive program. This means that curriculums must be developed which offer the bright child the challenge and, at the same time and in the same school, offer the reluctant or limited learner a challenge and an opportunity for success. It is irresponsible to require of tenth grade students to study their English or their biology from the same books and meet the requirements of the same curriculum. It is inconceivable that under that kind of condition each child would have the opportunity to develop as an individual. Instead, we need differentiated curriculums with success opportunities requiring of the student respectable effort, but giving him at the same time a truly realistic opportunity for success. When a student is faced with requirements far beyond his reach, he realizes that his situation is hopeless, the result is a helpless student. A truly comprehensive high school can under one roof, on one campus, offer a broad enough program to give each child who can come to school and adjust to group living an opportunity for success in a competitive program.

Our last imperative, and probably the most important, is to make more effective the transmission of our culture, our ideals, our way of life to our youth.

Joseph Wood Krutch writing in his book *The Measure of Man* states, "the most stupendous of man's inventions was not the wheel, or the wedge or the lever, but the values by which he has lived. In the future as in the past what becomes of him will depend less on what machines he invents but rather more on what values he creates for living." The permanence of a society is predicated on its values.

The youths of America are testing our system. They appear to be tearing at the ideals we have treasured. Are they, then, a declining generation? I think not. To the contrary, I believe this generation of young people today, because of the depth of their knowledge and the breadth of their concerns, is the greatest generation of all time.

They are, however, a new and vastly different group of people. Unseasoned by time and experience, they have seen first hand an incredible array of history unfold before them. They, probably better than the general public, comprehend change and accept its inevitability. We hear of a generation gap and that we cannot communicate with our youth. Probably our greatest mistake is not to assume with equal grace both roles in communication—that of sender and receiver. We must hear our youths if we expect them to hear us. We must talk *with* them as well as *to* them. Moreover, we need to demonstrate to our young men and women a steadfastness to those enduring and persisting ideals that have made our country great. We need courage to say no and the fortitude to make it stick. We must teach our youths by word and example that we do not have rights that supersede duties; that we must defend our country not destroy it; that we cannot, outside the framework of our government, be ourselves the arbiters of our laws.

We must be a society in debate and not defiance. Ours is a government of consent not of dissent. We must demonstrate respect for our institutions and our elected officials or our youth will, as a result of our own inconsistencies, seek to form their own codes and new institutions.

These are our imperatives, our measure of what will be the course of public education for the immediate years. We will make education more relevant, more permanent and more exciting and efficient. We will bring a competitive education within the grasp of most of the children and youth of all the people, and we will, using our public schools in the future as we have in the past, make firm the allegiance of our youth to this Nation under God indivisible with liberty and justice for all.

VIII. The Philosophies

Before taking over his first class, even while preparing his first lesson, a teacher must make important decisions about what to teach and how to teach it. Implicitly or explicitly, he must have a philosophy of education. Whatever decisions he makes stem from a system of values with which he has grown up; but as a teacher he must examine these values and think through their ramifications in terms of his own classroom behavior. As a step toward this necessary soul searching, the objectives of education were discussed in Part II.

You will recall that the material on goals divided neatly into two distinct points of view—one conservative, another liberal. In classical philosophical terms, these positions are more often identified as the traditional and the experimental. In general, the traditionalist believes the end of education is the acquisition of knowledge, that is, the training of the intellect, and that the end is what is important. The experimentalist believes the end of education is to shape both man's cognitive *and* affective behavior and that the ends and the means of achieving them are equally important. Within these two basic philosophical positions, there are a number of subtle but important differences and emphases. Thus, among traditionalists we find exponents of idealism, realism, and scholasticism; among the experimentalists, progressivism and existentialism. Again referring to Part II, Koerner and Rafferty would represent the traditionalist view, both idealistic and realistic, of education; Bruner would represent progressivism, and Carl Rogers and Paul Goodman existentialism. These schools of philosophy are important historically in understanding today's school practices.

In this chapter, idealism is represented by Earle F. Zeigler's "Idealism in Education," the realistic school by Harry S. Broudy's "Realism in American Education," and the scholastic school by Justin A. Driscoll's "A Philosophy of Catholic Education in a Time of Change."

For a clear statement of the experimentalist school of philosophy, we have included Phyllis Sullivan's "John Dewey's Philosophy of Education." While there are literally hundreds of articles on John Dewey, all but a few deal with only one minor aspect of his total philosophy. We found Sulli-

467

van's article to be the most comprehensive and also the most appropriate statement of Dewey's thinking for new teachers.

In "Existentialism and Educational Theory," C. A. Bowers describes the philosophy of existentialism in straightforward, nontechnical language; he also discusses the educational effect of the philosophy.

Most teachers are eclectics—some of what we espouse and do is the traditionalist in us, some of what we espouse and do is the experimentalist in us. And the same is true of the school program we are expected to implement. A review of the conflict among the various philosophical positions as they relate to the school curriculum is offered in "Philosophies and Aims of Education," which reflects on the ways teachers are able to have conflicting philosophies and the effect this position has on the public schools.

49. Idealism in Education

Earle F. Zeigler

To the idealist it is not the civilization or the society that is, or seems to be, of greatest importance. He believes that it is true that civilizations do develop personalities, "but in a larger sense it is true that personalities make civilizations." In both the lower and higher types of civilizations, the personality (or leader) shines through. "No civilization or culture of a people surpasses that of its greatest leader." Idealistic values achieved in the past may be lost through incompetent and uninspired leadership. *The important thing, however, is that in a purposeful, spiritual environment the individual personality develops; in this light, society appears to be a means to a higher goal.*

Society, School, and the Individual

. . . There appears to be a great deal of the "idealistic superstructure" left in modern America. The influence of Protestant Christianity is still very great, and . . . it is ungirded by absolute or objective idealism, the various branches of which see the Absolute as Spirit, as Intelligence, and as Intelligent Personal Self or Will, respectively.

Social and Cultural Heritage Are Passed On. Idealism, as well as realism, takes the position that the institution of education is necessary, because man needs a culture in which to develop, and it is the function of education to see to it that the social and cultural heritage is passed on to each human born therein. Idealism believes further that education gives God the opportunity to reveal Himself to man so that man may know the Divine through such an education. [Herman Harrell] Horne believes that we should educate in a social milieu, because it is the best place. "If we rightly educate there," we may expect a "transformed society, composed of

SOURCE: Earle F. Zeigler, *Philosophical Foundations for Physical, Health, and Recreation* (Englewood Cliffs, N.J.: Prentice-Hall, 1964), pp. 186–96. Copyright © 1964. Reprinted by permission of Prentice-Hall, Inc., Englewood Cliffs, New Jersey.

transformed individuals." [1] Education is therefore formalized through a school system.

Education and Future Progress. The idealistic position is that schools are established and supported by a society that sees the need to preserve its particular culture and to plan for its progress in the future. Schools reflect the society in which they are established. The school is one influence, albeit a very important one, that makes a society what it is. In this approach the school has a social and a communicative function; it should also develop an individual's and the society's ability to reason and plan. The question of progress is seen differently depending on the philosophical orientation of the society. Idealists, with their great concern for individual personality, see history as more than the influence of outstanding leaders on other men and the culture. Horne sees "the great man himself as an expression of some immanent purpose in the world." For him the "principle of cosmic personality" is the real explanation of progress. It gives us "a spiritual, as distinguished from a material, interpretation of history." [2]

It is interesting to note further that idealists, according to Horne, see education's function as being much more than "mere preservation of the cultural heritage." In the first place, he suggests that the school can improve society by suggesting desirable lines of future growth. It can "educate for leadership and followership." Another function would be to "express appreciation for right social emphases and criticism of misplaced emphases." It "can assist in handling social problems in a scientific way." And lastly, it "can assist in transmitting the established values of the past." [3]

The Supreme Importance of Individual Personality. Idealists have traditionally shown a great concern for the moral and spiritual values in society. Although the school should work for an ideal social order, the reasoning behind this is so that timeless values may be brought into the lives of mortal man. According to a recent report of the Educational Policies Commission of the National Education Association, "the basic moral and spiritual value in American life is the supreme importance of the individual personality." [4] To bring about the realization of this fundamental value the Commission is in favor of plans of school organization and administration in which the curriculum meets the many needs, interests, and aspirations of students. This belief is summed up as follows:

In educational terms, this value requires a school system which, by making

[1] Horne, *Forty-first Yearbook,* Part I, p. 173.

[2] *Ibid.,* p. 175.

[3] *Ibid.,* pp. 176–178.

[4] Educational Policies Commission, *Moral and Spiritual Values in the Public Schools* (Washington, D.C.: National Education Association of the United States, 1951), p. 18.

freely available the common heritage of human association and human culture, opens to every child the opportunity to grow to his full physical, intellectual, moral, and spiritual stature.[5]

An Intermediate Position. Progressivists feel that the school "should dare to create a new social order." [Kenneth H.] Hansen asks the question, "Does society determine what the school should be, and the school then simply follow the dictates of society?" [6] He answers his own question when he explains that this is the way that it has always been in the history of the world. Idealists appear to take an intermediate position in answering this question. They want to "preserve and transmit the established values of the past"; yet, they show great concern for future growth and the "handling of social problems in a scientific way." They insist that the best is yet to come.

Education's True Function. [Theodore M.] Greene's liberal approach to idealism is one in which there is a division of labor between the school and the other agencies of society. He urges the school to leave "certain vital functions" to society's other important institutions. If the school becomes involved in too many tasks, Greene is afraid that it will be less efficient and will neglect its true function. This he visualizes as follows:

. . . the preservation, dissemination, and extension of man's knowledge of himself and his total environment, along with all the techniques of teaching and learning.[7]

In speaking of the role of the school in our society, he does see *three* major responsibilities. First, the school should teach "the basic structure and essential processes of a democratic community." Our young people need to acquire an understanding of, and a devotion to, the freedoms that we have in this evolving democracy. But, he urges, secondly, that "there is nothing sacrosanct or absolute in any form of social and political democracy, including our own." Lastly, one of Greene's great concerns is that we infuse students with a passion for social justice.[8] Thus, it can be said that Greene believes that the school, as the only agency whose primary responsibility is education, should "stress knowledge and the development of the mind." [9] In fairness to his beliefs, however, it must be pointed out that he conceives the term *mind* as "man's *total* cognitive equipment."

---

[5] *Ibid.*, p. 19.

[6] Hansen, *Philosophy for American Education*, p. 187.

[7] Greene, *Fifty-fourth Yearbook*, Part I, p. 116.

[8] *Ibid.*, p. 133.

[9] *Ibid.*, p. 117.

Educational Aims and Objectives

·   ·   ·   ·   ·

Idealism versus Realism. In relationship to the other essentialistic positions in education, idealism is considered by some to be "on the border
line." [10] Whereas it may be said that idealism was responsible for a good
share of educational change in the nineteenth century, this is not true when
we consider certain educational innovations of the twentieth century. Because idealism does place great emphasis on freedom and development of
the personality, however, there do seem to be certain features of idealistic
philosophy of education which are quite close to progressivistic views. It is
true also that idealists and realists disagree on many points. For example:
idealism allows for more personal freedom; it views the world quite opti-
mistically; it is inclined toward a monistic outlook of the universe; and its
system of reality is based on God's spiritual mind. Yet despite all these
dissimilarities, [Theodore] Brameld believes that:

. . . modern realism and modern idealism belong to a united front; they are
engaged in a task so momentous as to require the talents and interests of both:
the task of constructing the intellectual and moral foundations for a modern
culture common to both.[11]

A Moral Imperative on Education. Idealistic philosophy of education
stresses that the developing organism becomes what it latently is. All education may be said to have a religious significance, which means that there
is a "moral imperative" on education. As man's mind strives to realize itself, there is the possibility of realization of the Absolute within the individual mind. Horne explains this approach somewhat more specifically by
explaining that education's aim is to help the child adjust to "these essential realities that the history of the race has disclosed." [12] These "essential
realities" (or spiritual ideals) are truth, beauty, and goodness—the permanent values of the race experience that must be inculcated.

The Idealistic Educational Plan. The idealistic view urges very strongly
that personality has ultimate worth. An understanding of this interesting
concept offers us clear insight into the educational plan of the idealist.
Horne clarifies this phase of the idealistic position as follows:

But the growth of the person, or the spirit, in man is even more marvelous

---

[10] John S. Brubacher, *Modern Philosophies of Education,* 2nd ed. (New York:
McGraw-Hill Book Company, Inc., 1950), p. 309.

[11] Theodore Brameld, *Philosophies of Education in Cultural Perspective* (New York:
The Dryden Press, Inc., 1955), p. 268.

[12] Herman Harrell Horne, *The Philosophy of Education,* rev. ed. (New York: The
Macmillan Company, 1930), p. 102.

[than the growth of the physical organism] . . . The person seems endowed with unlimited capacities for growth in the attainment of knowledge and wisdom, in the production and enjoyment of the beautiful, and in the acquisition of the ideal virtues of understanding, sympathy, coöperation, forgiveness, and self-sacrifice.[13]

Further insight into the educational goals of the idealist may be gained from a description of the *idealistic pupil* who aims for the stars in everything he undertakes:

The idealistic pupil is characterized by that admirable trait, the will to perfection. Whatever he does, he does as well as he can. He is ambitious to deserve honors in scholarship. He wants to grow in knowledge and wisdom, to appreciate the aesthetic things in life, to deserve approbation, and to be a worthy person. He seeks to cultivate social responsiveness and responsibility and those skills and techniques necessary for effective action. He strives for perfection because the ideal person is perfect. His motives may be misunderstood by some of his fellows but he is not disturbed thereby and goes on his straight course the best he can. He has the secret satisfaction of having aimed high and striven hard. This type of pupil is not a trouble-maker for teacher or parent or police officer, though at times he may exhibit the defect of his quality and become fanatical, ecstatic, or visionary.[14]

A Hierarchy of Educational Values. Our next step in this inquiry into the idealistic philosophy of education may well be into the realm of educational values. If we determine that the highest good in life is based on a particular view of human nature, it is then possible to enumerate the various objectives of living (and learning) into some sort of a hierarchy of values. The idealist is vitally concerned with man's effort to realize his absolute goal—the establishment of his likeness to the spiritual order.

Horne's Basic Values of Human Living. Again we must turn to Herman Harrell Horne for help, since he has enumerated what he has called "the requirements of human nature, . . . the characteristics of a truly-educated person," and "the educational objectives of the perfectly integrated individual" on a number of occasions. The following, then, is Horne's list of the basic values of human living: health, character, social justice, skill, art, love, knowledge, philosophy, and religion.[15]

If we were to scale some of these educational objectives as to their importance, *the most important one would be an understanding of worship* which brings man into a conscious relation with the infinite spirit of the universe. Secondly, the development of "character in the individual and justice in society" must be attended to in the best possible way. Very im-

[13] Horne, *Forty-first Yearbook,* Part I, p. 154.

[14] *Ibid.,* pp. 156–157

[15] *Ibid.,* p. 181.

portant also is a knowledge of how to produce and enjoy the beautiful; this is followed closely by knowledge about the structure of the universe. Although the idealist would be one of the first to argue that man cannot live by bread alone, still he is most anxious that a man attain the skill requisite to one's economic independence. And finally, in what must not be construed as a complete list of objectives in a hierarchical arrangement, we find *good health at the bottom*. Horne does say, however, that we can "yet esteem it highly as a basic value for all the others, . . ." [16] Education for the idealist can therefore be said to be *ideal-centered* rather than child-centered, or curriculum-centered, or society-centered.

A Cultivated Vocationalist. Idealists differ somewhat in their beliefs about the importance of vocational education in comparison to liberal education, but it may safely be said that their typical position is more progressive in this matter than that of the other essentialists. Horne refers to the educated person as a "cultivated vocationalist," but he does place higher emphasis on the fact that he should become a "cultivated human being." [17] Greene stresses the importance of a liberal education, also. He calls "knowledge and the development of the mind" the "central concern" in the entire educational process, but he is quick to point out that he is referring to "man's total cognitive equipment" when he attempts to define "mind." [18] When he speaks about the total preparation of the individual, it may be stated that he is taking [what he himself calls] a liberal idealistic position. Many idealists would designate the following statement as perhaps too progressive for them:

. . . so-called 'liberal education' and 'vocational training' should be conceived of neither as hostile rivals nor as mutually exclusive enterprises but, on the contrary, as two essential and complementary aspects of the total preparation of the individual for his total life. . . . If these two equally essential preparations for life are thus divorced, a *merely* liberal education will indeed tend to be useless, and a *merely* vocational training, crass.[19]

Eliminate Distinction. Greene takes a further stand on this question, which will prove most interesting to professionals in physical, health, and recreation. He urges strongly that the distinction between curricular and extracurricular activities should be eliminated forthwith; such an idea, he states, can only hurt the total personality development of the individual.[20] This belief very definitely represents a radical departure from the typical essentialistic position on this matter.

[16] *Ibid.*, p. 186.
[17] *Ibid.*, p. 161.
[18] Greene, *Fifty-fourth Yearbook*, Part I, p. 117.
[19] *Ibid.*, pp. 118–119.
[20] *Ibid.*, pp. 119–120.

Horne's Definition. It seems only appropriate to conclude this section on idealistic aims and objectives of education with Horne's classic definition of the educational process:

Education is the eternal process of superior adjustment of the physically and mentally developed, free, conscious, human being to God, as manifested in the intellectual, emotional, and volitional environment of man.[21]

The Process of Education

Now that we have considered the relationship that should exist among school, society, and individual and the aims and objectives of education according to the idealist, we are faced with the questions which relate to the actual educational process. What kind of activities do students engage in according to these beliefs (and in what way) in order that the end result will be satisfactory and rewarding to all those who are concerned?

The Idealistic Curriculum. The idealistic curriculum should be based on (1) the child's needs and interests; (2) the worthwhile demands of society; and (3) the type of universe in which we live.[22] Furthermore, it should offer a "rounded view of man in his world, a taste for the best things in life, and the ability to take one's own practical part in the world." [23] To bring about the desired result, there are certain essential studies. Horne divides the curriculum into three parts: the sciences; the fine arts; and the practical arts. For Greene the essential curriculum is divided as follows: formal disciplines (language, logic, and mathematics); the factual disciplines (the natural sciences and increasingly the social sciences); the normative disciplines (certain branches of philosophy such as ethics and aesthetics, artistic and literary criticism, and religion); and the synoptic disciplines (history, geography, and the remainder of philosophy).[24]

Greene on Classroom Skills. Greene believes that there are some *skills* (as he designates them) that can be directly taught in a rather formal classroom situation. These skills relate directly to the disciplines presented immediately above. The student should learn how to think clearly and consistently and to use the language. Secondly, he can be taught a great many facts about the natural and social sciences. Next, he should learn how to evaluate all the situations he encounters in the world around him accord-

---

[21] Horne, *The Philosophy of Education*, p. 285.

[22] Horne, *Forty-first Yearbook*, Part I, p. 159.

[23] *Ibid.*, p. 160.

[24] Greene, *Fifty-fourth Yearbook*, Part I, pp. 121–123.

ing to a set of standards or values. Lastly, he needs to acquire the skill necessary to see the world and its people "on balance." This latter skill will help him to avoid narrowness of perspective.

Attitude Development Can't Be Taught. But despite the fact that the above skills can be taught to a varying degree to the learner, depending on his native ability, Greene asserts that it is not possible to teach fundamental attitudes or values directly. How then is it possible to teach a passion for clear thinking and a love of language; or a respect and a keen desire for fact; or a respect for values and a desire to evaluate situations sensitively; or an understanding and abhorrence of a narrow-minded approach to the world which prevents one from seeing various relationships in broad perspective? The idealist's answer is that this type of attitudinal development must come about in children and youth indirectly "by example, inspiration, and contagion." [25]

The Idealistic Teacher. The idealist believes, therefore, that the teacher's personality is tremendously important! Such a teacher, as the idealist pictures him, is central and is the key to the entire educative process; he determines the pattern of education, arranges the environment, conceives objectives, and organizes the arrangement of the subject matter. The various idealistic educational philosophers paint such absolutely magnificent pictures of the qualities that the idealistic teacher should possess that one cannot help but believe that such a teacher could accomplish a great deal working with children. In fact, although idealists say that their curriculum is ideal-centered, it may well be stated that it is teacher-centered to a certain degree as well. For example, Horne describes this personality as follows:

The idealistic teacher, like the idealistic pupil, pursues the method of perfecting and the ideal of a cultivated personality. The things that are dear to him are self-consciousness, self-direction, self-activity, selfhood, inner spiritual growth . . . The infinite and the eternal, though he does not fully comprehend them, mean more to him than the finite and the temporal. His mind seems to rise naturally to the heavenly places. Plato and Emerson inspire him. He is much interested in understanding others through social intercourse. He feels the need for his pupils even as they feel there is something satisfying about him, as though he answered their deepest questions and satisfied their highest cravings. . . . Thus, teacher and pupils grow together as he awakens the dormant powers in younger selves. The sense of companionship in spiritual growth is dear to him. He is a life-sharer.[26]

[25] *Ibid.,* p. 123.
[26] Horne, *Forty-first Yearbook,* Part I, p. 157.

Such a teacher would no doubt have a great influence on many of his pupils, but the true idealistic teacher (according to Horne) does not give children *the* answers to questions; he tells them what the *possible* answers are, and they must come to their own conclusions. Any other approach would negate the respect that an idealistic teacher should have for the child's personality and intelligence. He does point out the weaknesses of other positions, but he would never superimpose his own will on the learner. It is presumed that "infinite time" may be necessary for all to see the truth as it really is.

Ever-Broadening Understanding. Believing that "the organism already latently is what it is to become," the idealist's education begins with the "self" (the individual person); it is more than a behavioral process. "The mind is the source of its own reactions to the world." [27] As [J. Donald] Butler indicates, "growth can only come through self-activity." [28] From an understanding of himself the student reaches out for an understanding of the world outside himself. Brameld explains the relationship of idealistic learning to the Gestalt theory as follows:

It follows that idealism often tends to respect and to stress subjective psychological ideas and processes. Introspection and tuition, for example, are more congenial to it than realism. Moreover, the capacity of the mind—in idealistic theory—to combine related parts into qualitative wholes of meaning suggests that idealism thus far anticipates the Gestalt approach to learning.[29]

But we cannot forget the importance of the "gradual acquiescence" of the learner (who has, to be sure, begun with himself) as he acquires a greater sense of understanding and a "feeling of oneness" with God. Once this relationship to Spirit is felt and appreciated, the result is a much greater self-understanding.

Importance of Imitation. In this theory of learning, imitation is natural and should actually be used as a method in the work of the school. Idealists place great emphasis on the influence of outstanding personalities on students at all levels. This is one of the ways by which youth grows to maturity, and it is a much more powerful influence than we realize at times.

Interest and Effort. Idealists believe further that interest is an extremely important factor in bringing about education, but they are not willing to

[27] Horne, *The Philosophy of Education*, p. 170.
[28] Butler, *Four Philosophies*, p. 251.
[29] Brameld, *Philosophies of Education in Cultural Perspective*, p. 242.

rest their entire case on this one factor alone. Horne has said that "effort leads to interest," and this maxim of learning should not be forgotten. If this is true, a certain amount of discipline at particular stages of learning may be necessary. Horne is more interested in a free discipline as an end product. Mankind starting with freedom has laboriously gained disciplined accomplishment. It is possible for education to speed up this process in the young by beginning with a certain amount of coercion. The end result, of course, is a student who has developed his selfhood and who is able to achieve what it is in him to become. During this process it is fortunate that individual interests are typically not at odds with group interests. It is helpful also that a certain amount of the subject matter included in the curriculum has formal disciplinary value. At this point it may be helpful to mention what Greene calls the "principle of flexible adaptation" to specific needs as part of the educational process.[30] Physical educators in recent years have known this principle as *the growth-and-development approach* in education. As the student matures, there are points along the way in which certain educational material may be introduced at an appropriate time in relationship to his developmental pattern. Such articulation of the various curriculum materials will tend to evoke the student's interest in the curriculum plan at hand.

A Common Core of Knowledge, Skills, and Attitudes. As for the curriculum itself, we have mentioned above the various disciplines of which it should be composed and also the concept of the "cultivated vocationalist." The idealist feels that there should be sufficient objective content—a common core of knowledge, skills, and attitudes—to pass on the racial (social) inheritance. To construct a curriculum we must understand man and his ideal character as well as those characteristics which an ideal society should possess. The development of an idealistic curriculum would involve a "coöperative pooling of experience and knowledge" on the part of the teachers concerned.[31] It would be quite difficult for students to share in this process to any great extent inasmuch as the cultural heritage and the requirements of human nature (and the resultant hierarchy of educational values) have determined the objectives of living and learning. The ideals of man to be realized in the schools of American democracy must be achieved if we ever hope that his nature will be complete. These cannot be left to chance despite the concept of individual differences. One such ideal might be the Jeffersonian conception of democracy, which is explained as:

. . . the sound democratic principle of helping each individual, without regard to race, color, or creed, to make the most of himself, to rise as high in the scale of values as his native endowment permits. . . .[32]

[30] Greene, *Fifty-fourth Yearbook*, Part I, p. 127.
[31] Horne, *Forty-first Yearbook*, Part I, p. 159.
[32] Greene, *Fifty-fourth Yearbook*, Part I, p. 129.

This is explained by Greene as a "fusion of objective aristocracy and social democracy."

Teaching Methodology. The teaching methodology employed by the idealistic teacher is not easily identified. Many might insist that they create their own teaching methods and do not wish to be bound by any particular approach. The typical idealistic teacher might stress drill as important, but he would be very careful that the repetition not become dull. He would stress that transfer of training may be explained through the whole-part relationship; thus, the teacher should be careful to point out the similarities and relations between the parts and the whole. Lecture certainly has a legitimate place as a method for the idealist, but it should involve much more than mere repetition of facts and ideas. There should be ample opportunity for questions and answers (a sort of informal dialectic). Even the project method of the progressives would not be out of bounds for the idealist. It would be very important to allow for as much flexibility as possible and certain alternative courses from which the student may choose. Good teachers create suspense whenever possible; they encourage the students to make decisions; they avoid wholesale indoctrination if they are liberal; and they encourage active effort at all times.

50. Realism in American Education

Harry S. Broudy

"Realism" is a pigeonhole in which one might find the names of John Wild, Jacques Maritain, Robert M. Hutchins, Mortimer J. Adler, I. L. Kandel, William C. Bagley, Gilbert Highet, Mark Van Doren, H. C. Morrison, Ross L. Finney, Plato, Aristotle, St. Augustine, St. Thomas Aquinas, Erasmus, Vives, Rabelais, Castiglione, Elyot, Montaigne, Milton, Bacon, and Comenius among half a hundred others. This is a motley crew of schoolmen, indeed. What, then, might make it appropriate to dub them all "Realists"?

If I had to pick one generic characteristic, it would be a belief in some kind of thoroughly objective anchorage for the enterprise of thought, conduct, and education. Special kinds of Realism differ as to what is taken as

SOURCE: *School and Society*, LXXXVII, 2145 (January 17, 1959), 11–14. Reprinted by permission of the publisher.

objective. In educational thought, for example, there has been a belief in and a passion for such objectivities as: things rather than words, traditions, ideals, intellectual disciplines, classics, natural law, God, innate capacities, human nature, the social order, the natural sciences, the folkways and mores, and cultural demands.

If the reader compares this assortment of beliefs with the list of names cited above, he will find that not every name shares every belief, and that those who do share a belief may not do so for the same reasons.

However, all unite against views that deny independent status or validity to every truth and every norm; against those who hold that all truths and all standards are matters of local time, place, and circumstance; that any man whatever is the measure of all things; that this man, though he is the only measure, himself has no stable generic human nature. In other words, they reject any *thoroughgoing* relativism, whether it be cultural, intellectual, esthetic, or moral.

I take it that, when we ask about the status of Realism in current education, we mean to inquire about its influence upon theory and practice in the conduct of schools. Influence in this sense comes from many sources. Into a wide-mouthed hopper are tossed theories, textbooks, teacher-training courses, editorials, speeches by indignant admirals and industrialists, and snide and derisive comments by liberal arts college professors, politicians, and assorted taxpayers. From the narrow end of the hopper emerge schools with a complement of teachers and pupils in some sort of transaction with a curriculum. The attempt to trace specific connection between input and output is futile, but we can distinguish three levels of influence.

Farthest from the practice is what might be called the BMIC (big man in the community) level of influence or that of the intelligent, successful layman. Next is a layer represented by the college professors, and the third is constituted by the personnel and the institutions that prepare people for teaching, educational administration, and supervision.

Realism is represented on all of these levels of influence, but the emphasis is not equally strong at each level nor is it manifested in the same way. Right now, of course, the influential laymen are notably vociferous in their Realism. They want "hard" subjects like science, mathematics, and languages in a prescribed curriculum and no coddling of either low or high I.Q.'s. They want an intellectual elite in order to maintain leadership in war and peace. They are Realists not simply because they face "unpleasant reality" but also because, if really hard pressed to justify their proposals, they might admit that they believe people who can learn hard subjects are "better" than those who cannot and that a society is bound to go to pot if it is not led by such "better" people. What sort of democratic design will fit these beliefs is either ignored, postponed, or improvised.

It is to be expected, perhaps, that this level of influence in education should be on the side of Realism. Its representatives have attended schools operated on this philosophy, and their position in the social order is hardly conducive to a passion for egalitarianism. They sense rather than understand that changes in educational values portend changes in the social system—changes that threaten the elite rather than the masses. Unfortunately, their partisanship in educational controversy beclouds the merits of the issue. For these merits are to be judged on theoretical grounds, and of these the successful man on the street, like his less successful counterpart, is usually innocent. If they are for the "right" things in education, it is usually for the wrong reasons, or for no reason at all.

On the second level of influence are the liberal arts faculties and, to some extent, their colleagues in the universities. Here we find Realism in at least two senses of the term. First of all, college professors want college freshmen to be well grounded in the skills and knowledge required for college study. They feel that it would be "unrealistic" to give priority to any other educational outcome. In this narrow phase of their Realism, they join with certain generals and admirals in agreeing that the only education that amounts to anything is a liberal arts training. Their naïveté about education for the non-college bound is always impressive.

More broadly, however, the liberal arts professors who vent their thoughts and especially their feelings about public education do have a genuine and rational commitment to a system of values. It is a commitment to the values exemplified by the intellectual disciplines of Western civilization, viz., the sciences and the humanities.

For the college professors in the liberal arts, education comes to have the meaning given to paideia by Werner Jaeger, i.e., a taking on by the new generation of the noblest and best elements of Western culture. This is regarded as good in itself apart from any vocational usefulness or uselessness.

Unfortunately, much of the writing of this group, e.g., Mortimer Smith, Arthur Bestor, and others, is devoted to derisive gibes at the "Educationists" whom they perceive as threats to their own value commitment. This preoccupation with the alleged foibles of the Educationists obscures the merits of their own position and blinds them and their followers to the real problem of our times, viz., how can the intellectual disciplines be transformed into a program of general education in a democratic society.

These people exert influence through institutions as well as through ideas. By their ability to influence admission requirements for college, they can affect the curriculum of the secondary school.

Finally, but not at all unimportant, is the fact that the liberal arts professors tend to get the lion's share of what little prestige education enjoys in our culture. At their best, they exemplify their own theory and, like all cultivated minds and personalities, exude a special sort of charm that gives them a power all out of proportion to their numbers.

This influence is never wholly extinguished in the lives of school teachers and administrators who received their undergraduate work at good liberal arts colleges. Their talk is the talk of the schools of education, but their hearts are likely to be with their first *alma mater*.

We now come to the Educationists themselves. I refer to the teachers of teachers and to the authors who write the books used in the training of educational workers, including the books dealing with the philosophy of education. Realism here is likely to have one of three emphases: cultural, religious, philosophical.

The cultural variety puts its stress on the reality of social institutions and tradition and their demands upon the individual. To meet these demands essential skills and bodies of knowledge are required and, therefore, should be taught to all and, if possible, mastered by all. Essentialism, one variant of this type of Realism, while not conspicuous in the current literature under this name, is still a strong and influential movement manifesting in school practice the theoretical positions of William C. Bagley, I. L. Kandel, and others. By not closing the door to innovations of method and to the influence of the social sciences, by finding a place for tradition and modernism, fixity and change, democracy and authority, it has won many friends and alienated relatively few.

Religious Realism makes central the objective truth of a specific creed and constructs an educational philosophy that it regards as consistent with this truth. As might be expected, the theology of the Western religions has utilized the language and concepts of realistic philosophy, especially that of Plato and Aristotle, from which fact the conclusion has too hastily been drawn that all realistic philosophies of education have religious commitments.

In our country Catholic education is the most prominent example of religious Realism in educational thought, but Judaism, Lutheranism, Episcopalianism, and many other religious denominations that conduct schools of one sort or another are no less realistic. They certainly would all agree that God and the Scriptures are not an hypothesis to be tested by social experiments, nor merely an invention of the human mind. Nevertheless, not all religious Realists come out with, nor do they logically have to come out with, the same designs for life and schooling.

Jacques Maritain, Martin Buber, Bernard Iddings Bell, and Reinhold Niebuhr are all religious Realists, but their views as to what is central in the good life certainly would not be mistaken for each other. Some religious educational philosophers are Classical Humanists with the benefit of Revelation; others regard the emotional commitments to the Faith as central with intellectual attainments in a distinctly subordinate role.

Estimating the influence of philosophical Realism presents a problem, first because there is so great a variety of views, *e.g.,* Neo-Realism, Critical Realism, some types of Organism, logical Realism, epistemological Realism, metaphysical Realism, etc. Because every sane philosophy would like to believe that it was saying something significant about an objective world, all philosophies make some claim to Realism. In the second place, not all of these varieties have ingressed into educational thinking and certainly not to the same degree.

Perhaps the most influential writer devoting himself consciously to a systematic philosophy of education in the realistic fashion has been and probably still is Robert Maynard Hutchins. The spectacle of a brilliant scholar, at the head of a great university, at one and the same time fearlessly battling for academic freedom and proposing a new organization of American education in the language of Aristotle and the Schoolmen, exerts a peculiar fascination. By and large, however, his writings have done more to reveal the weaknesses of American education than to provide workable remedies for them.[1]

His work did highlight, however, the old Classic Realistic belief that without assuming that man has a nature which is in some sense constant and knowable, and that the norms for the good life and the good society are not merely cultural accidents, even democracy and science, the twin deities of Pragmatism, have their feet in fluid clay. Others have tried to work out a design for democratic education consonant with these principles.[2]

As to the other brands of philosophical Realism, they have not as yet found their way significantly into educational philosophy. However, as the "classic" Instrumentalism of John Dewey is subjected to scrutiny, it is reasonable to believe that many variants of Realism will be tried on for size.[3]

Despite these manifestations of Realism in educational theorizing, by and large, the dominant influence in this domain still is Pragmatism and especially its Instrumentalist version in the works of John Dewey. It has taught several generations of educational workers its concepts, vocabulary, and ideals. The passing of many of its "giants" from active teaching has left Instrumentalism rich in disciples but without any one dominant per-

---

[1] Cf., R. M. Hutchins, "The Higher Learning in America" (New Haven: Yale University Press, 1936); "Morals, Religion, and Higher Education" (Chicago: University of Chicago Press, 1950); and "The Conflict in Education in a Democratic Society" (New York: Harper, 1953).

[2] Cf., the writer's "Building a Philosophy of Education" (New York: Prentice-Hall, 1954) and the chapter by John Wild in "Modern Philosophies and Education," 54th Yearbook, National Society for the Study of Education, Part I, 1955. The work of Abraham H. Maslow, "Motivation and Personality" (New York: Harper, 1954), may yet give strong empirical evidence for this belief.

[3] I find in Frederick S. Breed's "Education and the New Realism" (New York: Macmillan, 1939) little educational theory that depends directly on philosophical neo-Realism. However, there is a current flirtation with Whitehead that may prove significant, e.g., Frank C. Wegener's "The Organic Philosophy of Education" (Dubuque: Brown, 1957); and essays by George E. Axtelle and Joe R. Burnett of New York University and others. Cf., issues of Educational Theory. In another direction are the attempts of Richard D. Mosier to formulate some kind of Transcendental Realism for education.

sonality in the position of leadership. This, no doubt, has encouraged some deviationism, but it is still a powerful movement precisely because it does have a taproot in truth. That there may be other taproots and that one may not be enough is what the current scrutiny of Instrumentalist theory may well disclose.

When the debates are over and the smoke of theoretical battles has cleared, the real test of Realism's influence is the degree to which school practice has been affected by it.

Schools are realistic in the shabby meaning of Realism—namely, in not being unduly insistent on ideals, principles, and theoretical consistency. Schools tend to be "realistic" in trying to satisfy all the pressures and demands brought upon them by the community. But whereas some philosophies of education make a virtue out of this kind of accommodation by calling it "flexibility" or "democratic control" of the schools, Realism in its higher meaning is more likely to deplore it.

The reason for this is clear if the realistic emphasis on a constant structure of human nature, its capacities, and needs is kept in mind. It holds out rather grimly, therefore, even in the face of the social "facts" for a set of knowledges and learning arts that it believes everyone should learn. How to translate this into a program that does not do violence to individual differences in abilities and interests is the major problem for a realistic philosophy of education.

To do this Realism has to define generic capacities and needs in such a way that they transcend individual differences. Yet, these generic capacities must be so defined that they can be identified and the effects of learning on the realization of these capacities observed and measured. Otherwise, all talk about capacities and human nature, in education at least, is vague "palaver."

As to the influence of Realism on the thought and personality of the teacher, one can only guess that by virtue of its religious affiliations, if nothing else, Realism is probably at the core of the beliefs held by most public-school teachers explicitly or implicitly. Yet, if they have attended schools of education, they have absorbed the doctrines and the language of Pragmatism more or less thoroughly. What happens when these two ways of thinking interact can only be guessed at, but it might not be far from the truth to say that the teachers experience personally the same conflicts that the school manifests institutionally. This conflict has been stated in many ways: between divergent theories of democracy; between classical liberalism and the "new" liberalism; between the equalitarianism of democratic theory and the hierarchical structure of our economic institutions.

Yet, educationally the conflict always resolves itself into debates as to who shall decide *what* pupils shall be taught, *how* they shall be taught, and for *which goals*. On the whole, Realism would throw its philosophic weight behind the belief that the school, although created by society, gains authority as it develops a class of educationists, if you like, whose primary concern is to discover and apply knowledge about the educative enterprise. If human nature and the good life have any stable pattern, such knowledge is possible, and to the extent that it is achieved, it becomes *de jure,* if rarely *de facto,* the final authority on matters educational.

Thoroughgoing relativism furnishes the other party to the conflict, but it is not my task to expound it, even if it were necessary to do so. Each side has its theoretical difficulties, but the actual struggle takes place in the school board meeting, the classroom, and in the heart and mind of every thoughtful teacher.

51. A Philosophy of Catholic Education in a Time of Change

Right Reverend Monsignor Justin A. Driscoll

A vital issue in this day of ferment and stress is the philosophy of Catholic education. In surveying current literature—books, abstracts, and periodicals—one finds a broad spectrum of writings on Catholic education. Some of the literature is interesting and stimulating, but too much is unimaginative, pessimistic, or boring. Several articles have hinted at the need for new goals and objectives in Catholic education, but none has provided specific directives for such implementation.

Dr. William H. Conley, the first director of the Notre Dame study in Catholic education, stated this issue very well in his editorial in the September 1966 issue of *The Catholic School Journal:*

The first task before Catholic education is the development of a new statement of philosophy and objectives for the United States during this period in history. It must answer the question, "Why should Catholic schools exist in the United States?" The answers given to this question fifty years ago, or even twenty-five years ago, will not satisfy today. They will not be adequate for the coming decades. The essentials of a Catholic philosophy of education based on

SOURCE: *The Catholic School Journal* (November 1967), 29–33. Copyright © 1967 by CCM Professional Magazines, Inc. All rights reserved. Reprinted by permission of the publisher.

the nature of God, the nature of man and his dependence upon God, the nature of truth and man's relation to it and the ability to attain it, have of course, not changed. But the expansion of knowledge and the social developments which have taken place require new emphases. The objections which are the specifying or detailing of goals cannot have meaning or relevance in this drastically changing world unless there is adaptation to the change.[1]

In outlining a philosophy of Catholic education, even in this scientific and psychological age, the educator must have a clear concept of the nature of the children he teaches. Through the guided experiences offered in the school, the goals based on a true philosophy of Catholic education are achieved.

Basic Principles of Catholic Education

IN TERMS OF THE INDIVIDUAL

The broad outlines of the Catholic philosophy of education were sketched over thirty years ago by Pope Pius XI in his encyclical *Divini Illius Magistri* in a statement which is still vital: The "proper and immediate end of Christian education is cooperation with Divine grace in forming the true and perfect Christian, that is, to form Christ Himself in those regenerated by baptism." The Holy Father defined the limits within which our work as educators is operative: "Christian education takes the whole aggregate of human life, physical and spiritual, intellectual and moral, individual, domestic, and social."

The encyclical spelled out carefully the type of Christian we are expected to produce through the Catholic school: "The supernatural man who thinks, judges, and acts constantly and consistently in accordance with right reason illumined by the supernatural light of the example and teaching of Christ."

When we speak of the philosophy of Catholic education, we are mindful of the type of Christian we wish to educate. We recognize certain qualities about that person: he is composed of both matter and spirit, created by a personal God, and endowed with many natural powers. These powers—intellectual, volitional, emotional, and physical—are good when developed and controlled, and they enable him to know and desire the good and the true. Since he is a social being, it is necessary that he communicate with others. Through baptism, his fallen nature is raised to the dignity of a "child of God." Therefore the goal of Christian education is that of character in action; of Christian living in relation to God and the Church, to fellowman, and to nature.

[1] Conley, William H., "Renewal of Catholic Education," *The Catholic School Journal,* Vol. 66, No. 7, September, 1966, p. 4.

The Christian citizen that the Catholic school is expected to fashion is well grounded in the teachings of his faith, soundly formed in the rules of morality, intellectually prepared to participate in the functions of society, happily introduced to the ways of the ascetical and mystical life, and properly oriented towards rational integration of the person—he is a true citizen of the city of man and the city of God. Far from being a utopian ideal which we more or less hopefully strive to accomplish, this is a very definite and specific goal to which our efforts must unceasingly be directed.

IN TERMS OF THE COMMUNITY

Historically, and especially since 1900, Catholics of America have tended to emphasize the individual or the family aspect of living, rather than the community. Father Roman A. Bernert, formerly of Marquette University, observed that Catholics tended to be upright citizens who obeyed the law, but were hesitant in becoming shapers of the law. He noted that Catholic education was similarly colored by this tendency, which emphasized the salvation of one's soul rather than the salvation history of God's people. Thomas Jefferson, in a treatise on government, expressed a similar emphasis when he said that "two principles should govern the behavior of the individuals—reason and self-interest." [2]

Paraphrasing William Osborne in applying this Jeffersonian concept to the Church's treatment of minority groups, Father Bernert remarked that American Catholicism emphasized "the *individual* nature of evil as distinct from *institutional* or *cultural* evil, and the frequent reception of the sacraments as the keystone of salvation of one's soul." He commented that "the responsibility of bishops and priests was restricted almost entirely to the 'salvation process' . . . they provided churches, priests, novenas, retreats, and a Catholic education for the Negro (and other minority groups) but did very little for their socio-economic welfare." Only one thing seemed clear, the salvation of souls was the Supreme Law. [3]

The main objective which received nearly all the attention and effort of Catholic educators seemed to be the first commandment, with an emphasis on the formation of successful, individualistic, capitalistic, *laissez-faire,* progressive businessmen who on Sundays could feel reasonably comfortable in church as long as they "loved the Lord their God with their whole hearts, with their whole souls, and with their whole minds" (Mt 22, 27). However, small concern and effort were expended on the second commandment, which is like the first, "Thou shalt love thy neighbor as thyself." [4]

---

[2] Bernert, Rev. Roman A., S.J., "Catholic School Objectives: Do We Need a New Approach?," *The Catholic School Journal,* Vol. 66, No. 7, September, 1966, p. 50.

[3] Osborne, William, "The Church and the Negro: A Crisis in Leadership," *Cross Currents,* Vol. XV, No. 2, Spring, 1965, p. 133.

[4] Bernert, *op. cit.,* p. 51.

This idea was also one of the negative conclusions of the Greeley-Rossi study: "In the general population there was only very weak association (less than 11 percent) between religious education and enlightened social attitudes." [5]

Behind this type of emphasis was the assumption that society will be Christian if the individuals in it are Christian. Although the individual is the basic unit of the family, and the family of society, will the world be brought to Christianity by working on the individual as an individual? One might wonder if the "true and perfect Christian," the product of a Christian education, will be formed by emphasizing the individual; or will this tend to make him more self-centered, introspective, individualized, and selfish?

The Declaration on Christian Education by Vatican II makes it clear that much greater emphasis must be placed on the *social character* of Christian education.

Its [the school's] proper function is to create for the school community a special atmosphere animated by the Gospel spirit of freedom and charity, to help youth grow according to the new creatures they were made through baptism as they develop their own personalities, and finally to order the whole of human culture to the news of salvation so that the knowledge the students gradually acquire of the world life, and man is illumined by faith. So indeed the Catholic school, while it is open, as it must be, to the condition of the contemporary world, leads its students to promote efficaciously the good of the earthly city and also prepare them for service in the spread of the Kingdom of God. . . .[6]

Declaration on Christian Education

Vatican II marked a new positive period. It laid the foundation for future planning in education as well as in other fields. In the words of Pope Paul VI, the Council gave to the life of the Church new attitudes of mind, new aims, new standards of behavior; and rediscovered a spiritual beauty in all its aspects.

In the *Declaration on Christian Education* some major changes in our viewpoints on Catholic education are emphasized.

1. Basic Right to Education. All men of every race, condition, and age enjoy the dignity of human persons and may rightfully be educated according to their talents, culture, and ancestry, the Council tells us. Through association in brotherhood, genuine unity and earthly peace will be promoted, and the total good of society will be strengthened. To this end,

[5] Greeley, Andrew M., and Rossi, Peter H., *The Education of Catholic Americans* (Chicago: Aldine Publishing Co.), p. 220.

[6] *Declaration on Christian Education* by Vatican II, para. 7.

Catholics must give a wholehearted attention, and they must do it *soon*. With the latest scientific advances, the young can be assisted in developing their physical, moral, and intellectual qualities. By proper instruction in necessary and useful skills, they can become worthy members of a community, always recognizing and working toward the common good of every man. It is our duty to work for the spread of education for *every* person. This will call for sacrifice and service.

2. *Universal Education.* Catholics are exhorted to become concerned with the whole of man's life. They are especially urged to see that the educational needs of all men in all parts of the world are fulfilled. Ever-increasing efforts are to be made to promote the works of education.

3. *Ultimate Purpose.* A true education—Christian in all aspects—must enable the baptized person to give witness to the faith received. Through liturgical worship and a life of righteousness and sanctity, the individual must assist in promoting the Christian transformation of the world. Pastors of souls must make every effort to see that all the faithful, especially the young, have an opportunity for a suitable education—one in which truth and love are harmoniously developed.

4. *Parental Responsibility.* Since parents have brought life to their children, it is their responsibility, first and foremost, to provide and supervise the education of their children. It is a parental duty to create an atmosphere of love and reverence for God and a wholesome respect for their neighbor. It is through the family that children develop those social virtues necessary to belong to the People of God.

Since parents are the first teachers, they must enjoy true freedom in founding and choosing schools for their children. With the assistance of the government, whose duty it is to oversee and defend the liberties of its citizens, adequate schooling should be provided for every child, without unjust economic burdens placed upon parents who choose a Christian education.

All the faithful should assist in advancing the whole function of the school, especially in providing the young with authentic moral training.

5. *Assisting Agency—The Church.* As a human society capable of educating, the Church seeks to give all men an education penetrated with the spirit of Christ. She also offers her services to everyone by promoting the full development of the human person.

The Church is eager to employ modern methods and techniques in educating, especially that catechetical training which provides a knowledgeable active participation in the liturgy leading to apostolic action. She encourages the use of all other media of social communication and the formation of groups devoted to spiritual and physical development.

Because she desires to serve all humanity, the Church is deeply concerned about the religious education of those students who attend schools other than Catholic. She exhorts the teachers of these children to witness affection and helpfulness in transmitting in a suitable manner the doctrine of salvation.

6. *Assisting Agency—The School.* Animated by the spirit of freedom and charity found in the Gospels, the Catholic school seeks to hand on the cultural heritage of the past and to develop the intellectual powers of the students in preparing them for professional life.

Because of the differing backgrounds and temperaments of the students, the school can foster a willingness toward understanding. It is also the duty of the school to match the student's growth as God's new creature with that of his human personality. While pursuing cultural goals and natural development, the school strives to have the light of faith illumine the student's knowledge so that he can become the saving leaven of mankind.

Catholic schools—of every kind and at every level—should take on different forms in keeping with local circumstances. Elementary and secondary schools are still regarded as the foundations of education, but professional and technical schools, centers for adult education and social welfare, and schools for those requiring special care, are to be founded and fostered.

All schools should be centers whose work is the concern of families, teachers, civil society, and the entire community.

7. *The Teacher.* Co-partners with the parents in Christian education are the teachers who possess special qualities of mind and heart and who, through careful preparation, have the ability to renew and to adapt. All teachers should realize that *they* determine whether the goals of the school are fruitful.

Each teacher must be prepared in secular and religious knowledge, appropriately certified, and equipped with the best modern educational skills. By witnessing Christ in their teaching and in their lives, teachers stimulate students to personal initiative. After graduation of their students, teachers should continue to assist them with advice and friendship. The work of teaching is a true apostolate, most necessary for our times, and one which renders an authentic service to society. Young people should become aware of its importance, and should consider making it their life's vocation.

8. *Higher Learning.* Catholic colleges and universities are to be schools of excellence in which the graduates become Christian witnesses, who accept the challenge of true research in the pursuit of knowledge. These centers of higher learning are called upon to cooperate and collaborate with

all other educational institutions in molding men outstanding in training, who are ready to undertake the responsibilities of society and to witness the faith to the world. These institutions should be concerned with excellence rather than with enrollment. A mutual sharing within and between colleges and universities is called for. Together they can promote international gatherings, share scientific inquiry, communicate discoveries, and exchange professors.

Since the future of society and of the Church depends upon the young who are engaged in higher studies, it is imperative that the spiritual life of these students be so developed that they become true leaders who are at the same time truly Christian.

9. *The Student.* With the aid of the latest advances in psychology and in teaching, children and young people must be assisted in acquiring a mature sense of responsibility. In every phase of education, teachers must work with parents to provide for the individual differences of each child. A positive and prudent education in sex should be given according to the needs of the students. They should be trained to participate actively in community organizations, to discourse openly with others, and to be always willing to promote the common good.

10. *The Poor.* All Christians are especially urged to foster the education of the young, but of special concern are the needs of those who are poor or without a family. No sacrifice is to be spared in helping the school provide suitable training for these and for the non-Catholic. Promising students with slight means, and those from the newer countries, such as those lately established in the African nation, should have an opportunity for Catholic higher education.

The welfare of *all* children is to be served, not only for the salvation of souls, but also for the good of the earthly society and for the building of a better world.

The Church, through the *Declaration on Christian Education,* indicates that she has no desire to remain away *from* the world in a form of isolation, but that Christian education is *in* the world, and *for* the world, since man must always work out his salvation in the concrete situation in which God has placed him, and must achieve this not by protection but by contributing to the whole human community, of which he is an integral and inseparable part.

Other Decrees of Vatican II

Another document which throws new light on Catholic education is the *Decree on the Apostolate of the Laity.* The laity, as the People of God, are co-responsible with bishops, priests, and religious in presenting God's word by means of catechetical instructions. Parents should be the first to teach the faith to their children, and to educate them in a Christian manner through word and example. Training for the apostolate must start with the child's earliest education, so they in turn can be true witnesses to Christ among their companions. They should be taught to go beyond the family circle and become involved in community and parish affairs, conscious that they are living and active members of God's family.

Schools, colleges, and other Catholic institutions are also responsible for developing a Catholic sense and apostolic activity in young people. Teachers and educators should have the learning and skills that are needed for imparting effective apostolic training. Lay people are urged to participate in study sessions, congresses, meetings, and conferences, and to be acquainted with pertinent books and periodicals.

All men, especially those Catholics skilled in public affairs and Christian doctrine, should work together to preserve in civil legislation the rights of the family regarding the education of their children.

If taken seriously, this decree will bring invaluable benefits to the world. This is already evident in the more prominent role of the lay teacher, participation of parish members in teacher-aide programs, and leadership of laymen in parish and diocesan boards of education.

William B. Ball in "Justice in Federal Aid After Vatican II" states:

If Catholic schools are to provide education for the world, if they are to have profound relevance to all of the concerns of the secular city, then the particular insights and contributions of the apostolic layman as to education will be indispensable. Catholic education will have the objective of forming apostolic lay people, not defensive, ghettoized Catholics, not Catholics obsequious in the presence of authority, but real sowers of seed, leaders, teachers, and transformers of the times.[7]

COOPERATING WITH OTHERS

The *Decree on Ecumenism* tells us that we must not only come to understand the outlook of our separated brethren, but that we must participate in activities and enterprises that help foster unity among Christians. We are urged to avoid those expressions, judgments, and actions which militate against this unity. Study that is pursued with truth and good will enables Catholics to appreciate the distinctive doctrines of those not of our faith. The history, spiritual and liturgical life, religious psychology, and cultural backgrounds of those of other faiths need understanding.

After Catholic beliefs are explained more carefully in terms that our

[7] Ball, William B., "Justice in Federal Aid After Vatican II," *Catholic Mind,* Vol. LXIV, No. 1207, November, 1966, p. 30–34.

separated brethren can comprehend, dialogue will take place. From such encounters the true position of the Catholic Church will emerge, and there will be a better knowledge of the attitudes of all.

Cooperation among Christians contributes to a greater appreciation of the dignity of the human person, promotes peace, applies the principles of the Gospel to social life, and advances the arts and sciences. Such unity also makes possible the relief of affliction and illiteracy, and leads to an enriched understanding of one another.

Also of importance to the mission of the school is the *Declaration on the Relationship of the Church to Non-Christian Religions*. Catholics are told to forget past differences and become forward-looking by striving sincerely for that mutual understanding and respect which are the results of biblical and theological studies and of brotherly dialogues. Anything that is true and holy in non-Christian religions is to be accepted, for these views reflect that Truth which enlightens all men. It is through dialogue with these brothers that we recognize and promote their spiritual and moral values and those of their society and culture. The decree tells us to be careful—to "take pains"—that our teaching and preaching conform to the truth of the Gospel and to the spirit of Christ.

Unless all peoples work together, think together, and act together, they will not be able to improve extensively their relationships among all mankind.

As far as the long-range position of the Catholic school is concerned, Mr. Ball calls these two decrees (ecumenical and relation to non-Christian religions) the most important of all the Vatican II documents.

They are proving to be catalysts, not only among Catholics, but among all the American people. . . . The hand of God is not evident in the whole wonderful development. The image of Catholic exclusiveness is starting a promised, gradual disappearance, because the fact of exclusiveness is starting to break down. Dialogue and cooperation are evident everywhere. Love is begetting love. We have not, however, even begun to see the results of the ecumenical movement. Wait till the first Christ-Council generation of Americans comes of age: they will be people of whom this country has not seen the like. Likely they will be people much farther removed from the prejudices of our day than we are from those of a century ago. Hopefully, they will be as strange to some of the tensions that have stopped us as we are from feelings over Free Silver or the Stamp Tax.[8]

FREEDOM IN EDUCATION

Vatican II in the *Declaration on Religious Freedom* has opened a way towards new confidence in ecumenical relationships, and a new straightfor-

[8] *Ibid.*

wardness in affinity between the Church and the world. As the teachings in our schools begin to reflect not only ecumenism, but also religious liberty, alarm over a religiously oriented education will lessen. This in turn will help the Catholic people achieve, in the public forum, a great measure of justice for their children.

The declaration specifically vindicates freedom in education as a significant aspect of religious freedom. It states that the government must acknowledge the parent's right to make a free choice of schools without imposing unjust burdens or forcing children to attend instructions not in agreement with their beliefs. It also asserts that a single educational system which excludes all religion is not to be imposed on all peoples. Religious bodies also have a right to teach publicly and witness to the truth, both through speaking and writing. They are encouraged to hold meetings and to establish educational, cultural, charitable, and social organizations.

The Council urges everyone, especially those charged with the task of educating others, to do their utmost in forming persons who respect the moral order and are obedient to lawful authority.

It is hoped that the implications of this teaching of a most respected document will not be lost upon our brothers of other faiths.[9]

The development of relevant objectives which flow from our philosophy is not without its obstacles in this age. The secular trend in philosophy— the God-is-dead issue, secular humanism, existentialism, and situationism —these are all built upon the assumption that man can get along without God. Are we aware that in education the drift is away from God? There is evident necessity that Catholic schools must hold fast to their position and to their essential traditions. Catholic educators must take a stand on fundamentals, making a positive plan for renewal, remaining steadfastly aware of the unchangeable in a changing world. It is now time to plan realistically for such a renewal, proposing objectives that are relevant to our educational world of the here and now.

[9] *Ibid.*

52. John Dewey's Philosophy of Education

Phyllis Sullivan

Introduction

During the period between 1870–1910 radical changes were taking place in American society: there was an accelerating scientific and technological revolution; vast manufacturing centers were developing; new machines were bringing about industrial changes; railroad networks were binding nations together; and there was growth of a world-wide market. The new emphasis on industry brought an influx of population to the urban areas and a new problem to educators. Within these forty years, population doubled due to immigration and natural causes.

While these scientific, technological, and population changes were taking place, a revolution in education was also in the making. Previous to this period, education was received from the home and some public institutions. With the rapidly growing urban communities and the increase in population, the existing schools and the home were totally inadequate to provide the type of education demanded by the society. Since education must fill the needs and desires of society, the inadequacy of and discontent with the then present educational procedures fostered a system of education which was "a positive and constructive development of purposes, methods, and subject matter on the foundation of a theory of experience and its educational potentialities." [1] This system was based upon John Dewey's philosophy of education. Dewey felt that democracy depended upon education by the school and family to insure its growth, and that due to cultural inertia, education had lagged behind the social movement. America was a democracy, but education remained undemocratic. To force children to

[1] Joseph Ratner (ed.), *Intelligence in the Modern World—John Dewey's Philosophy* (New York: The Modern Library, 1939), p. 659.

SOURCE: *The High School Journal*, XL, 8 (May 1966), 391–97. Reprinted by permission of the publisher, The University of North Carolina Press.

study a standard course of material previously devised was against the democratic principle of life.[2]

Dewey's Philosophy of Education

THE PRINCIPLES OF EDUCATION

With the principles of democracy as a basis, Dewey developed a new concept of education emphasizing experience and growth. He defined the educational process as a process of growth and development by reorganizing or reconstructing of experiences which increased an individual's ability to direct subsequent experiences. Education has no end beyond itself. It should not be preparation solely for the future, but rather living every stage of present development. By giving the child command of himself starting in the present, the future will take care of itself. Education should not be the pouring of knowledge into a child, but supplying its growth from within. Growth meant to Dewey a movement toward a later result. Education should provide conditions for growth not only in school but also in adult life.[3] What then are the conditions necessary for growth?

Education must begin by understanding a child's capacities, interests, habits, and instincts. A child's nature is naturally active; therefore, Dewey's democratic school emphasized activities, not an inflexible or set curriculum. By participating in activities based upon his own interests, capacities, and previous experiences, a child learns through "direct living" and life.[4] The types of activities used to initiate growth vary with age, intellectual capacities, prior experiences, and social opportunity. Each activity should appeal to the child's present interest and needs.[5] A good activity is long enough so that several endeavors are involved and sufficiently complex so that several children can make many different responses. The initial desire for the activity must stem from the individual, and each step should help to raise a new question and a demand for more knowledge.[6] Some educators would call this the project method of teaching.

Experience as mentioned in Dewey's definition of education is a social

[2] John Dewey, *The Educational Situation* (Chicago: The University of Chicago Press, 1902), pp. 25–26.

[3] Joe Park (ed.), *Selected Readings in the Philosophy of Education* (New York: The Macmillan Company, 1958), pp. 21–81.

[4] Martin S. Dworkin (ed.), "The School and Society," *Dewey on Education* (New York: Bureau of Publications, Teachers College, Columbia University, 1959), pp. 41–46.

[5] Ratner, *op. cit.*, pp. 607–618.

[6] Martin S. Dworkin (ed.), "Progressive Education and the Science of Education," *Dewey on Education* (New York: Bureau of Publications, Teachers College, Columbia University, 1959), pp. 122–123.

process involving interaction of an individual with his environment. An experience includes initial confusion, tentative hypothesis, investigation, elaboration of hypothesis, and action to bring about results. Mere activity does not constitute an experience. The connection between performing an act and the consequence establishes the value of the activity.[7] Each activity should provide experiences upon which new experiences can be based. A good experience is a moving force which arouses interest, promotes activity, and sets up desires which are strong enough to get a person over the uninteresting aspects of the investigation to reach his final goal.[8] Experiences must be based on interest; interest not as a bait for unpleasant material, but actions which are connected with present mental powers and previous experiences.[9]

THE FUNCTION OF THE SCHOOL

What then is the function of the schools in promoting the democratic system of education? The traditional school with its physical arrangement intended for listening, its imposed discipline to get all students to learn the same material, its emphasis on conformity, its acquiring rather than inquiring atmosphere, and its set curriculum are totally inadequate to promote the spirit of social cooperation and the democratic concept. In the ideal school the child learns through social exchanges with others. When he has misconceptions, they are corrected. Good habits are acquired by carrying out activities for the common good of the group. Participation in activities provides opportunity for gaining knowledge. This type of learning is an extension of home training.[10] Education must create real life situations to provide appropriate experiences which suit the child's mental powers, interests and needs; to awaken new needs, raise new questions, and to provide the conditions necessary to develop all of the native capacities.[11] Discipline which was needed in the traditional school to enforce learning is not necessary in a democratic school. The social need for working together enforces control. Interest is a requisite for self-discipline, which is the ability to stick to an activity and carry it through to completion.[12] The only true discipline is that which comes through life, not imposed discipline. The child learns only those things which he experiences.[13]

---

[7] Park, op. cit., pp. 93–94.

[8] Ratner, op. cit., pp. 666–670.

[9] Park, op. cit., p. 91.

[10] Dworkin, "The School and Society," op. cit., pp. 51–53.

[11] John Dewey, Education Today (New York: G. P. Putnam's Sons, 1940), p. 209.

[12] Park, op. cit., pp. 77–93.

[13] Dworkin, "The School and Society," op. cit., p. 41.

THE CURRICULUM

There should be no set succession of studies. The social life of a child provides the background and unity for all of his education. The child should engage in constructive, expressive activities originating from his own social activities and relating to his previous experiences.[14] The activities could be associated with occupations or activities selected by the teachers and students as needs and interests arise. The activities should always start with the capacities and experiences already developed and be selected on the criterion of presenting new problems which stimulate new ways of observation and judgment.[15]

THE TEACHER

The teacher is concerned with ways in which a subject can become part of those experiences the child has had, how to use these experiences, and how he may assist in interpreting the child's needs and interests to place him in appropriate conditions for experiencing. Without relating the subject matter to experience, the material is purely symbolic and formal. Symbols which have no meaning because they are not connected with experience make education dead. When symbols are presented externally, motivation is lacking; there is no need for facts, no former experience with which to assimilate the new symbols. When former experiences are considered, subject matter can be an outgrowth of present activities. This in itself provides the motive or the need for learning.[16]

It is the teacher's obligation to know each child intimately. By knowing each child's needs, interests, and capacities the teacher can guide activities through discussions and suggestions. He can help find projects which lead by orderly inter-connection with other subject matter to adequate, realistic goals, and shape the end result through development of intermediate steps leading to it.[17] The teacher has subject matter at his finger tips and is therefore free from occupation with subject matter to observe pupil's attitudes, present needs, and capabilities.[18]

[14] Martin S. Dworkin (ed.), "My Pedagogic Creed," *Dewey on Education* (New York: Bureau of Publications, Teachers College, Columbia University, 1959), pp. 25–27.

[15] Ratner, *op. cit.*, pp. 674–675.

[16] Martin S. Dworkin (ed.), "The Child and the Curriculum," *Dewey on Education* (New York: Bureau of Publications, Teachers College, Columbia University, 1959), pp. 106–107.

[17] Ratner, *op. cit.*, pp. 624–626.

[18] Park, *op. cit.*, pp. 102–103.

Summary and Conclusions

Dewey's system of education is sometimes called progressive, sometimes called the new education. Dewey himself often hesitated to be classed with other so-called progressives because he didn't agree with their methods. His concept of progressive education was a revision of the curriculum and methods, not eliminating subject matter. He was against the child-centered concept because a child was a social being and therefore not self-centered as the term implied. He felt that education was a social task. Its purpose was not to carry on present societal concepts through future generations, but rather to educate for a better society, eliminating the undesirable in the environment and stressing the good to provide a better society. Education was to be carried out by using the democratic principle of life, by promoting freedom of activities and thought and stressing individuality, and by learning self-discipline through first-hand experiences.

The activities in the progressive schools were not just haphazard attempts to master subject matter as some educators have said. Each activity had specific goals to be reached through intermediate steps developed by inter-connecting, related subject matter to reach the solution.

Dewey has received vehement criticism both good and bad. Because of his democratic principles and humane methods, many educators lauded his attempts. His methods enriched the curriculum and allowed a student to carry a problem through to completion without division of subject matter. If nothing else, Dewey's philosophy brought the urgency of the educational problem to the attention of the American people. What better way to teach democracy than to put it to use in education!

Dewey encountered several problems in administering his system of education. The physical set up in most schools was for a passive system of education. Existing schools were resistant to change. Whenever money ran short, the "frills" were dropped, and the progressive type classes were considered "frills." There was also a tendency to be more critical of an innovation than of traditional education. Whenever a student had a shortcoming, it was blamed on the new method.

Dewey was criticized for trying to take a short cut to education. Without formal subjects his system of education appeared to be only trial and error. He neglected to develop his concept of subject matter content, its selection, development, and organization. The concepts that were written often lacked clarity, thus leading to misinterpretation. Whatever the criticisms for or against Dewey, it would appear obvious that he contributed many thought-provoking questions for traditional educators.

It is difficult to evaluate how many of Dewey's concepts have carried

TRADITIONAL VERSUS DEWEY'S PROGRESSIVE EDUCATION *

Concept	Traditional	Progressive
1. The aim of classroom conduct is	conformity.	individuality and freedom.
2. The method of teaching is	constant drill and repetition.	activities appealing to thought.
3. The emphasis on individuality is	brushed aside.	stressed.
4. Activities and experiences are	imposed from without.	built on previous experiences.
5. The structure of subject matter is	systematized.	based on interests.
6. A typical classroom is	passive and designed for listening.	active where talking and conferring are engaged in.
7. Students are grouped	through tests.	for social purposes.
8. Special talents are	overlooked.	used in cooperative experiences.
9. The purpose of education is	to perpetuate present social order.	to perpetuate a better social order.
10. The educational atmosphere is	acquiring.	inquiring.
11. Natural inquisitiveness is	ignored.	used as a starting point for investigations.
12. The curriculum is	uniform.	not a set series of studies.
13. The emphasis on experience is	outside of the child.	within the child.
14. The social impulses of creating and producing are	neglected.	stressed.
15. The school is	not a social institution which functions with other social institutions.	is a social institution which functions and interacts with other social institutions.
16. The aim of education is	getting the child ready for later life.	utilizing present life opportunities.

* The facts for this compilation have been taken from all of the sources listed in the bibliography and synthesized for this chart.

over into present-day education. Certainly the project method is used in modern-day classrooms. Activity courses such as home economics and industrial arts would seem to get their impetus from Dewey. The concept of first-hand experiences is evident in the laboratory sciences, library research, language laboratories, and field trips. The core concept also was an effort to correlate related subjects to make education more cohesive.

It would seem that America is again at a crossroads in education. With the accelerating pace of technology, education in 1966 is inadequate to prepare students for a technological life without education beyond high school. The dropout problem is of prime importance to modern educators. School methods and discipline are not sufficient to keep the interest of all students; thus, America is losing valuable manpower through the dropout. Dewey's activity method based on students' interests and capabilities might be a step in curbing the dropout problem and providing more adequate preparation for a more technological life.

Dewey's concept of learning in small segmented parts has been accepted as an important method of learning. Only one application of this theory of learning is B. F. Skinner's teaching machine based on this concept.

Whatever the reader's opinion of John Dewey, it would seem that one thing could be agreed upon. Without studying Dewey's philosophy of education, a very important aspect of the historical foundations of education would be omitted.

Bibliography

Dewey, John. *Education Today*. New York: G. P. Putnam's Sons, 1940. 370 pp.

Dewey, John. *The Educational Situation*. Chicago: The University of Chicago Press, 1902. 104 pp.

Dworkin, Martin S. (ed.) "The Child and the Curriculum," *Dewey on Education*. New York: Bureau of Publications, Teachers College, Columbia University, 1959. pp. 91–111.

Dworkin, Martin S. (ed.). "My Pedagogic Creed," *Dewey on Education*. New York: Bureau of Publications, Teachers College, Columbia University, 1959. pp. 19–32.

Dworkin, Martin S. (ed.). "Progressive Education and the Science of Education," *Dewey on Education*. New York: Bureau of Publications, Teachers College, Columbia University, 1959. pp. 113–126.

Dworkin, Martin S. (ed.). "The School and Society," *Dewey on Education*. New York: Bureau of Publications, Teachers College, Columbia University, 1959. pp. 33–90.

Park, Joe (ed.). *Selected Readings in the Philosophy of Education.* New York: The Macmillan Company, 1958. 440 pp.

Ratner, Joseph (ed.). *Intelligence in the Modern World—John Dewey's Philosophy.* New York: The Modern Library, 1939. 1077 pp.

53. Existentialism and Educational Theory[1]

C. A. Bowers

Existentialism has been defined as an attempt at philosophizing from the standpoint of the actor instead of, as has been customary, from that of the spectator.[2] It can be further differentiated from the traditional metaphysical approach to philosophy by an examination of the different modes of inquiry they respectively pursue. By raising questions about the existence of universals and the nature of truth, substance, and causality, the metaphysician seeks rational answers which will give an objective picture of the universe and man's place in it. Consequently, his attention is focused on the "reality" lying behind or beyond immediate experience, but not directly on experience itself. The existentialist wants to answer questions that are more relevant to human experience. Thus, he wants to know what gives meaning to man's existence; he explores the nature of freedom and its impact on the form of life man accepts for himself; and he seeks to understand the forces that cause man to become alienated from himself and his environment. The answer to these questions, he informs us, can only be found through an introspective examination of one's own experience. His answers will thus lack the universality of the metaphysician's; they will be,

[1] This paper was originally presented at the annual meeting of the Canadian Association of Professors of Education, Charlottetown, Prince Edward Island, 1964.

[2] E. L. Allen, *Existentialism from Within* (London: Routledge and Kegan Paul, Ltd., 1953), p. 3.

SOURCE: *Educational Theory,* XV, 3 (July 1965), 222–29. Reprinted by permission of the author, C. A. Bowers, Chairman, Department of Educational Foundations, University of Oregon, and the publisher.

in fact, entirely subjective. The Logical Positivists, along with John Dewey, have shown that the questions raised by the metaphysician reach beyond experience; therefore his answers cannot be proven either true or false by empirical methods of verification. This fact has caused some educational theorists to recognize that it is unfruitful to justify educational goals and procedures with metaphysical arguments. Others, however, continue the sterile practice of deducing educational principles from the traditional philosophical categories—Idealism, Realism, Rationalism, etc.

Kierkegaard's definition of a philosopher as a man who built a magnificent palace and then went to live in a hovel somewhere on the grounds is therefore relevant today. The educational philosophies we carefully deduce from traditional philosophical categories are in many ways just as irrelevant as the philosopher's magnificent palace. Although the public tolerates our speculative efforts, it requires us to inhabit a dwelling not made to our specifications. If educational theorists are going to be taken seriously by the public, they will have to turn their attention to the problems of human existence when attempting to justify their programs. A number of educational theorists have already rejected the metaphysician's interests as irrelevant, and are turning to the needs of society in order to justify educational programs that teach specific skills and social values. This approach, which is characteristic of both pragmatism and social reconstructionism, is inadequate because it emphasizes only the social side of man's nature, it ignores the inner man, the solitariness of one's being, where significant decisions are made. Existentialism is the only philosophical point of view which stresses this aspect of man's reality.

Existentialism represents a form of philosophical inquiry which cannot be easily categorized according to traditional modes of Western thought. Yet it is possible to find its position represented throughout Western history by men who, rejecting metaphysical speculation as too abstract and sterile, sought the meaning of existence in experience. The roots of existentialism can be traced from Socrates through St. Augustine, Pascal, Nietzsche, and Kierkegaard, but it is only in recent years that it has become an important movement. It has traditionally been a form of reaction against the submergence of the individual in a system; philosophical, religious, political, technological. It is still, in part, a philosophy of revolt. If one looks only at what the existentialist opposes, he cannot help but gain the impression that existentialism offers a nihilistic outlook, and therefore can give little positive direction in the formulation of one's philosophy. Today the existentialist is rebelling against large segments of our social life: the dehumanizing practice of reducing people to numbers that can be easily manipulated and controlled, the tendency to regard the individual as a means to a commercial or political end, our preoccupation with triviality, and our deliberate state of mental unawareness which is encouraged by so many social agencies—to name just a few. However, when the existentialist revolts against a social evil, he is in the same act, as Albert Camus has poignantly shown, affirming another value as being more worthwhile.[3] In saying "no" to mental or physical servitude he is, at the same time, committing himself to the value of individual freedom. The social practices against which the existentialist is revolting are real; to avoid contributing inadvertently to them we must examine both the reasons for his protest and the values he wants society to recognize. Moreover, a clearer understanding of what the existentialist calls the human condition may contribute to the revision of our present philosophies of education, which are largely derived from theories that tend to limit man within the confines of a definition.

The most significant idea advanced by the existentialist, though the religious existentialist would vigorously dispute it, is that "man first of all exists, encounters himself, surges up in the world—and defines himself afterwards." [4] This declaration that man first exists and then creates his own essence is in marked contrast to the position that man's essence is a universal existing prior to the individual. By rejecting the idea of pre-determination, which has been upheld for centuries by the followers of Plato and Aristotle, the existentialist is saying, in effect, that man is totally free to become the kind of person he proposes. The essence he creates is a product of his choices and will vary from individual to individual. Although we are not always aware of it, each moment confronts us with the necessity of choosing between alternative courses of action—and we can neither escape the burden of decision making nor the responsibility for the choice that is finally made. For example, we are constantly making decisions of a minor nature—the color of tie to wear, the route we will take to work—and less frequently, decisions of major significance: should one openly declare himself against racial prejudice or is it better to avoid getting involved personally? The paradox presented us by the existentialist is that each individual is free, whether he wants to be or not, to make a choice that only he can determine. But he must bear in solitude the anguish which accompanies his choice. Contrary to the belief of many, religion does not offer an escape from the burden of freedom. Abraham experienced the anguish of decision making when he had to decide whether it was really the voice of an angel or a figment of his imagination that commanded him to sacrifice his son. He was alone with the evidence and free to make his own interpretation; his freedom of choice was inescapable. The solitariness of decision making and the anguish of uncertainty are constant themes in existentialist literature. Critics have been quick to point to this as an example of the tragic image of man which existentialism pro-

---

[3] Albert Camus, *The Rebel* (New York: Vintage Books, 1956), p. 14.

[4] Jean-Paul Sartre, "Existentialism Is a Humanism" from *Existentialism from Dostoevsky to Sartre* by Walter Kaufmann (New York: Meridian Books, 1956), p. 290.

jects. They have, unfortunately, failed to see that the existentialist is not counselling flight and despair, but affirmation of life and reconciliation with oneself.[5]

If the individual does not possess a universal human nature, the question arises as to how he obtains his identity. Does he define himself or do the institutions within society tell him what he is and what is expected of him? If he is defined by social institutions or by another individual, part of his total self will be abstracted to fit the label given him: taxpayer, Jew, student, Protestant, black. The value of the individual's uniqueness is either generalized away or completely ignored; he becomes real to others as a label only. Because of the impossibility of doing justice to the uniqueness of the total self, both realized and potential, the existentialist wants each individual to come to terms with the meaning of his own existence. A new school of psychology, including Abraham Maslow, Gordon Allport and Viktor Frankl, is now trying to give this viewpoint a theoretical foundation. Frankl claims that "man's search for meaning is a primary force in his life and not a 'secondary rationalization of instinctual drives.' " [6] Both the existentialist and the "third force" psychologist are aware that the process of self-identification is an unending task: to define man is to limit him.

In contrast to the philosophers who have ignored the dilemma of human existence, the existentialist is the only one who has had anything important to say about the problem of alienation. Educational theorists like John Dewey and Robert M. Hutchins have also disregarded its significance even though many of the conflicting demands made on the school are a result of this social problem. Alienation is a characteristic of the human condition that manifests itself in a variety of ways. For our purpose of gaining insights that can serve as guides to new educational goals, it will suffice to indicate that the most common form of alienation is the individual's inability to have deep feelings for, or to derive significant meanings from, the experiences he undergoes. Or the individual may attach a meaning to an object and make the mistake of assuming the meaning he gives represents all the meaning and value the object possesses. This practice results in imposing on that which is the center of experience a reality and truth which may be only peripheral.[7] Furthermore, we become alienated from ourselves when we live without knowing why, and when we try to avoid present realities by living for the future or in the past. Alienation from our fellow man takes the form of treating him as an object to be manipulated for one's own psychological ends; while alienation from one's environment

[5] Norman N. Greene, *Jean-Paul Sartre: The Existentialist Ethic* (Ann Arbor: The University of Michigan Press, 1960), p. 9.

[6] Viktor Frankl, *Man's Search for Meaning* (New York: Washington Square Press, Inc., 1963), p. 154.

[7] Martin Buber, *I and Thou* (New York: Charles Scribner's Sons, 1958), pp. 22–23.

is manifested by a lack of awareness and sensitivity towards one's surroundings. Consuming without enjoying, evaluating an experience only in monetary terms, and acquiring friends on a basis other than mutual interest, are all common examples of alienation. In being alienated from oneself, the individual fails to discover what he values and believes in; according to Erich Fromm, when this happens his only haven is in conformity.[8] He will then look to others to find out who he is, what he should value, and how he should respond in different situations.

The existentialist has in effect drawn our attention to a new kind of universal. Unlike the universal forms and values of the metaphysician which were the absolutes from which we could draw a feeling of certainty, the existentialist speaks of the universal condition of man. Everybody, the world over, is confronted with the challenge of discovering his own identity. Moreover, we are all confronted with a basic decision which we have the freedom to make: the decision of settling for a life pre-occupied with triviality or one that is characterized by a stubborn search for a deeper truth and meaning. The universals of the human condition—the challenge and responsibility of using one's freedom, the search for the meaning of one's existence, and the problem of alienation—should be the center of attention for those educators who are sincerely concerned with providing learning experiences which contribute to the development of a free and morally responsible being. The use of the existentialist's concept of a universal, as opposed to that of the metaphysician, has the salutary advantage of allowing us to justify educational programs on philosophical grounds which do not contain a final definition of man. Instead of justifying the development of the individual's powers of reasoning on the grounds that man is a "rational animal"—a definition that tends to limit man by ignoring his other capacities—the existentialist would justify it with the argument that the ability to think rationally gives the individual a greater degree of freedom to choose and realize the kind of life that is determined from within.

When determining what should be taught and how, the existentialist claims we must take into consideration the ontological nature of man's freedom. Although freedom always exists in some form for the individual, we become aware of it only when we realize that to be alive means assuming the responsibility for making our own decisions. Freedom has been referred to as the methodological principle of the fulfilled human life. You do not "explain" freedom but use it to achieve other goals or ends.[9] Implicit here is the idea that one is not only conscious of his freedom but is also knowledgeable about the choices which are available. Without knowledge of desirable ends, freedom becomes a chaotic and disruptive force.

[8] Erich Fromm, *The Sane Society* (New York: Holt, Rinehart and Winston, 1955), p. 155.

[9] *Manus,* Volume XVII, No. 2 (January 8, 1964), p. 1.

Giving the student an awareness of the scope of his own freedom and the enlarged powers of reasoning necessary for its intelligent use should be considered a goal of an educational program. A number of practices in the field of education suggest this is not one of our present objectives. We teach the student how to fit into the group and how to conform to the expectations of society, but we do not make an equal effort to inform him that inherent in each situation are alternative choices and that his final choice should in the end be a private one, even if the choice is to conform to the group's mode of action. Nor do we make a significant effort to inform him that a morally responsible being is one who has developed his own inner core of values and who acts according to them even though the group pressures him to conform to its standards. The teaching of moral values in the classroom has become largely a matter of indoctrinating the student with particular values society expects him to live by. We have made social and economic efficiency the goal of education, and have ceased to think seriously about the type of education which liberalizes the individual.

The purpose of education, as seen from the existentialist point of view, is to enable the individual to understand his own culture so thoroughly he is no longer swayed unconsciously by its premises. With this understanding the individual becomes a free agent, knowing when and why he is conforming with or dissenting from the rest of his society. This educational goal cannot be achieved, however, as long as teachers themselves are unaware that they are being swayed by their culture. The dilemma is an existential one each teacher must face. He must become aware of the meaning of freedom in his own life before he can help the student to achieve the same state of awareness; self-deception on the part of the teacher can only thwart the student's powers of self-understanding and direction.

The quest for self-identity, which, according to the existentialist, has been largely ignored by our society, must also be considered as a central objective of any educational program. Discovery of self is primarily an educational process, and its importance has been recognized throughout Western history by individuals who have echoed the Socratic dictum: "Know thyself." Unfortunately their number has been small. For the most part, men have accepted from others—from teachers, philosophers, priests and politicians—instruction in who and what they are. This has led to frustration and conflict as they have tried to express their individuality in situations that required conformity from them. If, as the existentialist declares, we become alive at the center of our being only when we try to define who and what we are, should not the schools contribute intentionally to this form of learning?

References to the discovery of self as a worthwhile educational objective are scarce in recent educational literature. The lack of concern for this form of educational experience suggests that the schools are captives of the dominant social values; and these are, unfortunately, not the values of an introspective populace. What one finds are references to the learning of techniques: the technique of getting along with others, the technique of the market place, and the technique of conceptualizing in the traditional and socially accepted way. John Dewey, with his instrumentalist approach to both knowledge and value, epitomizes in many ways the North American society which has raised technique and process to a paramount position in social life. The existentialist is quick to point out that the limitations of Dewey's position are also the limitations of the general social outlook which he largely reflects. In commenting on Dewey's philosophy, one writer observed that pragmatism is afraid to face the ultimate puzzle of human individuality. Although the individual and his activities are what pragmatism is supposed to devote itself to, it is the adjusted individual, the stereotyped individual, the individual who has forgotten how to be an individual, that pragmatism celebrates.[10] The existentialist is not only criticizing Dewey for not having anything to say about the meaning of human existence, he is also indirectly challenging us to justify our educational program on the grounds of how much it contributes toward this form of understanding. In addition he might ask us to explain how the individual who has not been taught to think independently is going to resist the pressures of society. Albert Einstein's statement, "External compulsion can, to a certain extent, reduce but never cancel the responsibility of the individual," strikes a chord common to both the advocate of democracy and the existentialist.

When theorizing about the aims of education we cannot ignore the existential problem of alienation, for it is both an educational and a psychological problem. Formal education can reduce the degree of alienation by creating a frame of mind that is more open to the possibilities of experience and more sensitive to its meaning. It can also contribute to the alienation of the individual. This is done by indoctrinating him with the socially acceptable way of interpreting experience, and with the values which should be placed on experience. Harold Taylor, a former president of Sarah Lawrence College, observed that much of our education is devoted to teaching students how not to be themselves; by being taught a vocabulary acceptable to most people and a set of "facts" which are generally known, the student can go through life without ever having to express what he really thinks or feels.[11] He may know the prevailing social definition of truth and beauty, but unless he has done his own thinking in these areas he will not understand why something should be regarded as beautiful or true.

[10] Marjorie Grene, *Dreadful Freedom: A Critique of Existentialism* (Chicago: The University of Chicago Press, 1948), pp. 27–28.

[11] Harold Taylor, *Art and the Intellect* (New York: The Museum of Modern Art, 1960), pp. 20–21.

Our current tendency to place a positive value on education because it enables us to "get ahead" is a case in point. An education may be valuable for other reasons as well, but many people have mistaken the current popular value to be the only one that it can have. Unless the individual understands why he thinks or feels a certain way, he can never become the "majority of one" that Henry David Thoreau honors. Moreover, value judgments represent an authentic expression only when they come from within the individual; truth must also be an individual pursuit. We become pilgrims on the surface of life when we forget this fundamental truth. And it is this surface existence that characterizes the alienated person.

Educators cannot directly solve the problem of alienation, as it is an individual matter that is overcome as a greater understanding of self is attained. They can, however, indirectly assist the student by challenging him to examine the assumptions underlying the values and ideas which he learns from his culture. Arousing the student's curiosity and making him aware that an experience becomes fuller when it is entered into with an open mind, will help him to become less alienated from himself and his environment. This approach may be disconcerting to many teachers and administrators who fear the consequences that might result from the student's awareness of his own freedom and responsibility for self-discovery. Unorthodoxy in tastes, values and ideas all too often threatens the teacher's own unexamined position. Teachers frequently attempt to avoid this threat by indoctrinating the student with their own values and ideas. While such an approach will make easier the task of a certain kind of teacher, it has the effect of smothering the individuality of the student and thus contributes to his alienation. If we are sincere about the values of creativity, individualism, and a pluralistic society, we must avoid forcing our answers upon the student as a form of absolute truth.

An educational program based on the principles of existentialism might suggest to some the abandonment of systematic learning, a return to the days of the child-centered school. Such should not be the case. Self-determination presupposes that the individual understands his culture thoroughly enough to know when and why he is dissenting or conforming. The humanities, as well as the social and physical sciences, would therefore form the basis of the curriculum. These areas of study would also contribute to the formation of the student's own sense of identity by providing the opportunity to discover the emotional and intellectual responses which the cultural and physical environment evoke in him. When he develops strong feelings toward his surroundings and seeks to understand the nature of these feelings, he will be more likely to commit himself to values that enhance the well being of others and, in the end, himself. This is the real test of the adequacy of a curriculum. If the curriculum does not contribute to an understanding of the danger of having no commitment beyond self and the danger of commitments that imperil self, its value must be seriously questioned.

Subject matter is the grindstone upon which the student hones his intellect and refines his standards of taste. But it cannot be dispensed only through the method of telling and listening. The existentialist favors the Socratic method whereby the teacher draws the information from the student by means of skillful questioning. This method, which actively involves both teacher and student, has the advantage of causing the student to see meanings and relationships for himself; thus he begins to organize his own body of knowledge. Moreover, it should teach him to discriminate between a significant and a trivial question; his ability to cope with basic existential problems will depend upon his skill in raising important questions.

The school's task, according to the existentialist, is to make itself expendable. It does this by making the student self-reliant in the area of ideas and values. At one time cultural tradition and institutions took care of making decisions that democracy has only recently made the responsibility of the individual. There are other important areas which buttress the existentialist's claim that the good life must be fashioned from within. Social progress is dependent upon individuals who sense the importance of an idea or value and have the courage to stand alone if necessary in its defense. Creativity, which is part of this process, is also dependent upon intellectual vitality and freedom. Other areas that are interrelated with the aims of education derived from existentialism are politics and morality; individual commitment to a political or moral value means something only as the individual develops the ability to think for himself.

When viewed as part of the tradition of Western humanism, we can see that the values which the existentialist wants us to incorporate into a philosophy of education have always been at hand. In recent years, our search for a philosophy of education has been very much like the search for fire in the famous Zen Buddhist story:

> It is too clear and so it is hard to see.
> A man once searched for a fire with a lighted lantern.
> Had he known what fire was,
> He could have cooked his rice much sooner.

54. Philosophies and Aims of Education

J. Cecil Parker, T. Bentley Edwards, and William H. Stegeman

The Philosophic Conflict

It is easily seen that when people with different philosophies reach such different conclusions with respect to education, conflict must arise. People have a strong emotional attachment for their own system of values. Hence the conflict often becomes heated. Such conflict is part of the American scene and it is generally regarded as one of the great strengths of our particular brand of democracy. Elements of realism, idealism, and pragmatism can be found in different school systems throughout the United States, and indeed in any particular school system. A realist can criticize the idealist elements, an idealist can criticize the realist elements, and both can unite in condemning the pragmatical elements.

In the nature of things, the pragmatical elements are most clearly in evidence. Faced with the conflict of values just described, and prevented by law from adopting the viewpoint of a particular religious group, the schools in America are denied access, as a body, to the philosophies of realism, or of idealism. They are also denied access to pragmatism as a philosophical system because the great majority of Americans, both in and out of schools, hold metaphysical beliefs and pragmatism holds that a metaphysical position is not necessary for the conduct of a good life. Along with their metaphysical beliefs, but neatly compartmentalized, the majority of Americans hold a firm belief in the efficacy of science as a method of investigation. Schools and school people use the scientific method to solve problems. They also use methods of teaching that have proved themselves when investigated scientifically. These methods are consonant with empiri-

SOURCE: J. Cecil Parker, T. Bentley Edwards, and William H. Stegeman, *Curriculum in America* (New York: Thomas Y. Crowell Co., 1962), pp. 43–46. Copyright © 1962 by Thomas Y. Crowell Company. Reprinted by permission of the publisher.

cally tested facts in psychology and sociology. They are different from methods in use half a century ago. From the viewpoint of an idealist or a realist they are therefore suspect. But the methods cannot be attacked directly, for this can only be possible scientifically, that is, by introducing the results of empirical investigation or, if necessary, by conducting fresh investigations. They are therefore seen as pragmatical and are attacked indirectly by an attack on the axiology of pragmatism. Hence, the school people enter battle with their hands tied, and the critics of the school have a gun in each hand. School people cannot jump to the defense of pragmatism for they themselves are not, generally speaking, motivated by the axiology of pragmatism. And the critics refuse to discuss scientific evidence.

Critics of pragmatism say that the pragmatic rejection of absolute truth, and refusal to accept a body of knowledge which can be regarded as indispensable to man anywhere, anytime, is destroying the curriculum. Pragmatic axiology is attacked on the grounds that it places values in dependence upon expediency and provides no stable and suitable aims for education; and that while the scientific method does an admirable job of describing "What is?" it completely begs the question, "What ought to be?" They say that the concept of change and relativity, as applied to education, provides no stable standard by which to judge progress, and that Dewey's concept of education as growth fails to answer the question, "Growth toward what?" All of which is largely irrelevant when directed specifically at pragmatism, for the questions of the pragmatists leave intact those ideals about which most men agree, and it is irrelevant when directed specifically at the schools, for the schools are not dominated by the axiology of pragmatism.

Currently, the schools, and the American people generally, are attempting to survive the effects of a social earthquake brought about through the application of an extremely powerful method—the method of science—with the aid of various axiologies which do not incorporate that method into their system. Unfortunately, motives derived from a metaphysical position and acceptance of the results of scientific investigation cannot remain in watertight compartments. Sooner or later, parts of the metaphysical position are undermined by the scientific investigation, and either the metaphysical position must be modified, or the findings of science rejected. These two poles provide a dimension that is clearly evident in the present philosophic conflict. A system of education which is free from domination by a particular sect needs to devote much of its attention to the development and retention of a strong moral position. We are of the opinion that an emphasis in schools on the processes involved in the making of choices is the only device possible whereby free men can develop and retain a strong morality.

Much of the current criticism of education practice in the United States stems from an attitude of philosophic realism. This attitude produces a demand for more emphasis upon subject matter and higher standards of intellectual discipline, and accordingly the charges that today's schools do not maintain discipline and develop good work habits, that the schools are turning out individuals who lack respect for authority, and that society is not getting its money's worth from its educational institutions. The launching of "Sputnik" drew forth the demand that the schools produce more scientists and mathematicians, because society has great need for such. This is characteristic of a philosophy of social realism, which holds that man exists to serve society and should be fitted for that purpose above all else. Oddly enough, this is the philosophy underlying the ideology which we, as a nation, fear most, that of Soviet Communism.

Three major criticisms of current educational practices seem to stem from philosophical idealism. The contention that teachers need to be thoroughly educated individuals and that this education should include mastery of subjects they are teaching in order to inspire pupils to learn seems to derive from the philosophy that the teachers should be imitated. The demand for better treatment of individual differences seems to come from the idealist concept that the purpose of education is to develop individual personality. And the criticisms of inadequate attention to moral and spiritual values appear to be derived from the idealist axiology which holds that the purpose of this life and of all education is preparation of the individual for immortality.

The solution to the philosophic conflict seems to be found in developing a curriculum for decision-making, wherein the students learn through the application of critical thinking to make decisions that are compatible with democratic society's many conflicting philosophies. By learning to make decisions in a variety of contexts, it is believed that students later will be in a position to solve future problems of society in the best interests of themselves and society.

IX. The System

Every practicing teacher is an employee of a system, whether it is a one-teacher system or one that embraces several thousand professional members working under highly organized conditions with firmly established policies and practices. As an important part of a school system, the teacher has some definite responsibilities and obligations to it; in turn, the system has responsibilities and obligations to the teacher. An understanding of the system in which he is employed will increase the employee's success and happiness in his work.

The teacher should have a knowledge and understanding of the system's instructional and organizational design, financial structure, and personnel policies and procedures. These, of course, vary widely in the fifty state systems and the individual systems or districts within the states, so no attempt has been made here to present a description of a particular system. Besides, even if a typical system existed, so much space would be required to describe its various aspects that it would probably constitute an entire volume.

Teachers should investigate thoroughly any system in which they are considering employment before they place their signatures on teaching contracts. Most districts provide printed and verbal information about their school system and the community in which it is located. This information is normally available to teachers, especially if requested. Also, most modern school districts provide several days of orientation for new teachers prior to school openings so that they can get better acquainted with their new places of employment.

This part has to do in a general way with the school systems, or certain aspects of these systems, in the United States. The lead article, for instance, which was written early in 1969 when Richard Nixon was beginning his term of office as President, reveals his concern for education and for the public schools. After pledging that his administration would be "second to none" in its concern for education, the President then proposed and discussed several questions and issues of education for the 1970s, and gave special attention to the roles of each level of government in the enterprise of education.

Three ideas fundamental to public school financial activity aimed at eliminating certain fiscal disparities are discussed by David K. Cohen in "The Economics of Inequality." They are that support for public schools should not follow such systematic lines of social division as race, wealth, or residence; that the agency best able to remedy differences in districts within states is each state government; and that the existing inequalities may violate the Fourteenth Amendment.

"Teachers Belong in the Classroom," by Milton A. Kaplan, pinpoints one of education's major problems today: the confusion of roles of various personnel in the system. The reward system that takes good teachers and promotes them out of the classroom to administration is one of the problems discussed here. The article proposes several solutions to the system's staffing dilemmas.

Helen Robison, in "School Practices That Cause Failure," suggests that, where formerly it was children who failed, it now is the schools that are failing. Miss Robison, through her rhetorical queries, reveals deficiencies in the American school systems.

Abraham S. Fischler and James E. Smith describe in their short selection, "Educational Parks," a new concept in district organization— especially in large city systems—in which children's education could be continuous from preschool through Grade 12. They also describe other goals of this organizational structure.

Many other innovative practices in school systems are described in educational literature; in fact, the professional journals are replete with selections concerning such ideas and plans as nongrading, team teaching, "systems" approach to organization and instruction, learning centers, and individualized instruction. The central theme in most of the articles is an emphasis on individualizing instruction and making learning relevant to individual human beings. To pursue this current emphasis, the editors present three articles dealing with innovative practices that attempt to individualize instruction. They deal with Project PLAN, Individually Prescribed Instruction, and learning centers.

55. When I Look at American Education

Richard M. Nixon

From among his many achievements Thomas Jefferson, toward the close of his life, personally selected two he most wanted to be remembered by. He wanted to be remembered as the author of the Declaration of Independence and as founder of the University of Virginia.

Jefferson knew that the destiny of America was inseparable from education—that education would be the key to the fulfillment of the promise of this new nation. We have tried hard to hold to Jefferson's ideal. We have seen our schools and colleges flourish and grow, ever enriching our heritage.

Now, almost a century and a half after Jefferson, we know a sterner truth. The philosopher and educator, Alfred North Whitehead, has warned: "In the conditions of modern life, the rule is absolute: The race which does not value trained intelligence is doomed." So education, long the key to opportunity and fulfillment, is today also the key to survival.

Because my administration will be second to none in its concern for America, I pledge that it will be second to none in its concern for education.

As we move together into the 1970's, we will have to be bold. Like Thomas Jefferson, we in our time must have the courage to be founders, to devise new answers. Let us ask ourselves:

How can we devise more equitable methods of school support to overcome imbalances among school districts, particularly in urban areas?

How can our basic subjects, the intellectual tools of our civilization, be taught better?

Since diversity is inseparable from freedom itself, how can we encourage the growth of variety and flexibility, even as our society grows more complex?

SOURCE: *Today's Education*, LVIII, 1 (January 1969), 21–22. Reprinted by permission of the author and publisher.

How can we bring the schools closer to the people of our communities?

How can we rejuvenate vocational education so that it will be relevant not only to the jobs of today but to those of five and ten years from now?

How can we make the education of our teachers commensurate with the demands of the space age and how can we provide more incentive and greater professional recognition for our teachers?

What role can the miracles of technology play in the schools of tomorrow?

How can we best preserve the traditions of our civilization?

One of the great issues of the 1970's will be to determine the distinctive role of each level of government in the enterprise of education. I consider education a federal concern, a state responsibility, and a local function. I believe that a philosophy of encouraging the maximum local control and local participation will provide the answers the times demand.

The needs of children in a small New England town must not be presumed to be the same as those of children in downtown Detroit; and the needs of both may differ from those of a child in suburban Los Angeles or in rural Tennessee. The situation does not call for rigid blueprints or inflexible guide lines.

I saw a recent study of the ten "best high schools in America," and while each had an outstanding record in preparing its students for college, each had an approach, a technique, an attitude of its own. We must guard and cherish these qualities or in time we will become deadened by conformity and will lose the creativity and the innovative abilities that are the key to our future progress.

To this end, I believe it is vitally important that local school boards and local and state governments have the primary responsibility and the primary right to dispense funds. I will press, therefore, for a federal program to turn back to state and local control, through bloc grants, such funds as are required to upgrade their educational performance. Bloc grants, administered at state and local levels, provide greater flexibility than any other assistance. The federal government, with its ability to raise funds on a national basis, should aim at reducing the discrepancies among the various states in their resources for the support of education.

State government must bear the legal responsibility of setting standards for attendance, teacher certification, per-pupil expenditure, and the development of long-range plans. Local school systems should be responsible for developing specific projects and programs, and they should be permitted maximum flexibility, subject only to the broadest of policy definitions.

I believe that to prepare for the 1970's we should accord the highest priority to many needed changes on state and local levels.

First of all, serious imbalances exist in the financial support available to many school districts. In many states, the system of support for schools needs drastic revision. School districts have often developed haphazardly

—some in residential areas, some in commercial or industrial sections, and still others in poverty areas. Many are in transition from one phase to another. As a result, the tax base differs from district to district, and many schools suffer from too little support. It is imperative that state governments take the initiative here, for it is plainly wrong for the funds to any school to remain indefinitely below an acceptable minimum.

A second necessary move is to employ a variety of means to bring the schools closer to the people in order to relax the tense atmosphere of alienation and mistrust that prevails in some urban neighborhoods among students, parents, and teachers. Within broad limits, curriculums can be tailored to the needs of different groups. One school, for example, could emphasize Spanish history and culture, and another school, African culture. Members of the community could play an important part in the daily program—by serving as teaching assistants, for instance.

The individuals who make up a community must be involved with the schools. Parents need to find out what their children are learning. Are they learning things that not only interest them but also are relevant to our history and our civilization? It is up to the local communities to see that education is a living and relevant thing, and that it uses the past in ways which enrich the present.

The communities of America need to stand behind the teachers insofar as discipline is concerned. This view is not a punitive one toward students, but recognition that good education requires an environment of reason and order.

Another essential move is to make a serious and comprehensive effort to rejuvenate the teaching profession at the elementary and secondary levels. Everyone knows that the key to learning is the gifted teacher, but too often the gifted teacher is numbed by routine and stifled by red tape; too often the incentive to excellence succumbs to a system that fails to distinguish and reward superior performance.

We must level with ourselves, all across the country, about teachers' salaries. We tend to fancy that we have done very well in providing for these men and women who play such a critical role in our society, yet I know one teacher in an eastern school who receives only $5,400 a year after 30 years of teaching elementary pupils. I say this is wrong for America and a reflection on our sense of values.

It is essential that our universities take more seriously their obligations in the area of teacher education. The goal must be to produce teaching scholars and not educational technicians. The education of our teachers deserves equal emphasis with other disciplines within the university structure. Their training needs to be regarded as an enterprise as serious and exacting as the training of a nuclear physicist or a heart surgeon.

We must take a searching look at vocational education. Too often such training is geared to jobs that are obsolescent or in short supply. Too often, students lose interest, seeing, correctly, that there is little connection between what they are learning and the realities of the job market.

Private industry and business can play a genuinely creative role here. I would urge the leaders of state governments to call for the formation of task forces of knowledgeable citizens in business and industry and in the academic world who would ascertain what the job market is likely to be five or ten years hence. Then, with the aid of tax incentives, business and industry in each state could cooperate with the schools to prepare young people for the real jobs that will await them.

As students move through vocational training, they should spend part of the time on the actual jobs for which they are being trained. The goal of vocational education should be a flexible system of training and part-time work experience that each year would enable millions of young people with varying abilities, inclinations, and habits to make an effective transition from full-time schooling to full-time productive employment.

Increasing numbers of jobs in our economy require training and education beyond that available in most secondary schools, yet do not demand a college or professional degree. To meet the expanding demand for skilled technicians and semiprofessional workers and to offer the high school graduate a choice other than ending his formal education or pursuing a four-year program, I will press for the expansion and strengthening of two-year technical institutes and community junior colleges.

Even though education is and should remain the responsibility of the state and local community, the federal government must still play a vital supporting role. To this end, the new administration will seek to:

1. Create a National Institute for the Educational Future to serve as a clearinghouse for ideas in elementary and secondary education and to explore the revolutionary possibilities that modern science and technology are making available to education.

2. Maintain our national commitment to preschool education, expanding as necessary such programs as Head Start and Follow Through.

3. Create a National Teachers Corps, to bring carefully selected college and high school students into action as tutors in the core-city schools.

4. Encourage diversity by urging states to present plans for the distribution by the states of federal assistance to nonpublic school children and for the inclusion of nonpublic school representatives in the planning process.

5. Help encourage the growth of our private colleges and universities by allowing tax advantages for donations up to a specified level.

6. Propose the formation of community resource units composed of individuals, organizations, and groups within the community who will make their experience available for the encouragement of education.

7. Devise new ways by which, through long-term loans, the federal government can further assist students to gain a higher education, and devise new ways by which private capital can expand its participation in the support of students who need assistance.

When I look at American education, I do not see schools, but young Americans who deserve the chance to make a life for themselves and ensure the progress of their country. If we fail in this, no success we have is worth the keeping, but I say to you that we will not fail.

56. The Economics of Inequality

David K. Cohen

It is hardly news that some schools are rich and others poor; nor is it a surprise that the rich ones are likely to be found in well-to-do communities, and the poor ones in less affluent places. The news is that efforts are now underway to eliminate such differences in school expenditures.

During the past three or four decades, many states have sought to reduce financial disparities among school districts through "foundation" or "equalization" programs that provided aid to local districts. But large inequalities persisted. In recent months, however, lawsuits have been filed in six states that seek to compel the states to assume responsibility for eliminating differences in per pupil expenditures among rich and poor districts. These court actions raise a number of fundamental issues, both economic and educational.

The disparities around which all this activity centers are considerable. In Arkansas (the state with the lowest average expenditure for public schooling), the highest-spending 10 per cent of the districts in 1961 devoted $160 or more per pupil to the education of their charges, and the lowest 10 per cent spent $99 or less per pupil; in New York (the state with the highest average outlay for schooling), the top 10 per cent of the dis-

SOURCE: *Saturday Review,* April 19, 1969, pp. 64-65, 76–80. Copyright © 1969 Saturday Review, Inc. Reprinted by permission of the author, David K. Cohen, Associate Professor at the Harvard Graduate School of Education, and the publisher.

tricts spent $465 or more, and the lowest 10 per cent spent $333 or less on each student. Studies in individual states since then show that such disparities persist.

Local tax revenues, which cause part of the problem, are unequal for two main reasons. First, the central cities usually experience more than average competition for tax dollars; they have more problems which local taxation is supposed to alleviate (poverty, aging, ill health), and they provide services for people who work there, but live elsewhere (fire and police protection, sanitation). Thus, a smaller proportion of the average property tax dollar is available for spending on schools in central cities than in their neighboring suburbs. One recent study showed that although central cities raised more than $90 per capita in property taxes to their suburbs average of more than $70, the suburbs spent an average of $60 per capita on schools excluding capital outlays, while the cities spent about $50.

But even if municipal overburden did not exist, the same tax rates would not raise the same amount of money in all communities. Those with more rundown and unproductive land tend to have lower assessed valuations than communities with more well-kept and productive property. Many communities of the first sort are rural (with depleted farmland and underpopulated hamlets), but many others are urban, replete with slums, decaying business districts, and industrial wastelands. The problems of a weakening urban tax base often are compounded by fear of losing the existing jobs and tax revenue entirely.

In any event, when communities with different assessed valuations are taxed at the same rate, the per capita revenue yield varies; communities with the lower valuations raise less even though they make the same tax effort. And when the lower-assessed valuations are found in communities with the greatest poverty and social decay, the result is devastating. For instance, the average affluent homeowner in a well-to-do community is required to sacrifice a smaller proportion of his income to pay his share of an $800 annual per pupil outlay, than would a less well-off homeowner in a central city or depressed rural area. Affluent communities can raise more money for schools at lower tax rates than poor communities can at higher rates. Add to this the heavy burden of municipal services, and the fiscal problems of city schools are compounded.

Programs of state foundation and equalization aid could eliminate these local differences, but generally they do not. The reasons vary from state to state, but a few basic ones are similar. In many states, the aid formulas were designed decades ago to help finance the nonurban districts, which at the time were disadvantaged. Over the years, many of the rural areas became affluent suburbs, and many of the cities grew relatively poor. The state aid formulas, however, have not always been updated. In many metropolitan areas, state school aid programs deliver more dollars per pupil to suburban than to central-city schools. In 1964, for example, Detroit received $189 per pupil from Michigan, while the average suburban receipt per pupil was $240.

But even in those states where efforts have been made to reverse these trends the remedies are only partly effective, because state education departments are reluctant to equalize completely the tax burden among rich and poor districts. It is still easier to raise money for schooling in suburban places like Brookline than it is in Boston. The reluctance to correct this situation, of course, is political. State education departments are answerable to legislatures, which in turn must account to constituents. Parents and schoolmen who are relatively well-off may pay lip service to the idea of equal educational opportunity, but they also will use the political process to protect their advantage and that of their children.

The disparities, then, result both from variations in the wealth of local communities, and from the historic tendency of state education departments to adjust only partly for these local variations. The current burst of activity aimed at eliminating these disparities rests on a few common ideas. One is that levels of support for public schools should not follow such systematic lines of social division as race, wealth, or residence. A second is that the agency best able to remedy differences among districts within states is the state government itself. But it is generally agreed that state government is not likely to resolve fully the issue through the political process, and there is little reason to be any more hopeful about the Congress. Therefore, it is not surprising that the third common idea is that the existing inequalities may violate the Fourteenth Amendment.

The long process of court action has only begun, yet, it appears that if ever there were an idea whose time had come, this would seem to be the idea and ours the time. Since the mid-Fifties, American law and politics have been increasingly occupied with problems of inequality. The concern with intrastate school financing disparities is only the most recent extension of this trend. There is, however, another less apparent reason for its appeal. The last decade of struggle over schools saw efforts at desegregation founder on white resistance and bureaucratic inertia, and programs of compensatory education produce nothing more useful than debates in the liberal press. Lacking any noticeable improvements in either the quality or outcome of slum schools, many of the interested parties (parents, teachers, semi-professional school reformers, and community activists) are abandoning past cooperation in seeking more money or other improvements; instead, they increasingly have fallen to fighting among themselves over who should manage the educational enterprise. This has had a number of disquieting consequences for liberals; they are ideologically fragmented over the question of separatism or integration. Whatever other drawbacks the new lawsuits may have, they are blissfully neutral on the question of who shall control what in the cities.

All of these factors augur well for the proliferation of lawsuits, research, and organizations concerned with intrastate disparities in expenditures for public education. But if the existence of the differences is admitted on all sides, there is no such agreement on whether—or how—they should be eliminated.

The rationales for eliminating the inequities boil down to two. The first is that differences in school expenditures cause differences in the quality of education, and these in turn harm children's achievement, and thus their chances for success. The second is that irrespective of damage to anyone's education, the state has no business making distinctions based on such educationally irrelevant considerations as race, place, or community wealth, as is currently done in nearly all the aid formulas.

The arguments against eliminating the differences follow roughly the same lines. One is that the state aid programs do provide a minimally satisfactory education, and that high-expenditure districts offer not discrimination but leadership. Without beacons of educational excellence, general upgrading of the educational system would be impossible. The other is that neither courts nor legislatures have any business meddling with how much money parents choose to spend on their children's schooling; this is held to reflect an individual's ability and willingness to pay taxes, his concern for education, and his taste in the style of education offered. Any effort to eliminate the differences would infringe individual liberties.

What does the available evidence suggest concerning the merits of these positions?

If one argues—as Arthur Wise seems to, in *Rich Schools, Poor Schools* —that *all* intrastate differences in outlays for schooling must be eliminated, the "beacons of educational excellence" argument becomes a formidable obstacle. The supply of money available for public education is distinctly limited; compelling all districts within a state to spend roughly the same amount would be more likely to level them toward the mean, than to raise all of them up to the top. But the opposition between "beacons of educational excellence" and equalization is not inevitable; it exists only if educational excellence is identified as maintaining the advantages that current school financing arrangements extend to private wealth. One could as well argue that there is nothing intrinsically wrong with spending more on some children than others, as long as the difference results from the free choice of their parents and neighbors. From this view, government is not obliged to make all districts spend the same amount, but only to eliminate any dependence their spending may have upon such things as the personal income of parents, differences in communities' ability to raise taxes, or the formulas under which states aid local school districts.

Remedy, then, would consist of reducing to zero the correlation between measures of community wealth and school expenditures. This would make it as hard for affluent suburbs to spend $800 per pupil per year as it presently is for poor cities or depressed rural towns. Taxation and revenue distribution would have to be a good deal more redistributive than they are, but there is no inherent necessity for sameness. This would doubtless increase fiscal pain in the suburbs and reduce it in the cities, but equal pain in raising money is not the same thing as educational leveling. The second reduces variety, whereas the first only means that it comes no more easily to the wealthy than to the poor.

We can show that irrational disparities can be eliminated without suffocating variety—as is commonly found within American school systems—but it is another matter to prove that this does not infringe liberty. As a matter of fact, it is impossible to prove this point, for the simple reason that equalizing expenditures would indeed infringe liberty. The liberties in question, however, appear to consist of the freedom of those who *have* more to *get* more for less effort, through a system of government taxation and revenue distribution. Thus, the issue is not whether liberties are infringed, but whether they are the sort of liberties that can be allowed to permeate the workings of government.

It is hard to find very poor people who support the liberty of the rich to get more for less effort with the help of government, and it is nearly as difficult to find affluent people who take the view that they should be so taxed as to eliminate the very advantages over less fortunate folk which they either inherited or struggled most of their lives to attain. For this reason, when serious redistribution is sought (whether it be in votes, access to criminal justice, or school finance), it is found mainly through the courts. And the courts have become increasingly skeptical of liberties attained at the expense of others when a) the others are systematically disadvantaged in the economic or political struggle for equality, and b) when the relative disadvantage seems to have obvious and substantial support from agencies of government.

Therefore, it would be no great surprise if the egalitarian revolution were extended to intrastate variations in public school support. But assuming the courts found existing schemes of school support unconstitutional, what would be put in their place?

All the litigation presents dollar disparities as the chief evidence of evil, and there is consequently a profound bias toward conceiving good as the absence of dollar inequalities. Much of the litigation suggests such a remedy. One expression of this view has been proposed by John Coons, which he calls power equalizing. The idea is roughly as follows. A state decides that it wants to divorce variations in expenditures on education from differences in community wealth, and make them depend instead upon community interest in schooling. It decides to use local fiscal effort—the rate at which each community taxes itself for education—as the most convenient indicator of interest in schooling. The state then computes the average assessed valuation (making sure it is assessed uniformly) and determines the state average support for schools. It then arranges the formulas for collecting and distributing aid to education in such a way that districts that tax themselves at or above the state average rate, but fail to raise the state average expenditure per pupil, will receive aid sufficient to make up the difference. Districts that tax at the state average effort (or below) and raise *more* than the average revenue per pupil will turn back some of the excess dollars to the state.

For every bit of effort a district makes above the state average, it could either receive or contribute to state matching funds depending on its wealth. Thus, consider two hypothetical districts—one rich, one poor—both taxed at one mill above average. Let us say the poor one raised $10 per student with its extra effort, and the rich one raised $20. The state would adjust aid so that (in effect) $5 per student was taken from the rich district and assigned to the poor one; equal effort to attain above average schools would be rewarded with equal dollars to spend toward that end.

Of course, this example involves only one possible application of the idea that spending on schools should not be a function of local wealth. The system could as easily be keyed to the highest districts as to the average (which would simply raise all expenditures more), and state reimbursement for above average effort could provide greater or less encouragement of school expenditures by varying the level at which the state matched funds raised by above average local effort.

What is more, dollar equalization would not be irrevocably tied to local tax effort. States could decide to eliminate the local property tax entirely and fund education through state revenues. Or, they could devise some combination of local and state funding, under which individual districts would raise only a statutory minimum, and the state would supply the remainder up to some mandated maximum. In theory, at least, there are many alternative schemes for eliminating the association between community wealth and school expenditures.

There are, however, two substantial objections to any dollar-equalizing scheme. They have both been raised in the cases filed against the Michigan and the California State Departments of Education. The California suit hints that providing equal dollars to districts within a state is no guarantee that equal resources can be purchased, because prices vary from place to place. And both complaints suggest that educational resources should not be allocated on the basis of dollar equality, but educational need. Just as the cost of educational goods and services varies among districts, so does the need for education. Districts where costs are higher, or needs greater, should get more money.

Can variations in the cost of education be adequately measured and priced? Can education be provided on the basis of need? Measuring the cost of anything is no more or less precise than the calculations that lie just behind the dollar signs. It would, for example, be easy to measure interdistrict variations in the cost of teachers, if all we cared about was their height, weight, years of experience, tenure, or certification. But the teacher attributes that produce better student achievement are mysterious. Educational research shows little relationship between their experience, certification, tenure, and salary, and their students' achievement.

There is some evidence that teachers' expectations for their students' performance may influence how well the children do, but this presents other problems. We haven't the faintest idea of whether teachers with more productive expectations cost more; we don't know what a "more productive expectation" actually is; and finally, even if the solutions to these puzzles were as clear as daylight, there is no system of attitude measurement that is both sufficiently precise to single out those teachers whose expectations are the most productive, and sufficiently discreet to avoid the moral and constitutional problems that might attend rating employees of the state on the basis of their attitudes.

Thus, the objective characteristics we can easily measure and price seem of dubious educational value, and the subjective attributes—which may have some causal connection with achievement—provide no handles for effective measurement or pricing.

These conclusions bear directly on the notion of providing state aid on the basis of educational need. The great public concern about poverty has accustomed us to the notion that poor children require more education than the children of the well-to-do. Since more of anything costs more, this notion translated into the idea that effective education for the children of poverty means more money for their schools. On this basis Title I of the Elementary and Secondary Education Act and hundreds of similar state and local programs have been organized and funded, and it is on the same basis that attorneys in Illinois, California, and Michigan have argued that city schools should receive more money than districts with mostly advantaged children.

Because poor children are thought to need more education than other children in order to do as well, the more-than-average education is seen as a condition of producing average achievement. Therefore, the notion of assigning funds on the basis of need is simply a different way of saying that school districts should have some common performance standard.

However, educational research suggests that the present differences in schools' quality produce little difference in their students' achievement. And the recently instituted programs of compensatory education seem only to confirm this finding. Of course, in most cases the variations in school quality are small, and hardly provide a full test of the notion that schools could make a difference. But to a court or a legislature seeking to decide whether (or how) to allocate state funds on the basis of need, these research results might well have a mystifying and disquieting effect. They suggest, simply enough, that schoolmen and researchers haven't much evidence about the educational techniques that might satisfy a need criterion, or how much they might cost. Such news is bound to dampen judicial or legislative enthusiasm for such a criterion of resource allocation.

Finally, all of this assumes that there is something special about school achievement. Although that idea received almost religious attention in the late Fifties, the system of achievement-worship may be breaking down. No one has shown that student achievement is the sole useful criterion of schools' accomplishments. To do so we would have to a) demonstrate that achievement strongly affects adult occupation, income, etc., and b) secure some consensus that these things are more important than such other presumed outcomes of schooling as independence, creativity, or social integration. But the evidence that school achievement adds to the impact of preschool ability upon adult status is slim, and there is a growing agreement that performance on middle-class-oriented achievement tests is not the sole important outcome of schooling.

This leaves educational and political taste as the basis on which to select criteria for measuring school quality. Lacking agreement on the outcomes, we will fight about what's important to measure, and in the absence of measurement systems, we will have no solid basis on which to rest state aid formulas.

Of course, the absence of precise knowledge has never paralyzed state legislatures and school agencies before. They have been organizing and regulating education on the basis of insufficient knowledge for generations. Legislators could decide that it was important to allocate more money to teachers' salaries in rural areas, or to poor schools in cities. The point, however, is that this would be an act of political wisdom or mercy, not educational expertise.

There are other questions, which have little to do with the technologies of educational or social measurement. There is, for instance, no compelling evidence that state money should go to school districts instead of parents. Such a system might introduce more competition among schools, while increasing the alternatives to families, and in turn, this might result in greater efficiency and differentiation among schools.

A more difficult and complex question that arises is whether the equalization schemes discussed here really would make it as easy for the poor to purchase quality education as it now is for the affluent. There is, after all, more to poverty than the assessed valuation of a person's house; the fact that a given amount of tax effort produces the same dollars for education does not mean that they are equivalent for the poor and the rich. If, for example, the property tax takes a larger proportion of the personal income of the poor than the rich, then the rich still would be less constrained in extending above average effort. And even if aid formulas could take this into account, it would still be easier for the rich to invest around the margins of public education—for books, tutors, etc. It is not clear that the state could compensate for this situation since it would be necessary for the family, not the school district, to be the unit receiving state aid. But none of these points mean that remedy is either unreasonable or unfeasible. They suggest that a dollar-equalization scheme is probably feasible, but that its effect would be limited.

The only question that goes to the heart of the matter is whether dollar equalization would make any difference. An affirmative decision in these cases would set loose profound changes in our system of public finance; the courts would be less likely to take the step if they thought that the only point at issue was discrimination which had no educational impact. Unfortunately, it is not clear whether eliminating existing disparities would produce much change in schools or children. My earlier examples showed that the dollar difference between the lowest- and highest-spending 10 per cent of the school districts in Arkansas was no less than about $60 per pupil per year, and in New York no less than about $130. The evidence from children in programs of compensatory education which cost about that much is that their achievement was no better than that of comparable children who had no more money spent on them. And some programs (such as the More Effective Schools program in New York City) have invested much more—up to $500 per pupil per year; the evidence there is mixed, but even the most enthusiastic reading indicates that it reveals only a small achievement gain.

Of course, these programs often have been done badly, quickly, and many have not been sustained. It is conceivable that the same amount of money applied more steadily, over more years, might have better results. It could be that more money would offer a basis for innovation and experimentation, which might lead to better schools and higher achievement. It is possible that if equalization were keyed to the highest spending district rather than the average, the greater money would produce greater achievement. But if the available evidence does not controvert such statements, neither does it provide much support or encouragement.

Since the evidence is so mixed, and Americans are such devout believers in the efficacy of schooling, litigation to reduce the dependence of school expenditures on district wealth may well meet with success. If it does, many useful results would follow: the existing irrational and discriminatory inequalities in school support would be reduced or eliminated, which would provide a sound basis for federal efforts to reduce wealth-related disparities among states; it also might help build judicial barriers against the use of federal revenue sharing, or bloc grant schemes, to perpetuate or magnify existing intrastate inequalities. Finally, were any or all of these to occur, a more solid and equitable floor upon which to build compensatory efforts would have been constructed.

All these results would be positive. But there is no clear evidence that they would meet the two central problems of public education in our time

—its organization along racial lines and its apparent inability to reduce racial and class disparities in school outcomes. In fact, it seems apparent that much of the interest in intrastate fiscal disparities arises precisely from despair over the evident failure of efforts to resolve these central problems. It is more than a little ironic that fourteen years after *Brown,* after years of struggle to improve achievement in slum schools, the newest dimension in efforts to secure equal educational opportunity reminds us as much of the *Plessy* doctrine of separate-but-equal as anything more recent. In a way, of course, that is unfair: these suits do represent a new dimension, undreamed of in the world of *Plessy;* they begin to reach beyond race to the economic determinants of school quality. But in another sense it is not unfair; it reminds us that this new dimension of equal educational opportunity seems to touch the school problems which presently preoccupy us in only an oblique and incomplete fashion.

57. Teachers Belong
in the Classroom

Milton A. Kaplan

One of the tragic ironies in education today is that the school administration, which is charged with the responsibility of obtaining better teachers and improving teaching methods, is often responsible for doing just the opposite. With one hand it recruits frantically for teaching talent, and with the other hand it plucks that talent out of the classroom and allows the inexperienced and the inferior to do the actual teaching.

Let us examine the basis for this charge. As our schools increase in size —even in the outlying rural areas, the central school, fed by the school bus, has become a highly complex and organized society—more and more services are required. Secretaries are needed for clerical work of every kind and description. Guidance counsellors direct students along the intricate network of roads leading to a diploma. Deans exert pressure on the students' pattern of behavior. Psychologists examine the problems that rise

SOURCE: *The Educational Forum,* November 1968, pp. 49–54. Reprinted by permission of Kappa Delta Pi, an Honor Society in Education, owners of the copyright.

from the conflicts that are found in schools and in children. Chairmen train and supervise teachers and manage departments of study. Curriculum coordinators evaluate and shape the course of study. Assembly coordinators plan programs for auditorium exercises. Principals and assistant principals administer schools that present concerts, plays, and athletic contests; that conduct extracurricular activities every day—and sometimes every night—of the week, at the same time offering regular courses in academic, commercial, and industrial work and often special courses for retarded students and advanced courses for bright ones. All these students have to be taught, advised, guided, admonished, exercised, influenced, tested, entertained, and fed. The modern school, therefore, becomes a complex of activities that start early in the morning, when trucks roll up to deliver vegetables, meat, fruit, milk, ice cream, and pastry for the cavernous lunchroom and end late at night, when students straggle out of the auditorium, their faces still smeared with the traces of stage makeup.

All these activities need managers, responsible people who can supervise, superintend, and expedite. Where do they come from? The logical procedure would be to hire people for specific jobs, but logic is not always found in the formal administration of education. The tradition that shaped the small school of thirty or forty years ago still governs the burgeoning schools of today. Since, one, the administrative details must be handled, and since, two, outside personnel is rarely hired, teachers must be called on to shoulder the burden. Since, three, the administrative burden in a school is a heavy one, teachers must be released from some of their teaching duties. Since, four, the schools are growing larger and larger and the responsibilities of these schools more comprehensive, more and more teachers are being drafted for nonteaching duties. Since, five, these duties are important for the administration of the school, the more competent teachers are usually selected for these jobs and are replaced by younger, less experienced teachers.

Perhaps the best way to indicate the scope of these administrative duties and the number of teachers involved in the program is to take an English Department in a city high school and to list all the teachers in the department who participated in the administration of the school:

1. The program director, who taught two instead of the customary five classes
2. The assistant program director, who taught three classes
3. The college adviser, who taught two classes
4. The assistant college adviser, who taught three classes
5. The chairman, who taught one class
6. A guidance counsellor, who taught three classes
7. A guidance counsellor, who taught four classes
8. The assistant dean, who taught four classes
9. The director of the Honor School, who taught four classes.

That meant that a total of nineteen classes of English were removed from the program of these skilled and experienced English teachers. That meant, in turn, that four other, less experienced teachers had to be obtained to instruct these classes.

To give the magnitude of the administrative load, let us list all the positions in a metropolitan high school that involve some exemption from teaching duties:

Guidance Counsellors (12)
Employment Counsellor
College Adviser
Assistant College Adviser
Boys' Dean—A.M. Session
Assistant Boys' Dean—A.M. Session
Girls' Dean—A.M. Session
Assistant Girls' Dean—A.M. Session
Boys' Dean—P.M. Session
Assistant Boys' Dean—P.M. Session
Girls' Dean—P.M. Session
Assistant Girls' Dean—P.M. Session
Lateness Coordinator
Attendance Coordinator—A.M. Session
Attendance Coordinator—P.M. Session
Dean of Seniors
Chairmen of Departments (12)
Administrative Assistants (2)
Assistant to the Administrative Assistant Treasurer
Faculty Adviser to the Student Organization
Mimeographing Coordinator
Cafeteria Supervisor
Chairman of the Program Committee
Assistant Chairman of the Program Committee
Principal

It can thus be seen that forty-nine teachers—the principal is considered a teacher, too—are removed from at least one class of instruction. The principal and the administrative assistants do not teach any classes at all. The chairmen rarely teach more than one or two classes. In all fairness we must point out that the faculty totals almost 200, but even so, more than twenty-five percent of the faculty is on a part-time basis. As we examine the roster of schools throughout the country, we note that there is a growing tendency to release teachers from classroom duties for administrative functions as well as, often, coaching of teams, supervising of publications, and directing of plays.

The anomaly of the situation cannot be placed at the door of the principal. He must administer a school. Because the structure of the organization is not sufficiently flexible, he is forced to use stopgap tactics. Let us see how that works in practice.

One of the most agonizing problems facing the high school student is getting into a good college, or, failing that, getting into any college. He needs advice and direction from a person who knows him and who knows, at the same time, the varying requirements of the colleges. To find a person to fill this niche, the principal looks for a teacher who is intelligent and capable, who knows her students and their abilities, who can teach and influence them, who can be depended on for judgment and incisiveness, and who can write succinctly and well. To find a person with all these qualifications, he turns to one of his best teachers and makes her the college adviser. Because she is overwhelmed by applications, by requests for interviews and guidance, by numerous parental visits, and by the thousand-and-one details that flow in an endless stream from the multiple college applications each student feels impelled to make, Miss College Adviser is relieved of one of her subject classes, then another. Finally, she teaches but one or two classes. The rest of the time she can be found in the College Office, her shoulders weighed down by clerical minutiae. Very often she does not even know the students for whom she has to file official school recommendations. The school has thus gained a conscientious college adviser and lost an excellent classroom teacher. The regrettable feature in the situation is that a bright college graduate could learn to handle the duties of the office and thus release the teacher for more creative work. Unfortunately, no provision is made for this simple solution.

In the elementary school, in the junior high school, and in the senior high school, the same process goes on. The school lunchroom, to cite another instance, seats hundreds of students. Some schools are so large that several shifts have to be scheduled. Because the lunch period releases the students from the tensions of formal instruction, a moderating influence is needed, and teachers are therefore assigned to patrol the lunchroom while the students are eating. To organize and supervise all these students and teachers, one teacher is removed from the classroom for a few periods and made lunchroom coordinator. Because the duties of this position require a person who is both tactful and forceful, the principal once more selects a good teacher for the job, even though the loss in the classroom may be grievous. For example, in one of the high schools in Brooklyn, a mathematics teacher was chosen to administer the lunchroom, despite the fact that there was an acute shortage of mathematics teachers and his services were urgently needed in the classroom.

Since the qualities needed for a good guidance counsellor are those needed for a good teacher, the classroom once more loses the teacher to the administration. Carrying the process to its logical extreme, we find our best teachers in the college office, the curriculum office, the examiners' offices, the superintendents' offices, the school lunchroom, the audio-visual aids department, the program office—any place but in the classroom. The classroom is sacrificed to the demands of the administration.

The policy, unfortunately, is a short-sighted one for a number of reasons. First, in education the teacher must be the pivotal factor. He comes in close contact with his students five days a week for fifteen to twenty weeks each semester. If he is a good teacher, his influence is incalculable. If he is a bad teacher, his influence is equally incalculable. How can we tolerate a system, therefore, that invariably takes good teachers out of the classroom and replaces them with teachers who are generally less experienced and often less capable? If two alert teachers in, say, the Social Studies Department are relieved of a total of five classes to perform the duties of dean or lunchroom supervisor, 100 to 175 students every semester must forego the instruction that is rightly theirs, for these social studies teachers are trained in their field, skillful in their techniques, and perceptive in their attitude toward students, the very qualities that made the administrator pick them for their new jobs. In one school, a fine social studies teacher, who has an electrifying influence in her classes, spends most of her time in the program office supervising the scheduling of classes. Here in the midst of a shortage of teachers, especially good teachers, we find a policy that aggravates the shortage.

The policy has further insidious effects. Once the teacher has been tapped, he may no longer feel like a teacher. He is a guidance counsellor, an attendance coordinator, an assistant dean. The title has the ring of authority and prestige. The teacher now focuses his time and energy on the new job. When the bell rings for the start of his teaching session, he often is in the midst of a welter of details or a conference with a parent, which he abandons reluctantly for the chores of the classroom. In other words, teaching becomes a sideline, and too often the teacher-administrator finds that on a part-time basis, he can no longer give the classroom the concentration that made him a good teacher. There are numerous exceptions of course, but the psychological effect of promoting a teacher to an administrative post invests the new job with a glamour that belittles the work in the classroom. This attitude is intensified by a procedure in many schools that excuses administrators, especially guidance counsellors and members of the program committee, from all teaching duties during the first and last few days of each term to assist in the process of organizing the school.

Even if the teacher remains a good teacher in the two or three classes he finds on his program, his promotion is a wasteful one, for his new job is awarded to him only because there is no provision for employing specialized personnel trained to do the job. Let us present a graphic instance of how good teachers are thrown into the teeth of expediency. Because the regular attendance of students is important for educational and financial reasons—state aid for education is usually based on the figures of the actual attendance of pupils—schools find it advisable to appoint a teacher as attendance coordinator, sometimes on a full-time basis and more often on a part-time arrangement. This coordinator tries to improve attendance records by every means at his disposal. He investigates absences, telephones the home, and confers with pupils, parents, and social agencies. Sometimes, especially in large schools, several teachers assist in this project, and a full-time teaching position is thus used for this purpose. The school, therefore, is prepared to pay a full teacher's salary—sometimes over $12,000 a year—for a job that can be done expeditiously by an intelligent clerk for far less money and with no disruption of the teaching process.

Someone has to supervise the lunchroom—therefore a teacher is taken. Someone has to run the school store—a teacher is drafted. Someone has to direct the employment bureau—a teacher is appointed. We can go through the long list of positions that excuse teachers from classroom duty and rarely do we find a position that cannot be filled by a full-time clerk or assistant, who could devote all his time to his duties and, incidentally, save the educational system thousands of dollars and, incidentally again, restore the teacher to the classroom, where he is needed.

Principals may shake their heads sagely and say: "This is all very well in theory, but in practice, teachers want to leave the classroom. They consider the administrative assignment a promotion." Since teachers are quick to recognize that merit is rewarded by reduction of teaching load, it becomes obvious that an administrative assignment *is* a promotion. Things have reached such a pass that in contract negotiations the United Federation of Teachers persuaded the Board of Education of New York City to agree to rotate these positions among those teachers who are qualified. That means that at one time or another, qualified teachers will be relieved of some of their classes. That leaves the dismaying conclusion that those who are not considered qualified will have a full complement of classes. Something is radically wrong with a system if the reward for good service in the classroom is removal from that classroom. If we promote a good teacher by exempting him from teaching, we are contemptuous of the profession. Apparently many regard teaching as a means to an end, the end being administrative work. In a town near Elmira, New York, the elementary school boasts a large number of men teachers, an unusual but desirable situation in the primary grades. Investigation reveals, however, that every one of the men is studying "administration" and aiming to be a principal. A teacher, after all, does not earn the salary and the dignity of a principal.

Obviously, the situation cries for drastic revision. Physicians aren't pulled out of medical practice to perform administrative duties that could be assigned to less skilled personnel. By the same token, teachers who are trained to teach should teach, and administrative work, whenever possible, should be assigned to personnel trained to do that work. Many of the administrative functions of the school can be performed by a good office manager, who can concentrate on his job with the efficiency that we are told we find in the business world. At present, throughout the country there are signs that specialists are being trained specifically for the tasks demanded of them. Guidance counsellors in many systems are exclusively guidance counsellors and not part-time teachers, although first they are required to be teachers. In many schools, clerks are called on to handle the problems of attendance and employment placement. In New York City, teacher aides are being appointed to take over the so-called building assignments that ordinarily fall to the lot of the teachers—patrol of the lunchroom and the corridors, for example.

These are steps in the right direction, but we need more steps. Administration and supervision must not be the only avenues of promotion and reward open to teachers. Another avenue must be created in the classroom itself, because the educational system needs teachers desperately and cannot afford to reward teachers by exempting them from teaching. Let us reward the teacher by keeping him in the classroom and making his difficult task as pleasant as possible. Let us release him from as much clerical and routine work as possible. Let us pay him more, too, giving the experienced and capable teacher a salary that matches the administrator's. Let us reward our master teachers by using them for teaching. That means releasing them from home-room duty and patrol of the halls, and that means making the walls of the classroom the boundaries of their domain. Then they can teach without harassment or interruption. Then they can work with student teachers, giving these apprentices the good and focused training Dr. Conant recommends. Then the master teachers can help our younger instructors by giving them the benefit of their advice, skill, and experience. Perhaps additional categories in the salary scale could be created to allow the better teachers to qualify for the higher salaries now offered to supervisors and holders of higher degrees. Perhaps classes could be made so small and manageable that teachers would prefer to remain in the comfort of the classroom instead of looking toward administration as the refuge from the wear and tear of the educational process. Whatever method we use, and we may have to use many methods, our aim must be to keep our best teachers where they belong, in the classroom.

58. School Practices
That Cause Failure

Helen F. Robison

It used to be children who failed. Now the failure is seen to be school failure. When the failures were thought to be children, schools were not expected to change. But school failure calls for considerable change. In fact, it is probable that a substantial transformation of the school will have to be achieved in order to decrease school failure to minimal levels. The idea of a "community school," long in discard, seems to be reemerging. This time, however, while the school is not viewed as a substitute for all other community institutions, it is expected to take a more extended, collaborative and comprehensive view of its responsibilities and possibilities.

School failure rates are swollen by many factors, including administrative, teaching, curricular and interpersonal elements. It is not possible to pinpoint one factor as the most crucial and pivotal, since in reality a combination of interacting elements appears to be the matrix in which failure finds nutrient.

What Quality of School Leadership?

Administrative factors are important in all aspects of school operation, since leadership and school arrangements necessarily affect all else. Everywhere there are some school principals who are deluged with teacher applicants and others who are not. There are differences here which need study and evaluation—the quality of school leadership; its pervasive influence on teachers, parents and children; and the relationship of children's learning to the human, technical and procedural variations which flow from such leadership. New demands are being voiced for "school account-

Source: *Childhood Education*, XLIV, 3 (November 1967), 155–58. Copyright © 1967 by the Association. Reprinted by permission of the author and the Association for Childhood Education International, 3615 Wisconsin Avenue, N.W., Washington, D.C.

ability," "school production of results," and comparisons of school results on reading scores and other quantified devices. These urgencies, arising out of frustration, despair and fears that schools are failing at an accelerating rate, cannot be brushed aside as irrelevant and presumptuous. They must be met by sincere but realistic plans for change which promise to reverse the frightening failure-rates which exist.

Essential is clear recognition that schools are not analagous to competitive private commercial institutions. The schools are not selling a product for profit. More often, the schools are asked to turn very unprofitable prospects into more hopeful ones. This is not a competitive effort but one which requires a higher degree of cooperation than has been realized in the past. Too little recognition has been given to the fact that the schools in the nation's urban centers have been blamed for inability to offer instant compensation to children from blighted rural areas, from families with generations of educational and economic neglect. The problems are gigantic and will not be solved in a moment by emotion and instant action. Progress in resolving these problems requires generous financial support and considerable community confidence in the school's leadership, with better evaluative procedures to gauge change, avoiding more simplistic types of assessment. In fact, some broad form of school accountability is inevitable, if only to speed up needed changes and keep problems of school failure in a position of high priority on the school's agenda.

Can Administrative Practices Produce Failure?

A broad gamut of administrative practices feeds failure, including such easily remedied actions as discourtesy to parents and visitors from school clerical staffs to rigid insistence that all teachers use a specified reading method. Other practices administratively determined include grading and retention policies which brand children publicly as failures, in lieu of diagnosing and treating their problems. The school forfeits its power of educational redemption when it conveys worthlessness to a child. Grouping practices of certain types, tracking and oversized classes can contribute substantially to school failures, as do all arrangements which obscure the unique individuality of each child's history and current educational needs.

The school's value system is largely determined by administrative policies. If the school conveys values of quiet, obedience, cleanliness and orderliness, the turbulence and unpredictability of children's self-propelled learning will surely be squeezed out. Will the school value a child's intensity of effort or his drive to realize some urgency to learn which may diverge from the program specified in the syllabus? Conformity (whether in children's dress, behavior or learning styles) when enshrined as a school value leaves little tolerance for natural diversity of children or creative variations in teaching.

What Kind of Supervision?

The character of supervision available to the teaching staff is often as important to experienced teachers, who may need reorientation to changing programs and procedures, as to new teachers requiring initiation into their first professional responsibility and inservice guidance to develop their potential ability. If this supervision is essentially judgmental and non-informative, teaching may suffer from hostility, resentment, insecurity and uncertainty, adding undesirable types of affect to the classroom atmosphere. *If supervision is supportive, instructive, extending, reassuring and collaborative, enormous improvements in teaching may be possible.* Teachers require support not only to implement standard school programs but also to feel free to innovate or to try out an exemplary model. Freedom to innovate must mean freedom to fail. An off-with-her-head attitude only encourages teachers to keep within safe limits and avoid new programs.

Do Teachers Hinder Progress?

What about the teacher's share of responsibility for school failures? Do teachers have the professional attitudes required for their own self-improvement and for the children's needed progress? Are they able to ask for needed assistance (in personnel, services or supervision) as they see the need? Do they keep abreast of their fields? Are they open to new ideas or do they dismiss innovative possibilities in advance? Are parents to be blamed for the children's shortcomings or are cooperative procedures followed for interchange of information, aspirations and results? Humane teachers and supportive administrators and supervisors set the stage for improving children's educational experiences. *Teacher humaneness and kindness are absolutely necessary ingredients for satisfying the relationship needs of children and for offering worthy adult models for children's social and interpersonal learning.* But more is needed to prevent failure.

What about Quality of Curriculum?

What about curricular procedures? Is curriculum development based on knowledge of the most significant and relevant recent research? Is it flexibly adaptable to local, classroom and individual needs? Equally important, does it serve the diagnosed needs of the child population in the school?

Are teachers knowledgeable about diagnostic testing of children's cognitive levels and learning needs? Can they spark children's self-motivated learning toward conceptualization, analysis, synthesis and evaluation? Do teachers know how to help children find the mainstreams of culture in our time and wade in to whatever depths they can manage? What good is a 3-R education in an age of cybernetics, of explosive growth in scientific knowledge and technology, and of planetary needs to cope with such complex issues as population, food supply and man's survival on the earth? Educational aspirations are higher today for more children than ever before, because what enabled our grandparents to survive may be our undoing today.

What about the quality of the curriculum offered to children? Is it dull? Is it permeated by drill and workbook experiences? Can children find relationships between the school experience and the most intense issues in their lives? How relevant to life do children feel their schooling to be? What aspects in school offer, in addition to functional and practical experience, visions of exciting esthetic experience, of moral issues men live and die for, or of human striving for the unknown and the unknowable? How does school help conscience grow to a moral plane where it is based on logical reasoning, or "lawfulness" in the broadest and best sense, combining individual responsibility with well-developed moral fibre? Does the curriculum offer stimulation and satisfaction to slow students as well as gifted ones?

Generally, most teachers teach what they know and they do this to the best of their ability. Could this dedication become an instrument for improved education, by helping teachers to "know" more, to know and to use more information about knowledge, about technology and about teaching? To this end, the schools need help from all sources, including the universities, state and federal educational authorities, professional organizations, and research organizations now involved in developing and testing new types of curriculum and teaching methodology.

What Kinds of School and Teaching Arrangements?

Many school arrangements have become so deeply embedded in tradition that neither administrative, supervisory nor teacher personnel find it easy to initiate or support change. The self-contained classroom has become a nonsupportable slogan which needs discarding. With increasing availability of technology, teachers increasingly need to ease the curricular burden with television, movies, language laboratories, recordings and many other inputs now available from outside the classroom. Not only technological products but technical and professional personnel need readier access to classrooms. Teachers can find stimulation, support, challenge and rich stores of new information from audiovisual supervisors, librarians, music and art specialists, mathematics and science specialists, and social scientists. Researchers, educators, psychologists, anthropologists and political scientists are increasingly appreciative of invitations to work with teachers in schools, and new forms of collaboration and interdisciplinary study and demonstrations are going on. Teachers can contribute to more significant forms of research while acquiring for themselves some of the rigor, discipline and tentativeness which scholarship brings to bear on all forms of inquiry.

While teaching arrangements themselves do not offer panaceas for education, they can add facilitating, satisfying or additional possibilities to teaching which offer important emphases on real individualization. Team teaching, internships, ungraded classes; grade planning and evaluation, intervisitation plans, sharing of closed circuit television teaching models within the school or use of videotaping for teacher self-evaluation or group sharing, and well-planned use of teacher aides in the classroom, all suggest additional possibilities for teaching to become more relevant to each child and more specific to releasing his potential for self-maximization.

Interpersonal Relationships Valued

Finally, it must be stressed that *no system can be successful in reducing school failure unless all interpersonal relationships are valued above objects and events.* Truly, teachers cannot reduce failures without appropriate assortments of books, other teaching materials and equipment, and adequate architectural space. No matter how high the "per pupil expenditure" may go, it will not pay for excellent education unless children perceive themselves as appreciated and valued; unless teachers sense satisfaction, appreciation and enjoyment of good relationships in school and community; and unless parents feel confidence in the school staff's use of the educational establishment.

Parents have a right to demand the best of the schools. Schools have a right to use their educational expertise in ways that seem optimum to educators. A healthy relationship between school and community, which could result in lower rates of school failure, requires mutual respect, considerable cooperation and interchange, and much more communication. Of all the tensions growing out of the current drive by minority groups for economic and social betterment, the prime responsibility for educational improvement is properly the school's. But the school can only make substantial improvement in children's education with the wholehearted support and assistance of the community. Reduction of school failure may require novel, experimental forms of community-school partnership, with new roles for parents and teachers in sharing plans and procedures for better education for all children.

59. Educational Parks

Abraham S. Fischler and James E. Smith

There is a great deal of talk today about educational parks, especially by school officials associated with large city schools; few people are willing to even try to define them. However, the major justification for the park seems not to be on educational grounds, but rather on the basis that it will solve our de facto segregation problem in the inner cities. The educational park also seems to encompass community services as well. It incorporates large facilities for community productions, recreation, adult education, and clinics, both psychiatric and public health. Many articles have been written and linear cities devised as a strategy for the educational park.

The time has come to see if one can state the educational requirements for an educational park and attempt to justify the park concept on the basis of the educational opportunities it affords to all students, "womb through tomb." Therefore, the following represents the authors' opinions on these requirements, established as a minimum.

Educational Parks—Characteristics

An educational park should involve a preshool through twelfth grade population as a minimum. These grades represent (a) that which seems to be indicated in the research about "early learning" and (b) the commitment of the public to the educational development of all children. Since we have laws that make it mandatory for all children to remain in school through age sixteen, it appears that we should talk about an educational park that incorporates at least the mandatory ages as a minimum.

SOURCE: *California Elementary Administrator*, XXXI, 3 (May–June 1968), 36–37. Reprinted by permission of the publisher.

Needless to say, the park would bring together students from a wider geographic area and socioeconomic range than the usual neighborhood school. This provides more opportunity for cross-grouping on the basis of socio-economic level. The advantages here would be to have students examine their own values as they relate to a common problem.

It is essential that the total park be under the direction of one administrator. Whether he is called an assistant superintendent or a director does not make any difference. Of import is that there be one person, with the aid of a staff, who sets the philosophy which will permeate the educational program for all children. This administrative director should have a curriculum staff concerned with the education of all students, from preshool through the twelfth grade. This means that an assistant director in charge of curriculum is responsible for the complete educational program of the park. It is not enough to have three or more buildings in close proximity, each having its own principal and developing its own educational philosophy. By establishing an administrative structure which permeates the total educational endeavor, a continuity of philosophy and commitment is ensured.

A Continuous Educational Program

Another area of concern is that the program provided for the students is a continuous one. By continuous, we mean that it provides an opportunity for students to move at their own pace and level through a program which makes known to the students its sequence and its behavioral expectations. The work is divided into small learning units in order for the student to proceed systematically. Each unit provides for the student the choice of his own media, mode, and content through which he can acquire the desired behaviors. Each unit includes self-assessment, so that the student can assess himself prior to the teacher evaluation. It provides opportunities for the student to go into depth, some working on a theoretical level, others at a quite pragmatic level. It enables the student to make a variety of choices, thus providing for the teacher a cognitive map for each child. Each child also sets for himself his rate and level of learning within a particular field. The reward system is one of positive, rather than negative, reinforcement. At the present time, tests begin at 100 percent; missing one question brings the grade to 95. The philosophy with the park is one which says, "Every time the student reaches success, he is rewarded and proceeds to the next learning unit."

In order to provide the opportunity for each student to move at his own pace, utilizing his own styles, a master schedule of resources for the total park must be developed which will facilitate the above. We feel that in most school systems, especially at the secondary level, the schedule hinders what can be accomplished. It is essential that a schedule be developed which will provide each student the opportunity to differentiate the amount of time he would like to spend in different fields of study. To produce a self-directed learner, the opportunity must be provided within the school to give the youngsters time to develop the skills and necessary priorities which are essential for his adult life. Under the present situation, a student is scheduled all day (each day) until he reaches eighteen or is graduated from high school. From that point on, he is supposedly free to make his own decisions. If he goes on to college, the freshman year is most difficult because now he has to learn to proportion his time in relation to the tasks assigned. If he obtains employment, he has even more important decisions to make. Where in his high school training did he acquire any of these skills? We believe that the educational park schedule should allow the student to learn to make decisions as to how and where he can most appropriately utilize his time.

Once accepting the above, proper facilities have to be then made available. This means that laboratories (science, yes; but also English, math, social studies, etc.) instead of being built for 24 students are actually built for 50 or 60 students. Although 24 might be scheduled through the laboratory at any one time, we would like to see other students have the opportunity to come there for any part of the day in which they feel they would like to work in science. The same is true for other resource centers. A student should be free to go to a resource center and to work on his own with the materials he needs available.

It would be advantageous to have an information retrieval system, a system which enables students to dial and receive tapes, films, or film strips. This is feasible today and will likely be found in most schools within two decades. Teachers should make audio tapes of certain materials so that students, when they reach a certain point within any unit, can listen to a tape if they wish.

All of the above implies a new type of teacher, one who is *not* teller, informer or lecturer, or the only source of information. Rather, the teacher becomes a goal setter, a diagnostician, and a prescriber. He has the opportunity, as students are working individually, to move about and talk to each student as need arises. He has the opportunity to determine whether the student is setting realistic goals for himself. He can call together eight or ten youngsters at any particular time in order to aid them to analyze, synthesize, and develop judgment in relation to what they are learning. In assessing the types of student decisions, the teachers can diagnose certain learning difficulties, as well as learning styles. Once this information is available, he can prescribe to a student more accurately what he should be doing and how he might be doing it in order to achieve greater success and self-satisfaction.

Every test given should serve three functions. First, it should test the ability of the student to demonstrate his performance within this unit module. Second, it should test the retention of some of the behaviors which the student supposedly acquired in previous learning modules. Lastly, it should have a diagnostic component to determine to which of the next modules the student should proceed.

Summary

In summary, then, an educational park should provide for the continuous education of students from preschool through the twelfth grade. It should have one director of the total enterprise, as well as curriculum people concerned with the continuous progress of students. The program should provide for students to move at their own pace and level, utilizing their own learning styles. The schedule should facilitate this movement, and the teachers should develop the skills necessary to be goal setters, diagnosticians, and prescribers. The facilities should provide the space, the technology, and the opportunity for different size groups to meet at different times for different purposes with different kinds of equipment. Finally, the outcome should produce a self-directed learner—a person capable of making decisions based on his values, as well as his system of priorities.

60. Talent + Plan = A New Humanism

Helen P. Foster

humanism, *n. 1. the quality of being human; human nature. 2. any system or way of thought or action concerned with the interests and ideals of people.*

Webster's 20th Century Dictionary

To meet the national need for better education, and for the selection and evaluation of new, more personalized learning methods and materials, a

SOURCE: *Greater Pittsburgh*, September 1967. Reprinted by permission of the author and the publisher.

functioning model of an educational system for the 1970's—Project PLAN—is being put into operation this September by the American Institutes for Research in the Behavioral Sciences, the Westinghouse Learning Corporation, and twelve cooperating school systems of the United States.

Three of these school districts to pioneer with PLAN are in Western Pennsylvania: the Pittsburgh public schools, and the schools of Bethel Park and Penn-Trafford.

In a time of exploding populations, overcrowded schools and classrooms —of too many kids and not enough teachers—and vastly increasing technical information to be assimilated and mastered by students, Americans have in the past few years become increasingly aware of the need for major changes in the present educational system.

The last fifteen years have seen attempts to improve education by drastically revising specific courses, by instituting ungraded schools, and increasing provisions for independent study, by developing programmed learning materials and related teaching machines, and by introducing many new audio-visual techniques including language laboratories and educational television.

However, the physical appurtenances of good education are probably of small importance, and some educators' judgments can be faulty— Abraham Lincoln received his education in a rude log cabin; Thomas Edison was believed by some of his teachers to be retarded; Winston Churchill flunked English three times; and Albert Schweitzer's scholastic record in primary and secondary schools was very poor. Recorded history is studded with such disadvantaged or misunderstood schoolchildren.

Too often in the past twenty years inadequacies of staff, time, and working space have forced American children into unsuitable class—and mass—educational experiences, with indifferent or unhappy results, rather than providing education tailored—however modestly—to suit the needs and abilities of the individual child.

Jimmy Jones is not like Jimmy Smith—nor does Jamie Judson resemble in abilities, talents, and direction his classmate Georgie Jones.

Current educational programs in the elementary and secondary schools make inadequate provision for the very large individual differences to be found in any age or grade group in today's schools. These differences exist not only in academic ability and achievement, but also in individual patterns of special aptitudes and talents which, because of the exigencies of group needs, must frequently be ignored.

Jimmy Jones often gets lost in the shuffle.

Present educational programs are especially deficient in providing appropriate educational opportunities both for gifted children and for the 30 per cent of each age group who, under present circumstances, fail to complete the twelfth grade.

In addition, the demands of the information explosion will require future students to learn 1½ to 2 times as much as most American school children are now learning, and that the learning be tailored specifically to individual need.

The inadequacies of present-day education have created a strong feeling among American educators that revolutionary changes must be searched out and that new procedures must be evolved to enable the students of tomorrow's generation to keep pace with the information explosion, and to learn a great deal more from the same effort than did their parents.

The new approach pioneered by the American Institutes of Research and the Westinghouse Learning Corporation—called Project PLAN (Program for Learning in Accordance with Needs)—is a systematic one which uses the student and his individual needs as the basic unit in the system, and emphasizes evaluation of his progress at all stages of his educational development.

The functional model of PLAN begins with a tentative plan for the educational objectives to be attained by the student, then assists him in attaining these objectives through the use of specially designed modular segments of learning activities, and continuously monitors his progress with respect to the attainment of these objectives.

In this process the student—Jimmy Jones—and his teacher are provided with the services of a computer as a flexible tool for information processing, storage and retrieval. Stored in the computer is detailed information on Jimmy Jones' special aptitudes, patterns of learning, interests and background. In addition, a record is kept of the skills and knowledge Jimmy has acquired prior to reaching any given decision point. The computer also stores a complete file listing instructional materials in the form of modules or manageable segments which may be called "teaching-learning units." These are systematically indexed in terms of what Jimmy is expected to learn from them, what the prerequisites are, and for what other type of student and situation this unit is especially well-suited.

Under the direction of Dr. John Flanagan, chairman of the American Institutes for Research in the Behavioral Sciences, and Donald H. McGannon, chairman of the Westinghouse Learning Corporation, the development of the new components was initiated through two conferences in Palo Alto, California, attended by representatives of AIR, Westinghouse Learning Corporation, and teachers, superintendents, principals, and supervisors from the participating school districts. Among those also in attendance at the working sessions, held early this year, were leading behavioral scientists from the University of Pittsburgh, as well as such universities as Stanford, Illinois, Pennsylvania, California, Washington and Harvard, and participants from the United States Office of Education.

Project PLAN establishes twelve demonstration centers to augment the vital role of the teacher under advanced educational technologies.

The worth of any educational system is the excellence—or lack of excellence—of creative rapport between the student and the teacher in it. Education is part of the human experience—and it is the communication of learning from one human to another, from teacher to student, and the human exchange of ideas and ideals between the two, that creates good education. No computer can replace the creative ability of a good teacher.

Here and now, with the computer assuming the bulk of clerical and analytical activities, the teacher is freed to again devote his attention to teaching—to the selection and preparation of materials, and—most important of all—to the individual learning needs and objectives of that all-important student Jimmy Jones.

The system of PLAN is completely flexible and adaptive, designed for installation in today's schools, and for implementation in current classroom facilities. The major piece of equipment involved, the computer, is located at the AIR headquarters in Palo Alto, and connected directly to the schools via individualized terminals.

On the basis of Jimmy Jones' tentative goals and the estimates of his present knowledge, Jimmy and his teacher will receive descriptions from the computer of the two or three teaching-learning units in each of the various fields which appear best suited to his learning style, interests, and special aptitudes. Together Jimmy and his teacher will select the specific teaching-learning units on which he will start the year's work in each field. They will then receive a statement of the learning materials to be used and the knowledge and behavior changes to be learned. The plan for Jimmy will suggest reading to be done, workbook and other questions and exercises to be completed, and audio-visual materials to be added. The teacher is given suggestions as to specific points to check regarding Jimmy's progress, possible difficulties which may require his assistance, and some hints and suggestions for handling specific problems which may develop in Jimmy's work on the unit.

Project PLAN is based on the "success" principle. It is intended that Jimmy and other students be assigned only objectives which he and they can achieve at their present individual stages of learning and development.

In this way it is proposed that instead of the decrease in eagerness to learn which now takes place so often in the schools as a student proceeds from the first to the twelfth grades, the new approach of PLAN should result in an increasing desire on the part of Jimmy Jones to develop his skills, acquire knowledge, and prepare himself for living and learning in our society.

During the past 20 years, the American Institutes for Research in the Behavioral Sciences, a non-profit research and development organization, has completed a number of important research programs in the field of education. AIR, with principal offices located in Pittsburgh, Palo Alto, California, and Washington, D.C., is currently engaged in programs of research in instructional methods, and social, educational and mental health projects supported by government, industry, and foundation grants.

The Westinghouse Learning Corporation, a subsidiary of Westinghouse Electric Corporation, is devoted to broad-based activities in the field of education. Headquartered in New York City, the Learning Corporation maintains additional research, training and service facilities in Pittsburgh, Albuquerque, Washington, D.C., and San Francisco.

Westinghouse Learning Corporation activities include training of Peace Corpsmen assigned to Iran, Chile and Micronesia; advanced training programs at the Capital Job Corps Center in Washington, D.C. for selected "graduates" of the Job Corps; experimental projects in learning programs and computer-based teaching systems in conjunction with the University of Pittsburgh; development of audio-visual educational materials; and intensive research in the learning process at the Westinghouse Learning Behavior Systems Division in Albuquerque.

Project PLAN grew directly out of the findings of Project TALENT, conceived by the American Institutes for Research in the Behavioral Sciences ten years ago.

Project TALENT developed from efforts to assist high school students in the increasingly complex task of planning their educational development and preparing themselves to make full use of their individual abilities and special talents. After three years of planning, support from the Cooperative Research Program of the United States Office of Education made it possible to obtain detailed information during a two-day period from a representative sample of 440,000 students in the 9th, 10th, 11th, and 12th grades in public, private, and parochial schools throughout the United States.

In addition to the value of the original survey data concerning the achievements of these students, they were followed up one year after their graduation from high school, and are again being evaluated five years later, to determine the extent of their additional education, its value to them, and the occupations in which they are now engaged. Further evaluation of their development will be made ten and twenty years after graduation from high school to obtain additional data for improving both guidance and educational programs for the next generation of students.

Findings from Project TALENT have already had an important impact on policies regarding school size, class size, scholarship requirements, and vocational education.

More consideration is being given to guiding the student in planning for an appropriate occupational role, preparing him for the responsibilities of citizenship—including personal and social development—and helping him find the avenues leading to the deeply satisfying activities promised by increased leisure time.

The first school year of PLAN tryouts, 1967–68, is limited to grades one, five and nine. The system will be extended to grades two, six and ten in September 1968, moving on to the next higher grades in September 1969 and 1970, so that students in grades one through twelve will be using the new system by 1970.

Advocates of individualism and disciples of the humanistic approach in education have long regretted the un-human applications and efficiencies of the computer. Now, through utilization of the computer, individualized instruction which educators have been advocating can again be given.

As the Renaissance in Western Europe was born from the humanism of mediaeval philosophers and educators, is it not possible that the re-emergence of the importance of the individual in teaching programs, with the return to the humanistic approach which PLAN affords, can in the future be evaluated as a giant step in a continuously evolving and improving program of education?

Project PLAN offers the practical and pragmatic value of providing immediate benefits in improved education, and at the same time promises a blueprint for greater education for the future.

61. As Fast As Your Brain Knows How

William A. Coleman

Linda-Lee Bauer, 10, and her brother Cameron, 8, home from school for lunch, were rushing through the meal. "Take your time," said Linda Bauer, their mother. "The school won't run away." But the kids kept right on eating fast and in a few minutes sped out the door with a "So long, mom."

"Well," said a visitor, "I've never seen children that anxious to get back to school."

"They can't wait," Mrs. Bauer explained. "They love the school and they love the teacher. I sometimes think it's magic."

SOURCE: *Parade Magazine*, September 29, 1968, pp. 4–5. Reprinted by permission of the author and the publisher.

Revolutionary System

The Bauer children are normal, healthy, ordinary youngsters, but their school—Oakleaf Elementary in the Pittsburgh suburban district of Baldwin-Whitehall—is something else. It's the nation's pioneer in use of a revolutionary type of education known as Individually Prescribed Instruction (IPI). In this system each child advances at his own speed, and in extremely close personal relationship with his teacher. The traditional classroom concept, with all pupils studying the same thing at the same time, is out. Under IPI, education is a personal achievement and, usually, a personal triumph. Children judged immature and scheduled to be "left back" at other schools have become fine students at Oakleaf. And it wasn't too surprising that Mrs. Bauer thought of IPI as "magic." For, when Oakleaf pupils competed in a science test against forty-five University of Pittsburgh freshmen, fourth graders tied the collegians and sixth graders beat them!

The U.S. Office of Education, which is promoting IPI and has installed it in nearly 100 elementary schools across the country, says that without question it's *the* thing of the future. More than 2000 school districts are now on a growing waiting list, anxious for the special principal and elementary teacher training that's needed. And federal officials are already planning an IPI network in seventeen high schools to start next year in autumn.

The first thing that strikes you about IPI instruction is its informality. Two or three school grades may be grouped together in a suite of cheery rooms, working under two teachers and a librarian who act as tutors and coordinators. Special assistants take care of all grading and other paper work, leaving the teachers free to devote themselves to the youngsters.

Pupils are in no sense in competition. If one is two weeks behind another in arithmetic, there's no stigma. Each is learning at his own pace and each will get there in the end. In a typical classroom scene, a child has been started off on a certain learning project by the teacher and then left alone to progress on his own momentum. He may do this by writing on a worksheet at a desk. Or reading. Or watching motion pictures. Or engage in group discussion. Or listen to recordings. Or carry out scientific experiments at the direction of a recorder.

Under IPI, instruction is tailored to the individual pupil. Each one gets a daily prescription of instruction that is exactly what he is ready for. There's very little problem of discipline, apparently because the youngsters are activists in their own education, not simply receivers of instruction in a teacher-dominated classroom.

And an important fringe benefit of IPI comes when a child returns to school after an absence. He's not immediately faced with that sometimes hopeless challenge to "catch up to the class." He simply resumes his education at the point of interruption.

IPI was developed by Robert Glaser, John O. Bolvin and C. Mauritz Lindvall, professors at the University of Pittsburgh Learning, Research and Development Center, and installed at Oakleaf in 1963.

Johnny K. and Jimmy H. are two fifth graders who transferred recently to Oakleaf after having troubles at another school. Johnny complained of too much "useless homework" and said he "always felt stupid." Jimmy suffered from pressure, often had stomach pains. At Oakleaf, both were given two weeks of placement tests to determine where they stood in various subjects. It developed that in arithmetic their progress was about equal and they were started off at the same point in that subject.

Right at Home

Johnny felt right at home with IPI and within two weeks was insisting on a maximum of independence from the teacher. Jimmy took twice as long to catch on but he obviously was happy in IPI and had no more pains. In a month Johnny had mastered 13 separate arithmetic achievements, Jimmy about half that many. Progress was measured by periodic tests. If the boy scored 85 or better, he was passed on to a new skill. If he didn't make 85, he repeated study of the skill—but from a slightly different approach. According to his exact personal needs, the teacher assigned him to small-group instruction, or teacher tutoring, or a film strip—any of a variety of instructional variations.

"Sometimes," says an IPI teacher, "we find that a child has a block against learning something under one form of instruction but takes it in easily under another form. That's where the individual prescription comes in."

With IPI now flourishing from Connecticut to California—and one Hawaiian school is using it—federal officials believe it will be in universal use in U.S. public schools within five years. At that point all of our children will have the advantages of IPI which were described so eloquently by a little Oakleaf girl, "As fast as your brain knows how to go, that's how fast you go in school."

62. The Magic
of the Learning Center

Patricia Clark

The conversation between the teacher and the support team was brief and to the point: *Donald was in the eighth grade—approaching high school—and he could not read a single word.*

When he registered in this school last spring, his meager records indicated that he'd been enrolled in a number of special programs at two other school districts.

But with high school entrance rushing up to meet him, there wasn't much time left to tackle a problem that spelled "instant dropout." The work had to be done swiftly and it had to be done well.

At 8 o'clock the next morning, the teacher went through a "debriefing" session with the team's psychologist. She shared with him through records, anecdotal files, work samples and narrative, the picture she'd been able to form of Donald up to this point.

Watching the tall, withdrawn boy at school, as he worked with his classmates and different kinds of instructional media, the psychologist added another dimension to the profile. Now he needed evidence to determine whether or not his tentative diagnosis was correct. The tests he selected to use with Donald pointed solidly to the fact that he was verbally retarded. He had virtually no auditory memory. And for years his records indicated teachers had been trying to teach him to read through the phonics method. The tests also pointed to a certain visual acuity. He had good retention for visual stimuli. The psychologist prepared his report.

Up to this point, we have the type of situation that occurs daily in hundreds of schools across the country. And what happens after the psychologist gives the child a test and reports to the teacher? "Yes—he's got a problem all right . . . but . . ."

If we're really honest with ourselves, we know these kids usually go

Source: *CTA Journal,* LXV, 2 (March 1969), 16–19. Copyright © California Teachers Association 1969. Reprinted by permission of the author, Patricia Clark, Administrative Assistant, Fountain Valley School District, Fountain Valley, California, and the publisher.

back to being part of the glossed-over milieu. We try to do something for them—but we have twenty-nine others in the class—and they all have their special problems.

If instruction is going to be tailored to *Donald's* needs—or Janet's or Sam's or Mary Ann's—then a teacher must know exactly what those needs are. Have teachers been trained as *diagnosticians?* Can they determine curricular *prescriptions?* Do they have the tools to *evaluate?*

The problems that youngsters such as Donald bring to our classrooms mandate a close look at the answers we're able to give to these questions. As teachers of children, we share the *most* important problems of our society. And we've shared them since the first common school opened its doors to children who were then preparing for life in an agrarian society. But things have changed. To bridge the mammoth gap between the "pot-bellied stove" age to our present "push-button" age, we need a new kind of school, one with these characteristics:

· one that has learning centers that are equipped with a range of materials and the latest technology available
· one with master teachers, who are trained in diagnosis, prescription, and evaluation, to assist the classroom teachers and coordinate learning programs for children
· one with specialists, such as psychologist and learning disability teacher, right at the school, to diagnose and follow-up special problems
· and one with teacher aides to take over the burden of clerical duties and other time-consuming, non-professional tasks.

Why would these elements provide the bridge we need?

· because the classroom teacher must have more of an "even chance" at managing the problem of working effectively and efficiently with children —and this system "equalizes the odds."
· because these different staff members, through their training and talents and responsibilities, can bring to bear a team effort to solve problems related to working with children.
· because educators need extra space and specialized supplies and equipment if they're going to do the job—and a Learning Center provides them.

An educational plan has been developed in Fountain Valley to include the elements of the school situation described above. The design of the school has been modified and new roles have been spelled out in a staffing pattern to keep the schools "childworthy."

Fountain Valley's twelve schools, all constructed since 1963, resulted from a building program designed to facilitate the learning process. School buildings here are not merely protective shelters, but educational tools. Space has been reorganized so that six or eight classrooms are clustered about a core room, called a Learning Center.

The learning center functions as a resource center for diagnostic materials, electronic teaching devices, a bank of tape recordings, art materials, test banks, science equipment, audio-visual materials, study carrels and a library. This is the base of operations for the classroom teacher's support team. It's also a place for independent study, as well as guided lessons for individuals and small groups. "A little boy came in the other day," reports coordinating teacher Betty Christianson, "and said, 'Boy! this is a *neat* room. Look at all the stuff there is to do!' "

The learning center is organized so that several activities can continue at once. In one corner of the room, a small group of children may be working on a math lesson with tape recorder and head sets. At another table, a group from several classrooms and grade levels might be using programmed reading materials. One child might have a science experiment in progress, while art activities hold the attention of several other youngsters. An educational television program may have attracted several viewers, and it's very likely that there will be a group of children selecting books from the library shelves.

The coordinating teacher works with his team of teachers in deciding how the learning center will be used. The "Modified Teaching Day" provides time for the educational team to work together. Schedules have been adjusted in many of the schools to dismiss the children early one day each week to provide for a block of professional planning time. At this time, teachers will identify children from different rooms and grade levels who have a common need. These children are then scheduled to work together in a directed lesson or other activity with the coordinating teacher in the learning centers.

In this program, children are involved in making decisions, too. They have some "say," for example, in how the learning center will be used. A little boy came bouncing in to the center last week and said, "I'm going to the pretend corner and I didn't even have to ask my teacher!"

One of the key members of the support team is the learning analyst, a role filled by the school psychologist in this staffing plan. Whereas the school psychologist has typically been "locked in" to a three-step process of referral, case study, and report, his role here encompasses much more.

Ken Ortiz, a dynamic young psychologist who formerly served as a rehabilitation counselor at the Veteran's Hospital, sees his position of learning analyst as being right in the middle of the child's school world. He believes there's more to educational psychology than eight hours a day in his office administering tests and writing reports. To whatever extent is possible he works with all the people in the child's world, particularly staff, peers and parents.

Ortiz believes that extensive formal testing fits in "when you don't know what's causing a problem, or when you need more evidence to support your hypothesis." But extensive testing isn't warranted automatically with each referral. "It's *that* kind of procedure that needlessly consumes time."

Ortiz feels strongly that the psychologist should be a physical member of the school staff. There should be a relaxed relationship between him and other staff members. He says, "As a psychologist I should be *of* the school—not just *in* it."

Occupying a pivotal position on the professional team, the coordinating teacher serves as troubleshooter, problem-solver, consultant, demonstration teacher, and research scientist. He is a master teacher, who has demonstrated proficiency in individualizing instruction and who knows how to share that skill with the teachers on his team.

Mrs. Betty Christianson is one educator who *literally* has gone from the pot-bellied stove to the push-button era. In 1944, at age 18, the principal source of heat in her one-room school was the little stove in the corner. Today, as one of three coordinating teachers at her school of 770 students, most of her time is spent in a modern learning center, scheduling, teaching, organizing interest centers for children, building test and tape banks and working with other members of the team on curriculum projects.

Diagnosis and prescription is a key element of the coordinating teacher's role and is usually a cooperative venture, often involving all the members of the team. Task forces have been and still are involved in assembling banks of diagnostic instruments and cataloguing by concept files of worksheets, reading materials and audio-visual media. The modified teaching day has facilitated this process for several teams.

In Lois Thompson's primary learning center, she and psychologist Dixie Hoffman invested a considerable amount of time testing twenty children whose teachers suspected perceptual difficulties. Those children with actual diagnosed needs are now being treated through the use of Frostig materials prescribed by Mrs. Hoffman. Their progress will be evaluated cooperatively by classroom teachers, coordinating teacher, and psychologist.

Dramatic changes in technology, modification in curriculum content and research findings in methodology have become so prolific and rapid that adaptation to change has become a constant.

"There's a high level of constructive discontent among my teachers," says Mrs. Christianson, "because we know things can always be better than they are. They're constantly searching and they become frustrated and dissatisfied when they can't do it. . . . That's when I become most valuable—as they see the need for me—a resource, another source of talent for them to break out."

Another coordinating teacher, Pat Taylor, concurs. "One of the most important things I do is to help the teachers I work with become better teachers. In Fountain Valley, we have an unusual situation because of our sudden growth and our instructional point of view." (The district has grown 3500% in the last six years, and individualized instruction is the cornerstone of the educational program.) "We have some new teachers who are just learning what it means to adjust objectives, materials and rate to individual specifications. There are times when a teacher will ask me to come into her classroom almost in a student teaching relationship. I've spent days of demonstrating, observing, analyzing, discussing, and giving hints. They feel it's important to them to draw on my repertoire of experiences and ideas. And sometimes you really need to spell things out."

Miss Taylor brings home another point. "I believe it's my job to make these people comfortable so they feel good about themselves and their work. If that doesn't happen, we've cut down on their effectiveness."

The coordinating teacher is the frontline lieutenant just outside the classroom door—who sets the scene for total team effort in an atmosphere of cooperation, flexibility, and good communication. Mrs. Christianson describes it this way: "I think it's very important that we have rapport with our teachers. We're a team. I'm not a threat to them. I don't evaluate them. They can come to me and say, 'I've just had it. I can't seem to get through to this child.' And the support members of the team can help to redirect the child's experiences. It's too bad, but I think educators have established a false concept—that if we can't make it with one child, we're a failure. I think the learning center plan—with a team of professionals who have different kinds of responsibilities—works to alleviate that concept. Among other things, it acts as a 'big shoulder.' "

Frequently, children with perceptual difficulties or other serious physical, emotional or psychological problems are scheduled to work with another vital member of the learning center team: the "EH teacher." This teacher provides special attention to a small group of "educationally handicapped" children who can then work without distraction on their learning disabilities. He works closely with the classroom teacher and the coordinating teacher in evaluation and classroom carry-over.

To free the professional staff to attend to all of these responsibilities, teacher aides have been employed (one for each learning center). The four hours they work each day are devoted to fulfilling any of the non-teaching tasks related to the instructional program. Under supervision of the coordinating teacher, they check out library books for children, set up projectors, gather equipment, type ditto masters and duplicate worksheets, and other clerical tasks.

Unfortunately, Fountain Valley shares a problem that is common to so many other school districts: it's a bedroom community, with lots of children, but very little industry. Result: the amount of money behind each child in the schools is about one-half of the state average. With champagne objectives and a lemonade budget, the district has had to tap all possible sources of assistance.

To supplement the paid teacher aide program, 1400 Fountain Valley parents have formed a squadron of volunteers providing services to teachers and children. They do everything from processing library books and typing dittos to handmaking manipulative learning devices and instructional games at the district's curriculum materials center.

They frequently volunteer to work in the learning centers, setting up equipment, mixing paint, organizing files, and doing the little tasks that would normally subtract from the teacher's teaching time. Last year, their work saved the district $19,323 in services.

The real test of any innovation—whether it's a staffing pattern or new textbooks—comes when the question is asked: what significant differences does this kind of a program make for children? How is their instruction improved because of this change?

"We're really trying to meet the needs—and that's not just a phrase—of kids and teachers," says Lois Thompson. "When I think of the learning center and the things we're trying to do, I really believe we have a comprehensive-program that fits into all the areas that are an extension of the classroom."

"There's a shift here in the role of the teacher," says Betty Christianson. "The emphasis is on the learner, instead of one teacher on a pedestal spoon-feeding a group of thirty children that happen to be in her class. Sometimes I feel as though if I were able to raise the floor of the learning center, I'd be watching the action on a stage. The children flow into the center from their classrooms and begin immediately to get out equipment for a science experiment, to look things up in the library, to watch films, to talk about their work with each other. The *children* are performing instead of the teacher on *this* stage."

As Mrs. Christianson says, "It's all there. It's all inside these little people. We've just got to unlock it—let it out." But while we're unleashing the child's initiative and creativity, we owe it to him to help develop his sense of responsibility and self-discipline. We must help him define the framework of society's structure in which he'll have to operate. He needs both feet and wings.

A zest for learning—a curiosity, a willingness to investigate, an excitement about exploring "new territory"—is an important goal for learners which is facilitated by this program. The skills and attitudes are built in the classroom. The learning center is a place where children can "test their mettle."

In an art lesson in her learning center, Coordinating Teacher Erin Stewart asked a tiny, 8-year-old Oriental girl, "Do you know what happens when you mix red and blue together?" With brown eyes beaming and pigtails bouncing, Sarah rubbed her hands together excitedly and sang out! "I don't *know* but I'm gonna *find out!*"

And what do the children say about the learning center team approach? We asked some students at the Wardlow School. Eighth-level student Leilani McMillan recalls, "I used to feel funny about going in to a new place.

But I don't mind walking into the learning center when there are other people around, because I feel at home there. I know Mrs. Stewart and Miss Taylor [the coordinating teachers] aren't going to bite my head off. They're glad to see me. So I like going there. I feel like the teachers in there are my friends and they're showing me how to do something. You can go to them with your problems."

And Donald. . . . Donald has built his vocabulary up to 87 words in two months. He's reading for the first time in his life and his relationship with the Coordinating Teacher is something a professional treasures. A new world has been opened up for Donald, the first of many he'll feel confident enough now to conquer.

X. The Profession

For this final part, we have selected nine articles—by the best-known authorities in the field—because of our belief in the importance of this topic. We believe that teaching is the mother profession—the one on which all others depend—and that it behooves its practitioners and society in general to believe similarly, to act accordingly, and to bestir themselves to make teaching move in the direction of greater professional autonomy, status, and recognition.

Lester Seth Vander Werf's article, "Improving the Status of Teachers," tackles the status problem head-on, declaring that the solution is the assumption of a greater measure of responsibility by teachers themselves. He describes the realities that hinder the drive to raise the status of teaching and proposes specific local action to meet these problems—action, unfortunately, as necessary and appropriate today as it was the day the article was written.

Other realities and needed actions at both state and national levels are analyzed and recommended by T. M. Stinnett, long-time executive secretary of the NEA TEPS Commission during the time that organization was the leader in the national drive for higher professional standards for teachers. Stinnett focuses on the necessity for autonomy in the management of professional affairs and improved teacher welfare. He puts autonomy ahead of welfare, thus underscoring what is typically the reverse of what usually happens when most teachers and their professional organizations act. His concluding statement is beautiful: "The great question is not whether teaching *can* become a profession, but whether teachers can be persuaded to *act* like professionals." Amen!

What is most likely to ensure the realization of professional autonomy is accreditation of the institutions that prepare the practitioners. Experience has clearly documented the fact that the process of accreditation has been the single most important vehicle used by the other learned professions to achieve quality control. "Why Accredit Teacher Education?" is forcefully reasoned by William K. Selden, an authority on the entire process of accreditation and former executive secretary of the National Commission on

Accrediting, the body that coordinates the work of all accrediting agencies in the United States.

Closely linked to accreditation in the drive for professional autonomy is the process of certification—a state's stamp of approval on the qualifications of each individual who is going to engage in professional practice. Lucien Kinney's article on certification practices in secondary schools takes a look at the problem from a national point of view. His view differs from those of most writers on the subject, who have concerned themselves primarily with the problems of particular states. Kinney discusses broadly the certification process and national trends, pleading for the profession to establish a licensing system of its own that would be in addition to certification by each state. To do otherwise, he warns, is to "revert to the status of a craft under civil service"—the position teaching is in now in a number of states.

While the intracampus wars in teacher education are still raging, a new breed of teachers and new ways to recruit and train them are being demanded everywhere. There is also a demand—the loudest and least heeded—for personnel to teach the disadvantaged. The times call for bold new answers to an age-old training problem. George Denemark analyzes teacher education alternatives—in the colleges and universities—in "Repair, Reform, or Revolution." Perhaps the answer is not in the colleges and universities, but in the creation of new institutions and the development of new alliances. James Stone's idea for a new institution—the Education Professions Institute, a community-controlled, client-centered training agency—was described in Part VI. The notion of new alliances—for example, one between big business and education—is David Bickimer's proposal in his previously unpublished article, "Industry and the Education of Teachers."

Who speaks for the teaching profession? Certainly not the institutions who do the training or the schools who do the employing. The obvious, too obvious, answer is the practitioners. But there are questions: Which association of practitioners—the National Education Association or the American Federation of Teachers? Where does each organization stand on such crucial matters as "collective negotiations," "sanctions," and "strikes"? The historical rivalry between the two national organizations is rooted in their differences on the theory and nature of collective negotiations. The different traditions and goals of the two organizations can be seen most clearly in the collective negotiations arena. However, as each group has become more deeply involved in local issues, their strategies and tactics have become similar. The NEA spokesman is Allen M. West, an assistant executive secretary of that organization; the AFT spokesman is Charles Cogen, a former president of the organization. The AFT position on strikes is well known, and the NEA's most recent statement on its position in this rapidly changing arena is the policy adopted recently by its

Board of Directors. While recommending that "every effort be made to avoid the strike as a procedure for the resolution of impasse," the Board went on to state that "under conditions of severe stress, causing deterioration of the educational program, and when good faith attempts at resolution have been rejected, strikes have occurred and may occur in the future. In such instances, the NEA will offer all of the services at its command to the affiliate concerned to help resolve the impasse."

Finally, Part X, and the book, end on a philosophical note concerning the profession and the future. No one can do this better than Arthur F. Covey, the dynamic former executive secretary of the California Teachers' Association. His article, "Educational Power and the Teaching Profession," brings the book to a fitting climax with a challenge: Can any group develop or maintain professional status when its right or competence to have the major voice in basic decisions regarding its own work is denied?

63. Improving the Status of Teachers

Lester Seth Vander Werf

Many years ago Mary Follett defined a profession as a group which:

> Establishes its own standards
> Maintains its own standards
> Improves its own standards
> Keeps its members up to standards
> Educates the public to appreciate the standards
> Protects the public from those not meeting the standards
> Protects individual members from each other.

In the light of this definition the reader is asked to consider the following propositions, descriptive of teachers in a general way:

1. Teachers tend to be more docile than other groups in the United States. In contrast to laborers, for example, teachers are reluctant to stand together on salary demands, issues of national importance, standards of preparation and admission to professional societies. Teachers rarely agree on anything and everybody knows it. As a consequence, their influence is far less effective than it could be.

2. Teachers are inadequately organized. Teachers have more organizations than most occupational groups but no organization. New organizations appear constantly with sacking of an established one an unusual occurrence. Thus teachers proliferate their energies and duplicate their discussions, making their total organizational effort rather feeble.

3. Teachers are not well enough prepared for their functions. Many Americans are pleased when teachers can be hired with minimum standards or less. Yet, anyone who has been in the business of preparing teachers, or hiring them once they were "prepared," would admit that four

SOURCE: *American School Board Journal,* CXLIII, 3 (September 1961), 14–16. Reprinted by permission.

years is an inadequate preparation period for a profession like teaching. Six years could be used and eight would approximate more nearly a desirable and effective basic condition.

So firmly rooted is the idea that teaching is really not a profession that when a shortage occurs, as in the case of the last decade or so, there is a natural and easy truncation of standards, both in time and quality. Yet evidence of studies across the nation indicates that circumventing any standards helps not at all. In fact the higher the standards, the more young people are attracted to teaching. Who, after all, wishes to be associated with a field attainable by everyone?

A correlative to these ideas is the assumption that teachers will complete their education in service. Teachers forget, however, that learning at a fraction of the in-service rate inevitably means falling increasingly farther behind since at no time can it be truthfully said that teachers have "caught up" with their fields.

4. *Teachers do not as a group represent enough ability for their proper functioning in a complicated world.* Independent and governmental studies and experience have shown the following: too many teachers are no brighter than the average pupils they teach; too few people of top ability enter teaching as compared with other professions; in many colleges and universities prospective teachers are in general near the bottom groups in the institution as a whole in general ability, even in doctoral programs; except in isolated communities there seems to be no element of pride that comes from association with people of intellectual power and ability.

5. *Teachers are uncritical of other teachers' work, the books they write, the research they do.* Rarely does a professional book receive anything but glowing tributes in the professional journals. Critiques of research studies are rarely even attempted except by college staffs, that is, professors of education, and most of these are largely emotional. There is one exception. Let a nonprofessional write a book criticizing education as a field and the guns go to work. The shots are straight and direct hits. It is too bad that such trenchancy is not interactive.

Another side of this coin is equally devastating. Professional books tend to mimic each other in form and content, leaving the significant books few and far between. It may be that both editors and publishers are somewhat to blame. Often editors are authors, and may use their own works as criteria for the field. Publishers in their own way, of course, cannot risk an investment in a book either too different from, or superior to, the competition. Judgment of this kind may ultimately reflect upon the potential purchasers. All of these considerations suggest that the really prize books in education are relatively unknown or are avoided as too difficult, too theoretical or too controversial.

6. *Teachers have not kept up with their fields.* There is no professional group that escapes this charge to some degree. With advancements coming in all fields at such atomic rates, keeping abreast is a genuinely common complaint among practitioners. Yet, of whom except teachers can it be said that they are fifty years behind the times as suggested by the Physical Science Study Committee with reference to the teaching of physics.

Many are the reasons that can be suggested for this state of affairs: poor quality of teachers, inadequate preparation in which scholarship and general alertness are not prized,[1] salaries low enough to make the purchase of books and magazines a real burden, and uncertain status with a resulting uneven set of professional expectations.

7. *Teachers control relatively few of the conditions under which they work.* Required working hours, salary, awarding of increments, vacations, student load, matching preparation to assignment, fields and sub-segments of fields that must be taught, all are defined by state law or school board regulation. It is true that minimum salary laws have been enacted upon pressure by teachers. It is also true that tenure is a result of requests by teachers and with good reason. While petty school board members have wreaked havoc on many teachers, not all teachers currently favor tenure. Yet, tenure should be favored for the protection it affords the superior teacher who has courage to try the new, and who resists psychological slavery.

All in all teachers have a long road ahead if they are to become professional in truth as well as in name. Specifically they must assume much more responsibility for themselves. What follows may be suggestive of a partial program.

At the National Level

It would seem justified to indicate that states and local districts have failed to maintain a consistently high level of education, a thesis which has many implications for school finance and control.

Nonetheless, teachers or public education needs a much more aggressive leadership at the national level. The National Education Association has generally had excellent people in its service, but rarely if ever a person who was nationally prominent in the sense of outstanding labor leaders, politicians, musicians or athletes. A person who could maintain entree anywhere on the strength of his own personal accomplishments would probably have to be prominent to begin with and ought to be paid a stupen-

[1] Many are asked to teach subjects with little or no preparation. As a result they are forced to spend their time keeping a day ahead of their students.

dously high salary. If the leadership were to have influence, relationships with the very top of the nation's power strucure would have to be made and maintained.

The national leadership would in the first place work to improve teacher education. While the National Commission for Teacher Education and Professional Standards through its many conferences and programs has made some progress, the progress is not in proportion to the need. Again composed and headed by excellent people, the NCTEPS simply has not the prestige or power to make effective headway even with its own professional relatives.

The national leadership should encourage the voluntary but effective use of national guide lines for school programs. Such guide lines may take the following forms:

General Outlines. These may be roughly comparable to a good syllabus, may suggest topics, problems, sequence in one field, for one grade or several grades. Proved methods and techniques would be helpful.

Specific Concepts. One thinks immediately of the development in mathematics (probability or sets, for example) and science (wave theory). These statements might be issued in regular bulletins with notations as to where in the program they could be placed and what eliminated to make room.

Evidence of Controversial Matters. Here it would be necessary for experts to review research findings and draw cautious conclusions helpful to the teachers. One thinks, for example, of the teaching of formal grammar, the application of the Rule of One or the Rule of Two in working with double digit divisors, or factors which have controlled or may control inflation. Some NEA research materials are a desirable but inadequate start in this direction.

Subjective Material. Experts could be of real service here. One thinks of the relation of the social studies to patriotism. Since patriotism is largely emotional, we need authoritative statements drawn from the best writers, if for no other reason than to support those teachers who refuse to knuckle under crackpot pressure groups. One thinks, too, of reading. While there is much available research on the teaching of reading which could be published under the previous category, it is included here for its susceptibility to misinterpretation. The Council for Basic Education has questioned the concept of readiness. Somehow this objection must be reconciled if not adequately answered.

The national leadership should work to improve the national organization. Much could be done. With the coming of higher standards for teacher education some incentive would be provided to raise the standards of membership. Membership in professional organizations is not something which should have to be sold but something prized and purchased through desire to meet professional standards.

The national leadership should work toward one nationally consistent, if not nationally operated, measure of teacher competence. At the moment the only instrument available is the National Teacher Examination produced by Education Testing Service and administered annually in a number of centers around the country. While any national testing deserves the most cautious consideration, teachers' urging of some such program has dimensions other than a mandatory testing by the federal government.

The national leadership, working toward improvement of Teacher Education, teacher organizations and criteria of membership, guide lines for school programs, and common evaluation of teacher competence, would serve to enhance the status and financing of teaching. While it may be true that teachers have acquired some additional status in recent years, one could argue that the causes lie in the market place of short supply. One must be suspicious of any increased prestige wrought by economic factors alone. Actually, of course, teachers must eventually assume responsibility for matching supply with demand, must control the market place themselves, or their position will remain precarious and subject to the whims of state, national, or international forces.

A Local Program

In addition to the national program necessary to raise the status of teaching to a professional level, much can be done at the local level. Every school or school district, depending upon size, should organize two committees, a Professional Standards Committee and a Research-Curriculum Committee.

The Professional Standards Committee should be composed of the most respected teachers, about whom there is no question either in the community or among the staff; teachers, furthermore, who have the best education and are obviously using it. What would this committee do?

The Professional Standards Committee should first solicit co-operation from the administration in its desire to upgrade standards. There are, presumably, few superintendents who would not welcome such mature responsibility. The committee would recommend, as vacancies occur, the criteria to be used for appointing a candidate, would, by sub-committee or specially appointed ad hoc committee as needed, carry on initial screening of candidates, recommend one or more candidates who satisfactorily meet the originally specified criteria.

On the other hand the Professional Standards Committee should implement state and national codes of ethics, help enforce certification laws which are sometimes circumvented, and recommend the dismissal of poor teachers when necessary. This does not mean that the committee members must look under desks for evidence or be obnoxiously "snoopervisory" in other ways. It does mean that eyes and ears will be tuned in to incompetence implied by the teacher himself, the students, and the administration.

While most school systems are relatively free of politics, buying favors, promotions, and appointments occurs enough to place suspicion everywhere. The Professional Standards Committee should make periodic public reports indicating the "health" of the local political environment. The committee should make direct contact with the school superintendent and the school board to follow through. Getting nowhere, the committee should present the matter to the teaching staff as a whole to seek support for recommended or new action consistent with other policies. It is difficult to understand how professional teachers can accept political manipulation in silence.

Lastly, this committee should assume some responsibility for raising the standard of teacher education programs in their vicinity. It would make good sense to have this committee plan in-service programs to meet the variety of needs the staff may have, and encourage teachers to pursue further study in the light of school system needs (see Research Committee functions which follow). Encouraging programs of further study is not enough, however. Teachers have an obligation to report to institutions when courses and programs are either beneficial or completely innocuous. It is incomprehensible that teachers should avoid difficult courses or others which require final examinations. Yet this behavior is too common among teachers. When an institution or an instructor acquires the reputation for being "easy," teachers should so report. Deans, I believe, would welcome these reports. While teachers may justify the choice of weak courses on a number of grounds, they might consider how they appear to their own students to whom they grant no such choice.

The Research and Curriculum Committee should be composed of those teachers who are interested in research and experimentation, those who are leaders in formulating ideas, the most creative thinkers. Since it is unfortunate that creative people are not always the most respected in our society a distinction between the members of the two committees seems essential. The Research and Curriculum Committee likewise has much to achieve.

Since its basic purpose is to improve the instructional program, there will be much reading to be done. Continuous surveying of all types of educational literature is in order. Included here would be important studies completed or in progress, findings in subject matter fields as well as books and articles criticial of school practices. The committee could recommend visits to other schools where significant programs are in progress and, when necessary, suggest how time could be saved by eliminating some kinds of useless learnings as well as finding room for new learnings.

Second, the Research and Curriculum Committee should lend its energy to finding answers to local problems. This might be accomplished by designing local research studies with the hoped-for result of discovering how better teaching makes for better programs and better over-all planning leads to better teaching. It is even possible that teachers may find ways to save money. Even a few hundred dollars saved would enhance the attitude of the public to the teaching staff. On the other hand, while investment in education normally yields dividends in proportion to the amount spent, teachers should protect the public expenditure in return for the responsibility assumed.

Third, and equally important, objectives of education must be continuously appraised and the consistency of program in relation to objectives assayed. At times alternatives may be recommended or experimentation suggested to determine closer correlation between learning experiences and objectives, and tying in with research function mentioned above.

Lastly, this committee would evaluate the competencies of staff members in relation to school system need for specialists. Now it has been assumed normally that when a school system desired a specialist, one would be hired. While this may make sense in a large school system, forgetting for the moment that specialists so hired may make little if any impression, it is extremely expensive for small systems. Thus teachers may increase the effectiveness of the staff while at the same time extending their own expertness. Here, of course, the committee would co-ordinate activities with the Professional Standards Committee. Kinds of expertness should encompass the major subject fields such as mathematics, science, art and music, as well as so-called professional fields like research and measurement, psychology, reading and finance. Reading may be offered as an example of the nature of a new kind of expertness needed in today's schools. A reading specialist ought to bring together the disciplines of literature, linguistics, semantics, foreign language, and psychology as well as the methodological and clinical study and experience. Too often in the past the reading supervisor has had little preparation aside from methods courses.

So far only national and local action have been reviewed. What of the state level? Both local and national pressure should be exerted to change the composition of state boards of education so that they are populated by classroom teachers who would be known for their courage and integrity as well as their scholarship and would be expected to work closely with national boards to interpret and implement the guide lines for state and local programs.

The sum total of the program represents greatly increased responsibility on the part of teachers. Before the American people, or even teachers for that matter, will accept this change of direction, a major confusion must be overcome, namely, that the public decides *what* must be taught, while teachers determine *how* the teaching is done. There are inherent in this duality so many inconsistencies that it hardly seems necessary to delineate them. But briefly let this be said. How can one teach students *how* to read or *how* to think in isolation from the *what?* With whom does one check for approval of substance, the local D.A.R., the fire chief or the school custodian? If the American people do not trust educators to perform this as well as the other functions listed above indeed we are all in a sad way.

Since teachers are now largely ineffective in directing their own rise in status and welfare, it is somewhat ridiculous to talk about salaries in isolation, as great as the salary priority is. Perhaps better salaries would encourage teachers to assume more responsibility for quality of admission and quality of performance. It may, on the other hand, be fully as true that the assumption of responsibility in these two related professional conditions will lead to substantially augmented compensation levels. As it now stands, salary disparities among teachers' groups are subject to emergencies of the market place. Thus, if all teachers expect to gain in equivalent manner, the supply may have to be regulated in relation to emergency market pressures. For several years now the National Education Association has published annual supply and demand studies, suggesting that the basic information is available. When teachers finally recognize that it is well nigh impossible to educate those that control their destiny, they could chalk up one giant step.

64. Teacher Professionalization: Challenge and Promise

T. M. Stinnett

This topic is a timely one. Even the casual observer of the current educational scene cannot but be impressed with the restiveness, the ferment of ideas, and the fervent groping for a new and more satisfying status among teachers in the United States. These are, of course, most pronounced (at least most publicized) among teachers in the lower schools and especially in the large cities. I suspect

SOURCE: School of Education, Indiana University, *Bulletin*, XL, 5 (September 1964), 9–20. Reprinted by permission of the publisher.

that some degree of restiveness also abounds in higher education, but this can only be surmised.

What are the causal factors involved? And why have they coalesced into action at this precise moment in our history? These stirrings are, in part, a concomitant of the "agonizing reappraisal" of education which has been in process in this country now for about a decade. This reappraisal inevitably engendered an introspective examination by teachers of their own caliber and status. It is impossible for a society to give, as ours has, frenzied testament to the essential role of education, to its sense of well being, its survival, and its future stature without the idea getting through to teachers that perhaps their role needs to be elevated and their circumstances need to be upgraded drastically. I do not mean by this that the introspection has given exclusive emphasis to welfare and economic status. Again, even the casual observer in the last year could fairly draw this inference.

The welfare aspects are important in the current emerging aggressiveness of teachers, but they are not necessarily paramount. No, the basic problem is much broader, much more complex. The problem involves, first of all, the means by which the caliber of teachers and the quality of teaching services can be made consonant with the new demands upon education. And it involves, quite naturally, the search for means by which teaching can range alongside the so-called prestige professions in intellectual respect and economic rewards.

Too, a new public climate is emerging with reference to public employees. The President's [Kennedy] directive regarding the rights of bargaining for federal employees is an example. The strikes of doctors in Saskatchewan and Italy are evidences of new attitudes by the professions. Also, the influence of urbanization has served to produce a new militancy among teachers.

Any discussion of this problem must acknowledge some obvious realities and attempt some definitions and some delimitations.

Regarding the realities, there is the widespread dissent to the idea that the word "profession" should be associated with teaching. The difficulty here is three-fold: (1) The word "profession" has come to be so loosely used in recent years as to become somewhat meaningless; (2) the concept is held by many that it is fruitless to talk about teaching in the lower schools being or becoming a profession in the best sense of the word; and (3) there is general impatience of college teachers, both with the designation of themselves as teachers and with the idea that they are members of the profession.

With respect to the first of these difficulties, it would not seem productive for me to attempt to clarify the meaning of profession for this audience. There would be, I suppose, some points of difference, but the basic factors or characteristics or marks of a profession are quite generally fixed in most minds.

As to the aspirations of teachers for professional status, I can illustrate the dissent by two quotes. At the Denver NEA Convention in the summer of 1962, a labor leader sneered at the idea, saying:

One of the prime troubles, if not the chief curse of the teaching profession, is precisely that word "profession." That term, as it is used so frequently here, implies that your craft is somewhat above this world of ours; it implies a remoteness from the daily battle of the streets, the neighborhood, and the cities . . . American teachers are learning painfully and slowly that professionalism is too often used as a substitute for economic dignity. . . . There is more and more evidence that teachers cannot afford integrity and honesty.

In another passage this speaker referred to "the teaching industry." [1]

A fair interpretation of this speaker's comments would not be that he was condemning integrity and honesty. Taken in the full context, I think his meaning was that teachers must drop their kid-glove, soft-handed approach to economic rewards, which he apparently equates with the professions; must cease their obsession with the inevitable and intangible rewards, in this world or the next, for doing good in the world; and must become tough-minded and tough-acting and demand the rewards of the here and now. Certainly there can be no misinterpretation of his disdain of teaching as a profession. To me, the answer is to find the middle ground. I would agree that the posture of quiet supplication must give way to a more realistic and more aggressive posture. But I draw back from the notion that this posture should give way to one of exclusive obsession with economic returns.

Dr. Arthur Bestor has also expressed himself with sarcasm regarding the aspirations of teachers for professional status:

Educationists are morbidly self-conscious about the standing of their profession. They exhort one another to be "professional-minded" and each one feels his pulse from time to time to make sure it has the right professional beat. Beneath it all, however, lies a frightened uncertainty concerning the exact nature of a profession, and a desperate longing for palpable tokens of salvation. [2]

Regarding the third obstacle, the reluctance of college teachers to be associated with the word "profession" or the teaching profession, the reasons are too well known to require elaboration here. Perhaps this illustration will suffice. At the National TEPS Conference last June, an eminent physicist, one whom I know well and respect highly said: "In twenty-five

---

[1] Carey, James B., in an address before the NEA Representative Assembly, Denver, Colorado, July 3, 1962 (unpublished).

[2] Bestor, Arthur, *The Restoration of Learning*, Alfred A. Knopf, New York, 1955, p. 269.

years of attending meetings of my discipline, I have never heard one individual or speaker refer to my field as a profession."

Therefore, although I do so reluctantly, I shall confine my discussion to the attempts to professionalize teaching in the lower schools; and, to further delimit the topic, I shall confine it to public schools.

Two Frontier Thrusts

As I see it, if teaching is to become a recognized profession in every valid connotation of the word, there are two broad areas—two broad frontier thrusts for the future. These are basic, but not all-inclusive.

The first is in the area of achieving professional autonomy, a drive which is just beginning to take shape, the outlines of which have been spelled out by the New Horizons Task Force of NCTEPS.[3] The second is in the area of improved teacher welfare, which is beginning to shape up under the impact of several developments.

The first is a natural outgrowth of the Professional Standards Movement, which began as a formalized movement with the establishment of NCTEPS in 1946. The second is in part a concomitant of this movement, in part a result of the upsurge of our economy and serious imbalance in the status of teachers in relation to that of other professional workers and of workers in general. The latter is an inevitable companion piece to the former, which I shall try to demonstrate in a moment. At this point, however, I should be less than fair if I did not indicate that the New York City developments in the last two years added great momentum to the emerging drive for better economic status for teachers.

This was not the impelling consideration, but that it stepped up the tempo of the effort cannot, in my judgment, be denied. I think it is fair to say that, whatever one may think about the developments in New York City, the upheaval there served to symbolize the existing unrest among teachers. Also, I think it would be fair to say that it served as a warning that the status quo in teacher-society relationships is in for a drastic overhauling.

Professional Autonomy

The surest approach, at least in my opinion, to the achievement of the status of a profession for teaching and to the long-overdue upgrading of the economic conditions of teachers is the drive for professional autonomy.

[3] See Lindsey, Margaret, editor, *New Horizons for the Teaching Profession,* National Commission on Teacher Education and Professional Standards, National Education Association, The Association, Washington, D.C., 1961, 243 pp.

I know full well that this is a word charged with emotional overtones. I have sought more effective terminology, such as a self-managing profession, an inner-directed profession, but I always come back to autonomy. I should, therefore, seek to make clear the meaning of the word as I use it.

By professional autonomy, I mean that the teaching profession must be so firmly ensconced in the power structure of education that it is clearly and firmly in charge of those aspects which can be characterized as professional concerns. By this I mean in charge of determining the standards and seeing to their enforcement; for selection and admission to teacher education programs; for guidance, screening, and retention during preparation; for accreditation of teacher education institutions; for licensure and revocation of licensure; for professional growth; for working conditions; for protecting its members against unjust and capricious treatment; and for disciplining its members for unethical or unprofessional conduct.

In other words, professional autonomy to me means control by the profession of those standards by which the profession can undertake to assume responsibility for guaranteeing the competence of each member admitted to practice and permitted to continue in practice. This would be done through policy-making machinery that reflects the will of the profession, including adequate checks and balances by which different segments are protected.

Such a posture would enable the profession to guarantee the competence to perform the service assigned to it by society. And incidentally, this is the prime purpose, the basic rationale for teaching or any other profession demanding these rights from society. A related, but secondary, purpose is to safeguard the welfare of those practitioners who meet these standards, to protect them from substandard, unqualified competition.

As I have said, in my judgment here is the most fruitful approach to teacher welfare and economic status. An inner-directed profession, solidly in charge of these matters, first of all is in a position to shut off at the source the substandard teachers, the incompetents, the inferior performers who tend to perpetuate in the public mind the shibboleth that "anybody can teach." Moreover, it would be the greatest single step toward achieving such levels of excellence in teacher performance as to justify public respect and increased public support.

Logically, such a program would inevitably tend to guarantee a reasonable balance in teacher supply and demand. Beyond these, professional autonomy would tend toward the elimination of what at present amounts to anarchy in the control of the educational process. The intolerable conditions we have witnessed developing in the last decade of curriculum-making by headlines, methodology imposed by Madison Avenue hard selling, textbooks selected by wild-eyed pressure groups, certification requirements fixed by the expediency of the moment, and school financing geared to bargain basement rummage sales.

Moreover, so specialized has the work of the individual become, so fragmented and decentralized has society become as a result, that it seems obvious to me that the professional mind and the professional integrity must be mobilized to save us from a runaway trend. Life and death decisions in our society are going to be political decisions; and unless professions are prepared to participate in these decisions, they are relatively helpless. The fear motivations, under the aegis of suave public relations programs of the military-defense industry complex, threatens a dangerous road ahead for this country. Need I add that these fear motivations are becoming increasingly predominant in education. Perhaps I am too optimistic about the effect of the professional mind in education and in other fields. Obviously, I do not think so. But if I am, then I do not visualize the remedy for the threats to our future. If I seem to be an alarmist, read Fred Coak's recent book, *The Warfare State*.

The drive for substantial control over the standards by which the profession will undertake to guarantee to the public the competence of teachers admitted to practice—which is another way of saying by which the profession will seek to gain autonomy in the management of its professional affairs—may be encompassed under the following categories: teacher education (pre-service and in-service), accreditation, certification, and legal standards boards. I shall add to this the means for assuring a professional working climate, although this area is usually categorized as teacher welfare. I class it here because, to me, it is an integral part of the effort to guarantee competent practitioners.

Teacher education. The current goal is for universal adoption by the states of the five-year, pre-service program of teacher education. This goal, which is expected to be well toward implementation by the end of the 1960's, has been much more generally endorsed and much more enthusiastically received than was the four-year policy enumerated by NCTEPS in 1948. At that time, only about fifteen states were enforcing the degree requirement for elementary school teachers. This year forty-four states are enforcing it and three others have set deadlines for its enforcement. At present, nine states are mandating the fifth year of preparation by the end of a specified (usually five-year) period of initial teaching service with the bachelor's degree. Of course, the predominant practice will first become the mandated fifth year after the probationary period. Then the states will begin prescribing the five-year, pre-service requirement. Already, three states have adopted this for high school teachers, of which two apply it to both elementary and high school teachers.

The teacher education program. A five-year (master's degree), pre-service period of college and university preparation for the beginning teacher is advocated. And this is, in time, to be integrated with a sixth year of practical internship, subsequent to student teaching, as a part of the teacher education program. In this year the intern will be paid as a full-time teacher but will be functioning under the joint supervision of the preparing institution and the employing school and practicing under an apprentice certificate. The basis of this proposed regimen of preparation is to be a broad grounding in liberal education, with greater concentration in the specialized teaching fields. Professional preparation is to be woven into the full program, with heavy emphasis upon the graduate and intern year.

In addition, I think we shall move quickly to the six-year preparation requirement for special-school-service personnel. Seven states now have this requirement for superintendents, and one has the doctor's degree requirement. My information is that at least 20 additional states are fairly well set to institute the six-year requirement.

Accreditation. Except for teaching, the principle of a national accrediting process, largely in the hands of the profession, has long since been accepted as appropriate and essential. Teaching is well across the threshold of this achievement through the National Council for the Accreditation of Teacher Education. The nearly 400 accredited institutions are producing about 75 per cent of the new teachers each year. But there are 750 non-accredited institutions. In order that a quality floor of preparation can be assured, this must be extended until all institutions are accredited. I well know, of course, this is a controversial viewpoint, but I think I also know that professionalization of teaching is just a dream without it.

Teacher certification. To put legal undergirding under its prescribed standards of preparation, emphasis must be given to goals of licensure. The TEPS New Horizons Task Force Report advocates state licensure as the badge of admission to the profession, with one credential bearing appropriate endorsements of teaching fields or levels, instead of the confusing multitude of specialized certificates now the common practice among the states, the process to be in the hands of the profession itself, through the creation of proposed legal professional boards.

There are several crucial aspects of this recommendation. In the first place, the great diversity existing among the states in the number of separate-name certificates (totaling 579, or an average of 11 per state), ranging from one to sixty-eight, creates a chaotic situation, confusing both to the profession and to laymen. The effect of this practice has been to tend to fragment the teaching profession into many professions, with each specialty insisting upon its specialized certificate, with its separate name, thus setting each specialty apart as a separate entity. All other professions in America have only one basic legal license.

The specialties in these other professions are certified by the respective national professional associations rather than by the legal agencies, usually upon the completion of prescribed additional preparation and a qualifying examination. It will take some time for this goal to be realized in teaching, but there is already a decided trend in this direction. The intermediary step to this goal, in my opinion, will be perhaps two broad areas of certification: (1) for the classroom teacher (two forms), and (2) for special-school-service personnel (including administration and non-teaching specialties).

Secondly, the process of certification almost exclusively vested in lay state boards of education has resulted in bypassing the standards of the profession by the issuance of so-called emergency or substandard certificates. Currently, almost 100,000 of these certificates are issued annually to people who have not completed prescribed preparation programs. This means that about one in fourteen employed teachers in the United States is unqualified by standards of the profession; yet they operate with legal recognition. No other profession would tolerate such flaunting of its established standards, such violation of the rights of qualified practitioners to protection from substandard competition.

Some time in the future, what A. M. Carr-Saunders termed "closure" must be added to licensure. By closure he meant legal assignment of certain functions to a profession and exclusion of all others from performing this function.

Legal professional standards boards. To vest in the profession substantial, if not complete, controls over the licensing process, it is proposed that the respective states create by law professional standards boards. These boards, which would be adjuncts of the state departments of education, would be charged with developing criteria and procedures for the approval of teacher education programs, with developing and enforcing certification requirements to undergird the teacher education programs, and perhaps with authority to recommend revocation of certificates. I would like to be able to add that they would be autonomous but, realistically, I believe their recommendations would be subject to approval and, in some cases, to veto by the lay state boards of education.

Under these conditions, it may be reasonably asked: What is the difference between this proposal and what we now have? In my opinion, the creation of these legal, professional boards would be extremely effective. To illustrate, since 1933, advisory councils on teacher education and certification have been developed by the states. These advisory bodies, of which 11 have legal status, now exist in 47 states, the remaining being extra-legal. Over the years, these bodies have had profound influence on the upgrading of certification requirements and procedures, on a purely voluntary basis. State boards of education have quite generally followed their recommendations.

The chief remaining weakness, as I have said, is the general resort to the emergency certificate practice. How would making the boards legal bodies, with the power of veto still residing in the lay state boards of education improve the situation? The very fact that these professional boards are given legal status would be an indication that the legislatures intend to vest broad powers in the teaching profession for admission to practice. If this assumption is correct, then it may be surmised that state boards of education will exercise the power only in extreme cases.

Protection. Now I add to this first sweep forward—to that of the drive for professional autonomy—the area of protecting and disciplining members of the profession and that of enforcing a professional climate of working conditions. Properly conceived, I believe, these belong in the category of professional autonomy. Many, however, would class them in the second broad area of the forward thrust—that of teacher welfare.

As to protection, I shall state it as a blunt thesis that every practitioner of any profession worthy of the name should have quick and sure recourse to his professional colleagues if and when that practitioner is unjustly or capriciously treated. This could occur in dismissals in which due process has not been observed. It could occur in harassment and mis-assignment to induce resignations. It could occur in undue restraints or in the overt violation of academic freedom. I shall discuss the specifics available to professional organizations when I come to sanctions.

There must be machinery established and funds accumulated to buttress this proposition. The NEA National Commission on Professional Rights and Responsibilities is charged with this responsibility at the national level. The movement is now well underway for the creation of parallel state Professional Rights and Responsibilities Commissions, so that every aggrieved teacher has quick access to this recourse.

To implement this vital work, there are several supplementary factors:

1. Tenure or continuing contract provisions must be made available to all teachers, or in a given school district written personnel policies must be adopted which establish "due process" in the employment, retention, promotion, and dismissal of employees. Otherwise, the teacher is largely without job equity and job protection.

2. The profession itself must develop and seek implementation of a broad program of teacher evaluation in order to improve the quality of teaching services and to weed out the incompetent practitioner. Unless this is done, there will be increased resistance to tenure provisions and increased demands for merit salary schedules.

3. The profession must establish a fund from which monies can be provided, both for subsistence and for legal assistance, in the case of a discharged teacher. The NEA has established the Dushane Defense Fund. The Fund now consists of $100,000 with $10,000 annual appropria-

tions for current cases. However, in my judgment this figure should be built up to not less than $1,000,000, and perhaps to several million dollars to guarantee the equitable handling of distress cases of large groups of teachers.

Disciplining. As for the disciplining of members of the profession, this is perhaps the toughest of all the imperatives for the professionalization of teaching. Police work among friends or colleagues is a cruel sort of business. But this responsibility, however onerous, cannot be avoided by the profession. We cannot in good grace ask for professional autonomy without being willing to accept the total range of responsibilities.

Of course, the fundamental approach to this problem, as it probably is to the protective aspects, is the exercise of careful controls over admission to practice. The more the profession can assure the admission of carefully screened, well-prepared, competent people to teaching, the fewer protection and discipline cases it will have with which to contend. The weapons for disciplining members are censure, expulsion from professional membership, and the ultimate weapon of revocation of licensure. The first two, especially expulsion from membership, are powerful weapons, much more powerful than we have assumed. Revocation of licensure is the ultimate weapon and by far the most difficult to effect. The profession has been most laggard in this area, but it is now moving toward the development of one Code of Ethics and a series of interpretations of the Code to get itself into a positive posture.

Improved Teacher Welfare

The effort to become an inner-directed profession is one side of the coin of professionalization. The other side is teacher welfare. The two are indispensable components, each of which complements the other. The first, autonomy, I have indicated, is basic; the other, welfare, follows in part and must be forced in part. The first puts the profession in a position to regulate a balance in supply and demand, to eliminate substandard competition and prevent the operation of Gresham's Law applied to personnel policies; to include adequate welfare provisions as an integral part of the climate for professional services, and to elevate its quality to permit the enforcement of fair economic demands.

The teaching profession has lagged in the drive in the area of teacher welfare, I think, precisely because it has been so slow in demanding the power to put its own house in order. We are at the end of the beginning of this effort, opening the way for a realistic sweep toward gaining economic justice.

As I have said, the New York City situation was a symbol—a symbol of unrest among teachers about their economic status, especially in the large cities. It was neither the beginning nor the apex of this drive. The drive for teacher welfare has been proceeding, albeit at a measured pace, for years. In this drive are encompassed many aspects other than salary. Basic is the aspect that every teacher should have tenure status, either by tenure legislation or by continuing contract provisions. This is basic because without job equity teachers will be timid about demanding their rightful welfare status. The NEA has been working on this since 1921; and at present 43 states have such legislation (36 with tenure laws and 7 with continuing contract laws). Other aspects of teacher welfare include a reasonable work load, with free periods for lunch and for preparation; academic freedom; and protection against unfair or capricious dismissal— the right to "due process."

Partly as a result of the New York City situation, but more important, as a result of the emergence in dramatic form of an idea whose time has come, the 1962 NEA Representative Assembly took two significant steps. The first was the adoption of a resolution calling for the legal right of teachers to negotiate with school boards regarding working conditions and salaries. The second was a resolution specifying the use of sanctions to settle impasses.

The resolution on negotiations contemplates state legislation spelling out this right of teachers or local board action doing the same thing. Admittedly, the state legislation approach will be gradual—I would surmise, at the moment, not more than a half-dozen states are ready for such legislation. By far, the predominant procedure will be local board action. Hundreds of local school districts are already observing this right and this procedure but have not formalized them. So the first drive will be to get formal policies adopted by school boards.

Professional sanctions. The sanction most often referred to as a weapon to be used by teachers to get economic justice is that of the witholding or withdrawing of services of teachers. But this is only one of many sanctions which the profession has available. For example, accreditation of teacher education institutions, prerequisites based on national accreditation of the preparing institutions for certification, and, in time, for employment are powerful sanctions which most other professions have long used. Then there is the one that makes of sanctions a two-way street—the censure, expulsion from professional membership, and revocation of licensure, which can be applied to teachers themselves.

But the sanction of withdrawal of services to a school district is the major weapon for achieving economic gains. It is the one which has caused wide discussion in newspaper editorials (aroused by the Little Lake School District Case in California) and among superintendents and school boards. The public question is raised: How does this differ from the strike? Some newspapers, with their quick alertness to protect the helpless taxpayers, have already dubbed it as worse than the strike.

There are vast differences between this process and the strike. It does not interrupt services to children during a current school year. It does not violate an existing contract. It does not violate existing laws. It is not applied at the whim of a local group of teachers, out of quick anger or quarrels over petty matters. It will only be applied after thorough investigation and publicizing of the facts by responsible members of the state education associations and by the NEA. And it will be applied in most cases where the facts will be so overwhelmingly adverse to the school district that the clientele of that school district will demand remedial action. Finally, when applied, it will be the judgment and will of the total profession, not of an isolated segment of it. As a matter of fact, the threat of this sanction will, in my judgment, be so potent that there will be few cases in which it will be necessary to invoke it.

And it should be pointed out that there are several steps (or degrees) in the invoking of the withdrawal sanction. The first is the relatively simple one of withdrawal of placement services, that of the appropriate state education associations and such other agencies as they can persuade to cooperate. A second step is to advise the members of the state association, or the NEA, or both, who are employed elsewhere or are beginning teachers, not to apply for or accept employment in the offending school district until and unless the ban is lifted. The third step is to request members employed both in the offending district and elsewhere not to accept employment there in the ensuing year.

The fourth and final phase, the ultimate one, is for the association to declare it a violation of professional ethics for any of its members to remain in the employment of or to accept the proffer of employment in the school district until the ban is lifted. This final step will be rarely used. I know of only one such precedent case. Any one of these steps may be applied, or they all may be applied progressively, or they could all be involved at once.

The NEA has applied this sanction in only one case (North College Hill, Ohio) and in a matter of a day or so the conditions were corrected and the sanction lifted. Cases in which state education associations have invoked this sanction are Kelso, Washington; Poulson, Montana; and West Haven, Connecticut; and in each case it was effective. Now we have the much publicized case of Little Lake, California, the outcome of which yet remains to be seen.

What about the charge that this weapon is as bad or worse than the strike? If the charge were worded to mean "as effective or more effective," I think I would not quibble over that. But the district will be put on notice several months in advance of the application of the sanction. It will specify in detail the conditions which, in the judgment of the profession, make professional services for children impossible. It will, with such specifics, give the people of the district full opportunity to evaluate whether they will choose to continue conditions of inferior service to their children. And if they make this choice, substandard teachers can undoubtedly be found or non-members of professional organizations can be employed to staff their classrooms. At any rate, the decision will be made by the people of the district. And if the decision is for inferior service, then that decision is on their heads and not on the profession.

Conclusion

These two broad sweeps—the drive for professional autonomy and the drive for adequate welfare provisions—are waves of the future in the professionalization of teaching.

Obviously, there are other important factors the discussion of which time does not permit. Increasing the proportion of men in teaching is one factor of great importance. If the teaching staff of the nation is to be stabilized, becoming predominantly a life career, this is indispensable. The curing of the dual-control situation in large cities, in which school boards make the budget which is subject to approval or veto by a politically motivated city hall, is another. The reduction in the number of school districts (to 10,000 or fewer), to the point that each is large enough to provide the total range of services to children and large enough to be conducive to the maintenance of a professional working climate for teaching, is still another.

The completion of legislative reapportionment, by which ultraconservative rural domination of school policies and finance will diminish, will have profound influence. Finally, the posture of teachers as political eunuchs must give way to one of aggressive participation in government at all levels, with special emphasis upon influenceing educational legislation.

The great question is not whether teaching can become a profession, but whether teachers can be persuaded to act like professionals. There are, in this regard, centuries of inertia to overcome, but unless I am totally misreading the signs, this, too, shall pass away.

65. Why Accredit Teacher Education?

William K. Selden

The concept of accreditation, which in itself is difficult to comprehend, is complicated by the frequent confusion between accreditation and licensure or certification. Accreditation is the process whereby an organization or agency recognizes a college or university or program of study as having met certain predetermined qualifications or standards and then publishes publicly a list of those institutions which have have met the qualifications. Most commonly the organization or agency is a voluntary, extra-legal association either of institutions, individuals or both.

In contrast to accreditation, licensure is the process of approving an individual to perform certain functions, such as to practice a profession. The act of licensure is a legal responsibility of government pursued for the protection of the public. Among the professions from which the public obviously needs protection are architecture, dentistry, engineering, medicine, nursing, optometry, and the like. The public also needs protection from incompetent lawyers, but in law one is technically not licensed, but admitted to the bar by the Court, in a manner generally similar to licensure in the other professions. For permission to teach in elementary and secondary schools in the United States, one must usually obtain a license, but the term employed in this profession is certification. And, as with licensure in the other professions, this is a legal function assumed by each of the several states.

Although accreditation and licensure or certification are distinct and separate operations, they do depend somewhat on each other. In most states permission to take the state licensure examination is dependent upon several requirements, one of which relates frequently to graduation of the candidate from an approved program of study. In many cases there are alternate provisions which stipulate that the candidate who has not studied in such an institution may be admitted to take the examination after a longer period of apprenticeship or after completion of some other more exacting requirement.

SOURCE: *Journal of Teacher Education,* XI, 2 (June 1960), 185–90. Reprinted by permission of the author and publisher.

In practice the state licensure boards, which possess the legal responsibility of deciding which programs of study are to be approved, rely regularly on the list of programs of study accredited by the national professional accrediting agency in the appropriate field of study. These professional agencies may be organized in a number of different ways. Some may be associations only of practitioners; some, only representatives of professional schools; some, a combination of both; and others, a combination of both plus representatives of state licensing offices. In only two cases, pharmacy and teacher education, are specific provisions made for representation of the central administrations of colleges and universities. Among the prerequisites for accreditation by most of the professional agencies, such as teacher education, is the stipulation that an institution must first be accredited by one of the six regional associations of colleges and universities.

Extra-Legal Accreditation

In the United States we have developed the method of extra-legal accreditation as our major method of establishing and maintaining academic standards, in contrast to the situation in every other country in the world, where different methods are employed. In other countries, ministries of education with varying degrees of legal authority serve an important place in the maintenance of standards. In addition, external examining bodies frequently exist and, equally important, the creation or chartering of universities and teacher training institutions is severely restricted, in comparison with the almost profligate manner by which such institutions have been allowed to be chartered in this country.

To compensate for our lack of a ministry of education and non-use of external examinations, the colleges and universities in a manner consistent with our political heritage banded together to form associations, six of which are known as regional accrediting agencies. In various ways and at different times they all have assumed the function of accrediting as a means of establishing basic standards. Lest we think of this activity as only an altruistic function, that is, one of protection of the public welfare, it should be pointed out that accrediting, even though based on valid philosophical principles, has also served the purpose of self-protection for the institutions already accredited. The history of the slow acceptance of teacher education institutions proves this point.

The North Central Association of Colleges and Secondary Schools, which was founded in 1895 and which issued its first list of accredited higher institutions in 1913, did not adopt standards for admission of teachers colleges until 1918. And then these institutions faced a decade of struggle for real understanding of their problems on the part of those who then controlled accrediting and who in most cases had little knowledge of education for prospective public school teachers. Likewise, the issue over acceptance of teachers colleges made its first appearance at the initial meeting of the Middle States Association in 1887, and it was not until 1934, thirteen years after its first list of accredited higher institutions, that this agency would accredit colleges for teachers.

Accreditation of Teacher Education

With examples such as these, it is understandable that the teachers college people felt ostracized at the very time when they were attempting to help meet an ever growing demand for teachers in an expanding population with a corresponding increase in school enrollments. Because of compulsory attendance laws, the number of high-school students who did not expect to pursue higher education increased greatly, and the prospective teachers needed to be taught how to teach many poorly motivated and inadequately endowed young people. Lest we think, in a period of rapidly rising college and university enrollments, that the situation which I describe is past and gone, let it be noted that one fourth of New York City's present elementary-school pupils speak no English. Since 1950, 650,000 Negroes and Puerto Ricans, many culturally depressed, have moved into this large city and today these groups comprise 70 per cent of the school population. When one realizes that 30 per cent of the juvenile delinquency cases in that city presently involve Puerto Ricans, transplanted and unprepared for a new and frequently degrading cultural and vocational environment, it is not difficult to understand that the teachers in these and other schools need to know not merely the subjects they are to teach but how to teach these students, as well as how to protect themselves from physical harm.

Conditions such as these have generally been ignored by the liberal arts faculties as they all too often have tended to do nothing more than criticize, in their sometimes isolated ignorance. And yet these very criticisms fortunately are now being heard and are having their influence. We should be grateful for the public attention which is being attracted by such men as our professors of history and vice admirals to the need for an increase in the national effort toward a much higher academic quality throughout our entire educational system. In their criticisms they may sometimes display a lack of balanced judgment and of knowledge of social developments, and they may all too glibly place the blame for our contemporary educational deficiencies on too narrow a segment of society. Nevertheless, as catalysts they are serving a useful purpose. Partially as a result of their comments those who are responsible for the accreditation of programs in teacher education are placing increasing emphasis on the qualifications in subject matter education of those preparing to teach.

This trend must continue, even be accelerated among teacher education faculties. For all too long many on these faculties have been so engrossed in teaching the principles of operating a school and the techniques of teaching a class that they have placed an inadequate emphasis on the general or liberal education of the prospective teachers. The accumulation of credit points has too often been employed as the false measure of the educated teacher. Fortunately both subject matter and teacher education specialists realize that their two groups must work much more closely and harmoniously together for the sake of all teachers and our society.

The NCATE

In the American tradition the major method of establishing and maintaining academic standards has been through accreditation. Teacher education adopted this method a quarter of a century ago, many years after medicine near the turn of the century initiated this practice in a professional field of study. Many of the critics of the National Council for Accreditation of Teacher Education, which was organized in 1952 and is now a recognized accrediting agency, assumed that since this specific organization began its accrediting functions in 1954, this was the year that accrediting of teacher education by a national agency was begun.

Actually, the first national association of teachers colleges was formed in 1855, and accrediting by one of its successor organizations was begun in the 1920's. The present American Association of Colleges for Teacher Education later performed this function until 1954 when NCATE took over the accrediting responsibilities. NCATE was formed for the purpose of providing a broader representative base than was possible through AACTE alone, even though AACTE is obtaining a rapidly increasing membership of liberal arts colleges and complex universities. In addition to AACTE, the organizations which were included in the creation of this new agency, NCATE, were: the Council of Chief State School Officers, the National Association of State Directors of Teacher Education and Certification, the National Commission on Teacher Education and Professional Standards of the National Education Association, and the National School Boards Association. It might be emphasized that official participation of the Association of American Colleges were sought in order to include direct representation of the liberal arts colleges. This attempt, however, which has been repeated several times, has been unsuccessful for three reasons.

In the first place, the liberal arts people, at least up until a few years ago, frequently objected to the argument that teaching is a profession like medicine or law. For one group of teachers to claim that teaching is not a profession is to proclaim a denial of their own birthright. Teaching shares an ancient heritage of professional status with theology, law, and medicine. Even though teaching in this country does not presently enjoy the preferred economic or social status of law or medicine, the facts of contemporary political life are clear that without an organized presentation of professional goals, improved social and economic status will not likely be attained. Consequently, the attack of some liberal arts people, in which they denied the premise that teaching is a profession, merely served to strengthen the hands of the National Education Association, regional and state associations of public-school teachers, and other similar organizations in the determination of teachers to gain professional stature. To the profound disappointment of teachers, again they were experiencing not merely no assistance but criticisms from liberal arts professors as the public school teachers and teacher education people were endeavoring to attain what to them was a laudable ambition—the achievement of professional status and sound academic improvement.

A second contention shared by many liberal arts people was that the extension of professional accrediting into this area of teacher education was completely unnecessary since it could be adequately served by the regional associations. This argument fails to take into account the fact that all professions, as early as medieval times, have sought to control the preparation for and admission to their ranks. In our country, as medicine has so successfuly proved, accreditation has been one of the important mechanisms employed in this procedure. Admission in many of the states to many of the state licensure examinations, as has already been mentioned, not only in medicine but in a number of professions, is partially based on graduation from an approved professional school, and in practically all cases the lists of nationally accredited institutions serve this purpose better than the lists of regionally accredited colleges and universities. Here again teacher education has initiated no new departure but has merely followed the examples of its peers, in which the professions are not willing to rely on the lists of regionally accredited institutions for approval of professional programs of study. What is more, there is not likely to be any change in this attitude among the well recognized professions.

Dilemmas of the NCA

At this point it seems appropriate to include several comments about some of the dilemmas which the National Commission on Accrediting has had to face. Recognizing that an unlimited increase in the number of professional accrediting agencies would lead only to impossible difficulties for all of higher education, the Commission has succeeded in preventing the introduction of accrediting into a number of different additional fields of study. At the same time the Commission is aware that an inequity does exist, since accrediting is pursued in several academic fields which would probably not be permitted to assume this function if activity had not begun prior to the creation of the National Commission. Another dilemma relates to the strength and growth of the regional associations of colleges and secondary schools. Recognizing that these accrediting agencies are independent and autonomous, even though collectively they comprise a membership of higher institutions which is almost identical with that of the National Commission, the NCA has been able to urge an improvement in their practices and a strengthening of their policies only in an indirect manner. The successes which have been attained by the regional associations in these respects have been gained by them largely without the assistance of the presidents, vice presidents, deans and professors of liberal arts in the country's major universities and liberal arts colleges. Without the support of these educational leaders, necessary advances in the policies and practices of accrediting will be indefinitely delayed.

This comment leads to the third and last major argument of the liberal arts people against NCATE. Their contention that NCATE as originally organized did not provide for a proper and appropriate balance of control was sound. Since the teacher education people had generally been anxious to have liberal arts participation in this new accrediting organization, there was comparatively little difficulty in reaching an agreement on a revised structure. The real difficulty was, and in fact still is, to find a constructive method whereby liberal arts individuals can be appointed to the Council. Several years ago, when NCATE was recognized by the National Commission, a temporary method for selecting liberal arts individuals was devised. Now we are in the process of finding an improved and more substantial procedure. Although all parties directly concerned are sincerely anxious to work together congenially and constructively, the solution to this problem is not easy.

Joint Responsibilities of Liberal Arts and Teacher Education

It may be noticed that up to this point nothing has been written about the standards or requirements for accreditation in teacher education, nothing about the accreditation procedures to be followed, nor the composition of the visiting teams and the committees of review. Reference to these factors has intentionally been left to the end of this article. These are the areas in which both liberal arts and teacher education people can collectively exert a positive influence for good. But the influence of the liberal arts people will be negative if they incorrectly assume that teacher education has no place in the total education of teachers; or if they blatantly criticize schools of education for sometimes having been a haven for the less academically competent without recognizing that their own sometimes derogatory approach has often been a partial influence in encouraging this situation. In the same way the influence of the teacher education people will be harmful if they over-emphasize the importance of teacher education courses and if they subordinate academic accomplishment and intellectual stimulation to such factors as social adjustment and playground supervision.

All of us, whether in the liberal arts or teacher education fields, must recognize our responsibilities for the education of future teachers, and we must assume the obligations that rest on all of us as educators. In a time of such rapid social and technological change the education of teachers for the uncertainties of the future is a grave responsibility. In meeting this responsibility, neither the teacher education specialists nor the subject matter professors can successfully fulfill their social and professional obligations without working harmoniously and closely with each other. Most of all, the individuals actively involved in the National Council for Accreditation of Teacher Education fully recognize this point. The rapid transformation of the old normal schools, and now the teachers colleges, into general colleges and even into universities, is not only the result of a desire for greater prestige. An equally propelling force is the conviction that a future teacher will obtain a sounder education and be a better teacher when intimately exposed to the liberal arts subjects.

History has proved that the moral and ethical traditions of civilization can best be transmitted through a study of the liberal arts, especially when taught with a breadth of understanding and a depth of conviction. Experience has equally proved that a well trained teacher can usually instill enthusiasm and inspiration for these liberal arts courses among his students. Even though some excellent teachers are "just born," the unprecedented increase in the school population of the onrushing years does not permit us the luxury of relying on the fortunes of birth alone. Nature is in need of immediate assistance from both liberal arts people of understanding and teacher education people of ability. These two groups sharing the responsibility for teacher education will not merely provide stronger visiting teams and committees of review, as well as more constructive standards for accreditation, but better education for future generations of teachers.

66. Trends in Certification Practices for Secondary Schools

Lucien B. Kinney

Certification activities since World War II have followed an interesting cycle. General dissatisfaction with prescription and restriction during the 'fifties led to extensive modifications, culminating around 1960 when three-fourths of the 52 certificating units (the fifty states, Puerto Rico, and District of Columbia) were engaged in major revision of their credential structures. This activity has now subsided, and credential requirements and procedures are again subject to criticism, differing from that of the 'fifties mainly in specificity, vehemence, and breadth of participation.

An exploration for trends to identify current changes or lack of them should include not only the requirements themselves, but also the factors that have determined them, and may influence them in the future. Thus we shall be concerned here with trends in:

a. Nature of certification requirements;
b. Criticisms, challenges and attacks in the literature;
c. Influence of certification on quality of programs of teacher preparation; and
d. Role of the organized profession of education in certification revision.

Certification Requirements

Revisions in certification requirements reveal a continuing trend toward (a) a growing emphasis on academic preparation; (b) an increasing multiplicity of positions for which specific preparation is required.

Certification requirements are of two kinds: *general,* as age, citizenship, loyalty oath, license fees, etc., and *preparatory,* with which we are concerned here, including the amount and nature of professional course work

SOURCE: *The High School Journal,* L, 6 (March 1967), 316–23. Reprinted by permission of the North Carolina Press.

and student teaching, liberal education, and academic specialization in subjects to be taught at the secondary level. These are spelled out more or less in detail in the requirements of each state. The heightened interest of the public in academic preparation is revealed in newly-established regulations such as more rigid requirements that a teacher be assigned to the field in which he is prepared to teach; establishment of semester hour requirements for professional work as maxima as well as minima; requirements that applicants for administration credential hold either an elementary teaching credential (with an academic major), or a secondary teaching credential in an academic field. These are, of course, isolated actions, but as straws in the wind they reveal the continued influence of Sputnik on our programs of education.

Another trend in requirements is the growing multiplicity of positions requiring specific certification. These are being defined in increasing detail with respect to (a) levels in the school system, as elementary, secondary, junior high school, and junior college; (b) teaching fields, as academic, vocational, art, etc.; (c) various administrative and supervisory fields; and (d) special services other than supervisory or administrative. Until recently this increasing multiplicity could be measured by the number of different credentials required by a given state. Today, however, this measure is no longer available, since the policy of *endorsing* a given credential to delimit the teaching field or other position for which the holder meets specific preparation requirements, multiplies each credential into a category, or *credential type*. Thus a secondary teaching credential is multiplied, by endorsement, into a series of specialized subject-matter credentials.

Outside the personnel in instructional and administrative positions in the public schools there is wide diversity in practices with respect to certification. Requirements of certification of private and parochial school teachers, and of teachers at nursery school, kindergarten, junior college and teachers college levels vary among the states. Some states require certification of school personnel who have professional preparation in fields other than education, as school nurses, physicians, dental hygienists and social workers. Various non-professional categories are certificated in certain states, including senior school secretary, teacher-clerk, bus drivers, and school census takers. There are indications of a long-term trend toward definition and regularization of employment through certification in all public-school positions on a civil-service basis.

Behind this imposing facade of definitions and requirements, however, there still remains in the emergency credential a backdoor entrance to public-school employment. Emergency certification is as old as certification itself. The "emergency" situation is the normal situation. At present about one teacher in 16 has substandard preparation, as measured by certification requirements. This proportion, somewhat lower than in the immediate postwar years, has held steady for about a decade. Three-fourths of the emergency teachers are teaching in the grades, and a greater proportion are employed in the rural rather than in the metropolitan areas.

Attacks and Criticisms

Perhaps the most significant of current trends is a broadening and intensification of interest in certification, extending to the public as well as the profession. The public has long had a childlike faith in certification as a means for guaranteeing quality in the program of public education. Any suspicion of scholastic inadequacy in the staff, or evidence of improper staff assignments, has led to demands for revision in certification requirements. Doubts raised by Sputnik heightened public attention to certification, and gave it a political value which was not neglected by legislators in recent revision activities. The consequences of these revisions are still the subject of public interest which provide critics in the field with an audience.

The recent publication by Conant [1] is somewhat above the average among the vigorous reactions of college staff in the academic fields. Disturbed by bureaucratic controls of programs for teacher preparation he calls for a housecleaning in specific certification requirements, reducing prescription of content to a bachelor's degree and a course in student teaching. Others share his vigor, but have different points of view. Among the most interesting are those that reflect the belief that certification requirements are a creation of the "establishment" in education, variously defined as schools of education, the NEA, or state departments of education, to maintain control of the program of education. More specifically, the conspiracy may be to promote the flow of students in education, or to maintain a monopoly on teaching positions.

These flights of fancy would be fatally restricted if the writers were required to answer the question, Who is responsible for definition of certification requirements? In actual fact, the legislature in each state has the ultimate authority. It may delegate certain responsibilities to the state board of education, or its equivalent, on occasion, leaving administrative details to the state department of education. But whatever role the profession of education plays is strictly in an advisory capacity. Certification is a lay, not a professional operation.

It is typical of the discussion and debate in this field that no attention has been paid to the question, What is the purpose of certification? and, How can it best be designed to serve that purpose? Each writer tends to base his arguments and recommendations on implied purposes agreeable to

---

[1] James Conant, *The Education of American Teachers*, New York: McGraw-Hill, 1963.

himself. Until these are examined critically and some logical consensus is developed, further study of the literature can have little merit.

Certification and Quality of Programs

How valid is the public confidence that certification provides a guarantee of quality in the program of public education? Unfortunately, nothing in current requirements presents any assurance of quality in programs for preparation of teachers. Few will argue that prescription of course titles and semester hours is a means to that end. Content of a course entitled: *Educational psychology, 3 hours,* for example, will vary widely, even within the same institution, depending on who teaches it. It is not at all unusual for a college student inadvertently to repeat a course under a different instructor, without discovering the repetition until he checks his transcript.

Equally meaningless is popular demand for a course in student teaching. Among the variables that determine its value are:
Breadth and variety of student activities;
Support from college staff and master teacher; and
Integration of student teacher experiences within the overall program of teacher preparation.

Clearly, an applicant for a credential, in presenting a transcript showing fulfillment of a student teaching requirement, answers none of these questions. To enhance the quality of preparation for teaching, programs must incorporate what has been learned from intensive research on programs for preparation of teachers conducted during the past fifteen years. The variables listed above, for example, refer to factors experimentally determined as significant to the efficacy of student teaching. Yet it is notable that neither in the stages of planning and discussion, or in the completed requirements, have the findings of research influenced certification requirements. One must agree with Conant when he brands specificity in certification requirements as a "bankrupt process."

Quality in programs of preparation has high priority in the concerns of all professions. In professions other than education, flexibility and adaptability to more effective program designs are obtained by placing responsibility for program development on the staff of the preparing institution. Assignment of responsibility is always coupled with accountability for results—accountability both to the profession and to the public. By all major professions the process utilized to make the staff responsible for results in program building is professional accreditation. This procedure includes:

Establishment and publication of standards by the professional accrediting
agency;

Systematic appraisal by a committee of the agency visiting the campus;

Study of the committee report, and approval (or disapproval) of the program
by the agency.

The classic example of effectiveness of the professional accrediting agency
in program improvement is the revolution it brought about in the medical
schools early in the present century.

The National Council on Accreditation in Teacher Education, commonly referred to as NCATE, established in 1952 by NEA as the accrediting agency for the profession, has not become an integral part of the
certification process. It is true that 414 of the 1173 institutions for teacher
preparation are accredited by NCATE, and that these institutions prepare
70 per cent of the teachers certificated each year. This proportion has remained static for about ten years. In no state is responsibility for program
development assigned to staff, who are then held accountable for results
through accreditation.

Resistance from outside the profession, as well as apathy from within,
account for lack of progress. In recent years, NCATE has come in for bitter criticism, especially from college staff and from college and university
administrators. It is readily understandable that a university president,
after visitations of accrediting committees representing medicine, law,
journalism, nursing, pharmacy, dentistry, librarians, architects, veterinari-
ans, and optometry might begin to wonder who was running his institution.
He probably would resent the addition of education to the list. Conant reflects an administrator's disenchantment when he recommends in his recent
book that NCATE should be relegated to an advisory role, and—in later
statements—that it should be abolished. To be logical his recommendation
should be extended to all the professional accrediting agencies listed
above.

Professional Interest in Certification

The organized profession in education aspires to improve the efficacy of
certification as a process of professional licensure. The National Commission on Teacher Education and Professional Standards (NCTEPS) was created by NEA after World War II to provide leadership in advancing professional standards. More recently, the New Horizons Project was formed
by NCTEPS to spearhead this activity.

The efforts to reshape certification to serve as licensure have aroused
vigorous reaction. As is stated in the current *Manual*,[2] "One would have

[2] Earl Armstrong and T. M. Stinnett, *Certification Requirements for School Personnel in the United States.* Washington, D.C.: NCTEPS, NEA, 1964, p. 1.

to characterize the years between the 1961 and 1964 editions of the *Manual* as a period of aggressive, widely publicized attacks on the efforts of the teaching profession to gain control over its professional house through teacher education, accreditation, and certification."

Several crucial questions have been overlooked both by the profession and by their critics in this imbroglio. Is certification the licensure process for education? Can it and should it be redesigned to serve that purpose more efficiently?

Licensure practices vary among the professions. Yet while differing in detail, the overall programs for preparation and admission in all professions have these common features, which are interdependent and mutually supporting:

a. Responsibility for developing, testing, and validating programs of preparation rests with the college staff.
b. A professional accrediting agency of the profession systematically appraises the program of each college.
c. A licensure board composed of professional personnel, appointed by the state, screens the graduates of accredited institutions for admission to the profession.

Certification practices, when compared with licensure, reveal striking differences and few similarities: differences in purpose, in the role of the organized profession, and in the nature of the process itself. We have mentioned these unique features in passing, but it will be useful to summarize them here.

a. Contrasts in purposes. Professional licensure is designed to identify as members of the profession those qualified to practice, and to exclude the unqualified. Certification provides no assurance as to preparation—it has always been the practice to admit sufficient teachers with substandard preparation to staff the classes. On the other hand, practitioners from other professions as well as non-professional personnel are certificated, while many fully qualified practicing members of the profession are not certificated—in many private schools, nursery schools, kindergartens, and colleges other than junior colleges. Certification is not, and never was designed to be a badge of professional membership.

b. Role of the profession. The profession in education has no role in certification comparable to that of the licensure board in other professions. Whatever role it plays is advisory.

c. Differences in nature of the process. These differences in purpose and control result in an operation totally different from professional licensure. A few illustrations will serve to point up this fact:

Classification and definition of positions, in terms intelligible for administration by a clerical staff;

Admission requirements that prescribe patterns of preparation;

Restriction of duties of a given practitioner to those of a given classified position;

Incorporation of all purposes of professional standards into admission procedures.

These unique characteristics of certification are too fundamental to be viewed as differences in degree. They are differences in kind: certification is a civil service operation, not a process of professional licensure. It was designed, and is still essential, to regularize employment of public school personnel, not to screen candidates for admission to a profession.

Should attempts be continued to modify certification so as to incorporate the necessary features of licensure? That anything useful could or should come from this line of action is doubtful. Licensure requires joint responsibility and joint action by the state and the organized profession. No legislature could or should delegate any part of this important responsibility to the organized profession. The civil service features of certification, properly limited, are of tremendous significance in a state enterprise so extensive as public education.

The profession has evidently been fighting the wrong war. Through NCTEPS, it has been attempting not only the impossible but the undesirable in trying to convert certification into licensure. The efforts wasted in this direction, if directed to clarifying the importance of professional accreditation in teacher education, might have served a useful purpose. Professional accreditation is the keystone in the structure of professional standards. If licensure is limited to graduates of an accredited program, and becomes a legal prerequisite to certification, professional status has been achieved. Restrictive certification requirements will then become unnecessary, obsolete, and a thing of the past.

Largely because of the preoccupation of its membership with certification, education today presents the anomaly of a profession without licensure. It probably cannot remain at that status. It will either establish itself as a profession with licensure, or revert to the status of a craft under civil service. The choice will depend on the quality of professional leadership that emerges in the next few years.

67. Teacher Education:
Repair, Reform, or Revolution?

George W. Denemark

"Education is beyond repair! What is needed is radical reform. . . . Today, the alternative to reform is revolution." [1] Strong words, especially as they come not from some isolated critic outside of the educational establishment but from the report of a distinguished task force of educators commissioned by the American Association of Colleges for Teacher Education. Strong, perhaps, but straight to the point.

The experience of the past decade should make it clear to all that the demands upon America's schools have resulted in stresses requiring more than the occasional oiling of the squeaky wheel or the frustrated kick that constitutes the home repair technology familiar to most of us. Hopefully, these challenges can be met short of revolution, with its accompanying violent rejection of our system of education and the possible transfer of power to other agencies and personnel with little commitment to our democratic traditions.

What is true for American education in general is true in particular for teacher education. The quality and character of our elementary and secondary schools are dependent largely upon the quality and character of the teachers who staff them. The teachers, in turn, strongly reflect the strengths and shortcomings of the colleges that recruit them and provide initial preparation, the school systems that employ them and continue their training, and the professional organizations that supplement such formal training through a broad range of activities. If schools must change to meet the challenges of our times, the education of teachers must change as well. Recognition of the need for radical reform in both schools and

[1] *Teachers for the Real World,* Washington, D.C.: American Association of Colleges for Teacher Education, 1969, p. 9.

SOURCE: *Educational Leadership,* XXVII, 6 (March 1970), 539–43. Copyright © 1970 by the Association for Supervision and Curriculum Development. Reprinted by permission of the author and the Association for Supervision and Curriculum Development.

teacher preparation need not diminish our regard for the splendid heritage of either. Instead, reforming our institutions to meet our nation's needs can be viewed as a reflection of the special genius claimed for a democratic society.

What are the weaknesses in the education of American teachers which demand basic reform or threaten revolution?

1. *Inadequacies and irrelevance of much that presently constitutes the general studies or liberal education component.* In terms of both content and process, general studies often fail to provide students with opportunities to experience what is involved in decision making and choice, the establishment of meaning, the use of evidence and logic, and collaboration toward proximate goals. Instead, they afford narrow, formalized introductions to a string of disconnected subjects, superficially considered through emphasis upon nomenclature, classification systems, or the manipulation of paraphernalia. Separation of information and the problems and issues to which it applies unfortunately still characterizes segments of American higher education. This dichotomy represents a serious shortcoming in the education of any college student. For the prospective teacher it is of critical importance, for he will himself soon become an agent of general education in the elementary or secondary school and likely perpetuate the splintering of knowledge and the gap between ideas and action.

Reexamination of the traditional separation of liberal or general studies from professional studies is long overdue. The career concerns of students can motivate liberal studies and provide an avenue for understanding important concepts. And liberal education can invest professional studies with more personal and humane qualities.

2. *The hostile academic atmosphere in which teacher education is conducted.* Some colleges and universities have long been so hostile and grudging toward teacher education that many college students are negatively inclined toward their professional studies before even commencing them. Certain college professors feel no qualms about advising able students that they would be "wasting" their talents by going into preparation for elementary or secondary teaching. Although the financial survival of many small colleges is dependent upon their programs and enrollments in teacher education, budget allocations seldom reflect this, and priorities for staff and facilities point elsewhere.

Little wonder that James Stone describes teacher education as a "stepchild," unwanted by the colleges,[2] and Hobert Burns urges that we ". . . consider transferring much of the responsibility from colleges and universities to the public schools" since "many colleges, per-

[2] James C. Stone. *Breakthrough in Teacher Education.* San Francisco: Jossey-Bass Inc., Publishers, 1968.

haps even most, have not taken seriously the obligation to teacher education. . . ." [3]

3. *Lack of conceptual frameworks for teacher education.* Without the identification of some unifying theories or conceptual frameworks for structuring teacher education, most of our efforts at improvement result in mere "tinkering." An appropriate balance must be struck between theory and practice. Adequate recognition must be given to the broad range of objectives in teacher preparation from fundamental beginning skills to a body of systematized knowledge that permits teachers to become analysts and diagnosticians of the teaching-learning process—to become teacher-scholars.

We have been prone too often to regard the almost infinite number of minor variations from program to program as positive evidence of institutional initiative and concern for individuality. Instead, such variations are more likely to represent evidence of grossly inadequate attention to basic principles and of breakdowns in the communication process among professionals across institutional and sometimes even departmental boundary lines.

4. *Simplistic views of teaching and teacher education.* "Teachers should be taught as they are expected to teach." "What does it matter how much a person knows of a subject if he can't build an effective relationship with children?" The first oft-repeated viewpoint sounds appealing until one begins to reflect on the differences in experience level, motivation, capacity to handle abstractions, etc., between kindergartners and doctoral students. Few thoughtful persons would quarrel over the importance of reaching and relating to children. Need we choose, however, between that ability and such other important qualities as a broad concept of the world, ability to distinguish fact from opinion, or the capacity to pose open rather than closed structure questions which elicit higher order thinking among students? Teaching is a complex, demanding profession which is demeaned by those who would suggest that *only* affection for children or subject matter knowledge or specific teaching skills are sufficient. All these and more are necessary for the effective teacher.

Another evidence of a simplistic approach in teacher education is the almost childlike faith some have evinced in the efficacy of laboratory experiences. Whatever the scope, quality, duration, and structure of such experiences, some persons have equated improved teacher education with more of these and less of whatever else was being done. But unplanned laboratory experiences can turn out to be little more than "rubber-necking" or wasteful repetition of a narrow band of

[3] Hobert Burns. "Teacher Education Programs—Their Structure and Flexibility." NDEA *Special Bulletin*, December 1967. In: *Ibid.*, pp. 187–88.

teaching behavior and student response sandwiched between large slices of coming and going.

5. *Inadequate interlacing of theoretical and practical study.* Effective teachers interpret classroom events by means of theoretical knowledge but gain an appreciation of the significance of key concepts as they see them applied in school situations. It is essential, therefore, that teacher preparation programs give attention to each and to their appropriate integration.

Criticism continues that teacher education is too theoretical. Perhaps, to the contrary, it may not be *sufficiently* theoretical. Simply because training programs fail to reflect reality adequately does not *per se* make them too theoretical. Rather they may only be out of touch with reality—an equally serious but very different problem. Much of what currently passes for theory is simply outdated specific knowledge —for which there should be little room in the teacher education curriculum.

Improved opportunities to see teaching ideas in action and thus better understand them is highly important. But there is no magic in field experience. It is not meaningful simply because it is "out there." Rather, it is meaningful as it is carefully planned, structured, interpreted, and linked with theoretical or foundational studies. Contact with reality without the perspective of theory fosters adjustment to what *is* rather than stimulating realization of what *could be.* Beginning teachers must be able to survive in the classroom as it is, but if education is to improve—a matter we judge to be imperative—they must also have the vision of its potentialities and the skills to alter its course.

The development of educational media makes possible a linking of theoretical knowledge with real situations which illustrate its use. As pointed out in *Teachers for the Real World,* teaching behavior ". . . cannot be studied in the classroom because behavior perishes as it happens and nothing is left to analyze except the memory or a check sheet." [4] Utilization of video and audio tapes of behavior can capture the reality of classroom and community and permit its analysis in a manner that will help teachers become skillful interpreters of teaching and learning.

6. *Continued acceptance of the single model, omnicapable teacher.* Nearly all teachers are still prepared to work as isolated adults with standard size groups of children. Instead, we should be preparing them to assume different roles as members of instructional teams. Such roles might include aides, assistants, interns, beginning teachers, ancillary specialist personnel, coordinating teachers, and more. While

[4] *Teachers for the Real World, op. cit.,* p. 52.

colleges producing professional teachers may not engage in training all such personnel, they should clearly participate in the design of appropriate instructional staffing patterns and ensure that the preparation of those they do train provides for their effective integration in an instructional team.

7. *Low selection and retention standards for teacher candidates.* Operating in an economy of scarcity, teacher preparation programs frequently admitted, retained, and recommended for teaching licenses, persons woefully weak in handling ideas, oral and written communication, sensitivity to others, and management of their own personal lives. With many subject fields now producing more teachers than there are job openings, there is urgent need for the development of more effective means of predicting teaching success and of screening out those with a low probability of effective performance.

8. *Schedule rigidities and cumbersome procedures for curriculum change.* Many opportunities for relating on-campus and field experiences are blocked because college scheduling practices cut days into fifty-minute fragments. Block scheduling of general education and professional sequences, provision for dividing academic terms into on-campus and field experience segments, utilization of intersession or between semester periods, and other alternatives must be explored. Sensible ideas cannot continue to be impeded because of mechanical rigidities.

The system of curriculum change in most colleges is extremely cumbersome, clearly one which was designed originally to "keep the lid on" and maintain tight controls over programs. With the rapidity of contemporary societal changes, however, it seems essential that curricular change be facilitated rather than retarded. College faculties seldom utilize the "broken front" approach to curriculum improvement which their curriculum specialists urge upon lower school faculties. To speed change and to facilitate experimentation rather than wholesale installation of programs, procedures must permit small groups of school system and college staff to design and implement promising programs with adequate provision for evaluation and for communication of experience.

9. *Absence of student opportunities for exploration and inquiry.* Most teacher educators talk about the need for teachers to be experimental and exploratory in their work. Training programs, however, are often narrowly prescriptive and didactic in form. If we take our own words seriously, we must develop beginning competence in some of the research and inquiry skills among undergraduates preparing to teach.

Prospective teachers must be placed in situations that will afford them opportunities to act like researchers. To those who fear this is beyond them, there is considerable evidence to suggest that we have long been expecting too little of our students and that these low expectations may have conditioned the performance levels of many.

10. *Schizophrenic role expectations for teacher education departments.* Professors of pedagogy are frequently pressured by their university colleagues to accept a conventional academic view of their role, emphasizing basic scholarship while keeping school and community service commitments to a minimum. At the same time they are beleaguered by school systems wanting them to become involved more directly in the problems of inner city and suburbia, of gifted and disadvantaged, of individualization in a mass culture.

Mounting financial pressures on higher education and the growing problems of schools could bring about a redirection of teacher education that would probably take the form of school systems undertaking the professional training of teachers while the colleges would focus entirely upon academic studies. While doubtless appealing to some, such a development would destroy some of the advantages of the present plan. It would tend to base the preparation of new teachers on the patterns of the present—patterns which have already been shown to be seriously inadequate to the challenges of the times. It would lend support to the concept of teaching as a modestly demanding craft learned relatively easily through an apprenticeship rather than a complex profession demanding high levels of analysis, diagnosis, and planning ability. Separation of knowledge from application and thinking from doing would seem to be a third serious limitation of such a division of labor.

Schools of education should represent a bridge between formal academic studies in the university and the application of this knowledge to school and community problems. While these schools often fail in this role, it would still seem wise to attempt their reform rather than precipitate their abandonment. Universities need to become more directly concerned with the problems of the community, and schools need teachers capable of interpreting experience within frameworks of theory and principle.

The plea for resisting the full scale transfer of teacher education to the schools does not deny the critical need for new and more effective cooperative arrangements between schools and colleges. As James Stone concluded in *Breakthrough in Teacher Education,*

We are shadow-boxing with the real problem unless we are willing to develop new structures for bringing together the groups necessary for the education of our teachers—the schools, the colleges, and the communities in which schools are located.[5]

[5] Stone, *op. cit.,* p. 190.

The challenge of American teacher education today is that of building into its structure the capacity for adaptability to the rapidly changing needs of our schools and communities. Rather than a monolithic resisting force irrelevant to current problems and ultimately a stimulus for irrational, violent change, teacher education must find ways of anticipating and facilitating orderly change for the years ahead. In reforming itself it can help to reform all of education.

68. Industry and the Education of Teachers

David A. Bickimer

There is a story going around about the well-to-do parents who took their "hippie" son to the family analyst to "shape him up." The analyst, after skillfully removing the parents from the initial interview scene (no mean task), asked the boy some rather straightforward questions. And the session went something like this:

THE ANALYST: "Do you love your Mother?"
    The youth shook his "down to there" hair and thoughtfully said . . . . . "Sometimes."
THE ANALYST: "Do you hate your Father?"
    The advocate of the Rolling Stones, fingered his beads a bit and said . . . . . "Sometimes."
THE ANALYST: "Do you believe in God?"
    The groovy soul, taking a drag on his suspiciously sweet-smelling cigarette . . . . said, "Sometimes."

Any further conclusion to the story is never really considered by those who tell it. Presumably, the listener is left to contemplate the wisdom or banality of the client and the total effect of his responses on all those concerned. Similarly, when those who are interested in industry and the education of teachers are asked if they really believe that industry can educate teachers to a significant degree, in wisdom or banality, they seem to be saying, "Sometimes."

SOURCE: Address presented to the California Council on the Education of Teachers (mimeographed), Yosemite, California, November 2, 1969.

The Present State of Affairs

Perhaps, if this question—can industry educate teachers to a significant degree?—had been asked a few years ago, the answer would have been "Absolutely." At that time many were caught up in the potential "takeover" of the massive forces of big industries like Xerox, Raytheon, Time, and General Electric moving into an area fraught with frustration. Surely, it was felt, with all the resources at their disposal, these capitalistic giants would bring us the leverage needed to budge the educational universe in the "right" direction . . . on all fronts . . . including teacher education. But, and this point has been well documented and proved in daily experience, the "takeover" has not occurred. Education has learned that it is in many ways, including financially, bigger than business. The "takeover," welcomed or feared, has not and will not occur.

There is another story going the rounds of the airlines set about the announcement that came over the intercom aboard a typically tedious transcontinental flight. After about an hour of flight, the captain addressed the passengers as follows: "Ladies and Gentlemen, I have two things to tell you. The first thing is bad news, the second is good news. The bad news is that, I am sorry to report, we are lost. But take heart, the good news is that, although lost, we are right on schedule."

For some reason, this story is particularly humorous to pilots, but the layman wonders how one can be lost and still on schedule. And yet, it seems that the condition of being lost but on schedule approximates a description of the so-called "new" education industry as it tentatively moves into the arena of teacher education.

Indeed, the write-ups of the industry in *The New York Times* dutifully give reports of progress and failure on fronts such as computerized instruction, and many times end with an expression of interest on the part of firms in teacher education. But there are few if any reports of success or failure . . . just interest. Behind the interest is the lost condition of probing, questioning, and offering suggestions. Despite the host of questions, there is a feeling that the industry, in this regard, is right on schedule. For prior to this "period of inquiry," a groundwork was laid from which the questions might be asked.

A Willingness to Cooperate

For there is little doubt that industry can make a meaningful contribution to teacher education. This is the "word," at least; from practicing administrators like Bernard Watson, Associate Superintendent of Schools in Philadelphia; it is the "word" from directors of teacher education like

James Stone at Berkeley and presidents of corporations like Francis Keppel.

It is also the "word" from professional associations like the Associated Organizations for Teacher Education. There is now, clearly, a willingness to invite, however cautiously, industry into the arena of teacher education. Both industry and education must be grateful to the men who laid this foundation, who scheduled us all into our present question-filled, "lost," confused, state. Today, right on schedule, we can look to just a few of the questions one hears across the country. We might also hint at a few ways to answer the questions.

Some Goals for Industry

The general question is what can industry offer teacher education? Specifically, this general question becomes:

Shall industry offer products—films, tapes, filmstrips—which teacher educators select and incorporate into their programs? *Or* shall industry offer whole programs, or systems for teacher education . . . and should these systems be for the pre-service or in-service education of teachers?

In a recent article, Benjamin Wright and Shirley Tuska state that there is clear evidence of two problems which might well confront in-service teacher education.[1] Of the teachers who end up "out there" after pre-service training, too many of them are leaving. Moreover, of those who remain, too many of them, after the first few years, rigidify, lose their flexibility in front of the room, become classroom managers more than teachers. Too many fail to adapt to the individual student. A disproportionate number call upon the norms of scholarship rather than the norms of learning. A great number of teachers have a tendency to place the onus of failure too much on the student rather than on themselves. This being the case, products or systems developed by industry might aim (a) at increasing the length of teacher tenure and (b) at sustaining teacher flexibility in the classroom. Are these appropriate educational goals for industry to seek if it develops products or whole systems?

Teacher Flexibility and Products

What would the products or systems look like? If teacher flexibility, for example, is a desired goal, then materials dealing with alternative modes of behavior may be appropriate. And so, one might look to industry to

[1] Benjamin D. Wright and Shirley A. Tuska, "From Dream to Life in the Psychology of Becoming a Teacher," *The School Review*, LXXVI, 3 (September, 1968), 253–54.

furnish systems of model teaching techniques like the Far West Lab's mini-course [2] or aspects of Stanford's micro-teaching protocol.[3] Then, too, contingency management [4] teacher strategies might be a welcome addition to in-service programs. Simulation packages [5] would seem appropriate. All such "systems" or packages would hopefully yield greater teacher flexibility when used in the in-service situation. But, note, almost "to a man," these products are the result of the behavioral school of thought. What of the "inquiry" or "heuristic" school of thought of teacher education? Inquiry teaching is certainly an alternative strategy of teaching. How can industry aid us to provide the schools, perhaps for the first time, with the inquiry teacher, the "individualized" teacher, the "structure" teacher?

Pursuing the general question of what industry might offer teacher education, it may also be asked: Is the real potential to be found, not so much in products per se as in the service-process of *dissemination?* To help gain an understanding of dissemination, a look at an innovation like the Education Professions Institute helps.

Industrial Service for Teacher Educators

At the conclusion of his report of Ford-funded programs in teacher education,[6] James Stone proposes the Education Professions Institute. Funded and managed by the state, the EPI would be a new kind of educational institution, laden with prestige, and focusing on teacher development on the job.

The EPI is an intriguing institution. Suppose it is attempted by one state—California, for example. Suppose five years from now that the EPI exists, and the research shows it to be a resounding success. Will it remain only in California? Who will tell New York State about it? Who will help New York State assess its strengths and weaknesses, who will assess New York's "readiness," who will assist New York in its implementation, who will aid New York in its evaluation? And what about the other states?

One can suggest universities, but are they not already swamped with their own in-state problems? One can say the government but there is sen-

---

[2] McGraw-Hill is publishing the first fully developed mini-courses.

[3] General Learning Corporation is the publisher of *Teaching Skills for Elementary and Secondary School Teachers,* a multimedia program derived from work at Stanford University in New York City.

[4] Professor Paul Graubard of Yeshiva University in New York City has a proposal for a series of films on contingency management techniques.

[5] Science Research Associates, Chicago, Ill., has published *Teaching Problems Laboratory* and *Inner-City Simulation Laboratory.*

[6] James C. Stone, *Breakthrough in Teacher Education* (San Francisco: Jossey-Bass Inc., 1968), pp. 188–89.

timent to the effect that the Regional Lab, admirable in so many ways, can not disseminate on the national level as hoped. One can say industry, through a nationwide network of communication, utilizing up-to-date information-processing techniques, providing highly trained and sensitized personnel, providing products and services necessary to the dissemination of the EPI.

It is important to note that the word used here is *dissemination . . .* not *marketing . . .* for there is a world of difference. Glen Heathers [7] has, in a scholarly fashion, spoken to the need for a sophisticated dissemination process in education including teacher education.

Educational dissemination is more than advertising, more than promotion, more than slick packaging and selling. Educational dissemination is, rather, the final phase of the innovation (or research and development process) whereby schoolmen such as teacher educators are helped to (a) decide on the benefits of an innovation, (b) decide whether or not appropriate resources are at hand for the adoption of the innovation, (c) place the innovation in action, and (d) evaluate the outcomes of the innovation.

Are these four elements of dissemination the contribution which industry can bring to the education of our teachers?

To recapitulate: there is willingness in the teacher education profession to invite big business into the arena. There is an atmosphere conducive to asking some rather difficult questions. The questions deal with the goals appropriate to business in contributing to teacher education. Three possible goals are (a) tangible products which can be of assistance, (b) whole systems which can be adopted, and (c) the relatively "intangible" goal of a sophisticated dissemination process.

Obstacles to Goals

Even if these three goals are appropriate, there are obstacles to their accomplishment. While a general feeling of good will exists between industry and education, good will is frequently mesmerized by the tensions that intricate relationships inevitably produce. Organizational theorists have often testified to the huge potential for human cooperation in shaping man's environment but also document the conflicts inherent in complex relationships. Industry, as it seeks to create products or systems, knows full well that it can not work alone.

To create products in teacher education, industry must have access to the wisdom and expertise of the professional community of scholars. There seems little need to discuss the difficulties of this relationship as it now ex-

[7] Glen Heathers, "Influencing Change at the Elementary Level," *Perspectives on Educational Change,* ed. Richard I. Miller (New York: Appleton-Century-Crofts, 1967) pp. 45–52.

ists. It has been said that scholars must always be dissatisfied with their publishers and vice versa. As disheartening as this view is, it would appear that the situation has not been intolerable. If industry's contributions are to be primarily in publishing texts, and films and slides in teacher education, perhaps we can rely on some pretty standard experiences of the past. But moving to considerations of publishing whole systems and especially to considerations intrinsic to dissemination, the old publisher-scholar relationship begins to pale in its appropriateness as a model. For to publish a book is not to publish a system; to announce a system is not to *disseminate* it.

Dissemination Difficulties

It will be remembered that dissemination is essentially a service. Dissemination helps a schoolman to understand innovation. The disseminator gives advice to a schoolman (for example, a director of in-service education) on whether or not the schoolman is "ready" for the innovation. Dissemination assists the schoolman in using the innovation. Dissemination seeks to guarantee the "take" of the innovation through a knowledgeable monitoring process.

Were industry to disseminate, then schoolmen would accept the "disseminator" as a new kind of schoolman. Put another way, if industry sets for its goal dissemination of innovation as scholars have described it, the so-called "new" education industry, in this regard, would become a *new educational institution for profit*.

Moreover, from the other point of view, the businessman would accept a schoolman as a new kind of entrepreneur—an entrepreneur who might at seemingly unpredictable times shun publicity, a marketing agent who would spurn advertising. Such a schoolman-businessman might stand firm in a goal that no standard market analysis would justify, or he might openly delineate the weaknesses of a product or system. This educator-disseminator-salesman might refuse to "sell" because the "customer" wasn't ready, or he might advise a customer to buy another firm's products. This combination Dewey-Onassis might invest seemingly unreasonable amounts of time and money to guarantee the "take" of an innovation. He would devote scarce time and monies to high-level evaluation of the outcomes of an innovation.

Given some possible teacher education goals for industry, then, there are clearly the potential problems of whether an educator will accept the industrialist as a peer educator and whether the industrialist will accept the educator as a peer industrialist. These problems are potential obstacles in the path of industry's entry into the field of teacher education. The men who have laid the foundations for the present good will between industry and education are now beginning to experience these problems.

Anecdotes abound about and from both parties—each seems to be saying to the other . . . . "Great stuff . . . . but don't be too successful." Since the evidence here is largely anecdotal, it seems appropriate to desist from further observations and move to considerations appropriate to warding off the potential dilemma.

The Communication Difficulty

Chester Barnard, an ace at organizational theorizing, pointed out, as early as the thirties, that there were three elements to successful human cooperation. In *The Functions of the Executive*, he delineates these three elements as purpose, communication, and willingness to cooperate.[8]

The purposes of industry in teacher education have already been discussed. The willingness to cooperate on the part of industry and the teacher education profession is a matter of fact. What can now be discussed, in the context of avoiding a complex dilemma, is communication.

The potential problems of the marriage of education and industry in teacher education can be approached through increased communication between the two groups in question. This communication can be multivariate . . . i.e., through journals, speeches such as this one, conferences between industry and authors, etc. But there is a need for more intense in-depth communication so that better understanding can result. Speeches and articles in journals are insufficient. They are formal, abstract, and do not convey the intricacies of both parties' mutual milieux. Rather, the communication called for is a communication which allows each to feel the other's informal organization, the thousand and one nuances and innuendos known only to teacher educators . . . the thousand and one nuances known only to businessmen.

These nuances, these fine points, these truths, are not visible on organization charts nor even in journals and speeches. Rather, to know them, one must experience them.[9] It is one thing to know that a supervisor can foster the acquisition of a skill that a student teacher must have for tomorrow's lesson; it is another to teach that skill, to adapt to the student teacher's unique style, to subjectively sense the acquisition or nonacquisition of the skill in the context of a whole class of thirty individuals. Then, too, it is one thing to look at a business plan . . . it is another to develop one

---

[8] Chester I. Barnard, *The Functions of the Executive* (Cambridge: Harvard University Press, 1964), p. 82.

[9] At issue here is the whole question of *informal* organization and how one gets to know it. Cf. *Ibid.* and *passim.*

. . . . to try to "psyche out" a market, to conjecture about the size of the market, to agonize over the problem of control in dissemination.

Such experiential knowledge of each other's milieu might well occur right now. In this way, at least, there might be some confidence that the two parties will understand each other's unsystematized, existential, and very real ways of life. Two ways, at least, of achieving such a "soul-session" communication between industry and teacher educators seem fairly readily possible.

Two Ways to Communicate

The first way is the establishment of internships for teacher educators in industry and for businessmen in teacher education. These internships might occur in various ways and might even result in two new career patterns for teacher educators. What would such internships look like? What would such career patterns entail?

INTERNSHIPS FOR NEOPHYTES

The internships in question would have as their purpose the acquiring of the intuitive, behavioral knowledge of industry on the part of teacher educators. This intuitive "industrial feel" would assist the teacher educator in translating his professional language into that of the manager. Thus, for example, six months might find a Ph.D. candidate camped at McGraw-Hill or Motorola or Time, Inc., in a meaningful position in which he is not too swamped with responsibility, to the detriment of his learning about industry. On the other hand, most of the industries in question have some sort of management trainee program. Being complex firms, they feel the need to expose their own fledglings to the various potential places for them in the company. Not trusting to talks and articles and books, the training departments assign these trainees for months at a time to the various divisions where, although some responsibility is placed on them, the trainee's chief task is to find out what Division X is really all about. It seems the time to encourage management to assign the trainees, those curious about or those definitely interested in teacher education, to internships in schools of education, or in school districts which have an identifiable in-service training program.

"EXPERIENCED" INTERNSHIPS

These two types of internships concern themselves with the neophytes of both professions, business and teacher education. Nothing in them seems intrinsically opposed to the notion that experienced teacher educators and experienced businessmen might undergo a similar experience in each other's camp. This latter consideration opens up the possibility of a new career line for both sides.

It would seem to be beneficial, for example, for a practicing director of teacher education, of a director of curriculum and supervision to spend a year in industry. Thus, as part of a normal career pattern, an educator would enter the business world for a period of time and, having experienced at first hand the workings of the profit-motive and the pressures of corporate existence, the teacher educator would then return to the educational milieu as we know it.

A second possible career line would be that of the teacher educator who entered industry and stayed there becoming a businessman but remaining an educator. The value of such a person to increased communication would be great, at least at face value.

Preparation for New Career Lines

Thus, two career lines seem worthy of further examination. The specifications of these two career lines would have to be carefully marked off and the strengths and dangers of each clearly delineated. Perhaps the most crucial consideration in contemplating such career lines rest around concerns dealing with preparation programs for them. For should further consideration reveal that such career patterns would be helpful, and should such career options be delineated, then, as professional careers, they would require professional preparation. How would we ready a man to enter industry as an educator? How would we prepare an educator to enter industry even for a year or two? It doesn't seem fair to place an educator in such a position unless he knows the language of the profession he is entering and unless he knows at least the formal side of life in business. Such a man, for example, upon arriving at his business office the first day, can be expected to be asked questions like . . . "What products and services are now available in the in-service education of teachers?" "Who produces them?" How many of education professors could answer these questions right now? What kind of a course sequence would get a person ready to answer such reasonable questions?

If advantage is to be taken of the shared purpose and good will which now exists between industry and the teacher education profession, we are going to have to face the problem of communication. Perhaps imaginative internships for educators and for businessmen will help solve the communication dilemma. Perhaps actual new career lines must open up for educators and, of course, for buinessmen. Whatever occurs will have to be reflected in the preinternship or precareer experience of the educators and businessmen who share in this bold communications venture. New preparatory courses, seminars, books, simulations, etc., would seem to be called for.

Summary

Big business is not going to take over the education of teachers. Apparently, however, it would like to enter into a partnership with individuals and agencies already involved in the education of teachers. These individuals and agencies seem willing to invite business into the teacher education arena. Still to be resolved, however, is the specific contribution that industry can bring to the education of teachers. Should it proffer products, systems, a sophisticated dissemination process or what? Whatever is decided, the problem is one of communication.

Things have reached the point where formal communication and knowledge of each other is insufficient and unsatisfactory to each party. For further progress in cooperation, roles and role expectation for businessmen and educators alike will probably have to change. To a certain degree, educators may have to accept a new breed of educator among them. . . . to a certain degree, businessmen may have to accept a new breed of businessman among them. For the businessman-educator and the educator-businessman to appear on the scene and "make a difference," the informal, fluid, intuitive attitudes and norms of each profession must be communicated from one party to the other. To accomplish this goal, new types of internships and, perhaps, actual new career lines might occur. These new internships and new career lines will, should they emerge, call for new programs of preparation. In this way, perhaps, industry may make a more-than-sometime-thing contribution to teacher education and the present enigma of "being lost but on schedule" may be resolved.

69. The NEA and
Collective Negotiations[1]

Allan M. West

A planning committee recently discussed at considerable length whether to make the title of an assigned conference speech "The Teacher Rebellion" or "Why Are Teachers Raising Hell?"

I find there is a good deal of misunderstanding about the answer to this question. Some would dismiss the current ferment among teachers as a jurisdictional fight between two organizations. Others have said that it is being caused by a group of young radicals trying to wrest control of the schools from the elected authorities. Both of these views are superficial and false.

The current unrest among teachers is a natural response to a combination of a number of social forces in our society. And since the public school is society in miniature, these forces are having some profound effects upon schools and those of us who work in them.

If we are going to deal with these forces successfully, we must take a hard look at our present practices and be prepared to make some changes in our thinking and in the way that we work with each other. Let me identify briefly a few of the developments which illustrate why collective action in public education is a timely topic, and why we must change some of our old concepts and methods.

In the first place, our public school enrollments are growing rapidly. Between 1930 and 1964 our pupil population increased from 26 million to 42 million. But this is only part of the picture. While our elementary pop-

---

[1] Paper presented on April 2, 1965 at the Midwest Administration Center, University of Chicago, Chicago, Illinois. Allan M. West is Deputy Executive Secretary, National Education Association, Washington, D.C.

ulation was increasing from 22 to 27 million, our high school population increased from 4 to 15 million, and it costs more—about one and one-half times more—to educate a high school pupil than an elementary pupil.

Increased enrollments have caused a corresponding increase in the size of our teaching staff, and most of these new teachers are recent college graduates coming in at the bottom of the salary scale. This means that the average age of our teaching staff is being reduced. In the five years between 1956 and 1961, the average age of our teaching staff was reduced by two years. Moreover, during this same five-year period the proportion of men teachers has increased from 27.5 per cent to 31.3 per cent of the total teaching staff. In 1956, 53 per cent of the men teachers were under thirty-five. In 1961, 62 per cent were under thirty-five.

Today's teachers have more college training and fewer hold substandard credentials. The proportion of our teaching staff holding bachelor's degrees or better has increased from 60 per cent in 1947–48 to 90 per cent in 1963. The proportion holding master's degrees or higher in that same period has increased from 15 per cent to 25 per cent.

So our younger teaching staff is also better trained and more masculine. Today's teachers have a new spirit which is demanding a voice in determining what goes on in the classroom. They want to be full-fledged members of the school team. They want to be treated as responsible professionals. They want to be consulted about problems which affect them. They are saying: If we can be trusted to teach the boys and girls of the community, we should be trusted to help make the policies which determine the quality of education which they receive.

This need for recognition, this desire to play a more responsible role in school policy making, is at the bottom of many of the eruptions that have taken place in the past few months. This new breed of teacher is impatient. He does not want to wait for the benefits which he honestly thinks he deserves. He is not aware of the battles that have been fought and won in the past. He wants benefits now. He is more concerned with what an organization can do for him in the next six months than he is in what it has done for him in the past century.

School systems are also changing. Thirty years ago we had about 130,-000 school systems in the United States. Today there are only about 25,-000. Illinois offers a dramatic example of the changes taking place in our school systems. Since 1940 the number of school districts in Illinois has been reduced from 12,000 to 1,390.

Today's school is larger and more impersonal. The social distance between the classroom teacher and the administrator is greater. In larger school systems we tend to have less confidence in each other. We do not know each other well. We communicate in writing where formerly a teacher and an administrator could iron out problems with a personal conference. As systems become larger we become inhibited by rules. The superintendent ceases to be an individual; he is a name on the bottom of a memorandum. Bigness, depersonalizing of the school system, and bureaucracy have given greater significancc to the local unit. More teachers feel powerless as individuals to change conditions. Formal grievance procedures are needed to correct gripes that at one time could be settled informally.

There are also important changes taking place in the culture of our local communities. In rural areas with the mechanization of the farms young people have left to seek their fortunes in the cities and suburban areas.

In the growing urban and suburban areas problems are more complex. Large urban communities are more bureaucratic, less responsive to the needs of the citizens, and a new culture and a different scale of values is developing.

There are fewer white Anglo-Saxon Protestants, and more Jews, Negroes and Catholics with different social philosophies. There are greater demands for services because of growth, and there are greater frustrations due to inability of the community to respond to the needs of the citizens. The changing population is bringing with it needs for more water systems, rapid transit lines, welfare services, police, fire and health protection. All of these demands bring with them greater competition for the tax dollar, and in many communities frustration is a way of life for all who seek to meet new conditions with outmoded governmental machinery.

There was a time when most problems which teachers faced could be solved by the state associations through legislative action. Minimum salary laws were enacted requiring the local board of education to meet certain minimum requirements by statute. Mandatory minimum increments were added.

Tenure laws and retirement laws were passed by the legislature at the initiative of state education associations. This left little in the salary area for the local associations to do in areas when districts were small. But as districts have become larger, teachers are finding a need for a more vigorous and articulate voice in the local community to deal with the more impersonal board of education and administration, and to persuade the local community to recognize and meet school and teacher needs.

Current social changes also reveal some weaknesses in our past legislative approaches. Traditionally we have made allocations in terms of so many dollars per child, or classroom units. We now see that some children require more dollars than others. The question, therefore, is not simply one of equalizing educational opportunities through the distribution of a certain uniform number of dollars per child. It is also a matter of measuring differences in needs among children to be served by the public schools, and providing the dollars necessary to compensate for past failures of the home, church and community, if we are to meet the individual needs of pupils.

These are just a few of the forces which in combination account for the emergence of proposals to formalize procedures and tap the resources of our teaching staff. These are the forces which cause teachers to insist upon their recognition as full-fledged members of the school team with some assurance that their voice can be heard where policy decisions are made. These are some of the forces which have moved them to insist that they be considered in policy making as a *right,* rather than as a favor bestowed upon them by a benevolent administration or board of education. It is a matter of self-respect.

In the past few months we have seen explosions in big cities, suburban and even rural areas. In my opinion these explosions have taken place as a result of one or a combination of the following factors: accumulated frustrations of teachers because of their inability to meet their own standards in the classroom, a desire for a stronger voice in policy making, a protest against the impersonality of bigness and bureaucracy, a protest against arbitrary administration, or a protest against community inaction in the face of mounting school needs.

Traditional Approaches

Both professional organizations and teachers' unions exist to bring about changes. Obviously the methods used by each group will be different, since the philosophies which motivate the two groups are different.

Traditionally the union has devoted its efforts almost exclusively to the local school system. On the other hand, the professional organizations have emphasized action on *all three levels*—LOCAL, STATE and NATIONAL.

State associations exist in every state. Each has a paid staff, and in most states the "teachers' lobby" is numbered among the most effective lobbies on Capitol Hill.

The nature of the school enterprise is such that more than two dollars out of every three available to the schools for operation and maintenance go into the salary budget. It is just that kind of an operation. Therefore, if the legislatures can be persuaded to appropriate more dollars to schools, a good share of them will go into the salary budget. A school is a service enterprise in which professionally trained people provide services to children. It is therefore, appropriate that the salary category should account for most of the operating budget. There is little flexibility in the typical school budget. Maintenance of buildings can be postponed. But it is a small part of the total budget and a short-sighted way to "save" money. It has been the policy of professional organizations to work aggressively with state legislatures and the federal Congress to put more dollars in the hands of local boards of education. Local units then have had the task of seeing that teachers' salaries receive a fair share of the revenue.

Therefore, by joining with other organizations interested in the schools including the administration and local school board, the chief task of the state association has been to promote legislation which would improve the financing of the schools, protect the tenure of teachers, provide adequately for their retirement, protect against legislation which will cripple the schools, and promote that which will improve the quality of the school program. These services of the state associations have been backed up by the Research Division of the National Education Association and the work of a host of state and national committees and commissions which provide specialized information and a forum for sharing successful experiences and developing uniform legislative goals. Local associations have been involved in the legislative effort by taking part actively in the election of legislators, persuading them after election to support good school measures, and making certain that teachers share equitably in the fruits of the legislation.

These state legislative programs must continue and remain strong. The constitutions of the several states place the primary responsibility for schools upon the state legislature. Teachers must continue to have an articulate voice in its deliberations. They must also be active in the political arena to elect legislators who will support good school legislation. In recent years the importance of strong leadership at the national level to secure good school legislation from the federal Congress has become dramatically clear and increasingly important. While federal funds still comprise a small share of total school revenues, the percentage of federal funds has increased significantly.

The growing size, complexity and impersonality of local school systems have added a new and important dimension to that traditionally performed by the local unit. It is clear that professional associations must devote more effort to strengthening local associations and improving community relationships. This has been recognized and a great deal of effort is now being made by professional associations to strengthen them. Local units must engage in a growing variety of activities required to give a voice to teachers in the local community above and beyond that required to support state and national programs.

The unions have approached the problem differently. They have borrowed procedures from industry through which to apply pressure on the local board of education. The theory is that if sufficient pressure is applied locally, and, if the local board of education cannot grant the relief requested, it will be sufficiently uncomfortable to seek relief from the higher levels of government.

Unions are not equipped to work on all three levels. They do not have either the organization or the strength. They have no state organizations in most states, and none which are comparable in strength to the state education associations. If the president of the American Federation of Teachers accurately defines the policy of the AFT, there appears to be little distinction between the procedures which it considers to be appropriate for industry and those which are appropriate for teaching in the public service. Charles Cogen, in an interview with Peter A. Janssen of *The Philadelphia Inquirer,* following his election in 1964, said that he hopes ". . . to use all of the devices available to trade unions because after all we are a trade union. These include strikes if necessary, picketing and rallies."

Because of the great differences in the purposes, resources, philosophies and structures of the two organizations, it is not surprising that they should adopt different methods of operation. The union relies chiefly on force applied at the local level. The professional association relies chiefly on persuasion at all three levels—local, state and national.

It is only natural that the associations see strength in the cooperative approach to the solution to school problems. It is based on the belief that teachers, school boards and school administrators have differences, but they also have many common and overriding mutual interests. It is, therefore, possible to agree to disagree on some things, and to agree to cooperate on others.

The professional organization believes that it can serve teachers best by remaining independent of organic connections and resulting loyalties to noneducational organizations. Such ties inhibit its policies and prevent it from putting the interests of teachers and education *first* in its considerations. Affiliations with labor organizations also carry with them obligations which are frequently in conflict with the first-priority goals of teachers. It is also our belief that by remaining independent of other groups the professional organization will have the freedom to work for school and teacher advancement with any and all interested groups, including organized labor. Such independence makes it possible for the professional organizations to focus upon and give top priority to matters of education, and education alone. It also relieves the professional organization of any obligation to support noneducation programs and to respect picket lines on questions which are external to the schools, and that might alienate groups which otherwise might be persuaded to support school measures.

An example is the recent action by the American Federation of Teachers to have removed from the schools textbooks and encyclopedia sets produced by the Kingsport Press of Kingsport, Tennessee. Included in the AFT's blacklist of 170 titles are such well-known and reputable publishers of textbooks as: Grossett and Dunlap; Harper and Row; Holt, Rinehart and Winston; Alfred A. Knopf; J. B. Lippincott; McGraw Hill; Charles E. Merrill; Random House; Charles Scribner and Sons; Field Enterprises Educational Corporation; and Grolier, Inc.

The reason given by AFT to ban these books from schools was their disagreement with the labor policy of the Kingsport Press. This action by the 49th convention of AFT was obviously taken to pay the debt incurred by the teachers' union for the acceptance of financial and other help from the other AFL-CIO unions. This obligation which unionized teachers assume is too high a price to pay. And it is not necessary. Independent teacher groups the nation over are negotiating better contracts without sacrificing their professional integrity.

Albert Shanker, president of the United Federation of Teachers, in response to a letter published in the *New York World-Telegram and Sun* of April 8, 1965 stated that unionized teachers must help other unions achieve their objectives so that they can get the support which teachers need when they are in trouble. Charles Cogen, president of AFT, stated this policy in his address to the 49th convention in August, 1965 in these words:

Every AFT member knows the practical need for making sure that our brothers and sisters in other unions are "there" when we need them. They will be ready to help us if we are "there" when they need *our* support. Such solidarity is imperative, even though we know that the labor movement, including ourselves, has some shortcomings.

I believe in trade unions. I believe in collective bargaining. But I believe that trade unions are wrong for teachers because the cost of labor support can be the loss of the teachers' professional integrity and freedom to teach. This is illustrated by the Kingsport Press incident.

Some Indications for the Future

In the past two years approximately 400 formal agreements have been negotiated, establishing a procedure for employer-employee relationships in school systems throughout the country. A greater proportion of those recently negotiated are Level Three agreements. By this I mean agreements which contain a complete procedure involving (1) a recognition of the association as the spokesman for all teachers; (2) a definition of the procedures under which negotiation with the board of education and administration shall take place; and (3) a provision for resolving an impasse if it should develop. It is no secret that considerable resistance has come from school boards based chiefly on the claim that give-and-take negotiation and advisory appeals procedures encroach upon the legal prerogatives of the board.

Recently Commissioner Arvid Anderson of the Wisconsin Employment Relations Board said:

. . . examples are evident that governmental units at all levels, both with and without express legislative sanction, have been engaged in the practice of collective bargaining in the manner described for a long time. The best example is the fact that [President Kennedy] issued Executive Order 10988. . .[2]

Acceleration of the adoption of formalized procedures by boards of education can be expected. I also see a lessening of resistance to procedures for the resolving of an impasse as an encroachment upon the legal authority of the board of education. Boards of education have the legal responsibility for the adoption of school policy, but boards of education can arrive at that policy in any way they choose. In the days ahead I see an acceptance of the idea of give-and-take discussions for negotiations by boards of education recognizing that teachers have a right to participate in a responsible way in the formulation of school policy. I think our experience to date shows that the powers of boards of education are broad enough to permit them to involve teachers in the decision-making process if they want to do it. The legal argument is usually an expression of the reluctance of the board to give up the practice of unilateral decision making.

LEGISLATION FOR PROFESSIONAL NEGOTIATION

Some form of professional negotiation legislation was proposed in at least fourteen states in 1965. New laws were passed by legislatures in eight states. Let me suggest five reasons why I think that more and more states will turn to the legislative route.

1. State legislation will increase the number of agreements much more rapidly than is possible under the voluntary approach. With legislation, school board acceptance of professional negotiation will be a matter of compliance rather than a matter of choice. Legislation will also permit separate treatment for school personnel rather than blanketing them into laws which do not recognize the special character of the school. An important example is the law passed by the 1965 Washington State Legislature. This law provides for (1) the inclusion of all certificated personnel in the negotiating unit; (2) a broad definition of the subject matter of the negotiation which goes beyond the limits of the narrow definition of the labor law; and (3) a procedure for resolving an impasse which is separate and apart from the channels provided by the state labor law.

2. The voluntary approach has more appeal for those districts with the most enlightened personnel policies. Therefore those systems which need professional negotiation most are likely to be the last to adopt it voluntarily.

3. State laws assure teachers of their *right* to take an active part in the process of school policy making. They recognize that teachers have a legit-

---

[2] Arvid Anderson, "The Developing State of Collective Bargaining for Public Employees." Address to Conference on Public Employment and Collective Bargaining, University of Chicago, February 5, 1965.

imate role to play in the formulation of the policies which affect them. They give teachers greater on-the-job dignity, security, and independence in performing their functions at the heart of the public education process.

4. Legislation can establish a uniform set of rules for the procedure of give-and-take negotiations to operate, which will apply in all school systems in the state. A uniform set of conditions will stimulate the perfection of the process by permitting sharing of experiences among the different school systems.

5. The establishment of legal authority for the meaningful participation of teachers in policy making removes the legal, or sovereignty, argument which has been a major obstacle to securing voluntary acceptance of professional negotiation.

UNIT DEFINITION

A question which has arisen in the past, and will likely arise in the future, concerns the appropriate definition of the negotiating unit. Ideally all members of the professional staff have an identity of interest centering on (1) the skills and training which are common to all; (2) the professional commitment to a high-quality school program; (3) the agreed-upon standards of professional practice; and (4) salary and fringe benefits which apply to all professional personnel such as retirement, insurance, and sick leave (all of which override partisan interest generated by their positions in the school hierarchy).

To the extent that this identity of interest prevails, the conclusions seem inescapable: all persons holding professional certificates or permits issued by the state agency, with a possible exception of the superintendent, should be members of the unit, even though they may perform supervisory or administrative functions. This principle was followed in all referendums held in Connecticut, and is practiced by the teachers in Canada.

However, in many school districts, particularly large ones, realities may not conform to the ideal. Classroom teachers may desire representation independent of administrators. The determining factor in any school system should be the desires of the professional personnel concerned. Custom, established practice and membership patterns usually provide the evidence of the desires of the membership.

Some will argue that an all-inclusive unit is inappropriate. And in some instances it is. However, this decision should follow the desires of the local members. Great strength can be given to an organization if an all-inclusive unit can be formed with complete freedom for teachers to participate in discussions without inhibitions. Some will argue that a classroom-teacher-only unit will be more militant.

In the last year one of the most militant demonstrations of determination on the part of educators to improve their conditions was the effort made by the Utah Education Association. It would be difficult to find a person more militant than the president of that association. He was a high school principal. Yet the policy-making apparatus of that association is in the firm control of classroom teachers. The inclusion of administrators in its membership and in active participation has given strength to the organization. At the height of the activity, boards of education, not classroom teachers, attempted to force administrators out of the association. Some boards of education tried to insist that administrators give their complete loyalty to them and withdraw from the association. But the administrators held their ground and remained in the association. The association enrolls better than 90 per cent of all certified personnel in the state. This solidarity gave great strength to the organization in the legislative and political activities which led to the substantial improvement of the school program and paved the way for the removal of national sanctions on March 15, 1965.

Some unions have had similar experience with all-inclusive units—notably the Typographical Workers and the Building Trades. Efforts have been made by management to force the separation of supervisory employees, but without success. Forcing a uniform standard upon all local units *could be* playing management's game rather than serving the best interests of the employees.

The National Union of Teachers in Great Britain is an independent professional organization enrolling over 242,000 school personnel. It has a long record of militant action to improve the status of teachers and promote popular education. Reference is made to the source of NUT's militance in an article in the *Monthly Labor Review* for September, 1964, as follows:

. . . Two-thirds of all NUT members are women teachers, but it is the head teachers of both primary and secondary schools who, though numerically a much smaller group, dominate the national executive of the Union and also play a leading part in local association politics. The drive towards "trade union" tactics, and towards militancy, comes mainly (though not exclusively) from assistant masters who comprise an important section of the Union, while this insistence on "professionalism" and respectability stems largely, though by no means entirely, from those enjoying the highest status in the profession—the headmasters and headmistresses. This is as far as broad generalization can go . . .[3]

Separate units for classroom teachers and administrators is justified if teachers feel that their active participation in organization affairs is being restricted in the all-inclusive unit. Separation can also be justified if administrators attempt to use their administrative authority to influence asso-

---

[3] Walter Roy, "Reaction of Organized Teachers to Crisis," *Monthly Labor Review*, September, 1964, p. 1022.

ciation policy. But the mere inclusion of administrative personnel in the unit does not prevent it from being militant in the pursuit of its goals. Moreover, those who argue against the inclusion of administrators fail to recognize that when employees become more highly skilled or professionally trained, they tend to identify more closely with the purposes of an enterprise, and differences become less marked as skills and training increase.

EXCLUSIVE REPRESENTATION

The organization which has the support of the majority of the professional staff should be their exclusive representative. The professional negotiation process seeks agreement on policy matters. Since there can be only one policy, there should be only one teacher representative. I suggest that we will see wide acceptance of this principle as more and more teacher organizations press for formalized procedures.

The chief strength of the concept of exclusive representation is that it encourages responsible behavior. Experiences of the past three years with joint committees or a multiplicity of organizations speaking only for their members argue for the selection of an exclusive representative. Joint committees are torn with organizational rivalries. They frequently provide a forum for minority groups to make unreasonable demands in an effort to attract membership from the uncommitted.

The designation of an exclusive representative to represent all teachers of a school system does not prevent the minority organization from pressing its views with the superintendent and board of education.

Experience indicates that the minority organization does not dissolve when a majority organization is awarded exclusive representation rights. For example, in Detroit where the professional association lost an election last year it has increased its membership and it is a stronger organization now than it was before the election.

SCOPE OF THE NEGOTIATIONS

If we are to attract the kind of imaginative, creative and resourceful teacher we would like for our schools, we must create the conditions which will attract this kind of individual. The truly professional teacher wants freedom to exercise independent judgment as a professional. Teachers as other persons will generally react in terms of the way in which they are treated.

Dr. Francis S. Chase, in a study of over 200 school systems in 43 states, sought to determine what administrative polices and practices tend to increase the satisfactions which teachers experience in their work. From replies from 1784 teachers he generalized that:

One of the most important contributors to the satisfaction which teachers take in their work and the enthusiasm which they feel for the system in which they are working is a sense of professional status, responsibility, and freedom. Freedom to plan one's own work was rated as the most important potential source of satisfaction by all groups of respondents. It was given the highest possible rating for satisfaction by 77 per cent of teachers in elementary schools, 75 per cent of those in secondary schools, 69 per cent of the men teachers, 78 per cent of the women teachers, over 80 per cent of the superior teachers, and nearly 69 per cent of the below-average teachers.

The interviews supplied further evidence of the importance of this factor. Again and again teachers who were enthusiastic about the system in which they were working praised their freedom to experiment, to adapt programs to the needs of their pupils; or cited as important to satisfaction the fact that they were regarded as competent to make their own decisions and to work out their own procedures.

. . . Freedom to plan one's own work is given the highest possible rating by more than three-fourths of all respondents, and achieves a considerably higher average rating than any other factor.[4]

While I think most teachers desire to participate in the establishment of salary schedules, class size and other conditions of work, they also want a voice in other aspects of the program which influence the quality of education.

Precedents, traditions and habits have grown up in industry concerning the subject matter of negotiations. Certain subjects have been labeled management prerogatives. Others have been designated areas in which workers have a legitimate interest. Generally speaking, employees in industry have the legal right to negotiate only on those subjects which come under the general heading of wages, hours and working conditions.

When it comes to education, these precedents, traditions and habits are irrelevant. One of the earmarks of a professional group is the recognition of its responsibilities beyond the limits of self-interest. This includes the responsibility to the general welfare of the school system. A professional group should be permitted to negotiate with the board of education on matters which affect the quality of education other than those covered by the narrow definitions in labor law. This philosophy is based on the belief that the case for improved teacher welfare rests on the necessity for improving the quality of public education generally. Teachers have an interest in the conditions which attract and retain a better teaching force. They are concerned with in-service training programs, class size, selection of textbooks, the kinds of programs available for emotionally disturbed, physically handicapped children, and other matters which go beyond the limited industrial definition. In a recent survey in one big-city school system it

[4] Francis S. Chase, "Factors for Satisfaction in Teaching," *Phi Delta Kappan*, November, 1951, p. 130.

was found that the one problem which was of greatest concern to teachers was the lack of adequate provision for emotionally disturbed children. Professional associations are uniquely equipped and backed by resources to bring to bear on negotiations the expert services necessary to make good decisions. The specialized services of the many departments, special projects, and research departments of the state and national associations enable the association to make contributions in many areas having a bearing on the quality of education which are not available to any other organization.

SANCTIONS

Sanctions have proved to be effective. We have recently had four dramatic examples of the success of sanctions in winning results for teachers without violating professional responsibilities. In Utah; Waterbury, Connecticut; Little Lake, California; and Oklahoma, sanctions focused public attention on conditions in the schools which needed correction. This ability to capture public attention and define school problems in concert with effective public relations programs and political action made it possible for the people of Little Lake, California, to turn out of office a majority of the school board, secure the resignation of the superintendent, and remove the conditions for which the sanction was applied. In Waterbury the sanction defined the issues which made it possible for the people of Waterbury to elect a new mayor and secure through political action the remedies needed to correct the situation which called for the sanction.

In Utah the sanction was a means of dramatizing the problem and appealing to the pride of the people to take corrective action. They responded by electing a new governor and a majority of the legislature in a campaign which emphasized education. The legislation is estimated to provide a $450 increase for teachers this year, $250 more next year, and it will add other benefits which will affect the quality of education. This is in addition to the more than $600 received last year.

Speaking to a statewide meeting of Utah teachers on March 19, 1965, Governor Calvin Rampton acknowledged that sanctions had brought about an awareness of the needs of education and the kinds of problems to be faced.

In Oklahoma sanctions provided the stimulation whereby both legislative action and a successful referendum made it possible to correct the conditions which caused their imposition.

At the beginning of the 1965 legislative session the Governor of Oklahoma offered the Oklahoma Education Association an increase of $50 per teacher. Instead of this token $50 raise, every teacher in Oklahoma will get a minimum salary increase of $350 and many of those in large school systems will receive $800–$1,000 and more.

Sanctions do not violate the provisions of teaching contracts. They are completely under the control of the teaching profession. They can be escalated in stages. Safeguards are built into the sanctions to provide that they be applied only after an investigation or field study has been made by a competent national agency. They are applied only as a last resort and after opportunity has been provided for corrective action.

As we work with sanctions I expect that we will learn a great deal through experience. It is, therefore, important that we proceed with a pragmatic view toward them. However, on the basis of experience to date, they show great promise as a means of securing public attention for school problems and providing a motivating force to bring about corrective action.

The effectiveness of sanctions emphasizes the need for responsibility in their use. The association does not assume this responsibility lightly.

GRIEVANCE PROCEDURES

There is a need, especially in our larger school systems, for improved and more effective formal grievance procedures. I am convinced that some of the explosions that are occurring in education are a result of the accumulated frustrations of teachers. Many of these frustrations could be relieved if teachers had easy access to machinery for resolving problems which result from differences in the interpretation or administration of school policies. Little problems become big problems if they go unresolved.

School systems without satisfactory provisions for handling grievances run the risk of having dissatisfaction become acute and explode into a major incident. Moreover, the lack of grievance procedures can outweigh and cause teachers to forget about many favorable conditions. Often school administrators are unaware of the needs for grievance procedures. When one becomes an administrator, he no longer participates in the boiler-room sessions where grievances are aired.

A grievance procedure should have six general characteristics:

1. The term "grievance" should be clearly defined so that a teacher may have fair notice of when the procedure can be invoked.

2 The procedure should be easily accessible to any person who thinks he has a grievance, and its use should be encouraged by the administration.

3. The procedure should have prescribed time limits within which the grievance must be processed at each stage.

4. The procedure should guarantee the grievant independent representation at all stages.

5. The procedure should guarantee the grievant protection from administrative coercion, interference, restraint, discrimination or reprisal by reason of having filed and processed his grievance.

6. The procedure should terminate in a full and fair review, where the grievant so desires, by an agency which is in no way beholden to or prejudiced against any party in interest.

The needs for formalized employer-employee relationships *are coming*. They are coming because they are necessary to personalize and make more effective employer-employee relationships in education. The task of teachers, administrators and school boards alike is to devote our best thinking to the task of developing procedures which will recognize the unique nature of schools, and best represent sound public policy. None of us has yet had enough experience to be confident that we have *all* the answers. But pioneering can be an exciting adventure.

70. The American Federation of Teachers and Collective Negotiations*

Charles Cogen

In April, 1965, as president of the American Federation of Teachers, I addressed a telegram to the president of the Department of Classroom Teachers of the National Education Association. I proposed that the DCT and the AFT engage in a dialogue for the purpose of establishing a nationwide "Code of Observance" for the conduct of teacher representation elections. What we in the AFT were seeking was a united front of teachers in

---

* An address by Charles Cogen, President of the American Federation of Teachers from 1964 to 1968, on July 8, 1965, to the National Institute on Collective Negotiations in Public Education cosponsored by Phi Delta Kappa and Rhode Island College, Providence, R.I.

SOURCE: Charles Cogen, "The American Federation of Teachers and Collective Negotiations," in Stanley Elam, Myron Lieberman, and Michael Moskow, eds., *Readings on Collective Negotiations in Public Education* (New York: Rand McNally & Company, 1967), pp. 162–72. Copyright © 1967 by Rand McNally & Company. Reprinted by permission of the publisher.

establishing uniform rules for choosing local exclusive negotiating representative organizations, regardless of whether the organization chosen by the teachers was an AFT local or an association affiliated with NEA or its state branches.

Increasingly, educational commentators have proposed that the AFT and the NEA merge into one organization. We would not rule out such a possibility. The AFT favors "teacher unity"—but there are fundamental points at issue between the two organizations, and many of these revolve around the question of the proper relationship between teachers and their employing boards of education. We reasoned that if teacher unity in an organizational sense is not possible, at least we ought to be able to agree on the rights which teachers have, and we should stand united in our insistence that these rights be recognized by boards of education. Within this framework the two organizations could then compete for teacher support.

Our efforts to establish a common framework of teachers' rights as employees were rebuffed by the Department of Classroom Teachers. Instead, the DCT supports legislation defining the negotiating relationship on a state-by-state basis. We consider this action irresponsible and harmful to teachers. It seems motivated more by the desire of the associations to maintain the organizational status quo than by any consideration for improving the status of teaching as a profession. At best the state-by-state approach can only result in a patchwork of unsatisfactory compromises, achieved after decades of effort, and it is likely to lead to a prolonged guerilla war in which teachers become embroiled in unproductive attacks against each other while the great issues confronting the schools are neglected.

If there were to be a nationwide negotiating code, what would it look like?

What a National Code for Teacher Negotiations Would Include

In general, the AFT favors the same sort of relationship between teachers and their boards of education as that which has been established for employees in the private sector through the National Labor and Management Relations Act.

We favor the principle of exclusive recognition of a single bargaining agent. We are opposed to "members only" bargaining, in which two or more organizations have separate but equal rights to negotiate with the board. We are opposed to "joint committees," whether they are chosen on an organization basis or by direct election of individual committee members.

We favor recognition of the organization which achieves a majority of those voting in a secret ballot election, where there are two or more organizations vying for such recognition. We are opposed to recognition on the basis of membership lists, except where only one organization is seeking exclusive recognition. Even here, due notice should be given so that any other organization could force an election upon making a sufficient showing of interest.

We favor "continuing recognition" until such time as a significant proportion of the members of the negotiating unit petition for a new election. We are opposed to required annual or biennial elections of negotiating agents.

We favor negotiating units composed of non-supervisory educational employees only. We are opposed to units composed of "all certificated employees," including principals and other administrators and supervisors.

We would place no limit on the scope of negotiations the items which are subject to the bargaining process. Anything on which the two parties can agree should become a part of the agreement; anything on which they cannot agree will, of course, not appear.

We favor written agreements between boards of education and negotiating agents. These agreements should be legally binding.

We favor development of a code of unfair labor practices and definitions of what constitutes good faith negotiations.

We favor according teachers the right to strike; we are opposed to anti-strike laws, and we are opposed to the use of injunctions in teacher-board disputes.

We favor the use of skilled mediators to resolve impasses. We are opposed to compulsory arbitration of negotiable items.

We favor individual grievance procedures, with outside arbitration as the final step. We oppose grievance procedures which place the board or the superintendent in the position of final arbiter.

Any nationwide teacher-board relations code would include the items I have noted. Many variations in detail are possible and these we are perfectly willing to discuss and even compromise on, but it is obvious that even the compromises least advantageous to teachers and most favorable to those who are in the management end of the school enterprise would constitute a tremendous advance in teachers' rights. Neither the AFT nor the DCT-NEA could bind its local units to any such code, of course, nor would agreement between the two teacher organizations mean that all boards of education would accept the code. Most local teacher organizations, however, want guidance, and many boards of education are willing to help establish some order in what is now a chaotic situation. At the very least we have an obligation to set standards of right and wrong in this field.

Appropriateness of Labor-Management Concepts to Education

Some educational commentators decry the trend toward collective negotiations on grounds that bargaining between teachers and their employer is not appropriate to education. Teaching, they say, is a profession, and education is not a business. Now, some might deny that teaching is, at present, a profession, and everyone can agree that education is not a business in the usual sense, but semantic arguments of this sort advance us very little.

Teachers certainly are *employees* of the board of education, regardless of their professional status or the lack of it, and if one were to place a schematic drawing of the staff structure of a typical private business corporation of comparable size, the little boxes and circles would be about the same for each. The same stresses, strains, and conflicts which exist in such structures in private enterprise are also to be found in enterprises owned by the public, whether they be school systems, fire departments, or bus lines.

The "non-profit" argument, too, is fallacious. Schools are just as much in the marketplace for their share of consumer dollars as any manufacturer of automobiles or safety pins. People pay taxes because they want schools, just as they put up $3,000 for a new automobile or 10¢ for a packet of pins because they want these things. Boards of education and superintendents are elected and employed to produce education, and their obligation is even set forth by law. Their success, like that of private managers, is measured by an equation in which public approval is balanced against costs.

Many superintendents, principals, and other supervisors and administrators resent efforts to classify them as "management," as though there were something disgraceful about the term, and most of the opposition to applying established labor-management concepts to education comes from this quarter. Their attitude is reflected by the non-union associations, and a large "literature" of circumlocutions, rationalizations, and anti-labor propaganda has emerged from the effort to avoid labor-management terms and concepts. Yet, ironically, one of the most widely read educational magazines among administrators and school board members is *School Management*.

Supervisors and Administrators Should Not Be in Teachers' Units

A basic labor relations tenet is that management employees should not be in the same bargaining units as non-supervisory employees. There can be no question about the predominantly managerial status of a school superintendent. Even legislation sponsored by the various non-union state associations excludes superintendents from the bargaining—or negotiating —unit. As to principals and others in middle management, the determining questions are "how much discretionary power?" and "with whom does he identify?" Two categories are debatable. Teaching department heads, for instance, who have little discretionary power and who in the main are treated as teachers, probably should be included in the bargaining unit. Assistant principals, who usually exercise the authority of the principal, and who are usually paid or given other benefits based upon those given principals, probably should be excluded.

Only in a few of our largest cities is there anything approaching a civil service merit system for the selection of administrative personnel, and even where such a system operates the superintendent retains a great amount of power in determining who gets promoted. The standard practice in private enterprise of allowing the chief executive a free hand in the selection of his subordinates has been applied to the educational enterprise. The increasing tendency to require specialized certificates changes the status and power factors very little. Getting a certificate is a matter of getting the credits. In some cases, acting appointments are made and then confirmed after the person chosen has acquired his certificate.

Basing the salaries of administrative personnel on percentages of the teacher salary, or "indices," does not materially change the concept we have been discussing. True, under an index, every time the teachers get a raise the administrators get one too, which ought to produce friendly feelings toward teacher salary campaigns. But when hard negotiations begin, or a strike occurs, and the order comes down from the superintendent to tighten the rules or cross the picket line, it is a rare administrator who will uphold the teachers cause.

The supervisors' salary index idea is bitterly resented by many teachers because the very people who try to curb teacher action end up by benefiting the most from teacher success. Also, the index freezes a status relationship which many teachers do not acknowledge.

The relationship existing now between supervisory personnel and teachers is superordinate-subordinate, not primarily collegial.

In normal employee-employer relations, those who have authority to hire and fire, settle grievances, or make specific job assignments are excluded from the employee bargaining unit. Placing these positions firmly on the management side acts to check possible abuses of power, and allows non-supervisory employees to make group decisions without being subjected to undue influence and undemocratic pressures from supervisors. We would see no objection to middle management administrators and supervisors forming bargaining units of their own, but these should be separate from those for non-supervisory personnel.

We in the AFT think it unwise—even downright silly—to ignore the experience which has been amassed in labor-management relations over the years. The principles and concepts which have evolved apply to industries of widest possible diversity, and there is no reason to segregate educational employees and attempt to establish a new body of rules for them. In fact, teachers can only lose from such a development.

Organization, Negotiation, and Professionalism

Effective organization, negotiating rights, and greater professionalism are all parts of the same problem with which teachers are now confronted. It is worse than useless to have the *right* to negotiate where teachers have no *power* to negotiate, and the development of rights and power by teachers must be accompanied by a much higher degree of involvement in matters of professional concern.

Most administrators would agree with this last statement, at least in principle; where they would disagree is on the question of priority. The administrators would say, as some Southern governors say about civil rights: "They aren't ready for it. First they have to show that they know how to handle these rights and privileges."

Many of us in the AFT might, in turn, agree that teachers must be much more willing to accept responsibility for matters which they all too often abjure, but progress in this direction will come as a concomitant to the increased power and rights of teachers rather than as a prerequisite. As teachers achieve improved status, more able and aggressive individuals will be attracted to enter—and remain in—the profession. As teachers become more "professional," they will achieve greater power and more rights. I do not want to add to the torrent of definitions of professionalism which has spewed forth from lecturers, panelists, writers, and after-dinner speakers over the decades. When I use the term I am referring to our commitment as teachers to accept responsibility, to welcome innovation, and to be firm in our insistence on proper standards so that the quality and quantity of education is constantly improved and enlarged.

This sort of professionalism can develop only in a society of equals, in which all have an equal responsibility in the common enterprise.

Collective negotiation is the logical, practical, and meaningful way to develop greater professionalism among teachers. In the past, when teachers depended primarily upon public relations, research, lobbying, and paternalism, their progress toward professionalism was tortuously slow. As they assume the new rights and responsibilities which go with collective bargaining—or collective negotiation—their progress is speeded up.

Those who seek to place limits on the scope of teacher bargaining are basically anti-professional. A professional insists on professional standards

—conditions of work which permit him to use his professional skills to the greatest advantage. In New York City, the Board of Education representatives take the position that the proper size of a class is not a proper subject for negotiations, while the union asserts the right of its members to exercise their collective professional judgment on this question. Would a doctor allow a hospital superintendent to determine the time he can spend with each patient, or the number of patients on whom he must operate in an hour?

What should be the "professional" role of the superintendent of schools in the negotiating process? The NEA, in its rapidly expanding literature on "professional negotiation," talks of the "dual role" of the superintendent. The superintendent does have a "dual role"—but the duality is not quite the kind meant by the NEA. Rather than one role as advisor of the board and another as advisor of the teachers, the two roles of the superintendent are both management in function. On the one hand he is an administrator, responsible for the efficient operation of the educational enterprise. On the other he is an educational leader, responsible for making policy recommendations to the board of education. The superintendent has as great an obligation to negotiate on professional matters as on business affairs.

In a clothing factory, the workers negotiate about wages, fringe benefits, and conditions of work but garment workers are not expected to set clothing styles. Teachers, however, as professionals, have an obligation to exercise their professional judgment—to share the educational policy-making function.

I look for a great expansion in the effective scope of negotiations between teachers and school management. Obviously class size, number of classes taught, curriculum, hiring standards, textbooks and supplies, extracurricular activities—in fact, anything having to do with the operation of the school—is a matter for professional concern and should thus be subject to collective bargaining. The fact that these items also involve budgetary arrangements is an added reason for including them in the scope of bargaining.

Teachers can, through local and eventually state-wide and possibly national negotiation, even use their collective power to control standards of entry into the profession.

Some Legal Problems

In many states during the past few years we have run into legal obstacles to establishing the right of teachers to negotiate. Sometimes these obstacles have been created by boards of education and sometimes they have been created by the non-union associations.

In Taylor Township, Michigan, a teacher, using the same law firm retained by the Michigan Education Association, obtained a restraining order prohibiting recognition of any exclusive bargaining representative which might be chosen as a result of a forthcoming election. The election was held, after a two-month delay, but on an advisory basis only. The Board of Education has thus far refused to enter into an agreement with the Taylor Federation of Teachers, which received a majority of the votes.

In Detroit, legal obstacles to exclusive recognition delayed a representation election in 1964 and nearly precipitated a strike. The election was held, and the union won, but one of the stipulations under which the election was authorized by the Detroit Board of Education was that a new election would be held in a year. On the eve of the second election, the Detroit Education Association sought a court order to grant administrative and supervisory personnel the right to vote in the election. When the judge refused to rule immediately, the DEA withdrew from the ballot, and a committee representing the union was then recognized as the exclusive bargaining agent for the teachers. The legality of any agreement in Michigan is still in doubt. Yet peculiarly enough, in April, 1965, in Hamtramck, Michigan, the board ratified a written agreement reached between its negotiating committee and that of the union.

In New York, the status of the exclusive recognition of the United Federation of Teachers has been upheld by the State Commissioner of Education, but the contract between the board and the union has not yet been tested in court. This is probably due to the fact that the contract contains a compulsory arbitration feature on grievances, as a final step, which tends to make it self-enforcing, and also to the no-strike clause, which is the union's *quid pro quo* in making the contract. If the board breached the contract, the union could consider itself free of its agreement not to strike during the duration of the contract.

Many boards of education fall back on the doctrine of "sovereignty" to deny teachers bargaining rights. They say that signing a contract would restrict their freedom to act during the duration of the contract. Not infrequently, as in St. Louis, Missouri, associations have reinforced the board's view that exclusive recognition is illegal.

There are really very few recent court decisions as to the legality of exclusive recognition. Unfortunately, state attorneys general tend to repeat court doctrine and opinions of their predecessors in office which were handed down prior to the growth of unionism among government employees during the past decade.

The fact remains that in spite of adverse legal opinions, the number of written and unwritten collective bargaining agreements based on exclusive recognition is increasing at a very rapid rate. We in the AFT are inclined to proceed on the assumption that boards of education can enter into exclusive bargaining agreements if they want to, and that in most states attempts to obtain statutory sanction for such arrangements are apt to raise more problems than they solve.

The Impasse Problem

I wish to conclude my remarks by stating our view toward the problem of resolution of impasses in negotiations. We believe that work stoppages by teachers should be a last resort in attempting to resolve such impasses. Every possible effort to reach an agreement should be made before a work stoppage occurs. However, we also believe, as does the NEA, as evidenced by its sanctions policy, that work stoppages by teachers are morally justifiable under certain circumstances.

AFT locals are urged to follow the normal procedure of collective bargaining. When an impasse occurs, they usually resort to some sort of public appeal—a public demonstration; informational picketing; leaflets; newspaper, radio, and television advertisements; and marshaling of support from the labor movement and parent and civic organizations. If these efforts fail to move the board from its position, the members often set a strike date.

We strongly advocate the use of skilled mediators in attempting to resolve negotiating impasses. In addition to his experience and skill, the impartiality of the mediator must be above question. We do not think that most state superintendents of public instruction qualify for the mediation role on either count. Few have had mediation training or experience, and even the "fairest" state superintendent is apt to have a pro-management bias. Perhaps standing educational mediation panels could be approved by state teacher organizations and the state school boards association. Mediators for any particular situation could then be chosen from this panel.

In most cases when a strike date is set, a settlement is reached before the deadline. However, there are occasional impasses which are settled only after the walkout occurs. Few of these work stoppages have lasted more than a day or so. Teachers have shown great reluctance to use the strike to resolve an impasse, and one reason for this hesitancy is that in most states a strike by public employees is enjoinable, either under a specific anti-strike statute or under common law. The lurking fear of court action, added to the distaste of many teachers for such drastic action, has limited the willingness of teachers to strike. Teachers' strikes tend to be more in the nature of demonstrations to call public attention to the points at issue.

Legally, no one can be forced to work. A group of public employees who are determined enough can withstand court fines and jailings of their leaders and threatened loss of vested rights, just as the social workers in the New York City Welfare Department did in January of 1965, and when they do, they usually win. However, teacher groups are only now approaching such solidarity. In the meantime, methods of avoiding the legal entanglements of anti-strike laws and injunctions should be explored.

The most desirable step toward giving teachers bargaining power in negotiations would be to outlaw the use of the injunction in teacher-board disputes, just as the Norris-La Guardia Act outlaws injunctions in labor disputes in the private sector. The Michigan Board of Education recently declared in favor of granting teachers the right to strike, but widespread acceptance of the right to strike is not an immediate likelihood.

Perhaps the best avenue to explore is the "no contract, no work" concept.

When teachers understand that they are to work only under the terms and conditions of a collective bargaining contract—or professional negotiation agreement, if you prefer—no formal action would be required to set a deadline for a work stoppage. Lack of contract or the acceptance of a contract is a self-evident fact, and teachers would simply act accordingly. Certain types of picketing, advertising, and communications are usually subject to court restraint, but no court can force a union to sign an agreement. So long as teachers remain true to the no-contract-no-work principle, a legally permissible work stoppage can be carried on.

In some respects the no-contract-no-work policy is similar to the code of ethics approach of Myron Lieberman and others, and it also bears strong resemblance to the sanctions approach of the NEA, at least as projected in the Utah and Oklahoma situations.

If teachers have a code of ethics involving standards of salaries, class sizes, teaching program loads, and other vital matters, and agree that they will teach only under these ethical conditions, a work stoppage is implicit when conditions fail to meet these standards. The difficulty with this approach lies in its rigidity. There is such a variation in the ability of local school districts to provide adequate professional conditions that either exceptions would have to be made or the code itself would be so substandard as to be meaningless in many situations. The code of ethics could have meaning if considered in conjunction with local collective negotiations and the no-contract-no-work principle, however.

The sanctions approach of the NEA has possibilities for development into an effective professional weapon, but in its present formulation it has many pitfalls and drawbacks. The basic idea underlying sanctions—that teachers should not work in districts which do not maintain adequate professional standards—is sound. It is the same principle underlying the no-contract-no-work idea. However, if a district is not a fit place in which to teach, all teachers—those presently employed as well as applicants for teaching positions—should refuse to teach there. We see no moral or logical defense for condoning teaching by those who are already there while new applicants are urged to go elsewhere.

Furthermore, this strangulation approach is unduly attenuated and a great deal of harm can be done to the children and to public education in general while the process runs its course.

Another problem with the sanctions idea is that of "who invokes and who revokes." An impasse occurs in local negotiations, or in a state educational program. The local or state association declares in favor of sanctions. Then an investigating team comes in, ostensibly to make an evaluation of the professional conditions which prevail. In actuality the "evaluation" is a sort of under-the-table negotiation in which local teachers as a collective force are removed from the process. Let us presume, however, that following the evaluation sanctions are applied in their most extreme forms and teachers are encouraged to pick up their goods and chattels and teach elsewhere (a vengeance harder on the avenger than the avengee). Who decides the point at which conditions have become acceptable? And then does everybody move back into town?

Compared with a strike or a no-contract-no-work policy as a way of resolving an impasse, sanctions are slow, uncertain, potentially harmful to children and the schools, difficult to enforce, a hindrance to teacher involvement in the problems which concern them, and lacking in democratic controls. If sanctions procedures could be modified to correct these defects, what would emerge would be essentially, a no-contract-no-work policy.

In all the foregoing I have avoided mention of arbitration as a method of settling negotiating impasses. While we favor arbitration to enforce an agreement once it is negotiated, as a final step of a grievance procedure, we are opposed to its use in negotiations for a variety of reasons which are too lengthy to go into here, and which I have outlined in a brief policy paper available from our office.

Conclusion

I now come back to my original thesis: The principles involved in establishing collective negotiation are too important to be settled on the basis of organizational advantage. Rather, the two organizations ought to make every effort to agree on these principles and mutually uphold them. We must never lose sight of the fact that it is the *teachers* whom we represent and serve. Any temporary organizational advantage which might seem possible by pursuing some expediential course which is contrary to sound principles of teacher-board relationships will be swept aside as teachers march toward their goal of greater dignity and professional status.

71. Educational Power and the Teaching Profession

Arthur F. Corey

The constant use of the term "black power" has given a new connotation to a word that has in the past usually derived its meaning from the context in which it was used. Yesterday one might have asked, "What kind of power?" Today the word "power" is defined as the organization and implementation of the activities and influence of a somewhat homogeneous group in an attempt to gain conscious and desirable ends.

We often find illustration or parallel for human relations in mechanical principles. In the physical world, raw force is usually disorganized and uncoordinated energy. A tornado, an earthquake, or a huge waterfall exert unbelievable amounts of energy. They possess great force, but in a mechanical sense they develop no power. Natural sources of energy—that is, natural forces—must be concentrated and organized and channeled to accomplish desired ends before they can accurately be called "power."

In human relations, individuals have influence. Personal influence is social energy; it is tremendous force. When personal influence is so organized and concentrated and directed that it affects other people, it can rightfully be called "power." Good teachers have unique opportunity to exert such power over their students. If children are significantly different because of the influence of a teacher, then that teacher is truly "powerful." This is what Thomas Jefferson meant in ascribing to William Small, one of his teachers at the College of William and Mary, a "powerful" effect on all his later life.

Teachers have opportunity for "power" in all their personal relations. They can affect the opinions and attitudes of their family, neighbors, friends, tradesmen, and parents of their pupils. They may even have acquaintances within the power structure of the community. They can, if they will, have influence with a congressman, a state legislator, a city coun-

SOURCE: *Phi Delta Kappan*, XLIX, 6 (February 1968), 331–34. Reprinted by permission of the author and publisher.

cilman, or a school board member. In all these relationships there is the possibility of "power." One of the negative aspects of today's larger school districts is the fact that personal relationships are less intimate—more tenuous and fragile—and therefore personal "power" is more difficult to establish and maintain.

It is not to deprecate the challenging possibilities of the influence of the individual teacher to accept the fact that the profession cannot be effective in directing changes in the schools unless these "units" of individual influence are organized, concentrated, and directed to desired ends.

The term "pressure group" is an epithet which has no definite meaning, usually applied to a group with which one disagrees and which one wishes to castigate. Most organized groups have common interests to advance and protect, and so long as their activities are honest there is nothing inimical or unethical in group activity. It must be expected that evil men will get together to further their nefarious ends. Edmund Burke once said, "When bad men combine, the good must associate." In fact, the political chicanery of certain economic groups was rampant until thwarted by the emergence of other groups strong and courageous enough to thwart them. Pure democracy in which every man as a unit speaks his own mind and controls his own destiny is a political ideal never yet approximated, and more and more difficult of realization as society becomes more complex. The play of group against group is the process of modern democracy. There is little profit in decrying this condition. We must be interested in making it more effective for the common good.

The only possible cure for the evils of organized pressure is more and better organization among honest and intelligent men and women of good will. We can be sure that economic interests will continue to organize for pressure and we accept their right to do so. Professional groups have also learned to organize to accomplish their cherished objectives. The real danger in American life is that large segments of our people will continue to be unorganized, and will have no effective voice in government and public affairs. The man who has no share in organized "power" is certainly not independent of it. He is consistently the victim of the organized pressures which shape his way of life. The teacher who wishes to have real influence must get himself into an effective group and work in it.

Tyranny, in modern times, begins by exploiting the unorganized mass and then uses this instrument to destroy all other organizations. The strongest guarantee against authoritarianism is the presence in society of many strong, voluntary organizations. The most corrupt political machines usually have developed where the unorganized mass is largest. Huey Long's reign in Louisiana is an excellent example. The decline in the power of Tammany Hall resulted from the development of many voluntary pressure groups that could not easily be exploited. Organization that is voluntarily supported by its members, and whose program is cooperatively

ity of teachers. The schism between teachers and administrators, with the latter often maintaining independent representation at the capitol, has also tarnished the image of the united profession. In spite of these negative factors, the legislative record of state teachers associations has remained dramatically successful in the fields of school finance and teacher welfare.

The sad truth is that money for schools and economic security for teachers will not be enough in themselves to create the kind of schools which America now needs. These factors are basic and necessary, but well-financed schools with well-paid, secure teachers can still be woefully inadequate.

Educational power demands not only unity but commitment. Legislators have learned by experience that teachers really care about their own welfare, but lawmakers are not yet convinced that teachers are deeply motivated toward educational innovation and instructional improvement. This was painfully evident in the 1961 session of the California legislature.

Senator Fisher, and the Democratic Party which he represented, had no reason to believe that the members of the California Teachers Association would be vitally interested in a bill which sought to revolutionize the preparation of teachers. Assemblyman Casey had no reason to believe that the profession would be angered by his legislation, which mandated curricular detail. In opposing these bills, the CTA was operating outside its traditional sphere and legislators simply didn't take the opposition seriously. If these bills had attempted to weaken tenure, reduce retirement allowances, or cut state aid, they would have been killed in committee or never given a hearing. The politicians couldn't believe that the teachers back home really cared about certification or curricular detail. The fact that Senator Fisher, by his own admission, was defeated for reelection by angry teachers and that Assemblyman Casey is no longer in the legislature may be some slight assistance in correcting such legislative miscalculation in the future. However, educational power cannot be built by the occasional defeat of a recalcitrant legislator. The commitment of teachers to educational improvement must become traditional and hence accepted.

In an age of transience, society cannot permit a lag of a generation between important social and economic change and the resultant adjustment in education. The teaching profession must, through its organizational structure, be far more active in leading, or if necessary pushing, the reorganization of educational objectives, curriculum content, and teaching method.

With the collapse of space and time, we must give relatively more importance to the future than the past. The traditional argument that one learns to understand the future by knowing about the past has lost much of its validity. There is little precedent in the past for what our children face in the future. This fact is profoundly disturbing to many people and gives

developed by those members, is the only thing in modern life which we can justly call self-government. Self-government is the essence of individual liberty.

The professional not only knows his field; he applies his knowledge to the control and direction of some aspects of the lives of others. In short, the conception of a profession, when expressed in terms of its function as it bears on others in a society, implies that, in relating thought to action, power is exercised in a certain way in that society.

If in more and more areas of life today people are discovering that they can get more dependably what they most basically want by forging more effective power structures, the profession of teaching should develop, with some clarity, ideas about where its weight is to be felt.

Despite some recognition in our literature that the work of a profession involves the use of power, the analysis of power as it is related to the knowledge and service of the professions, especially the teaching profession, has been neglected. This neglect has meant that efforts to professionalize teaching have had no theory of power to support and guide them. They have had no theoretical analysis sufficient to discriminate between the functions of power in different contexts and no analysis to identify its uses and abuses.

Power obviously presents awkward problems for a community which abhors its existence and disavows its possession but values its exercise. Despite this convention of reticence and understatement, which seems to outlaw ostensible pursuit of power and which leads to a constant search for euphemisms to disguise its possession, there is no indication that, as a profession, we are averse to power. On the contrary, few things are more valued and more jealously guarded by their possessors in our society.

Teachers, like other Americans, are in fact very eager for power. They enjoy its possession, but would prefer to wield it quietly behind the scenes. This reticence has a basis in the fact that many teachers have a somewhat uneasy conscience based upon the assumption that organized power and democracy are not compatible. The truth is that democracy cannot function without organized power. Our political parties, the foundation stones of our representative government, are in themselves examples of organized power.

Many teachers seem to assume a scarcity theory about power. This theory is not dissimilar to the now outmoded scarcity theory of wealth. It was long thought that the only way in which one man or one social segment could improve his or its economic status was to lower the economic status of someone else in society. Just so, the scarcity theory of power unconsciously held by many assumes that the amount of power in society is a fixed quantity and therefore, when it is assumed by one group, it is *ipso facto* removed from some other group.

With obeisance toward these complexities, we shall take "power" to refer to organized and sustained social influence or control exerted by persons or groups on the decisions and actions of others. It relates to effectiveness in influencing action, decision, and policy in the entire range of human association. However, it is with the political aspect of power that this statement addresses itself.

America probably faces a generation of unprecedented political turmoil. The great issues will have to do with educational and social objectives and increasingly the people will begin to see that the kind of society they are to have is inescapably linked with the kind of education offered. America is heavily committed to more and more education for more of its people, but there is little consensus about what kind and quality of education this is to be.

Alvin Toffler [1] in a recent article calls the years between now and the turn of the century "The Age of Transience." Says he, "Rapid change will characterize every aspect of life. Time and space will collapse." People and things will come and go—in and out of one's life—at a faster rate than ever before. Man must learn to live with impermanence. There is ample evidence that even our ideas about goodness and badness—our sense of values—will change along with our environment. Impermanence will be further accelerated as science and technology advance and transience will permeate every aspect of life. The significant thing for us today is that in 1968 this acceleration is just barely beginning. The next third of a century will almost certainly be marked by scientific and social changes so severe that we must virtually abandon our habitual ways of thinking and doing and feeling. When society changes, education must inevitably change, and it will require great quantities of "educational power" to win this race with catastrophe. If teachers are to lead educational change, or even influence it, they will do it through political power.

Teachers have been distressingly naive in their insistence that "schools must be kept out of politics." It may be that such people tend to confuse "politics" with patronage. Politics is the science of determining *who* gets *what* and *when*. No segment of American government is so thoroughly political as the public schools.

There is nothing inherently unethical in political power if it is broadly based, consistent, and responsible. The insistence that group power must be broadly based leads many into erroneous conclusions. Not every member of a large group can vote on every issue, but all must still be involved in decision making. Power, to be effective, must be applied speedily and effectively and by responsible leaders, but must be based upon generalizations which have been picked in advance with the broadest possible group participation. The platform of an organization, broad-based and democrat-

[1]Alvin Toffler, "Can We Cope with Tomorrow?," *Redbook Magazine,* Jan., 1966

ically determined, should be comprehensive enough to guide the on-the-spot decisions which must be made by its leaders.

Politics is the process through which organized power is, in the final analysis, applied in a free society. The effective methods for group political action have drastically changed in California in recent years. There was probably never a teachers' organization in America which enjoyed the political power possessed by the California Teachers Association (CTA) a generation ago. However, exactly the same methods would today be completely ineffective. The abolition of cross-filing, the sharp increase in the number of voters in legislative constituencies, and the unbelievable rise in campaign costs have combined to force groups which aspire to operate within the power structure to share the high campaign costs which otherwise keep all but the rich from running for legislative office. Time was when a pleasant letter praising a legislator for his support of public education was appreciated and was accepted as support. Those times are gone. Political support of public education is often measured in dollars, and if teachers are to stay in the game they must play the game under the new rules. This is the practical condition which gives rise to professional political action arms. Political forces are in flux. Labor and agriculture are gradually losing dominant places they once held in American politics. The present moment is indeed auspicious for the expansion and refinement of "educational power."

The expansion of educational power must be viewed and defended in terms of its objectives. Such power seeks to improve the quality of the educational experiences offered to American children. The ultimate end must always be improvement in the school program. Politicians instinctively respect that which they fear. They respect "power."

In the past the state teachers associations have generally been considered to be among the most effective groups in the legislative field. California has been no exception. The Golden State may also be typical of new conditions and new factors which must be faced if educational power is to be effective enough to give the profession some voice in educational decisions which may determine the nation's future.[2]

The unity which characterized professional legislative programs during the last decade is no longer so evident to legislators and to the public. The teachers union has been more disruptive to these programs than have the activities of organizations which have traditionally opposed public education. Although notoriously unsuccessful in attaining its own legislative objectives, the union has given legislatures the image of a house divided against itself and the excuse to defeat programs favored by a large major-

[2] "Legislative Policies and Procedures Used by State Teachers Associations," Corey and Strickland, an unpublished dissertation, University of Southern California, 1956.

rise to the irrational demand from the far right that we continue to educate for life in a kind of world which has ceased to exist. It will require educational power to counter these misguided pressures.

The most important change in professional association programs in the immediate future must be increased involvement in the improvement of instruction. This responsibility has long been recognized, but it must be given high priority in teacher association budgets and hence in program emphasis. No group can develop or maintain professional status when its right or competence to have a voice in basic decisions regarding its own work is challenged or denied.

The teaching profession must assert that education in America is too important to leave in the hands of the prejudiced or the uninformed. It is a specialized field, the details of which are far too complex to leave to the average citizen. When professional organizations show as much interest in improving instruction as they now do in improving salaries, the public will be more willing to accord the profession a voice in determining educational policy. This is to say that if professional organizations really assert themselves in stimulating innovation and improving instruction, this very activity will be self-serving in that it will go far in developing the professional power to secure acceptance of their proposals.

	STONE & SCHNEIDER *Foundations of Education,* 2d ed. Crowell, 1971	RAGAN & HENDERSON *Foundations of American Education* Harper & Row, 1970	KNELLER *Foundations of Education,* 2d ed. Harper & Row, 1967
Text chs.	Related Articles in *Readings in the Foundations of Education,* 2d ed.		
1	1–6	2, 4, 5	44, 48
2	7–14	7	54
3	15–20	6, 9, 10, 12, 17, 21	49, 50
4	22, 24, 25	44–48	13, 14, 51–54
5	21, 23, 26, 28	7–14	
6	27, 29, 30, 31	27, 31	56, 65, 69, 70
7	37, 38	3, 11, 39	51
8	32–36, 39–43	57–60	4, 7, 66, 67
9	41–48	61–62	9, 56, 63, 68
10	49–54	64–67	1, 2, 11, 25, 26, 35, 38, 39, 41
11	55–62	32, 33, 36, 41	1, 2, 3, 5, 24, 34
12	63–71	33, 35, 37, 42, 56	31, 50, 61
13		43, 56, 59	13, 14, 19, 27, 29
14		16, 34, 38, 42	28, 30, 32–39
15		1, 2, 4, 6	7, 8, 37, 55, 57–60, 62
16		9, 14, 22	10, 14–17, 24, 28, 30, 40, 49–54
17		12, 13, 23, 24, 48, 55, 63, 64, 71	18, 20, 25, 27–31, 57, 59, 61, 62
18			11, 18, 27, 29, 30, 57, 59

Education Texts Published or Revised since 1967

	HASKEW & MCLENDON *This Is* *Teaching,* 3d ed. Scott Foresman, 1968	DEYOUNG & WYNN *American Education,* 6th ed. McGraw-Hill, 1968	RICHEY *Planning for Teaching,* 4th ed. McGraw-Hill, 1968
Text chs.	Related Articles in *Readings in the Foundations of Education,* 2d ed.		
1	6, 15, 20, 25, 57, 71	2, 5, 7, 9, 11, 13, 14, 23, 24, 39	6–9, 11, 14, 15, 26, 40–71
2	18, 20	4, 41, 55, 56, 67	15, 17
3	2, 27, 31, 33, 34	46, 47	43, 63–68
4	4, 5, 7, 9, 10, 32–43	44	15, 16, 63
5	15, 16, 29, 30, 60–61	16, 32, 36, 45, 57–59	15, 16, 18, 22, 26, 57, 63, 64
6	6, 17, 19	27, 31	15–20, 24, 25, 58–62
7	28, 58, 62	20, 25, 31, 58, 60–63	8, 22, 26, 63–71
8	55, 56	6, 11, 16, 18, 24, 29, 33, 37, 40	22, 26, 63, 68
9	22, 26, 57, 63, 64, 68, 71	5, 6, 8, 10, 21, 23, 49–54, 65–67	69, 70
10	8, 40, 43, 65–71	1, 24, 43	57, 58, 63, 64, 69, 70
11	12, 49–54	11, 21, 23, 27, 29, 33, 34, 38, 39	7, 55, 57–62
12	44–48	15, 17, 18, 22, 26, 40, 63, 64, 67	69, 70
13	1–3, 7, 9, 11, 13, 14	69, 70	44–48
14		6, 7, 10, 13, 14, 16, 18–20, 24, 25, 28, 34, 45, 49–55	49–54
15		20, 25, 28, 45, 59, 60–62	1–6
16		7, 56, 68–71	7–14
17		2, 3, 5, 6, 9–11, 13, 16, 19, 21, 23, 24, 36–39, 41, 42, 56, 71	3, 5, 6, 9–11, 13, 15, 16, 18, 19, 21, 23, 25, 32–43, 55, 62
18			12, 17, 26, 57, 63, 64, 67, 71